Commentaries on the Constitution of the United States

Volume III

Commentaries on the Constitution of the United States

Volume III

with a Preliminary Review of
the Constitutional History of the
Colonies and States Before the
Adoption of the Constitution

JOSEPH STORY

COSIMOCLASSICS

NEW YORK

Commentaries on the Constitution of the United States with a Preliminary Review of the Constitutional History of the Colonies and States Before the Adoption of the Constitution, Volume III
Originally published in 1833 by Hilliard, Gray and Company, Boston.
This edition published by Cosimo Classics in 2020.

ISBN: 978-1-64679-217-7

This edition is a replica of a rare classic. As such, it is possible that some of the text might be blurred or of reduced print quality. Thank you for your understanding, and we wish you a pleasant reading experience.

Cosimo aims to publish books that inspire, inform, and engage readers worldwide. We use innovative print-on-demand technology that enables books to be printed based on specific customer needs. This approach eliminates an artificial scarcity of publications and allows us to distribute books in the most efficient and environmentally sustainable manner. Cosimo also works with printers and paper manufacturers who practice and encourage sustainable forest management, using paper that has been certified by the FSC, SFI, and PEFC whenever possible.

Ordering Information:
Cosimo publications are available at online bookstores. They may also be purchased for educational, business, or promotional use:
  Bulk orders: Special discounts are available on bulk orders for reading groups, organizations, businesses, and others.
  Custom-label orders: We offer selected books with your customized cover or logo of choice.

For more information, contact us at www.cosimobooks.com

COMMENTARIES.

CHAPTER XVI.

POWER OVER NATURALIZATION AND BANKRUPTCY.

§ 1097. The next clause is, that congress "shall have " power to establish an uniform rule of naturalization, " and uniform laws on the subject of bankruptcies " throughout the United States."

§ 1098. The propriety of confiding the power to establish an uniform rule of naturalization to the national government seems not to have occasioned any doubt or controversy in the convention. For aught that appears on the journals, it was conceded without objection.[1] Under the confederation, the states possessed the sole authority to exercise the power; and the dissimilarity of the system in different states was generally admitted, as a prominent defect, and laid the foundation of many delicate and intricate questions. As the free inhabitants of each state were entitled to all the privileges and immunities of citizens in all the other states,[2] it followed, that a single state possessed the power of forcing into every other state, with the

---

[1] Journ. of Convention, 220, 257. — One of the grievances stated in the Declaration of Independence was, that the king had endeavoured to prevent the population of the states by obstructing the laws for naturalization of foreigners.

[2] The Confederation, art. 4.

enjoyment of every immunity and privilege, any alien, whom it might choose to incorporate into its own society, however repugnant such admission might be to their polity, conveniencies, and even prejudices. In effect every state possessed the power of naturalizing aliens in every other state ; a power as mischievous in its nature, as it was indiscreet in its actual exercise. In one state, residence for a short time might, and did confer the rights of citizenship. In others, qualifications of greater importance were required. An alien, therefore, incapacitated for the possession of certain rights by the laws of the latter, might, by a previous residence and naturalization in the former, elude at pleasure all their salutary regulations for self-protection. Thus the laws of a single state were preposterously rendered paramount to the laws of all the others, even within their own jurisdiction.[1] And it has been remarked with equal truth and justice, that it was owing to mere casualty, that the exercise of this power under the confederation did not involve the Union in the most serious embarrassments.[2] There is great wisdom, therefore, in confiding to the national government the power to establish a uniform rule of naturalization throughout the United States. It is of the deepest interest to the whole Union to know, who are entitled to enjoy the rights of citizens in each state, since they thereby, in effect, become entitled to the rights of citizens in all the states. If aliens might be admitted indiscriminately to enjoy all the rights of citizens at the will of a single state, the Union might itself be endangered by an influx of foreigners, hostile to its institutions, ignorant of its powers, and incapable of a due estimate of its privileges.

[1] The Federalist, No. 42.   [2] Ibid.

§ 1099. It follows, from the very nature of the power, that to be useful, it must be exclusive; for a concurrent power in the states would bring back all the evils and embarrassments, which the uniform rule of the constitution was designed to remedy. And, accordingly, though there was a momentary hesitation, when the constitution first went into operation, whether the power might not still be exercised by the states, subject only to the control of congress, so far as the legislation of the latter extended, as the supreme law ;[1] yet the power is now firmly established to be exclusive.[2] The Federalist, indeed, introduced this very case, as entirely clear, to illustrate the doctrine of an exclusive power by implication, arising from the repugnancy of a similar power in the states. "This power must necessarily be exclusive," say the authors ; "because, if each state had power to prescribe a distinct rule, there could be no uniform rule."[3]

[1] *Collet* v. *Collet*, 2 Dall. R. 294 ; *United States* v. *Villato*, 2 Dall. 270; Sergeant on Const. Law, ch. 28, [ch. 30, 2d. edit.]
[2] See The Federalist, No. 32, 42 ; *Chirac* v. *Chirac*, 2 Wheat. R. 259, 269 ; Rawle on the Const. ch. 9, p. 84, 85 to 88 ; *Houston* v. *Moore*, 5 Wheat. R. 48, 49 ; *Golden* v. *Prince*, 3 Wash. Cir. Ct. R. 313, 322 ; 1 Kent's Comm. Lect. 19, p. 397 ; 1 Tuck. Black. Comm. App. 255 to 259; 12 Wheat. R. 277, per. Johnson J. ; but see Id. 307, per Thompson J. — A question is often discussed under this head, how far a person has a right to throw off his national allegiance, and to become the subject of another country, without the consent of his native country. This is usually denominated the right of expatriation. It is beside the purpose of these Commentaries to enter into any consideration of this subject, as it does not properly belong to any constitutional inquiry. It may be stated, however, that there is no authority, which has affirmatively maintained the right, (unless provided for by the laws of the particular country,) and there is a very strong current of reasoning on the other side, independent of the known practice and claims of the nations of modern Europe. See Rawle on the Constitution, ch. 9, p. 85 to 101 ; Sergeant on Const. Law, ch. 28, [ch. 30.] ; 2 Kent's Comm. Lect. 25, p. 35 to 42.
[3] The Federalist, No. 32.

§ 1100. The power, to pass laws on the subject of bankruptcies was not in the original draft of the constitution. The original article was committed to a committee together with the following proposition : "to establish uniform laws upon the subject of bankruptcies, and respecting the damages arising on the protest of foreign bills of exchange." The committee subsequently made a report in favour of incorporating the clause on the subject of bankruptcies into the constitution ; and it was adopted by a vote of nine states against one.[1] The brevity, with which this subject is treated by the Federalist, is quite remarkable. The only passage in that elaborate commentary, in which the subject is treated, is as follows: "The power of establishing uniform laws of bankruptcy is so intimately connected with the regulation of commerce, and will prevent so many frauds, where the parties or their property may lie, or be removed into different states, that the expediency of it seems not likely to be drawn in question."[2]

§ 1101. The subject, however, deserves a more exact consideration. Before the adoption of the constitution the states severally possessed the exclusive right, as matter belonging to their general sovereignty, to pass laws upon the subject of bankruptcy and insolvency.[3] Without stopping at present to consider, what is the precise meaning of each of these terms, as contradistinguished from the other ; it may be stated, that the general object of all bankrupt and insolvent laws is, on the one hand, to secure to creditors an ap-

---

[1] Journ. of Convention, 220, 305, 320, 321, 357.

[2] The Federalist, No. 42.

[3] *Sturgis* v. *Crowninshield,* 4 Wheat. R. 122, 203, 204 ; Rawle on the Constitution, ch. 9, p. 101, 102.

propriation of the property of their debtors *pro tanto* to the discharge of their debts, whenever the latter are unable to discharge the whole amount ; and, on the other hand, to relieve unfortunate and honest debtors from perpetual bondage to their creditors, either in the shape of unlimited imprisonment to coerce payment of their debts, or of an absolute right to appropriate and monopolize all their future earnings. The latter course obviously destroys all encouragement to industry and enterprize on the part of the unfortunate debtor, by taking from him all the just rewards of his labour, and leaving him a miserable pittance, dependent upon the bounty or forbearance of his creditors. The former is, if possible, more harsh, severe, and indefensible.[1] It makes poverty and misfortune, in themselves sufficiently heavy burthens, the subject or the occasion of penalties and punishments. Imprisonment, as a civil remedy, admits of no defence, except as it is used to coerce fraudulent debtors to yield up their present property to their creditors, in discharge of their engagements. But when the debtors have no property, or have yielded up the whole to their creditors, to allow the latter at their mere pleasure to imprison them, is a refinement in cruelty, and an indulgence of private passions, which could hardly find apology in an enlightened despotism; and are utterly at war with all the rights and duties of free governments. Such a system of legislation is as unjust, as it is unfeeling. It is incompatible with the first precepts of Christianity ; and is a living reproach to the nations of christendom, carrying them back to the worst ages of paganism.[2]

---

[1] See 1 Tuck. Black Comm. App. 259.
[2] See 2 Black. Comm. 471, 472, 473. See also 1 Tuck. Black. Comm. App. 259.

One of the first duties of legislation, while it provides
amply for the sacred obligation of contracts, and the
remedies to enforce them, certainly is, *pari passu*, to relieve the unfortunate and meritorious debtor from a
slavery of mind and body, which cuts him off from a
fair enjoyment of the common benefits of society, and
robs his family of the fruits of his labour, and the benefits
of his paternal superintendence. A national government, which did not possess this power of legislation,
would be little worthy of the exalted functions of guarding the happiness, and supporting the rights of a free
people. It might guard against political oppressions,
only to render private oppressions more intolerable,
and more glaring.

§ 1102. But there are peculiar reasons, independent
of these general considerations, why the government
of the United States should be entrusted with this
power. They result from the importance of preserving harmony, promoting justice, and securing equality
of rights and remedies among the citizens of all the
states. It is obvious, that if the power is exclusively
vested in the states, each one will be at liberty to frame
such a system of legislation upon the subject of bankruptcy and insolvency, as best suits its own local interests, and pursuits. Under such circumstances no uniformity of system or operations can be expected. One
state may adopt a system of general insolvency ; another, a limited or temporary system ; one may relieve
from the obligation of contracts ; another only from
imprisonment ; another may adopt a still more restrictive course of occasional relief ; and another may refuse to act in any manner upon the subject. The
laws of one state may give undue preferences to one
class of creditors, as for instance, to creditors by bond, or

judgment; another may provide for an equality of debts, and a distribution *pro ratâ* without distinction among all. One may prefer creditors living within the state to all living without; securing to the former an entire priority of payment out of the assets. Another may, with a more liberal justice, provide for the equal payment of all, at home and abroad, without favour or preference. In short, diversities of almost infinite variety and object may be introduced into the local system, which may work gross injustice and inequality, and nourish feuds and discontents in neighbouring states. What is here stated, is not purely speculative. It has occurred among the American states in the most offensive forms, without any apparent reluctance or compunction on the part of the offending state. There will always be found in every state a large mass of politicians, who will deem it more safe to consult their own temporary interests and popularity, by a narrow system of preferences, than to enlarge the boundaries, so as to give to distant creditors a fair share of the fortune of a ruined debtor. There can be no other adequate remedy, than giving a power to the general government, to introduce and perpetuate a uniform system.[1]

§ 1103. In the next place it is clear, that no state can introduce any system, which shall extend beyond its own territorial limits, and the persons, who are subject to its jurisdiction. Creditors residing in other states cannot be bound by its laws; and debts contracted in other states are beyond the reach of its legislation. It can neither discharge the obligation of such contracts, nor touch the remedies, which relate to them in any other jurisdiction. So that the most meri-

---

[1] See Mr. Justice Johnson's Opinion in *Ogden* v. *Saunders*, 12 Wheat. R. 274, 275.

torious insolvent debtor will be harassed by new suits, and new litigations, as often as he moves out of the state boundaries.[1] His whole property may be absorbed by his creditors residing in a single state, and he may be left to the severe retributions of judicial process in every other state in the Union. Among a people, whose general and commercial intercourse must be so great, and so constantly increasing, as in the United States, this alone would be a most enormous evil, and bear with peculiar severity upon all the commercial states. Very few persons engaged in active business will be without debtors or creditors in many states in the Union. The evil is incapable of being redressed by the states. It can be adequately redressed only by the power of the Union. One of the most pressing grievances, bearing upon commercial, manufacturing, and agricultural interests at the present moment, is the total want of a general system of bankruptcy. It is well known, that the power has lain dormant, except for a short period, ever since the constitution was adopted; and the excellent system, then put into operation, was repealed, before it had any fair trial, upon grounds generally believed to be wholly beside its merits, and from causes more easily understood, than deliberately vindicated.[2]

---

1 2 Kent's Comm. Lect. 37, p. 323, 324 : Sergeant on Const. Law, ch. 28, [ch. 30 :] Mr. Justice Johnson in 12 Wheat. R. 273 to 275.

2 See the Debate on the Bankrupt Bill in the House of Representatives in the winter session of 1818 : Webster's Speeches, p. 510, &c. — It is matter of regret, that the learned mind of Mr. Chancellor Kent should have attached so much importance to a hasty, if not a petulant, remark of Lord Eldon on this subject. There is no commercial state in Europe, which has not, for a long period, possessed a system of bankrupt or insolvent laws. England has had one for more than three centuries. And at no time have the parliament or people shown any intention to abandon the system. On the contrary, by recent acts of parlia-

§ 1104. In the next place, the power is important in regard to foreign countries, and to our commercial credits and intercourse with them. Unless the general government were invested with authority to pass suitable laws, which should give reciprocity and equality in cases of bankruptcies here, there would be danger, that the state legislation might, by undue domestic preferences and favours, compel foreign countries to retaliate; and instead of allowing creditors in the United States to partake an equality of benefits in cases of bankruptcies, to postpone them to all others. The existence of the power is, therefore, eminently useful; first, as a check upon undue state legislation; and secondly, as a means of redressing any grievances sustained by foreigners in commercial transactions.

§ 1105. It cannot but be matter of regret, that a power so salutary should have hitherto remained (as has been already intimated) a mere dead letter. It is extraordinary, that a commercial nation, spreading its enterprise through the whole world, and possessing such an infinitely varied, internal trade, reaching almost to every cottage in the most distant states, should voluntarily surrender up a system, which has elsewhere enjoyed such general favour, as the best security of creditors against fraud, and the best protection of debtors against oppression.

ment, increased activity and extent have been given to the bankrupt and insolvent laws. It is easy to exaggerate the abuses of the system, and point out its defects in glowing language. But the silent and potent influences of the system in its beneficent operations are apt to be overlooked, and are rarely sufficiently studied. What system of human legislation is not necessarily imperfect? Yet who would, on that account, destroy the fabric of society? — 2 Kent's Comm. Lect. 37, p. 321 to 324, and note (b) id. (2d edit. p. 391, 392.)

§ 1106. What laws are to be deemed bankrupt laws within the meaning of the constitution has been a matter of much forensic discussion and argument. Attempts have been made to distinguish between bankrupt laws and insolvent laws. For example, it has been said, that laws, which merely liberate the person of the debtor, are insolvent laws, and those, which discharge the contract, are bankrupt laws. But it would be very difficult to sustain this distinction by any uniformity of laws at home or abroad. In some of the states, laws, known as insolvent laws, discharge the person only; in others, they discharge the contract. And if congress were to pass a bankrupt act, which should discharge the person only of the bankrupt, and leave his future acquisitions liable to his creditors, there would be great difficulty in saying, that such an act was not in the sense of the constitution a bankrupt act, and so within the power of congress.[1] Again; it has been said, that insolvent laws act on imprisoned debtors only at their own instance; and bankrupt laws only at the instance of creditors. But, however true this may have been in past times, as the actual course of English legislation,[2] it is not true, and never was true, as a distinction in colonial legislation. In England it was an accident in the system, and not a material ground to discriminate, who were to be deemed in a legal sense

---

1 *Sturgis* v. *Crowninshield*, 4 Wheat. R. 122, 194, 202.

2 It was not true in England at the time of the American revolution; for under the insolvent act, commonly called the "Lords' Act of 32 Geo. 2, ch. 28," the creditors of the insolvent were equally with himself entitled to proceed to procure the benefit of the act *ex parte*. See 3 Black. Comm. 416, and note 3 of Mr. Christian. The present system of bankruptcy in England has been enlarged, so as now to include voluntary and concerted cases of bankruptcy. And the insolvent system is applied to all other imprisoned debtors, not within the bankrupt laws. See Petersdorff's Abridgment, titles, *Bankrupt* and *Insolvent*.

insolvents, or bankrupts. And if an act of congress should be passed, which should authorize a commission of bankruptcy to issue at the instance of the debtor, no court would on this account be warranted in saying, that the act was unconstitutional, and the commission a nullity.[1] It is believed, that no laws ever were passed in America by the colonies or states, which had the technical denomination of "bankrupt laws." But insolvent laws, quite co-extensive with the English bankrupt system in their operations and objects, have not been unfrequent in colonial and state legislation. No distinction was ever practically, or even theoretically attempted to be made between bankruptcies and insolvencies. And an historical review of the colonial and state legislation will abundantly show, that a bankrupt law may contain those regulations, which are generally found in insolvent laws; and that an insolvent law may contain those, which are common to bankrupt laws.[2]

§ 1107. The truth is, that the English system of bankruptcy, as well as the name, was borrowed from the continental jurisprudence, and derivatively from the Roman law. "We have fetched," says Lord Coke, " as well the name, as the wickedness of bankrupts, from foreign nations; for *banque* in the French is *mensa*, and a banquer or eschanger is *mensarius;* and *route* is a sign or mark, as we say a cart route is the sign or mark, where the cart hath gone. Metaphorically it is taken for him, that hath wasted his estate, and removed his bank, so as there is left but a mention thereof. Some say it should be derived from *banque* and *rumpue*, as he that

---

[1] *Sturgis* v. *Crowninshield*, 4 Wheat. R. 122, 194.
[2] *Sturgis* v. *Crowninshield*, 4 Wheat. R. 122, 194, 198, 203; 2 Kent's Comm. Lect. 37, p. 321, &c.

hath broken his bank or state.[1] Mr. Justice Blackstone
inclines strongly to this latter intimation, saying, that the
word is derived from the word *bancus*, or *banque*, which
signifies the table or counter of a tradesman, and *ruptus*,
broken; denoting thereby one, whose shop or place of
trade is broken and gone. It is observable, that the
first statute against bankrupt, is 'against such persons,
as do make bankrupt,' (34 Hen. 8, ch. 4,) which is a
literal translation of the French idiom, *qui font banque
route*."[2]

§ 1108. The system of discharging persons, who
were unable to pay their debts, was transferred from
the Roman law into continental jurisprudence at an
early period. To the glory of Christianity let it be said,
that the law of cession (*cessio bonorum*) was introduced
by the Christian emperors of Rome, whereby, if a debt-
or ceded, or yielded up all his property to his creditors,
he was secured from being dragged to gaol, *omni quo-
que corporali cruciatu semoto;* for as the emperor
(Justinian) justly observed, *inhumanum erat spoliatum
fortunis suis in solidum damnari;*[3] a noble declaration,
which the American republics would do well to follow,
and not merely to praise. Neither by the Roman, nor
the continental law, was the *cessio bonorum* confined to
traders, but it extended to all persons. It may be added, that the *cessio bonorum* of the Roman law, and that,
which at present prevails in most parts of the continent
of Europe, only exempted the debtor from imprison-

---

1 4 Inst. ch. 63.

2 2 Black. Comm. 472, note; Cooke's Bankr. Laws, Introd. ch. 1.— The
modern French phrase in the Code of Commerce is *la banqueroute.*
"Tout commerçant failli, &c. est en etat de banqueroute." Art. 438.

3 2 Black. Comm. 472, 473; Cod. Lib. 7, tit. 71, *per totum*, Ayliffe's
Pandects, B. 4, tit. 14.

ment. It did not release or discharge the debt, or exempt the future acquisitions of the debtor from execution for the debt. The English statute, commonly
called the "Lords' Act," went no farther, than to discharge the debtor's person. And it may be laid down,
as the law of Germany, France, Holland, Scotland, and
England, that their insolvent laws are not more extensive in their operation, than the *cessio bonorum* of the
civil law. In some parts of Germany, we are informed
by Huberus and Heineccius, a *cessio bonorum* does
not even work a discharge of the debtor's person, and
much less of his future effects.[1] But with a view to
the advancement of commerce, and the benefit of creditors, the systems, now commonly known by the name
of "bankrupt laws," were introduced; and allowed a
proceeding to be had at the instance of the creditors
against an unwilling debtor, when he did not choose to
yield up his property; or, as it is phrased in our law,
bankrupt laws were originally proceedings *in invitum*.
In the English system the bankrupt laws are limited to
persons, who are traders, or connected with matters of
trade and commerce, as such persons are peculiarly
liable to accidental losses, and to an inability of paying
their debts without any fault of their own.[2] But this is
a mere matter of policy, and by no means enters into
the nature of such laws. There is nothing in the nature,
or reason of such laws to prevent their being applied
to any other class of unfortunate and meritorious debtors.[3]

---

[1] 1 Kent's Comm. Lect. 19, p. 336; 1 Domat, B. 4, tit. 5, § 1, 2.

[2] 2 Black. Comm. 473, 474.

[3] See Debate on the Bankr. Bill in the House of Representatives, Feb.
1818, 4 Elliot's Debates, 282 to 284. — Perhaps as satisfactory a description of a bankrupt law, as can be framed, is, that it is a law for the

§ 1109. How far the power of congress to pass uniform laws on the subject of bankruptcies supersedes the authority of state legislation on the same subject, has been a matter of much elaborate forensic discussion. It has been strenuously maintained by some learned minds, that the power in congress is exclusive of that of the states; and, whether exerted or not, it supersedes state legislation.[1] On the other hand, it has been maintained, that the power in congress is not exclusive; that when congress has acted upon the subject, to the extent of the national legislation the power of the states is controlled and limited; but when unexerted, the states are at liberty to exercise the power in its full extent, unless so far as they are controlled by other constitutional provisions. And this latter opinion is now firmly established by judicial decisions.[2] As this doctrine seems now to have obtained a general acquiescence, it does not seem necessary to review the reasoning, on which the different opinions are founded; although, as a new question, it is probably as much open

benefit and relief of creditors and their debtors, in cases, in which the latter are unable, or unwilling to pay their debts. And a law on the subject of bankruptcies, in the sense of the constitution, is a law making provisions for cases of persons failing to pay their debts. An amendment was proposed by the state of New-York to the constitution at the time of adopting it, that the power of passing uniform bankrupt laws should extend only to merchants and other traders; but it did not meet general favour.*

1 See *Golden* v. *Prince*, 3 Wash. Circ. R. 313; *Ogden* v. *Saunders*, 12 Wheat. R. 264, 267 to 270, per Washington J. It is well known, that Mr. Justice Washington was not alone in the Court in this opinion in the original case, (*Sturgis* v. *Crowninshield*, 4 Wheat. R. 122,) in which it was first decided.

2 *Sturgis* v. *Crowninshield*, 4 Wheat. R. 122, 191 to 196; Id. 198 to 202; *Ogden* v. *Saunders*, 12 Wheat. R. 273, 275, 280, 306, 310, 314, 335, 369.

to controversy, as any one, which has ever given rise to judicial argumentation. But upon all such subjects it seems desirable to adopt the sound practical maxim, *Interest reipublicæ, ut finis sit litium.*

§ 1110. It is, however, to be understood, that although the states still retain the power to pass insolvent and bankrupt laws, that power is not unlimited, as it was before the constitution. It does not, as will be presently seen, extend to the passing of insolvent or bankrupt acts, which shall discharge the obligation of antecedent contracts. It can discharge such contracts only, as are made subsequently to the passing of such acts, and such, as are made within the state between citizens of the same state. It does not extend to contracts made with a citizen of another state within the state, nor to any contracts made in other states.[1]

---

[1] *Ogden* v. *Saunders*, 12 Wheat. R. 122, 369 ; *Boyle* v. *Zacharie*, 6 Peters's R. 348 ; 2 Kent. Comm. Lect. 37, p. 323, 324 ; Sergeant on Const. Law, ch. 28, p. 309, [ch. 30, p. 322 ;] Rawle on the Constitution, ch. 9, p. 101, 102.

CHAPTER XVII.

POWER TO COIN MONEY AND FIX THE STANDARD OF
WEIGHTS AND MEASURES.

§ 1111. The next power of congress is "to coin "money, regulate the value thereof, and of foreign coin, "and fix the standard of weights and measures."

§ 1112. Under the confederation, the continental congress had delegated to them, "the sole and exclusive right and power of regulating the alloy and value of coin struck by their own authority, or by that of the states," and "fixing the standard of weights and measures throughout the United States." It is observable, that, under the confederation, there was no power given to regulate the value of foreign coin, an omission, which in a great measure would destroy any uniformity in the value of the current coin, since the respective states might, by different regulations, create a different value in each.[1] The constitution has, with great propriety, cured this defect; and, indeed, the whole clause, as it now stands, does not seem to have attracted any discussion in the convention.[2] It has been justly remarked, that the power "to coin money" would, doubtless, include that of regulating its value, had the latter power not been expressly inserted. But the constitution abounds with pleonasms and repetitions of this nature.[3]

§ 1113. The grounds, upon which the general power to coin money, and regulate the value of foreign and

1 The Federalist, No. 42.
2 Journ. of Convention, 220, 257, 357.
3 Mr. Madison's Letter to Mr. Cabell, 18th Sept. 1828.

domestic coin, is granted to the national government, cannot require much illustration in order to vindicate it. The object of the power is to produce uniformity of value throughout the Union, and thus to preclude us from the embarrassments of a perpetually fluctuating and variable currency. Money is the universal medium or common standard, by a comparison with which the value of all merchandise may be ascertained, or, it is a sign, which represents the respective values of all commodities.[1] It is, therefore, indispensable for the wants and conveniencies of commerce, domestic as well as foreign. The power to coin money is one of the ordinary prerogatives of sovereignty, and is almost universally exercised in order to preserve a proper circulation of good coin of a known value in the home market. In order to secure it from debasement it is necessary, that it should be exclusively under the control and regulation of the government ; for if every individual were permitted to make and circulate, what coin he should please, there would be an opening to the grossest frauds and impositions upon the public, by the use of base and false coin. And the same remark applies with equal force to foreign coin, if allowed to circulate freely in a country without any control by the government. Every civilized government, therefore, with a view to prevent such abuses, to facilitate exchanges, and thereby to encourage all sorts of industry and commerce, as well as to guard itself against the embarrassments of an undue scarcity of currency, injurious to its own interests and credits, has found it necessary to coin money, and affix to it a public stamp and value, and to regulate the introduction and use of foreign coins.[2] In England, this

1 1 Black. Comm. 276.

2 Smith's Wealth of Nations, B. 1, ch. 4.

prerogative belongs to the crown ; and, in former ages, it was greatly abused ; for base coin was often coined and circulated by its authority, at a value far above its intrinsic worth ; and thus taxes of a burthensome nature were laid indirectly upon the people.[1] There is great propriety, therefore, in confiding it to the legislature, not only as the more immediate representatives of the public interests, but as the more safe depositaries of the power.[2]

§ 1114. The only question, which could properly arise under our political institutions, is, whether it should be confided to the national, or to the state government. It is manifest, that the former could alone give it complete effect, and secure a wholesome and uniform currency throughout the Union. The varying standards and regulations of the different states would introduce infinite embarrassments and vexations in the course of trade ; and often subject the innocent to the grossest frauds. The evils of this nature were so extensively felt, that the power was unhesitatingly confided by the articles of confederation exclusively to the general government,[3] notwithstanding the extraordinary jealousy, which pervades every clause of that instrument. But the concurrent power thereby reserved to the states, (as well as the want of a power to regulate the value of foreign coin,) was, under that feeble pageant of sovereignty, soon found to destroy the whole importance of the grant. The floods of depreciated paper money, with which most of the states of the Union, during the last war, as well as the revolutionary war with England, were inundated, to the dismay of the traveller and

---

[1] 1 Black. Comm. 278 ; Christian's note, 21 ; Davies's Rep. 48 ; 1 Hale's Pl. Cr. 192 to 196.

[2] 1 Tucker's Black. Comm. App. 261.   [3] Art. 9.

the ruin of commerce, afford a lively proof of the mischiefs of a currency exclusively under the control of
the states.[1]

§ 1115. It will be hereafter seen, that this is an exclusive power in congress, the states being expressly
prohibited from coining money. And it has been said by
an eminent statesman,[2] that it is difficult to maintain, on
the face of the constitution itself and independent of
long continued practice, the doctrine, that the states,
not being at liberty to coin money, can authorize the
circulation of bank paper, as currency, at all. His reasoning deserves grave consideration, and is to the following effect. The states cannot coin money. Can
they, then, coin that, which becomes the actual and
almost universal substitute for money? Is not the right
of issuing paper, intended for circulation in the place,
and as the representative of metallic currency, derived
merely from the power of coining and regulating the
metallic currency? Could congress, if it did not possess the power of coining money and regulating the
value of foreign coins, create a bank with the power to
circulate bills? It would be difficult to make it out.
Where, then, do the states, to whom all control over
the metallic currency is altogether prohibited, obtain
this power? It is true, that in other countries, private

---

1 During the late war with Great Britain, (1812 to 1814,) in consequence of the banks of the Middle, and Southern, and Western states
having suspended specie payments for their bank notes, they depreciated
as low as 25 per cent. discount from their nominal value. The duties on
inports were, however, paid and received in the local currency ; and the
consequence was, that goods imported at Baltimore paid 20 per cent.
less duty, than the same goods paid, when imported into Boston. This
was a plain practical violation of the provision of the constitution, that all
duties, imports, and excises shall be *uniform*.

2 Mr. Webster's Speech on the Bank of the United States, 25th and
28th of May, 1832.

bankers, having no legal authority over the coin, issue notes for circulation. But this they do always with the consent of government, express or implied; and government restrains and regulates all their operations at its pleasure. It would be a startling proposition in any other part of the world, that the prerogative of coining money, held by government, was liable to be defeated, counteracted, or impeded by another prerogative, held in other hands, of authorizing a paper circulation. It is further to be observed, that the states cannot issue bills of credit; not that they cannot make them a legal tender; but that they cannot issue them at all. This is a clear indication of the intent of the constitution to restrain the states, as well from establishing a paper circulation, as from interfering with the metallic circulation. Banks have been created by states with no capital whatever, their notes being put in circulation simply on the credit of the state. What are the issues of such banks, but bills of credit issued by the state?[1]

§ 1116. Whatever may be the force of this reasoning, it is probably too late to correct the error, if error there be, in the assumption of this power by the states, since it has an inveterate practice in its favour through a very long period, and indeed ever since the adoption of the constitution.

§ 1117. The other power, "to fix the standard of "weights and measures," was, doubtless, given from like motives of public policy, for the sake of uniformity, and the convenience of commerce.[2] Hitherto, however, it has remained a dormant power, from the many

---

[1] This opinion is not peculiar to Mr. Webster. It was maintained by the late Hon. Samuel Dexter, one of the ablest statesmen and lawyers, who have adorned the annals of our country.

[2] The Federalist, No. 42.

difficulties attendant upon the subject, although it has been repeatedly brought to the attention of congress in most elaborate reports.[1] Until congress shall fix a standard, the understanding seems to be, that the states possess the power to fix their own weights and measures ;[2] or, at least, the existing standards at the adoption of the constitution remain in full force. Under the confederation, congress possessed the like exclusive power.[3] In England, the power to regulate weights and measures is said by Mr. Justice Blackstone to belong to the royal prerogative.[4] But it has been remarked by a learned commentator on his work, that the power cannot, with propriety, be referred to the king's prerogative ; for, from Magna Charta to the present time, there are above twenty acts of parliament to fix and establish the standard and uniformity of weights and measures.[5]

§ 1118. The next power of congress is, " to provide "for the punishment of counterfeiting the securities and "current coin of the United States." This power would naturally flow, as an incident, from the antecedent powers to borrow money, and regulate the coinage ; and, indeed, without it those powers would be without any adequate sanction. This power would seem to be exclusive of that of the states, since it grows out of the constitution, as an appropriate means to carry into effect other delegated powers, not antecedently existing in the states.[6]

---

[1] Among these, none are more elaborate and exact, than that of Mr. Jefferson and Mr. J. Q. Adams, while they were respectively at the head of the department of state.

[2] Rawle on the Constitution, ch. 9, p. 102.   [3] Art. 9.

[4] 1 Black. Comm. 276.

[5] 1 Black. Comm. 276 ; Christian's note, (16.)

[6] See Rawle on Constitution, ch. 9, p. 103; The Federalist, No. 42.

CHAPTER XVIII.

POWER TO ESTABLISH POST-OFFICES AND POST-
ROADS.

§ 1119. The next power of congress is, "to estab-
"lish post-offices and post-roads." The nature and
extent of this power, both theoretically and practically,
are of great importance, and have given rise to much
ardent controversy. It deserves, therefore, a deliberate examination. It was passed over by the Federalist
with a single remark, as a power not likely to be disputed in its exercise, or to be deemed dangerous by its
scope. The "power," says the Federalist, "of establishing post-roads must, in every view, be a harmless
power; and may, perhaps, by judicious management,
become productive of great public conveniency. Nothing, which tends to facilitate the intercourse between
the states, can be deemed unworthy of the public care."[1]
One cannot but feel, at the present time, an inclination
to smile at the guarded caution of these expressions,
and the hesitating avowal of the importance of the power. It affords, perhaps, one of the most striking proofs,
how much the growth and prosperity of the country
have outstripped the most sanguine anticipations of our
most enlightened patriots.

§ 1120. The post-office establishment has already
become one of the most beneficent, and useful establishments under the national government.[2] It circulates
intelligence of a commercial, political, intellectual, and

---

[1] The Federalist, No. 42.
[2] 1 Tuck. Black. Comm. App. 265; Rawle on the Const. ch. 9, p. 103.

private nature, with incredible speed and regularity. It thus administers, in a very high degree, to the comfort, the interests, and the necessities of persons, in every rank and station of life. It brings the most distant places and persons, as it were, in contact with each other ; and thus softens the anxieties, increases the enjoyments, and cheers the solitude of millions of hearts. It imparts a new influence and impulse to private intercourse; and, by a wider diffusion of knowledge, enables political rights and duties to be performed with more uniformity and sound judgment. It is not less effective, as an instrument of the government in its own operations. In peace, it enables it without ostentation or expense to send its orders, and direct its measures for the public good, and transfer its funds, and apply its powers, with a facility and promptitude, which, compared with the tardy operations, and imbecile expedients of former times, seem like the wonders of magic. In war it is, if possible, still more important and useful, communicating intelligence vital to the movements of armies and navies, and the operations and duties of warfare, with a rapidity, which, if it does not always ensure victory, at least, in many instances, guards against defeat and ruin. Thus, its influences have become, in a public, as well as private view, of incalculable value to the permanent interests of the Union. It is obvious at a moment's glance at the subject, that the establishment in the hands of the states would have been wholly inadequate to these objects ; and the impracticability of a uniformity of system would have introduced infinite delays and inconveniences ; and burthened the mails with an endless variety of vexatious taxations, and regulations. No one, accustomed to the retardations of the post in passing through independent states on the continent of Europe, can fail to appreciate the benefits of a power, which pervades the Union. The national government is that alone, which can safely or effectually execute it, with equal promptitude and cheapness, certainty and uniformity. Already the post-office establishment realizes a revenue exceeding two millions of dollars, from which it defrays all its own expenses, and transmits mails in various directions over more than one hundred and twenty thousand miles. It transmits intelligence in one day to distant places, which, when the constitution was first put into operation, was scarcely transmitted through the same distance in the course of a week.[1] The rapidity of its movements has been in a general view doubled within the last twenty years. There are now more than eight thousand five hundred post-offices in the United States; and at every session of the legislature new routes are constantly provided for, and new post-offices established. It may, therefore, well be deemed a most benefi-

[1] In the American Almanac and Repository published at Boston, in 1830, (a very valuable publication,) there is, at page 217, a tabular view of the number of post-offices, and amounts of postage, and net revenue and extent of roads in miles travelled by the mail for a large number of years between 1790 and 1828. In 1790 there were seventy-five post-offices, and the amount of postage was $37,935, and the number of miles travelled was 1875. In 1828 there were 7530 post-offices, and the amount of postage was $1,659,915, and the number of miles travelled was 115,176. See also American Almanac for 1832, p. 134. And from Dr. Lieber's Encyclopædia Americana, (article *Posts*,) it appears, that in 1831, the amount of postage was $1,997,811, and the number of miles travelled 15,468,692. The first post-office, ever established in America, seems to have been under an act of parliament, in 1710. Dr. Lieber's Encyc. Amer. article *Posts*.

In Mr. Professor Malkin's introductory Lecture on History, before the London University, in March, 1830, he states, (p. 14,) " It is understood, that in England the first mode adopted for a proper and regular conveyance of letters was in 1642, weekly, and on horseback to every part of the kingdom. The present improved system by mail-coaches was not introduced until 1782."

cent power, whose operations can scarcely be applied, except for good, and accomplish in an eminent degree some of the high purposes set forth in the preamble of the constitution, forming a more perfect union, providing for the common defence, and promoting the general welfare.

§ 1121. Under the confederation, (art. 9,) congress was invested with the sole and exclusive power of " establishing and regulating post-offices *from one state to another* throughout the United States, and exacting such postage on the papers passing through the same, as may be requisite to defray the expenses of the said office."[1] How little was accomplished under it will be at once apparent from the fact, that there were but seventy-five post-offices established in all the United States in the year 1789; that the whole amount of postage in 1790 was only $37,935; and the number of miles travelled by the mails only 1875.[2] This may be in part attributable to the state of the country, and the depression of all the commercial and other interests of the country. But the power itself was so crippled by the confederation, that it could accomplish little. The national government did not possess any power, except to establish post-offices from state to state, (leaving perhaps, though not intended, the whole interior post-offices in every state to its own regulation,) and the postage, that could be taken, was not allowed to be be-

---

[1] There is, in Bioren and Duane's Edition of the Laws of the United States, (Vol. 1, p. 649, &c.) an account of the post-office establishment, during the revolution and before the constitution was adopted. Dr. Franklin was appointed in July, 1775, the first Postmaster General. The act of 1782 directed, that a mail should be carried at least once in every week to and from each stated post-office.

[2] American Almanac, 1830, p. 217; Dr. Lieber's Encyc. Amer. article *Posts*, ante, vol. iii. p. 24, note.

yond the actual expenses; thus shutting up the avenue
to all improvements. In short, like every other power
under the confederation, it perished from a jealousy,
which required it to live, and yet refused it appropriate
nourishment and sustenance.[1]

§ 1122. In the first draft of the constitution, the
clause stood thus, "Congress shall have power to establish post-offices." It was subsequently amended by
adding the words "and post-roads," by the vote of six
states against five; and then, as amended, it passed
without opposition.[2] It is observable, that the confederation gave only the power to establish and regulate
post-offices; and therefore the amendment introduced
a new and substantive power, unknown before in the
national government.

§ 1123. Upon the construction of this clause of the
constitution, two opposite opinions have been expressed. One maintains, that the power to establish post-
offices and post-roads can intend no more, than the
power to direct, where post-offices shall be kept, and
on what roads the mails shall be carried.[3] Or, as it
has been on other occasions expressed, the power to
establish post-roads is a power to designate, or point out,
what roads shall be mail-roads, and the right of passage
or way along them, when so designated.[4] The other
maintains, that although these modes of exercising the
power are perfectly constitutional; yet they are not the
whole of the power, and do not exhaust it. On the
contrary, the power comprehends the right to make, or
construct any roads, which congress may deem proper

1 See Sergeant on Const. Introduction, p. 17, (2d Edition.)
2 Journal of Convention, 220, 256, 257, 261, 357.
3 4 Elliot's Debates, 279.
4 4 Elliot's Debates, 354; Ibid. 233.

'or the conveyance of the mail, and to keep them in due repair for such purpose.

§ 1124. The grounds of the former opinion seem to be as follows. The power given under the confederation never practically received any other construction. Congress never undertook to make any roads, but merely designated those existing roads, on which the mail should pass. At the adoption of the constitution there is not the slightest evidence, that a different arrangement, as to the limits of the power, was contemplated. On the contrary, it was treated by the Federalist, as a harmless power, and not requiring any comment.[1] The practice of the government, since the adoption of the constitution, has conformed to this view. The first act passed by congress, in 1792, is entitled " an act to establish post-offices and post-roads." The first section of this act established many post-offices as well as post-roads. It was continued, amended, and finally repealed, by a series of acts from 1792 to 1810; all of which acts have the same title, and the same provisions declaring certain roads to be post-roads. From all of which it is manifest, that the legislature supposed, that they had established post-roads in the sense of the constitution, when they declared certain roads, then in existence, to be post-roads, and designated the routes, along which the mails were to pass. As a farther proof upon this subject, the statute book contains many acts passed at various times, during a period of more than twenty years, discontinuing certain post-roads.[2] A strong argument is also derivable from the practice of continental Europe, which must be presumed to have been known to the framers of the constitution. Different

[1] The Federalist, No. 42.   [2] 4 Elliot's Debates, 354.

nations in Europe have established posts, and for mutual convenience have stipulated a free passage for the posts arriving on their frontiers through their territories. It is probable, that the constitution intended nothing more by this provision, than to enable congress to do by law, without consulting the states, what in Europe can be done only by treaty or compact. It was thought necessary to insert an express provision in the constitution, enabling the government to exercise jurisdiction over ten miles square for a seat of government, and of such places, as should be ceded by the states for forts, arsenals, and other similar purposes. It is incredible, that such solicitude should have been expressed for such inconsiderable spots, and yet, that at the same time, the constitution intended to convey by implication the power to construct roads throughout the whole country, with the consequent right to use the timber and soil, and to exercise jurisdiction over them. It may be said, that, unless congress have the power, the mail-roads might be obstructed, or discontinued at the will of the state authorities. But that consequence does not follow ; for when a road is declared by law to be a mail-road, the United States have a right of way over it ; and, until the law is repealed, such an interest in the use of it, as that the state authorities could not obstruct it.[1] The terms of the constitution are perfectly satisfied by this limited construction, and the power of congress to make whatever roads they may please, in any state, would be a most serious inroad upon the rights and jurisdiction of the states. It never could have been contemplated.[2]

---

[1] 4 Elliot's Debates, 354, 355.

[2] Aware of the difficulties attendant upon this extremely strict construction, another has been attempted, which is more liberal, but which

§ 1125. The grounds, upon which the other opinion is maintained, are as follows: This is not a question of implied power ; but of express power. We are

---

it has been thought (as will be hereafter seen) to surrender the substance of the argument. It will be most satisfactory to give it in the very words of its most distinguished advocate:

"The first of these grants is in the following words: 'Congress shall 'have power to establish post-offices and post-roads.' What is the just import of these words, and the extent of the grant? The word 'establish' is the ruling term ; 'post-offices and post-roads' are the subjects, on which it acts. The question, therefore, is, what power is ganted by that word? The sense, in which words are commonly used, is that, in which they are to be understood in all transactions between public bodies and individuals. The intention of the parties is to prevail, and there is no better way of ascertaining it, than by giving to the terms used their ordinary import. If we were to ask any number of our most enlightened citizens, who had no connexion with public affairs, and whose minds were unprejudiced, what was the import of the word 'establish,' and the extent of the grant, which it controls, we do not think, that there would be any difference of opinion among them. We are satisfied, that all of them would answer, that a power was thereby given to congress to fix on the towns, court-houses, and other places, throughout our Union, at which there should be post-offices ; the routes, by which the mails should be carried from one post-office to another, so as to diffuse intelligence as extensively, and to make the institution as useful, as possible ; to fix the postage to be paid on every letter and packet thus carried to support the establishment ; and to protect the post-offices and mails from robbery, by punishing those, who should commit the offence. The idea of a right to lay off the roads of the United States, on a general scale of improvement ; to take the soil from the proprietor by force ; to establish turnpikes and tolls, and to punish offenders in the manner stated above, would never occur to any such person. The use of the existing road, by the stage, mail-carrier, or post-boy, in passing over it, as others do, is all, that would be thought of ; the jurisdiction and soil remaining to the state, with a right in the state, or those authorized by its legislature, to change the road at pleasure.

"The intention of the parties is supported by other proof, which ought to place it beyond all doubt. In the former act of government, (the confederation,) we find a grant for the same purpose, expressed in the following words: "The United States, in congress assembled, shall have the sole and exclusive right and power of establishing and regulating post-offices from one state to another, throughout the United States, and of exacting such postage on the papers passing through the same, as

not now looking to what are properly incidents, or means to carry into effect given powers; but are to construe the terms of an express power. The words o.

---

may be requisite to defray the expenses of the said post-office.' The term 'establish' was likewise the ruling one, in that instrument, and was evidently intended, and understood, to give a power simply and solely to fix where there should be post-offices. By transferring this term from the confederation into the constitution, it was doubtless intended, that it should be understood in the same sense in the latter, that it was in the former instrument, and to be applied alike to post-offices and post-roads. In whatever sense it is applied to post-offices, it must be applied in the same sense to post-roads. But it may be asked, if such was the intention, why were not all the other terms of the grant transferred with it? The reason is obvious. The confederation being a bond of union between independent states, it was necessary, in granting the powers, which were to be exercised over them, to be very explicit and minute in defining the powers granted. But the constitution, to the extent of its powers, having incorporated the states into one government, like the government of the states, individually, fewer words, in defining the powers granted by it, were not only adequate, but perhaps better adapted to the purpose. We find, that brevity is a characteristic of the instrument. Had it been intended to convey a more enlarged power in the constitution, than had been granted in the confederation, surely the same controlling term would not have been used; or other words would have been added, to show such intention, and to mark the extent, to which the power should be carried. It is a liberal construction of the powers granted in the constitution, by this term, to include in it all the powers, that were granted in the confederation by terms, which specifically defined, and (as was supposed) extended their limits. It would be absurd to say, that, by omitting from the constitution any portion of the phraseology, which was deemed important in the confederation, the import of that term was enlarged, and with it the powers of the constitution, in a proportional degree, beyond what they were in the confederation. The right to exact postage and to protect the post-offices and mails from robbery, by punishing the offenders, may fairly be considered, as incidents to the grant, since, without it, the object of the grant might be defeated. Whatever is absolutely necessary to the accomplishment of the object of the grant, though not specified, may fairly be considered as included in it. Beyond this the doctrine of incidental power cannot be carried.

"If we go back to the origin of our settlements and institutions, and trace their progress down to the Revolution, we shall see, that it was in this sense, and in none other, that the power was exercised by all our

the constitution are , "Congress shall have power to "establish post-offices and post-roads." What is the true meaning of these words ? There is no such known

---

colonial governments. Post-offices were made for the country, and not the country for them. They are the offspring of improvement. They never go before it. Settlements are first made ; after which the progress is uniform and simple, extending to objects in regular order, most necessary to the comfort of man ; schools, places of public worship, court-houses, and markets ; post-offices follow. Roads may, indeed, be said to be coeval with settlements. They lead to all the places mentioned, and to every other, which the various and complicated interests of society require.

"It is believed, that not one example can be given, from the first settlement of our country to the adoption of this constitution, of a post-office being established, without a view to existing roads ; or of a single road having been made by pavement, turnpike, &c. for the sole purpose of accommodating a post-office. Such, too, is the uniform progress of all societies. In granting then this power to the United States, it was, undoubtedly, intended by the framers and ratifiers of the constitution, to convey it in the sense and extent only, in which it had been understood and exercised by the previous authorities of the country.

"This conclusion is confirmed by the object of the grant and the manner of its execution. The object is the transportation of the mail throughout the United States, which may be done on horse-back, and was so done, until lately, since the establishment of stages. Between the great towns, and in other places, where the population is dense, stages are preferred, because they afford an additional opportunity to make a profit from passengers. But where the population is sparse, and on cross roads, it is generally carried on horseback. Unconnected with passengers and other objects, it cannot be doubted, that the mail itself may be carried in every part of our Union, with nearly as much economy, and greater despatch, on horseback, than in a stage ; and in many parts with much greater. In every part of the Union, in which stages can be preferred, the roads are sufficiently good, provided those, which serve for every other purpose, will accommodate them. In every other part, where horses alone are used, if other people pass them on horseback, surely the mail-carrier can. For an object so simple and so easy in the execution, it would, doubtless, excite surprise, if it should be thought proper to appoint commissioners to lay off the country on a great scheme of improvement, with the power to shorten distances, reduce heights, level mountains, and pave surfaces.

"If the United States possessed the power contended for under this grant, might they not, in adopting the roads of the individual states for

sense of the word " establish," as to " direct," " designate," or " point out."   And if there were, it does not follow, that a special or peculiar sense is to be given to the words, not conformable to their general meaning, unless that sense be required by the context, or, at least, better harmonizes with the subject matter, and objects of the power, than any other sense.   That cannot be pretended in the present case.   The received general meanings, if not the only meanings of the word " establish," are, to settle firmly, to confirm, to fix, to form or modify, to found, to build firmly, to erect permanently.[1] And it is no small objection to any construction, that it requires the word to be deflected from its received and usual meaning; and gives it a meaning unknown to, and unacknowledged by lexicographers. Especially is it objectionable and inadmissible, where the received and common meaning harmonizes with the subject matter; and if the very end were required, no more exact expression could ordinarily be used.   In legislative acts, in state papers, and in the constitution itself, the word is found with the same general sense now insisted on; that is, in the sense of, to create, to form, to make, to construct, to settle, to build up with a view to permanence.   Thus, our treaties speak of establishing reg-

the carriage of the mail, as has been done, assume jurisdiction over them, and preclude a right to interfere with or alter them? Might they not establish turnpikes, and exercise all the other acts of sovereignty, above stated, over such roads, necessary to protect them from injury, and defray the expense of repairing them? Surely, if the right exists, these consequences necessarily followed, as soon as the road was established.   The absurdity of such a pretension must be apparent to all, who examine it.   In this way, a large portion of the territory of every state might be taken from it; for there is scarcely a road in any state, which will not be used for the transportation of the mail.   A new field for legislation and internal government would thus be opened." President Monroe's Message, of 4th May, 1822, p. 24 to 27.

[1] Johnson's Dict. *ad verb.* ; Webster's Dict. ibid.

ulations of trade. Our laws speak of *establishing* navy-hospitals, where land is to be purchased, work done, and buildings erected; of *establishing* trading-houses with the Indians, where houses are to be erected and other things done. The word is constantly used in a like sense in the articles of confederation. The authority is therein given to congress of *establishing* rules in cases of captures; of *establishing* courts of appeal in cases of capture; and, what is directly in point, of *establishing* and *regulating post-offices*. Now, if the meaning of the word here was simply to point out, or designate post-offices, there would have been an end of all further authority, except of regulating the post-offices, so designated and pointed out. Under such circumstances, how could it have been possible under that instrument (which declares, that every power not *expressly* delegated shall be retained by the states) to find any authority to carry the mail, or to make contracts for this purpose? much more to prohibit any other persons under penalties from conveying letters, despatches, or other packets from one place to another of the United States? The very first act of the continental congress on this subject was, " for *establishing* a post," (not a post office ;) and it directed, " that a line of posts be appointed under the direction of the postmaster general, from Falmouth, in New-England, to Savannah, in Georgia, with as many cross-posts, as he shall think fit ; " and it directs the necessary expenses of the "*establishment*" beyond the revenue to be paid out by the United Colonies.[1] Under this, and other supplementary acts, the establishment continued until October, 1782, when, under the articles of confederation,

---

[1] Ordinance of 26th July 1775; 1 Journal of Congress, 177, 178.

the establishment was re-organized, and, instead of a
mere appointment and designation of post-offices, provision was made, " that a continued communication of
posts throughout the United States shall be *established*
and maintained," &c.; and many other regulations
were made wholly incompatible with the narrow construction of the words now contended for.[1]

§ 1126. The constitution itself also uniformly uses
the word "establish" in the general sense, and never
in this peculiar and narrow sense. It speaks in the
preamble of one motive being, "to *establish* justice,"
and that the people do *ordain* and *establish* this constitution. It gives power to *establish* an uniform rule
of naturalization and uniform laws on the subject of
bankruptcies. Does not this authorize congress to
make, create, form, and construct laws on these subjects? It declares, that the judicial power shall be vested
in one supreme court and in such inferior courts, as
congress may, from time to time, *ordain* and *establish*.
Is not a power to *establish* courts a power to create, and
make, and regulate them? It declares, that the ratification of nine states shall be sufficient for the *establishment* of this constitution between the states so ratifying
the same.[2] And in one of the amendments, it provides, that congress shall make no law respecting an
establishment of religion. It is plain, that to construe
the word in any of these cases, as equivalent to *designate*, or *point out*, would be absolutely absurd. The
clear import of the word is, to create, and form, and fix
in a settled manner. Referring it to the subject matter, the sense, in no instance, can be mistaken. To

---

[1] Ordinance, 18 Oct. 1782; 1 U. S. Laws, (Bioren & Duane,) 651;
7 Journ. of Congress, 503.
[2] See 4 Elliot's Debates, 356.

establish courts is to create, and form, and regulate them. To establish rules of naturalization is to frame and confirm such rules. To establish laws on the subject of bankruptcies is to frame, fix, and pass them. To establish the constitution is to make, and fix, and erect it, as a permanent form of government. In the same manner, to establish post-offices and post-roads is to frame and pass laws, to erect, make, form, regulate, and preserve them. Whatever is necessary, whatever is appropriate to this purpose, is within the power.

§ 1127. Besides; upon this narrow construction, what becomes of the power itself? If the power be to *point out*, or *designate post-offices*, then it supposes, that there already exist some offices, out of which a designation can be made. It supposes a power to select among things of the same nature. Now, if an office does not already exist at the place, how can it be designated, as a post-office? If you cannot create a post-office, you can do no more, than mark out one already existing. In short, these rules of strict construction might be pressed still farther; and, as the power is only given to designate, not offices, but post-offices, the latter must be already in existence; for otherwise the power must be read, to designate what offices shall be used, as post-offices, or at what places post-offices shall be recognised; either of which is a departure from the supposed literal interpretation.

§ 1128. In the next place, let us see, what upon this narrow interpretation becomes of the power in another aspect. It is to establish post-offices. Now, the argument supposes, that this does not authorize the purchase or erection of a building for an office; but it does necessarily suppose the authority to erect or create an office; to regulate the duties of the officer; and to fix

a place, (*officina*) where his business is to be performed.
It then unavoidably includes, not merely a power to
designate, but a power to create the thing intended,
and to do all other acts to make the thing effectual ; that
is, to create the whole system appropriate to a post-
office establishment.   Now, this involves a plain departure from the very ground of the argument.   It is no
longer a power to designate a thing, or mark out a
route ; but it is a power to create, and fix every other
thing necessary and appropriate to post-offices.   The
argument, therefore, resorts to implications in order to
escape from its own narrow interpretation ; and the
very power to designate becomes a power to create
offices and frame systems, and institute penalties, and
raise revenue, and make contracts.   It becomes, in
fact, the very thing, which the other argument supposes to be the natural sense, viz. the power to erect,
and maintain a post-office establishment.

§ 1129. Under any other interpretation, the power
itself would become a mere nullity.   If resort be had to
a very strict and critical examination of the words, the
power "to establish post-offices" imports no more,
than the power to create the offices intended ; that
done, the power is exhausted ; and the words are satisfied.   The power to create the office does not necessarily include the power to carry the mail, or regulate
the conveyance of letters, or employ carriers.   The
one may exist independently of the other.   A state
might without absurdity possess the right to carry the
mail, while the United States might possess the right to
designate the post-offices, at which it should be opened,
and provide the proper officers ; or the converse powers might belong to each.   It would not be impracticable, though it would be extremely inconvenient and

embarrassing. Yet, no man ever imagined such a construction to be justifiable. And why not? Plainly, because constitutions of government are not instruments to be scrutinized, and weighed, upon metaphysical or grammatical niceties. They do not turn upon ingenious subtleties; but are adapted to the business and exigencies of human society; and the powers given are understood in a large sense, in order to secure the public interests. Common sense becomes the guide, and prevents men from dealing with mere logical abstractions. Under the confederation, this very power to establish post-offices was construed to include the other powers already named, and others far more remote. It never entered into the heads of the wise men of those days, that they possessed a power to create post-offices, without the power to create all the other things necessary to make post-offices of some human use. They did not dream of post-offices without posts, or mails, or routes, or carriers. It would have been worse than a mockery. Under the confederation, with the strict limitation of powers, which that instrument conferred, they put into operation a large system for the appropriate purposes of a post-office establishment.[1] No man ever doubted, or denied the constitutionality of this exercise of the power. It was largely construed to meet the obvious intent, for which it was delegated. The words of the constitution are more extensive, than those of the confederation. In the latter, the words to establish *"post-roads"* are not to be found. These words were certainly added for some purpose. And if any, for what other purpose, than to enable congress to lay out and make roads?[2]

---

[1] See Act of 18th of October, 1782.
[2] 4 Elliot's Debates, 356.

§ 1130. Under the constitution congress has, without any questioning, given a liberal construction to the power to establish post-offices and post-roads. It has been truly said, that in a strict sense, "this power is executed by the single act of making the establishment. But from this has been inferred the power and duty of carrying the mail along the post-road from one post-office to another. And from this implied power has been again inferred the right to punish those, who steal letters from the post-office, or rob the mail. It may be said with some plausibility, that the right to carry the mail, and to punish those, who rob it, is not indispensably necessary to the establishment of a post-office and a post-road. This right is indeed essential to the beneficial exercise of the power; but not indispensably necessary to its existence."[1]

§ 1131. The whole practical course of the government upon this subject, from its first organization down to the present time, under every administration, has repudiated the strict and narrow construction of the words above mentioned.[2] The power to establish post-offices and post-roads has never been understood to include no more, than the power to point out and designate post-offices and post-roads. Resort has been constantly had to the more expanded sense of the word "establish;" and no other sense can include the objects, which the post-office laws have constantly included. Nay, it is not only not true, that these laws have stopped short of an exposition of the words sufficiently broad to justify the making of roads; but they have included exercises of power far more remote from the

1 M'Culloch v. Maryland, 4 Wheat. R. 316, 417.
2 See the laws referred to in Post-Master-General v. Early, 12 Wheat. R. 136, 144, 145.

immediate objects. If the practice of the government is, therefore, of any weight in giving a constitutional interpretation, it is in favour of the liberal interpretation of the clause.

§ 1132. The fact, if true, that congress have not hitherto made any roads for the carrying of the mail, would not affect the right, or touch the question. It is not doubted, that the power has been properly carried into effect, by making certain state roads post-roads. When congress found those roads suited to the purpose, there could be no constitutional reason for refusing to establish them, as mail-routes. The exercise of authority was clearly within the scope of the power. But the argument would have it, that, because this exercise of the power, clearly within its scope, has been hitherto restrained to making existing roads post-roads, therefore congress cannot proceed constitutionally to make a post-road, where no road now exists. This is clearly what lawyers call a *non sequitur*. It might with just as much propriety be urged, that, because congress had not hitherto used a particular means to execute any other given power, therefore it could not now do it. If, for instance, congress had never provided a ship for the navy, except by purchase, they could not now authorize ships to be built for a navy, or *à converso*. If they had not laid a tax on certain goods, it could not now be done. If they had never erected a custom-house, or court-house, they could not now do it. Such a mode of reasoning would be deemed by all persons wholly indefensible.

§ 1133. But it is not admitted, that congress have not exercised this very power with reference to this very object. By the act of 21st of April, 1806, (ch. 41,) the president was authorized to cause to be opened a

road from the frontier of Georgia, on the route from
Athens to New-Orleans; and to cause to be opened a
road or roads through the territory, then lately ceded
by the Indians to the United States, from the river
Mississippi to the Ohio, and to the former Indian boundary line, which was established by the treaty of Green-
ville; and to cause to be opened a road from Nashville,
in the state of Tennessee, to Natchez, in the Mississippi territory.   The same remark applies to the act of
29th of March, 1806, (ch. 19,) "to regulate the laying
"out and making a road from Cumberland, in the state
"of Maryland, to the state of Ohio."   Both of these
acts were passed in the administration of President
Jefferson, who, it is well known, on other occasions
maintained a strict construction of the constitution.

§ 1134. But passing by considerations of this nature,
why does not the power to establish post-offices and
post-roads include the power to make and construct
them, when wanted, as well as the power to establish a
navy-hospital, or a custom-house, a power to make and
construct them?   The latter is not doubted by any
persons; why then is the former?   In each case, the
sense of the ruling term "establish" would seem to be
the same; in each, the power may be carried into effect
by means short of constructing, or purchasing the things
authorized.   A temporary use of a suitable site or
buildings may possibly be obtained with, or without
hire.   Besides; why may not congress purchase, or
erect a post-office building, and buy the necessary
land, if it be in their judgment advisable?   Can there
be a just doubt, that a power to establish post-offices
includes this power, just as much, as a power to establish custom-houses would to build the latter?   Would
it not be a strange construction to say, that the abstract

office might be created, but not the officina, or place, where it could be exercised? There are many places peculiarly fit for local post-offices, where no suitable building might be found. And, if a power to construct post-office buildings exists, where is the restraint upon constructing roads?

§ 1135. It is said, that there is no reason, why congress should be invested with such a power, seeing that the state roads may, and will furnish convenient routes for the mail. When the state-roads do furnish such routes, there can certainly be no sound policy in congress making other routes. But there is a great difference between the policy of exercising a power, and the right of exercising it. But, suppose the state-roads do not furnish (as in point of fact they did not at the time of the adoption of the constitution, and as hereafter, for many exigencies of the government in times of war and otherwise, they may not) suitable routes for the mails, what is then to be done? Is the power of the general government to be paralyzed? Suppose a mail-road is out of repair and founderous, cannot congress authorize the repair of it? If they can, why then not make it originally? Is the one more a means to an end, than the other? If not, then the power to carry the mails may be obstructed; nay, may be annihilated by the neglect of a state.[1] Could it have been the intention of the constitution, in the exercise of this most vital power, to make it dependent upon the will, or the pleasure of the states?

§ 1136. It has been said, that when once a state-road is made a post-road by an act of congress, the national government have acquired such an interest in

---

[1] 4 Elliot's Debates, 356.

the use of it, that it is not competent for the state
authorities to obstruct it.   But how can this be made
out?   If the power of congress is merely to select or
designate the mail-roads, what interest in the use is
acquired by the national government any more, than by
any travellers upon the road?   Where is the power
given to acquire it?   Can it be pretended, that a state
may not discontinue a road, after it has been once
established, as a mail-road?   The power has been
constantly exercised by the states ever since the adoption of the constitution.   The states have altered, and
discontinued, and changed such roads at their pleasure.   It would be a most truly alarming inroad upon
state sovereignty to declare, that a state-road could
never be altered or discontinued after it had once become a mail-road.   That would be to supersede all state
authority over their own roads.   If the states can discontinue their roads, why not obstruct them?   Who
shall compel them to repair them, when discontinued,
or to keep them at any time in good repair?   No one
ever yet contended, that the national government possessed any such compulsive authority.   If, then, the
states may alter or discontinue their roads, or suffer
them to go out of repair, is it not obvious, that the
power to carry the mails may be retarded or defeated
in a great measure by this constitutional exercise of
state power?   And, if it be the right and duty of congress to provide adequate means for the transportation
of the mails, wherever the public good requires it, what
limit is there to these means, other than that they are
appropriate to the end?[1]

---

[1] 4 Elliot's Debates, 356.

§ 1137. In point of fact, congress cannot be said, in any exact sense, to have yet executed the power to establish post-roads, if by that power we are to understand the designation of particular state-roads, on which the mails shall be carried. The general course has been to designate merely the towns, between which the mails shall be carried, without ascertaining the particular roads at all. Thus, the Act of 20th of February, 1792, ch. 7, (which is but a sample of the other acts,) declares, that "the following roads be established, as post-roads, namely, from Wiscasset in the District of Maine to Savannah in Georgia, by the following route, to wit : Portland, Portsmouth, Newburyport, Ipswich, Salem, Boston, Worcester," &c. &c.; without pointing out any road between those places, on which it should be carried. There are different roads from several of these places to the others. Suppose one of these roads should be discontinued, could the mail-carriers insist upon travelling it ?

§ 1138. The truth is, that congress have hitherto acted under the power to a very limited extent only ; and will forever continue to do so from principles of public policy and economy, except in cases of an extraordinary nature. There can be no motive to use the power, except for the public good ; and circumstances may render it indispensable to carry it out in particular cases to its full limits. It has already occurred, and may hereafter occur, that post-roads may be important and necessary for the purpose of the Union, in peace as well as in war, between places, where there is not any good state-road, and where the amount of travel would not justify any state in an expenditure equal to the construction of such a state-road.[1] In such cases, as the benefit is for the Union, the burthen ought to be borne by the Union. Without any invidious distinction, it may be stated, that the winter mail-route between Philadelphia, and Baltimore, and Washington, by the way of the Susquehannah and Havre de Grace, has been before congress under this very aspect. There is no one, who will doubt the importance of the best post-road in that direction ; (the nearest between the two cities ;) and yet it is obvious, that the nation alone can be justly called upon to provide the road.

§ 1139. Let a case be taken, when state policy or state hostility shall lead the legislature to close up, or discontinue a road, the nearest and the best between two great states, rivals perhaps for the trade and intercourse of a third state, shall it be said, that congress has no right to make, or repair a road for keeping open for the mail the best means of communication between those states ? May the national government be compelled to take the most inconvenient and indirect routes for the mail ?[2] In other words, have the states a power to say, how, and upon what roads the mails shall, and shall not travel ? If so, then in relation to post-roads, the states, and not the Union, are supreme.

§ 1140. But it is said, that it would be dangerous to allow any power in the Union to lay out and construct post-roads ; for then the exercise of the power would supercede the state jurisdiction. This is an utter mistake. If congress should lay out and construct a post-road in a state, it would still be a road within the ordinary territorial jurisdiction of the state. The state could not, indeed, supercede, or obstruct, or discon-

---

1 See Rawle on the Constitution, ch. 9, p. 103, 104.
2 4 Elliot's Debates, 356.

tinue it, or prevent the Union from repairing it, or the mails from travelling on it. But subject to these incidental rights, the right of territory and jurisdiction, civilly and criminally, would be complete and perfect in the state. The power of congress over the road would be limited to the mere right of passage and preservation. That of the state would be general, and embrace all other objects. Congress undoubtedly has power to purchase lands in a state for any public purposes, such as forts, arsenals, and dock-yards. So, they have a right to erect hospitals, custom-houses, and court-houses in a state. But no person ever imagined, that these places were thereby removed from the general jurisdiction of the state. On the contrary, they are universally understood for all other purposes, not inconsistent with the constitutional rights and uses of the Union, to be subject to state authority and rights.

§ 1141. The clause respecting cessions of territory for the seat of government, and for forts, arsenals, dock-yards, &c. has nothing to do with the point. But if it had, it is favourable to the power. That clause was necessary for the purpose of ousting the state jurisdiction in the specified cases, and for vesting an *exclusive* jurisdiction in the general government. No general or *exclusive* jurisdiction is either required, or would be useful in regard to post-roads. It would be inconvenient for congress to assemble in a place, where it had not exclusive jurisdiction. And an exclusive jurisdiction would seem indispensable over forts, arsenals, dock-yards, and other places of a like nature. But surely it will not be pretended, that congress could not erect a fort, or magazine, in a place within a state, unless the state should cede the territory. The only effect would be, that the jurisdiction in such a

case would not be exclusive. Suppose a state should
prohibit a sale of any of the lands within its boundaries
by its own citizens, for any public purposes indispensable for the Union, either military or civil, would not
congress possess a constitutional right to demand, and
appropriate land within the state for such purposes,
making a just compensation? Exclusive jurisdiction
over a road is one thing ; the right to make it is quite
another. A turnpike company may be authorized to
make a road; and yet may have no jurisdiction, or at
least no exclusive jurisdiction over it.

§ 1142. The supposed silence of the Federalist [1]
proves nothing. That work was principally designed to
meet objections, and remove prejudices. The post-
office establishment in its nature, and character, and
purposes, was so generally deemed useful and convenient, and unexceptionable, that it was wholly unnecessary to expound its value, or enlarge upon its benefits.

§ 1143. Such is a summary of the principal reasoning on each side of this much contested question. The
reader must decide for himself, upon the preponderance of the argument.

§ 1144. This question, as to the right to lay out
and construct post-roads, is wholly distinct from that of
the more general power to lay out and make canals,
and military and other roads. The latter power may
not exist at all ; even if the former should be unquestionable. The latter turns upon a question of
implied power, as incident to given powers.[2] The
former turns upon the true interpretation of words
of express grant. Nobody doubts, that the words
" establish post-roads," may, without violating their re-

---

1 No. 42.   2 See Rawle on the Constitution, ch. 9, p. 104.

ceived meaning in other cases, be construed so, as to include the power to lay out and construct roads. The question is, whether that is the true sense of the words, as used in the constitution. And here, if ever, the rule of interpretation, which requires us to look at the nature of the instrument, and the objects of the power, as a national power, in order to expound its meaning, must come into operation.

§ 1145. But whatever be the extent of the power, narrow or large, there will still remain another inquiry, whether it is an exclusive power, or concurrent in the states. This is not, perhaps, a very important inquiry, because it is admitted on all sides, that it can be exercised only in subordination to the power of congress, if it be concurrent in the states. A learned commentator deems it concurrent, inasmuch as there seems nothing in the constitution, or in the nature of the thing itself, which may not be exercised by both governments at the same time, without prejudice or interference; but subordinate, because, whenever any power is expressly granted to congress, it is to be taken for granted, that it is not to be contravened by the authority of any particular state. A state might, therefore, establish a post-road, or post-office, on any route, where congress had not established any.[1] On the other hand, another learned commentator is of opinion, that the power is exclusive in congress, so far as relates to the conveyance of letters, &c.[2] It is highly improbable, that any state will attempt any exercise of the power, considering the difficulty of carrying it into effect, without the co-operation of congress.

---

[1] 1 Tuck. Black. Comm. App. 265.
[2] Rawle on the Constitution, ch. 9, p. 103, 104.

CHAPTER XIX.

POWER TO PROMOTE SCIENCE AND USEFUL ARTS.

§ 1146. THE next power of congress is, " to promote " the progress of science and the useful arts, by secur- "ing, for limited times, to authors and inventors the "exclusive right to their respective writings and dis- " coveries."

§ 1147. This power did not exist under the confed- eration ; and its utility does not seem to have been questioned. The copyright of authors in their works had, before the revolution, been decided in Great Britain to be a common law right ; and it was regulated and limited under statutes passed by parliament upon that subject.[1] The right to useful inventions seems, with equal reason, to belong to the inventors ; and, accord- ingly, it was saved out of the statute of monopolies in the reign of King James the First, and has ever since been allowed for a limited period, not exceeding four- teen years.[2] It was doubtless to this knowledge of the common law and statuteable rights of authors and in- ventors, that we are to attribute this constitution- al provision.[3] It was beneficial to all parties, that the national government should possess this power ; to authors and inventors, because, otherwise, they would have been subjected to the varying laws and systems of the different states on this subject, which would im-

[1] 2 Black. Comm. 406, 407, and Christian's note, (5); 4 Burr. R. 2303 ; Rawle on Const. ch. 9, p. 105, 106 ; 2 Kent's Comm. Lect. 36, p. 306, 307, 314, 315.
[2] 2 Black. Comm. 407, and Christian's note, (8) ; 4 Black. Comm. 159 ; 2 Kent's Comm. Lect. 36, p. 299 to 306.
[3] The Federalist, No. 43.

pair, and might even destroy the value of their rights; to the public, as it would promote the progress of science and the useful arts, and admit the people at large, after a short interval, to the full possession and enjoyment of all writings and inventions without restraint. In short, the only boon, which could be offered to inventors to disclose the secrets of their discoveries, would be the exclusive right and profit of them, as a monopoly for a limited period. And authors would have little inducement to prepare elaborate works for the public, if their publication was to be at a large expense, and, as soon as they were published, there would be an unlimited right of depredation and piracy of their copyright. The states could not separately make effectual provision for either of the cases;[1] and most of them, at the time of the adoption of the constitution, had anticipated the propriety of such a grant of power, by passing laws on the subject at the instance of the continental congress.[2]

§ 1148. The power, in its terms, is confined to authors and inventors; and cannot be extended to the introducers of any new works or inventions. This has been thought by some persons of high distinction to be a defect in the constitution.[3] But perhaps the policy of further extending the right is questionable; and, at all events, the restriction has not hitherto operated as any discouragement of science or the arts. It has been doubted, whether congress has authority to decide the fact, that a person is an author or inventor in the sense of the

---

[1] 2 Kent's Comm. Lect. 36, p. 298, 299.

[2] The Federalist, No. 43; See also 1 Tuck. Black. Comm. App. 265, 266; Rawle on Const. ch. 9, p. 105, 106; See Hamilton's Report on Manufactures, § 8, p. 235, &c.

[3] Hamilton's Rep. on Manufactures, § 8, p. 235, 236.

constiution, so as to preclude that question from judicial inquiry. But, at all events, such a construction ought never to be put upon the terms of any general act in favour of a particular inventor, unless it be inevitable.[1]

§ 1149. It has been suggested, that this power is not exclusive, but concurrent with that of the states, so always, that the acts of the latter do not contravene the acts of congress.[2] It has, therefore, been asserted, that where congress go no farther than to secure the right to an author or inventor, the state may regulate the use of such right, or restrain it, so far as it may deem it injurious to the public. Whether this be so or not may be matter for grave inquiry, whenever the question shall arise directly in judgment. At present, it seems wholly unnecessary to discuss it theoretically. But, at any rate, there does not seem to be the same difficulty in affirming, that, as the power of congress extends only to authors and inventors, a state may grant an exclusive right to the possessor or introducer of an art or invention, who does not claim to be an inventor, but has merely introduced it from abroad.[3]

§ 1150. In the first draft of the constitution the clause is not to be found ; but the subject was referred to a committee, (among other propositions,) whose report was accepted, and gave the clause in the very form, in which it now stands in the constitution.[4] A more extensive proposition, " to establish public institutions, " rewards, and immunities for the promotion of agricul-

1 *Evans v. Eaton*, 3 Wheat. R. 454, 513.
2 1 Tuck. Black. Comm. App. 265, 266; *Livingston v. Van Ingen*, 9 John. R. 507.
3 *Livingston v. Van Ingen*, 9 John. R. 507 ; Sergeant on Const. ch. 28, [ch. 31.]
4 Journ. of Convention, 260, 327, 328, 329.

ture, commerce, and manufactures" was (as has been before stated) made, and silently abandoned.[1] Congress have already, by a series of laws on this subject, provided for the rights of authors and inventors ; and, without question, the exercise of the power has operated as an encouragement to native genius, and to the solid advancement of literature and the arts.

§ 1151. The next power of congress is, "to consti-"tute tribunals inferiour to the Supreme Court." This clause properly belongs to the third article of the constitution ; and will come in review, when we survey the constitution and powers of the judicial department. It will, therefore, be, for the present, passed over.

---

[1] Journal of Convention, 261.

CHAPTER XX.

POWER TO PUNISH PIRACIES AND FELONIES.

§ 1152. The next power of congress is. " to define " and punish piracies and felonies committed on the " high seas, and offences against the law of nations."

§ 1153. By the confederation the sole and exclusive power was given to congress " of appointing courts for the trial of piracies and felonies committed on the high seas." [1] But there was no power expressly given to define and punish piracies and felonies.[2] Congress, however, proceeded to pass an ordinance for the erection of a court for such trials, and prescribed the punishment of death upon conviction of the offence.[3] But they never undertook to define, what piracies or felonies were. It was taken for granted, that these were sufficiently known and understood at the common law ; and that resort might, in all such cases, be had to that law, as the recognised jurisprudence of the Union.[4]

§ 1154. If the clause of the constitution had been confined to piracies, there would not have been any necessity of conferring the power to define the crime,

---

[1] Art. 9.   [2] The Federalist, No. 42.

[3] See Ordinance for trial of piracies and felonies, 5th April, 1781 ; 7 Journ. Cong. 76.

[4] A motion was made in Congress to amend the articles of confederation, by inserting in lieu of the words, as they stand in the instrument, the following, " declaring what acts committed on the high seas shall be deemed piracies and felonies. It was negatived by the vote of nine states against two. The reason, probably, was the extreme reluctance of congress to admit any amendment after the project had been submitted to the states.*

*1 Secret Journals of Congress, 384, June 25, 1778.

since the power to punish would necessarily be held to include the power of ascertaining and fixing the definition of the crime.   Indeed, there would not seem to be the slightest reason to define the crime at all; for piracy is perfectly well known and understood in the law of nations, though it is often found defined in mere municipal codes.[1] By the law of nations, robbery or forcible depredation upon the sea, *animo furandi*, is piracy. The common law, too, recognises, and punishes piracy as an offence, not against its own municipal code, but as an offence against the universal law of nations; a pirate being deemed an enemy of the human race.[2] The common law, therefore, deems piracy to be robbery on the sea; that is, the same crime, which it denominates robbery, when committed on land.[3] And if congress had simply declared, that piracy should be punished with death, the crime would have been sufficiently defined. Congress may as well define by using a term of a known and determinate meaning, as by an express enumeration of all the particulars included in that term; for that is certain, which, by reference, is made certain. If congress should declare murder a felony, no body would doubt, what was intended by murder. And, indeed, if congress should proceed to declare, that homicide, " with malice aforethought," should be deemed murder, and a felony; there would still be the same necessity

1 The Federalist, No. 42; Rawle on Const. ch. 9. p. 107; 2 Elliot's Debates, 389, 390.

2 4 Black. Comm. 71 to 73.

3 Mr. East says, " The offence of piracy, by the common law, consists in committing those acts of robbery and depredation upon the high seas, which, if committed upon land, would have amounted to felony there." *
In giving this definition he has done no more than follow the language of preceding writers on the common law.†

* 2 East, P. C. 796.   † 4 Black. Comm. 71 to 73.

of ascertaining, from the common law, what constituted malice aforethought. So, that there would be no end to difficulties or definitions; for each successive definition might involve some terms, which would still require some new explanation. But the true intent of the constitution in this part, was, not merely to define piracy, as known to the law of nations, but to enumerate what crimes in the national code should be deemed piracies. And so the power has been practically expounded by congress.[1]

§ 1155. But the power is not merely to define and punish piracies, but *felonies*, and *offences* against *the law of nations;* and on this account, the power to define, as well as to punish, is peculiarly appropriate. It has been remarked, that felony is a term of loose signification, even in the common law; and of various import in the statute law of England.[2] Mr. Justice Blackstone says, that felony, in the general acceptation of the English law, comprises every species of crime, which occasioned at common law the forfeiture of lands and goods. This most frequently happens in those crimes, for which a capital punishment either is, or was liable to be inflicted. All offences now capital by the English law are felonies; but there are still some offences, not capital, which are yet felonies, (such as suicide, petty larceny, and homicide by chance medley;[3]) that is, they subject the committers of them to some forfeiture, either of lands or goods.[4] But the idea of capital punishment has now become so associated, in the English law, with the idea of felony, that if an act of parliament makes a new offence felony, the

---

1 *United States* v. *Smith,* 5 Wheat. R. 153, 158 to 163.
2 The Federalist. No. 42; 2 Elliot's Deb. 389, 390.
3 Co. Litt. 391.   4 4 Black. Comm. 93 to 98.

law implies, that it shall be punished with death, as well as with forfeiture.[1]

§ 1156. Lord Coke has given a somewhat different account of the meaning of felony; for he says "*ex vi termini significat quodlibet capitale crimen felleo animo perpetratum;*" (that is, it signifies every capital offence committed with a felonious intent;) "in which sense murder is said to be done *per feloniam,* and is so appropriated by law, as that *felonice* cannot be expressed by any other word.[2] This has been treated as a fanciful derivation, and not as correct, as that of Mr. J. Blackstone, who has followed out that of Spelman.[3]

§ 1157. But whatever may be the true import of the word felony at the common law, with reference to municipal offences, in relation to offences on the high seas, its meaning is necessarily somewhat indeterminate; since the term is not used in the criminal jurisprudence of the Admiralty in the technical sense of the common law.[4] Lord Coke long ago stated, that a pardon of felonies would not pardon piracy, for "piracy or robbery on the high seas was no felony, whereof the common law took any knowledge, &c.; but was only punishable by the civil law, &c.; the attainder by which law wrought no forfeiture of lands or corruption of blood."[5]   And he added, that the statute of 28 Henry 8, ch. 15, which created the High Commission Court for the trial of "all treasons, felonies, robberies, murders, and confederacies, committed in or upon the high sea, &c.," did not alter

---

[1] 4 Black. Comm. 98 ; See also 1 Hawk. P. C. ch. 37, (Curwood's Edit. ch. 7.)
[2] Co. Litt. 391 ; 1 Hawk. P. C. ch. 37.
[3] See 1 Curwood's Hawk. P. C. ch. 7, note p, 71.
[4] *United States* v. *Smith,* 5 Wheat. R. 153, 159.
[5] 3 Inst. 112.

the offence, or make the offence felony, but left the offence as it was before the act, viz. felony only by the civil law.[1]

§ 1158. Offences against the law of nations are quite as important, and cannot with any accuracy be said to be completely ascertained, and defined in any public code, recognized by the common consent of nations. In respect, therefore, as well to felonies on the high seas, as to offences against the law of nations, there is a peculiar fitness in giving to congress the power to define, as well as to punish. And there is not the slightest reason to doubt, that this consideration had very great weight with the convention, in producing the phraseology of the clause.[2] On either subject it would have been inconvenient, if not impracticable, to have referred to the codes of the states, as well from their imperfection, as their different enumeration of the offences. Certainty, as well as uniformity, required, that the power to define and punish should reach over the whole of these classes of offences.[3]

§ 1159. What is the meaning of "high seas" within the intent of this clause does not seem to admit of any serious doubt. The phrase embraces not only the waters of the ocean, which are out of sight of land, but the waters on the sea coast below low water mark, whether within the territorial boundaries of a foreign nation, or of a domestic state.[4] Mr. Justice Blackstone has remarked, that the *main sea* or high sea begins at the low water mark. But between the high water

[1] 3 Inst. 112; Co. Lect. 391, a.

[2] *United States* v. *Smith*, 5 Wheat. R. 153, 159.

[3] The Federalist, No. 42 ; Sergeant on Const. ch. 28, (ch. 30;) Rawle on Const. ch. 9, p. 107.

[4] *United States* v. *Pirates*, 5 Wheat. R. 184, 200, 204, 206 ; *United States* v. *Willberger*, 5 Wheat. R. 76, 94.

mark and the low water mark, where the tide ebbs and flows, the common law and the admiralty have *divisum imperium*, an alternate jurisdiction, one upon the water, when it is full sea; the other upon the land, when it is an ebb.[1] He doubtless here refers to the waters of the ocean on the sea-coast, and not in creeks and inlets. Lord Hale says, that the sea is either that, which lies within the body of the county or without. That, which lies without the body of a county, is called the main sea, or ocean.[2] So far, then, as regards the states of the Union, "high seas" may be taken to mean that part of the ocean, which washes the sea-coast, and is without the body of any county, according to the common law; and, so far as regards foreign nations, any waters on their sea-coast, below low-water mark.[3]

§ 1160. Upon the propriety of granting this power to the national government, there does not seem to have been any controversy; or if any, none of a serious nature. It is obvious, that this power has an intimate connexion and relation with the power to regulate commerce and intercourse with foreign nations, and the rights and duties of the national government in peace and war, arising out of the law of nations. As the United States are responsible to foreign governments for all violations of the law of nations, and as the welfare of the Union is essentially connected with the conduct of our citizens in regard to foreign nations, congress ought to possess the power to define and

---

[1] 1 Black. Comm. 110; Constable's case, 5 Co. R. 106; 3 Inst. 113; 2 East's P. C. 802, 803.

[2] Hale in Harg. Law Tracts, ch. 4, p. 10; 1 Hale P. C. 423, 424.

[3] See Rawle on the Const. ch. 9, p. 107; Sergeant on the Const. ch. 28, [ch. 30;] 1 Kent's Comm. Lect. 17, p. 342, &c.; *United States v. Grush*, 5 Mason's R. 290.

punish all such offences, which may interrupt our inter-course and harmony with, and our duties to them.[1]

§ 1161. Whether this power, so far as it concerns the law of nations, is an exclusive one, has been doubt-ed by a learned commentator.[2] As, up to the present time, that question may be deemed for most purposes to be a mere speculative question, it is not proposed to discuss it, since it may be better reasoned out, when it shall require judicial decision.

§ 1162. The clause, as it was originally reported in the first draft of the constitution, was in substance, though not in language, as it now stands. It was sub-sequently amended; and in the second draft stood in its present terms.[3] There is, however, in the Supple-ment to the Journal, an obscure statement of a question put, to strike out the word "punish," seeming to refer to this clause, which was carried in the affirmative by the vote of six states against five.[4] Yet the constitu-tion itself bears testimony, that it did not prevail.

---

1 See 1 Tucker's Black. Comm. App. 268, 269; Rawle on Const. ch. 9, p. 108.

2 Rawle on Const. ch. 9, p. 108.

3 Journal of Convention, 221, 257 to 259, 357.

4 Journal of Convention, p. 375, 376.

CHAPTER XXI.

THE POWER TO DECLARE WAR AND MAKE CAPTURES.

§ 1163. The next power of congress is to "declare "war, grant letters of marque and reprisal, and make "rules concerning captures on land and water."

§ 1164. A similar exclusive power was given to congress by the confederation.[1] That such a power ought to exist in the national government, no one will deny, who believes, that it ought to have any powers whatsoever, either for offence or defence, for the common good, or for the common protection. It is, therefore, wholly superfluous to reason out the propriety of granting the power.[2] It is self-evident, unless the national government is to be a mere mockery and shadow. The power could not be left without extreme mischief, if not absolute ruin, to the separate authority of the several states; for then it would be at the option of any one to involve the whole in the calamities and burthens of warfare.[3] In the general government it is safe, because there it can be declared only by the majority of the states.

§ 1165. The only practical question upon this subject would seem to be, to what department of the national government it would be most wise and safe to confide this high prerogative, emphatically called the last resort of sovereigns, *ultima ratio regum*. In Great Britain it is the exclusive prerogative of the crown;[4] and in

---

[1] Art. 9; The Federalist, No. 41.
[2] See The Federalist, No. 23, 41.
[3] 1 Tucker's Black. Comm. App. 271.
[4] 1 Black. Comm. 257, 258.

other countries, it is usually, if not universally, confided to the executive department. It might by the constitution have been confided to the executive, or to the senate, or to both conjointly.

§ 1166. In the plan offered by an eminent statesman in the convention, it was proposed, that the senate should have the sole power of declaring war.[1] The reasons, which may be urged in favour of such an arrangement, are, that the senate would be composed of representatives of the states, of great weight, sagacity, and experience, and that being a small and select body, promptitude of action, as well as wisdom, and firmness, would, as they ought, accompany the possession of the power. Large bodies necessarily move slowly ; and where the co-operation of different bodies is required, the retardation of any measure must be proportionally increased. In the ordinary course of legislation this may be no inconvenience. But in the exercise of such a prerogative, as declaring war, despatch, secresy, and vigour are often indispensable, and always useful towards success. On the other hand it may be urged in reply, that the power of declaring war is not only the highest sovereign prerogative ; but that it is in its own nature and effects so critical and calamitous, that it requires the utmost deliberation, and the successive review of all the councils of the nation. War, in its best estate, never fails to impose upon the people the most burthensome taxes, and personal sufferings. It is always injurious, and sometimes subversive of the great commercial, manufacturing, and agricultural interests. Nay, it always involves the prosperity, and not unfrequently the existence, of a

---

[1] Mr. Hamilton's Plan, Journal of Convention, p. 131.

nation. It is sometimes fatal to public liberty itself, by introducing a spirit of military glory, which is ready to follow, wherever a successful commander will lead ; and in a republic, whose institutions are essentially founded on the basis of peace, there is infinite danger, that war will find it both imbecile in defence, and eager for contest. Indeed, the history of republics has but too fatally proved, that they are too ambitious of military fame and conquest, and too easily devoted to the views of demagogues, who flatter their pride, and betray their interests. It should therefore be difficult in a republic to declare war ; but not to make peace. The representatives of the people are to lay the taxes to support a war, and therefore have a right to be consulted, as to its propriety and necessity. The executive is to carry it on, and therefore should be consulted, as to its time, and the ways and means of making it effective. The co-operation of all the branches of the legislative power ought, upon principle, to be required in this the highest act of legislation, as it is in all others. Indeed, there might be a propriety even in enforcing still greater restrictions, as by requiring a concurrence of two thirds of both houses.[1]

§ 1167. This reasoning appears to have had great weight with the convention, and to have decided its choice. Its judgment has hitherto obtained the unqualified approbation of the country.[2]

---

[1] Several of the states proposed an amendment to the constitution to this effect. But it was never adopted by a majority.* Under the confederation, the assent of nine states was necessary to a declaration of war, (Art. 9.)

[2] 1 Tucker's Black. Comm. App. 269 to 272 ; Rawle on the Const. ch. 9, p. 109.

* 1 Tucker's Black. Comm. App. 271, 272, 374.

§ 1168. In the convention, in the first draft of the constitution, the power was given merely "to make war." It was subsequently, and not without some struggle, altered to its present form.[1] It was proposed to add the power " to make peace ;" but this was unanimously rejected ;[2] upon the plain ground, that it more properly belonged to the treaty-making power. The experience of congress, under the confederation, of the difficulties, attendant upon vesting the treaty-making power in a large legislative body, was too deeply felt to justify the hazard of another experiment.[3]

§ 1169. The power to declare war may be exercised by congress, not only by authorizing general hostilities, in which case the general laws of war apply to our situation; or by partial hostilities, in which case the laws of war, so far as they actually apply to our situation, are to be observed.[4] The former course was resorted to in our war with Great Britain in 1812, in which congress enacted, " that war be, and hereby is declared to exist, between the United Kingdom of Great Britain and Ireland and the dependencies thereof, and the United States of America and their territories."[5] The latter course was pursued in the qualified war of 1798 with France, which was regulated by divers acts of congress, and of course was confined to the limits prescribed by those acts.[6]

§ 1170. The power to declare war would of itself carry the incidental power to grant letters of marque

---

1 Journal of Convention, 221, 258, 259, 327, 328.

2 Ibid, 259.

3 The Federalist, No. 64. See also Rawle on the Const. ch. 9, p. 110; North Amer. Rev. Oct. 1827, p. 263.

4 *Talbot* v. *Seeman*, 1 Cranch's R. 1, 28; *Bas* v. *Tingey*, 4 Dall. 37.

5 Act of 1812, ch. 102.

6 Rawle on the Const. ch. 9, p. 109; Sergeant on Const. ch. 28, [ch. 30;] *Bas* v. *Tingey*, 4 Dall. R. 37.

and reprisal, and make rules concerning captures. It is most probable, that an extreme solicitude to follow out the powers enumerated in the confederation occasioned the introduction of these clauses into the constitution. In the former instrument, where all powers, not *expressly* delegated, were prohibited, this enumeration was peculiarly appropriate. But in the latter, where incidental powers were expressly contemplated, and provided for, the same necessity did not exist. As has been already remarked in another place, and will abundantly appear from the remaining auxiliary clauses to the power to declare war, the constitution abounds with pleonasms and repetitions, sometimes introduced from caution, sometimes from inattention, and sometimes from the imperfections of language.[1]

§ 1171. But the express power " to grant letters of marque and reprisal " may not have been thought wholly unnecessary, because it is often a measure of peace, to prevent the necessity of a resort to war. Thus, individuals of a nation sometimes suffer from the depredations of foreign potentates ; and yet it may not be deemed either expedient or necessary to redress such grievances by a general declaration of war. Under such circumstances the law of nations authorizes the sovereign of the injured individual to grant him this mode of redress, whenever justice is denied to him by the state, to which the party, who has done the injury, belongs. In this case the letters of marque and reprisal (words used as synonymous, the latter (reprisal) signifying, a taking in return, the former (letters of marque) the passing the frontiers in order to such taking,) contain an authority to seize the bodies or goods of the subjects of the offending state, wherever they may

[1] See Mr. Madison's Letter to Mr. Cabell., 18th Sept. 1828.

be found, until satisfaction is made for the injury.[1] This power of reprisal seems indeed to be a dictate almost of nature itself, and is nearly related to, and plainly derived from that of making war. It is only an incomplete state of hostilities, and often ultimately leads to a formal denunciation of war, if the injury is unredressed, or extensive in its operations.[2]

§ 1172. The power to declare war is exclusive in congress; and (as will be hereafter seen,) the states are prohibited from engaging in it, unless in cases of actual invasion or imminent danger thereof. It includes the exercise of all the ordinary rights of belligerents; and congress may therefore pass suitable laws to enforce them. They may authorize the seizure and condemnation of the property of the enemy within, or without the territory of the United States; and the confiscation of debts due to the enemy. But, until laws have been passed upon these subjects, no private citizens can enforce any such rights; and the judiciary is incapable of giving them any legitimate operation.[3]

§ 1173. The next power of congress is "to raise and "support armies; but no appropriation of money to that "use shall be for a longer term than two years."

§ 1174. The power to raise armies is an indispensable incident to the power to declare war; and the latter — would be literally *brutum fulmen* without the former, a means of mischief without a power of defence.[4] Under the confederation congress possessed no power whatsoever to raise armies; but only "to

---

[1] 1 Black. Comm. 258, 259.
[2] 1 Black. Comm. 258, 259; Bynkershoek on War, ch. 24, p. 182, by Duponceau; Valin Traité des Prises, p. 223, 321; 1 Tuck. Black. Comm. App. 271; 4 Elliot's Deb. 251.
[3] *Brown* v. *United States*, 8 Cranch's R. 1.
[4] 4 Elliot's Deb. 220, 221.

agree upon the number of land forces, and to make requisitions from each state for its quota, in proportion to the number of white inhabitants in such state ;" which requisitions were to be binding ; and thereupon the legislature of each state were to appoint the regimental officers, raise the men, and clothe, arm, and equip them in a soldier-like manner, at the expense of the United States.[1] The experience of the whole country, during the revolutionary war, established, to the satisfaction of every statesman, the utter inadequacy and impropriety of this system of requisition. It was equally at war with economy, efficiency, and safety.[2] It gave birth to a competition between the states, which created a kind of auction of men. In order to furnish the quotas required of them, they outbid each other, till bounties grew to an enormous and insupportable size. On this account many persons procrastinated their enlistment, or enlisted only for short periods. Hence, there were but slow and scanty levies of men in the most critical emergencies of our affairs ; short enlistments at an unparalleled expense ; and continual fluctuations in the troops, ruinous to their discipline, and subjecting the public safety frequently to the perilous crisis of a disbanded army. Hence also arose those oppressive expedients for raising men, which were occasionally practised, and which nothing, but the enthusiasm of liberty, could have induced the people to endure.[3] The burthen was also very

---

[1] Art. 9 ; Art. 7.

[2] 1 American Museum, 270, 273, 283 ; 5 Marshall's Life of Washington, App. note 1.

[3] The Federalist, No. 22, 23. — The difficulties connected with this subject will appear still more striking in a practical view from the letters of General Washington, and other public documents at the period. See 5 Marshall's Life of Washington, ch. 3, p. 125, 126 ; ch. 5, p. 212 to 220 ; ch. 6, p. 238 to 248. See 6 Journals of Congress in 1780 *passim.* Circular Letter of Congress, in May, 1779 ; 5 Jour. of Cong. 224 to 231.

unequally distributed.   The states near the seat of war, influenced by motives of self-preservation, made efforts to furnish their quotas, which even exceeded their abilities ; while those at a distance were exceedingly remiss in their exertions.   In short, the army was frequently composed of three bodies of men ; first, raw recruits ; secondly, persons, who were just about completing their term of service ; and thirdly, of persons, who had served out half their term, and were quietly waiting for its determination.   Under such circumstances, the wonder is not, that its military operations were tardy, irregular, and often unsuccessful ; but, that it was ever able to make head-way at all against an enemy, possessing a fine establishment, well appointed, well armed, well clothed, and well paid.[1]   The appointment, too, by the states, of all regimental officers, had a tendency to destroy all harmony and subordination, so necessary to the success of military life.

§ 1175.   There is great wisdom and propriety in relieving the government from the ponderous and unwieldy machinery of the requisitions and appointments under the confederation.   The present system of the Union is *general* and direct, and capable of a uniform organization and action.   It is essential to the common defence, that the national government should possess the power to raise armies ; build and equip fleets ; prescribe rules for the government of both ; direct their operations ; and provide for their support.[2]

§ 1176.   The clause, as originally reported, was "to raise armies ; " and subsequently it was, upon the report of a committee, amended, so as to stand in its present

---

[1] The Federalist, No. 22, 23.
[2] The Federalist, No. 23 ; 2 Elliot's Debates, 92, 93.

form; and as amended it seems to have encountered no opposition in the convention.[1] It was, however, afterwards assailed in the state conventions, and before the people, with incredible zeal and pertinacity, as dangerous to liberty, and subversive of the state governments. Objections were made against the general and indefinite power to raise armies, not limiting the number of troops; and to the maintenance of them in peace, as well as in war.

§ 1177. It was said, that congress, having an unlimited power to raise and support armies, might, if in their opinion the general welfare required it, keep large armies constantly on foot, and thus exhaust the resources of the United States. There is no control on congress, as to numbers, stations, or government of them. They may billet them on the people at pleasure. Such an unlimited authority is most dangerous, and in its principles despotic; for being unbounded, it must lead to despotism. We shall, therefore, live under a government of military force.[2] In respect to times of peace, it was suggested, that there is no necessity for having a standing army, which had always been held, under such circumstances, to be fatal to the public rights and political freedom.[3]

§ 1178. To these suggestions it was replied with equal force and truth, that to be of any value, the power must be unlimited. It is impossible to foresee, or define the extent and variety of national exigencies, and the correspondent extent and variety of the national means necessary to satisfy them. The power must be co-extensive with all possible combinations of circum-

[1] Journal of Convention, 221, 327, 328.
[2] 2 Elliot's Debates, 2-5, 286, 307, 308, 430.
[3] 2 Elliot's Debates, 307, 308, 430.

stances, and under the direction of the councils entrusted with the common defence. To deny this would be
to deny the means, and yet require the end. These
must, therefore, be unlimited in every matter essential
to its efficacy, that is, in the formation, direction, and
support of the national forces.[1] This was not doubted
under the confederation; though the mode adopted to
carry it into effect was utterly inadequate and illusory.[2]
There could be no real danger from the exercise of the
power. It was not here, as in England, where the executive possessed the power to raise armies at pleasure; which power, so far as respected standing armies
in time of peace, it became necessary to provide by the
bill of rights, in 1688, should not be exercised without
the consent of parliament.[3] Here the power is exclusively confined to the legislative body, to the representatives of the states, and of the people of the states.
And to suppose it will not be safe in their hands,
is to suppose, that no powers of government, adapted
to national exigencies, can ever be safe in any political body.[4] Besides, the power is limited by the
necessity (as will be seen) of biennial appropriations.[5]
The objection, too, is the more strange, because there
are but two constitutions of the thirteen states, which
attempt in any manner to limit the power; and these
are rather cautions for times of peace, than prohibitions.[6]
The confederation itself contains no prohibition or
limitation of the power.[7] Indeed, in regard to times of
war, it seems utterly preposterous to impose any limit-

1 The Federalist, No. 23; 2 Elliot's Debates, 92, 93, 438.
2 2 Elliot's Debates, 438.   3 1 Black. Comm. 262, 413.
4 The Federalist, No. 23, 26.   5 The Federalist, No. 24, 25.
6 The Federalist, No. 24, and note; Id. No. 26.
7 The Federalist, No. 24; 2 Elliot's Debates, 438.

ations upon the power; since it is obvious, that emergencies may arise, which would require the most various, and independent exercises of it. The country would otherwise be in danger of losing both its liberty and its sovereignty, from its dread of investing the public councils with the power of defending it. It would be more willing to submit to foreign conquest, than to domestic rule.

§ 1179. But in times of peace the power may be at least equally important, though not so often required to be put in full exercise. The United States are surrounded by the colonies and dependencies of potent foreign governments, whose maritime power may furnish them with the means of annoyance, and mischief, and invasion. To guard ourselves against evils of this sort, it is indispensable for us to have proper forts and garrisons, stationed at the weak points, to overawe or check incursions. Besides; it will be equally important to protect our frontiers against the Indians, and keep them in a state of due submission and control.[1] The garrisons can be furnished only by occasional detachments of militia, or by regular troops in the pay of the government. The first would be impracticable, or extremely inconvenient, if not positively pernicious. The militia would not, in times of profound peace, submit to be dragged from their occupations and families to perform such a disagreeable duty. And if they would, the increased expenses of a frequent rotation in the service; the loss of time and labour; and the breaking up of the ordinary employments of life; would make it an extremely ineligible scheme of military power. The true and proper recourse should, there-

---

[1] The Federalist, No. 24, 25; 2 Elliot's Debates, 292, 293.

fore, be to a permanent, but small standing army for
such purposes.[1] And it would only be, when our neighbours should greatly increase their military force, that
prudence and a due regard to our own safety would
require any augmentation of our own.[2] It would be
wholly unjustifiable to throw upon the states the defence of their own frontiers, either against the Indians,
or against foreign foes. The burthen would often be
disproportionate to their means, and the benefit would
often be largely shared by the neighbouring states.
The common defence should be provided for out of the
common treasury. The existence of a federal government, and at the same time of military establishments
under state authority, are not less at variance with each
other, than a due supply of the federal treasury, and
the system of quotas and requisitions.[3]

§ 1180. It is important also to consider, that the surest
means of avoiding war is to be prepared for it in peace.
If a prohibition should be imposed upon the United
States against raising armies in time of peace, it would
present the extraordinary spectacle to the world of a
nation incapacitated by a constitution of its own choice
from preparing for defence before an actual invasion.
As formal denunciations of war are in modern times often
neglected, and are never necessary, the presence of an
enemy within our territories would be required, before
the government would be warranted to begin levies of
men for the protection of the state. The blow must
be received, before any attempts could be made to
ward it off, or to return it. Such a course of conduct
would at all times invite aggression and insult; and
enable a formidable rival or secret enemy to seize upon

1 The Federalist, No. 24 ; 2 Elliot's Debates, 292, 293.
2 The Federalist, No. 24, 41.   3 Id. No. 25.

the country, as a defenceless prey ; or to drain its resources by a levy of contributions, at once irresistible
and ruinous.[1]   It would be in vain to look to the militia
for an adequate defence under such circumstances.
This reliance came very near losing us our independence, and was the occasion of the useless expenditure of many millions.   The history of other countries,
and our past experience, admonish us, that a regular
force, well disciplined and well supplied, is the cheapest,
and the only effectual means of resisting the inroads of
a well disciplined foreign army.[2]   In short, under such
circumstances the constitution must be either violated,
(as it in fact was by the states under the confederation,[3])
or our liberties must be placed in extreme jeopardy.
Too much precaution often leads to as many difficulties,
as too much confidence.   How could a readiness for
war in time of peace be safely prohibited, unless we
could in like manner prohibit the preparations and
establishments of every hostile nation ?   The means of
security can be only regulated by the means and the
danger of attack.   They will, in fact, ever be determined by these rules, and no other.   It will be in vain
to oppose constitutional barriers to the impulse of self-
preservation.[4]

§ 1181. But the dangers from abroad are not alone
those, which are to be guarded against in the structure of
the national government.   Cases may occur, and indeed
are contemplated by the constitution itself to occur, in
which military force may be indispensable to enforce
the laws, or to suppress domestic insurrections. Where
the resistance is confined to a few insurgents, the sup-

[1] The Federalist, No. 25 ; 2 Elliot's Debates, 92, 93.
[2] The Federalist, No. 25, 41.   [3] Id. 25.
[4] The Federalist, No. 41 ; 3 Elliot's Debates, 305.

pression may be ordinarily, and safely confided to the
militia.   But where it is extensive, and especially if it
should pervade one, or more states, it may become important and even necessary to employ regular troops,
as at once the most effective, and the most economical
force.[1]   Without the power to employ such a force in
time of peace for domestic purposes, it is plain, that the
government might be in danger of being overthrown
by the combinations of a single faction.[2]

§ 1182. The danger of an undue exercise of the
power is purely imaginary.   It can never be exerted,
but by the representatives of the people of the states;
and it must be safe there, or there can be no safety at
all in any republican form of government.[3]   Our notions,
indeed, of the dangers of standing armies in time of
peace, are derived in a great measure from the principles and examples of our English ancestors.   In England, the king possessed the power of raising armies
in the time of peace according to his own good pleasure.   And this prerogative was justly esteemed dangerous to the public liberties.   Upon the revolution of
1688, parliament wisely insisted upon a bill of rights,
which should furnish an adequate security for the future.
But how was this done?   Not by prohibiting standing
armies altogether in time of peace; but (as has been
already seen) by prohibiting them *without the consent of
parliament.*[4]   This is the very proposition contained in
the constitution; for congress can alone raise armies;
and may put them down, whenever they choose.

1 The Federalist, No. 28, 26.
2 2 Elliot's Debates, 92, 93.
3 The Federalist, No. 23, 26, 28.
4 The Federalist, No. 26; 1 Black. Comm. 413.

§ 1183. It may be admitted, that standing armies may prove dangerous to the state. But it is equally true, that the want of them may also prove dangerous to the state. What then is to be done? The true course is to check the undue exercise of the power, not to withhold it.[1] This the constitution has attempted to do by providing, that "no appropriation of money "to that use shall be for a longer term than two years." Thus, unless the necessary supplies are voted by the representatives of the people every two years, the whole establishment must fall. Congress may indeed, by an act for this purpose, disband a standing army at any time ; or vote the supplies only for one year, or for a shorter period. But the constitution is imperative, that no appropriation shall prospectively reach beyond the biennial period. So that there would seem to be every human security against the possible abuse of the power.[2]

§ 1184. But, here again it was objected, that the executive might keep up a standing army in time of peace, notwithstanding no supplies should be voted. But how can this possibly be done? The army cannot go without supplies; it may be disbanded at the pleasure of the legislature ; and it would be absolutely impossible for any president, against the will of the nation, to keep up a standing army in *terrorem populi*.[3]

§ 1185. It was also asked, why an appropriation should not be annually made, instead of biennially, as is the case in the British parliament.[4] The answer is, that congress may in their pleasure limit the appropriation

---

[1] The Federalist, No. 41 ; 2 Elliot's Debates, 93, 308, 309.
[2] The Federalist, No. 26, 41.
[3] The Federalist, No. 26.
[4] 1 Tucker's Black. Comm. App. 272; 1 Black. Comm. 414, 415.

to a single year ; but exigencies may arise, in which, with a view to the advantages of the public service and the pressure of war, a biennial appropriation might be far more expedient, if not absolutely indispensable. Cases may be supposed, in which it might be impracticable for congress, in consequence of public calamities, to meet annually for the despatch of business. But the supposed example of the British parliament proves nothing. That body is not restrained by any constitutional provision from voting supplies for a standing army for an unlimited period. It is the mere practice of parliament, in the exercise of its own discretion, to make an annual vote of supplies. Surely, if there is no danger in confiding an unlimited power of this nature to a body chosen for seven years, there can be none in confiding a limited power to an American congress, chosen for two years.[1]

§ 1186. In some of the state conventions an amendment was proposed, requiring, that no standing army, or regular forces be kept up in time of peace, except for the necessary protection and defence of forts, arsenals, and dockyards, without the consent of two thirds of both houses of congress.[2] But it was silently suffered to die away with the jealousies of the day. The practical course of the government on this head has allayed all fears of the people, and fully justified the opinions of the friends of the constitution. It is remarkable, that scarcely any power of the national government was at the time more strongly assailed by

---

[1] The Federalist, No. 41.
[2] 1 Tucker's Black. Comm. App. 271, 272, 379.—An attempt was also made in the convention, to insert a clause, limiting the number of the army in time of peace to a —— number ; but it was negatived. Journal of Convention, p. 262

appeals to popular prejudices, or vindicated with more full and masculine discussion. The Federalist gave it a most elaborate discussion, as one of the critical points of the constitution.[1] In the present times the subject attracts no notice, and would scarcely furnish a topic, even for popular declamation. Ever since the constitution was put into operation, congress have restrained their appropriations to the current year; and thus practically shown the visionary nature of these objections.

§ 1187. Congress in 1798, in expectation of a war with France, authorized the president to accept the services of any companies of volunteers, who should associate themselves for the service, and should be armed, clothed, and equipped at their own expense, and to commission their officers.[2] This exercise of power was complained of at the time, as a virtual infringement of the constitutional authority of the states in regard to the militia; and, as such, it met with the disapprobation of a learned commentator.[3] His opinion does not, however, seem since to have received the deliberate assent of the nation. During the late war with Great Britain, laws were repeatedly passed, authorizing the acceptance of volunteer corps of the militia under their own officers; and eventually, the president was authorized, with the consent of the senate, to commission officers for such volunteer corps. These laws exhibit the decided change of the public opinion on this subject; and they deserve more attention, since the measures were promoted and approved under the auspices of the very

[1] The Federalist, No. 24 to 29.

[2] Act of 28th of May, 1798, ch. 64 ; Act of 22d of June, 1798, ch. 74 ; Act of 2d of March, 1799, ch. 187.

[3] 1 Tucker's Black. Comm. App. 273, 274, 329, 330. See also Virginia Report and Resolutions, 9th of January, 1800, p. 53 to 56.

party, which had inculcated an opposite opinion.[1]   It is proper to remark, that the Federalist maintained, that the disciplining and effective organization of the whole militia would be impracticable; that the attention of the government ought particularly to be directed to the formation of a select corps of moderate size, upon such principles, as would really fit them for service in case of need; and that such select corps would constitute the best substitute for a large standing army, and the most formidable check upon any undue military powers; since it would be composed of citizens well disciplined, and well instructed in their rights and duties.[2]

§ 1188. The next power of congress is " to provide and maintain a navy."

§ 1189. Under the confederation congress possessed the power " to build and equip a navy."[3]   The same language was adopted in the original draft of the constitution; and it was amended by substituting the present words, apparently without objection, as more broad and appropriate.[4]   In the convention, the propriety of granting the power seems not to have been questioned. But it was assailed in the state conventions as dangerous. It was said, that commerce and navigation are the principal sources of the wealth of the maritime powers of Europe; and if we engaged in commerce, we should soon become their rivals.   A navy would soon be

---

[1] See Act of 8th of Feb. 1812, ch. 22; Act of 6th of July, 1812, ch. 138; Act of 24th of Feb. 1814, ch. 75; Act of 30th of March, 1814, ch. 96; Act of 27th of Jan. 1815, ch. 178.   See also Act of 24th of Feb. 1807, ch. 70.

[2] The Federalist, No. 29.

[3] Art. 9.

[4] Journ. of Convention, 221, 262.

thought indispensable to protect it. But the attempt
on our part to provide a navy would provoke these
powers, who would not suffer us to become a naval
power. Thus, we should be immediately involved in
wars with them. The expenses, too, of maintaining a
suitable navy would be enormous ; and wholly disproportionate to our resources. If a navy should be provided at all, it ought to be limited to the mere protection of our trade.[1] It was further urged, that the
Southern states would share a large portion of the burthens of maintaining a navy, without any corresponding
advantages.[2]

§ 1190. With the nation at large these objections
were not deemed of any validity. The necessity of a
navy for the protection of commerce and navigation
was not only admitted, but made a strong ground for
the grant of the power. One of the great objects of
the constitution was the encouragement and protection of navigation and trade. Without a navy, it
would be utterly impossible to maintain our right to the
fisheries, and our trade and navigation on the lakes, and
the Mississippi, as well as our foreign commerce. It
was one of the blessings of the Union, that it would be
able to provide an adequate support and protection for
all these important objects. Besides ; a navy would be
absolutely indispensable to protect our whole Atlantic
frontier, in case of a war with a foreign maritime power.
We should otherwise be liable, not only to the invasion
of strong regular forces of the enemy ; but to the attacks and incursions of every predatory adventurer.
Our maritime towns might all be put under contribu-
tion ; and even the entrance and departure from our

---

[1] 2 Elliot's Deb. 224, 319, 320.
[2] 2 Elliot's Deb. 319, 320.

own ports be interdicted at the caprice, or the hostility of a foreign power. It would also be our cheapest, as well as our best defence ; as it would save us the expense of numerous forts and garrisons upon the sea-coast, which, though not effectual for all, would still be required for some purposes. In short, in a maritime warfare without this means of defence, our commerce would be driven from the ocean, our ports would be blockaded, our sea-coast infested with plunderers, and our vital interests put at hazard.[1]

§ 1191. Although these considerations were decisive with the people at large in favour of the power, from its palpable necessity and importance to all the great interests of the country, it is within the memory of all of us, that the same objections for a long time prevailed with a leading party in the country,[2] and nurtured a policy, which was utterly at variance with our duties, as well as our honour. It was not until during the late war with Great Britain, when our little navy, by a gallantry and brilliancy of achievement almost without parallel, had literally fought itself into favour, that the nation at large began to awake from its lethargy on this subject, and to insist upon a policy, which should at once make us respected and formidable abroad, and secure protection and honour at home.[3] It has been proudly said

---

[1] The Federalist, No. 11, 24, 41. See also 1 Tucker's Black. Comm. App. 272.

[2] See 5 Marshall's Life of Washington, ch. 7, p. 523 to 531.

[3] Lest it should be supposed, that these remarks are not well founded, the following passage is extracted from the celebrated Report and Resolutions of the Virginia legislature, of 7th and 11th Jan. 1800, which formed the text-book of many political opinions for a long period. " With respect to the navy, it may be proper to remind you, that whatever may be the proposed object of its establishment, or whatever the prospect of temporary advantages resulting therefrom, it is demonstrated by the experience of all nations, who have adventured far into naval

by a learned commentator on the laws of England, that the royal navy of England hath ever been its greatest defence and ornament. It is its ancient and natural strength; the floating bulwark of the island; an army, from which, however strong and powerful, no danger can be apprehended to liberty.[1] Every American citizen ought to cherish the same sentiment, as applicable to the navy of his own country.

§ 1192. The next power of congress is " to make " rules for the government and regulation of the land and " naval forces." This is a natural incident to the preceding powers to make war, to raise armies, and to provide and maintain a navy. Its propriety, therefore, scarcely could be, and never has been denied, and need not now be insisted on. The clause was not in the original draft of the constitution; but was added without objection by way of amendment.[2] It was without question borrowed from a corresponding clause in the articles of confederation,[3] where it was with more propriety given, because there was a prohibition of all implied powers. In Great Britain, the king, in his capacity of generalissimo of the whole kingdom, has the sole power of regulating

---

policy, that such prospect is ultimately delusive; and that a navy has ever in practice been known more as an instrument of power, a source of expense, and an occasion of collisions and wars with other nations, than as an instrument of defence, of economy, or of protection to commerce. Nor is there any nation, in the judgment of the general assembly, to whose circumstances this remark is more applicable, than to the United States." p. 57, 58. And the senators and representatives were instructed and requested by one of the resolutions " to prevent any augmentation of the navy, and to promote any proposition for reducing it, as circumstances will permit, within the narrowest limits compatible with the protection of the sea-coasts, ports, and harbours of the United States." p. 59.

[1] 1 Black. Comm. 418.
[2] Journal of Convention, p. 221, 262.
[3] Art. 9.

fleets and armies.[1] But parliament has repeatedly interposed ; and the regulation of both is now in a considerable measure provided for by acts of parliament.[2]
The whole power is far more safe in the hands of congress, than of the executive ; since otherwise the most
summary and severe punishments might be inflicted at
the mere will of the executive.

§ 1193. It is a natural result of the sovereignty over
the navy of the United States, that it should be exclusive. Whatever crimes, therefore, are committed
on board of public ships of war of the United States,
whether they are in port or at sea, they are exclusively
cognizable and punishable by the government of the
United States. The public ships of sovereigns, wherever they may be, are deemed to be extraterritorial,
and enjoy the immunities from the local jurisdiction
belonging to their sovereign.[3]

---

[1] 1 Black. Comm. 262, 421.
[2] 1 Black. Comm. 413, 414, 415, 420, 421.
[3] See *United States* v. *Bevans*, 3 Wheaton's R. 336, 390. *The Schr.
Exchange*, 7 Cranch's R. 116.

CHAPTER XXII.

POWER OVER THE MILITIA.

§ 1194. THE next power of congress is " to provide " for calling forth the militia to execute the laws of the " Union, suppress insurrections, and repel invasions."

§ 1195. This clause seems, after a slight amendment, to have passed the convention without opposition.[1] It cured a defect severely felt under the confederation, which contained no provision on the subject.

§ 1196. The power of regulating the militia, and of commanding its services to enforce the laws, and to suppress insurrections, and repel invasions, is a natural incident to the duty of superintending the common defence, and preserving the internal peace of the nation. In short, every argument, which is urged, or can be urged against standing armies in time of peace, applies forcibly to the propriety of vesting this power in the national government. There is but one of two alternatives, which can be resorted to in cases of insurrection, invasion, or violent opposition to the laws ; either to employ regular troops, or to employ the militia to suppress them. In ordinary cases, indeed, the resistance to the laws may be put down by the *posse comitatus*, or the assistance of the common magistracy. But cases may occur, in which such a resort would be utterly vain, and even mischievous ; since it might encourage the factious to more rash measures, and prevent the application of a force, which would at once destroy the hopes, and crush the efforts of the disaffected. The

---

[1] Journal of Convention, 221, 283.

general power of the government to pass all laws
necessary and proper to execute its declared powers,
would doubtless authorize laws to call forth the *posse
comitatus,* and employ the common magistracy, in cases,
where such measures would suit the emergency.[1]   But
if the militia could not be called in aid, it would be absolutely indispensable to the common safety to keep up a
strong regular force in time of peace.[2] The latter would
certainly not be desirable, or economical ; and therefore
this power over the militia is highly salutary to the public repose, and at the same time an additional security
to the public liberty.   In times of insurrection or invasion, it would be natural and proper, that the militia
of a neighbouring state should be marched into another
to resist a common enemy, or guard the republic against
the violences of a domestic faction or sedition.   But it
is scarcely possible, that in the exercise of the power
the militia should ever be called to march great distances, since it would be at once the most expensive and
the most inconvenient force, which the government
could employ for distant expeditions.[3] The regulation
of the whole subject is always to be in the power of
congress ; and it may from time to time be moulded so,
as to escape from all dangerous abuses.

§ 1197. Notwithstanding the reasonableness of
these suggestions, the power was made the subject of
the most warm appeals to the people, to alarm their fears,
and surprise their judgment.[4] At one time it was said,

[1] 2 Elliot's Debates, 300, 304, 305, 308, 309.
[2] The Federalist, No. 29 ; 2 Elliot's Debates, 292, 293, 294, 308, 309.
[3] The Federalist, No. 29 ; 2 Elliot's Deb. 92, 107, 108, 292, 293, 294,
308, 309 ; 3 Elliot's Deb. 305, 306.
[4] 2 Elliot's Deb. 66, 67, 307, 310, 314, 315 ; The Federalist, No. 29 ;
Luther Martin's Address, Yates's Minutes ; 4 Elliot's Deb. 33, 34.

that the militia under the command of the national government might be dangerous to the public liberty; at
another, that they might be ordered to the most distant
places, and burthened with the most oppressive services; and at another, that the states might thus be
robbed of their immediate means of defence.[1] How
these things could be accomplished with the consent of
both houses of congress, in which the states and the
people of the states are represented, it is difficult to
conceive. But the highly coloured and impassioned
addresses, used on this occasion, produced some propositions of amendment in the state conventions,[2] which,
however, were never duly ratified, and have long since
ceased to be felt, as matters of general concern.

§ 1198. The next power of congress is, " to provide
" for organizing, arming, and disciplining the militia, and
" for governing such part of them, as may be employed
" in the service of the United States; reserving to the
" states respectively the appointment of the officers,
" and the authority of training the militia according to
" the discipline prescribed by congress."

§ 1199. This power has a natural connexion with
the preceding, and, if not indispensable to its exercise,
furnishes the only adequate means of giving it promptitude and efficiency in its operations. It requires no
skill in the science of war to discern, that uniformity in
the organization and discipline of the militia will be
attended with the most beneficial effects, whenever
they are called into active service. It will enable them
to discharge the duties of the camp and field with mutual intelligence and concert, an advantage of peculiar

---

[1] See the Federalist, No. 29; 2 Elliot's Deb. 285, 286, 287, 289, 307,
310.
[2] 1 Tucker's Black. Comm. App. 273.

moment in the operations of an army ; and it will enable them to acquire, in a much shorter period, that
degree of proficiency in military functions, which is
essential to their usefulness.   Such an uniformity, it is
evident, can be attained only through the superintending power of the national government.[1]

§ 1200. This clause was not in the original draft of
the constitution; but it was subsequently referred to a
committee, who reported in favour of the power ; and
after considerable discussion it was adopted in its present shape by a decided majority.   The first clause in
regard to organizing, arming, disciplining, and governing
the militia, was passed by a vote of nine states against
two ; the next, referring the appointment of officers to
the states, after an ineffectual effort to amend it by
confining the appointment to officers under the rank of
general officers, was passed without a division ; and the
last, referring the authority to train the militia according to the discipline prescribed by congress, was passed by a vote of seven states against four.[2]

§ 1201. It was conceived by the friends of the constitution, that the power thus given, with the guards,
reserving the appointment of the officers, and the training of the militia to the states, made it not only wholly
unexceptionable, but in reality an additional security to
the public liberties.[3]   It was nevertheless made a topic
of serious alarm and powerful objection.   It was suggested, that it was indispensable to the states, that they
should possess the control and discipline of the militia.

1 The Federalist, No. 4, 29 ; 1 Tucker's Black. Comm. App. 273,
274 ; 5 Marshall's Life of Washington, ch. 1, p. 54. See Virginia Report and Resolutions, 7 Jan. 1800, p. 54 to 57.
2 Journal of Convention, 221, 263, 272, 280, 281, 282, 357, 376, 377.
3 2 Elliot's Deb. 92, 301, 310, 312, 314, 317.

Congress might, under pretence of organizing and disciplining them, inflict severe and ignominious punishments on them.[1] The power might be construed to be exclusive in congress. Suppose, then, that congress should refuse to provide for arming or organizing them, the result would be, that the states would be utterly without the means of defence, and prostrate at the feet of the national government.[2] It might also be said, that congress possessed the exclusive power to suppress insurrections, and repel invasions, which would take from the states all effective means of resistance.[3] The militia might be put under martial law, when not under duty in the public service.[4]

§ 1202. It is difficult fully to comprehend the influence of such objections, urged with much apparent sincerity and earnestness at such an eventful period. The answers then given seem to have been in their structure and reasoning satisfactory and conclusive: But the amendments proposed to the constitution (some of which have been since adopted [5]) show, that the objections were extensively felt, and sedulously cherished. The power of congress over the militia (it was urged) was limited, and concurrent with that of the states. The right of governing them was confined to the single case of their being in the actual service of the United States, in some of the cases pointed out in the constitution. It was then, and then only, that they could be subjected by the general government to

1 2 Elliot's Debates, 301, 307, 310, 312.
2 2 Elliot's Debates, 145, 290, 310, 311, 312 ; Luther Martin's Address, Yates's Minutes ; 4 Elliot's Debates, 34, 35.
3 2 Elliot's Debates, 310, 311, 312, 314, 315, 316, 317, 318.
4 2 Elliot's Debates, 287, 288, 294.
5 1 Tuck. Black. Comm. App. 273.

martial law.[1]   If congress did not choose to arm, organize, or discipline the militia, there would be an inherent
right in the states to do it.[2]   All, that the constitution
intended, was, to give a power to congress to ensure
uniformity, and thereby efficiency. But, if congress
refused, or neglected to perform the duty, the states
had a perfect concurrent right, and might act upon it
to the utmost extent of sovereignty.[3] As little pretence was there to say, that congress possessed the
exclusive power to suppress insurrections and repel
invasions. Their power was merely competent to
reach these objects; but did not, and could not, in
regard to the militia, supersede the ordinary rights of
the states. It was, indeed, made a duty of congress
to provide for such cases ; but this did not exclude the
co-operation of the states.[4] The idea of congress inflicting severe and ignominious punishments upon the
militia in times of peace was absurd.[5] It presupposed,
that the representatives had an interest, and would intentionally take measures to oppress them, and alienate
their affections. The appointment of the officers of
the militia was exclusively in the states ; and how
could it be presumed, that such men would ever consent to the destruction of the rights or privileges of
their fellow-citizens.[6] The power to discipline and

1 2 Elliot's Debates, 299, 311.
2 2 Elliot's Debates, 293, 294, 312, 313, 314, 326, 327, 439 ; 1 Tuck.
Black. Comm. App. 272, 273; Rawle on the Constitution, ch. 9, p. 111,
112; *Houston* v. *Moore*, 5 Wheat. R. 1, 21, 45, 48 to 52.
3 *Houston* v. *Moore*, 5 Wheat. R. 1, 16, 17, 21, 22, 24, 32, 51, 52, 56 ;
3 Sergeant & Rawle, 169.
4 2 Elliot's Debates, 312, 313, 316, 317, 318, 368 ; Rawle on the Constitution, ch. 9, p. 111.
5 2 Elliot's Debates, 304, 309.
6 2 Elliot's Debates, 368 ; Rawle on the Constitution, ch. 9, p. 112.

train the militia, except when in the actual service of the United States, was also exclusively vested in the states; and under such circumstances, it was secure against any serious abuses.[1] It was added, that any project of disciplining the whole militia of the United States would be so utterly impracticable and mischievous, that it would probably never be attempted. The most, that could be done, would be to organize and discipline select corps ; and these for all general purposes, either of the states, or of the Union, would be found to combine all, that was useful or desirable in militia services.

§ 1203. It is hardly necessary to say, how utterly without any practical justification have been the alarms, so industriously spread upon this subject at the time, when the constitution was put upon its trial. Upon two occasions only has it been found necessary on the part of the general government, to require the aid of the militia of the states, for the purpose of executing the laws of the Union, suppressing insurrections, or repelling invasions. The first was to suppress the insurrection in Pennsylvania in 1794;[3] and the other, to repel the enemy in the recent war with Great Britain. On other occasions, the militia has indeed been called into service to repel the incursions of the Indians; but in all such cases, the injured states have led the way, and requested the co-operation of the national government. In regard to the other power of organizing, arming, and disciplining the militia, congress passed an act in 1792,[4] more effectually to

---

[1] See The Federalist, No. 29; 1 Tucker's Black. Comm. App. 274 ; Rawle on the Constitution, ch. 9, p. 112.

[2] The Federalist, No. 29.

[3] 5 Marsh. Life of Washington, ch. 8, p. 576 to 592 ; 2 Pitk. Hist. ch. 23, p. 421 to 428.

[4] Act of 8th May, 1792, ch. 33.

provide for the national defence, by establishing a uniform militia throughout the United States. The system provided by this act, with the exception of that portion, which established the rules of discipline and field service, has ever since remained in force. And the militia are now governed by the same general system of discipline and field exercise, which is observed by the regular army of the United States.[1] No jealousy of military power, and no dread of severe punishments are now indulged. And the whole militia system has been as mild in its operation, as it has been satisfactory to the nation.

§ 1204. Several questions of great practical importance have arisen under the clauses of the constitution respecting the power over the militia, which deserve mention in this place. It is observable, that power is given to congress "to *provide* for calling forth the militia "to execute the laws of the Union, suppress insurrec- "tions, and repel invasions." Accordingly, congress in 1795, in pursuance of this authority, and to give it a practical operation, provided by law, "that whenever the United States shall be invaded, or be in imminent danger of invasion from any foreign nation or Indian tribe, it shall be lawful for the president to call forth such number of the militia of the state, or states most convenient to the place of danger, or scene of action, as he may judge necessary, to repel such invasion, and to issue his order for that purpose to such officer or officers of the militia, as he shall think proper." Like provisions are made for the other cases stated in the constitution.[2] The constitutionality of this act has not

---

[1] Act of 1820, ch. 97; Act of 1821, ch. 68.
[2] Act of 1795, ch. 101.

been questioned,[1] although it provides for calling forth
the militia, not only in cases of invasion, but of imminent danger of invasion; for the power to repel invasions
must include the power to provide against any attempt
and danger of invasion, as the necessary and proper
means to effectuate the object. One of the best means
to repel invasion is, to provide the requisite force for action, before the invader has reached the territory of the
nation.[2] Nor can there be a doubt, that the president,
who is (as will be presently seen) by the constitution
the commander-in-chief of the army and navy of the
United States, and of the militia, when called into the
actual service of the United States, is the proper
functionary, to whom this high and delicate trust ought
to be confided. A free people will naturally be jealous
of the exercise of military power; and that of calling
forth the militia is certainly one of no ordinary magnitude. It is, however, a power limited in its nature to
certain exigencies; and by whomsoever it is to be executed, it carries with it a corresponding responsibility.[3]
Who is so fit to exercise the power, and to incur the
responsibility, as the president?

§ 1205. But a most material question arises: By
whom is the exigency (the *casus fœderis*, if one may
so say) to be decided? Is the president the sole and
exclusive judge, whether the exigency has arisen, or
is it to be considered, as an open question, which
every officer, to whom the orders of the president are

1 *Houston* v. *Moore*, 5 Wheat. R. 1, 60; *Martin* v. *Mott*, 12 Wheat. R.
19; *Houston* v. *Moore*, 3 Sergeant & Rawle, 169; *Duffield* v. *Smith*,
3 Sergeant & Rawle, 590; *Vanderheyden* v. *Young*, 11 Johns. R. 150.
2 *Martin* v. *Mott*, 12 Wheat. R. 19, 29.
3 *Martin* v. *Mott*, 12 Wheat. R. 19, 29; Rawle on Constitution, ch. 13,
p. 155, &c.

addressed, may decide for himself, and equally open to be contested by every militia-man, who shall refuse to obey the orders of the president?[1]   This question was much agitated during the late war with Great Britain, although it is well known, that it had been practically settled by the government, in the year 1794, to belong exclusively to the president;[2] and no inconsiderable diversity of opinion was then manifested in the heat of the controversy, *pendente lite, et flagrante bello.*   In Connecticut and Massachusetts, it was held, that the governors of the states, to whom orders were addressed by the president to call forth the militia on account of danger of invasion, were entitled to judge for themselves, whether the exigency had arisen; and were not bound by the opinion or orders of the president.[3] This doctrine, however, was disapproved elsewhere. It was contested by the government of the United States;[4] and was renounced by other states.[5]

§ 1206. At a very recent period, the question came before the Supreme Court of the United States for a judicial decision; and it was then unanimously determined, that the authority to decide, whether the exigency has arisen, belongs exclusively to the president;

---

1 *Martin* v. *Mott*, 12 Wheat. R. 19, 29, 30.

2 See *Houston* v. *Moore*, 5 Wheat. R. 37.

3 1 Kent's Comm. Lect. 12, p. 244 to 250; 8 Mass. R. Suppt. 547 et seq.; Rawle on the Constitution, ch. 13, p. 155, &c. — At a later period this doctrine seems to have been abandoned by Massachusetts. See Report and Resolves of Massachusetts, June 12, 1818, and February 15, 1830. See also Resolutions of Maine Legislature in 1820.

4 See President Madison's Message of 4th November, 1812, and President Monroe's Message, and other documents stated in Report and Resolves of Massachusetts, 15th February, 1830.

5 See *Vanderheyden* v. *Young*, 11 Johns. R. 150; Rawle on the Constitution, ch. 13, p. 155 to 160; *Duffield* v. *Smith*, 3 Sergeant & Rawle, 590.

and that his decision is conclusive upon all other persons. The court said, that this construction necessarily resulted from the nature of the power itself, and from the manifest objects contemplated by the act of congress. The power itself is to be exercised upon sudden emergencies, upon great occasions of state, and under circumstances, which may be vital to the existence of the Union. A prompt and unhesitating obedience to orders is indispensable to the complete attainment of the object. The service is a military service, and the command of a military nature; and in such cases, every delay and every obstacle to an efficient and immediate compliance would necessarily tend to jeopard the public interests. While subordinate officers or soldiers are pausing to consider, whether they ought to obey, or are scrupulously weighing the facts, upon which the commander-in-chief exercises the right to demand their services, the hostile enterprize may be accomplished, without the means of resistance. If the power of regulating the militia, and of commanding its services in times of insurrection and invasion, are, as it has been emphatically said, they are,[1] natural incidents to the duties of superintending the common defence, and of watching over the internal peace of the confederacy, these powers must be so construed, as to the modes of their exercise, as not to defeat the great end in view. If a superior officer has a right to contest the orders of the president, upon his own doubts, as to the exigency having arisen, it must be equally the right of every inferior officer and soldier. And any act done by any person in furtherance of such orders would subject him to responsibility in a civil suit, in which his

---

[1] The Federalist, No. 29.

defence must finally rest upon his ability to establish
the facts by competent proofs. Besides ; in many instances the evidence, upon which the president might
decide, that there was imminent danger of invasion,
might be of a nature not constituting strict technical
proof; or the disclosure of the evidence might reveal
important state secrets, which the public interest, and
even safety, might imperiously demand to be kept in
concealment.[1] The act of 1795 was manifestly framed upon this reasoning. The president is by it necessarily constituted, in the first instance, the judge
of the existence of the exigency, and is bound to act
according to his belief of the facts. If he does so act,
and decides to call out the militia, his orders for this
purpose are in strict conformity to the law ; and it
would seem to follow, as a necessary consequence, that
every act done by a subordinate officer in obedience
to such orders is equally justifiable. The law contemplates, that under such circumstances orders shall be
given to carry the power into effect ; and it cannot be,
that it is a correct inference, that any other person has
a right to disobey them. No provision is made for an
appeal from, or review of the president's opinion. And
whenever a statute gives a descretionary power to
any person to be exercised by him upon his own
opinion of certain facts, the general rule of construction
is, that he is thereby constituted the sole and exclusive
judge of the existence of those facts.[2]

§1207. It seems to be admitted, that the power to
call forth the militia may be exercised either by requisitions upon the executive of the states ; or by orders

---

1 *Martin v. Mott*, 12 Wheat. R. 30, 31.
2 *Martin v. Mott*. 12 Wheat. R. 19, 31, 32.

directed to such executive, or to any subordinate officers of the militia. It is not, however, to be understood,
that the state executive is in any case bound to leave
his executive duties, and go personally into the actual
service of the United States.[1]

§ 1208. The power to govern the militia, when in
the actual service of the United States, is denied by no
one to be an exclusive one. Indeed, from its very nature, it must be so construed; for the notion of distinct
and independent orders from authorities wholly unconnected, would be utterly inconsistent with that unity of
command and action, on which the success of all military operations must essentially depend.[2] But there is
nothing in the constitution, which prohibits a state from
calling forth its own militia, not detached into the service of the Union, to aid the United States in executing
the laws, in suppressing insurrections, and in repelling
invasions. Such a concurrent exercise of power in no
degree interferes with, or obstructs the exercise of the
powers of the Union. Congress may, by suitable laws,
provide for the calling forth of the militia, and annex
suitable penalties to disobedience of their orders, and
direct the manner, in which the delinquents may be
tried. But the authority to call forth, and the authority
exclusively to govern, are quite distinct in their nature.
The question, when the authority of congress over the
militia becomes exclusive, must essentially depend upon
the fact, when they are to be deemed in the actual service of the United States. There is a clear distinction
between calling forth the militia, and their being in

---

[1] See *Houston* v. *Moore*, 5 Wheat. R. 1, 15, 16, and Mr. J. Johnson's
Opinion, Id. 36, 37, 40, 46.

[2] The Federalist, No. 9, 29; *Houston* v *Moore*. 5 Wheat. R. 1, 17, 53,
54, 55, 56, 61, 62.

actual service. ' These are not contemporaneous acts, nor necessarily identical in their constitutional bearings. The president is not commander-in-chief of the militia, except when in actual service ; and not, when they are merely ordered into service. They are subjected to martial law only, when in actual service, and not merely when called forth, before they have obeyed the call. The act of 1795, and other acts on this subject, manifestly contemplate and recognise this distinction. To bring the militia within the meaning of being in actual service, there must be an obedience to the call, and some acts of organization, mustering, rendezvous, or marching, done in obedience to the call, in the public service.[1]

§ 1209. But whether the power is exclusive in congress to punish delinquencies in not obeying the call on the militia, by their own courts-martial, has been a question much discussed, and upon which no inconsiderable contrariety of opinion has been expressed. That it may, by law, be made exclusive, is not denied. But if no such law be made, whether a state may not, by its own laws, constitute courts-martial to try and punish the delinquencies, and inflict the penalties prescribed by the act of congress, has been the point of controversy. It is now settled, that, under such circumstances, a state court-martial may constitutionally take cognizance of, and inflict the punishment. But a state cannot add to, or vary the punishments inflicted by the acts of congress upon the delinquents.[2]

---

[1] *Houston* v. *Moore*, 5 Wheat. R. 1, 17, 18, 20, 53, 60, 61, 63, 64 ; Rawle on Const. ch. 13.p. 159.

[2] *Houston* v. *Moore*, 5 Wheat. R. 1, 2, 3, 24, 28, 44, 69 to 75 ; Rawle on Const. ch. 13, p. 158, 159 ; *Houston* v. *Moore*, 3 Serg. & Rawle, 169 ; *Duffield* v. *Smith*, 3 Serg. & R. 590 ; 1 Kent's Comm. Lect. 12, p. 248, 249, 250 ; Serg. on Const. ch. 28, [ch. 30] ; *Meade's case*, 5 Hall's Law Journ. 536 ; *Bolton's case*, 3 Serg. & Rawle, 176, note.

§ 1210. A question of another sort was also made during the late war with Great Britain; whether the militia, called into the actual service of the United States, were to be governed and commanded by any officer, but of the same militia, except the president of the United States; in other words, whether the president could delegate any other officer of the regular army, of equal or superior rank, to command the militia in his absence. It was held in several of the Eastern states, that the militia were exclusively under the command of their own officers, subject to the personal orders of the president; and that he could not authorize any officer of the army of the United States to command them in his absence, nor place them under the command of any such officer.[1] This doctrine was deemed inadmissible by the functionaries of the United States. It has never yet been settled by any definitive judgment of any tribunal competent to decide it.[2] If, however, the doctrine can be maintained, it is obvious, that the public service must be continually liable to very great embarrassments in all cases, where the militia are called into the public service in connexion with the regular troops.

---

[1] 8 Mass. Rep. Supp. 549, 550; 5 Hall's Amer. Law Journ. 495; 1 Kent's Comm. Lect. 12, p. 244 to 247.

[2] 1 Kent's Comm. Lect. 12, p. 244 to 247.

CHAPTER XXIII.

POWER OVER SEAT OF GOVERNMENT AND OTHER CEDED PLACES.

§1211. The next power of congress is, " to exercise " exclusive legislation in all cases whatsoever over such " district, not exceeding ten miles square, as may, by "cession of particular states and the acceptance of con- " gress, become the SEAT OF THE GOVERNMENT of the " United States ; and to exercise like authority over all " places purchased by the consent of the legislature of " the state, in which the same shall be, for the erection "of FORTS, MAGAZINES, ARSENALS, and other needful " BUILDINGS."

§ 1212. This clause was not in the original draft of the constitution ; but was referred to a committee, who reported in its favour ; and it was adopted into the constitution with a slight amendment without any apparent objection.[1]

§ 1213. The indispensable necessity of complete and exclusive power, on the part of the congress, at the seat of government, carries its own evidence with it. It is a power exercised by every legislature of the Union, and one might say of the World, by virtue of its general supremacy. Without it not only the public authorities might be insulted, and their proceedings be interrupted with impunity ; but the public archives might be in danger of violation, and destruction, and a dependence of the members of the national government on the state authorities for protection in the discharge of their functions be created, which would bring on the national councils the imputation of being subjected

---

[1] Journ. of Convent. 222, 260. 328, 329, 358.

to undue awe and influence, and might, in times of high excitement, expose their lives to jeopardy. It never could be safe to leave in possession of any state the exclusive power to decide, whether the functionaries of the national government should have the moral or physical power to perform their duties.[1] It might subject the favoured state to the most unrelenting jealousy of the other states, and introduce earnest controversies from time to time respecting the removal of the seat of government.

§ 1214. Nor can the cession be justly an object of jealousy to any state; or in the slightest degree impair its sovereignty. The ceded district is of a very narrow extent; and it rests in the option of the state, whether it shall be made or not. There can be little doubt, that the inhabitants composing it would receive with thankfulness such a blessing, since their own importance would be thereby increased, their interests be subserved, and their rights be under the immediate protection of the representatives of the whole Union.[2] It is not improbable, that an occurrence, at the very close of the revolutionary war, had a great effect in introducing this provision into the constitution. At the period alluded to, the congress, then sitting at Philadelphia, was surrounded and insulted by a small, but insolent body of mutineers of the continental army. Congress applied to the executive authority of Pennsylvania for defence; but, under the ill-conceived constitution of the state at that time, the executive power was vested in a council consisting of thirteen members; and they possessed, or exhibited so little energy, and such apparent intimidation, that congress indignantly removed to New-Jersey,

---

[1] The Federalist, No. 43; 2 Elliot's Deb. 92, 321, 322, 326.

[2] The Federalist, No. 43; 2 Elliot's Deb. 92, 321, 322, 326, 327.

whose inhabitants welcomed them with promises of defending them. Congress remained for some time at Princeton without being again insulted, till, for the sake of greater convenience, they adjourned to Annapolis. The general dissatisfaction with the proceedings of Pennsylvania, and the degrading spectacle of a fugitive congress, were sufficiently striking to produce this remedy.[1] Indeed, if such a lesson could have been lost upon the people, it would have been as humiliating to their intelligence, as it would have been offensive to their honour.

§ 1215. And yet this clause did not escape the common fate of most of the powers of the national government. It was represented, as peculiarly dangerous. It may, it was said, become a sort of public sanctuary, with exclusive privileges and immunities of every sort. It may be the very spot for the establishment of tyranny, and of refuge of the oppressors of the people. The inhabitants will be answerable to no laws, except those of congress. A powerful army may be here kept on foot; and the most oppressive and sanguinary laws may be passed to govern the district.[2] Nay, at the distance of fourteen years after the constitution had quietly gone into operation, and this power had been acted upon with a moderation, as commendable, as it ought to be satisfactory, a learned commentator expressed regret at the extent of the power, and intimated in no inexplicit terms his fears for the future. "A system of

1 Rawle on Const. ch. 9, p. 112, 113.

2 2 Elliot's Debates, 320, 321, 323, 324, 325, 326; Id. 115. — Amendments limiting the power of congress to such regulations, as respect the police and good government of the district, were proposed by several of the states at the time of the adoption of the constitution. But they have been silently abandoned. 1 Tucker's Black. Comm. App. 276, 374.

laws," says he, "incompatible with the nature and principles of a representative democracy, though not likely to be introduced at once, may be matured by degrees, and diffuse its influence through the states, and finally lay the foundation of the most important changes in the nature of the federal government. Let foreigners be enabled to hold lands, and transmit them by inheritance, or devise; let the preference to males, and the rights of primogeniture be revived with the doctrine of entails; and aristocracy will neither want a ladder to climb by, nor a base for its support.[1]"

§ 1216. What a superstructure to be erected on such a narrow foundation! Several of the states now permit foreigners to hold and transmit lands; and yet their liberties are not overwhelmed. The whole South, before the revolution, allowed and cherished the system of primogeniture; and yet they possessed, and transmitted to their children their colonial rights and privileges, and achieved under this very system the independence of the country. The system of entails is still the law of several of the states; and yet no danger has yet assailed them. They possess, and enjoy the fruits of republican industry and frugality, without any landed or other aristocracy. And yet the petty district of ten miles square is to overrule in its policy and legislation all, that is venerable and admirable in state legislation! The states, and the people of the states are represented in congress. The district has no representatives there; but is subjected to the exclusive legislation of the former. And yet congress, at home republican, will here nourish aristocracy. The states will here lay the foundation for the destruction of their

---

[1] 1 Tucker's Black. Comm. App. 277.

own institutions, rights, and sovereignty. At home, they will follow the legislation of the district, instead of guiding it by their precept and example. They will choose to be the engines of tyranny and oppression in the district, that they may become enslaved within their own territorial sovereignty. What, but a disposition to indulge in all sorts of delusions and alarms, could create such extraordinary flights of imagination? Can such things be, and overcome us, like a summer's cloud, without our special wonder? At this distance of time, it seems wholly unnecessary to refute the suggestions, which have been so ingeniously urged. If they prove any thing, they prove, that there ought to be no government, because no persons can be found worthy of the trust.

§ 1217. The seat of government has now, for more than thirty years, been permanently fixed on the river Potomac, on a tract of ten miles square, ceded by the states of Virginia and Maryland. It was selected by that great man, the boast of all America, the first in war, the first in peace, and the first in the hearts of his countrymen. It bears his name; it is the monument of his fame and wisdom. May it be for ever consecrated to its present noble purpose, *capitoli immobile saxum!*

§ 1218. The inhabitants enjoy all their civil, religious, and political rights. They live substantially under the same laws, as at the time of the cession, such changes only having been made, as have been devised, and sought by themselves. They are not indeed citizens of any state, entitled to the privileges of such; but they are citizens of the United States. They have no immediate representatives in congress. But they may justly boast, that they live under a paternal government, attentive to their wants, and zealous for their welfare. They, as yet, possess no local legislature; and have, as yet, not desired to possess one. A learned commentator has doubted, whether congress can create such a legislature, because it is the delegation of a delegated authority.[1] A very different opinion was expressed by the Federalist; for it was said, that "a municipal legislature for local purposes, derived from their own suffrages, will of course be allowed them."[2] In point of fact, the corporations of the three cities within its limits possess and exercise a delegated power of legislation under their charters, granted by congress, to the full extent of their municipal wants, without any constitutional scruple, or surmise of doubt.

§ 1219. The other part of the power, giving exclusive legislation over places ceded for the erection of forts, magazines, &c., seems still more necessary for the public convenience and safety. The public money expended on such places, and the public property deposited in them, and the nature of the military duties, which may be required there, all demand, that they should be exempted from state authority. In truth, it would be wholly improper, that places, on which the security of the entire Union may depend, should be subjected to the control of any member of it. The power, indeed, is wholly unexceptionable; since it can only be exercised at the will of the state; and therefore it is placed beyond all reasonable scruple.[3] Yet, it did not escape without the scrutinizing jealousy of the opponents of the constitution, and was denounced, as dangerous to state sovereignty.[4]

---

[1] 1 Tucker's Black. Comm. App. 278.

[2] The Federalist, No. 43.

[3] The Federalist, No. 43. See also *United States v. Bevans*, 3 Wheat. R. 336, 388.

[4] 2 Elliot's Debates, 145.

§ 1220. A great variety of cessions have been made by the states under this power. And generally there has been a reservation of the right to serve all state process, civil and criminal, upon persons found therein. This reservation has not been thought at all inconsistent with the provision of the constitution; for the state process, *quoad hoc*, becomes the process of the United States, and the general power of exclusive legislation remains with congress. Thus, these places are not capable of being made a sanctuary for fugitives, to exempt them from acts done within, and cognizable by, the states, to which the territory belonged; and at the same time congress is enabled to accomplish the great objects of the power.[1]

§ 1221. The power of congress to exercise exclusive jurisdiction over these ceded places is conferred on that body, as the legislature of the Union; and cannot be exercised in any other character. A law passed in pursuance of it is the supreme law of the land, and binding on all the states, and cannot be defeated by them. The power to pass such a law carries with it all the incidental powers to give it complete and effectual execution; and such a law may be extended in its operation incidentally throughout the United States, if congress think it necessary so to do. But if intended to have efficiency beyond the district, language must be used in the act expressive of such an intention; otherwise it will be deemed purely local.[2]

---

[1] *Commonwealth v. Clary*, 8 Mass. R. 72; *United States v. Cornell*, 2 Mason R. 60; Rawle on Constitution, ch. 27, p. 238; Sergeant on Constitution, ch. 28, [ch. 30;] 1 Kent's Comm. Lect. 19, p. 402 to 404.

[2] *Cohens v. Virginia*, 6 Wheat. R. 264, 424, 425, 426, 427, 428; Sergeant on Constitution, ch. 28, [ch. 30;] 1 Kent. Comm. Lect. 19, p. 402 to 404; Rawle on Constitution, ch. 27, p. 238, 239; *Loughborough v. Blake*, 5 Wheat. R. 322, 324.

§ 1222. It follows from this review of the clause, that the states cannot take cognizance of any acts done in the ceded places after the cession; and, on the other hand, the inhabitants of those places cease to be inhabitants of the state, and can no longer exercise any civil or political rights under the laws of the state.[1] But if there has been no cession by the state of the place, although it has been constantly occupied and used, under purchase, or otherwise, by the United States for a fort, arsenal, or other constitutional purpose, the state jurisdiction still remains complete and perfect.[2]

§ 1223. Upon a recent occasion, the nature and effect of the exclusive power of legislation, thus given by the constitution in these ceded places, came under the consideration of the Supreme Court, and was much discussed. It was argued, that all such legislation by congress was purely local, like that exercised by a territorial legislature; and was not to be deemed legislation by congress in the character of the legislature of the Union. The object of the argument was to establish, that a law, made in or for such ceded places, had no extra-territorial force or obligation, it not being a law of the United States. The reasoning of the court affirming, that such an act was a law of the United States, and that congress in passing it acted, as the legislature of the Union, can be best conveyed in their own language, and would be impaired by an abridgment.

---

[1] 8 Mass. R. 72; 1 Hall's Journal of Jurisp. 53; 1 Kent's Comm. Lect. 19, p. 403, 404.

[2] *The People* v. *Godfrey*, 17 Johns. R. 225; *Commonwealth* v. *Young*, 1 Hall's Journal of Jurisp. 47; 1 Kent's Comm. Lect. 19, p. 403, 404; Sergeant on Constitution, ch. 28, [ch. 30;] Rawle on Constitution, ch. 27, p. 238 to 240.

§ 1224. "In the enumeration of the powers of congress, which is made in the eighth section of the first article, we find that of exercising exclusive legislation over such district, as shall become the seat of government. This power, like all others, which are specified, is conferred on congress, as the legislature of the Union ; for, strip them of that character, and they would not possess it. In no other character can it be exercised. In legislating for the district, they necessarily preserve the character of the legislature of the Union ; for it is in that character alone, that the constitution confers on them this power of exclusive legislation. This proposition need not be enforced. The second clause of the sixth article declares, that 'this constitution, and the laws of the United States, which shall be made in pursuance thereof, shall be the supreme law of the land.' The clause, which gives exclusive jurisdiction, is unquestionably a part of the constitution, and, as such, binds all the United States. Those, who contend, that acts of congress, made in pursuance of this power, do not, like acts made in pursuance of other powers, bind the nation, ought to show some safe and clear rule, which shall support this construction, and prove, that an act of congress, clothed in all the forms, which attend other legislative acts, and passed in virtue of a power conferred on, and exercised by congress, as the legislature of the Union, is not a law of the United States, and does not bind them.

§ 1225. "One of the gentlemen sought to illustrate his proposition, that congress, when legislating for the district, assumed a distinct character, and was reduced to a mere local legislature, whose laws could possess no obligation out of the ten miles square, by a reference to the complex character of this court. It is, they say, a court of common law, and a court of equity. Its character, when sitting as a court of common law, is as distinct from its character, when sitting as a court of equity, as if the powers belonging to those departments were vested in different tribunals. Though united in the same tribunal, they are never confounded with each other. Without inquiring, how far the union of different characters in one court may be applicable, in principle, to the union in congress of the power of exclusive legislation in some places, and of limited legislation in others, it may be observed, that the forms of proceedings in a court of law are so totally unlike the forms of proceedings in a court of equity, that a mere inspection of the record gives decisive information of the character, in which the court sits, and consequently of the extent of its powers. But if the forms of proceeding were precisely the same, and the court the same, the distinction would disappear.

§ 1226. "Since congress legislates in the same forms, and in the same character, in virtue of powers of equal obligation conferred in the same instrument, when exercising its exclusive powers of legislation, as well as when exercising those, which are limited, we must inquire, whether there be any thing in the nature of this exclusive legislation, which necessarily confines the operation of the laws, made in virtue of this power, to the place, with a view to which they are made. Connected with the power to legislate within this district, is a similar power in forts, arsenals, dock-yards, &c. Congress has a right to punish murder in a fort, or other place within its exclusive jurisdiction; but no general right to punish murder committed within any of the states. In the act for the punishment of crimes against the United States, murder

committed within a fort, or any other place or district
of country, under the sole and exclusive jurisdiction of
the United States, is punished with death. Thus congress legislates in the same act, under its exclusive and
its limited powers.

§ 1227. "The act proceeds to direct, that the body
of the criminal, after execution, may be delivered to a
surgeon for dissection, and punishes any person, who
shall rescue such body during its conveyance from the
place of execution to the surgeon, to whom it is to be
delivered. Let these actual provisions of the law, or
any other provisions, which can be made on the subject, be considered with a view to the character, in
which congress acts, when exercising its powers of exclusive legislation. If congress is to be considered
merely as a local legislature, invested, as to this object,
with powers limited to the fort, or other place, in which
the murder may be committed, if its general powers cannot come in aid of these local powers, how can the offence
be tried in any other court, than that of the place, in
which it has been committed? How can the offender
be conveyed to, or tried in, any other place? How can
he be executed elsewhere? How can his body be
conveyed through a country under the jurisdiction of
another sovereign, and the individual punished, who,
within that jurisdiction, shall rescue the body? Were
any one state of the Union to pass a law for trying a
criminal in a court not created by itself, in a place
not within its jurisdiction, and direct the sentence
to be executed without its territory, we should all
perceive, and acknowledge its incompetency to such
a course of legislation. If congress be not equally
incompetent, it is, because that body unites the powers of local legislation with those, which are to op-

erate through the Union, and may use the last in aid of the first; or, because the power of exercising exclusive legislation draws after it, as an incident, the power of making that legislation effectual; and the incidental power may be exercised throughout the Union, because the principal power is given to that body, as the legislature of the Union.

§ 1228. "So, in the same act, a person, who, having knowledge of the commission of murder, or other felony, on the high seas, or within any fort, arsenal, dockyard, magazine, or other place, or district of country within the sole and exclusive jurisdiction of the United States, shall conceal the same, &c. he shall be adjudged guilty of misprision of felony, and shall be adjudged to be imprisoned, &c. It is clear, that congress cannot punish felonies generally; and, of consequence, cannot punish misprision of felony. It is equally clear, that a state legislature, the state of Maryland for example, cannot punish those, who, in another state, conceal a felony committed in Maryland. How, then, is it, that congress, legislating exclusively for a fort, punishes those, who, out of that fort, conceal a felony committed within it?

§ 1229. "The solution, and the only solution of the difficulty, is, that the power vested in congress, as the legislature of the United States, to legislate exclusively within any place ceded by a state, carries with it, as an incident, the right to make that power effectual. If a felon escape out of the state, in which the act has been committed, the government cannot pursue him into another state, and apprehend him there; but must demand him from the executive power of that other state. If congress were to be considered merely, as the local legislature for the fort, or other place, in which the offence might be committed, then this principle would apply to them, as to other local legislatures; and the felon, who should escape out of the fort, or other place, in which the felony may have been committed, could not be apprehended by the marshal, but must be demanded from the executive of the state. But we know, that the principle does not apply; and the reason is, that congress is not a local legislature, but exercises this particular power, like all its other powers, in its high character, as the legislature of the Union. The American people thought it a necessary power, and they conferred it for their own benefit. Being so conferred, it carries with it all those incidental powers, which are necessary to its complete and effectual execution.

§ 1230. "Whether any particular law be designed to operate without the district or not, depends on the words of that law. If it be designed so to operate, then the question, whether the power, so exercised, be incidental to the power of exclusive legislation, and be warranted by the constitution, requires a consideration of that instrument. In such cases the constitution and the law must be compared and construed. This is the exercise of jurisdiction. It is the only exercise of it, which is allowed in such a case." [1]

---

1 *Cohens* v. *Virginia*, 6 Wheat. R. 424 to 429.

CHAPTER XXIV.

POWERS OF CONGRESS — INCIDENTAL.

§ 1231. THE next power of congress is, "to make "all laws, which shall be *necessary* and *proper* for "carrying into execution the foregoing powers, and "all other powers vested by this constitution in the "government of the United States, or in any depart-"ment, or officer thereof."

§ 1232. Few powers of the government were at the time of the adoption of the constitution assailed with more severe invective, and more declamatory intemperance, than this.[1] And it has ever since been made a theme of constant attack, and extravagant jealousy.[2] Yet it is difficult to perceive the grounds, upon which it can be maintained, or the logic, by which it can be reasoned out. It is only declaratory of a truth, which would have resulted by necessary and unavoidable implication from the very act of establishing the national government, and vesting it with certain powers. What is a power, but the ability or faculty of doing a thing? What is the ability to do a thing, but the power of employing the *means* necessary to its execution? What is a legislative power, but a power of making laws? What are the means to execute a legislative power, but laws? What is the power for instance, of laying and collecting taxes, but a legislative power, or a power to make laws to lay and collect taxes? What

[1] The Federalist, No. 33, 44 ; 1 Elliot's Deb. 293, 294, 300 ; 2 Elliot's Deb. 196, 342.
[2] 1 Tuck. Black. Comm. App. 286, 287 ; 4 Elliot's Deb. 216, 217, 224, 225.

are the proper means of executing such a power, but
necessary and proper laws? In truth, the constitutional operation of the government would be precisely the
same, if the clause were obliterated, as if it were repeated in every article.[1] It would otherwise result, that
the power could never be exercised; that is, the end
would be required, and yet no means allowed. This
would be a perfect absurdity. It would be to create
powers, and compel them to remain for ever in a torpid,
dormant, and paralytic state. It cannot, therefore, be
denied, that the powers, given by the constitution, imply
the ordinary means of execution;[2] for without the
substance of the power the constitution would be a
dead letter. Those, who object to the article, must
therefore object to the form, or the language of the
provision. Let us see, if any better could be devised.[3]

§ 1233. There are four possible methods, which the
convention might have adopted on this subject. First,
they might have copied the second article of the confederation, which would have prohibited the exercise
of any power not *expressly* delegated. If they had
done so, the constitution would have been construed
with so much rigour, as to disarm it of all real authority; or with so much latitude, as altogether to destroy
the force of the restriction. It is obvious, that no important power delegated by the confederation was, or
indeed could be executed by congress, without recurring
more or less to the doctrine of construction or implica-

[1] The Federalist, No. 33; 2 Elliot's Debates, 196; Hamilton on Bank,
1 Hamilton's Works, 121; M'Culloch v. Maryland, 4 Wheaton's R. 419.
[2] M'Culloch v. Maryland, 4 Wheat. R. 409; 4 Elliot's Debates, 217,
218, 220, 221.
[3] The Federalist, No. 44. See also President Monroe's Exposition
and Message, 4th of May, 1822, p. 47; 3 Elliot's Deb. 318.

tion.[1] It had, for instance, power to establish courts for the trial of prizes and piracies, to borrow money, and emit bills of credit. But how could these powers be put in operation without some other implied powers and means? The truth is, that, under the confederation, congress was from this very clause driven to the distressing alternative, either to violate the articles by a broad latitude of construction, or to suffer the powers of the government to remain prostrate, and the public service to be wholly neglected. It is notorious, that they adopted, and were compelled to adopt the former course; and the country bore them out in what might be deemed an usurpation of authority.[2] The past experience of the country was, therefore, decisive against any such restriction. It was either useless, or mischievous.[3]

§ 1234. Secondly. The convention might have attempted a positive enumeration of the powers comprehended under the terms, *necessary* and *proper*. The attempt would have involved a complete digest of laws on every subject, to which the constitution relates. It must have embraced all future, as well as all present exigencies, and been accommodated to all times, and all occasions, and all changes of national situation and character. Every new application of the general power must have been foreseen and specified; for the particular powers, which are the means of attaining the objects of the general power, must, necessarily, vary with those objects; and be often properly varied, when the objects

---

[1] The Federalist, No. 44.
[2] See The Federalist, No. 38, 44; 4 Wheat. R. 423; 4 Elliot's Deb. 218, 219.
[3] *M'Culloch v. Maryland*, 4 Wheat. R. 406, 407, 423.

remain the same.[1] Who does not at once perceive,
that such a course is utterly beyond human reach and
foresight?[2] It demands a wisdom never yet given
to man ; and a knowledge of the future, which belongs
only to Him, whose providence directs, and governs all.

§ 1235. Thirdly. The convention might have attempted a negative enumeration of the powers, by specifying the powers, which should be excepted from the
general grant. It will be at once perceived, that this
task would have been equally chimerical with the foregoing; and would have involved this additional objection, that in such a case, every defect in the enumeration would have been equivalent to a positive grant of
authority. If, to avoid this consequence, they had attempted a partial enumeration of the exceptions, and
described the residue by the general terms, "not necessary or proper," it must have happened, that the enumeration would comprehend a few exceptions only, and
those only, which were most prominent; and therefore
the least likely to be abused; and that others would be
less forcibly excepted under the residuary clause, than
if there had not been any partial enumeration of exceptions.[3]

§ 1236. Fourthly. The convention might have
been wholly silent on this head; and then (as has been
already seen) the auxiliary powers, or means to carry
into execution the general powers, would have resulted
to the government by necessary implication; for
wherever the end is required, the means are authorized; and wherever a general power to do a thing

1 The Federalist, No. 44 ; 2 Elliot's Deb. 223.
2 M'Culloch v. Maryland, 4 Wheat. R. 407 ; 4 Elliot's Deb. 223, 224 ;
Anderson v. Dunn, 6 Wheat. R. 204, 225, 226.
3 The Federalist, No. 44.

is given, every particular power necessary for doing it, is included. If this last course had been adopted, every objection, now urged against the clause, would have remained in full force ; and the omission might have been made in critical periods a ground to assail the essential powers of the Union.[1]

§ 1237. If, then, the clause imports no more, than would result from necessary implication, it may be asked, why it was inserted at all. The true answer is, that such a clause was peculiarly useful, in order to avoid any doubt, which ingenuity or jealousy might raise upon the subject. Much plausible reasoning might be employed by those, who were hostile to the Union, and in favour of state power, to prejudice the people on such a subject, and to embarrass the government in all its reasonable operations. Besides ; as the confederation contained a positive clause, restraining the authority of congress to powers expressly granted, there was a fitness in declaring, that that rule of interpretation should no longer prevail. The very zeal, indeed, with which the present clause has been always assailed, is the highest proof of its importance and propriety. It has narrowed down the grounds of hostility to the mere interpretation of terms.[2]

§ 1238. The plain import of the clause is, that congress shall have all the incidental and instrumental powers, necessary and proper to carry into execution all the express powers. It neither enlarges any power specifically granted ; nor is it a grant of any new power to congress. But it is merely a declaration for the removal of all uncertainty, that the means of carry-

---

[1] The Federalist, No. 44.
[2] The Federalist, No. 33, 44.

ing into execution those, otherwise granted, are included in the grant.[1] Whenever, therefore, a question arises concerning the constitutionality of a particular power, the first question is, whether the power be *expressed* in the constitution. If it be, the question is decided. If it be not *expressed*, the next inquiry must be, whether it is properly an incident to an express power, and necessary to its execution. If it be, then it may be exercised by congress. If not, congress cannot exercise it.[2]

§ 1239. But still a ground of controversy remains open, as to the true interpretation of the terms of the clause; and it has been contested with no small share of earnestness and vigour. What, then, is the true constitutional sense of the words "necessary and proper" in this clause? It has been insisted by the advocates of a rigid interpretation, that the word "necessary" is here used in its close and most intense meaning; so that it is equivalent to *absolutely and indispensably necessary.* It has been said, that the constitution allows only the means, which are *necessary;* not those, which are merely *convenient* for effecting the enumerated powers. If such a latitude of construction be given to this phrase, as to give any non-enumerated power, it will go far to give every one; for there is no one, which ingenuity might not

[1] Some few statesmen have contended, that the clause gave farther powers, than mere incidental powers. But their reasoning does not seem very clear or satisfactory. See Governor Randolph's Remarks, 2 Elliot's Debates, 342; Mr. Gerry's Speech in Febuary, 1791, 4 Elliot's Debates, 225, 227. These Speeches are, however, valuable for some striking views, which they present, of the propriety of a liberal construction of the words.

[2] See Virginia Report and Resolutions, Jan., 1800, p. 33, 34; 1 Tuck. Black. Comm. App. 287, 288; President Monroe's Exposition and Message, 4th of May, 1822, p. 47; 5 Marshall's Wash. App. note 3; 1 Hamilton's Works, 117, 121.

torture into a convenience in some way or other to some one of so long a list of enumerated powers. It would swallow up all the delegated powers, and reduce the whole to one phrase. Therefore it is, that the constitution has restrained them to the *necessary* means; that is to say, to those means, *without which the grant of the power would be nugatory.* A little difference in the degree of convenience cannot constitute the necessity, which the constitution refers to.[1]

§ 1240. The effect of this mode of interpretation is to exclude all choice of means; or, at most, to leave to congress in each case those only, which are most direct and simple. If, indeed, such implied powers, and such only, as can be shown to be indispensably necessary, are within the purview of the clause, there will be no end to difficulties, and the express powers must practically become a mere nullity.[2] It will be found, that the operations of the government, upon any of its powers, will rarely admit of a rigid demonstration of the necessity (in this strict sense) of the particular means. In most cases, various systems or means may be resorted to, to attain the same end; and yet, with respect to each, it may be argued, that it is not constitutional, because it is not indispensable; and the end may be obtained by other means. The consequence of such reasoning would be, that, as no means could be shown to be constitutional, none could be adopted.[3] For instance, con-

---

[1] 4 Jefferson's Corresp. 525, 526; 4 Elliot's Deb. 216, 217, 224, 225, 267; *M'Culloch* v. *Maryland,* 4 Wheat. R. 412, 413.

[2] Hamilton on Bank, 1 Hamilton's Works, 119; 5 Marshall's Wash. App. note 3, p. 9; Mr. Madison, 4 Elliot's Deb. 223.

[3] *United States* v. *Fisher,* 2 Cranch, 358; 1 Peters's Cond. R. 421; Hamilton on Bank, 1 Hamilton's Works, 119; 5 Marshall's Wash. note 3, p. 9, 10; Mr. Madison, 4 Elliot's Deb. 223.

gress possess the power to make war, and to raise armies, and incidentally to erect fortifications, and purchase cannon and ammunition, and other munitions of war. But war may be carried on without fortifications, cannon, and ammunition. No particular kind of arms can be shown to be absolutely necessary; because various sorts of arms of different convenience, power, and utility are, or may be resorted to by different nations. What then becomes of the power? Congress has power to borrow money, and to provide for the payment of the public debt; yet no particular method is indispensable to these ends. They may be attained by various means. Congress has power to provide a navy; but no particular size, or form, or equipment of ships is indispensable. The means of providing a naval establishment are very various; and the applications of them admit of infinite shades of opinion, as to their convenience, utility, and necessity. What then is to be done? Are the powers to remain dormant? Would it not be absurd to say, that congress did not possess the choice of means under such circumstances, and ought not to be empowered to select, and use any means, which are in fact conducive to the exercise of the powers granted by the constitution?[1] Take another example; congress has, doubtless, the authority, under the power to regulate commerce, to erect lighthouses, beacons, buoys, and public piers, and authorize the employment of pilots.[2] But it cannot be affirmed, that the exercise of these powers is in a strict sense necessary; or that the power to regulate commerce would be nugatory without establishments of this na-

---

[1] *United States* v. *Fisher*, 2 Cranch. R. 358; 1 Peters's Condens. R. 421.

[2] See 4 Elliot's Debates, 265, 280.

ture.[1] In truth, no particular regulation of commerce can ever be shown to be exclusively and indispensably necessary ; and thus we should be driven to admit, that all regulations are within the scope of the power, or that none are. If there be any general principle, which is inherent in the very definition of government, and essential to every step of the progress to be made by that of the United States, it is, that every power, vested in a government, is in its nature sovereign, and includes, by force of the term, a right to employ all the means requisite, and fairly applicable to the attainment of the end of such power; unless they are excepted in the constitution, or are immoral, or are contrary to the essential objects of political society.[2]

§ 1241. There is another difficulty in the strict construction above alluded to, that it makes the constitutional authority depend upon casual and temporary circumstances, which may produce a necessity to-day, and change it to-morrow. This alone shows the fallacy of the reasoning. The expediency of exercising a particular power at a particular time must, indeed, depends on circumstances ; but the constitutional right of exercising it must be uniform and invariable ; the same to-day as to-morrow.[3]

§ 1242. Neither can the degree, in which a measure is necessary, ever be a test of the legal right to adopt it. That must be a matter of opinion, (upon which different men, and different bodies may form opposite judgments,) and can only be a test of expediency.

---

1 Hamilton on Bank, 1 Hamilton's Works, 120.

2 Hamilton on Bank, 1 Hamilton's Works, 112.

3 Hamilton on Bank, 1 Hamilton's Works, 117 ; 5 Marshall's Wash. App. note 3. p. 8.

The relation between the measure and the end, between the nature of the means employed towards the
execution of a power, and the object of that power,
must be the criterion of constitutionality ; and not the
greater or less of necessity or expediency.[1] If the
legislature possesses a right of choice as to the means,
who can limit that choice ? Who is appointed an um-
pire, or arbiter in cases, where a discretion is confided
to a government ? The very idea of such a controlling
authority in the exercise of its powers is a virtual denial of the supremacy of the government in regard to
its powers. It repeals the supremacy of the national
government, proclaimed in the constitution.

§ 1243. It is equally certain, that neither the grammatical, nor the popular sense of the word, "necessary,"
requires any such construction. According to both,
"necessary" often means no more than *needful, requisite, incidental, useful,* or *conducive to.* It is a common
mode of expression to say, that it is necessary for a
government, or a person to do this or that thing, when
nothing more is intended or understood, than that the
interest of the government or person requires, or will
be promoted by the doing of this or that thing. Every
one's mind will at once suggest to him many illustrations of the use of the word in this sense.[2] To employ the means, necessary to an end, is generally understood, as employing any means calculated to produce
the end, and not as being confined to those single means,
without which the end would be entirely unattainable.

§ 1244. Such is the character of human language,

1 Hamilton on Bank, 1 Hamilton's Works, 119, 120; 5 Marshall's
Wash. App. note 3, p. 9, 10; *M'Culloch* v. *Maryland,* 4 Wheat. R. 423.
2 Hamilton on Bank, 1 Hamilton's Works, 118; 5 Marshall's Wash.
App. note 3. p. 9.

that no word conveys to the mind in all situations one single definite idea ; and nothing is more common, than to use words in a figurative sense. Almost all compositions contain words, which, taken in their rigorous sense, would convey a meaning, different from that, which is obviously intended. It is essential to just interpretation, that many words, which import something excessive, should be understood in a more mitigated sense ; in a sense, which common usage justifies. The word "necessary" is of this description. It has not a fixed character peculiar to itself. It admits of all degrees of comparison ; and is often connected with other words, which increase or diminish the impression, which the mind receives of the urgency it imports. A thing may be necessary, very necessary, absolutely or indispensably necessary. It may be little necessary, less necessary, or least necessary. To no mind would the same idea be conveyed by any two of these several phrases. The tenth section of the first article of the constitution furnishes a strong illustration of this very use of the word. It contains a prohibition upon any state to "lay any imposts or duties, &c. ex-"cept what may be *absolutely necessary* for executing "its inspection laws." No one can compare this clause with the other, on which we are commenting, without being struck with the conviction, that the word "*absolutely*," here prefixed to "necessary," was intended to distinguish it from the sense, in which, standing alone, it is used in the other.[1]

---

[1] *M'Culloch* v. *Maryland*, 4 Wheaton's R. 413 to 415. — In this case (4 Wheaton's R. 411 to 425,) there is a very elaborat argument of the Supreme Court upon the whole of this subject, a portion of which has been already extracted in the preceding Commentaries, on the rules of interpretation of the constitution.

§ 1245. That the restrictive interpretation must be abandoned, in regard to certain powers of the government, cannot be reasonably doubted. It is universally conceded, that the power of punishment appertains to sovereignty, and may be exercised, whenever the sovereign has a right to act, as incidental to his constitutional powers. It is a means for carrying into execution all sovereign powers, and may be used, although not indispensably necessary. If, then, the restrictive interpretation must be abandoned, in order to justify the constitutional exercise of the power to punish ; whence is the rule derived, which would reinstate it, when the government would carry its powers into operation, by means not vindictive in their nature ? If the word, "necessary" means *needful, requisite, essential, conducive to,* to let in the power of punishment, why is it not equally comprehensive, when applied to other means used to facilitate the execution of the powers of the government ?[1]

§ 1246. The restrictive interpretation is also contrary to a sound maxim of construction, generally admitted, namely, that the powers contained in a constitution of government, especially those, which concern the general administration of the affairs of the country, such as its finances, its trade, and its defence, ought to be liberally expounded in advancement of the public good. This rule does not depend on the particular form of a government, or on the particular demarcations of the boundaries of its powers ; but on the nature and objects of government itself. The means, by which national exigencies are provided for, national inconveniences obviated, and national prosperity pro-

[1] *M'Culloch* v. *Maryland,* 4 Wheat. R. 418.

moted, are of such infinite variety, extent, and complexity, that there must of necessity be great latitude of discretion in the selection, and application of those means. Hence, consequently, the necessity and propriety of exercising the authorities, entrusted to a government, on principles of liberal construction.[1]

§ 1247. It is no valid objection to this doctrine to say, that it is calculated to extend the powers of the government throughout the entire sphere of state legislation. The same thing may be said, and has been said, in regard to every exercise of power by implication and construction. There is always some chance of error, or abuse of every power; but this furnishes no ground of objection against the power; and certainly no reason for an adherence to the most rigid construction of its terms, which would at once arrest the whole movements of the government.[2] The remedy for any abuse, or misconstruction of the power, is the same, as in similar abuses and misconstructions of the state governments. It is by an appeal to the other departments of the government; and finally to the people, in the exercise of their elective franchises.[3]

§ 1248. There are yet other grounds against the restrictive interpretation derived from the language, and the character of the provision. The language is, that congress shall have power " to make all laws, which " shall be *necessary* and *proper*." If the word "necessary" were used in the strict and rigorous sense contended for, it would be an extraordinary departure from the usual course of the human mind, as exhibited in solemn instruments, to add another word "proper;"

---

[1] Hamilton on Bank, 1 Hamilton's Works, 120, 121.
[2] Hamilton on Bank, 1 Hamilton's Works, 122.
[3] The Federalist, No. 33, 44.

the only possible effect of which is to qualify that strict and rigorous meaning, and to present clearly the idea of a choice of means in the course of legislation.[1] If no means can be resorted to, but such as are indispensably necessary, there can be neither sense, nor utility in adding the other word; for the necessity shuts out from view all consideration of the propriety of the means, as contradistinguished from the former. But if the intention was to use the word "necessary" in its more liberal sense, then there is a peculiar fitness in the other word. It has a sense at once admonitory, and directory. It requires, that the means should be, *bonâ fide*, appropriate to the end.

§ 1249. The character of the clause equally forbids any presumption of an intention to use the restrictive interpretation. In the first place, the clause is placed among the powers of congress, and not among the limitations on those powers. In the next place, its terms purport to enlarge, and not to diminish, the powers vested in the government. It purports, on its face, to be an additional power, not a restriction on those already granted.[2] If it does not, in fact, (as seems the true construction,) give any new powers, it affirms the right to use all necessary and proper means to carry into execution the other powers; and thus makes an *express* power, what would otherwise be merely an *implied* power. In either aspect, it is impossible to construe it to be a restriction. If it have any effect, it is to remove the implication of any restriction. If a restriction had been intended, it is impossible, that the framers of the constitution should have concealed it

---

[1] *M'Culloch v. Maryland*, 4 Wheat. R. 418, 419.
[2] *M'Culloch v. Maryland*, 4 Wheat. R. 419, 420.

under phraseology, which purports to enlarge, or at least give the most ample scope to the other powers. There was every motive on their part to give point and clearness to every restriction of national power; for they well knew, that the national government would be more endangered in its adoption by its supposed strength, than by its weakness. It is inconceivable, that they should have disguised a restriction upon its powers under the form of a grant of power. They would have sought other terms, and have imposed the restraint by negatives.[1] And what is equally strong, no one, in or out of the state conventions, at the time when the constitution was put upon its deliverance before the people, ever dreamed of, or suggested, that it contained a restriction of power. The whole argument on each side, of attack and of defence, gave it the positive form of an express power, and not of an express restriction.

§ 1250. Upon the whole, the result of the most careful examination of this clause is, that, if it does not enlarge, it cannot be construed to restrain the powers of congress, or to impair the right of the legislature to exercise its best judgment, in the selection of measures to carry into execution the constitutional powers of the national government. The motive for its insertion doubtless was, the desire to remove all possible doubt respecting the right to legislate on that vast mass of incidental powers, which must be involved in the constitution, if that instrument be not a splendid pageant, or a delusive phantom of sovereignty. Let the end be legitimate; let it be within the scope of the constitution; and all means, which are appropriate, which are

---

1 *M'Culloch* v. *Maryland,* 4 Wheat. R. 420.

plainly adapted to the end, and which are not prohibited, but are consistent with the letter and spirit of the instrument, are constitutional.[1]

§ 1251. It may be well, in this connexion, to mention another sort of implied power, which has been called with great propriety a resulting power, arising from the aggregate powers of the national government. It will not be doubted, for instance, that, if the United States should make a conquest of any of the territories of its neighbours, the national government would possess sovereign jurisdiction over the conquered territory. This would, perhaps, rather be a result from the whole mass of the powers of the national government, and from the nature of political society, than a consequence or incident of the powers specially enumerated.[2] It may, however, be deemed, if an incident to any, an incident to the power to make war. Other instances of resulting powers will easily suggest themselves. The United States are nowhere declared in the constitution to be a sovereignty entitled to sue, though jurisdiction is given to the national courts over controversies, to which the United States shall be a party. It is a natural incident, resulting from the sovereignty and character of the national government.[3] So the United States, in their political capacity, have a right to enter into a contract, (although it is not expressly provided for by the constitution,) for it is an incident to their general right of sovereignty, so far as it is appro-

---

1 *M'Culloch* v. *Maryland*, 4 Wheat. R. 420, 421, 423. See also 4 Elliot's Debates, 220, 221, 222, 223, 224, 225; 2 Elliot's Debates, 196, 342; 5 Marsh. Wash. App. No. 3; 2 American Museum. 536; *Anderson* v. *Dunn*, 6 Wheat. R. 204, 225, 226; Hamilton on Bank, 1 Hamilton's Works, 111 to 123.

2 Hamilton on Bank, 1 Hamilton's Works, 115.

3 See *Dugan* v. *United States*, 3 Wheat. R. 173, 179, 180.

priate to any of the ends of the government, and within the constitutional range of its powers.[1] So congress possess power to punish offences committed on board of the public ships of war of the government by persons not in the military or naval service of the United States, whether they are in port, or at sea ; for the jurisdiction on board of public ships is every where deemed exclusively to belong to the sovereign.[2]

§ 1252. And not only may implied powers, but implied exemptions from state authority, exist, although not expressly provided for by law. The collectors of the revenue, the carriers of the mail, the mint establishment, and all those institutions, which are public in their nature, are examples in point. It has never been doubted, that all, who are employed in them, are protected, while in the line of their duty, from state control ; and yet this protection is not expressed in any act of congress. It is incidental to, and is implied in, the several acts, by which those institutions are created ; and is preserved to them by the judicial department, as a part of its functions.[3] A contractor for supplying a military post with provisions cannot be restrained from making purchases within a state, or from transporting provisions, to the place, at which troops are stationed. He could not be taxed, or fined, or lawfully obstructed, in so doing.[4] These incidents necessarily flow from the supremacy of the powers of the Union, within their legitimate sphere of action.

§ 1253. It would be almost impracticable, if it were not useless, to enumerate the various instances, in

[1] *United States* v. *Tingey*, 5 Peters's R. 115.
[2] *United States* v. *Bevans*, 3 Wheaton's R. 388 ; The Exchange, 7 Cranch, 116 ; S. C. 2 Peters's Cond. R. 429.
[3] *Osborn* v. *Bank of U. States*, 9 Wheat. R. 365, 366.
[4] Id. 367.

which congress, in the progress of the government, have made use of incidental and implied means to execute its powers. They are almost infinitely varied in their ramifications and details. It is proposed, however, to take notice of the principal measures, which have been contested, as not within the scope of the powers of congress, and which may be distinctly traced in the operations of the government, and in leading party divisions.[1]

---

[1] Some minor points will be found in the debates collected in 4 Elliot's Debates, 139, 141, 229, 234, 235, 238, 239, 240, 243, 249, 251, 252, 261, 265, 266, 270, 271, 280. There is no express power given by the constitution to erect forts, or magazines, or light-houses, or piers, or buoys, or public buildings, or to make surveys of the coast; but they have been constantly deemed incidental to the general powers. Mr. Bayard's Speech in 1807, (4 Elliot's Debates, 265;) Mr. Pickering's Speech, 1817, (4 Elliot's Debates, 280.)

CHAPTER XXV.

INCIDENTAL POWERS — NATIONAL BANK.

§ 1254. ONE of the earliest and most important measures, which gave rise to a question of constitutional power, was the act chartering the bank of the United States in 1791. That question has often since been discussed ; and though the measure has been repeatedly sanctioned by congress, by the executive, and by the judiciary, and has obtained the like favour in a great majority of the states, yet it is, up to this very hour, still debated upon constitutional grounds, as if it were still new, and untried. It is impossible, at this time, to treat it, as an open question, unless the constitution is for ever to remain an unsettled text, possessing no permanent attributes, and incapable of having any ascertained sense ; varying with every change of doctrine, and of party ; and delivered over to interminable doubts. If the constitution is to be only, what the administration of the day may wish it to be ; and is to assume any, and all shapes, which may suit the opinions and theories of public men, as they successively direct the public councils, it will be difficult, indeed, to ascertain, what its real value is. It cannot possess either certainty, or uniformity, or safety. It will be one thing to-day, and another thing to-morrow, and again another thing on each succeeding day. The past will furnish no guide, and the future no security. It will be the reverse of a law ; and entail upon the country the curse of that miserable servitude, so much abhorred and denounced, where all is vague and uncertain in the fundamentals of government.

§ 1255. The reasoning, upon which the constitutionality of a national bank is denied, has been already in
some degree stated in the preceding remarks. It turns
upon the strict interpretation of the clause, giving the
auxiliary powers necessary, and proper to execute the
other enumerated powers. It is to the following effect :
The power to incorporate a bank is not among those
enumerated in the constitution.` It is known, that the
very power, thus proposed, as a means, was rejected,
as an end, by the convention, which formed the constitution. A proposition was made in that body, to authorize congress to open canals, and an amendatory
one to empower them to create corporations. But the
whole was rejected ; and one of the reasons of the rejection urged in debate was, that they then would have
a power to create a bank, which would render the great
cities, where there were prejudices and jealousies on
that subject, adverse to the adoption of the constitution.[1]
In the next place, all the enumerated powers can be
carried into execution without a bank. A bank, therefore, is not *necessary*, and consequently not authorized by this clause of the constitution. It is urged,
that a bank will give great facility, or convenience to
the collection of taxes. If this were true, yet the
constitution allows only the means, which are *necessary*,
and not merely those, which are *convenient* for effecting the enumerated powers. If such a latitude of construction were allowed, as to consider convenience, as
justifying the use of such means, it would swallow up
all the enumerated powers.[2] Therefore, the constitution

[1] 4 Jefferson's Correspondence, 523, 526; Id. 506.
[2] Ibid; 4 Elliot's Debates, 219.

restrains congress to those means, without which the power would be nugatory.[1]

§ 1256. Nor can its convenience be satisfactorily established. Bank-bills may be a more convenient vehicle, than treasury orders, for the purposes of that department. But a little difference in the degree of convenience cannot constitute the necessity contemplated by the constitution. Besides; the local and state banks now in existence are competent, and would be willing to undertake all the agency required for those very purposes by the government. And if they are able and willing, this establishes clearly, that there can be no necessity for establishing a national bank.[2] If there would ever be a superior conveniency in a national bank, it does not follow, that there exists a power to establish it, or that the business of the country cannot go on very well without it. Can it be thought, that the constitution intended, that for a shade or two of convenience, more or less, congress should be authorized to break down the most ancient and fundamental laws of the states, such as those against mortmain, the laws of alienage, the rules of descent, the acts of distribution, the laws of escheat and forfeiture, and the laws of monopoly ? Nothing but a necessity, invincible by any other means, can justify such a prostration of laws, which constitute the pillars of our whole system of jurisprudence.[3] If congress have the power to create one corporation, they may create all sorts ; for the power is

---

[1] 4 Jefferson's Correspondence, 523, 525, 526 ; 5 Marsh. Wash. App. Note 3.

[2] Ibid ; 4 Elliot's Debates, 220.

[3] 4 Jefferson's Correspondence, 523, 526, 527 ; 5 Marsh. Wash. App. Note 3; 1 Hamilton's Works, 130.

no where limited ; and may even establish monopolies.[1]
Indeed this very charter is a monopoly.[2]

§ 1257. The reasoning, by which the constitutionality of the national bank has been sustained,
is contained in the following summary. The powers confided to the national government are unquestionably, so far as they exist, sovereign and supreme.[3] It is not, and cannot be disputed, that the
power of creating a corporation is one belonging to
sovereignty.   But so are all other legislative powers ;
for the original power of giving the law on any subject
whatever is a sovereign power. If the national government cannot create a corporation, because it is an exercise of sovereign power, neither can it, for the same
reason, exercise any other legislative power.[4]   This
consideration alone ought to put an end to the abstract
inquiry, whether the national government has power to
erect a corporation, that is, to give a legal or artificial
capacity to one or more persons, distinct from the natural capacity.[5]   For, if it be an incident to sovereignty, and it is not prohibited, it must belong to the
national government in relation to the objects entrusted
to it. The true difference is this ; where the authority
of a government is general, it can create corporations
in all cases ; where it is confined to certain branches
of legislation, it can create corporations only as to those
cases.[6] It cannot be denied, that implied powers may
be delegated, as well as express. It follows, that a

---

[1] 4 Elliot's Debates, 217, 219, 224, 225.
[2] 4 Elliot's Debates, 219, 220, 223.
[3] Hamilton on Bank, 1 Hamilton's Works, 113; 4 Wheat. R. 405, 406, 409, 410.
[4] M'Culloch v. Maryland, 4 Wheat. R. 409.
[5] Hamilton on Bank, 1 Hamilton's Works, 113, 114, 121.
[6] Hamilton on Bank, 1 Hamilton's Works, 113, 114, 131.

power to erect corporations may as well be implied, as any other thing, if it be an instrument or means of carrying into execution any specified power. The only question in any case must be, whether it be such an instrument or means, and have a natural relation to any of the acknowledged objects of government. Thus, congress may not erect a corporation for superintending the police of the city of Philadelphia, because they have no authority to regulate the police of that city. But if they possessed the authority to regulate the police of such city, they might, unquestionably, create a corporation for that purpose; because it is incident to the sovereign legislative power to regulate a thing, to employ all the means, which relate to its regulation, to the best and greatest advantage.[1]

§ 1258. A strange fallacy has crept into the reasoning on this subject. It has been supposed, that a corporation is some great, independent thing; and that the power to erect it is a great, substantive, independent power; whereas, in truth, a corporation is but a legal capacity, quality, or means to an end; and the power to erect it is, or may be, an implied and incidental power. A corporation is never the end, for which other powers are exercised; but a means, by which other objects are accomplished. No contributions are made to charity for the sake of an incorporation; but a corporation is created to administer the charity. No seminary of learning is instituted in order to be incorporated; but the corporate character is conferred to subserve the purposes of education. No city was ever built with the sole object of being incorporated; but it is incorporated as affording the best means of being well governed.

---

[1] Hamilton on Bank, 1 Hamilton's Works, 115, 116, 130, 131, 136.

So a mercantile company is formed with a certain capital for carrying on a particular branch of business. Here, the business to be prosecuted is the end. The association, in order to form the requisite capital, is the primary means. If an incorporation is added to the association, it only gives it a new quality, an artificial capacity, by which it is enabled to prosecute the business with more convenience and safety. In truth, the power of creating a corporation is never used for its own sake; but for the purpose of effecting something else. So that there is not a shadow of reason to say, that it may not pass as an incident to powers expressly given, as a mode of executing them.[1]

§ 1259. It is true, that among the enumerated powers we do not find that of establishing a bank, or creating a corporation. But we do find there the great powers to lay and collect taxes; to borrow money; to regulate commerce; to declare and conduct war; and to raise and support armies and navies. Now, if a bank be a fit means to execute any or all of these powers, it is just as much implied, as any other means. If it be "necessary and proper" for any of them, how is it possible to deny the authority to create it for such purposes?[2] There is no more propriety in giving this power in *express* terms, than in giving any other incidental powers or means in express terms. If it had been intended to grant this power generally, and to make it a distinct and independent power, having no relation to, but reaching beyond the other enumerated powers, there would then have been a propriety in giving it in express terms, for otherwise it would not

[1] *M'Culloch v. Maryland*, 4 Wheat. R. 411; Hamilton on Bank, 1 Hamilton's Works, 116, 117, 135.

[2] *M'Culloch v. Maryland*, 4 Wheat. R. 406, 407, 408, 409, 110. 411.

exist. Thus, it was proposed in the convention, to give a general power "to grant charters of incorporation;" — to "grant charters of incorporation in cases, where the pub-"lic good may require them, and the authority of a sin-"gle state may be incompetent;" [1] — and "to grant let-"ters of incorporation for canals, &c." [2] If either of these propositions had been adopted, there would have been an obvious propriety in giving the power in express terms; because, as to the two former, the power was general and unlimited, and reaching far beyond any of the other enumerated powers; and as to the latter, it might be far more extensive than any incident to the other enumerated powers.[3] But the rejection of these propositions does not prove, that congress in no case, as an incident to the enumerated powers, should erect a corporation; but only, that they should not have a substantive, independent power to erect corporations beyond those powers.

§ 1260. Indeed, it is most manifest, that it never could have been contemplated by the convention, that congress should, in no case, possess the power to erect a corporation. What otherwise would become of the territorial governments, all of which are corporations created by congress? There is no where an express power given to congress to erect them. But under the confederation, congress did provide for their erection, as a resulting and implied right of sovereignty, by the celebrated ordinance of 1787; and congress, under the

[1] Journ. of Convention, p. 260.
[2] Journ. of Convention, p. 376. — In the first congress of 1789, when the amendments proposed by congress were before the House of Representatives for consideration, Mr. Gerry moved to add a clause, "That congress erect no company of merchants with exclusive advantages of commerce." The proposition was negatived. 2 Lloyd's Deb. 257.
[3] M'Culloch v. Maryland, 4 Wheat. R. 421, 422.

constitution, have ever since, without question, and with the universal approbation of the nation, from time to time created territorial governments. Yet congress derive this power only by implication, or as necessary and proper, to carry into effect the express power to regulate the territories of the United States.[1]   In the convention, two propositions were made and referred to a committee at the same time with the propositions already stated respecting granting of charters, " to dispose of the unappropriated lands of the United States," and " to institute temporary governments for new states arising therein." Both these propositions shared the same fate, as those respecting charters of incorporation.   But what would be thought of the argument, built upon this foundation, that congress did not possess the power to erect territorial governments, because these propositions were silently abandoned, or annulled in the convention ?

§ 1261. This is not the only case, in which congress may erect corporations.   Under the power to accept a cession of territory for the seat of government, and to exercise exclusive legislation therein ; no one can doubt, that congress may erect corporations therein, not only public,but private corporations.[2]   They have constantly exercised the power ; and it has never yet been breathed, that it was unconstitutional.   Yet it can be exercised only as an incident to the power of general legislation. And if so, why may it not be exercised, as an incident to any specific power of legislation, if it be a means to attain the objects of such power ?

§ 1262. That a national bank is an appropriate means to carry into effect some of the enumerated powers of the

---

[1] *M'Culloch* v. *Maryland,* 4 Wheat. R. 422 ; Hamilton on Bank, 1 Hamilton's Works, 135, 136.

[2] Hamilton on Bank, 1 Hamilton's Works, 128, 129, 135.

government, and that this can be best done by erecting
it into a corporation, may be established by the most
satisfactory reasoning.   It has a relation, more or less
direct, to the power of collecting taxes, to that of borrowing money, to that of regulating trade between the
states, and to those of raising and maintaining fleets
and armies.[1]   And it may be added, that it has a most
important bearing upon the regulation of currency between the states.   It is an instrument, which has been
usually applied by governments in the administration of
their fiscal and financial operations.[2]   And in the present
times it can hardly require argument to prove, that it is
a convenient, a useful, and an essential instrument in
the fiscal operations of the government of the United
States.[3]   This is so generally admitted by sound and intelligent statesmen, that it would be a waste of time to
endeavour to establish the truth by an elaborate survey
of the mode, in which it touches the administration of all
the various branches of the powers of the government.[4]

---

[1] Hamilton on Bank, 1 Hamilton's Works, p. 138.
[2] Hamilton on Bank, 1 Hamilton's Works, p. 152, 153.
[3] M'Culloch v. Maryland, 4 Wheat. R. 422, 423.
[4] In Mr. Hamilton's celebrated Argument on the Constitutionality of
the Bank of the United States, in Feb. 1791, there is an admirable exposition of the whole of this branch of the subject.   As the document is
rare, the following passages are inserted :
    " It is presumed to have been satisfactorily shown, in the course of
the preceding observations, 1. That the power of the government, as to
the objects intrusted to its management, is, in its nature, sovereign.
2. That the right of erecting corporations, is one, inherent in, and inseparable from, the idea of sovereign power. 3. That the position, that
the government of the United States can exercise no power, but such as
is delegated to it by its constitution, does not militate against this principle. 4. That the word *necessary*, in the general clause, can have no
restrictive operation, derogating from the force of this principle ; indeed,
that the degree, in which a measure is, or is not necessary, cannot be a
test of *constitutional* right, but of expediency only. 5. That the power
to erect corporations is not to be considered, as an independent and

§ 1263. In regard to the suggestion, that a proposition was made, and rejected in the convention to confer this very power, what was the precise nature or ex-

---

substantive power, but as an incidental and auxiliary one ; and was,
therefore, more properly left to implication, than expressly granted.
6. That the principle in question does not extend the power of the government beyond the prescribed limits, because it only affirms a power
to incorporate for purposes *within the sphere of the specified powers.*
And lastly, that the right to exercise such a power, in certain cases, is
unequivocally granted in the most positive and comprehensive terms.
To all which it only remains to be added, that such a power has actually been exercised in two very eminent instances, namely, in the
erection of two governments ; one northwest of the river Ohio, and the
other southwest ; the last, independent of any antecedent compact.
And there results a full and complete demonstration, that the secretary
of state and attorney-general are mistaken, when they deny generally
the power of the national government to erect corporations.
   " It shall now be endeavoured to be shown, that there is a power to
erect one of the kind proposed by the bill.   This will be done by trac-
ing a natural and obvious relation between the institution of a bank, and
the objects of several of the enumerated powers of the government ; and
by showing, that, *politically* speaking, it is necessary to the effectual
execution of one or more of those powers.   In the course of this investigation various instances will be stated, by way of illustration, of a
right to erect corporations under those powers.   Some preliminary observations may be proper.   The proposed bank is to consist of an association of persons for the purpose of creating a joint capital to be employed, chiefly and essentially, in loans.   So far the object is not only
lawful, but it is the mere exercise of a right, which the law allows to
every individual.   The bank of New-York, which is not incorporated, is
an example of such an association.   The bill proposes, in addition, that
the government shall become a joint proprietor in this undertaking ; and
that it shall permit the bills of the company, payable on demand, to be
receivable in its revenues ; and stipulates, that it shall not grant privileges, similar to those, which are to be allowed to this company, to any
others.   All this is incontrovertibly within the compass of the discretion
of the government.   The only question is, whether it has a right to incorporate this company, in order to enable it the more effectually to
accomplish ends, which are in themselves lawful.   To establish such a
right, it remains to show the relation of such an institution to one or more
of the specified powers of the government.   Accordingly, it is affirmed,
that it has a relation, more or less direct, to the power of collecting taxes;
to that of borrowing money ; to that of regulating trade between the

tent of this proposition, or what were the reasons for refusing it, cannot now be ascertained by any authentic document, or even by any accurate recollection of the

---

states ; and to those of raising and maintaining fleets and armies. To the two former, the relation may be said to be immediate. And, in the last place, it will be argued, that it is clearly within the provision, which authorizes the making of all *needful rules* and *regulations* concerning the property of the United States, as the same has been practised upon by the government.

" A bank relates to the collection of taxes in two ways. *Indirectly*, by increasing the quantity of circulating medium, and quickening circulation, which facilitates the means of paying ; *directly*, by creating a *convenient species* of mediu , in which they are to be paid. To designate or appoint the money or thing, in which taxes are to be paid, is not only a proper, but a necessary, *exercise* of the power of collecting them. Accordingly, congress, in the law concerning the collection of the duties on imposts and tonnage, have provided, that they shall be payable in gold and silver. But while it was an indispensable part of the work to say in what they should be paid, the choice of the specific thing was mere matter of discretion. The payment might have been required in the commodities themselves. Taxes in kind, however ill-judged, are not without precedents even in the United States ; or it might have been in the paper money of the several states, or in the bills of the bank of North-America, New-York, and Massachusetts, all or either of them ; or it might have been in bills issued under the authority of the United States. No part of this can, it is presumed, be disputed. The appointment, then, of the money or *thing*, in which the taxes are to be paid, is an incident to the power of collection. And among the expedients, which may be adopted, is that of bills issued under the authority of the United States. Now the manner of issuing these bills is again matter of discretion. The government might, doubtless, proceed in the following manner: It might provide that they should be issued under the direction of certain officers, payable on demand ; and in order to support their credit, and give them a ready circulation, it might, besides giving them a currency in its taxes, set apart, out of any monies in its treasury a given sum, and appropriate it, under the direction of those officers, as a fund for answering the bills, as presented for payment.

" The constitutionality of all this would not admit of a question, and yet it would amount to the institution of a bank, with a view to the more convenient collection of taxes. For the simplest and most precise idea of a bank is, a deposit of coin or other property, as a fund for *circulating a credit* upon it, which is to answer the purpose of money. That such an arrangement would be equivalent to the establishment of a bank,

members.   As far as any document exists, it specifies
only canals.[1]   If this proves any thing, it proves no more,
than that it was thought inexpedient to give a power to

---

would become obvious, if the place, where the fund to be set apart was
kept, should be made a receptacle of the monies of all other persons, who
should incline to deposit them there for safe keeping; and would become still more so, if the officers, charged with the direction of the fund,
were authorized to make discounts at the usual rate of interest, upon
good security.   To deny the power of the government to add this ingredient to the plan, would be to refine away all government.   A further process will still more clearly illustrate the point.   Suppose, when
the species of bank, which has been described, was about to be instituted,
it were to be urged, that in order to secure to it a due degree of confidence, the fund ought not only to be set apart and appropriated generally, but ought to be specifically vested in the officers, who were to have
the direction of it, and in their successors in office, to the end, that it
might acquire the character of *private property*, incapable of being
resumed without a violation of the sanction, by which the rights of property are protected ; and occasioning more serious and general alarm :
the apprehension of which might operate as a check upon the government.   Such a proposition might be opposed by arguments against the
expediency of it, or the solidity of the reason assigned for it ; but it is
not conceivable, what could be urged against its constitutionality.   And
yet such a disposition of the thing would amount to the erection of a corporation ; for the true definition of a corporation seems to be this: It is
a *legal* person, or a person created by act of law ; consisting of one or
more natural persons, authorized to hold property or a franchise in succession, in a legal, as contradistinguished from a natural capacity.   Let
the illustration proceed a step further.   Suppose a bank, of the nature,
which has been described, without or with incorporation, had been instituted, and that experience had evinced, as it probably would, that being
wholly under a public direction, it possessed not the confidence requisite
to the credit of its bills.   Suppose also, that by some of those adverse
conjunctures, which occasionally attend nations, there had been a very
great drain of the specie of the country, so as not only to cause general
distress for want of an adequate medium of circulation; but to produce, in consequence of that circumstance, considerable defalcations in
the public revenues.   Suppose, also, that there was no bank instituted
in any state ; in such a posture of things, would it not be most manifest,
that the incorporation of a bank, like that proposed by the bill, would be
a measure immediately relative to the effectual collection of the taxes,

---

[1] Journal of Convention, p. 376.

incorporate for the purpose of opening canals generally
But very different accounts are given of the import of
the proposition, and of the motives for rejecting it.

---

and completely within the province of a sovereign power of providing, by all laws necessary and proper, for that collection.

"If it be said, that such a state of things would render that necessary, and therefore constitutional, which is not so now; the answer to this, (and a solid one it doubtless is,) must still be, that which ha b en already stated; circumstances may affect the *expediency* of the measure, but they can neither add to, nor diminish its *constitutionality*. A bank has a direct relation to the power of borrowing money, because it is an usual, and in sudden emergencies, an essential instrument, in the obtaining of loans to government. A nation is threatened with a war; large sums are wanted on a sudden to make the requisite preparations: taxes are laid for the purpose; but it requires time to obtain the benefit of them; anticipation is indispensable. If there be a bank, the supply can at once be had; if there be none, loans from individuals must be sought. The progress of these is often too slow for the exigency; in some situations they are not practicable at all. Frequently when they a e, it is of great consequence to be able to anticipate the product of them by advances from a bank. The essentiality of such an institution, as an instrument of loans, is exemplified at this very moment. An Indian expedition is to be prosecuted. The only fund, out of which the money can arise consistently with the public engagements, is a tax, which only begins to be collected in July next. The preparations, however, are instantly to be made. The money must, therefore, be borrowed; and of whom could it be borrowed, if there were no public banks? It happens, that there are institutions of this kind; but if there were none, it would be indispensable to create one. Let it then be supposed, that the necessity existed, (as but for a casualty would be the case,) that proposals were made for obtaining a loan; that a number of individuals came forward and said, we are willing to accommodate the government with this money; with what we have in hand, and the credit we can raise upon it, we doubt not of being able to furnish the sum required. But in order to this, it is indispensable, that we should be incorporated as a bank. This is essential towards putting it in our power to do what is desired, and we are obliged, on that account, to make it the *consider ation* or *condition* of the loan. Can it be believed, that a compliance with this proposition would be unconstitutional? Does not this alone evince the contrary? It is a necessary part of a power to borrow, to be able to stipulate the considerations or conditions of a loan. It is evident, as has been remarked elsewhere, that this is not confined to the mere stipulation of a franchise. If it may, (and it is not perceived why it may

Some affirm, that it was confined to the opening of
canals and obstructions of rivers ; others, that it embraced banks ; and others, that it extended to the

---

not,) then the grant of a corporate capacity may be stipulated, as a consideration of the loan. There seems to be nothing unfit, or foreign from
the nature of the thing, in giving individuality, or a corporate capacity,
to a number of persons, who are willing to lend a sum of money to the
government, the better to enable them to do it, and make them an ordinary instrument of loans in future emergencies of state.

"But the more general view of the subject is still more satisfactory.
The legislative power of borrowing money, and of making all laws necessary and proper for carrying into execution that power, seems
obviously competent to the appointment of the *organ*, through which the
abilities and wills of individuals may be most efficaciously exerted, for
the accommodation of the government by loans. The attorney-general
opposes to this reasoning the following observation. Borrowing money
presupposes the accumulation of a fund to be lent ; and is secondary to
the creation of an ability to lend. This is plausible in theory, but it is
not true in fact. In a great number of cases, a previous accumulation
of a fund, equal to the whole sum required, does not exist ; and nothing
more can be actually presupposed, than that there exists resources, which,
put into activity to the greatest advantage, by the nature of the operation with the government, will be equal to the effect desired to be produced. All the provisions and operations of government must be
presumed to contemplate things as they *really* are. The institution of a
bank has also a natural relation to the regulation of trade between the
states, in so far as it is conducive to the creation of a convenient medium of exchange between them, and to the keeping up a full circulation, by preventing the frequent displacement of the metals in reciprocal
remittances. Money is the very hinge on which commerce turns. And
this does not mean merely gold and silver ; many other things have
served the purpose with different degress of utility. Paper has been
extensively employed. It cannot, therefore, be admitted with the attorney-general, that the regulation of trade between the states, as it concerns the medium of circulation and exchange, ought to be considered
as confined to coin. It is even supposable, that the whole, or the greatest part, of the coin of the country, might be carried out of it. The secretary of state objects to the relation here insisted upon, by the following
mode of reasoning : To erect a bank, says he, and to regulate commerce,
are very different acts. He who erects a bank, creates a subject of
commerce. So does he, who raises a bushel of wheat, or digs a dollar
out of the mines ; yet neither of these persons regulates commerce
thereby. To make a thing, which may be bought and sold, is not to

power of incorporations generally. Some, again, allege, that it was disagreed to, because it was thought improper to vest in congress a power of erecting corporations ;

---

prescribe regulations for *buying* and *selling*. This is making the regulation of commerce to consist in prescribing rules for buying and selling. This, indeed, is a species of regulation of trade, but it is one, which falls more aptly within the province of the local jurisdictions, than within that of the general government, whose care they must have presumed to have been intended to be directed to those general political arrangements concerning trade, on which its aggregate interests depend, rather than to the details of buying and selling. Accordingly, such only are the regulations to be found in the laws of the United States ; whos objects are to give encouragement to the enterprise of our own merchants, and to advance our navigation and manufactures. And it is in reference to these general relations of commerce, that an establishment, which furnishes facilities to circulation, and a convenient medium of exchange and alienation, is to be regarded as a regulation of trade.

" The secretary of state further urges, that if this was a regulation of commerce, it would be *void*, as *extending* as much to the internal part of every state, as to its external. But what regulation of commerce does not extend to the internal commerce of every state ? What are all the duties upon imported articles, amounting, in some cases, to prohibitions, but so many bounties upon domestic manufactures, affecting the interest of different classes of citizens in different ways ? What are all the provisions in the coasting act, which relate to the trade between district and district of the same state ? In short, what regulation of trade between the states, but must affect the internal trade of each state ? what can operate upon the whole, but must extend to every part ? The relation of a bank to the execution of the powers, that concern the common defence, has been anticipated. It has been noted, that at this very moment, the aid of such an institution is essential to the measure to be pursued for the protection of our frontiers.

" It now remains to show, that the incorporation of a bank is within the operation of the provision, which authorizes congress to make all needful rules and regulations concerning the property of the United States. But it is previously necessary to advert to a distinction, which has been taken up by the attorney-general. He admits, that the word property may signify personal property, however acquired; and yet asserts, that it cannot signify money arising from the sources of revenue pointed out in the constitution, 'because,' says he, 'the disposal and regulation of money is the final cause for raising it by taxes.' But it would be more accurate, to say, that the *object* to which money is intended to be applied, is the *final cause* for raising it, than that the dis-

others, because they thought it unnecessary to specify
the power; and inexpedient to furnish an additional
topic of objection to the constitution.   In this state

---

posal and regulation of it, is such.   The support of a government, the
support of troops for the common defence, the payment of the public
debt, are the true final causes for raising money.   The disposition and
regulation of it, when raised, are the steps, by which it is applied to the
ends, for which it was raised, not the ends themselves.   Hence, therefore
the money to be raised by taxes, as well as any other personal property,
must be supposed to come within the meaning, as they certainly do within the letter, of authority to make all needful rules and regulations concerning the property of the United States.   A case will make this plainer.
Suppose the public debt discharged, and the funds now pledged for it,
liberated.   In some instances it would be found expedient to repeal the
taxes; in others, the repeal might injure our own industry, our agricul-
ture, and manufactures.   In these cases, they would, of course, be
retained.   Here, then, would be monies arising from the authorized
sources of revenue, which would not fall within the rule, by which the
attorney-general endeavours to except them from other personal property, and from the operation of the clause in question.   The monies
being in the coffers of government, what is to hinder such a disposition
to be made of them, as is contemplated in the bill; or what an incorporation of the parties concerned, under the clause, which has been cited.
    "It is admitted, that, with regard to the western territory, they give
a power to erect a corporation; that is, to constitute a government.
And by what rule of construction can it be maintained, that the same
words, in a constitution of government, will not have the same effect,
when applied to one species of property as to another, as far as the subject is capable of it?   Or that a legislative power to make all needful
rules and regulations, or to pass all laws necessary and proper concerning the public property, which is admitted to authorize an incorporation,
in one case, will not authorize it in another? will justify the institution
of a government over the Western Territory, and will not justify the
incorporation of a bank, for the more useful management of the money
of the nation?   If it will do the last as well as the first, then, under this
provision alone, the bill is constitutional, because it contemplates, that
the United States shall be joint proprietors of the stock of the bank.
There is an observation of the secretary of state, to this effect, which
may require notice in this place. — Congress, says he, are not to lay
taxes *ad libitum, for any purpose they please,* but only to pay the debts, or
provide for the welfare of the Union.   Certainly, no inference can be
drawn from this, against the power of applying their money for the institution of a bank.   It is true, that they cannot, without breach of trust,
lay taxes for any other purpose, than the general welfare; but so neither

of the matter, no inference whatever can be drawn from it.[1]   But, whatever may have been the private intentions of the framers of the constitution, which

---

can any other government.   The welfare of the community is the only legitimate end, for which money can be raised on the community.   Congress can be considered as only under one restriction, which does not apply to other governments.   They cannot rightfully apply the money they raise to any purpose, merely or purely local.   But with this exception, they have as large a discretion, in relation to the application of money, as any legislature whatever.

"The constitutional *test* of a right application, must always be, whether it be for a purpose of *general* or *local* nature.   If the former, there can be no want of constitutional power.   The quality of the object, as how far it will really promote, or not, the welfare of the Union, must be matter of conscientious discretion ; and the arguments for or against a measure, in this light, must be arguments concerning expediency or inexpediency, not constitutional right ; whatever relates to the general order of the finances, to the general interests of trade, &c., being general objects, are constitutional ones, for the *application of money.*   A bank, then, whose bills are to circulate in all the revenues of the country, is evidently a general object ; and for that very reason, a constitutional one, as far as regards the appropriation of money to it, whether it will really be a beneficial one or not, is worthy of careful examination ; but is no more a constitutional point, in the particular referred to, than the question, whether the western lands shall be sold for twenty or thirty cents per acre ?   A hope is entertained, that, by this time, it has been made to appear to the satisfaction of the President, that the bank has a natural relation to the power of collecting taxes ; to that of regulating trade ; to that of providing for the common defence ; and that, as the bill under consideration contemplates the government in the light of a joint proprietor of the stock of the bank, it brings the case within the provision of the clause of the constitution, which immediately respects the property of the United States.   Under a conviction, that such a relation subsists, the secretary of the treasury, with all deference, conceives, that it will result, as a necessary consequence from the position, that all the specified powers of government are sovereign, as to the proper objects, that the incorporation of a bank is a constitutional measure : and that the objections, taken to the bill in this respect, are ill-founded.

"But, from an earnest desire to give the utmost possible satisfaction to the mind of the president, on so delicate and important a subject, the

---

[1] Hamilton on Bank, 1 Hamilton's Works, 127.

can rarely be established by the mere fact of the'r
votes, it is certain, that the true rule of interpretation is to ascertain the public and just intention from

secretary of the treasury will ask his indulgence, while he gives some
additional illustrations of cases, in which a power of erecting corporations
may be exercised, under some of those heads of the specified powers of the
government, which are alleged to include the rightof incorporating a bank.
1. It does not appear susceptible of a doubt, that if congress had thought
proper to provide in the collection law, that the bonds, to be given for the
duties, should be given to the collector of the district A. or B. as the case
might require, to inure to him and his successors in office, in trust for
the United States; that it would have been consistent with the constitution to make such an arrangement. And yet this, it is conceived, would
amount to an incorporation. 2. It is not an unusual expedient of taxation, to farm particular branches of revenue; that is, to sell or mortgage
the product of them for certain definite sums, leaving the collection to
the parties, to whom they are mortgaged or sold. There are even examples of this in the United States. Suppose that there was any particular branch of revenue, which it was manifestly expedient to place on
this footing, and there were a number of persons willing to engage with
the government, upon condition that they should be incorporated, and
the funds vested in them, as well for their greater safety, as for the more
convenient recovery and management of the taxes; is it supposable
that there could be any constitutional obstacle to the measure? It is
presumed, that there could be none. It is certainly a mode of collection,
which it would be in the discretion of the government to adopt; though
the circumstances must be very extraordinary, that would induce the
secretary to think it expedient. 3. Suppose a new and unexplored
branch of trade should present itself with some foreign country Suppose it was manifest, that to undertake it with advantage, required a
union of the capitals of a number of individuals, and that those individ-
als would not be disposed to embark without an incorporation, as well to
obviate the consequences of a private partnership, which makes every
individual liable in his whole estate for the debts of the company to their
utmost extent, as for the more convenient management of the business;
what reason can there be to doubt, that the national government would
have a constitutional right to institute and incorporate such a company?
None. They possess a general authority to regulate trade with foreign
countries. This is a mean, which has been practised to that end by all
the principal commercial nations, who have trading companies to this
day, which have subsisted for centuries. Why may not the United
States *constitutionally* employ the means usual in other countries for
attaining the ends intrusted to them? A power to make all needful

the language of the instrument itself, according to the common rules applied to all laws. The people, who adopted the constitution, could know nothing of the

rules and regulations concerning territory, has been construed to mean a power to erect a government. A power to regulate trade is a power to make all needful rules and regulations concerning trade. Why may it not, then, include that of erecting a trading company, as well as in other cases to erect a government?

"It is remarkable, that the state conventions, who have proposed amendments in relation to this point, have most, if not all of them, expressed themselves nearly thus: Congress shall not grant monopolies, nor *erect any company* with exclusive advantages of commerce! Thus at the same time expressing their sense, that the power to erect trading companies, or corporations, was inherent in congress, and objecting to it no further, than as to the grant of *exclusive* privileges. The secretary entertains all the doubts, which prevail concerning the utility of such companies; but he cannot fashion to his own mind a reason to induce a doubt, that there is a constitutional authority in the United States to establish them. If such a reason were demanded, none could be given, unless it were this — that congress cannot erect a corporation; which would be no better, than to say, they cannot do it, because they cannot do it. First, presuming an inability without reason, and then assigning that inability, as the cause of itself. Illustrations of this kind might be multiplied without end. They will, however, be pursued no further.

"There is a sort of evidence on this point, arising from an aggregate view of the constitution, which is of no inconsiderable weight. The very general power of laying and collecting taxes, and appropriating their proceeds; that of borrowing money indefinitely; that of coining money and regulating foreign coins; that of making all needful rules and regulations respecting the property of the United States; — these powers combined, as well as the reason and nature of the thing, speak strongly this language; that it is the manifest design and scope of the constitution to vest in congress all the powers requisite to the effectual administration of the finances of the United States. As far as concerns this object, there appears to be no parsimony of power. To suppose, then, that the government is precluded from the employment of so usual, and so important an instrument for the administration of its finances, as that of a bank, is to suppose, what does not coincide with the general tenour and complexion of the constitution, and what is not agreeable to impressions, that any mere spectator would entertain concerning it. Little less, than a prohibitory clause, can destroy the strong presumptions, which result from the general aspect of the government. Nothing but demonstration should exclude the idea, that the power exists.

private intentions of the framers. They adopted it upon its own clear import, upon its own naked text. Nothing is more common, than for a law to effect more or less, than the intention of the persons, who framed it; and it must be judged of by its words and sense, and not by any private intentions of members of the legislature.[1]

§ 1264. In regard to the faculties of the bank, if congress could constitutionally create it, they might confer on it such faculties and powers, as were fit to make it an appropriate means for fiscal operations. They had a right to adapt it in the best manner to its end. No one can pretend, that its having the faculty

---

"In all questions of this nature, the practice of mankind ought to have great weight against the theories of individuals. The fact, for instance, that all the principal commercial nations have made use of trading corporations or companies, for the purpose of *external commerce*, is a satisfactory proof, that the establishment of them is an incident to the regulation of commerce. This other fact, that banks are an usual engine in the administration of national finances, and an ordinary, and the most effectual instrument of loans, and one, which, in this country, has been found essential, pleads strongly against the supposition, that a government clothed with most of the important prerogatives of sovereignty, in relation to its revenues, its debt, its credit, its defence, its trade, its intercourse with foreign nations, is forbidden to make use of that instrument, as an appendage to its own authority. It has been usual, as an auxiliary test of constitutional authority, to try, whether it abridges any pre-existing right of any state, or any individual. The proposed measure will stand the most severe examination on this point. Each state may still erect as many banks, as it pleases; every individual may still carry on the banking business to any extent he pleases. Another criterion may be this; whether the institution or thing has a more direct relation, as to its uses, to the objects of the reserved powers of the state government, than to those of the powers delegated by the United States? This rule, indeed, is less precise, than the former; but it may still serve as some guide. Surely, a bank has more reference to the objects intrusted to the national government, than to those left to the care of the state governments. The common defence is decisive in this comparison." 1 Hamilton's Works, 138 to 154.

[1] Hamilton on Bank, 1 Hamilton's Works, 127, 128.

of holding a capital; of lending and dealing in money; of issuing bank notes; of receiving deposits; and of appointing suitable officers to manage its affairs; are not highly useful and expedient, and appropriate to the purposes of a bank. They are just such, as are usually granted to state banks; and just such, as give increased facilities to all its operations. To say, that the bank might have gone on without this or that faculty, is nothing. Who, but congress, shall say, how few, or how many it shall have, if all are still appropriate to it, as an instrument of government, and may make it more convenient, and more useful in its operations? No man can say, that a single faculty in any national charter is useless, or irrelevant, or strictly improper, that is conducive to its end, as a national instrument. Deprive a bank of its trade and business, and its vital principles are destroyed. Its form may remain, but its substance is gone. All the powers given to the bank are to give efficacy to its functions of trade and business.[1]

§ 1265. As to another suggestion, that the same objects might have been accomplished through the state banks, it is sufficient to say, that no trace can be found in the constitution of any intention to create a dependence on the states, or state institutions, for the execution of its great powers. Its own means are adequate to its end; and on those means it was expected to rely for their accomplishment. It would be utterly absurd to make the powers of the constitution wholly dependent on state institutions. But if state banks might be employed, as congress have a choice of means, they had a right to choose a national bank, in preference to state banks, for the financial operations of the government.[2]

---

[1] *Osborn* v. *Bank of United States*, 9 Wheat. R. 861, 862 to 865.
[2] *M'Culloch* v. *Maryland*, 4 Wheat. R. 424.

Proof, that they might use one means, is no proof, that they cannot constitutionally use another means.

§ 1266. After all, the subject has been settled repeatedly by every department of the government, legislative, executive, and judicial. The states have acquiesced; and a majority have constantly sustained the power. If it is not now settled, it never can be. If it is settled, it would be too much to expect a re-argument, whenever any person may choose to question it.[1]

---

[1] See 4 Elliot's Debates, 216 to 229 ; *M'Culloch v. Maryland*, 4 Wheat. R. 316; *Osborn v. Bank of United States*, 9 Wheat. R. 738, 859; 1 Kent's Comm. Lect. 12, p. 233 to 239; Sergeant on Constitution, ch. 28, [ch. 30;] 5 Marsh. Wash. App. Note 3.

CHAPTER XXVI.

POWERS OF CONGRESS — INTERNAL IMPROVE-MENTS.

§ 1267. ANOTHER question, which has for a long time agitated the public councils of the nation, is, as to the authority of congress to make roads, canals, and other internal improvements.

§ 1268. So far, as regards the right to appropriate money to internal improvements generally, the subject has already passed under review in considering the power to lay and collect taxes. The doctrine there contended for, which has been in a great measure borne out by the actual practice of the government, is, that congress may appropriate money, not only to clear obstructions to navigable rivers; to improve harbours; to build breakwaters; to assist navigation; to erect forts, light-houses, and piers; and for other purposes allied to some of the enumerated powers; but may also appropriate it in aid of canals, roads, and other institutions of a similar nature, existing under state authority. The only limitations upon the power are those prescribed by the terms of the constitution, that the objects shall be for the common defence, or the general welfare of the Union. The true test is, whether the object be of a local character, and local use; or, whether it be of general benefit to the states.[1] If it be purely

---

[1] Hamilton's Report on Manufactures, 1791, 1 Hamilton's Works, 231, 232; 1 Kent's Comm. Lect. 12, p. 250, 251, (2 ed. p. 267, 268;) Sergeant on Constitution, ch. 28, [ch. 30;] President Monroe's Exposition and Message, 4th May, 1822, p. 38, 39.

local, congress cannot constitutionally appropriate money for the object. But, if the benefit be general, it matters not, whether in point of locality it be in one state, or several; whether it be of large, or of small extent; its nature and character determine the right, and congress may appropriate money in aid of it; for it is then in a just sense for the general welfare.

§ 1269. But it has been contended, that the constitution is not confined to mere appropriations of money; but authorizes congress directly to undertake and carry on a system of internal improvements for the general welfare; wherever such improvements fall within the scope of any of the enumerated powers. Congress may not, indeed, engage in such undertakings merely because they are internal improvements for the general welfare, unless they fall within the scope of the enumerated powers. The distinction between this power, and the power of appropriation is, that in the latter, congress may appropriate to any purpose, which is for the common defence or general welfare; but in the former, they can engage in such undertakings only, as are means, or incidents to its enumerated powers. Congress may, therefore, authorize the making of a canal, as incident to the power to regulate commerce, where such canal may facilitate the intercourse between state and state. They may authorize light-houses, piers, buoys, and beacons to be built for the purposes of navigation. They may authorize the purchase and building of custom-houses, and revenue cutters, and public warehouses, as incidents to the power to lay and collect taxes. They may purchase places for public uses; and erect forts, arsenals, dock-yards, navy-yards, and magazines, as incidents to the power to make war.

§ 1270. For the same reason congress may authorize the laying out and making of a military road, and acquire a right over the soil for such purposes; and as incident thereto they have a power to keep the road in repair, and prevent all obstructions thereto. But in these, and the like cases, the general jurisdiction of the state over the soil, subject only to the rights of the United States, is not excluded. As, for example, in case of a military road; although a state cannot prevent repairs on the part of the United States, or authorize any obstructions of the road, its general jurisdiction remains untouched. It may punish all crimes committed on the road; and it retains in other respects its territorial sovereignty over it. The right of soil may still remain in the state, or in individuals, and the right to the easement only in the national government. There is a great distinction between the exercise of a power, excluding altogether state jurisdiction, and the exercise of a power, which leaves the state jurisdiction generally in force, and yet includes, on the part of the national government, a power to preserve, what it has created.[1]

§ 1271. In all these, and other cases, in which the power of congress is asserted, it is so upon the general ground of its being an incidental power; and the course of reasoning, by which it is supported, is precisely the same, as that adopted in relation to other cases already considered. It is, for instance, admitted, that congress cannot authorize the making of a canal, except for some purpose of commerce among the states, or for some

---

[1] See 1 Kent's Comm. Lect. 12, p. 250, 251 ; Sergeant on Constitution, ch. 28, [ch. 30, ed. 1830;] 2 U. S. Law Journal, April, 1826, p. 251, &c.; 3 Elliot's Debates, 309, 310; 4 Elliot's Debates, 244, 265, 279, 291, 356 ; Webster's Speeches, p. 392 to 397.

other purpose belonging to the Union; and it cannot make a military road, unless it be necessary and proper for purposes of war. To go over the reasoning at large would, therefore, be little more, than a repetition of what has been already fully expounded.[1] The Journal of the Convention is not supposed to furnish any additional lights on the subject, beyond what have been already stated.[2]

§ 1272. The resistance to this extended reach of the national powers turns also upon the same general reasoning, by which a strict construction of the constitution has been constantly maintained. It is said, that such a power is not among those enumerated in the constitution; nor is it implied, as a means of executing any of them. The power to regulate commerce cannot include a power to construct roads and canals, and improve the navigation of water-courses in order to facilitate, promote, and secure such commerce, without a latitude of construction departing from the ordinary import of the terms, and incompatible with the nature of the constitution.[3] The liberal inter-

<hr>

[1] See *M'Culloch* v. *Maryland*, 4 Wheat. R. 406, 407, 413 to 421; Webster's Speeches, p. 392 to 397; 4 Elliot's Debates, 280.

[2] Journal of Convention, p. 260, 376.

[3] President Madison's Message, 3d March, 1817; 4 Elliot's Debates, 280, 281; President Monroe's Message, 4th May. 1822, p. 22 to 35; President Jackson's Message, 27th May, 1830; 4 Elliot's Debates, 333, 334, 335; 1 Kent's Comm. Lect. 12, p. 250, 251; 4 Elliot's Debates, 291, 292, 354, 355; Sergeant on Constitution, ch. 28, [ch. 30;] 4 Jefferson's Corresp. 421. — President Monroe, in his elaborate Exposition accompanying his Message of the 4th of May, 1822, denies the independent right of congress to construct roads and canals; but asserts in the strongest manner their right to *appropriate* money to such objects. His reasoning for the latter is thought by many to be quite irresistible in favour of the former. See the message from page 35 to page 47. One short passage may be quoted. "Good roads and canals will promote many very important national purposes. They will facilitate the opera-

pretation has been very uniformly asserted by congress; the strict interpretation has not uniformly, but has upon several important occasions been insisted upon by the executive.[1] In the present state of the controversy, the duty of forbearance seems inculcated upon the commentator; and the reader must decide for himself upon his own views of the subject.

§ 1273. Another question has been made, how far congress could make a law giving to the United States a preference and priority of payment of their debts, in cases of the death, or insolvency, or bankruptcy of their debtors, out of their estates. It has been settled, upon deliberate argument, that congress possess such a constitutional power. It is a necessary and proper power to carry into effect the other powers of the government. The government is to pay the debts of the Union; and must be authorized to use the means, which appear to itself most eligible to effect that object. It may purchase, and remit bills for this object; and it may take all those precautions, and make all those regulations, which will render the transmission safe. It may, in like manner, pass all laws to render effectual the collection of its debts. It is no objection to this right of priority, that it will interfere with the rights of the state sovereignties respecting the dignity of debts, and will defeat the measures, which they have a right

---

tions of war; the movements of troops; the transportation of cannon, of provisions and every warlike store, much to our advantage, and the disadvantage of the enemy in time of war. Good roads will facilitate the transportation of the mail, and thereby promote the purposes of commerce and political intelligence among the people. They will, by being properly directed to these objects, enhance the value of our vacant lands, a treasure of vast resource to the nation." This is the very reasoning, by which the friends of the general power support its constitutionality.

[1] 4 Jefferson's Corresp. 421; 1 Kent's Comm. Lect. 12, p. 250, 251.

154 CONSTITUTION OF THE U. STATES. [BOOK III.

to adopt to secure themselves against delinquencies on the part of their own revenue or other officers. This objection, if of any avail, is an objection to the powers given by the constitution. The mischief suggested, so far as it can really happen, is the necessary consequence of the supremacy of the laws of the United States on all subjects, to which the legislative power of congress extends.[1]

§ 1274. It is under the same implied authority, that the United States have any right even to sue in their own courts; for an express power is no where given in the constitution, though it is clearly implied in that part respecting the judicial power. And congress may not only authorize suits to be brought in the name of the United States, but in the name of any artificial person, (such as the Postmaster-General,[2]) or natural person for their benefit.[3] Indeed, all the usual incidents appertaining to a *personal* sovereign, in relation to contracts, and suing, and enforcing rights, so far as they are within the scope of the powers of the government, belong to the United States, as they do to other sovereigns.[4] The right of making contracts and instituting suits is an incident to the general right of sovereignty; and the United States, being a body politic, may, within the sphere of the constitutional powers confided to it, and through the instrumentality of the proper department, to which those powers are confided, enter into

---

[1] *United States* v. *Fisher*, 2 Cranch, 358; 1 Peters's Condensed Rep. 421; *Harrison* v. *Sterry*, 5 Cranch, 289; 2 Peters's Condensed Rep. 260; 1 Kent's Comm. Lect. 12, p. 229 to 233.

[2] *Postmaster-General* v. *Early*, 12 Wheat. R. 136.

[3] See *Dugan* v. *United States*, 3 Wheat. R. 173, 179; *United States* v. *Buford*, 3 Peters's R. 12, 30; *United States* v. *Tingey*, 5 Peters's R. 115, 127, 128.

[4] *Cox* v. *United States*, 6 Peters's R. 172.

contracts not prohibited by law, and appropriate to the just exercise of those powers ; and enforce the observance of them by suits and judicial process.[1]

§ 1275. There are almost innumerable cases, in which the auxiliary and implied powers belonging to congress have been put into operation. But the object of these Commentaries is, rather to take notice of those, which have been the subject of animadversion, than of those, which have hitherto escaped reproof, or have been silently approved.

§ 1276. Upon the ground of a strict interpretation, some extraordinary objections have been taken in the course of the practical operations of the government. The very first act, passed under the government, which regulated the time, form, and manner, of administering the oaths prescribed by the constitution,[2] was denied to be constitutional. But the objection has long since been abandoned.[3] It has been doubted, whether it is constitutional to permit the secretaries to draft bills on subjects connected with their departments, to be presented to the house of representatives for their consideration.[4] It has been doubted, whether an act authorizing the president to lay, regulate, and revoke, embargoes was constitutional.[5] It has been doubted, whether congress have authority to establish a military academy.[6] But these objections have been silently, or practically abandoned.

---

1 *United States* v. *Tingey*, 5 Peters's R. 115, 128.
2 Act of 1st June, 1789, ch. 1.
3 4 Elliot's Deb. 139, 140, 141; 1 Lloyd's Deb. 218 to 225.
4 4 Elliot's Debates, 238, 239, 240.
5 4 Elliot's Debates, 240. See Id. 265.
6 4 Jefferson's Corresp. 499.

CHAPTER XXVII.

POWERS OF CONGRESS — PURCHASES OF FOREIGN
TERRITORY — EMBARGOES.

§ 1277. But the most remarkable powers, which have been exercised by the government, as auxiliary and implied powers, and which, if any, go to the utmost verge of liberal construction, are the laying of an unlimited embargo in 1807, and the purchase of Louisiana in 1803, and its subsequent admission into the Union, as a state. These measures were brought forward, and supported, and carried, by the known and avowed friends of a strict construction of the constitution ; and they were justified at the time, and can be now justified, only upon the doctrines of those, who support a liberal construction of the constitution. The subject has been already hinted at ; but it deserves a more deliberate review.

§ 1278. In regard to the acquisition of Louisiana :— The treaty of 1803 contains a cession of the whole of that vast territory by France to the United States, for a sum exceeding eleven millions of dollars. There is a stipulation in the treaty on the part of the United States, that the inhabitants of the ceded territory shall be incorporated into the Union, and admitted, as soon as possible, according to the principles of the federal constitution, to the enjoyment of all the rights, advantages, and immunities of citizens of the United States.[1]

§ 1279. It is obvious, that the treaty embraced several very important questions, each of them upon the

---

[1] Art. 3.

grounds of a strict construction full of difficulty and delicacy. In the first place, had the United States a constitutional authority to accept the cession and pay for it? In the next place, if they had, was the stipulation for the admission of the inhabitants into the Union, as a state, constitutional, or within the power of congress to give it effect?

§ 1280. There is no pretence, that the purchase, or cession of any foreign territory is within any of the powers expressly enumerated in the constitution. It is no where in that instrument said, that congress, or any other department of the national government, shall have a right to purchase, or accept of any cession of foreign territory. The power itself (it has been said) could scarcely have been in the contemplation of the framers of it. It is, in its own nature, as dangerous to liberty, as susceptible of abuse in its actual application, and as likely as any, which could be imagined, to lead to a dissolution of the Union. If congress have the power, it may unite any foreign territory whatsoever to our own, however distant, however populous, and however powerful. Under the form of a cession, we may become united to a more powerful neighbour or rival; and be involved in European, or other foreign interests, and contests, to an interminable extent. And if there may be a stipulation for the admission of foreign states into the Union, the whole balance of the constitution may be destroyed, and the old states sunk into utter insignificance. It is incredible, that it should have been contemplated, that any such overwhelming authority should be confided to the national government with the consent of the people of the old states. If it exists at all, it is unforeseen, and the result of a sovereignty, intended to be limited, and yet not

sufficiently guarded. The very case of the cession of
Louisiana is a striking illustration of the doctrine. It
admits, by consequence, into the Union an immense
territory, equal to, if not greater, than that of all the
United States under the peace of 1783. In the natural progress of events, it must, within a short period,
change the whole balance of power in the Union, and
transfer to the West all the important attributes of the
sovereignty of the whole. If, as is well known, one
of the strong objections urged against the constitution
was, that the original territory of the United States was
too large for a national government; it is inconceivable,
that it could have been within the intention of the people, that any additions of foreign territory should be
made, which should thus double every danger from this
source. The treaty-making power must be construed, as
confined to objects within the scope of the constitution.
And, although congress have authority to admit new
states into the firm, yet it is demonstrable, that this clause
had sole reference to the territory then belonging to the
United States ; and was designed for the admission of
the states, which, under the ordinance of 1787, were
contemplated to be formed within its old boundaries. In
regard to the appropriation of money for the purposes
of the cession the case is still stronger. If no appropriation of money can be made, except for cases within
the enumerated powers, (and this clearly is not one,)
how can the enormous sum of eleven millions be justified for this object ? If it be said, that it will be " for
the common defence, and general welfare" to purchase
the territory, how is this reconcileable with the strict
construction of the constitution ? If congress can appropriate money for one object, because it is deemed
for the common defence and general welfare, why may

they not appropriate it for all objects of the same sort? If the territory can be purchased, it must be governed; and a territorial government must be created. But where can congress find authority in the constitution to erect a territorial government, since it does not possess the power to erect corporations?

§ 1281. Such were the objections, which have been, and in fact may be, urged against the cession, and the appropriations made to carry the treaty into effect. The friends of the measure were driven to the adoption of the doctrine, that the right to acquire territory was incident to national sovereignty ; that it was a resulting power, growing necessarily out of the aggregate powers confided by the federal constitution; that the appropriation might justly be vindicated upon this ground, and also upon the ground, that it was for the common defence and general welfare. In short, there is no possibility of defending the constitutionality of this measure, but upon the principles of the liberal construction, which has been, upon other occasions, so earnestly resisted.[1]

---

[1] See the Debates in 1803, on the Louisiana Treaty, printed by T. & G. Palmer in Philadelphia, in 1804, and 4 Elliot's Debates 257 to 260. — The objections were not taken merely by persons, who were at that time in opposition to the national administration. President Jefferson himself (under whose auspices the treaty was made,) was of opinion, that the measure was unconstitutional, and required an amendment of the constitution to justify it. He accordingly urged his friends strenuously to that course ; at the same time he added, "that it will be desirable for congress to do what is necessary in *silence* "; " whatever congress shall think necessary to do should be done with as *little debate as possible, and particularly so far as respects the constitutional difficulty.*" " I confess, then, I think it important in the present case, to set an example against *broad* construction by appealing for new power to the people. If, however, our friends shall think differently, certainly I shall acquiesce with satisfaction ; confiding, that the good sense of our country will correct the evil of construction, when it shall produce ill effects." What a latitude of interpretation is this ! The constitution may be over-

§ 1282. As an incidental power, the constitutional right of the United States to acquire territory would seem so naturally to flow from the sovereignty confided to it, as not to admit of very serious question. The constitution confers on the government of the Union the power of making war, and of making treaties; and it seems consequently to possess the power of acquiring territory either by conquest or treaty.[1] If the cession be by treaty, the terms of that treaty must be obligatory; for it is the law of the land. And if it stipulates for the enjoyment by the inhabitants of the rights, privileges, and immunities of citizens of the United States, and for the admission of the territory into the Union, as a state, these stipulations must be equally obligatory. They are within the scope of the constitutional authority of the government, which has the right to acquire territory, to make treaties, and to admit new states into the Union.[2]

§ 1283. The mere recent acquisition of Florida, which has been universally approved, or acquiesced in by all the states, can be maintained only on the same

---

leaped, and a *broad* construction adopted for favourite measures, and resistance is to be made to such a construction only, when it shall produce ill effects! His letter to Dr. Sibley (in June, 1803) recently published is decisive, that he thought an amendment of the constitution necessary. Yet he did not hesitate without such amendment to give effect to every measure to carry the treaty into effect during his administration. See 4 Jefferson's Corresp. p. 1, 2, 3, Letter to Dr. Sibley, and Mr. J. Q. Adams's Letter to Mr. Speaker Stevenson, July 11, 1832.

[1] *Amer. Insur. Co.* v. *Canter*, 1 Peters's Sup. R. 511, 512; Id. 517, note, Mr. Justice Johnson's Opinion.

[2] Ibid. — In the celebrated Hartford Convention, in January, 1815, a proposition was made to amend the constitution so, as to prohibit the admission of new states into the Union without the consent of two-thirds of both houses of congress. In the accompanying report there is a strong though indirect denial of the power to admit new states *without the original limits* of the United States.

principles; and furnishes a striking illustration of the truth, that constitutions of government require a liberal construction to effect their objects, and that a narrow interpretation of their powers, however it may suit the views of speculative philosophers, or the accidental interests of political parties, is incompatible with the permanent interests of the state, and subversive of the great ends of all government, the safety and independence of the people.

§ 1284. The other instance of an extraordinary application of the implied powers of the government, above alluded to, is the embargo laid in the year 1807, by the special recommendation of President Jefferson. It was avowedly recommended, as a measure of safety for our vessels, our seamen, and our merchandise from the then threatening dangers from the belligerents of Europe ;[1] and it was explicitly stated " to be a measure of precaution called for by the occasion ; " and " neither hostile in its character, nor as justifying, or inciting, or leading to hostility with any nation whatever."[2] It was in no sense, then, a war measure. If it could be classed at all, as flowing from, or as an incident to, any of the enumerated powers, it was that of regulating commerce. In its terms, the act provided, that an embargo be, and hereby is, laid on all ships and vessels in the ports, or within the limits or jurisdiction, of the United States, &c. bound to any foreign port or place.[3] It was in its terms unlimited in duration ; and could be removed only by a subsequent act of congress,

---

[1] 6 Wait's State Papers, 57.
[2] 7 Wait's State Papers, 25, Mr. Madison's Letter to Mr. Pinkney ; *Gibbons* v. *Ogden*, 9 Wheat. R. 191, 192, 193.
[3] Act, 22d December, 1807, ch. 5.

having the assent of all the constitutional branches of the legislature.[1]

§ 1285. No one can reasonably doubt, that the laying of an embargo, suspending commerce for a limited period, is within the scope of the constitution. But the question of difficulty was, whether congress, under the power to regulate commerce with foreign nations, could constitutionally suspend and interdict it wholly for an unlimited period, that is, by a permanent act, having no limitation as to duration, either of the act, or of the embargo. It was most seriously controverted, and its constitutionality denied in the Eastern states of the Union, during its existence. An appeal was made to the judiciary upon the question ; and it having been settled to be constitutional by that department of the government, the decision was acquiesced in, though the measure bore with almost unexampled severity, upon the Eastern states ; and its ruinous effects can still be traced along their extensive seaboard. The argument was, that the power to regulate did not include the power to annihilate commerce, by interdicting it permanently and entirely with foreign nations. The decision was, that the power of congress was sovereign, relative to commercial intercourse, qualified by the limitations and restrictions contained in the constitution itself. Non-intercourse and Embargo laws are within the range of legislative discretion ; and if congress have the power, for purposes of safety, of preperation, or counteraction, to suspend commercial intercourse with foreign nations, they are not limited, as to the du-

[1] In point of fact, it remained in force until the 28th of June, 1809, being repealed by an act passed on the first of March, 1809, to take effect at the end of the next session of congress, which terminated on the 28th of June, 1809.

ration, any more, than as to the manner and extent of the measure.[1]

§ 1286. That this measure went to the utmost verge of constitutional power, and especially of implied power, has never been denied. That it could not be justified by any, but the most liberal construction of the constitution, is equally undeniable. It was the favourite measure of those, who were generally the advocates of the strictest construction. It was sustained by the people from a belief, that it was promotive of the interests, and important to the safety of the Union.

§ 1287. At the present day, few statesmen are to be found, who seriously contest the constitutionality of the acts respecting either the embargo, or the purchase and admission of Louisiana into the Union. The general voice of the nation has sustained, and supported them. Why, then, should not that general voice be equally respected in relation to other measures of vast public importance, and by many deemed of still more vital interest to the country, such as the tariff laws, and the national bank charter? Can any measures furnish a more instructive lesson, or a more salutary admonition, in the whole history of parties, at once to moderate our zeal, and awaken our vigilance, than those, which stand upon principles repudiated at one time upon constitutional scruples, and solemnly adopted at another time, to subserve a present good, or foster the particular policy of an administration? While the principles of the constitution should be preserved with a most guarded caution, and a most sacred regard to the rights of the

---

[1] *United States* v. *The Brig William*, 2 Hall's Law Journal, 255; 1 Kent's Comm. Lect. 19, p. 405; Sergeant on Const. Law, ch. 28, (ch. 30;) *Gibbons* v. *Ogden*, 9 Wheat. R. 1, 191 to 193.

states; it is at once the dictate of wisdom, and enlightened patriotism to avoid that narrowness of interpretation, which would dry up all its vital powers, or compel the government (as was done under the confederation,) to break down all constitutional barriers, and trust for its vindication to the people, upon the dangerous political maxim, that the safety of the people is the supreme law, (*salus populi suprema lex;*) a maxim, which might be used to justify the appointment of a dictator, or any other usurpation.[1]

§ 1288. There remain one or two other measures of a political nature, whose constitutionality has been denied; but which, being of a transient character, have left no permanent traces in the constitutional jurisprudence of the country. Reference is here made to the Alien and Sedition laws, passed in 1798, both of which were limited to a short duration, and expired by their own limitation.[2] One (the Alien act) authorized the president to order out of the country such aliens, as he should deem dangerous to the peace and safety of the United States; or should have reasonable grounds to suspect to be concerned in any treasonable, or secret

---

1 Mr. Jefferson, on many occasions, was not slow to propose, or justify measures of a very strong character; and such as proceeded altogether upon the ground of implied powers. Thus, in writing to Mr. Crawford, on 20th of June, 1816, he deliberately proposed, with a view to enable us in future to meet any war, to adopt "the report of the then secretary of the war department, *for placing the force of the nation at effectual command,*" and to " ensure resources for money *by the suppression of all paper circulation during peace, and licensing that of the nation alone during war.*" 4 Jefferson's Corresp. 285. Whence are these vast powers derived? The latter would amount to a direct prohibition of the circulation of any bank notes of the state banks; and in fact would amount to a suppression of the most effective powers of the state banks.

2 Act of 25th of June, 1798, ch. 75; Act of 14th of July, 1798, ch. 91; 1 Tuck. Black. Comm. App. part 2, note G, p. 11 to 30.

machinations against the government of the United States, under severe penalties for disobedience. The other declared it a public crime, punishable with fine and imprisonment, for any persons unlawfully to combine, and conspire together, with intent to oppose any measure or measures of the United States, &c.; or with such intent, to counsel, advise, or attempt to procure any insurrection, unlawful assembly, or combination; or to write, print, utter, or publish, or cause, or procure to be written, &c., or willingly to assist in writing, &c., any false, scandalous, and malicious writing or writings against the government of the United States, or either house of congress, or the president, with intent to defame them, or to bring them into contempt, or disrepute, or to excite against them the hatred of the people, or to stir up sedition; or to excite any unlawful combination for opposing, or resisting any law, or any lawful act of the president, or to resist, oppose, or defeat any such law or act; or to aid, encourage, or abet any hostile designs of any foreign nations against the United States. It provided, however, that the truth of the writing or libel might be given in evidence; and that the jury, who tried the cause, should have a right to determine the law and the fact, under the direction of the court, as in other cases.

§ 1289. The constitutionality of both the acts was assailed with great earnestness and ability at the time; and was defended with equal masculine vigour. The ground of the advocates, in favour of these laws, was, that they resulted from the right and duty in the government of self-preservation, and the like duty and protection of its functionaries in the proper discharge of their official duties. They were impugned, as not conformable to the letter or spirit of the constitution;

and as inconsistent in their principles with the rights of
citizens, and the liberty of the press. The Alien act
was denounced, as exercising a power not delegated
by the constitution ; as uniting legislative and judicial
functions, with that of the executive ; and by this Union
as subverting the general principles of free government, and the particular organization and positive provisions of the constitution. It was added, that the Sedition act was open to the same objection, and was expressly forbidden by one of the amendments of the
constitution, on which there will be occasion hereafter
to comment.[1] At present it does not seem necessary
to present more than this general outline, as the measures are not likely to be renewed ; and as the doctrines,
on which they are maintained, and denounced, are not
materially different from those, which have been already
considered.[2]

---

[1] The Alien, and Sedition Acts were the immediate cause of the
Virginia Resolutions of December, 1798, and of the elaborate vindication of them, in the celebrated Report of the 7th of January, 1800. The
learned reader will there find an ample exposition of the whole constitutional objections. See also 4 Jefferson's Correspondence, 23, 27. The
reasoning on the other side may be found in the Debates in Congress,
at the time of the passage of these acts. It is greatly to be lamented,
that there is no authentic collection of all the Debates in congress, in a
form, like that of the Parliamentary Debates. See also 4 Elliot's Deb.
251, 252; Debates on the Judiciary, in 1802, Mr. Bayard's Speech,
p. 371, 372; Addison's Charges to the Grand Jury, No. 25, p. 270; Id.
No. 26 p. 289. These charges are commonly bound with Addison's
Reports. See also 1 Tuck. Black. Comm. 296 to 300; Id. Part 2, App.
note 6, p. 11 to 36; Report of Committee of House of Representatives
of congress, 25th February, 1799, and Resolve of Kentucky, of 1798, and
Resolve of Massachusetts, of 9th and 13th of February, 1799, on the same
subject.
[2] Mr. Vice President Calhoun, in his letter of the 28th of August,
1832, to Gov. Hamilton, uses the following language. "From the adop-
tion of the constitution we have had but one continued agitation of con|
stitutional questions, embracing some of the most important powers exercised by the government ; and yet, in spite of all the ability, and force

of argument, displayed in the various discussions, backed by the high authority, claimed for the Supreme Court to adjust such controversies, not a single constitutional question of a political character, which has ever been agitated during this long period, has been settled in the public opinion, *except that of the unconstitutionality of the Alien, and Sedition laws ;* and what is remarkable, that was settled *against the decision of the Supreme Court.*" Now, in the first place, the constitutionality of the Alien, and Sedition laws never came before the Supreme Court for decision ; and consequently, never was decided by that court. In the next place, what is meant by *public opinion* deciding constitutional questions? What public opinion? Where, and at what time delivered? It is notorious, that some of the ablest statesmen and jurists of America, at the time of the passage of these acts, and ever since, have maintained the constitutionality of these laws. They were upheld, as constitutional, by some of the most intelligent, and able state legislatures in the Union, in deliberate resolutions affirming their constitutionality. Nay more, it may be affirmed, that at the time, when the controversy engaged the public mind most earnestly upon the subject, there was, (to say the least of it) as great a weight of judicial, and professional talent, learning, and patriotism, enlisted in their favour, as there ever has been against them. If, by being settled by public opinion, is meant that all the people of America were united in one opinion on the subject, the correctness of the statement cannot be admitted; though its sincerity will not be questioned. It is one thing to believe a doctrine universally admitted, because we ourselves think it clear ; and quite another thing to establish the fact. The Sedition and Alien laws were generally deemed inexpedient, and therefore any allusion to them now rarely occurs, except in political discussions, when they are introduced to add odium to the party, by which they were adopted. But the most serious doubts may be entertained, whether even in the present day, a majority of constitutional lawyers, or of judicial opinions, deliberately hold them to be unconstitutional.

If public opinion is to decide constitutional questions, instead of the public functionaries of the government in their deliberate discussions and judgments, (a course quite novel in the annals of jurisprudence,) it would be desirable to have some mode of ascertaining it in a satisfactory, and conclusive form ; and some uniform test of it, independent of mere private conjectures. No such mode has, as yet, been provided in the constitution. And, perhaps, it will be found upon due inquiry, that different opinions prevail at the same time on the same subject, in the North, the South, the East, and the West. If the judgments of the Supreme Court (as it is more than hinted) have not, even upon the most deliberate *juridical* arguments, been satisfactory, can it be expected that *popular* arguments will be more so? It is said, that not a single constitutional question, except that of the Alien and Sedition laws, has ever been settled. If by this no more is meant, than that all minds have not acquiesced in the decisions, the statement must be admitted to be correct. And such must, under such a postulate, be for ever the case with all constitutional questions. It is utterly hopeless in any way to satisfy all minds upon such a subject. But if it be meant, that these decisions have not been approved, or acquiesced in, by a majority of the Union, as correct expositions of the constitution, that is a statement, which remains to be proved ; and is certainly not to be taken for granted. In truth, it is obvious, that so long as statesmen deny, that any decision of the Supreme Court is conclusive upon the interpretation of the constitution, it is wholly impossible, that any constitutional question should ever, in their view, be settled. It may always be controverted ; and if so, it will always be controverted by some persons. Human nature never yet presented the extraordinary spectacle of all minds, agreeing in all things ; nay not in all truths, moral, political, civil, or religious. Will the case be better, when twenty-four different states are to settle such questions, as they may please, from day to day, or year to year ; holding one opinion at one time, and another at another ? If constitutional questions are never to be deemed settled, while any persons shall be found to avow a doubt, what is to become of any government, national or state ? Did any statesmen ever conceive the project of a constitution of government for a nation or state, every one of whose powers and operations should be liable to be suspended at the will of any one, who should doubt their constitutionality? Is a constitution of government made only, as a text, about which, casuistry and ingenuity may frame endless doubts, and endless questions ? Or is it made, as a fixed system to guide, to cheer, to support, and to protect the people ? Is there any gain to rational liberty, by perpetuating doctrines, which leave obedience an affair of mere choice or speculation, now and for ever ?

CHAPTER XXVIII.

POWER OF CONGRESS TO PUNISH TREASON.

§ 1290. And here, in the order of the constitution, terminates the section, which enumerates the powers of congress. There are, however, other clauses detached from their proper connexion, which embrace other powers delegated to congress ; and which for no apparent reason have been so detached. As it will be more convenient to bring the whole in review at once, it is proposed (though it is a deviation from the general method of this work) to submit them in this place to the consideration of the reader.

§ 1291. The third section of the fourth article gives a constitutional definition of the crime of treason, (which will be reserved for a separate examination,) and then provides : " The congress shall have power to declare " the punishment of treason ; but no attainder of trea- " son shall work corruption of blood, or forfeiture, ex- " cept during the life of the person attainted."

§ 1292. The propriety of investing the national government with authority to punish the crime of treason against the United States could never become a question with any persons, who deemed the national government worthy of creation, or preservation. If the power had not been expressly granted, it must have been implied, unless all the powers of the national government might be put at defiance, and prostrated with impunity. Two motives, probably, concurred in introducing it, as an express power. One was, not to leave it open to implication, whether it was to be exclusively punishable with death according to the known rule of the common law, and with the barbarous accompaniments pointed out by it; but to confide the punishment to the discretion of congress. The other was, to impose some limitation upon the nature and extent of the punishment, so that it should not work corruption of blood or forfeiture beyond the life of the offender.

§ 1293. The punishment of high treason by the common law, as stated by Mr. Justice Blackstone,[1] is as follows: 1. That the offender be drawn to the gallows, and not be carried or walk, though usually (by connivance at length ripened into law) a sledge or hurdle is allowed, to preserve the offender from the extreme torment of being dragged on the ground or pavement. 2. That he be hanged by the neck, and cut down alive. 3. That his entrails be taken out and burned, while he is yet alive. 4. That his head be cut off. 5. That his body be divided into four parts. 6. That his head and quarters be at the king's disposal. These refinements in cruelty (which if now practised would be disgraceful to the character of the age) were, in former times, literally and studiously executed; and indicate at once a savage and ferocious spirit, and a degrading subserviency to royal resentments, real or supposed. It was wise to place the punishment solely in the discretion of congress; and the punishment has been since declared to be simply death by hanging;[2] thus inflicting death in a manner becoming the humanity of a civilized society.

§ 1294. It is well known, that corruption of blood, and forfeiture of the estate of the offender followed, as a necessary consequence at the common law, upon every attainder of treason. By corruption of blood all

---

[1] 4 Black. Comm. 92.   [2] Act of 30th April, 1790, ch. 36.

inheritable qualities are destroyed; so, that an attainted person can neither inherit lands, nor other hereditaments from his ancestors, nor retain those, he is already in possession of, nor transmit them to any heir. And this destruction of all inheritable qualities is so complete, that it obstructs all descents to his posterity, whenever they are obliged to derive a title through him to any estate of a remoter ancestor. So, that if a father commits treason, and is attainted, and suffers death, and then the grandfather dies, his grandson cannot inherit any estate from his grandfather; for he must claim through his father, who could convey to him no inheritable blood.[1] Thus the innocent are made the victims of a guilt, in which they did not, and perhaps could not, participate; and the sin is visited upon remote generations. In addition to this most grievous disability, the person attainted forfeits, by the common law, all his lands, and tenements, and rights of entry, and rights of profits in lands or tenements, which he possesses. And this forfeiture relates back to the time of the treason committed, so as to avoid all intermediate sales and incumbrances; and he also forfeits all his goods and chattels from the time of his conviction.[2]

§ 1295. The reason commonly assigned for these severe punishments, beyond the mere forfeiture of the life of the party attainted, are these : By committing treason the party has broken his original bond of allegiance, and forfeited his social rights. Among these social rights, that of transmitting property to others is deemed one of the chief and most valuable. Moreover, such forfeitures, whereby the posterity of the

---

[1] 2 Black. Comm. 252, 253 ; 4 Black. Comm. 388, 389.
[2] 4 Black. Comm. 381 to 388.

offender must suffer, as well as himself, will help to restrain a man, not only by the sense of his duty, and
dread of personal punishment, but also by his passions
and natural affections; and will interest every dependent and relation, he has, to keep him from offending.[1]
But this view of the subject is wholly unsatisfactory.
It looks only to the offender himself, and is regardless
of his innocent posterity. It really operates, as a post-
humous punishment upon them; and compels them to
bear, not only the disgrace naturally attendant upon
such flagitious crimes; but takes from them the common rights and privileges enjoyed by all other citizens,
where they are wholly innocent, and however remote
they may be in the lineage from the first offender. It
surely is enough for society to take the life of the
offender, as a just punishment of his crime, without
taking from his offspring and relatives that property,
which may be the only means of saving them from poverty and ruin. It is bad policy too; for it cuts off all
the attachments, which these unfortunate victims might
otherwise feel for their own government, and prepares
them to engage in any other service, by which their
supposed injuries may be redressed, or their hereditary
hatred gratified.[2] Upon these and similar grounds, it
may be presumed, that the clause was first introduced
into the original draft of the constitution; and, after some
amendments, it was adopted without any apparent resistance.[3] By the laws since passed by congress, it is
declared, that no conviction or judgment, for any capital
or other offences, shall work corruption of blood, or any

[1] 4 Black. Comm. 382. See also Yorke on Forfeitures.
[2] See Rawle on Const. ch. 11, p. 145, 146.
[3] Journal of Convention, 221, 269, 270, 271.

forfeiture of estate.[1]   The history of other countries abundantly proves, that one of the strong incentives to prosecute offences, as treason, has been the chance of sharing in the plunder of the victims.   Rapacity has been thus stimulated to exert itself in the service of the most corrupt tyranny ; and tyranny has been thus furnished with new opportunities of indulging its malignity and revenge ; of gratifying its envy of the rich, and good ; and of increasing its means to reward favourites, and secure retainers for the worst deeds.[2]

§ 1296. The power of punishing the crime of treason against the United States is exclusive in congress ; and the trial of the offence belongs exclusively to the tribunals appointed by them.   A state cannot take cognizance, or punish the offence ; whatever it may do in relation to the offence of treason, committed exclusively against itself, if indeed any case can, under the constitution, exist, which is not at the same time treason against the United States.[3]

---

[1] Act of 1790, ch. 36, § 24.

[2] See 1 Tuck. Black. Comm. App. 275, 276 ; Rawle on Const. ch. 11, p. 143 to 145.

[3] See *The People v. Lynch*, 11 Johns. R. 553 ; Rawle on Const. ch. 11, p. 140, 142, 143 ; Id. ch. 21, p. 207 ; Sergeant on Const. ch. 30, [ch. 32.]

CHAPTER XXIX.

POWER OF CONGRESS AS TO PROOF OF STATE
RECORDS AND PROCEEDINGS.

§ 1297. THE first section of the fourth article declares : "Full faith and credit shall be given in each
" state to the public acts, records, and judicial proceed
"ings of every other state. And the congress may by
" general laws prescribe the manner, in which such
"acts, records, and proceeding shall be proved, and
" *the effect thereof.*"

§ 1298. The articles of confederation contained a
provision on the same subject. It was, that "full faith
and credit shall be given in each of these states to the
records, acts, and judicial proceedings of the courts
and magistrates of every other state." [1] It has been
said, that the meaning of this clause is extremely indeterminate ; and that it was of but little importance
under any interpretation, which it would bear.[2] The
latter remark may admit of much question, and is certainly quite too loose and general in its texture. But
there can be no difficulty in affirming, that the authority
given to congress, under the constitution, to prescribe
the form and effect of the proof is a valuable improvement, and confers additional certainty, as to the true
nature and import of the clause. The clause, as reported in the first draft of the constitution, was, " that
full faith and credit shall be given in each state to the
acts of the legislature, and to the records and judicial
proceedings of the courts and magistrates of every
other state." The amendment was subsequently

[1] Art. 4.   [2] The Federalist, No. 42.

reported, substantially in the form, in which it now stands, except that the words, in the introductory clause, were, "Full faith and credit *ought to* be given, (instead of "shall"); and, in the next clause, the *legislature shall*, (instead of, the congress "*may*"); and in the concluding clause, "and the effect, which judgments obtained in one state shall have in another," (instead of, "*and the effect thereof.*") The latter was substituted by the vote of six states against three; the others were adopted without opposition; and the whole clause, as thus amended, passed without any division.[1]

§ 1299. It is well known, that the laws and acts of foreign nations are not judicially taken notice of in any other nation; and that they must be proved, like any other facts, whenever they come into operation or examination in any forensic controversy. The nature and mode of the proof depend upon the municipal law of the country, where the suit is depending; and there are known to be great diversities in the practice of different nations on this subject. Even in England and America the subject, notwithstanding the numerous judicial decisions, which have from time to time been made, is not without its difficulties and embarrassments.[2]

---

[1] Journal of Convention, p. 228, 305, 320, 321.

[2] See Starkie on Evid. P. 2, § 92, p. 251, and note to American ed. P. 4, p. 569; *Appleton* v. *Braybrook*, 6 M. & Selw. 34,; *Livingston* v. *Maryland Insurance Company*, 6 Cranch, 274; S. C. 2. Peters's Cond. R. 370; *Talbot* v. *Seeman*, 1 Cranch, 1, 38; S. C. 1 Peters's Cond. R. 229; *Raynham* v. *Canton*, 3 Pick. R. 293; *Conseequa* v. *Willings*, 1 Peters's Cir. R. 225, 229; *Church* v. *Hubbard*, 2 Cranch, 187, 238; S. C. 1 Peters's Cond. R. 385; *Yeaton* v. *Fry*, 5 Cranch, 335, 343; S. C. 2 Peters's Cond. R. 273; *Picton's case*, 24, Howell's State Trials, 494, &c.; *Vandervoorst* v. *Smith*, 3 Caine's R. 155; *Delafield* v. *Hurd*, 3 Johns. R. 310. See also Pardessus Cours de Droit. Comm.cr. P. 6. tit. 7, ch. 2, partout.

§ 1300. Independent of the question as to *proof*, there is another question, as to the *effect*, which is to be given to foreign judgments, when duly authenticated, in the tribunals of other nations, either as matter to maintain a suit, or to found a defence to a suit. Upon this subject, also, different nations are not entirely agreed in opinion or practice. Most, if not all of them, profess to give some effect to such judgments ; but many exceptions are allowed, which either demolish the whole efficiency of the judgment, as such, or leave it open to collateral proofs, which in a great measure impair its validity. To treat suitably of this subject would require a large dissertation, and appropriately belongs to another branch of public law.[1]

§ 1301. The general rule of the common law, recognised both in England and America, is, that foreign judgments are *primâ facie* evidence of the right and matter, which they purport to decide. At least, this may be asserted to be in England the preponderating weight of opinion ; and in America it has been held, upon many occasions,[2] though its correctness has been recently questioned, upon principle and authority, with much acuteness.[3]

§ 1302. Before the revolution, the colonies were deemed foreign to each other, as the British colonies

[1] See authorities in preceding note, and *Walker* v. *Whittier*, 1 Doug. R. 1 ; *Phillips* v. *Hunter*, 2 H. Bl. 409 ; Johnson's Dig. of New-York Rep. *Evid.* V ; Starkie on Evidence, P. 2, § 67, p. 206 : Id. § 68, p. 214 ; *Bissell* v. *Briggs*, 9 Mass. R. 462 ; Bigelow's Dig. *Evid. C.*, *Judgment*, D. E. F. H. I.; *Hitchcock* v. *Aickin*, 1 Caine's R. 460.

[2] See authorities in preceding notes ; and Starkie on Evid. P. 2, § 67 ; p. 206 to 216, and Notes of American Ed. ibid. ; *Plummer* v. *Woodbourne*, 4 Barn. Cresw. 625.

[3] Starkie on Evid. P. 2, § 67, p. 206 to 216 ; Bigelow's Dig. *Evid. C.* and cases cited in Kaims's Equity, B. 3, ch. 8, p. 375.

are still deemed foreign to the mother country, and, of
course, their judgments were deemed foreign judgments within the scope of the foregoing rule.[1] It followed, that the judgments of one colony were deemed
re-examinable in another, not only as to the jurisdiction
of the court, which pronounced them ; but also as to
the merits of the controversy, to the extent, in which
they were then understood to be re-examinable in England. In some of the colonies, however, laws had been
passed, which put judgments in the neighbouring colonies upon a like footing with domestic judgments, as to
their conclusiveness, when the court possessed jurisdiction.[2] The reasonable construction of the article of
the confederation on this subject is, that it was intended to give the same conclusive effect to judgments of
all the states, so as to promote uniformity, as well as
certainty, in the rule among them. It is probable, that
it did not invariably, and perhaps not generally, receive
such a construction ; and the amendment in the constitution was, without question, designed to cure the
defects in the existing provision.[3]

§ 1302. The clause of the constitution propounds three
distinct objects; first, to declare, that full faith and credit
shall be given to the records, &c. of every other state;
secondly, to prescribe the manner of authenticating
them ; and thirdly, to prescribe their effect, when so

---

[1] *Bissell* v. *Briggs*, 9 Mass. R. 462 ; *Commonwealth* v. *Green*, 17 Mass.
R. 515, 543.

[2] This was done in Massachusetts by the Provincial act of 14 Geo. 3,
ch. 2, as to judgments of the courts of the neighbouring colonies. See
Bissell v. *Briggs*, 9 Mass. R. 462, 465 ; Ancient Colony and Province
Laws, [ed. 1814,] p. 684.

[3] See *Kibbe* v. *Kibbe*, 1786, Kirby R. 119; *James* v. *Allen*, 1786, 1
Dall. R. 188 ; *Phelps* v. *Holker*, 1788, 1 Dall. R. 261 ; 3 Jour. of Cong.
12 Nov. 1777, p. 493 ; S. C. 1 Secret Journal, p. 366 ; *Hitchcock* v. *Aicken*,
1 Caine's R. 460, 478, 479.

authenticated. The first is declared, and established by
the constitution itself, and is to receive no aid, nor is it
susceptible of any qualification by congress. The other
two are expressly subjected to the legislative power.

§ 1303. Let us then examine, what is the true meaning and interpretation of each section of the clause.
"Full faith and credit shall be given in each state to
"the public acts, records, and judicial proceedings of
"every other state." The language is positive, and
declaratory, leaving nothing to future legislation. "Full
"faith and credit *shall* be given;" what, then, is
meant by full faith and credit? Does it import no
more than, that the same faith and credit are to be
given to them, which, by the comity of nations, is ordinarily conceded to all foreign judgments? Or is it
intended to give them a more conclusive efficiency,
approaching to, if not identical with, that of domestic judgments; so that, if the jurisdiction of the court
be established, the judgment shall be conclusive, as
to the merits? The latter seems to be the true object
of the clause; and, indeed, it seems difficult to assign
any other adequate motive for the insertion of the
clause, both in the confederation and in the constitution. The framers of both instruments must be presumed to have known, that by the general comity of
nations, and the long established rules of the common
law, both in England and America, foreign judgments
were *primâ facie* evidence of their own correctness.
They might be impugned for their injustice, or irregularity; but they were admitted to be a good ground of
action here, and stood firm, until impeached and overthrown by competent evidence, introduced by the
adverse party. It is hardly conceivable, that so much
solicitude should have been exhibited to introduce, as

between confederated states, much less between states
united under the same national government, a clause
merely affirmative of an established rule of law, and not
denied to the humblest, or most distant foreign nation.
It was hardly supposable, that the states would deal
less favourably with each other on such a subject, where
they could not but have a common interest, than with
foreigners. A motive of a higher kind must naturally
have directed them to the provision. It must have
been, "to form a more perfect Union," and to give to
each state a higher security and confidence in the
others, by attributing a superior sanctity and conclusiveness to the public acts and judicial proceedings of all.
There could be no reasonable objection to such a
course. On the other hand, there were many reasons
in its favour. The states were united in an indissoluble
bond with each other. The commercial and other intercourse with each other would be constant, and infinitely diversified. Credit would be every where given
and received ; and rights and property would belong to
citizens of every state in many other states than that, in
which they resided. Under such circumstances it could
scarcely consist with the peace of society, or with the interest and security of individuals, with the public or with
private good, that questions and titles, once deliberately
tried and decided in one state, should be open to litigation
again and again, as often as either of the parties, or their
privies, should choose to remove from one jurisdiction
to another. It would occasion infinite injustice, after
such trial and decision, again to open and re-examine
all the merits of the case. It might be done at a distance from the original place of the transaction ; after
the removal or death of witnesses, or the loss of other
testimony ; after a long lapse of time, and under cir-

cumstances wholly unfavourable to a just understanding of the case.

§ 1304. If it should be said, that the judgment might be unjust upon the merits, or erroneous in point in law, the proper answer is, that if true, that would furnish no ground for interference; for the evils of a new trial would be greater, than it would cure. Every such judgment ought to be presumed to be correct, and founded in justice. And what security is there, that the new judgment, upon the re-examination, would be more just, or more conformable to law, than the first? What state has a right to proclaim, that the judgments of its own courts are better founded in law or in justice, than those of any other state? The evils of introducing a general system of re-examination of the judicial proceedings of other states, whose connexions are so intimate, and whose rights are so interwoven with our own, would far outweigh any supposable benefits from an imagined superior justice in a few cases.[1] Motives of this sort, founded upon an enlarged confidence, and reciprocal duties, might well be presumed to have entered into the minds of the framers of the confederation, and the constitution. They intended to give, not only faith and credit to the public acts, records, and judicial proceedings of each of the states, such as belonged to those of all foreign nations and tribunals; but to give to them *full* faith and credit; that is, to attribute to them positive and absolute verity, so that they cannot be contradicted, or the truth of them be denied, any more than in the state, where they originated.[2]

---

[1] *Green* v. *Sarmiento*,1 Peters's Cir. R. 74,78 to 80; *Hitchcock* v. *Aicken*, 1 Caine's R. 462.

[2] *Green* v. *Sarmiento*, 1 Peters's Cir. R. 74, 80, 81 ; *Bissell* v. *Briggs*, 9 Mass. R. 462, 467; *Commonwealth* v. *Green*, 17 Mass. R. 515, 544, 545.

§ 1305. The next section of the clause is, "And "the congress may by general laws prescribe the man-"ner, in which such acts, records, and proceedings "shall be proved, — *and the effect thereof.*" It is obvious, that this clause, so far as it authorizes congress to prescribe the mode of authentication, is wholly beside the purpose of the preceding. Whatever may be the faith and credit due to the public acts, records, and proceedings of other states, whether *primâ facie* evidence only, or conclusive evidence ; still the mode of establishing them in proof is of very great importance, and upon which a diversity of rules exists in different countries. The object of the present provision is to introduce uniformity in the rules of proof, (which could alone be done by congress.) It is certainly a great improvement upon the parallel article of the confederation. That left it wholly to the states themselves to require any proof of public acts, records, and proceedings, which they might from time to time deem advisable ; and where no rule was prescribed, the subject was open to the decision of the judicial tribunals, according to their own views of the local usage and jurisprudence. Many embarrassments must necessarily have grown out of such a state of things. The provision, therefore, comes recommended by every consideration of wisdom and convenience, of public peace, and private security.

§ 1306. But the clause does not stop here. The words added are, "and the effect thereof." Upon the proper interpretation of these words some diversity of opinion has been judicially expressed. Some learned judges have thought, that the word "thereof" had reference to the proof, or authentication ; so as to read, "and to prescribe the effect of such proof, or authentication." Others have thought, that it referred to the

antecedent words, " acts, records, and proceedings;"
so as to read, "and to prescribe the effect of such
acts, records, and proceedings." [1] Those, who were
of opinion, that the preceding section of the clause
made judgments in one state conclusive in all others,
naturally adopted the former opinion; for otherwise
the power to declare the effect would be wholly
senseless; or congress could possess the power to repeal, or vary the full faith and credit given by that section. Those, who were of opinion, that such judgments
were not conclusive, but only *primâ facie* evidence, as
naturally embraced the other opinion ; and supposed,
that until congress should, by law, declare what the
effect of such judgment should be, they remained only
primâ facie evidence.

§ 1307. The former seems now to be considered
the sounder interpretation. But it is not, practically
speaking, of much importance, which interpretation
prevails ; since each admits the competency of congress to declare the effect of judgments, when duly
authenticated ; so always, that full faith and credit are
given to them ; and congress by their legislation have
already carried into operation the objects of the clause.
The act of 26th of May, 1790, (ch. 11,) after providing
for the mode of authenticating the acts, records, and
judicial proceedings of the states, has declared, "and
the said records and judicial proceedings, authenticated as aforesaid, shall have *such* faith and credit given
to them in every court within the United States, as
they have by law or usage in the courts of the state,

1 See *Bissell* v. *Briggs*, 9 Mass. R. 462, 467 ; *Hitchcock* v. *Aicken*, 1
Caine's R. 460 ; *Green* v. *Sarmiento*, 1 Peters's Circt. R. 74 ; *Field* v.
Gibbs, Id. 155 ; *Commonwealth* v. *Green*, 17 Mass. R. 515, 544, 545.

from whence the said records are or shall be taken." [1]
It has been settled upon solemn argument, that this
enactment does declare the effect of the records, as evidence, when duly authenticated. It gives them the
same faith and credit, as they have in the state court,
from which they are taken. If in such court they have
the faith and credit of the highest nature, that is to say,
of *record* evidence, they must have the same faith and
credit in every other court. So, that congress have
declared the *effect* of the records, by declaring, what
degree of faith and credit shall be given to them. If
a judgment is conclusive in the state, where it is pronounced, it is equally conclusive every where. If re-
examinable there, it is open to the same inquiries in every
other state. [2]   It is, therefore, put upon the same footing, as a domestic judgment. But this does not prevent an inquiry into the jurisdiction of the court, in
which the original judgment was given, to pronounce
it; or the right of the state itself to exercise authority
over the persons, or the subject matter. The constitution did not mean to confer a new power or jurisdiction; but simply to regulate the effect of the acknowledged jurisdiction over persons and things within the
territory. [3]

---

1 By the act of 27th March, 1804, ch. 56, the provisions of the act of
1790 are enlarged, so as to cover some omissions, such as state office-
books, the records of territorial courts, &c.

2 *Mills* v. *Duryee*, 7 Cranch. R. 481 ; *Hampden* v. *M'Connell*, 3 Wheat.
R. 234 ; 1 Kent's Comm. Lect. 12, p. 243, 244 ; Sergeant on Const.
ch. 31, [ch. 33.]

3 *Bissell* v. *Briggs*, 9 Mass. R. 462, 467 ; *Shumway* v. *Stillman*, 4 Cow-
en's R. 292 ; *Borden* v. *Fitch*, 13 Johns. R. 121.

CHAPTER XXX.

POWERS OF CONGRESS — ADMISSION OF NEW STATES,
AND ACQUISITION OF TERRITORY.

§ 1308. THE third section of the fourth article contains two distinct clauses. The first is — " New states " may be admitted by the congress into this Union. " But no new state shall be formed or erected within " the jurisdiction of any other state, nor any state be " formed by the jurisdiction of two or more states, or " parts of states, without the consent of the legislature " of the states concerned, as well as of the congress."

§ 1309. A clause on this subject was introduced into the original draft of the constitution, varying in some respects from the present, and especially in requiring the consent of two thirds of the members present of both houses to the admission of any new state. After various modifications, attempted or carried, the clause substantially in its present form was agreed to by the vote of eight states against three.[1]

§ 1310. In the articles of confederation no provision is to be found on this important subject. Canada was to be admitted of right, upon her acceding to the measures of the United States. But no other colony (by which was evidently meant no other British colony) was to be admitted, unless by the consent of nine states.[2] The eventual establishment of new states within the limits of the Union seems to have been wholly overlooked by the framers of that instrument.[3]   In the pro-

---

1 Journal of Convention, p. 222, 307, 308, 309, 310, 311, 365, 385.
2 Article 11.   3 The Federalist, No. 43.

gress of the revolution it was not only perceived, that from the acknowledged extent of the territory of several of the states, and its geographical position, it might be expedient to divide it into two states; but a much more interesting question arose, to whom of right belonged the vacant territory appertaining to the crown at the time of the revolution, whether to the states, within whose chartered limits it was situated, or to the Union in its federative capacity. This was a subject of long and ardent controversy, and (as has been already suggested) threatened to disturb the peace, if not to overthrow the government of the Union.[1] It was upon this ground, that several of the states refused to ratify the articles of confederation, insisting upon the right of the confederacy to a portion of the vacant and unpatented territory included within their chartered limits. Some of the states most interested in the vacant and unpatented western territory, at length yielded to the earnest solicitations of congress on this subject.[2] To induce them to make liberal cessions, congress declared, that the ceded territory should be disposed of for the common benefit of the Union, and formed into republican states, with the same rights of sovereignty, freedom, and independence, as the other states; to be of a suitable extent of territory, not less than one hundred, nor more than one hundred and fifty miles square; and that the reasonable expenses incurred by the state, since the commencement of the war, in subduing Brit-

---

[1] 2 Pitk. Hist. ch. 11, p. 17, 19, 24, 27, 28, 29 to 32; Id. 32 to 36; 1 Kent's Comm. Lect. 10, p. 197, 198. See also 1 Secret Journals of Congress in 1775, p. 368 to 386; Id. 433 to 438; Id. 445, 446.

[2] 1 Tuck. Black. Comm. App. 283, 284, 285, 286; 2 Pitkin's Hist. ch. 11, p. 33 to 36; 1 U. S. Laws, (Duane & Bioren's Edition,) p. 467, 472; ante vol. 1, § 227, 228.

ish posts, or in maintaining and acquiring the territory, should be reimbursed.[1]

§ 1311. Of the power of the general government thus constitutionally to acquire territory under the articles of the confederation, serious doubts were at the time expressed; more serious than, perhaps, upon sober argument, could be justified. It is difficult to conceive, why the common attribute of sovereignty, the power to acquire lands by cession, or by conquest, did not apply to the government of the Union, in common with other sovereignties; unless the declaration, that every power not *expressly* delegated was retained by the states, amounted to (which admitted of some doubt) a constitutional prohibition.[2] Upon more than one occasion it has been boldly pronounced to have been founded in usurpation. "It is now no longer," said the Federalist in 1788, "a point of speculation and hope, that the western territory is a mine of vast wealth to the United States; and although it is not of such a nature, as to extricate them from their present distresses, or for some time to come to yield any regular supplies for the public expenses; yet it must hereafter be able, under proper management, both to effect a gradual discharge of the domestic debt, and to furnish for a certain period liberal tributes to the federal treasury. A very large proportion of this fund has been already surrendered by individual states; and it may with reason be expected, that the remaining states will not persist in withholding similar proofs of their equity and generosity.

---

1 See 1 Secret Journals of Congress, 6th Sept. 1780. p. 440 to 444; 6 Journal of Congress, 10th Oct. 1780, p. 213; 2 Pitkin's Hist. ch. 11, p. 34, 35, 36; 7 Journal of Congress, 1st March, 1781, p. 43 to 48; Land Laws of U. S. Introductory chapter, 1 U. S. Laws, p. 452, (Duane & Bioren's Edition.)

2 See *Amer. Insur. Company* v. *Canter*, 1 Peters's Sup. R. 511, 542.

We may calculate, therefore, that a rich and fertile soil of an area equal to the inhabited extent of the United States will soon become a national stock. Congress have assumed the administration of this stock. They have begun to make it productive. Congress have undertaken to do more; they have proceeded to form new states; to erect temporary governments; to appoint officers for them; and to prescribe the conditions, on which such states shall be admitted into the confederacy. *All this has been done, and done without the least colour of constitutional authority.* Yet no blame has been whispered, and no alarm has been sounded."[1]

§ 1312. The truth is, that the importance, and even justice of the title to the public lands on the part of the federal government, and the additional security, which it gave to the Union, overcame all scruples of the people, as to its constitutional character. The measure, to which the Federalist alludes in such emphatic terms, is the famous ordinance of congress, of the 13th of July, 1787, which has ever since constituted, in most respects, the model of all our territorial governments; and is equally remarkable for the brevity and exactness of its text, and for its masterly display of the fundamental principles of civil and religious liberty. It begins by providing a scheme for the descent and distributions of estates equally among all the children, and their representatives, or other relatives of the deceased in equal degree, making no distinction between the whole and half blood; and for the mode of disposing of real estate by will, and by conveyances. It then proceeds to provide for the organization of the territorial

---

[1] The Federalist, No. 38. 42. 43.

governments, according to their progress in population, confiding the whole power to a governor and judges in the first instance, subject to the control of congress. As soon as the territory contains five thousand inhabitants, it provides for the establishment of a general legislature, to consist of three branches, a governor, a legislative council, and a house of representatives; with a power to the legislature to appoint a delegate to congress. It then proceeds to state certain fundamental articles of compact between the original states, and the people and states in the territory, which are to remain unalterable, unless by common consent. The first provides for freedom of religious opinions and worship. The second provides for the right to the writ of *habeas corpus;* for the trial by jury; for a proportionate representation in the legislature; for judicial proceedings according to the course of the common law; for capital offences being bailable; for fines being moderate, and punishments not cruel or unusual; for no man's being deprived of his liberty or property, but by the judgment of his peers, or the law of the land; for full compensation for property taken, or services demanded for the public exigencies; "and for the just preservation of "rights and property, that no law ought ever to be "made, or have force in the said territory, that shall "in any manner whatever *interfere with, or affect private* "*contracts or engagements, bonâ fide,* and without fraud "previously formed." The third provides for the encouragement of religion, and education, and schools, and for good faith and due respect for the rights and property of the Indians. The fourth provides, that the territory and states formed therein shall for ever remain a part of the confederacy, subject to the constitutional authority of congress; that the inhabitants shall be liable to be taxed proportionately for the public expenses; that the legislatures in the territory shall never interfere with the primary disposal of the soil by congress, nor with their regulations for securing the title to the soil to purchasers; that no tax shall be imposed on lands, the property of the United States; and nonresident proprietors shall not be taxed more than residents; that the navigable waters leading into the Mississippi and St. Lawrence, and the carrying places between the same shall be common highways, and for ever free. The fifth provides, that there shall be formed in the territory not less than three, nor more than five states with certain boundaries; and whenever any of the said states shall contain 60,000 free inhabitants, such state shall (and may before) be admitted by its delegates into congress on an equal footing with the original states in all respects whatever, and shall be at liberty to form a permanent constitution and state government, provided it shall be republican, and in conformity to these articles of compact. The sixth and last provides, that there shall be neither slavery nor involuntary servitude in the said territory, otherwise than in the punishment of crimes; but fugitives from other states, owing service therein, may be reclaimed.[1] Such is a brief outline of this most important ordinance, the effects of which upon the destinies of the country have already been abundantly demonstrated in the territory, by an almost unexampled prosperity and rapidity of population, by the formation of republican governments, and by an enlightened system of jurisprudence. Already three states, composing a part of that territory,

---

[1] See 3 Story's Laws of United States App. 2073, &c.; 1 Tucker's Black. Comm. App. 278, 282.

have been admitted into the Union ; and others are fast advancing towards the same grade of political dignity.[1]

§ 1313. It was doubtless with reference principally to this territory, that the article of the constitution, now under consideration, was adopted. The general precaution, that no new states shall be formed without the concurrence of the national government, and of the states concerned, is consonant to the principles, which ought to govern all such transactions. The particular precaution against the erection of new states by the partition of a state without its own consent, will quiet the jealousy of the larger states ; as that of the smaller will also be quieted by a like precaution against a junction of states without their consent.[2] Under this provision no less than eleven states have, in the space of little more than forty years, been admitted into the Union upon an equality with the original states. And it scarcely requires the spirit of prophecy to foretell, that in a few years the predominance of numbers, of population, and of power will be unequivocally transferred from the old to the new states. May the patriotic wish be for ever true to the fact, *felix prole parens.*

§ 1314. Since the adoption of the constitution large acquisitions of territory have been made by the United States, by the purchase of Louisiana and Florida, and by the cession of Georgia, which have greatly increased the contemplated number of states. The constitution-

---

[1] In Mr. Webster's Speech on Mr. Foote's Resolution, in Jan. 1830, there is a very interesting and powerful view of this subject, which will amply repay the diligence of a deliberate perusal. See Webster's Speeches, &c. p. 360 to 364; Id. 369. It is well known, that the ordinance of 1787 was drawn by the Hon. Nathan Dane of Massachusetts, and adopted with scarcely a verbal alteration by Congress. It is a noble and imperishable monument to his fame.

[2] The Federalist, No. 43.

ality of the two former acquisitions, though formerly much questioned, is now considered settled beyond any practical doubt.[1]

§ 1315. At the time, when the preliminary measures were taken for the admission of the state of Missouri into the Union, an attempt was made to include a restriction, prohibiting the introduction of slavery into that state, as a condition of the admission. On that occasion the question was largely discussed, whether congress possessed a constitutional authority to impose such a restriction, upon the ground, that the prescribing of such a condition is inconsistent with the sovereignty of the state to be admitted, and its equality with the other states. The final result of the vote, which authorized the erection of that state, seems to establish the rightful authority of congress to impose such a restriction, although it was not then applied. In the act passed for this purpose, there is an express clause, that in all the territory ceded by France to the United States under the name of Louisiana, which lies north of 36° 30′ N. Lat., not included within the limits of the state of Missouri, slavery and involuntary servitude, otherwise than in the punishment of crimes, whereof the parties shall have been duly convicted, shall be, and is hereby for ever prohibited.[2] An objection of a similar character was taken to the compact between Virginia and Kentucky upon the ground, that it was a restriction upon state sovereignty. But the Supreme Court had no hesita-

---

1 See Ante, Vol. iii. p. 156, § 1278 to § 1283; *American Insurance Company* v. *Canter*, 1 Peters's Sup. R. 511, 542.

2 Act. 6, March 1820, ch. 20. — The same subject was immediately afterwards much discussed in the state legislatures; and opposite opinions were expressed by different states in the form of solemn resolutions.

tion in overruling it, considering it as opposed by the
theory of all free governments, and especially of those,
which constitute the American Republics.[1]

---

[1] *Green* v. *Biddle*, 8 Wheat. R. 1, 87, 88.

CHAPTER XXXI.

POWERS OF CONGRESS — TERRITORIAL GOVERN-MENTS.

§ 1316. THE next clause of the same article is, "The "congress shall have power to dispose of and make all "needful rules and regulations respecting the territory "and other property belonging to the United States; "and nothing in this constitution shall be so construed, "as to prejudice any claims of the United States, or "of any particular state." The proviso thus annexed to the power is certainly proper in itself, and was probably rendered necessary by the jealousies and questions concerning the Western territory, which have been already alluded to under the preceding head.[1] It was perhaps suggested by the clause in the ninth article of the confederation, which contained a proviso, "that no state shall be deprived of territory for the benefit of the United States."

§ 1317. The power itself was obviously proper, in order to escape from the constitutional objection already stated to the power of congress over the territory ceded to the United States under the confederation. The clause was not in the original draft of the constitution; but was added by the vote of ten states against one.[2]

§ 1318. As the general government possesses the right to acquire territory, either by conquest, or by treaty, it would seem to follow, as an inevitable consequence,

---

[1] The Federalist, No. 43; ante, ch. 30.
[2] Journal of Convention, p. 228, 310, 311, 365.

that it possesses the power to govern, what it has so acquired. The territory does not, when so acquired, become entitled to self-government, and it is not subject
to the jurisdiction of any state. It must, consequently,
be under the dominion and jurisdiction of the Union, or
it would be without any government at all.[1]   In cases
of conquest, the usage of the world is, if a nation
is not wholly subdued, to consider the conquered
territory, as merely held by military occupation, until
its fate shall be determined by a treaty of peace.
But during this intermediate period it is exclusively subject to the government of the conqueror.
In cases of confirmation or cession by treaty, the
acquisition becomes firm and stable; and the ceded
territory becomes a part of the nation, to which it is
annexed, either on terms stipulated in the treaty, or on
such, as its new master shall impose. The relations of
the inhabitants with each other do not change; but
their relations with their former sovereign are dissolved;
and new relations are created between them and their
new sovereign. The act transferring the country trans-
fers the allegiance of its inhabitants. But the general
laws, not strictly political, remain, as they were, until
altered by the new sovereign. If the treaty stipulates,
that they shall enjoy the privileges, rights, and immunities of citizens of the United States, the treaty, as a
part of the law of the land, becomes obligatory in these
respects. Whether the same effects would result from
the mere fact of their becoming inhabitants and citizens
by the cession, without any express stipulation, may
deserve inquiry, if the question should ever occur.

---

[1] *American Insurance Company* v. *Canter*, 1 Peters's Sup. R. 511, 542,
543; Id. 517, Mr. Justice Johnson's Opinion.

But they do not participate in political power; nor can they share in the powers of the general government, until they become a state, and are admitted into the Union, as such. Until that period, the territory remains subject to be governed in such manner, as congress shall direct, under the clause of the constitution now under consideration.[1]

§ 1319. No one has ever doubted the authority of congress to erect territorial governments within the territory of the United States, under the general language of the clause, "to make all needful rules and regulations." Indeed, with the ordinance of 1787 in the very view of the framers, as well as of the people of the states, it is impossible to doubt, that such a power was deemed indispensable to the purposes of the cessions made by the states. So that, notwithstanding the generality of the objection, (already examined,) that congress has no power to erect corporations, and that in the convention the power was refused; we see, that the very power is an incident to that of regulating the territory of the United States; that is, it is an appropriate means of carrying the power into effect.[2] What shall be the form of government established in the territories depends exclusively upon the discretion of congress. Having a right to erect a territorial government, they may confer on it such powers, legislative, judicial, and executive, as they may deem best. They may confer upon it general legislative powers, subject only to the laws and constitution of the United

1 *American Insurance Company* v. *Canter*, 1 Peters's Sup. R. 511, 542, 543.
3 See ante, § 1260, 1261; 4 Jefferson's Corresp. 523, 525; Hamilton on the Bank of U. S., 1 Hamilton's Works, 121, 127 to 131; Id. 135, 147, 151; Id. 114, 115 Act of Congress, 7th Aug. 1789, ch. 8.

States.   If the power to create courts is given to the territorial legislature, those courts are to be deemed strictly territorial ; and in no just sense constitutional courts, in which the judicial power conferred by the constitution can be deposited.   They are incapable of receiving it.   They are legislative courts, created in virtue of the general right of sovereignty in the government, or in virtue of that clause, which enables congress to make all needful rules and regulations respecting the territory of the United States.[1]   The power is not confined to the territory of the United States; but extends to " other property belonging to the United States ; " so that it may be applied to the due regulation of all other personal and real property rightfully belonging to the United States.   And so it has been constantly understood, and acted upon.

§ 1320. As if it were not possible to confer a single power upon the national government, which ought not to be a source of jealousy, the present has not been without objection.   It has been suggested, that the sale and disposal of the Western territory may become a source of such immense revenue to the national government, as to make it independent of, and formidable to, the people.   To amass immense riches (it has been said) to defray the expenses of ambition, when occasion may prompt, without seeming to oppress the people, has uniformly been the policy of tyrants.   Should such a policy creep into our government, and the sales of the public lands, instead of being appropriated to the discharge of the public debt, be converted to a treasure in a bank, those, who, at any time, can command it, may be tempted to apply it to the most nefarious purposes.   The

[1] *American Insurance Company* v. *Canter*, 1 Peters's Sup. R. 511, 546.

improvident alienation of the crown lands in England has been considered, as a circumstance extremely favourable to the liberty of the nation, by rendering the government less independent of the people. The same reason will apply to other governments, whether monarchical or republican.[1]

§ 1321. What a strange representation is this of a republican government, created by, and responsible to, the people in all its departments! What possible analogy can there be between the possession of large revenues in the hands of a monarch, and large revenues in the possession of a government, whose administration is confided to the chosen agents of the people for a short period, and may be dismissed almost at pleasure? If the doctrine be true, which is here inculcated, a republican government is little more than a dream, however its administration may be organized; and the people are not worthy of being trusted with large public revenues, since they cannot provide against corruption, and abuses of them. Poverty alone (it seems) gives a security for fidelity; and the liberties of the people are safe only, when they are pressed into vigilance by the power of taxation. In the view of this doctrine, what is to be thought of the recent purchases of Louisiana and Florida? If there was danger before, how mightily must it be increased by the accession of such a vast extent of territory, and such a vast increase of resources? Hitherto, the experience of the country has justified no alarms on this subject from such a source. On the other hand, the public lands hold out, after the discharge of the national debt, ample revenues to be devoted to the cause of education and sound learning, and to internal improvements, without trenching upon the property, or

---

[1] 1 Tuck. Black. Comm. App. 284.

embarrassing the pursuits of the people by burthensome taxation. The constitutional objection to the appropriation of the other revenues of the government to such objects has not been supposed to apply to an appropriation of the proceeds of the public lands. The cessions of that territory were expressly made for the common benefit of the United States; and therefore constitute a fund, which may be properly devoted to any objects, which are for the common benefit of the Union.[1]

§ 1322. The power of congress over the public territory is clearly exclusive and universal; and their legislation is subject to no control; but is absolute, and unlimited, unless so far as it is affected by stipulations in the cessions, or by the ordinance of 1787, under which any part of it has been settled.[2] But the power of congress to regulate the other national property (unless it has acquired, by cession of the states, exclusive jurisdiction) is not necessarily exclusive in all cases. If the national government own a fort, arsenal, hospital, or lighthouse establishment, not so ceded, the general jurisdiction of the state is not excluded in regard to the site; but, subject to the rightful exercise of the powers of the national government, it remains in full force.[3]

§ 1323. There are some other incidental powers given to congress, to carry into effect certain other

---

1 1 Kent's Comm. Lect. 12, p. 242, 243; Id. Lect. 17, p. 359.
2 Rawle on Const. ch. 27, p. 237; 1 Kent's Comm. Lect. 12, p. 243; Id. Lect. 17, p. 359, 360.
3 Rawle on Const. ch. 27, p. 240; *The People* v. *Godfrey*, 17 Johns. R. 225; *Commonwealth* v. *Young*, 1 Hall's Journal of Jurisp. 47. — Sergeant on Const. ch. 31, [ch. 33.] — Whether the general doctrine in the case of *Commonwealth* v. *Young*, (1 Hall's Journal 47,) can be maintained, in its application to that case, is quite a different question.

provisions of the constitution. But they will most properly come under consideration in a future part of these Commentaries. At present, it may suffice to say, that with reference to due energy in the government, due protection of the national interests, and due security to the Union, fewer powers could scarcely have been granted, without jeoparding the whole system. Without the power of the purse, the power to declare war, or to promote the common defence, or general welfare, would have been wholly vain and illusory. Without the power exclusively to regulate commerce, the intercourse between the states would have been constantly liable to domestic dissensions, jealousies, and rivalries, and to foreign hostilities, and retaliatory restrictions. The other powers are principally auxiliary to these; and are dictated at once by an enlightened policy, a devotion to justice, and a regard to the permanence (may it ripen into a perpetuity!) of the Union.[1]

---

[1] Among the extraordinary opinions of Mr. Jefferson, in regard to government in general, and especially to the government of the United States, none strikes the calm observer with more force, than the cool and calculating manner, in which he surveys the probable occurrence of domestic rebellions. "I am," he says, "not a friend to a very energetic government. It is always oppressive. It places the governors, indeed, more at their ease, at the expense of the people. The late rebellion in Massachusetts (in 1787) has given more alarm, than I think it should have done. Calculate, that one rebellion in thirteen states, in the course of eleven years, is but one for each state, in a century and a half. *No country should be so long without one.* Nor will any degree of power in the hands of government prevent insurrections." Letter to Mr. Madison, in 1787, 2 Jefferson's Corresp. 276. Is it not surprising, that any statesman should have overlooked the horrible evils, and immense expenses, which are attendant upon every rebellion? The loss of life, the summary exercise of military power, the desolations of the country, and the inordinate expenditures, to which every rebellion must give rise? Is not the great object of every good government to

§ 1324. As there are incidental powers belonging to the United States in their sovereign capacity, so there are incidental rights, obligations, and duties. It may be asked, how these are to be ascertained. In the first place, as to duties and obligations of a public nature, they are to be ascertained by the law of nations, to which, on asserting our independence, we necessarily became subject. In regard to municipal rights and obligations, whatever differences of opinion may arise in regard to the extent, to which the common law attaches to the national government, no one can doubt, that it must, and ought to be resorted to, in order to ascertain many of its rights and obligations. Thus, when a contract is entered into by the United States, we naturally and necessarily resort to the common law, to interpret its terms, and ascertain its obligations. The same general rights, duties, and limitations, which the common law attaches to contracts of a similar character between private individuals, are applied to the contracts of the government. Thus, if the United States become the holder of a bill of exchange, they are bound to the same diligence, as to giving notice, in order to

preserve, and perpetuate domestic peace, and the security of property, and the reasonable enjoyment of private rights, and personal liberty? If a state is to be torn into factions, and civil wars, every eleven years, is not the whole Union to become a common sufferer? How, and when are such wars to terminate? Are the insurgents to meet victory or defeat? Has not history established the melancholy truth, that constant wars lead to military dictatorship, and despotism, and are inconsistent with the free spirit of republican governments? If the tranquillity of the Union is to be disturbed every eleventh year by a civil war, what repose can there be for the citizens in their ordinary pursuits? Will they not soon become tired of a republican government, which invites to such eternal contests, ending in blood, and murder, and rapine? One cannot but feel far more sympathy with the opinion of Mr. Jefferson, in the same letter, in which he expounds the great political maxim, "Educate and inform the whole mass of the people." 2 Jefferson's Corresp. 276.

change an indorser, upon the dishonour of the bill, as a private holder would be.[1] In like manner, when a bond is entered into by a surety for the faithful discharge of the duties of an office by his principal, the nature and extent of the obligation, created by the instrument, are constantly ascertained by reference to the common law; though the bond is given to the government in its sovereign capacity.[2]

---

[1] *United States* v. *Barker*, 12 Wheat. R. 559.

[2] See, among other cases, *United States* v. *Kirkpatrick*, 9 Wheat. R. 720; *Farrar* v. *United States*, 5 Peters's R. 373; *Smith* v. *United States*, 5 Peters's R. 294; *United States* v. *Tingey*, 5 Peters's R. 115; *United States* v. *Buford*, 3 Peters's R. 12, 30.

CHAPTER XXXII.

PROHIBITIONS ON THE UNITED STATES.

§ 1325. HAVING finished this review of the powers of congress, the order of the subject next conducts us to the prohibitions and limitations upon these powers, which are contained in the ninth section of the first article. Some of these have already been under discussion, and therefore will be pretermitted.[1]

§ 1326. The first clause is as follows: "The mi-" gration, or importation of such persons, as any of the "states now existing shall think proper to admit, shall "not be prohibited by the congress, prior to the year "one thousand eight hundred and eight; but a tax, "or duty, may be imposed on such importation, not "exceeding ten dollars for each person."

§ 1327. The corresponding clause of the first draft of the constitution was in these words: "No tax, or duty, shall be laid, &c. on the migration, or importation of such persons, as the several states shall think proper to admit; nor shall such migration, or importation be prohibited." In this form it is obvious, that the migration and importation of slaves, which was the sole object of the clause, was in effect perpetuated, so long, as any state should choose to allow the traffic. The subject was afterwards referred to a committee, who reported the clause substantially in its present shape; except that the limitation was the year one thousand eight hundred, instead of one thousand eight hun-

---

[1] Those, which respect taxation, and the regulation of commerce, have been considered under former heads; to which the learned reader is referred. Ante, Vol. II, ch. 14, 15.

dred and eight. The latter amendment was substituted by the vote of seven states against four; and as thus amended, the clause was adopted by the like vote of the same states.[1]

§ 1328. It is to the honour of America, that she should have set the first example of interdicting and abolishing the slave-trade, in modern times. It is well known, that it constituted a grievance, of which some of the colonies complained before the revolution, that the introduction of slaves was encouraged by the crown, and that prohibitory laws were negatived.[2] It was doubtless to have been wished, that the power of prohibiting the importation of slaves had been allowed to be put into immediate operation, and had not been postponed for twenty years. But it is not difficult to account, either for this restriction, or for the manner, in which it is expressed.[3] It ought to be considered, as a great point gained in favour of humanity, that a period of twenty years might for ever terminate, within the United States, a traffic, which has so long, and so loudly upbraided the barbarism of modern policy. Even within this period, it might receive a very considerable discouragement, by curtailing the traffic between for-

---

[1] Journ. of Convention, p. 222, 275, 276, 285, 291, 292, 358, 378; 2 Pitk. Hist. ch. 20, p. 261, 262. — It is well known, as an historical fact, that South-Carolina and Georgia insisted upon this limitation, as a condition of the Union. See 2 Elliot's Deb. 335, 336; 3 Elliot's Deb. 97.

[2] See 2 Elliot's Debates, 335; 1 Secret Journal of Congress, 378, 379.

[3] See 3 Elliot's Debates, 98, 250, 251; 3 Elliot's Debates, 335 to 338. —In the original draft of the Declaration of Independence by Mr. Jefferson, there is a very strong paragraph on this subject, in which the slave-trade is denounced, "as a piratical warfare, the opprobrium of infidel powers, and the warfare of the Christian king of Great Britain, determined to keep open a market, where men should be bought and sold;" and it is added, that "he has prostituted his negative for suppressing every legislative attempt to prohibit, or restrain this execrable commerce." 1 Jefferson's Corresp. 146, in the fac simile of the original.

eign countries; and it might even be totally abolished by
the concurrence of a few states.[1] " Happy," it was then
added by the Federalist, " would it be for the unfortunate Africans, if an equal prospect lay before them of
being redeemed from the oppressions of their European
brethren."[2]   Let it be remembered, that at this period
this horrible traffic was carried on with the encouragement and support of every civilized nation of Europe;
and by none with more eagerness and enterprize, than
by the parent country.   America stood forth alone, un-
cheered and unaided, in stamping ignominy upon this
traffic on the very face of her constitution of government, although there were strong temptations of interest to draw her aside from the performance of this
great moral duty.

§1329. Yet attempts were made to pervert this
clause into an objection against the constitution, by
representing it on one side, as a criminal toleration of
an illicit practice ; and on another, as calculated to
prevent voluntary and beneficial emigrations to America.[3]   Nothing, perhaps, can better exemplify the
spirit and manner, in which the opposition to the constitution was conducted, than this fact.   It was notorious, that the postponement of an immediate abolition
was indispensable to secure the adoption of the constitution.   It was a necessary sacrifice to the prejudices
and interests of a portion of the Southern states.[4] The
glory of the achievement is scarcely lessened by its
having been gradual, and by steps silent, but irresistible.

---

[1] The Federalist, No. 42.   [2] Ibid.
[3] The Federalist, No. 42; 2 Elliot's Debates, 335, 336 ; 3 Elliot's
Debates, 250, 251.
[4] 2 Elliot's Debates, 335, 336 ; 1 Lloyd's Deb. 305 to 313 ; 3 Elliot's
Debates, 97 ; Id. 250, 251 ; 1 Elliot's Debates, 60 ; 1 Tuck. Black. Comm·
App. 290.

§ 1330. Congress lost no time in interdicting the traffic, as far as their power extended, by a prohibition of American citizens carrying it on between foreign countries. And as soon, as the stipulated period of twenty years had expired, congress, by a prospective legislation to meet the exigency, abolished the whole traffic in every direction to citizens and residents. Mild and moderate laws were, however, found insufficient for the purpose of putting an end to the practice ; and at length congress found it necessary to declare the slave-trade to be a piracy, and to punish it with death.[1] Thus it has been elevated in the catalogue of crimes to this 'bad eminence' of guilt ; and has now annexed to it the infamy, as well as the retributive justice, which belongs to an offence equally against the laws of God and man, the dictates of humanity, and the solemn precepts of religion. Other civilized nations are now alive to this great duty ; and by the noble exertions of the British government, there is now every reason to believe, that the African slave-trade will soon become extinct ; and thus another triumph of virtue would be obtained over brutal violence and unfeeling cruelty.[2]

§ 1331. This clause of the constitution, respecting the importation of slaves, is manifestly an exception from the power of regulating commerce. Migration seems appropriately to apply to voluntary arrivals, as importation does to involuntary arrivals ; and so far, as an exception from a power proves its existence, this proves, that the power to regulate commerce applies equally to the regulation of vessels employed in trans-

[1] Act of 1820, ch. 113.
[2] See 1 Kent's Comm. Lect. 9, p. 179 to 187.

porting men, who pass from place to place voluntarily, as to those, who pass involuntarily.[1]

§ 1332. The next clause is, "The privilege of the "writ of habeas corpus shall not be suspended, unless "when, in cases of rebellion or invasion, the public "safety may require it."

§ 1333. In order to understand the meaning of the terms here used, it will be necessary to have recourse to the common law; for in no other way can we arrive at the true definition of the writ of habeas corpus. At the common law there are various writs, called writs of habeas corpus. But the particular one here spoken of is that great and celebrated writ, used in all cases of illegal confinement, known by the name of the writ of *habeas corpus ad subjiciendum*, directed to the person detaining another, and commanding him to produce the body of the prisoner, with the day and cause of his caption and detention, *ad faciendum, subjiciendum, et recipiendum*, to do, submit to, and receive, whatsoever the judge or court, awarding such writ, shall consider in that behalf.[2] It is, therefore, justly esteemed the great bulwark of personal liberty; since it is the appropriate remedy to ascertain, whether any person is rightfully in confinement or not, and the cause of his confinement; and if no sufficient ground of detention appears, the party is entitled to his immediate discharge. This writ is most beneficially construed; and is applied to every case of illegal restraint, whatever it may be; for every restraint upon a man's liberty is, in the eye of the law, an imprisonment, wherever may be the place, or whatever may be the manner, in which the restraint is effected.[3]

1 *Gibbons* v. *Ogden*, 9 Wheat. R. 1, 216, 217; Id. 206, 207.
2 3 Black. Comm. 131.
3 2 Kent. Comm. Lect. 24, p. 22, &c. (2 edit. p. 26 to 32.)

§ 1334. Mr. Justice Blackstone has remarked with great force, that "to bereave a man of life, or by violence to confiscate his estate without accusation or trial, would be so gross and notorious an act of despotism as must at once convey the alarm of tyranny throughout the whole kingdom. But confinement of the person by secretly hurrying him to gaol, where his sufferings are unknown or forgotten, is a less public, a less striking, and therefore a more dangerous engine of arbitrary force." [1] While the justice of the remark must be felt by all, let it be remembered, that the right to pass bills of attainder in the British parliament still enables that body to exercise the summary and awful power of taking a man's life, and confiscating his estate, without accusation or trial. The learned commentator, however, has slid over this subject with surprising delicacy. [2]

§ 1335. In England this is a high prerogative writ, issuing out of the Court of King's Bench, not only in term time, but in vacation, and running into all parts of the king's dominions ; for it is said, that the king is entitled, at all times, to have an account, why the liberty of any of his subjects is restrained. It is grantable, however, as a matter of right, *ex merito justitiæ*, upon the application of the subject. [3] In England, however, the benefit of it was often eluded prior to the reign of Charles the Second ; and especially during the reign of Charles the First. These pitiful evasions gave rise to the famous Habeas Corpus Act of 31 Car. 2, c. 2, which has been frequently considered, as another magna charta in that kingdom ; and has reduced the

[1] 1 Black. Comm. 136.   [2] 4 Black. Comm. 259.
[3] 4 Inst. 290 ; 1 Kent's Comm. Lect. 24, p. 22, (p. 26 to 32 ;) 3 Black. Comm. 133.

general method of proceedings on these writs to the true standard of law and liberty.[1] That statute has been, in substance, incorporated into the jurisprudence of every state in the Union; and the right to it has been secured in most, if not in all, of the state constitutions by a provision, similar to that existing in the constitution of the United States.[2] It is not without reason, therefore, that the common law was deemed by our ancestors a part of the law of the land, brought with them upon their emigration, so far, as it was suited to their circumstances; since it affords the amplest protection for their rights and personal liberty. Congress have vested in the courts of the United States full authority to issue this great writ, in cases falling properly within the jurisdiction of the national government.[3]

§ 1336. It is obvious, that cases of a peculiar emergency may arise, which may justify, nay even require, the temporary suspension of any right to the writ. But as it has frequently happened in foreign countries, and even in England, that the writ has, upon various pretexts and occasions, been suspended, whereby persons apprehended upon suspicion have suffered a long imprisonment, sometimes from design, and sometimes, because they were forgotten,[4] the right to suspend it is expressly confined to cases of rebellion or invasion, where the public safety may require it. A very just and wholesome restraint, which cuts down at a blow a fruitful means of oppression, capable of being abused in

---

[1] 3 Black. Comm. 135, 136 ; 2 Kent's Comm. Lect. 24, p. 22, 23, (2d edit. p. 26 to 32.)

[2] 2 Kent's Comm. Lect. 24, p. 23, 24, (2d edit. p. 26 to 32.)

[3] *Ex parte Bollman*, &c., 4 Cranch, 75 ; S. C. 2 Peters's Cond. R. 33.

[4] 3 Black. Comm. 137, 138 ; 1 Tuck. Black. Comm. App. 291, 292.

bad times to the worst of purposes. Hitherto no suspension of the writ has ever been authorized by congress since the establishment of the constitution.[1] It
would seem, as the power is given to congress to
suspend the writ of habeas corpus in cases of rebellion
or invasion, that the right to judge, whether exigency
had arisen, must exclusively belong to that body.[2]

§ 1337. The next clause is, "No bill of attainder
"or *ex post facto* law shall be passed."

§ 1338. Bills of attainder, as they are technically
called, are such special acts of the legislature, as inflict
capital punishments upon persons supposed to be guilty
of high offences, such as treason and felony, without
any conviction in the ordinary course of judicial proceedings. If an act inflicts a milder degree of punishment than death, it is called a bill of pains and penal-

---

[1] Mr. Jefferson expressed a decided objection against the power to
suspend the writ of habeas corpus in any case whatever, declaring himself in favour of "the eternal and unremitting force of the habeas corpus
laws." 2 Jefferson's Corresp. 274, 291. — "Why," said he on another
occasion, "suspend the writ of habeas corpus in insurrections and rebellions ?" — "If the public safety requires, that the government should
have a man imprisoned on less probable testimony in those, than in other emergencies, let him be taken and tried, *retaken and retried*, while
the necessity continues, only giving him redress against the government for damages." 2 Jefferson's Corresp. 344. — Yet the only attempt
ever made in congress to suspend the writ of habeas corpus was during
his administration on occasion of the supposed treasonable conspiracy of
Col. Aaron Burr. Mr. Jefferson sent a message to congress on the
subject of that conspiracy on 22d January, 1807. On the next day,
Mr. Giles of the senate moved a committee to consider the expediency
of suspending the writ of habeas corpus be appointed, and the motion
prevailed. The committee (Mr. Giles, chairman) reported a bill for this
purpose. The bill passed the senate, and was rejected in the house of
representatives by a vote of 113 for the rejection, against 19 in its favour.
See 3 Senate Journal, 22d January, 1807, p. 127; Id. 130, 131. 5 Journ.
of House of Representatives, 26th January, 1807, p. 550, 551, 552.

[2] *Martin v. Mott*, 12 Wheat. R. 19. See also 1 Tuck. Black. Comm.
App. 292 ; 1 Kent's Comm. Lect. 12, (2d edit. p. 262 to 265.)

ties.[1]   But in the sense of the constitution, it seems, that bills of attainder include bills of pains and penalties; for the Supreme Court have said, " A bill of attainder may affect the life of an individual, or may confiscate his property, or both." [2]   In such cases, the legislature assumes judicial magistracy, pronouncing upon the guilt of the party without any of the common forms and guards of trial, and satisfying itself with proofs, when such proofs are within its reach, whether they are conformable to the rules of evidence, or not. In short, in all such cases, the legislature exercises the highest power of sovereignty, and what may be properly deemed an irresponsible despotic discretion, being governed solely by what it deems political necessity or expediency, and too often under the influence of unreasonable fears, or unfounded suspicions.   Such acts have been often resorted to in foreign governments, as a common engine of state ; and even in England they have been pushed to the most extravagant extent in bad times, reaching, as well to the absent and the dead, as to the living. Sir Edward Coke [3] has mentioned it to be among the transcendent powers of parliament, that an act may be passed to attaint a man, after he is dead. And the reigning monarch, who was slain at Bosworth, is said to have been attainted by an act of parliament a few months after his death, notwithstanding the absurdity of deeming him at once in possession of the throne and a traitor.[4]   The punishment has often been inflicted without calling upon the party accused to

[1] 2 Woodeson's Law Lect. 625.
[2] *Fletcher* v. *Peck*, 6 Cranch, R. 138 ; S. C. 2 Peters's Cond. R. 322 ; 1 Kent's Comm. Lect. 19, p. 382.
[3] 4 Coke. Inst. 36, 37.
[4] 2 Woodeson's Lect. 622, 621.

answer, or without even the formality of proof; and sometimes, because the law, in its ordinary course of proceedings, would acquit the offender.[1] The injustice and iniquity of such acts, in general, constitute an irresistible argument against the existence of the power. In a free government it would be intolerable; and in the hands of a reigning faction, it might be, and probably would be, abused to the ruin and death of the most virtuous citizens.[2] Bills of this sort have been most usually passed in England in times of rebellion, or of gross subserviency to the crown, or of violent political excitements ; periods, in which all nations are most liable (as well the free, as the enslaved) to forget their duties, and to trample upon the rights and liberties of others.[3]

---

[1] 2 Woodeson's Lect. 624.

[2] Dr. Paley has strongly shown his disapprobation of laws of this sort. I quote from him a short but pregnant passage. " This fundamental rule of civil jurisprudence is violated in the case of acts of attainder or confiscation, in bills of pains and penalties, and in all *ex post facto* laws whatever, in which parliament exercises the double office of legislature and judge. And whoever either understands the value of the rule itself, or collects the history of those instances, in which it has been invaded, will be induced, I believe, to acknowledge, that it had been wiser and safer never to have departed from it. He will confess, at least, that nothing but the most manifest and immediate peril of the commonwealth will justify a repetition of these dangerous examples. If the laws in being do not punish an offender, let him go unpunished ; let the legislature, admonished of the defect of the laws, provide against the commission of future crimes of the same sort. The escape of one delinquent can never produce so much harm to the community, as may arise from the infraction of a rule, upon which the purity of public justice, and the existence of civil liberty, essentially depend."

[3] See 1 Tucker's Black. Comm. App. 292, 293 ; Rawle on Const. ch. 10, p. 119. See *Cooper* v. *Telfair*, 4 Dall. R. 14. — Mr. Woodeson, in his Law Lectures, (Lect. 41,) has devoted a whole lecture to this subject, which is full of instruction, and will reward the diligent perusal of the student. 2 Woodeson's Law Lect. 621. — During the American revolution this power was used with a most unsparing hand ; and it has

§ 1339. Of the same class are *ex post facto* laws, that is to say, (in a literal sense,) laws passed after the act done. The terms, *ex post facto* laws, in a comprehensive sense, embrace all retrospective laws, or laws governing, or controlling past transactions, whether they are of a civil, or a criminal nature. And there have not been wanting learned minds, that have contended with no small force of authority and reasoning, that such ought to be the interpretation of the terms in the constitution of the United States.[1] As an original question, the argument would be entitled to grave consideration; but the current of opinion and authority has been so generally one way, as to the meaning of this phrase in the state constitutions, as well as in that of the United States, ever since their adoption, that it is difficult to feel, that it is now an open question.[2] The general interpretation has been, and is, that the phrase applies to acts of a criminal nature only; and, that the prohibition reaches every law, whereby an act is declared a crime, and made punishable as such, when it was not a crime, when done; or whereby the act, if a crime, is aggravated in enormity, or punishment; or whereby different, or less evidence, is required to convict an offender, than was required, when the act was committed. The Supreme Court have given the following definition. "An *ex post facto* law is one, which ren-

been a matter of regret in succeeding times, however much it may have been applauded *flagrante bello.*

[1] Mr. Justice Johnson's Opinion in *Satterlee* v. *Mathewson*, 2 Peters's R. 416, and note, id. App. 681, &c.; 2 Elliot's Debates, 353; 4 Wheat. R. 578, note; *Ogden* v. *Saunders*, 12 Wheat. R. 286.

[2] See *Calder* v. *Bull*, 3 Dall. 386; *Fletcher* v. *Peck*, 6 Cranch, 138; S. C. 1 Peters's Cond. R. 172; 2 Peters's Cond. R. 308; The Federalist, No. 44, 84; Journ. of Convention, Supp. p. 431; 2 Amer. Mus. 536; 2 Elliot's Debates, 343, 352, 354; *Ogden* v. *Saunders*, 12 Wheat. R. 266, 303, 329, 330, 335; 1 Kent. Comm. Lect. 19, p. 381, 382.

ders an act punishable in a manner, in which it was not punishable, when it was committed." [1] Such a law may inflict penalties on the person, or may inflict pecuniary penalties, which swell the public treasury.[2] Laws, however, which mitigate the character, or punishment of a crime already committed, may not fall within the prohibition, for they are in favour of the citizen.[3]

§ 1340. The next clause (passing by such, as have been already considered) is, "No money shall be "drawn from the treasury but in consequence of ap- "propriations made by law. And a regular statement "and account of the receipts and expenditures of all "public money shall be published from time to time."

§ 1341. This clause was not in the original draft of the constitution; but the first part was subsequently introduced, upon a report of a committee; and the latter part was added at the very close of the convention.[4]

§ 1342. The object is apparent upon the slightest examination. It is to secure regularity, punctuality, and fidelity, in the disbursements of the public money. As all the taxes raised from the people, as well as the revenues arising from other sources, are to be applied to the discharge of the expenses, and debts, and other engagements of the government, it is highly proper, that congress should possess the power to decide, how and when any money should be applied for these purposes. If it were otherwise, the executive would

1 *Fletcher* v. *Peck*, 6 Cranch, 138; S. C. 2 Peters's Cond. R. 322.
2 Ibid.
3 Rawle on Constitution, ch. 10, p. 119; 1 Tuck. Black. Comm. App. 293; 1 Kent. Comm. Lect. 19, p. 381, 382; Sergeant on Constitution, ch. 28 [ch. 30]; *Calder* v. *Bull*, 3 Dall. R. 386.
4 Journal of Convention, 219, 328, 345, 358, 378.

possess an unbounded power over the public purse of
the nation ; and might apply all its monied resources
at his pleasure. The power to control, and direct the
appropriations, constitutes a most useful and salutary
check upon profusion and extravagance, as well as upon
corrupt influence and public peculation. In arbitrary
governments the prince levies what money he pleases
from his subjects, disposes of it, as he thinks proper,
and is beyond responsibility or reproof. It is wise to
interpose, in a republic, every restraint, by which
the public treasure, the common fund of all, should be
applied, with unshrinking honesty to such objects, as
legitimately belong to the common defence, and the
general welfare. Congress is made the guardian of
this treasure ; and to make their responsibility complete
and perfect, a regular account of the receipts and expenditures is required to be published, that the people
may know, what money is expended, for what purposes, and by what authority.

§ 1343. A learned commentator has, however, thought,
that the provision, though generally excellent, is defective in not having enabled the creditors of the
government, and other persons having vested claims
against it, to recover, and to be paid the amount judicially ascertained to be due to them out of the public
treasury, without any appropriation.[1] Perhaps it is
a defect. And yet it is by no means certain, that evils
of an opposite nature might not arise, if the debts,
judicially ascertained to be due to an individual by
a regular judgment, were to be paid, of course, out
of the public treasury. It might give an opportunity
for collusion and corruption in the management of
suits between the claimant, and the officers of the

---

[1] 1 Tuck. Black. Comm. App. 362 to 364.

government, entrusted with the performance of this
duty. Undoubtedly, when a judgment has been fairly
obtained, by which a debt against the government is
clearly made out, it becomes the duty of congress to
provide for its payment ; and, generally, though certainly with a tardiness, which has become, in some sort, a
national reproach, this duty is discharged by congress
in a spirit of just liberality. But still, the known fact,
that the subject must pass in review before congress,
induces a caution and integrity in making and substan-
tiating claims, which would in a great measure be done
away, if the claim were subject to no restraint, and no
revision.

§ 1344. The next clause is, " No title of nobility shall
" be granted by the United States ; and no person hold-
" ing any office of profit or trust under them shall, with-
" out the consent of the congress, accept of any present,
" emolument, office, or title of any kind whatever, from
" any king, prince, or foreign state.

§ 1345. This clause seems scarcely to require even
a passing notice. As a perfect equality is the basis of
all our institutions, state and national, the prohibition
against the creation of any titles of nobility seems proper, if not indispensable, to keep perpetually alive a
just sense of this important truth. Distinctions between
citizens, in regard to rank, would soon lay the foundation of odious claims and privileges, and silently subvert
the spirit of independence and personal dignity, which
are so often proclaimed to be the best security of
a republican government.[1]

§ 1346. The other clause, as to the acceptance of
any emoluments, title, or office, from foreign govern-

<hr>

[1] The Federalist, No. 84.

ments, is founded in a just jealousy of foreign influence of every sort. Whether, in a practical sense, it
can produce much effect, has been thought doubtful. A
patriot will not be likely to be seduced from his duties
to his country by the acceptance of any title, or present, from a foreign power. An intriguing, or corrupt
agent, will not be restrained from guilty machinations
in the service of a foreign state by such constitutional
restrictions. Still, however, the provision is highly important, as it puts it out of the power of any officer of
the government to wear borrowed honours, which shall
enhance his supposed importance abroad by a titular
dignity at home.[1] It is singular, that there should not
have been, for the same object, a general prohibition
against any citizen whatever, whether in private or
public life, accepting any foreign title of nobility. An
amendment for this purpose has been recommended
by congress ; but, as yet, it has not received the ratification of the constitutional number of states to make it
obligatory, probably from a growing sense, that it is
wholly unnecessary.[2]

---

[1] 1 Tuck. Black. Comm. App. 295, 296; Rawle on Constitution, ch.
10, p. 119, 120.
[2] Rawle on Constitution, ch. p. 10, 120.

CHAPTER XXXIII.

PROHIBITIONS ON THE STATES.

§ 1347. THE tenth section of the first article (to which we are now to proceed) contains the prohibitions and restrictions upon the authority of the states. Some of these, and especially those, which regard the power of taxation, and the regulation of commerce, have already passed under consideration ; and will, therefore, be here omitted. The others will be examined in the order of the text of the constitution.

§ 1348. The first clause is, " No state shall enter " into any treaty, alliance, or confederation ; grant " letters of marque or reprisal; coin money ; emit bills " of credit; make any thing but gold and silver coin a " tender in payment of debts ; pass any bill of attainder, " *ex post facto* law, or law impairing the obligation of " contracts, or grant any title of nobility." [1]

§ 1349. The prohibition against treaties, alliances, and confederations, constituted a part of the articles of confederation,[2] and was from thence transferred in substance into the constitution. The sound policy,

---

[1] In the original draft of the constitution, some of these prohibitory clauses were not inserted ; and, particularly, the last clause, prohibiting a state to pass any bill of attainder, *ex post facto* law, or law impairing the obligation of contracts. The former part was inserted by a vote of seven states against three. The latter was inserted in the revised draft of the constitution, and adopted at the close of the convention, whether with, or without opposition, does not appear.* It was probably suggested by the clause in the ordinance of 1787, (Art. 2,) which declared, " that no law ought to be made, &c., that shall interfere with, or affect private contracts, or engagements, *bonâ fide*, and without fraud, previously formed."

[2] Art. 6.

* Journal of Convention, p. 227, 302, 359, 377, 379.

nay, the necessity of it, for the preservation of any national government, is so obvious, as to strike the most careless mind. If every state were at liberty to enter into any treaties, alliances, or confederacies, with any foreign state, it would become utterly subversive of the power confided to the national government on the same subject. Engagements might be entered into by different states, utterly hostile to the interests of neighbouring or distant states ; and thus the internal peace and harmony of the Union might be destroyed, or put in jeopardy. A foundation might thus be laid for preferences, and retaliatory systems, which would render the power of taxation, and the regulation of commerce, by the national government, utterly futile. Besides ; the intimate dangers to the Union ought not to be overlooked, by thus nourishing within its own bosom a perpetual source of foreign corrupt influence, which, in times of political excitement and war, might be wielded to the destruction of the independence of the country. This, indeed, was deemed, by the authors of the Federalist, too clear to require any illustration.[1] The corresponding clauses in the confederation were still more strong, direct, and exact, in their language and import.

§ 1350. The prohibition to grant letters of marque and reprisal stands upon the same general ground ; for otherwise it would be in the power of a single state to involve the whole Union in war at its pleasure. It is true, that the granting of letters of marque and reprisal is not always a preliminary to war, or necessarily designed to provoke it. But in its essence, it is a hostile measure for unredressed grievances, real or supposed ;

---

[1] The Federalist, No. 44.

and therefore is most generally the precursor of an appeal to arms by general hostilities. The security (as has been justly observed) of the whole Union ought not to be suffered to depend upon the petulance or precipitation of a single state.[1] Under the confederation there was a like prohibition in a more limited form. According to that instrument, no state could grant letters of marque and reprisal, until after a declaration of war by the congress of the United States.[2] In times of peace the power was exclusively confided to the general government. The constitution has wisely, both in peace and war, confided the whole subject to the general government. Uniformity is thus secured in all operations, which relate to foreign powers; and an immediate responsibility to the nation on the part of those, for whose conduct the nation is itself responsible.[3]

§ 1351. The next prohibition is to coin money. We have already seen, that the power to coin money, and regulate the value thereof, is confided to the general government. Under the confederation a concurrent power was left in the states, with a restriction, that congress should have the exclusive power to regulate the alloy and value of the coin struck by the states.[4] In this, as in many other cases, the constitution has made a great improvement upon the existing system. Whilst the alloy and value depended on the general government, a right of coinage in the several states could have no other effect, than to multiply expensive mints, and diversify the forms and weights of the circulating coins. The latter inconvenience would defeat one

---

[1] 1 Tucker's Black. Comm. App. 310, 311.
[2] Article 6.
[3] The Federalist, No. 44; Rawle on Constitution, ch. 10, p. 136.
[4] Article 9.

main purpose, for which the power is given to the general government, viz. uniformity of the currency ; and the former might be as well accomplished by local mints established by the national government, if it should ever be found inconvenient to send bullion, or old coin for re-coinage to the central mint.[1] Such an event could scarcely occur, since the common course of commerce throughout the United States is so rapid and so free, that bullion can with a very slight expense be transported from one extremity of the Union to another. A single mint only has been established, which has hitherto been found quite adequate to all our wants. The truth is, that the prohibition had a higher motive, the danger of the circulation of base and spurious coin connived at for local purposes, or easily accomplished by the ingenuity of artificers, where the coins are very various in value and denomination, and issued from so many independent and unaccountable authorities. This subject has, however, been already enlarged on in another place.[2]

§ 1352. The prohibition to "emit bills of credit" cannot, perhaps, be more forcibly vindicated, than by quoting the glowing language of the Federalist, a language justified by that of almost every contemporary writer, and attested in its truth by facts, from which the mind involuntarily turns away at once with disgust and indignation. "This prohibition," says the Federalist, "must give pleasure to every citizen in proportion to his love of justice, and his knowledge of the true springs of public prosperity. The loss, which America has sustained since the peace from the pestilent effects of

---

[1] The Federalist, No. 44.
[2] 1 Tuck. Black. Comm. App. 311, 312; Id. 261. Ante, Vol. 3, p. 16 to 20.

paper money on the necessary confidence between man and man; on the necessary confidence in the public councils; on the industry and morals of the people; and on the character of republican government, constitutes an enormous debt against the states, chargeable with this unadvised measure, which must long remain unsatisfied; or rather an accumulation of guilt, which can be expiated no otherwise, than by a voluntary sacrifice on the altar of justice of the power, which has been the instrument of it. In addition to these persuasive considerations, it may be observed, that the same reasons, which show the necessity of denying to the states the power of regulating coin, prove with equal force, that they ought not to be at liberty *to substitute a paper medium, instead of coin.* Had every state a right to regulate the value of its coin, there might be as many different currencies, as states; and thus the intercourse among them would be impeded. Retrospective alterations in its value might be made; and thus the citizens of other states be injured, and animosities be kindled among the states themselves. The subjects of foreign powers might suffer from the same cause; and hence the Union be discredited and embroiled by the indiscretion of a single member. No one of these mischiefs is less incident to a power in the states to emit paper money, than to coin gold or silver." [1]

§ 1353. The evils attendant upon the issue of paper money by the states after the peace of 1783, here spoken of, are equally applicable, and perhaps apply with even

---

[1] The Federalist, No. 44; 2 Elliot's Debates, 83. — See in Mr. Webster's Speeches on the Bank of United States, in Senate, 25th and 28th of May, 1832, some cogent remarks on the same subject. See also Mr. Madison's Letter to Mr. C. J. Ingersoll, 2d of February, 1811.

increased force to the paper issues of the states and the Union during the revolutionary war. Public, as well as private credit, was utterly prostrated.[1] The fortunes of many individuals were destroyed; and those of all persons were greatly impaired by the rapid and unparalleled depreciation of the paper currency during this period. In truth, the history of the paper currency, which during the revolution was issued by congress alone, is full of melancholy instruction. It is at once humiliating to our pride, and disreputable to our national justice. Congress at an early period (November, 1775,) directed an emission of bills of credit to the amount of three millions of dollars; and declared on the face of them, that " this bill entitles the bearer to receive —— Spanish milled dollars, or the value thereof in gold or silver, according to a resolution of congress, passed at Philadelphia, November 29th, 1775." And they apportioned a tax of three millions on the states, in order to pay these bills, to be raised by the states according to their quotas at future designated periods. The bills were directed to be receivable in payment of the taxes; and the thirteen colonies were pledged for their redemption.[2] Other emissions were subsequently made. The depreciation was a natural, and indeed a necessary consequence of the fact, that there was no fund to redeem them. Congress endeavoured to give them additional credit by declaring, that they ought to be a tender in payment of all private and public debts; and that a refusal to receive the tender ought to be an extinguishment of the debt, and recommending the states to pass such tender laws. They went even farther, and

---

[1] See *Sturgis* v. *Crowninshield*, 4 Wheat. R. 204, 205.
[2] 1 Journal of Congress, 1775, p. 186, 280, 304.

thought proper to declare, that whoever should refuse to receive this paper in exchange for any property, *as gold and silver, should be deemed "an enemy to the liberties of these United States."* [1] This course of violence and terror, so far from aiding the circulation of the paper, led on to still farther depreciation. New issues continued to be made, until in September, 1779, the whole emission exceeded one hundred and sixty millions of dollars. At this time congress thought it necessary to declare, that the issues on no account should exceed two hundred millions ; and still held out to the public the delusive hope of an ultimate redemption of the whole at par. They indignantly repelled the idea, in a circular address, that there could be any violation of the public faith, pledged for their redemption ; or that there did not exist ample funds to redeem them. They indulged in still more extraordinary delusions, and ventured to recommend paper money, as of peculiar value. "Let it be remembered," said they, "that paper money is the only kind of money, which cannot make to itself wings and fly away." [2]

§ 1354. The states still continued to fail in complying with the requisitions of congress to pay taxes ; and congress, notwithstanding their solemn declaration to the contrary, increased the issue of paper money, until it amounted to the enormous sum of upwards of three hundred millions. [3] The idea was then abandoned of

---

[1] 2 Journal of Congress, 11th January, 1776, p. 21 ; 14th January, 1777 ; 3 Journal of Congress, p. 19, 20 ; 2 Pitk. Hist. ch. 16, p. 155, 156.

[2] See 4 Journal of Congress, 9th Dec. 1778, p. 742, and 5 Journal or Congress, 13th Sept. 1779, p. 341 to 353 ; 2 Pitk. Hist. ch. 16, p. 156, 157.

[3] In the American Almanac for 1830, p. 183, the aggregate amount is given at 357,000,000 of the old emission, and 2,000,000 of the new emission ; upon which the writer adds, "there was an average depreciation of two thirds of its original value." Mr. Jefferson has given an in-

any redemption at par. In March, 1780, the states
were required to bring in the bills at *forty for one;*
and new bills were then to be issued in lieu of them,
bearing an interest of five per cent., redeemable in six
years, to be issued on the credit of the individual states,
and guaranteed by the United States.[1] This new
scheme of finance was equally unavailing. Few of the
old bills were brought in; and of course few of the new
were issued. At last the continental bills became of
so little value, that they ceased to circulate; and in the
course of the year 1780, they quietly died in the hands
of their possessors.[2] Thus were redeemed the solemn
pledges of the national government![3] Thus, was a
paper currency, which was declared to be equal to gold
and silver, suffered to perish in the hands of persons
compelled to take it; and the very enormity of the

---

teresting account of the history of paper money during the revolution,
in an article written for the Encyclopédie Méthodique. 1 Jefferson's
Corresp. 398, 401, 411, 412.

1 6 Journal of Convention, 18th March, 1780, p. 45 to 48.

2 2 Pitkin's Hist. ch. 16, p. 156, 157; 1 Jefferson's Corresp. 401, 402,
411, 412.

3 The twelfth article of the confederation declares, "that all bills of
credit emitted, &c. by or under the authority of congress, &c. shall be
deemed and considered, as a charge against the United States, for payment and satisfaction whereof the said United States and the public
faith are hereby solemnly pledged." When was this pledge redeemed?
The act of congress of 1790, ch. 61, for the liquidation of the public
debt, directs bills of credit to be estimated at the rate of one hundred
dollars for one dollar in specie. In Mr. Secretary Hamilton's Report on
the public debt and credit in January, 1790, the unliquidated part of the
public debt, consisting chiefly of continental bills of credit, was estimated at two millions of dollars. What was the nominal amount of the bills of
credit, which this sum of two millions was designed to cover at its specie
value, does not appear in the Report. But in the debates in congress
upon the bill founded on it, it was asserted, that it was calculated, that
there were about 78 or 80 millions of paper money then outstanding,
valued at a depreciation of 40 for 1. 3 Lloyd's Deb. 282, 283, 288.

wrong made the ground of an abandonment of every attempt to redress it!

§ 1355. Without doubt the melancholy shades of this picture were deepened by the urgent distresses of the revolutionary war, and the reluctance of the states to perform their proper duty. And some apology, if not some justification of the proceedings, may be found in the eventful transactions and sufferings of those times. But the history of paper money, without any adequate funds pledged to redeem it, and resting merely upon the pledge of the national faith, has been in all ages and in all nations the same. It has constantly become more and more depreciated; and in some instances has ceased from this cause to have any circulation whatsoever, whether issued by the irresistible edict of a despot, or by the more alluring order of a republican congress. There is an abundance of illustrative facts scattered over the history of those of the American colonies, who ventured upon this pernicious scheme of raising money to supply the public wants, during their subjection to the British crown; and in the several states, from the declaration of independence down to the present times. Even the United States, with almost inexhaustible resources, and with a population of 9,000,000 of inhabitants, exhibited during the late war with Great-Britain the humiliating spectacle of treasury notes, issued and payable in a year, remaining unredeemed, and sunk by depreciation to about half of their nominal value!

§ 1356. It has been stated by a very intelligent historian, that the first case of any issue of bills of credit in any of the American colonies, as a substitute for money, was by Massachusetts to pay the soldiers, who returned unexpectedly from an unsuccessful expedition against Canada, in 1690. The debt, thus due to the soldiers, was paid by paper notes from two shillings to ten pounds denomination, which notes were to be received for payment of the tax, which was to be levied, and all other payments into the treasury.[1] It is added, that they had better credit than King James's leather money in Ireland about the same time. But the notes could not command money, nor any commodities at money price.[2] Being of small amount, they were soon absorbed in the discharge of taxes. At subsequent periods the government resorted to similar expedients. In 1714, there being a cry of a scarcity of money, the government caused £50,000 to be issued in bills of credit, and in 1716, £100,000 to be lent to the inhabitants for a limited period, upon lands mortgaged by them, as security, and in the mean time to pass as money.[3] These bills were receivable into the treasury in discharge of taxes, and also of the mortgage debts so contracted. Other bills were afterwards issued; and, indeed, we are informed, that, for about forty years, the currency of the province was in much the same state, as if £100,000 sterling had been stamped on pieces of leather or paper, of various denominations, and declared to be the money of the government, receivable in payment of taxes, and in discharge of private debts.[4] The consequence was a very great depreciation, so that an ounce of silver, which, in 1702, was worth six shillings and eight pence, was, in 1749, equal to fifty shillings of this paper currency.[5] It seems, that all the other

---

[1] 1 Hutch. Hist. ch. 3, p. 402.   [2] Ibid.

[3] 1 Hutch. Hist. ch. 3, p. 403, note; 2 Hutch. Hist. 208, 245, and note; Id. 380, 381, 403, 404.

[4] 1 Hutch. Hist. ch. 3, p. 402, 403, and note ibid.

[5] Ibid. — Hutchinson says, that, in 1747, the currency had sunk to sixty shillings for an ounce of silver. 2 Hutch. Hist. 438.

colonies, except Nova Scotia, at different times and for various purposes, authorized the issue of paper money.[1] There was a uniform tendency to depreciation, wherever it was persisted in.[2]

§ 1357. It would seem to be obvious, that, as the states are expressly prohibited from coining money, the prohibition would be wholly ineffectual, if they might create a paper currency, and circulate it as money. But, as it might become necessary for the states to borrow money, the prohibition could not be intended to prevent such an exercise of power, on giving to the lender a certificate of the amount borrowed, and a promise to repay it.

§ 1358. What, then, is the true meaning of the phrase "bills of credit" in the constitution? In its enlarged, and perhaps in its literal sense, it may comprehend any instrument, by which a state engages to pay money at a future day (and of course, for which it obtains a present credit ;) and thus it would include a certificate given for money borrowed. But the language of the constitution itself, and the mischief to be prevented, which we know from the history of our country, equally limit the interpretation of the terms. The word " emit " is never employed in describing those contracts, by which a state binds itself to pay money at a future day for services actually received, or for money borrowed for present use. Nor are instruments, executed for such purposes, in common language denominated "bills of credit." To emit bills of credit conveys to the mind the idea of issuing paper, intended to circulate through the community for its ordinary purposes, as money, which paper is redeemable at a future day. This is the sense,

---

[1] 1 Hutch. Hist. ch. 3, p. 402 403, and note ibid.
[2] 4 Peters's Sup. Ct. R. 435.

in which the terms of the constitution have been generally understood.[1] The phrase (as we have seen) was well known, and generally used to indicate the paper currency, issued by the states during their colonial dependence. During the war of our revolution the paper currency issued by congress was constantly denominated, in the acts of that body, bills of credit ; and the like appellation was applied to similar currency issued by the states. The phrase had thus acquired a determinate and appropriate meaning. At the time of the adoption of the constitution, bills of credit were universally understood to signify a paper medium intended to circulate between individuals, and between government and individuals, for the ordinary purposes of society. Such a medium has always been liable to considerable fluctuation. Its value is continually changing ; and these changes, often great and sudden, expose individuals to immense losses, are the sources of ruinous speculations, and destroy all proper confidence between man and man.[2] In no country, more than our own, had these truths been felt in all their force. In none had more intense suffering, or more wide-spreading ruin accompanied the system. It was, therefore, the object of the prohibition to cut up the whole mischief by the roots, because it had been deeply felt throughout all the states, and had deeply affected the prosperity of all. The object of the prohibition was not to prohibit the thing, when it bore a particular name ; but to prohibit the thing, whatever form or name it might assume. If the words are not merely empty sounds, the prohibition must comprehend the emission of any paper medium by a state government for the purposes

---

1 *Craig v. State of Missouri,* 4 Peters's Sup. Ct. R. 410, 432.
2 *Craig v. State of Missouri,* 4 Peters's Sup. Ct. R. 432, 441, 442.

of common circulation.[1] It would be preposterous to suppose, that the constitution meant solemnly to prohibit an issue under one denomination, leaving the power complete to issue the same thing under another. It can never be seriously contended, that the constitution means to prohibit names, and not things; to deal with shadows, and to leave substances. What would be the consequence of such a construction? That a very important act, big with great and ruinous mischief, and on that account forbidden by words the most appropriate for its description, might yet be performed by the substitution of a name. That the constitution, even in one of its vital provisions, might be openly evaded by giving a new name to an old thing. Call the thing a bill of credit, and it is prohibited. Call the same thing a certificate, and it is constitutional.[2]

§ 1359. But it has been contended recently, that a bill of credit, in the sense of the constitution, must be such a one, as is, by the law of the state, made a legal tender. But the constitution itself furnishes no countenance to this distinction. The prohibition is general; it extends to all bills of credit, not to bills of a particular description. And surely no one in such a case is at liberty to interpose a restriction, which the words neither require, nor justify. Such a construction is the less admissible, because there is in the same clause

---

[1] *Craig* v. *State of Missouri*, 4 Peters's Sup. Ct. R. 432, 441, 442.

[2] Id. 432, 433, 441, 442, 443. — An act of parliament was passed, (24 Geo. 2, ch. 53,) regulating and restraining the issues of paper money and bills of credit in the New-England colonies, in which the language used demonstrates, that bills of credit was a phrase constantly used and understood, as equivalent to paper money. The prohibitory clauses forbid the issue of " any paper bills, or bills of credit of any kind, or denomination whatsoever," &c., and constantly speak of " paper bills or bills of credit," as equivalents. See *Deering* v. *Parker*, 4 Dall. (July 1760,) p. xxiii.

an express and substantive prohibition of the enactment of tender laws. If, therefore, the construction were
admissible, the constitution would be chargeable with the
folly of providing against the emission of bills of credit,
which could not, in consequence of another prohibition,
have any legal existence. The constitution considers
the emission of bills of credit, and the enactment of
tender laws, as distinct operations, independent of each
other, which may be frequently performed. Both are
forbidden. To sustain the one, because it is not also
the other; to say, that bills of credit may be emitted,
if they are not made a tender in payment of debts, is,
in effect, to expunge that distinct, independent prohibition, and to read the clause, as if it had been entirely
omitted.[1] No principle of interpretation can justify
such a course.

§ 1360. The history of paper money in the American colonies and states is often referred to for the
purpose of showing, that one of its great mischiefs was
its being made a legal tender in the discharge of debts;
and hence the conclusion is attempted to be adduced,
that the words of the constitution may be restrained to
this particular intent. But, if it were true, that the evils
of paper money resulted solely from its being made a
tender, it would be wholly unjustifiable on this account
to narrow down the words of the constitution, upon a
mere conjecture of intent, not derivable from those
words. A particular evil may have induced a legislature to enact a law; but no one would imagine, that its
language, if general, ought to be confined to that single
case. The leading motive for a constitutional provision
may have been a particular mischief; but it may yet
have been intended to cut down all others of a like na-

---

[1] *Craig v. State of Missouri*, 4 Peters's Sup. Ct. R. 433, 434.

ture, leading more or less directly to the same general injury to the country. That the making of bills of credit a tender was the most pernicious of their characteristics, will not authorize us to convert a general prohibition into a particular one.[1]

§ 1361. But the argument itself is not borne out by the facts. The history of our country does not prove, that it was an essential quality of bills of credit, that they should be a tender in payment of debts ; or that this was the only mischief resulting from them. Bills of credit were often issued by the colonies, and by the several states afterwards, which were not made a legal tender ; but were made current, and simply receivable in discharge of taxes and other dues to the public.[2] None of the bills of credit, issued by congress during the whole period of the revolution, were made a legal tender ; and indeed it is questionable, if that body possessed the constitutional authority to make them such. At all events they never did attempt it ; but recommended, (as has been seen,) that the states should make them a tender.[3] The act of parliament

---

1 *Craig* v. *State of Missouri*, 4 Peters's Sup. Ct. R. 433, 434.

2 The bills of credit issued by Massachusetts in 1690 (the first ever issued in any colony) were in the following form : " No. —, 10s. This indented bill of ten shillings, due from the Massachusetts Colony to the possessor, shall be in value equal to money, and shall be accordingly accepted by the treasurer, and receivers subordinate to him, in all public payments, and for any stock at any time in the treasury, Boston, in New-England, Dec. the 10th, 1690. By order of the General Court: Peter Townsend, Adam Winthrop, Tim. Thornton, Committee." So, that it was not, in any sense, a tender, except in discharge of public debts. 3 Mass. Hist. Collections, (2d series,) p. 260, 261. The bills of credit of Connecticut, passed before the revolution, were of the same general character and operation. They were not made a tender in payment of private debts. The emission of them was begun in 1709, and continued, at least, for nearly a half century. The acts, authorizing the emission, generally contained a clause for raising a tax to redeem them.

3 *Craig* v. *State of Missouri*, 4 Peters's Sup. Ct. R. 434, 435, 436, 442, 443.

of 24 Geo. 2, ch. 53, is equally strong on this point. It prohibited any of the New-England colonies from issuing any new paper bills, or "bills of credit," except upon the emergencies pointed out in the act; and required those colonies to call in, and redeem all the outstanding bills. It then proceeded to declare, that after September, 1751, no "paper currency or bills of credit," issued, or created in any of those colonies, should be a legal tender, with a proviso, that nothing therein contained should be construed to extend to make any of the bills, then subsisting, a legal tender.

§ 1362. Another suggestion has been made; that paper currency, which has a fund assigned for its redemption by the state, which authorizes its issue, does not constitutionally fall within the description of "bills of credit." The latter words (it is said) appropriately import bills drawn on *credit merely*, and not bottomed upon any real or substantial fund for their redemption; and there is a material, and well known distinction between a bill drawn upon a fund, and one drawn upon credit only.[1] In confirmation of this reasoning, it has been said, that the emissions of paper money by the states, previous to the adoption of the constitution, were, properly speaking, bills of credit, not being bottomed upon any fund constituted for their redemption, but resting solely, for that purpose, upon the credit of the state issuing the same. But this argument has been deemed unsatisfactory in its own nature, and not sustained by historical facts. All bills issued by a state, whether special funds are assigned for the redemption of them or not, are in fact issued on the credit of the state. If these funds should from any cause fail, the bills would be still payable by the state.

[1] *Craig v. State of Missouri*, 4 Peters's Sup. Ct. R. 447.

If these funds should be applied to other purposes, (as
they may be by the state,) or withdrawn from the
reach of the creditor, the state is not less liable for their
payment. No exclusive credit is given, in any such
case, to the fund. If a bill or check is drawn on a fund
by a private person, it is drawn also on his credit, and
if the bill is refused payment out of the fund, the
drawer is still personally responsible. Congress has,
under the constitution, power to borrow money on the
credit of the United States. But it would not be less
borrowing on that credit, that funds should be pledged
for the re-payment of the loan; such, for instance, as
the revenue from duties, or the proceeds of the public
lands. If these funds should fail, or be diverted, the
lender would still trust to the credit of the government.
But, in point of fact, the bills of credit, issued by the
colonies and states, were sometimes with a direct or
implied pledge of funds for their redemption. The
constitution itself points out no distinction between
bills of the one sort or the other. And the act of 24
Geo. 2d. ch. 53 requires, that when bills of credit are
issued by the colonies in the emergencies therein stated, an ample and sufficient fund shall, by the acts authorizing the issue, be established for the discharge of
the same within five years at the farthest. So, that
there is positive evidence, that the phrase, " bills of
credit," was understood in the colonies to apply to all
paper money, whether funds were provided for the re-
payment or not.[1]

§ 1363. This subject underwent an ample discussion in a late case. The state of Missouri, with a view
to relieve the supposed necessities of the times, au-

___
[1] See 2 Hutch. Hist. 208, 381.

thorized the establishment of certain loan-offices to loan certain sums to the citizens of that state, for which the borrowers were to give security by mortgage of real estate, or personal property, redeemable in a limited period by instalments. The loans were to be made in certificates, issued by the auditor and treasurer of the state, of various denominations, between ten dollars and fifty cents, all of which, on their face, purported to be receivable at the treasury, or any of the loan offices of the state, in the discharge of taxes or debts due to the state for the sum of — with interest for the same at two per centum per annum. These certificates were also made receivable in payment of all salt at the salt springs ; and by all public officers, civil and military, in discharge of their salaries and fees of office. And it was declared, that the proceeds of the salt springs, the interest accruing to the state, and all estates purchased under the same act, and all debts due to the state, should be constituted a fund for the redemption of them. The question made was, whether they were "bills of credit," within the meaning of the constitution. It was contended, that they were not ; they were not made a legal tender, nor directed to pass as money, or currency. They were mere evidences of loans made to the state, for the payment of which specific and available funds were pledged. They were merely made receivable in payment of taxes, or other debts due to the state.

§ 1364. The majority of the Supreme Court were of opinion, that these certificates were bills of credit within the meaning of the constitution. Though not called bills of credit, they were so in fact. They were designed to circulate as currency, the certificates being to be issued in various denominations, not exceeding ten dollars, nor less than fifty cents. Under such circumstances, it was impossible to doubt their real character and object, as a paper currency. They were to be emitted by the government ; and they were to be gradually withdrawn from circulation by an annual withdrawal of ten per cent. It was wholly unnecessary, that they should be declared to be a legal tender. Indeed, so far as regarded the fees and salaries of public officers, they were so.[1] The minority were of a different opinion, upon various grounds. One was, that they were properly to be deemed a loan by the state, and not designed to be a circulating currency, and not declared to be so by the act. Another was, that they bore on their face an interest, and for that reason varied in value every moment of their existence, which disqualified them for the uses and purposes of a circulating medium. Another was, that all the bills of credit of the revolution contained a promise to pay, which these certificates did not, but were merely redeemable in discharge of taxes, &c. Another was, that they were not issued upon the mere credit of the state ; but funds were pledged for their redemption. Another was, that they were not declared to be a legal tender. Another was, that their circulation was not enforced by statutory provisions. No creditor was under any obligation to receive them. In their nature and character, they were not calculated to produce any of the evils, which the paper money issued in the revolution did, and which the constitution intended to guard against.[2]

---

[1] *Craig* v. *The State of Missouri*, 4 Peters's Sup.Ct. R. 410, 425 to 438.

[2] Some of these grounds apply equally to some of the " bills of credit," issued by the colonies. In fact, these certificates seem to have differed in few, if any essential circumstances, from those issued by the

§ 1365. The next prohibition is, that no state shall
" make any thing but gold and silver coin, a tender in
" payment of debts." This clause was manifestly founded in the same general policy, which procured the
adoption of the preceding clause. The history, indeed,
of the various laws, which were passed by the states
in their colonial and independent character upon this
subject, is startling at once to our morals, to our patriotism, and to our sense of justice. Not only was paper
money issued, and declared to be a tender in payment of
debts; but laws of another character, well known under the appellation of tender laws, appraisement laws,
instalment laws, and suspension laws, were from time
to time enacted, which prostrated all private credit,
and all private morals. By some of these laws, the
due payment of debts was suspended; debts were,
in violation of the very terms of the contract, authorized
to be paid by instalments at different periods; property of any sort, however worthless, either real or personal, might be tendered by the debtor in payment of
his debts; and the creditor was compelled to take the

Province of Massachusetts in 1714 and 1716, and had the same general
objects in view by the same means, viz. to make temporary loans to the
inhabitants to relieve their wants by an issue of paper money.* The
bills of credit issued by congress in 1780 were payable with interest.
So were the treasury notes issued by congress in the late war with
Great Britain. Yet both circulated and were designed to circulate as
currency. The bills of credit issued by congress in the revolution were
not made a legal tender.† It has also been already seen, that the first
bills of credit ever issued in America, in 1690, contained no promise of
payment by the state, and were simply receivable in discharge of public dues.‡ Mr. Jefferson, in the first volume of his Correspondence,
(p. 401, 402,) has given a succinct history of paper money in America,
especially in the revolution. It is a sad but instructive account.

* 1 Hutch. History, 402, 403, and note ; 2 Hutch. History, 208.
† Ante, § 1361.
‡ 3 Mass. Hist. Collection, (2d series,) 260, 261 Ante, § 1353, 1361. See 4 Mass. Hist. Coll.
(2d series,) 99.

property of the debtor, which he might seize on execution, at an appraisement wholly disproportionate to its known value.[1] Such grievances, and oppressions, and others of a like nature, were the ordinary results of legislation during the revolutionary war, and the intermediate period down to the formation of the constitution. They entailed the most enormous evils on the country ; and introduced a system of fraud, chicanery, and profligacy, which destroyed all private confidence, and all industry and enterprise.[2]

§ 1366. It is manifest, that all these prohibitory clauses, as to coining money, emitting bills of credit, and tendering any thing, but gold and silver, in payment of debts, are founded upon the same general policy, and result from the same general considerations. The policy is, to provide a fixed and uniform value throughout the United States, by which commercial and other dealings of the citizens, as well as the monied transactions of the government, might be regulated. For it may well be asked, why vest in congress the power to establish a uniform standard of value, if the states might use the same means, and thus defeat the uniformity of the standard, and consequently the standard itself? And why establish a standard at all for the government of the various contracts, which might be entered into, if those contracts might afterwards be discharged by a different standard, or by that, which is not money, under the authority of state tender laws? All these prohibitions are, therefore, entirely homogeneous, and are essential to the establishment of a uniform standard of value in the formation and discharge of contracts. For this reason, as well as others derived from the

1 3 Elliot's Debates, 144.
2 See *Sturgis* v. *Crowninshield*, 4 Wheat. R. 204.

phraseology employed, the prohibition of state tender laws will admit of no construction confining it to state laws, which have a retrospective operation.[1] Accordingly, it has been uniformly held, that the prohibition applies to all future laws on the subject of tender ; and therefore no state legislature can provide, that future pecuniary contracts may be discharged by any thing, but gold and silver coin.[2]

§ 1367. The next prohibition is, that no state shall "pass any bill of attainder, *ex post facto* law, or law "impairing the obligation of contracts." The two former require no commentary, beyond what has been already offered, under a similar prohibitory clause applied to the government of the United States. The same policy and principles apply to each.[3] It would have been utterly useless, if not absurd, to deny a power to the Union, which might at the same time be applied by the states, to purposes equally mischievous, and tyrannical ; and which might, when applied by the states, be for the very purpose of subverting the Union. Before the constitution of the United States was adopted, every state, unless prohibited by its own constitution, might pass a bill of attainder, or *ex post facto* law, as a general result of its sovereign legislative power. And such a prohibition would not be implied from a constitutional provision, that the legislative, executive, and judiciary departments shall be separate, and distinct ; that crimes shall be tried in the county, where they are committed ; or that the trial by jury shall remain invio-

[1] *Ogden* v. *Saunders*, 12 Wheat. R. 265, per Washington J.
[2] *Ogden* v. *Saunders*, 12 Wheat. R. 265, 269, 288, 289, 305, 306, 328, 335, 336, 339.
[3] See The Federalist, No. 44, 84.

late. The power to pass such laws would still remain, at least so far as respects crimes committed without the state.[1] During the revolutionary war, bills of attainder, and *ex post facto* acts of confiscation, were passed to a wide extent; and the evils resulting therefrom were supposed, in times of more cool reflection, to have far outweighed any imagined good.

---

[1] *Cooper* v. *Telfair*, 4 Dall. R. 14; S. C. 1 Peters's Cond. R. 211.

CHAPTER XXXIV.

§ 1368. The remaining clause, as to impairing the obligation of contracts, will require a more full and deliberate examination. The Federalist treats this subject in the following brief, and general manner. "Bills of attainder, *ex post facto* laws, and laws impairing the obligation of contracts are contrary to the first principles of the social compact, and to every principle of sound legislation. The two former are expressly prohibited by the declarations prefixed to some of the state constitutions; and all of them are prohibited by the spirit and scope of their fundamental character. Our own experience has taught us, nevertheless, that additional fences against these dangers ought not to be omitted. Very properly, therefore, have the convention added this constitutional bulwark, in favour of personal security, and private rights, &c. The sober people of America are weary of the fluctuating policy, which has directed the public councils. They have seen with regret and indignation, that sudden changes and legislative interferences in cases affecting personal rights became jobs in the hands of enterprising and influential speculators, and snares to the more industrious and less informed part of the community. They have seen, too, that one legislative interference is but the first link in a long chain of repetitions, every subsequent interference being naturally provoked by the effects of the preceding. They very rightly infer, therefore, that some thorough reform is wanting, which will banish speculations on public measures, inspire a general prudence and industry, and give a regular course to the business of society."[1]

§ 1369. With these remarks the subject is dismissed. And yet, perhaps, there is not a single clause of the constitution, which has given rise to more acute and vehement controversy; and the nature and extent of whose prohibitory force has called forth more ingenious speculation, and more animated juridical discussion.[2] What is a contract? What is the obligation of a contract? What is impairing a contract? To what classes of laws does the prohibition apply? To what extent does it reach, so as to control prospective legislation on the subject of contracts? These and many other questions, of no small nicety and intricacy, have vexed the legislative halls, as well as the judicial tribunals, with an uncounted variety and frequency of litigation and speculation.

§ 1370. In the first place, what is to be deemed a contract, in the constitutional sense of this clause? A contract is an agreement to do, or not to do, a particular thing;[3] or (as was said on another occasion) a contract is a compact between two or more persons.[4] A contract is either executory, or executed. An executory contract is one, in which a party binds himself to do, or not to do a particular thing. An executed contract is one, in which the object of the contract is performed. This differs in nothing from a grant;[5] for a contract

---

1 The Federalist, No. 44.

2 1 Kent's Comm. Lect. 19, p. 387.

3 *Sturgis* v. *Crowninshield*, 4 Wheaton's R. 197. See also *Green* v. *Biddle*, 8 Wheat. R. 92; *Ogden* v. *Saunders*, 12 Wheat. R. 256, 297, 302, 316, 335; *Gorden* v. *Prince*, 3 Wash. Cir. Ct. R. 319.

4 *Fletcher* v. *Peck*, 6 Cranch, 136; S. C. 2 Peters's Cond. R. 321.

5 Id. and 2 Black. Comm. 443.

executed conveys a chose in possession ; a contract executory conveys only a chose in action.[1] Since, then, a
grant is in fact a contract executed, the obligation of which
continues ; and since the constitution uses the general term, *contract*, without distinguishing between those,
which are executory and those, which are executed ; it
must be construed to comprehend the former, as well
as the latter. A state law, therefore, annulling conveyances between individuals, and declaring, that the grantors
should stand seized of their former estates, notwithstanding those grants, would be as repugnant to the
constitution, as a state law discharging the vendors
from the obligation of executing their contracts of sale
by conveyances. It would be strange, indeed, if a contract to convey were secured by the constitution, while
an absolute conveyance remained unprotected.[2] That
the contract, while executory, was obligatory ; but when
executed, might be avoided.

§ 1371. Contracts, too, are express, or implied.
Express contracts are, where the terms of the agreement are openly avowed, and uttered at the time of the
making of it. Implied contracts are such, as reason
and justice dictate from the nature of the transaction,
and which therefore the law presumes, that every man
undertakes to perform.[3] The constitution makes no
distinction between the one class of contracts and the
other. It then equally embraces, and applies to both.
Indeed, as by far the largest class of contracts in civil
society, in the ordinary transactions of life, are implied,
there would be very little object in securing the inviola-

---

[1] 2 Black. Comm. 443.
[2] *Fletcher* v. *Peck*, 6 Cranch's R. 137 ; S. C. 2 Peters's Cond. R. 321,
322.
[3] 2 Black. Comm. 443.

bility of express contracts, if those, which are implied, might be impaired by state legislation. The constitution is not chargeable with such folly, or inconsistency. Every grant in its own nature amounts to an extinguishment of the right of the grantor, and implies a contract not to re-assert it. A party is, therefore, always estopped by his own grant.[1] How absurd would it be to provide, that an express covenant by him, as a muniment attendant upon the estate, should bind him for ever, because executory, and resting in action; and yet, that he might re-assert his title to the estate, and dispossess his grantee, because there was only an implied covenant not to re-assert it.

§ 1372. In the next place, what is the obligation of a contract? It would seem difficult to substitute words more intelligible, or less liable to misconstruction, than these. And yet they have given rise to much acute disquisition, as to their real meaning in the constitution. It has been said, that right and obligation are correlative terms. Whatever I, by my contract, give another a right to require of me, I, by that act, lay myself under an obligation to yield or bestow. The obligation of every contract, then, will consist of that right, or power over my will or actions, which I, by my contract, confer on another. And that right and power will be found to be measured, neither by moral law alone, nor by universal law alone, nor by the laws of society alone; but by a combination of the three; an operation, in which the moral law is explained, and applied by the law of nature, and both modified and adapted to the exigencies of society by positive law. In an advanced

---

[1] *Fletcher* v. *Peck*, 6 Cranch's R. 137; S. C. 2 Peters's Cond. R. 321, 322; *Dartmouth College* v. *Woodward*, 4 Wheat. R. 657, 658, 688, 689.

state of society, all contracts of men receive a relative, and not a positive interpretation. The state construes them, the state applies them, the state controls them, and the state decides, how far the social exercise of the rights, they give over each other, can be justly asserted.[1] Again, it has been said, that the constitution distinguishes between a contract, and the obligation of a contract. The latter is the law, which binds the parties to perform their agreement. The law, then, which has this binding obligation, must govern and control the contract in every shape, in which it is intended to bear upon it.[2] Again, it has been said, that the obligation of a contract consists in the power and efficacy of the law, which applies to, and enforces performance of it, or an equivalent for non-performance. The obligation does not inhere, and subsist in the contract itself, *proprio vigore*, but in the law applicable to the contract.[3] And again, it has been said, that a contract is an agreement of the parties; and if it be not illegal, it binds them to the extent of their stipulations. Thus, if a party contracts to pay a certain sum on a certain day, the contract binds him to perform it on that day, and this is its obligation.[4]

§ 1373. Without attempting to enter into a minute examination of these various definitions, and explanations of the obligation of contracts, or of the reasoning, by which they are supported and illustrated; there are some considerations, which are pre-supposed by all

---

[1] Per Johnson J. in *Ogden* v. *Saunders*, 12 Wheat. R. 281, 282.

[2] Id. Washington J., p. 257, 258, 259; Thompson J., p. 300, 302; Trimble J., p. 316.

[3] Id. Trimble J., p. 317, 318.

[4] Id. Marshall C. J., p. 335, 344 to 346; *Sturgis* v. *Crowninshield*, 4 Wheat. R. 197; *Fletcher* v. *Peck*, 6 Cranch's R. 137.

of them; and others, which enter into some, and are excluded in others.

§ 1374. It seems agreed, that, when the obligation o contracts is spoken of in the constitution, we are to understand, not the mere moral, but the legal obligation of contracts. The moral obligation of contracts is, so far as human society is concerned, of an imperfect kind, which the parties are left free to obey or not, as they please. It is addressed to the conscience of the parties, under the solemn admonitions of accountability to the Supreme Being. No human lawgiver can either impair, or reach it. The constitution has not in contemplation any such obligations, but such only, as might be impaired by a state, if not prohibited.[1] It is the civil obligation of contracts, which it is designed to reach, that is, the obligation, which is recognised by, and results from the law of the state, in which it is made. If, therefore, a contract, when made, is by the law of the place declared to be illegal, or deemed to be a nullity, or a *nude pact*, it has no civil obligation, because the law in such cases forbids its having any binding efficacy, or force. It confers no legal right on the one party, and no correspondent legal duty on the other. There is no means allowed, or recognised to enforce it; for the maxim is, *ex nudo pacto non oritur actio*. But when it does not fall within the predicament of being either illegal, or void, its obligatory force is coextensive with its stipulations.

§ 1375. Nor is this obligatory force so much the result of the positive declarations of the municipal law, as of the general principles of natural, or (as it is some-

---

[1] *Ogden* v. *Saunders*, 12 Wheaton's R. 257, 258, 280, 281, 300, 316 to 318, 337, 338.

times called) universal law.   In a state of nature, independent of the obligations of positive law, contracts
may be formed, and their obligatory force be complete.[1]
Between independent nations, treaties and compacts
are formed, which are deemed universally obligatory;
and yet in no just sense can they be deemed dependent on municipal law.[2] Nay, there may exist (ab-
stractly speaking) a perfect obligation in contracts,
where there is no known and adequate means to enforce them.   As, for instance, between independent
nations, where their relative strength and power preclude the possibility, on the side of the weaker party,
of enforcing them.   So in the same government, where
a contract is made by a state with one of its own citizens, which yet its laws do not permit to be enforced
by any action or suit.   In this predicament are the
United States, who are not suable on any contracts
made by themselves; but no one doubts, that these are
still obligatory on the United States. Yet their obligation is not recognised by any positive municipal law in
a great variety of cases. It depends altogether upon
principles of public or universal law. Still, in these
cases there is a right in the one party to have the contract performed, and a duty on the other side to perform it. But, generally speaking, when we speak of
the obligation of a contract, we include in the idea some
known means acknowledged by the municipal law to
enforce it. Where all such means are absolutely denied, the obligation of the contract is understood to be
impaired, though it may not be completely annihilated.
Rights may, indeed, exist without any present adequate

---

[1] *Ogden* v. *Saunders,* 12 Wheat. R. 281, 282; Id. 344 to 346; Id. 350.
[2] *Ogden* v. *Saunders,* 12 Wheat. R. 280, 281, 344 to 346.

correspondent remedies between private persons. Thus, a state may refuse to allow imprisonment for debt; and the debtor may have no property. But still the right of the creditor remains; and he may enforce it against the future property of the debtor.[1] So a debtor may die without leaving any known estate, or without any known representative. In such cases we should not say, that the right of the creditor was gone; but only, that there was nothing, on which it could presently operate. But suppose an administrator should be appointed, and property in contingency should fall in, the right might then be enforced to the extent of the existing means.

§ 1376. The civil obligation of a contract, then, though it can never arise, or exist contrary to positive law, may arise or exist independently of it;[2] and it may be, exist, notwithstanding there may be no present adequate remedy to enforce it. Wherever the municipal law recognises an absolute duty to perform a contract, there the obligation to perform it is complete, although there may not be a perfect remedy.

§ 1377. But much diversity of opinion has been exhibited upon another point; how far the existing law enters into, and forms a part of the contract. It has been contended by some learned minds, that the municipal law of the place, where a contract is made, forms a part of it, and travels with it, wherever the parties to it may be found.[3] If this were admitted to be true, the consequence would be, that all the existing laws of a state, being incorporated into the contract, would con-

---

[1] See *Sturgis v. Crowninshield*, 4 Wheat. 200, 201; *Mason v. Haile*, 12 Wheat. R. 370.

[2] *Ogden v. Saunders*, 12 Wheat. R. 344 to 346; Id. 350.

[3] *Ogden v. Saunders*, 12 Wheat. R. 259, 260; Id. 297, 298, 302.

stitute a part of its stipulations, so that a legislative repeal of such laws would not in any manner affect it.[1] Thus, if there existed at the time a statute of limitations, operating on such contracts, or an insolvent act, under which they might be discharged, no subsequent repeal of either could vary the rights of the parties, as to using them, as a bar to a suit upon such contracts. If, therefore, the legislature should provide by a law, that all contracts thereafter made should be subject to the entire control of the legislature, as to their obligation, validity, and execution, whatever might be their terms, they would be completely within the legislative power, and might be impaired, or extinguished by future laws; thus having a complete *ex post facto* operation. Nay, if the legislature should pass a law declaring, that all future contracts might be discharged by a tender of any thing, or things, besides gold and silver, there would be great difficulty in affirming them to be unconstitutional; since it would become a part of the stipulations of the contract. And yet it is obvious, that it would annihilate the whole prohibition of the constitution upon the subject of tender laws.[2]

§ 1378. It has, therefore, been judicially held by a majority of the Supreme Court, that such a doctrine is untenable. Although the law of the place acts upon a contract, and governs its construction, validity, and obligation, it constitutes no part of it. The effect of such a principle would be a mischievous abridgment of legislative power over subjects within the proper jurisdiction of states, by arresting their power to repeal, or modify such laws with respect to existing contracts.[3]

---

[1] *Ogden* v. *Saunders*, 12 Wheat. R. 260, 261, 262, 284, 336 to 339.

[2] *Ogden* v. *Saunders*, 12 Wheat. R. 284, 324, 325, 336 to 339.

[3] *Ogden* v. *Saunders*, 12 Wheat. R. 343.

The law necessarily steps in to explain, and construe the stipulations of parties, but never to supersede, or vary them. A great mass of human transactions depends upon implied contracts, upon contracts, not written, which grow out of the acts of the parties. In such cases the parties are supposed to have made those stipulations, which, as honest, fair, and just men, they ought to have made. When the law assumes, that the parties have made these stipulations, it does not vary their contract, or introduce new terms into it; but it declares, that certain acts, unexplained by compact, impose certain duties, and that the parties had stipulated for their performance. The difference is obvious between this, and the introduction of a new condition into a contract drawn out in writing, in which the parties have expressed every thing, that is to be done by either.[1] So, if there be a written contract, which does not include every term, which is ordinarily and fairly to be implied, as accompanying what is stated, the law performs the office only of expressing, what is thus tacitly admitted by the parties to be a part of their intention. To such an extent the law acts upon contracts. It performs the office of interpretation. But this is very different from supposing, that every law, applicable to the subject matter, as a statute of limitations, or a statute of insolvency, enters into the contract, and becomes a part of the contract. Such a supposition is neither called for by the terms of the contract, nor can be fairly presumed to be contemplated by the parties, as matters *ex contractu*. The parties know, that they must obey the laws; and that

---

[1] *Ogden* v. *Saunders*, 12 Wheat. R. 341, 342.

the laws act upon their contracts, whatever may be their intention.[1]

§ 1379. In the next place, what may properly be deemed impairing the obligation of contracts in the sense of the constitution? It is perfectly clear, that any law, which enlarges, abridges, or in any manner changes the intention of the parties, resulting from the stipulations in the contract, necessarily impairs it. The manner or degree, in which this change is effected, can in no respect influence the conclusion; for whether the law affect the validity, the construction, the duration, the discharge, or the evidence of the contract, it impairs its obligation, though it may not do so to the same extent in all the supposed cases.[2] Any deviation from its terms by postponing, or accelerating the period of performance, which it prescribes; imposing conditions not expressed in the contract; or dispensing with the performance of those, which are a part of the contract; however minute or apparently immaterial in their effect upon it, impair its obligation.[3] *A fortiori*, a law, which makes the contract wholly invalid, or extinguishes, or releases it, is a law impairing it.[4] Nor is this all. Although there is a distinction between the obligation of a contract, and a remedy upon it; yet if there are certain remedies existing at the time, when it is made, all of which are afterwards wholly extinguished by new laws, so that there remain no means of enforcing its obligation, and no redress; such an abolition of all remedies, operating *in presenti*, is also an im-

---

[1] *Ogden* v. *Saunders*, 12 Wheat. R. 284, 324, 325, 338, 339, 340, 343, 354.

[2] Id. 256; Id. 327; *Golden* v. *Prince*, 3 Wash. Cir. R. 319.

[3] *Green* v. *Biddle*, 8 Wheat. R. 1, 84.

[4] *Sturgis* v. *Crowninshield*, 4 Wheat. R. 197, 198.

pairing of the obligation of such contract.[1] But every
change and modification of the remedy does not involve such a consequence. No one will doubt, that
the legislature may vary the nature and extent of remedies, so always, that some substantive remedy be in
fact left. Nor can it be doubted, that the legislature
may prescribe the times and modes, in which remedies
may be pursued; and bar suits not brought within such
periods, and not pursued in such modes. Statutes of
limitations are of this nature; and have never been
supposed to destroy the obligation of contracts, but to
prescribe the times, within which that obligation shall
be enforced by a suit; and in default to deem it either
satisfied, or abandoned.[2] The obligation to perform a
contract is coeval with the undertaking to perform it.
It originates with the contract itself, and operates anterior to the time of performance. The remedy acts
upon the broken contract, and enforces a pre-existing
obligation.[3] And a state legislature may discharge a
party from imprisonment upon a judgment in a civil
case of contract, without infringing the constitution; for
this is but a modification of the remedy, and does not
impair the obligation of the contract.[4] So, if a party
should be in gaol, and give a bond for the prison liberties, and to remain a true prisoner, until lawfully discharged, a subsequent discharge by an act of the legislature would not impair the contract; for it would be a
lawful discharge in the sense of the bond.[5]

---

[1] *Ogden* v. *Saunders*, 12 Wheat. R. 284, 285, 327, 349, 350, 351, 352,
353; *Sturgis* v. *Crowninshield*, 4 Wheat. R. 200, 201, 207.

[2] *Sturgis* v. *Crowninshield*, 4 Wheat. R. 200, 206, 207 : *Mason* v.
Haile, 12 Wheat. R. 370 380, 381 ; *Ogden* v. *Saunders*, 12 Wheat. R.
262, 263, 349, 350 ; *Hawkins* v. *Barney's Lessee*, 5 Peters's Sup. R. 457.

[3] *Ogden* v. *Saunders*, 12 Wheat. R. 349, 350.

[4] *Mason* v. *Haile*, 12 Wheat. R. 370.   [5] Ibid.

§ 1380. These general considerations naturally conduct us to some more difficult inquiries growing out of them ; and upon which there has been a very great diversity of judicial opinion. The great object of the framers of the constitution undoubtedly was, to secure the inviolability of contracts. This principle was to be protected in whatever form it might be assailed. No enumeration was attempted to be made of the modes, by which contracts might be impaired. It would have been unwise to have made such an enumeration, since it might have been defective ; and the intention was to prohibit every mode or device for such purpose. The prohibition was universal.[1]

§ 1381. The question has arisen, and has been most elaborately discussed, how far the states may constitutionally pass an insolvent law, which shall discharge the obligation of contracts. It is not doubted, that the states may pass insolvent laws, which shall discharge the person, or operate in the nature of a *cessio bonorum,* provided such laws do not discharge, or intermeddle with the obligation of contracts. Nor is it denied, that insolvent laws, which discharge the obligation of contracts, made antecedently to their passage, are unconstitutional.[2] But the question is, how far the states may constitutionally pass insolvent laws, which shall operate upon, and discharge contracts, which are made subsequently to their passage. After the most ample argument it has at length been settled by a majority of the Supreme Court, that the states may constitutionally pass such laws operating upon future contracts.

---

1 *Sturgis v. Crowninshield,* 4 Wheat. R. 199, 200.

2 *Sturgis v. Crowninshield,* 4 Wheat. R. 122; *Farmers and Mechanics Bank v. Smith,* 6 Wheat. R. 131 ; *Ogden v. Saunders,* 12 Wheat. R. 213.

§ 1382. The learned judges, who held the affirmative, were not all agreed, as to the grounds of their opinions. But their judgment rests on some one of the following grounds: (1.) Some of the judges held, that the law of the place, where a contract is made, not only regulates, and governs it, but constitutes a part of the contract itself; and, consequently, that an insolvent law, which, in the event of insolvency of the party, authorizes a discharge of the contract is obligatory as a part the contract. (2.) Others held, that, though the law of the place formed no part of the contract, yet the latter derived its whole obligation from that law, and was controlled by its provisions; and, consequently, that its obligation could extend no further, than the law, which caused the obligation ; and if it was subject to be discharged in case of insolvency, the law so far controlled, and limited its obligation. (3.) That the connexion with the other parts of the clause, (bills of attainder and *ex post facto* laws,) as they applied to retrospective legislation, fortified the conclusion, that the intention in this part was only to prohibit the like legislation. (4.) That the known history of the country, as to insolvent laws, and their having constituted a part of the acknowledged jurisprudence of several of the states for a long period, forbade the supposition, that under such a general phrase, as laws impairing the obligation of contracts, insolvent laws, in the ordinary administration of justice, could have been intentionally included. (5.) That, whenever any person enters into a contract, his assent may be properly inferred to abide by those rules in the administration of justice, which belong to the jurisprudence of the country of the contract. And, when he is compelled to pursue his debtor in other states, he is equally bound to acquiesce in the law of the latter, to which he subjects himself. (6.) That the law of the contract remains the same every where, and will be the same in every tribunal. But the remedy necessarily varies, and with it the effect of the constitutional pledge, which can only have relation to the laws of distributive justice, known to the policy of each state severally. These and other auxiliary grounds, which were illustrated by a great variety of arguments, which scarcely admit of abridgment, were deemed satisfactory to the majority of the court.

§ 1383. The minority of the judges maintained their opinions upon the following grounds :   (1.) That the words of the clause in the constitution, taken in their natural and obvious sense, admit of a prospective, as well as of a retrospective operation.   (2.) That an act of the legislature does not enter into the contract, and become one of the conditions stipulated by the parties ; nor does it act externally on the agreement, unless it have the full force of law.   (3.) That contracts derive their obligation from the act of the parties, and not from the grant of the government.   And the right of the government to regulate the manner, in which they shall be formed, or to prohibit such as may be against the policy of the state, is entirely consistent with their inviolability, after they have been formed.   (4.) That the obligation of a contract is not identified with the means, which government may furnish to enforce it.   And that a prohibition to pass any law impairing it does not imply a prohibition to vary the remedy. Nor does a power to vary the remedy imply a power to impair the obligation derived from the act of the parties.   (5.) That the history of the times justified this interpretation of the clause. The power of changing the relative situation of debtor and creditor, and of interfering with contracts,

had been carried to such an excess by the state legislature, as to break in upon all the ordinary intercourse
of society, and to destroy all private confidence. It
was a great object to prevent for the future such mischievous measures. (6.) That the clause, in its terms,
purports to be perpetual; and the principle, to be of
any value, must be perpetual. It is expressed in terms
sufficiently broad to operate in all future times; and the
just inference, therefore, is, that it was so intended.
But if the other interpretation of it be adopted, the
clause will become of little effect; and the constitution
will have imposed a restriction, in language indicating
perpetuity, which every state in the Union may elude
at pleasure. The obligation of contracts in force at
any given time is but of short duration; and if the prohibition be of retrospective laws only, a very short lapse
of time will remove every subject, upon which state
laws are forbidden to operate, and make this provision
of the constitution so far useless. Instead of introducing a great principle, prohibiting all laws of this noxious
character, the constitution will suspend their operation
only for a moment, or except pre-existing cases from
it. The nature of the provision is thus essentially
changed. Instead of being a prohibition to pass laws
impairing the obligation of contracts, it is only a prohibition to pass retrospective laws. (7.) That there is
the less reason for adopting such a construction, since
the state laws, which produced the mischief, were prospective, as well as retrospective.[1]

§ 1384. The question is now understood to be finally at rest; and state insolvent laws, discharging the
obligation of future contracts, are to be deemed consti-

---

[1] See *Ogden* v *Saunders*, 12 Wheat. R. p. 254 to 357.

tutional.   Still a very important point remains to be
examined; and that is, to what contracts such laws can
rightfully apply.   The result of the various decisions on
this subject is, (1.) That they apply to all contracts made within the state between citizens of the
state.   (2.) That they do not apply to contracts made
within the state between a citizen of a state, and a citizen of another state.   (3.) That they do not apply to
contracts not made within the state.   In all these cases
it is considered, that the state does not possess a jurisdiction, coextensive with the contract, over the parties;
and therefore, that the constitution of the United States
protects them from prospective, as well as retrospective
legislation.[1]   Still, however, if a creditor voluntarily
makes himself a party to the proceedings under an insolvent law of a state, which discharges the contract, and
accepts a dividend declared under such law, he will be
bound by his own act, and be deemed to have abandoned
his extra-territorial immunity.[2]   Of course, the constitutional prohibition does not apply to insolvent, or other
laws passed before the adoption of the constitution,
operating upon contracts and rights of property vested,
and in *esse* before that time.[3]   And it may be added,
that state insolvent laws have no operation whatsoever
on contracts made with the United States; for such
contracts are in no manner whatsoever subject to state
jurisdiction.[4]

§ 1385. It has been already stated, that a grant is a
contract within the meaning of the constitution, as much
as an unexecuted agreement.   The prohibition, there-

[1] *Ogden* v. *Saunders*, 12 Wheat. R. 353 ; *McMullan* v. *Neil*, 4 W heat.
R. 209.
[2] *Clay* v. *Smith*, 3 Peters's Sup. R. 411.
[3] *Owings* v. *Speed*, 5 Wheat. R. 420.
[4] *United States* v. *Wilson*, 8 Wheat. R. 253.

fore, equally reaches all interferences with private grants and private conveyances, of whatever nature they may be. But it has been made a question, whether it applies, in the same extent, to contracts and grants of a state created directly by a law, or made by some authorized agent in pursuance of a law. It has been suggested, that, in such cases, it is to be deemed an act of the legislative power; and that all laws are repealable by the same authority, which enacted them. But it has been decided upon solemn argument, that contracts and grants made by a state are not less within the reach of the prohibition, than contracts and grants of private persons; that the question is not, whether such contracts or grants are made directly by law in the form of legislation, or in any other form, but whether they exist at all. The legislature may, by a law, directly make a grant; and such grant, when once made, becomes irrevocable, and cannot be constitutionally impaired. So the legislature may make a contract with individuals directly by a law, pledging the state to a performance of it; and then, when it is accepted, it is equally under the protection of the constitution. Thus, where a state authorized a sale of its public lands, and the sale was accordingly made, and conveyances given, it was held, that those conveyances could not be rescinded, or revoked by the state.[1] So where a state, by a law, entered into a contract with certain Indians to exempt their lands from taxation for a valuable consideration, it was held, that the exemption could not be revoked.[2] And grants of land, once voluntarily made

---

[1] *Fletcher* v. *Peck*, 6 Cranch 87, 135; S. C. 2 Peters's Cond. R. 208; 1 Kent's Comm. Lect. 19, p. 388.

[2] *New Jersey* v. *Wilson*, 7 Cranch, 164; S. C. 2 Peters's Cond. R. 457; 1 Kent's Comm. Lect. 19, p. 389.

by a state, by a special law, or under general laws, when
once perfected, are equally as incapable of being resumed by a subsequent law, as those founded on a valuable
consideration.   Thus, if a state grant glebe lands, or
other lands to parishes, towns, or private persons gra-
tuitously, they constitute irrevocable executed contracts.[1]   And it may be laid down, as a general principle, that, whenever a law is in its own nature a contract, and absolute rights have vested under it, a repeal
of that law cannot divest those rights, or annihilate or
impair the title so acquired.   A grant (as has been
already stated) amounts to an extinguishment of the
right of the grantor, and implies a contract not to reassert
it.[2]

1386. The cases above spoken of are cases, in
which rights of property are concerned, and are,
manifestly, within the scope of the prohibition. But a
question, of a more nice and delicate nature, has been
also litigated; and that is, how far charters, granted by
a state, are contracts within the meaning of the constitution.   That the framers of the constitution did not
intend to restrain the states in the regulation of their
civil institutions, adopted for internal government, is
admitted ; and it has never been so construed. It has
always been understood, that the contracts spoken of
in the constitution were those, which respected property, or some other object of value, and which conferred rights capable of being asserted in a court of
justice.[3]   A charter is certainly in form and sub-

---

[1] *Terrett v. Taylor*, 9 Cranch, 52 ; S. C. 3 Peters's Cond. R. 259; *Town of Pawlet v. Clarke*, 9 Cranch, 535; S. C. 3 Peters's Cond. R. 408; 1 Kent's Comm. Lect. 19, p. 389.

[2] *Fletcher v. Peck*, 6 Cranch 87, 135 ; S. C. 2 Peters's Cond. R. 308 ; 1 Kent's Comm. Lect. 19, p. 38.

[3] *Dartmouth College v. Woodward*, 4 Wheat. R. 518, 629.

stance a contract; it is a grant of powers, rights, and privileges; and it usually gives a capacity to take and to hold property. Where a charter creates a corporation, it emphatically confers this capacity; for it is an incident to a corporation, (unless prohibited,) to take and to hold property. A charter granted to private persons, for private purposes, is within the terms, and the reason of the prohibition. It confers rights and privileges, upon the faith of which it is accepted. It imparts obligations and duties on their part, which they are not at liberty to disregard; and it implies a contract on the part of the legislature, that the rights and privileges, so granted, shall be enjoyed. It is wholly immaterial, in such cases, whether the corporation take for their own private benefit, or for the benefit of other persons. A grant to a private trustee, for the benefit of a particular *cestui que trust*, is not less a contract, than if the trustee should take for his own benefit. A charter to a bank, or insurance, or turnpike company, is certainly a contract, founded in a valuable consideration. But it is not more so, than a charter incorporating persons for the erection and support of a hospital for the aged, the sick, or the infirm, which is to be supported by private contributions, or is founded upon private charity. If the state should make a grant of funds, in aid of such a corporation, it has never been supposed, that it could revoke them at its pleasure. It would have no remaining authority over the corporation, but that, which is judicial, to enforce the proper administration of the trust. Neither is a grant less a contract, though no beneficial interest accrues to the possessor. Many a purchase, whether corporate or not, may, in point of fact, be of no exchangeable value to the owners; and yet the grants confirming them are not less within the protection of the constitution. All incorporeal hereditaments, such as immunities, dignities, offices, and franchises, are in law deemed valuable rights, and wherever they are subjects of a contract or grant, they are just as much within the reach of the constitution, as any other grants ; for the constitution makes no account of the greater, or less value of any thing granted. All corporate franchises are legal estates. They are powers coupled with an interest; and the corporators have vested rights in their character as corporators.[1]

§ 1387. A charter, then, being a contract within the scope of the constitution, the next consideration, which has arisen upon this important subject, is, whether the principle applies to all charters, public as well as private. Corporations are divisible into two sorts, such as are strictly public, and such as are private. Within the former denomination are included all corporations, created for public purposes only, such as cities, towns, parishes, and other public bodies. Within the latter denomination all corporations are included, which do not strictly belong to the former. There is no doubt, as to public corporations, which exist only for public purposes, that the legislature may change, modify, enlarge, and restrain them ; with this limitation, however, that property, held by such corporation, shall still be secured for the use of those, for whom, and at whose expense it has been acquired. The principle may be stated in a more general form. If a charter be a mere grant of political power, if it create a civil institution,

---

[1] *Dartmouth College* v. *Woodward,* 4 Wheat. R. 518, 629, 630, 636, 638, 644, 645, 646, 647, 653, 656, 657, 658, 697, 698, 699, 700, 701, 702.

[2] *Terrett* v. *Taylor,* 9 Cranch, 52 ; *Dartmouth College* v. *Woodward,* 4 Wheat. R. 663, 694.

to be employed in the administration of the government, or, if the funds be public property alone, and the government alone be interested in the management of them, the legislative power over such charter is not restrained by the constitution, but remains unlimited.[1] The reason is, that it is only a mode of exercising public rights and public powers, for the promotion of the general interest; and, therefore, it must, from its very nature, remain subject to the legislative will, so always that private rights are not infringed, or trenched upon.

§ 1388. But an attempt has been made to press this principle much farther, and to exempt from the constitutional prohibition all charters, which, though granted to private persons, are in reality trusts for purposes and objects, which may, in a certain sense, be deemed public and general. The first great case, in which this doctrine became the subject of judicial examination and decision, was the case of Dartmouth College. The legislature of New-Hampshire had, without the consent of the corporation, passed an act changing the organization of the original provincial charter of the college, and transferring all the rights, privileges, and franchises from the old charter trustees to new trustees, appointed under the act. The constitutionality of the act was contested, and after solemn argument, it was deliberately held by the Supreme Court, that the provincial charter was a contract within the meaning of the constitution, and that the amendatory act was utterly void, as impairing the obligation of that charter. The college was deemed, like other colleges of private foundation, to be a private eleemosynary institution,

---

[1] *Dartmouth College* v. *Woodward*, 4 Wheat. R. 518, 629, 630, 659, 663, 694, to 701.

endowed, by its charter, with a capacity to take property unconnected with the government. Its funds were bestowed upon the faith of the charter, and those funds consisted entirely of private donations. It is true, that the uses were in some sense public ; that is, for the general benefit, and not for the mere benefit of the corporators; but this did not make the corporation a public corporation. It was a private institution for general charity. It was not distinguishable in principle from a private donation, vested in private trustees, for a public charity, or for a particular purpose of beneficence. And the state itself, if it had bestowed funds upon a charity of the same nature, could not resume those funds. In short, the charter was deemed a contract, to which the government, and the donors, and the trustees of the corporation, were all parties. It was for a valuable consideration, for the security and disposition of property, which was entrusted to the corporation upon the faith of its terms ; and the trustees acquired rights under it, which could not be taken away; for they came to them clothed with trusts, which they were obliged to perform, and could not constitutionally disregard. The reasoning in the case, of which this is a very faint and imperfect outline, should receive a diligent perusal; and it is difficult to present it in an abridged form, without impairing its force, or breaking its connexion.[1] The doctrine is held to be equally applicable to grants of additional rights and privileges to an existing corporation, and to the original charter, by which a corporation is first brought into existence, and established. As soon as the latter become organ-

---

[1] *Dartmouth College* v. *Woodward*, 4 Wheat. R. 518, 624 et seq.; 1 Kent. Comm. Lect. 19, p. 389 to 392.

ized and in *esse*, the charter becomes a contract with the corporators.[1]

§ 1389. It has not been thought any objection to this interpretation, that the preservation of charters, and other corporate rights, might not have been primarily, or even secondarily, within the contemplation of the framers of the constitution, when this clause was introduced. It is probable, that the other great evils, already alluded to, constituted the main inducement to insert it, where the temptations were more strong, and the interest more immediate and striking, to induce a violation of contracts. But though the motive may thus have been to reach other more pressing mischiefs, the prohibition itself is made general. It is applicable to all contracts, and not confined to the forms then most known, and most divided. Although a rare or particular case may not of itself be of sufficient magnitude to induce the establishment of a constitutional rule; yet it must be governed by that rule, when established, unless some plain and strong reason for excluding it can be given. It is not sufficient to show, that it may not have been foreseen, or intentionally provided for. To exclude it, it is necessary to go farther, and show, that if the case had been suggested, the language of the convention would have been varied so, as to exclude and except it. Where a case falls within the words of a rule or prohibition, it must be held within its operation, unless there is something obviously absurd, or mischievous, or repugnant to the general spirit of the instrument, arising from such a construction.[2] No such

---

[1] *Dartmouth College* v. *Woodward*, 4 Wheat. R. 518, 624 et seq.; 1 Kent. Comm. Lect. 19, p. 389 to 392.

[2] *Dartmouth College* v. *Woodward*, 4 Wheat. 644, 645. See also *Sturgis* v. *Crowninshield*, 4 Wheat, R. 202.

absurdity, mischief, or repugnancy, can be pretended in the present case. On the contrary, every reason of justice, convenience, and policy unite to prove the wisdom of embracing it in the prohibition. An impregnable barrier is thus thrown around all rights and franchises derived from the states, and solidity and inviolability are given to the literary, charitable, religious, and commercial institutions of the country.[1]

§ 1390. It has also been made a question, whether a compact between two states, is within the scope of the prohibition. And this also has been decided in the affirmative.[2] The terms, compact and contract, are synonymous; and, when propositions are offered by one state, and agreed to and accepted by another, they necessarily constitute a contract between them. There is no difference, in reason or in law, to distinguish between contracts made by a state with individuals, and contracts made between states. Each ought to be equally inviolable.[3] Thus, where, upon the separation of Kentucky from Virginia, it was agreed by compact between them, that all private rights and interests in lands in Kentucky, derived from the laws of Virginia, should remain valid and secure under the laws of Kentucky, and should be determined by the laws then existing in Virginia; it was held by the Supreme Court, that certain laws of Kentucky, (commonly called the occupying claimant laws,) which varied and restricted the rights and remedies of the owners of

---

[1] 1 Kent. Comm. Lect. 19, p. 392.

[2] *Green* v. *Biddle*, 8 Wheat. R. 1; 1 Kent. Comm. Lect. 19, p. 393; Sergeant on Constitution, ch. 28 [ch. 30.]

[3] *Green* v. *Biddle*, 8 Wheat. R. 1, 92.

such lands, were void, because they impaired the obligation of the contract. Nothing (said the court) can be more clear upon principles of law and reason, than that a law, which denies to the owner of the land a remedy to secure the possession of it, when withheld by any person, however innocently he may have obtained it; or to recover the profits received from it by the occupant; or which clogs his recovery of such possession and profits, by conditions and restrictions, tending to diminish the value and amount of the thing recovered; impairs his right to, and interest in, the property. If there be no remedy to recover the possession, the law necessarily presumes a want of right to it. If the remedy afforded be qualified and restrained by conditions of any kind, the right of the owner may indeed subsist, and be acknowledged; but it is impaired, and rendered insecure, according to the nature and extent of such restrictions.[1] But statutes and limitations, which are mere regulations of the remedy, for the purposes of general repose and quieting titles, are not supposed to impair the right; but merely to provide for the prosecution of it within a reasonable period; and to deem the non-prosecution within the period an abandonment of it.[2]

§ 1391. Whether a state legislature has authority to pass a law declaring a marriage void, or to award a divorce, has, incidentally, been made a question, but has never yet come directly in judgment. Marriage, though it be a civil institution, is understood to constitute a solemn, obligatory contract between the parties. And it has been, *arguendo*, denied, that a state legislature

---

[1] *Green* v. *Biddle*, 8 Wheat. R. 1, 75, 76.

[2] *Hawkins* v. *Barney's Lessee*, 5 Peters's Sup. R. 457; *Bank of Hamilton* v. *Dudley's Lessee*, 2 Peters's Sup. R. 492.

constitutionally possesses authority to dissolve that
contract against the will, and without the default of
either party. This point, however, may well be
left for more exact consideration, until it becomes the
very ground of the *lis mota*.[1]

§ 1392. Before quitting this subject it may be proper
to remark, that as the prohibition, respecting *ex post
facto* laws, applies only to criminal cases; and the other
is confined to impairing the obligation of contracts;
there are many laws of a retrospective character, which
may yet be constitutionally passed by the state legislatures, however unjust, oppressive, or impolitic they
may be.[2] Retrospective laws are, indeed, generally unjust; and, as has been forcibly said, neither accord with
sound legislation, nor with the fundamental principles
of the social compact.[3] Still they are, with the exceptions above stated, left open to the states, according to
their own constitutions of government; and become
obligatory, if not prohibited by the latter. Thus, for
instance, where the legislature of Connecticut, in 1795,
passed a resolve, setting aside a decree of a court of
probate disapproving of a will, and granted a new
hearing; it was held, that the resolve, not being against
any constitutional principle in that state, was valid;
and that the will, which was approved upon the new
hearing, was conclusive, as to the rights obtained under
it.[4] There is nothing in the constitution of the United
States, which forbids a state legislature from exercising

[1] *Dartmouth College* v. *Woodward*, 4 Wheat. R. 629, 695. 696.
[2] See *Beach* v. *Woodhull*, 1 Peters's Cir. Ct. R.; 2 *Calder* v. *Bull*,
3 Dall. R. 386; *Satterlee* v *Mathewson*, 2 Peters's Sup. R. 380; *Wilkinson*
v. *Leland*, 2 Peters's Sup. R. 627, 661.
[3] Patterson J. in *Calder* v. *Bull*, 3 Dall. R. 397.
[4] *Calder* v. *Bull*, 3 Dall. R. 386.

judicial functions; nor from divesting rights, vested by law in an individual; provided its effect be not to impair the obligation of a contract.[1] If such a law be void, it is upon principles derived from the general nature of free governments, and the necessary limitations created thereby, or from the state restrictions upon the legislative authority, and not from the prohibitions of the constitution of the United States. If a state statute should, contrary to the general principles of law, declare, that contracts founded upon an illegal or immoral consideration, or otherwise void, should nevertheless be valid, and binding between the parties; its retrospective character could not be denied; for the effect would be to create a contract between the parties, where none had previously existed. Yet it would not be reached by the constitution of the United States; for to create a contract, and to impair or destroy one, can never be construed to mean the same thing. It may be within the same mischief, and equally unjust, and ruinous; but it does not fall within the terms of the prohibition.[2] So, if a state court should decide, that the relation of landlord and tenant did not legally subsist between certain persons; and the legislature should pass a declaratory act, declaring, that it did subsist; the act, so far as the constitution of the United States is concerned, would be valid.[3] So, if a state legislature should confirm a void sale, if it did not divest the settled rights of property, it would be valid.[4] Nor (as has been already seen) would a state law, discharging

---

1 *Satterlee v. Mathewson,* 2 Peters's Sup. R. 380, 413 ; *Calder v. Bull,* 3 Dall. R. 386. See *Olney v. Arnold,* 3 Dall. R. 308; *Wilkinson v. Leland,* 2 Peters's Sup. R. 627.

2 *Satterlee v. Mathewson,* 2 Peters's Sup. R. 380, 412, 413.

3 *Satterlee v. Mathewson,* 2 Peters's Sup. R. 380, 412, 413.

4 *Wilkinson v. Leland,* 2 Peters's Sup. R. 627, 661.

a party from imprisonment under a judgment upon a
contract, though passed subsequently to the imprisonment, be an unconstitutional exercise of power; for it
would leave the obligation of the contract undisturbed.
The states still possess the rightful authority to abolish
imprisonment for debt; and may apply it to present, as
well as to future imprisonment.[1]

§ 1393. Whether, indeed, independently of the
constitution of the United States, the nature of republican and free governments does not necessarily impose some restraints upon the legislative power, has
been much discussed. It seems to be the general
opinion, fortified by a strong current of judicial opinion,
that since the American revolution no state government can be presumed to possess the trancendental
sovereignty, to take away vested rights of property;
to take the property of A. and transfer it to B. by a
mere legislative act.[2] That government can scarcely
be deemed to be free, where the rights of property
are left solely dependent upon a legislative body, without any restraint. The fundamental maxims of a free
government seem to require, that the rights of personal
liberty, and private property, should be held sacred.
At least, no court of justice, in this country, would be
warranted in assuming, that any state legislature possessed a power to violate and disregard them; or that
such a power, so repugnant to the common principles
of justice and civil liberty, lurked under any general
grant of legislative authority, or ought to be implied
from any general expression of the will of the people,
in the usual forms of the constitutional delegation of

---

1 *Mason* v. *Haile*, 2 Peters's Sup. R. 870.
2 *Fletcher* v. *Peck*, 6 Cranch, 67, 134.

power. The people ought not to be presumed to part
with rights, so vital to their security and well-being,
without very strong, and positive declarations to that
effect.[1]

§ 1394. The remaining prohibition in this clause is,
that no state shall "grant any title of nobility." The
reason of this prohibition is the same, as that, upon
which the like prohibition to the government of the
nation is founded. Indeed, it would be almost absurd
to provide sedulously against such a power in the latter,
if the states were still left free to exercise it. It has
been emphatically said, that this is the corner-stone of
a republican government; for there can be little danger, while a nobility is excluded, that the government
will ever cease to be that of the people.[2]

---

* 1 *Wilkinson* v. *Leland*, 2 Peters's Sup. R. 627, 657.   See also *Satterlee*
v. *Mathewson*, 2 Peters's Sup. R. 380, 413, 414; *Fletcher* v. *Peck*,
6 Cranch, 67, 134; *Tenett* v. *Taylor*, 9 Cranch, 52; *Town of Pawlet*
v. *Clark*, 9 Cranch, 535.   See also Sergeant on Const. ch. 28, [ch. 30.]
   2 The Federalist, No. 84.

CHAPTER XXXV.

PROHIBITIONS ON THE STATES.

§ 1395. The next clause of the constitution is, " No state shall, without the consent of congress, lay " any duty on tonnage ; keep troops, or ships of war " in time of peace ; enter into any agreement or com- " pact with another state, or with a foreign power, or " engage in war, unless actually invaded, or in such " imminent danger, as will not admit of delay."

§ 1396. The first part of this clause, respecting lay- ing a duty on tonnage, has been already considered. The remaining clauses have their origin in the same general policy and reasoning, which forbid any state from entering into any treaty, alliance, or confederation; and from granting letters of marque and reprisal. In regard to treaties, alliances, and confederations, they are wholly prohibited. But a state may, *with the con- sent of congress*, enter into an agreement, or compact with another state, or with a foreign power. What precise distinction is here intended to be taken be- tween *treaties*, and *agreements*, and *compacts* is no- where explained ; and has never as yet been subjected to any exact judicial, or other examination. A learned commentator, however, supposes, that the former ordi- narily relate to subjects of great national magnitude and importance, and are often perpetual, or for a great length of time ; but that the latter relate to transitory, or local concerns, or such, as cannot possibly affect any other interests, but those of the parties.[1] But this

---

[1] 1 Tucker's Black. Comm. App. 310.

is at best a very loose, and unsatisfactory exposition, leaving the whole matter open to the most latitudinarian construction. What are subjects of great national magnitude and importance? Why may not a compact, or agreement between states, be perpetual? If it may not, what shall be its duration? Are not treaties often made for short periods, and upon questions of local interest, and for temporary objects?[1]

§ 1397. Perhaps the language of the former clause may be more plausibly interpreted from the terms used, "treaty, alliance, or confederation," and upon the ground, that the sense of each is best known by its association (*noscitur a sociis*) to apply to treaties of a political character; such as treaties of alliance for purposes of peace and war; and treaties of confederation, in which the parties are leagued for mutual government, political co-operation, and the exercise of political sovereignty; and treaties of cession of sovereignty, or conferring internal political jurisdiction, or external political dependence, or general commercial privileges.[2] The latter clause, "compacts and agreements," might then very properly apply to such, as regarded what might

---

[1] The corresponding article of the confederation did not present exactly the same embarrassments in its construction. One clause was, "No state, without the consent of the United States, in congress assembled, shall enter into any conference, agreement, alliance, or treaty with any king, prince, or state"; and "No two or more states shall enter into any treaty, confederation, or alliance whatever between them, without the consent of the United States, &c.; specifying accurately the purposes, for which the same is to be entered into, and how long it shall continue." Taking both clauses, it is manifest, that the former refers exclusively to foreign states, or nations; and the latter to the states of the Union.

[2] In this view, one might be almost tempted to conjecture, that the original reading was "treaties of alliance, or confederation;" if the corresponding article of the confederation (art. 6) did not repel it.

be deemed mere private rights of sovereignty; such as questions of boundary; interests in land, situate in the territory of each other; and other internal regulations for the mutual comfort, and convenience of states, bordering on each other. Such compacts have been made since the adoption of the constitution. The compact between Virginia and Kentucky, already alluded to, is of this number. Compacts, settling the boundaries between states, are, or may be, of the same character. In such cases, the consent of congress may be properly required, in order to check any infringement of the rights of the national government; and at the same time a total prohibition, to enter into any compact or agreement, might be attended with permanent inconvenience, or public mischief.

§ 1398. The other prohibitions in the clause respect the power of making war, which is appropriately confided to the national government.[1] The setting on foot of an army, or navy, by a state in times of peace, might be a cause of jealousy between neighbouring states, and provoke the hostilities of foreign bordering nations. In other cases, as the protection of the whole Union is confided to the national arm, and the national power, it is not fit, that any state should possess military means to overawe the Union, or to endanger the general safety. Still, a state may be so situated, that it may become indispensable to possess military forces, to resist an expected inva-

---

[1] There were corresponding prohibitions in the confederation, (art. 6,) which differ more in form, than in substance, from those in the constitution. No state was at liberty, in time of peace, to keep up vessels of war, or land forces, without the consent of congress. Nor was any state at liberty to engage in war without the consent of congress, unless invaded, or in imminent danger thereof.

sion, or insurrection. The danger may be too imminent
for delay; and under such circumstances, a state will
have a right to raise troops for its own safety, even
without the consent of congress. After war is once
begun, there is no doubt, that a state may, and indeed
it ought to possess the power, to raise forces for its
own defence; and its co-operation with the national
forces may often be of great importance, to secure
success and vigour in the operations of war. The
prohibition is, therefore, wisely guarded by exceptions
sufficient for the safety of the states, and not justly
open to the objection of being dangerous to the
Union.

§ 1399. In what manner the consent of congress is
to be given to such acts of the state, is not positively
provided for. Where an express consent is given, no
possible doubt can arise. But the consent of congress
may also be implied; and, indeed, is always to be implied, when congress adopts the particular act by
sanctioning its objects, and aiding in enforcing them.
Thus, where a state is admitted into the Union, notori-
ously upon a compact made between it and the state,
of which it previously composed a part; there the act of
congress, admitting such state into the Union, is an implied consent to the terms of the compact. This was
true, as to the compact between Virginia and Kentucky, upon the admission of the latter into the Union;[1]
and the like rule will apply to other states, such as
Maine, more recently admitted into the Union.

§ 1400. We have thus passed through the positive
prohibitions introduced upon the powers of the states.
It will be observed, that they divide themselves into

---

[1] *Green v. Biddle*, 8 Wheat. R. 1, 85, 86, 87.

two classes ; those, which are political in their character, as an exercise of sovereignty ; and those, which more especially regard the private rights of individuals.[1]   In the latter, the prohibition is absolute and universal.   In the former, it is sometimes absolute, and sometimes subjected to the consent of congress.   It will, at once, be perceived, how full of difficulty and delicacy the task was to reconcile the jealous tenacity of the states over their own sovereignty, with the permanent security of the national government, and the inviolability of private rights.   The task has been accomplished with eminent success.   If every thing has not been accomplished, which a wise forecast might have deemed proper for the preservation of our national rights and liberties, in all political events, much has been done to guard us against the most obvious evils, and to secure a wholesome administration of private justice.   To have attempted more, would probably have endangered the whole fabric ; and thus have perpetuated the dominion of misrule and imbecility.

§ 1401.   It has been already seen, and it will hereafter more fully appear, that there are implied, as well as express, prohibitions in the constitution upon the power of the states.   Among the former, one clearly is, that no state can control, or abridge, or interfere with the exercise of any authority under the national government.[2]   And it may be added, that state laws, as, for instance, state statutes of limitations, and state insolvent laws, have no operation upon the rights or contracts of the United States.[3]

---

[1] See *Ogden* v. *Saunders*, 12 Wheat. R. 334, 335.
[2] 1 Kent's Comm. Lect. 19, p. 382.
[3] *United States* v. *Wilson*, 8 Wheat. R. 253 ; *United States* v. *Hoar*, 2 Mason R. 311.

§ 1402. And here end our commentaries upon the first article of the constitution, embracing the organization and powers of the legislative department of the government, and the prohibitions upon the state and national governments. If we here pause, but for a moment, we cannot but be struck with the reflection, how admirably this division and distribution of legislative powers between the state and national governments is adapted to preserve the liberty, and promote the happiness of the people of the United States. To the general government are assigned all those powers, which relate to the common interests of all the states, as comprising one confederated nation. While to each state is reserved all those powers, which may affect, or promote its own domestic interests, its peace, its prosperity, its policy, and its local institutions. At the same time, such limitations and restraints are imposed upon each government, as experience has demonstrated to be wise to control any public functionaries, or as are indispensable to secure the harmonious operations of the Union.[1]

§ 1403. A clause was originally proposed, and carried in the convention, to give the national legislature a negative upon all laws passed by the states, contravening, in the opinion of the national legislature, the articles of the Union, and treaties subsisting under its authority. This proposition was, however, afterwards negatived ; and finally abandoned.[2] A more acceptable substitute

---

[1] 1 Tuck. Black. Comm. App. 314.

[2] Journal of Convention, 68, 86, 87, 104, 107, 136, 183, 283 ; North American Review, October, 1827, p. 264, 266 ; 2 Pitkin's History, 261. — This seems to have been a favourite opinion of Mr. Madison, as well as of some other distinguished statesmen. North American Review, October, 1827, p. 264, 265, 266 ; 2 Pitkin's History, 251, 259.

was found in the article, (hereafter to be examined,) which declares, that the constitution, laws, and treaties of the United States shall be the supreme law of the land.

CHAPTER XXXVI.

EXECUTIVE DEPARTMENT — ORGANIZATION OF.

§ 1404. In the progress of our examination of the constitution, we are now arrived at the second article, which contains an enumeration of the organization and powers of the executive department. What is the best constitution for the executive department, and what are the powers, with which it should be entrusted, are problems among the most important, and probably the most difficult to be satisfactorily solved, of all, which are involved in the theory of free governments.[1] No man, who has ever studied the subject with profound attention, has risen from the labour without an increased and almost overwhelming sense of its intricate relations, and perplexing doubts. No man, who has ever deeply read the human history, and especially the history of republics, but has been struck with the consciousness, how little has been hitherto done to establish a safe depositary of power in any hands; and how often in the hands of one, or a few, or many, of an hereditary monarch, or an elective chief, the executive power has brought ruin upon the state, or sunk under the oppressive burthen of its own imbecility. Perhaps our own history, hitherto, does not establish, that we have wholly escaped all the dangers ; and that here is not to be found, as has been the case in other nations, the vulnerable part of the republic.

§ 1405. It appears, that the subject underwent a very elaborate discussion in the convention, with much

---

[1] See 2 Elliot's Deb. 358 ; 1 Kent's Comm. Lect. 13, p. 255, 256.

diversity of opinion ; and various propositions were submitted of the most opposite character. The Federalist has remarked, that there is hardly any part of the system, the arrangement of which could have been attended with greater difficulty ; and none, which has been inveighed against with less candor, or criticised with less judgment.[1]

§ 1406. The first clause of the first section of the second article is as follows : " The executive power " shall be vested in a President of the United States " of America. He shall hold his office during the term " of four years ; and together with the Vice-President, " chosen for the same term, be chosen as follows."

§ 1407. Under the confederation there was no national executive. The whole powers of the national government were vested in a congress, consisting of a single body ; and that body was authorized to appoint a committee of the states, composed of one delegate from every state, to sit in the recess, and to delegate to them such of their own powers, not requiring the consent of nine states, as nine states should consent to.[2] This want of a national executive was deemed a fatal defect in the confederation.

§ 1408. In the convention, there does not seem to have been any objection to the establishment of a national executive. But upon the question, whether it should consist of a single person, the affirmative was carried by a vote of seven states against three.[3] The term of service was at first fixed at seven years, by a vote of five states against four, one being divided. The term was afterwards altered to four years, upon the report of a

1 The Federalist, No. 67.   2 Confederation, Art. 9, 10.
3 Journ. of Convention, 68, 89, 96, 136.

committee, and adopted by the vote of ten states against one.[1]

§ 1409. In considering this clause, three practical questions are naturally suggested : First, whether there should be a distinct executive department ; secondly, whether it should be composed of more than one person ; and, thirdly, what should be the duration of office.

§ 1410. Upon the first question, little need be said. All America have at length concurred in the propriety of establishing a distinct executive department. The principle is embraced in every state constitution ; and it seems now to be assumed among us, as a fundamental maxim of government, that the legislative, executive, and judicial departments ought to be separate, and the powers of one ought not to be exercised by either of the others. The same maxim is found recognised in express terms in many of our state constitutions. It is hardly necessary to repeat, that where all these powers are united in the same hands, there is a real despotism, to the extent of their coercive exercise. Where, on the other hand, they exist together, and yet depend for their exercise upon the mere authority of recommendation, (as they did under the confederation,[2]) they become at once imbecile and arbitrary, subservient to popular clamour, and incapable of steady action. The harshness of the measures in relation to paper money, and the timidity and vacillation in relation to military affairs, are examples not easily to be forgotten.

---

1 Journal of Convention, 90, 136, 211, 225, 324, 332, 333 ; 2 Pitkin's Hist. 252.
2 See 1 Jefferson's Corresp. 63.

§ 1411. Taking it, then, for granted, that there ought to be an executive department, the next consideration is, how it ought to be organized. It may be stated in general terms, that that organization is best, which will at once secure energy in the executive, and safety to the people. The notion, however, is not uncommon, and occasionally finds ingenious advocates, that a vigorous executive is inconsistent with the genius of a republican government.[1] It is difficult to find any sufficient grounds, on which to rest this notion; and those, which are usually stated, belong principally to that class of minds, which readily indulge in the belief of the general perfection, as well as perfectibility, of human nature, and deem the least possible quantity of power, with which government can subsist, to be the best. To those, who look abroad into the world, and attentively read the history of other nations, ancient and modern, far different lessons are taught with a severe truth and force. Those lessons instruct them, that energy in the executive is a leading character in the definition of a good government.[2] It is essential to the protection of the community against foreign attacks.

[1] See 2 American Museum, 427. — Milton was of this opinion; and triumphantly states, that "all ingenious and knowing men will easily agree with me, that a free commonwealth, without a single person or house of lords, is by far the best government, if it can be had." (Milton on the Ready and Easy Way to establish a Free Commonwealth.) His notion was, that the whole power of the government should centre in a house of commons. — Locke was in favour of a concentration of the whole executive and legislative powers in a small assembly; and Hume thought the executive powers safely lodged with a hundred senators. (Hume's Essays, Vol. 1, Essay 16, p. 526.) — Mr. Chancellor Kent has made some just reflections upon these extraordinary opinions in 1 Kent's Comm. Lect. 13, p. 264.

[2] 1 Kent's Comm. Lect. 13, p. 253, 254; Rawle on Const. ch. 12, p. 147, 148.

It is not less essential to the steady administration of the laws, to the protection of property against those irregular and high-handed combinations, which sometimes interrupt the ordinary course of justice, and to the security of liberty against the enterprises and assaults of ambition, of faction, and of anarchy.[1] Every man the least conversant with Roman history knows, how often that republic was obliged to take refuge in the absolute power of a single man, under the formidable name of a dictator, as well against the intrigues of ambitious individuals, aspiring to tyranny, and the seditions of whole classes of the community, threatening the existence of the government, as against foreign enemies, menacing the destruction an l conquest of the state.[2] A feeble executive implies a feeble execution of the government. A feeble execution is but another phrase for a bad execution ; and a government ill executed, whatever may be its theory, must, in practice, be a bad government.[3]

§ 1412. The ingredients, which constitute energy in the executive, are unity, duration, an adequate provision for its support, and competent powers. The ingredients, which constitute safety in a republican form of government, are a due dependence on the people, and a due responsibility to the people.[4]

§ 1413. The most distinguished statesmen have uniformly maintained the doctrine, that there ought to be a single executive, and a numerous legislature. They have considered energy, as the most necessary qualification of the power, and this as best attained by

---

[1] The Federalist, No. 70 ; Rawle on Const. ch. 12, p. 149.
[2] Ibid.   [3] Ibid.
[4] Ibid. 1 Kent's Comm. Lect. 13, p. 253, 254.

reposing the power in a single hand. At the same time, they have considered with equal propriety, that a numerous legislature was best adapted to the duties of legislation, and best calculated to conciliate the confidence of the people, and to secure their privileges and interests.[1] Montesquieu has said, that "the executive power ought to be in the hands of a monarch, because this branch of government, having need of despatch, is better administered by one, than by many. On the other hand, whatever depends on the legislative power is oftentimes better regulated by many, than by a single person. But if there were no monarch, and the executive power should be committed to a certain number of persons, selected from the legislative body, there would be an end to liberty; by reason, that the two powers would be united, as the same persons would sometimes possess, and would always be able to possess, a share in both."[2] De Lolme, in addition to other advantages, considers the unity of the executive as important in a free government, because it is thus more easily restrained.[3] "In those states," says he, "where the execution of the laws is entrusted to several different hands, and to each with different titles and prerogatives, such division, and such changeableness of measures, which must be the consequence of it, constantly hide the true cause of the evils of the state. Sometimes military tribunes, and at others consuls bear an absolute sway. Sometimes patricians usurp every thing; and at other times those, who are called nobles. Sometimes the people are oppressed by de-

[1] The Federalist, No. 70.
[2] Montesquieu's Spirit of Laws, B. 11, ch. 6.
[3] De Lolme on Const. of England, B. 2, ch. 2.

cemvirs ; and at others by dictators. Tyranny in such
states does not always beat down the fences, that are
set around it ; but it leaps over them. When men
think it confined to one place, it starts up again in another. It mocks the efforts of the people, not because
it is invincible, but because it is unknown. But the
indivisibility of the public power in England has constantly kept the views and efforts of the people directed to one and the same object."[1] He adds, in another place, " we must observe a difference between
the legislative and executive powers. The latter may
be confined, and even is the more easily so, when undivided. The legislature on the contrary, in order to
its being restrained, should absolutely be divided."[2]

§ 1414. That unity is conducive to energy will
scarcely be disputed. Decision, activity, secresy, and
despatch will generally characterise the proceedings of
one man in a much more eminent degree, than the
proceedings of a greater number ; and in proportion,
as the number is increased, these qualities will be diminished.[3]

§ 1415. This unity may be destroyed in two ways ;
first, by vesting the power in two or more magistrates
of equal dignity ; secondly, by vesting it ostensibly in
one man, subject, however, in whole or in part to the
control and advice of a council. Of the first, the
two consuls of Rome may serve, as an example in ancient times ; and in modern times, the brief and hasty

1 De Lolme on Const. of England, B. 2, ch. 2.
2 De Lolme on Const. of England, B. 2, ch. 3. See also, The Federalist, No. 70; 1 Kent's Comm. Lect. 13, p. 253 to 255. — The celebrated Junius (the great unknown) has pronounced De Lolme's work to be
at once " deep, solid, and ingenious."
3 The Federalist, No. 70 ; 1 Kent's Comm. Lect. 13, p. 253, 254.

history of the three consuls of France, during its short-lived republic.[1] Of the latter, several states in the Union furnish examples, as some of the colonies did before the revolution. Both these methods of destroying the unity of the executive have had their advocates. They are both liable to similar, if not to equal objections.[2]

§ 1416. The experience of other nations, so far as it goes, coincides with what theory would point out. The Roman history records may instances of mischiefs to the republic from dissensions between the consuls, and between the military tribunes, who were at times substituted instead of the consuls. Those dissensions would have been even more striking, as well as more frequent, if it had not been for the peculiar circumstances of that republic, which often induced the consuls to divide the administration of the government between them. And as the consuls were generally chosen from the Patrician order, which was engaged in perpetual struggles with the Plebeians for the preservation of the privileges and dignities of their own order; there was an external pressure, which compelled them to act together for mutual support and defence.[3]

§ 1417. But independent of any of the lights derived from history, it is obvious, that a division of the executive power between two or more persons must always tend to produce dissensions, and fluctuating councils. Whenever two or more persons are engaged

---

[1] 4 Jefferson's Corresp. 160, 161. — Propositions were made in the convention, for an executive composed of a plurality of persons.* They came from that party in the convention, which was understood to be favourable to a continuation of the confederation with amendments.†

[2] The Federalist, No. 70.   [3] Id.

in any common enterprise, or pursuit, there is always danger of difference of opinion. If it be a public trust, or office, in which they are clothed with equal dignity and authority, there are peculiar dangers arising from personal emulation, or personal animosity ; from superior talents on one side, encountering strong jealousies on the other; from pride of opinion on one side, and weak devotion to popular prejudices on the other; from the vanity of being the author of a plan, or resentment from some imagined slight by the approval of that of another. From these, and other causes of the like nature, the most bitter rivalries and dissensions often spring. Whenever these happen, they lessen the respectability, weaken the authority, and distract the plans and operations of those, whom they divide. The wisest measures are those often defeated, or delayed, even in the most critical moments. And what constitutes even a greater evil, the community often becomes split up into rival factions, adhering to the different persons, who compose the magistracy; and temporary animosities become thus the foundation of permanent calamities to the state.[1]   Indeed, the ruinous effects of rival factions in free states, struggling for power, has been the constant theme of reproach by the admirers of monarchy, and of regret by the lovers of republics.   The Guelphs and the Ghibelins, the white and the black factions, have been immortalized in the history of the Italian states; and they are but an epitome of the same unvarying scenes in all other republics.[2]

§ 1418. From the very nature of a free government, inconveniences resulting from a division of power must

---

[1] The Federalist, No. 70.
[2] De Lolme on Const. B. 2, ch. 1.

be submitted to, in the formation of the legislature. But it is unwise, as well as unnecessary, in the constitution of the executive. In the legislature promptitude of decision is not of great importance. It is more often an evil, than a benefit. Differences of opinion in that department may, indeed, sometimes retard salutary measures; but they often lead to more circumspection and deliberation, and to more perfection and accuracy in the laws. A resolution, once passed by a legislative body, becomes a law; and opposition to it is either illegal or impolitic. Before it becomes a law, opposition may diminish the mischiefs, or increase the good of the measure. But no favourable circumstances palliate, or atone for the disadvantages of dissension in the executive department. The evils are here pure and unmixed. They embarrass and weaken every plan, to which they relate, from the first step to the final conclusion. They constantly counteract the most important ingredients in the executive character, vigour, expedition, and certainty of operation. In peace, distraction of the executive councils is sufficiently alarming and mischievous. But in war, it prostrates all energy, and all security. It brings triumph to the enemy, and disgrace to the country.[1]

---

1 The Federalist, No. 70. — The learned commentator on Blackstone's Commentaries was of opinion, that an executive composed of a single delegate of each state, like the " committee of congress" under the confederation, would have been better, than a single chief magistrate for the Union. If such a scheme had prevailed, we should have had at this time an executive magistracy of twenty-four persons. See 1 Tuck. Black. Comm. App. 349, 350. Surely the experience of the country, under the confederation, must have been wholly forgotten, when this scheme approved itself to the judgment of the proposer. Mr. Jefferson has told us in an emphatic manner, that the " committee of congress immediately fell into schisms and dissensions, which became at length so inveterate, as to render all co-operation among them impracticable. They dissolved themselves,

§ 1419. Objections of a like nature apply, though in some respects with diminished force, to the scheme of an executive council, whose constitutional concurrence is rendered indispensable. An artful cabal in that council would be able to distract and enervate the whole public councils. And even without such a cabal, the mere diversity of views and opinions would almost always mark the exercise of the executive authority with a spirit of habitual feebleness and dilatoriness, or a degrading inconsistency.[1] But an objection, in a republican government quite as weighty, is, that such a participation in the executive power has a direct tendency to conceal faults, and destroy responsibility. Responsibility is of two kinds, to censure, and to punishment. The first is the more important of the two, especially in an elective government. Men in public trust will more often act in such a manner, as to render them unworthy of public favour, than to render themselves liable to legal punishment. But the multiplication of voices in the business of the executive renders it difficult to fix responsibility of either kind; for it is perpetually shifted from one to another. It often becomes impossible amidst mutual accusations to determine, upon whom the blame ought to rest.[4] A sense of mutual impropriety sometimes induces the parties to resort to plausible pretexts to disguise their misconduct; or a dread of public responsibility to cover up,

---

abandoning the helm of government; and it continued without a head, until congress met, in the ensuing winter. This was then imputed to the temper of two or three individuals. *But the wise ascribed it to the nature of man.*" 4 Jefferson's Corresp. 161.

[1] The Federalist, No. 70.

[2] The Federalist, No. 70; 3 Elliot's Deb. 99, 100, 103; Id. 272; 1 Kent's Comm. Lect. 13, p. 253, 254.

under the lead of some popular demagogue, their own
faults and vacillations. — Thus, a council often becomes
the means, either of shifting off all effective responsibility from the chief magistrate, or of intrigues and
oppositions, which destroy his power, and supplant his
influence.   The constant excuse, for want of decision
and public spirit on his part, will be, that he has been
overruled by his council; and on theirs, that he would
not listen to sound advice, or resisted a cordial co-operation.   In regard to the ordinary operations of government, the general result is to introduce a system of
bargaining and management into the executive councils ; and an equally mischievous system of corruption
and intrigue in the choice and appointment of counsel-
lors.   Offices are bestowed on unworthy persons to
gratify a leading member, or mutual concessions are
made to cool opposition, and disarm enmity.   It is but
too true, that in those states, where executive councils
exist, the chief magistrate either sinks into comparative
insignificance, or sustains his power by arrangements,
neither honourable to himself, nor salutary to the people.
He is sometimes compelled to follow, when he ought to
lead ; and he is sometimes censured for acts, over which
he has no control, and for appointments to office, which
have been wrung from him by a sort of political necessity.[1]

§ 1420. The proper conclusion to be drawn from
these considerations is, that plurality in the executive
deprives the people of the two greatest securities for the
faithful exercise of delegated power.   First, it removes
the just restraints of public opinion ; and, secondly, it
diminishes the means, as well as the power, of fixing
responsibility for bad measures upon the real authors.[2]

[1] The Federalist, No. 70.
[2] The Federalist, No. 70 ; 1 Kent's Comm. Lect. 13, p. 253, 254 ;
1 Tuck. Black. Comm. App. 318, 319 ; 3 Elliot's Deb. 99, 100.

§ 1421. The case of the king of Great Britain is adduced, as a proof the other way; but it is a case wholly inapplicable to the circumstances of our republic. In Great Britain there is an hereditary magistrate; and it is a settled maxim in that government, that he can do no wrong; the true meaning of which is, that, for the sake of the public peace, he shall not be accountable for his administration of public affairs, and his person shall be sacred. In that kingdom it is, therefore, wise, that he should have a constitutional council, at once to advise him in regard to measures, and to become responsible for those measures. In no other way could any responsibility be brought home to the executive department. Still the king is not bound by the advice of his council. He is the absolute master of his own conduct; and the only alternative left to the ministry is, to compel him to follow their advice, or to resign the administration of the government. In the American republic the case is wholly different. The executive magistrate is chosen by, and made responsible to, the people; and, therefore, it is most fit, that he should have the exclusive management of the affairs, for which he is thus made responsible. In short, the reason for a council in Great Britain is the very reason for rejecting it in America. The object, in such case, is to secure executive energy and responsibility. In Great Britain it is secured by a council. In America it would be defeated by one.[1]

§ 1422. The idea of a council to the executive, which has prevailed to so great an extent in the state constitutions, has, without doubt, been derived from that

---

[1] The Federalist, No. 70. See Rawle on Const. ch. 12, p. 147 to 150; North Amer. Review, Oct. 1827, p. 264, 265.

maxim of republican jealousy, which considers power as safer in the hands of a number of men, than of a single man. It is a misapplication of a known rule, that in the multitude of counsel there is safety. If it were even admitted, that the maxim is justly applicable to the executive magistracy, there are disadvantages on the other side, which greatly overbalance it. But in truth, all multiplication of the executive is rather dangerous, than friendly to liberty; and it is more safe to have a single object for the jealousy and watchfulness of the people, than many.[1] It is in the highest degree probable, that the peculiar situation, in which the American states were placed antecedently to the revolution, with colonial governors placed over them by the crown, and irresponsible to themselves, gave a sanction to the opinion of the value of an executive council, and of the dangers of a single magistrate, wholly disproportionate to its importance, and inconsistent with the permanent safety and dignity of an elective republic.[2]

§ 1423. Upon the question, whether the executive should be composed of a single person, we have already seen, that there was, at first, a division of opinion in the convention, which framed the constitution, seven states voting in the affirmative, and three in the negative; ultimately, however, the vote was unanimous in its favour.[3] But the project of an executive council was not so easily dismissed. It was renewed at different periods in various forms; and seems to have been finally, though

[1] The Federalist, No. 70; 1 Kent's Comm. Lect. 13, p. 253, 254; 3 Elliot's Deb. 99, 100.

[2] Mr. Chancellor Kent has, in his Commentaries, condensed the whole pith of the argument into two paragraphs of great brevity and clearness. 1 Kent's Comm. Lect. 13, p. 253, 254. See also Rawle on Const. ch. 12, p. 147, &c. 1 Tuck. Black. Comm. App. 316 to 318.

[3] Journal of Convention, p. 95, 96; Id. 183.

indirectly, disposed of by the vote of eight states against three.[1] The reasoning, which led to this conclusion, is understood to have been that, which has been already stated, and which is most elaborately expounded in the Federalist.[2]

§ 1424. The question as to the unity of the executive being disposed of, the next consideration is, as to the proper duration of his term of office. It has been already mentioned, that duration in office constitutes an essential requisite to the energy of the executive department. This has relation to two objects; first, the personal firmness of the chief magistrate in the employment of his constitutional powers; and, secondly, the stability of the system of administration, which may have been adopted under his auspices. With regard to the first, it is evident, that the longer the duration in office, the greater will be the probability of obtaining so important an advantage. A man will naturally be interested in whatever he possesses, in proportion to the firmness or precariousness of the tenure, by which he holds it. He will be less attached to what he holds by a momentary, or uncertain title, than to what he enjoys by a title durable, or certain; and of course he will be willing to risk more for the one, than for the other. This remark is not less applicable to political privilege, or honour, or trust, than to any article of ordinary property. A chief magistrate, acting under the consciousness, that in a very short time he must lay down office, will be apt to feel himself too little interested in it to hazard any material censure or perplexity from an independent exercise of his powers, or from those ill hu-

1 Journ. of Convention, p. 69, 104, 265, 278, 340, 341. See also 2 Amer. Museum, 435, 534, 537.
2 The Federalist, No. 70; 3 Elliot's Deb. 100.

mours, which are apt at times to prevail in all governments.   If the case should be, that he should, notwithstanding, be re-eligible, his wishes, if he should have
any for office, would combine with his fears to debase
his fortitude, or weaken his integrity, or enhance his
irresolution.[1]

§ 1425.   There are some, perhaps, who may be inclined to regard a servile pliancy of the executive to a
prevalent faction, or opinion in the community, or in the
legislature, as its best recommendation.   But such notions betray a very imperfect knowledge of the true
ends and objects of government.   While republican
principles demand, that the deliberate sense of the
community should govern the conduct of those, who
administer their affairs, it cannot escape observation,
that transient impulses and sudden excitements, caused
by artful and designing men, often lead the people
astray, and require their rulers not to yield up their
permanent interests to any delusions of this sort.   It is
a just observation, that the people commonly intend the
public good.   But no one, but a deceiver, will pretend,
that they do not often err, as to the best means of promoting it.   Indeed, beset, as they are, by the wiles of
sycophants, the snares of the ambitious and the avaricious, and the artifices of those, who possess their confidence more, than they deserve, or seek to possess it
by artful appeals to their prejudices, the wonder rather
is, that their errors are not more numerous and more
mischievous.   It is the duty of their rulers to resist
such bad designs at all hazards ; and it has not unfrequently happened, that by such resistance they have
saved the people from fatal mistakes, and, in their moments of cooler reflection, obtained their gratitude and

---

[1] The Federalist, No. 71.

their reverence.[1] But how can resistance be expected, where the tenure of office is so short, as to make it ineffectual and insecure?

§ 1426. The same considerations apply with increased force to the legislature. If the executive department were to be subservient to the wishes of the legislature, at all times and under all circumstances, the whole objects of a partition of the powers of government would be defeated. To what purpose would it be to separate the executive and judiciary from the legislature, if both are to be so constituted, as to be at the absolute devotion of the latter? It is one thing to be subordinate to the laws; and quite a different thing to be dependent upon the legislative body. The first comports with, the last violates, the fundamental principles of good government; and, in fact, whatever may be the form of the constitution, the last unites all power in the same hands. The tendency of the legislative authority to absorb every other has been already insisted on at large in the preceding part of these Commentaries, and need not here be further illustrated. In governments purely republican it has been seen, that this tendency is almost irresistible. The representatives of the people are but too apt to imagine, that they are the people themselves; and they betray strong symptoms of impatience and even disgust at the least resistance from any other quarter. They seem to think the exercise of its proper rights by the executive, or the judiciary, to be a breach of their privileges, and an impeachment of their wisdom.[2] If, therefore, the executive is

---

[1] The Federalist, No. 71.

[2] The Federalist, No. 71; Id. No. 73; Id. No. 51. — Mr. Jefferson says, "The executive in our governments is not the sole, it is scarcely the principal object of my jealousy. The tyranny of the legislatures is the most formidable dread at present, and will be for many years. That

to constitute an effective, independent branch of the government, it is indispensable to give it some permanence of duration in office, and some motive for a firm exercise of its powers.

§ 1427. The other ground, that of stability in the system of administration, is still more strikingly connected with duration in office. Few men will be found willing to commit themselves to a course of policy, whose wisdom may be perfectly clear to themselves, if they cannot be permitted to complete, what they have begun. Of what consequence will it be to form the best plans of executive administration, if they are perpetually passing into new hands, before they are matured, or may be defeated at the moment, when their reasonableness and their value cannot be understood, or realized by the public? One of the truest rewards to patriots and statesmen is the consciousness, that the objections raised against their measures will disappear upon a fair trial; and that the gratitude and affection the people will follow their labours, long after they have ceased to be actors upon the public scenes. But who will plant, when he can never reap? Who will sacrifice his present ease, and reputation, and popularity, and encounter obloquy and persecution, for systems, which he can neither mould so, as to ensure success, nor direct so, as to justify the experiment?

§ 1428. The natural result of a change of the head of the government will be a change in the course of administration, as well as a change in the subordinate persons, who are to act as ministers to the executive. A successor in office will feel little sympathy with the plans of his predecessor. To undo what has been

of the Executive will come in its turn ; but it will be at a remote period."
2 Jefferson's Corresp. 443.

done by the latter will be supposed to give proofs of his own capacity ; and will recommend him to all those, who were adversaries of the past administration ; and perhaps will constitute the main grounds of elevating him to office. Personal pride, party princi-ples, and an ambition for public distinction will thus naturally prompt to an abandonment of old schemes, and combine with that love of novelty so congenial to all free states, to make every new administration the founders of new systems of government.[1]

§ 1429. What should be the proper duration of office is matter of more doubt and speculation. On the one hand, it may be said, that the shorter the period of office, the more security there will be against any dangerous abuse of power. The longer the period, the less will responsibility be felt, and the more personal ambition will be indulged. On the other hand, the considerations above stated prove, that a very short period is, practically speaking, equivalent to a surrender of the executive power, as a check in government, or subjects it to an intolerable vacillation and imbecility. In the convention itself much diversity of opinion existed on this subject. It was at one time proposed, that the executive should be chosen during good be-haviour. But this proposition received little favour, and seems to have been abandoned without much effort.[2]

---

1 The Federalist, No 72.

2 This plan, whatever may now be thought of its value, was at the time supported by some of the purest patriots. Mr. Hamilton, Mr. Madison, and Mr. Jay were among the number. North American Review, Oct. 1827, p. 263, 264, 266 ; Journal of Convention, p. 130, 131, 185 ; 2 Pitk. Hist. 259, note. Mr. Hamilton, (it seems) at a subsequent period of the convention, changed his opinion on account of the increased danger to the public tranquillity, incident to the election of a magistrate to this

§ 1430. Another proposition was (as has been seen) to choose the executive for seven years, which at first passed by a bare majority ; [1] but being coupled with a clause, " to be chosen by the national legislature," it was approved by the vote of eight states against two.[2] Another clause, " to be ineligible a second time," was added by the vote of eight states against one, one being divided.[3] In this form the clause stood in the first draft of the constitution, though some intermediate efforts were made to vary it.[4] But it was ultimately altered upon the report of a committee so, as to change the mode of election, the term of office, and the re-eligibility, to their present form, by the vote of ten states against one.[5]

§ 1431. It is most probable, that these three propositions had a mutual influence upon the final vote. Those, who wished a choice to be made by the people, rather than by the national legislature, would naturally incline to a shorter period of office, than seven years. Those, who were in favour of seven years, might be willing to consent to the clause against re-eligibility, when they would resist it, if the period of office were reduced to four years.[6] And those, who favoured the latter, might more readily yield the prohibitory clause, than increase the duration of office. All this, however, is but conjecture ; and the most, that can be gathered

degree of permanency. 2 Pitk. Hist. 259, 260, note. Possibly, the same change may have occurred in the opinions of others. — Journal of Convention, p. 130, 131.

[1] Journal of Convention, p. 90.
[2] Id. 92, 136, 224, 225; Id. 286, 287.
[3] Id. 94, 204.
[4] Journal of Convention, 190, 191 to 196, 200 ; Id. 286, 287, 288.
[5] Id 225, 324, 330, 332, 337. See 2 Jefferson's Correspondence, p. 64, 65 ; 2 Pitk. Hist. 252, 253 ; Journal of Convention, 288, 289.
[6] See 1 Jefferson's Correspondence, p. 64, 65.

from the final result, is, that opinions, strongly maintained at the beginning of the discussion, were yielded
up in a spirit of compromise, or abandoned upon the
weight of argument.[1]

§ 1432. It is observable, that the period actually
fixed is intermediate between the term of office of the
senate, and that of the house of representatives. In the
course of one presidential term, the house is, or may be,
twice recomposed; and two-thirds of the senate changed, or re-elected. So far, as executive influence can be
presumed to operate upon either branch of the legislature unfavourably to the rights of the people, the latter
possess, in their elective franchise, ample means of
redress. On the other hand, so far, as uniformity and
stability in the administration of executive duties are
desirable, they are in some measure secured by the
more permanent tenure of office of the senate, which
will check too hasty a departure from the old system,
by a change of the executive, or representative branch
of the government.[2]

---

[1] 3 Elliot's Debates, 99, 100; 2 Id. 358; 1 Jefferson's Correspondence, 64, 65.

[2] Doctor Paley has condemned all elective monarchies, and, indeed,
all elective chief magistrates. " The confession of every writer on the
subject of civil government," says he, " the experience of ages, the
example of Poland, and of the Papal Dominions, seem to place this
amongst the few indubitable maxims, which the science of government
admits of. A crown is too splendid a prize to be conferred upon merit.
The passions, or interests of the electors, exclude all consideration of the
qualities of the competitors. The same observation holds concerning
the appointments to any office, which is attended with a great share of
power or emolument. Nothing is gained by a popular choice worth
the dissensions, tumults, and interruptions of regular industry, with
which it is inseparably attended." (Paley's Moral Philosophy, B. 6, ch.
7, p. 367.) Mr. Chancellor Kent has also remarked, that it is a curious
fact in European history, that on the first partition of Poland in 1773,
when the partitioning powers thought it expedient to foster and confirm
all the defects of its wretched government, they sagaciously demanded

§ 1433. Whether the period of four years will answer all the purposes, for which the executive department is established, so as to give it at once energy and safety, and to preserve a due balance in the administration of the government, is a problem, which can be solved only by experience. That it will contribute far more, than a shorter period, towards these objects, and thus have a material influence upon the spirit and character of the government, may be safely affirmed.[1] Between the commencement and termination of the period of office, there will be a considerable interval, at once to justify some independence of opinion and action, and some reasonable belief, that the propriety of the measures adopted during the administration may be seen, and felt by the community at large. The executive need not be intimidated in his course by the dread of an immediate loss of public confidence, without the power of regaining it before a new election ; and he may, with some confidence, look forward to that esteem and respect of his fellow-citizens, which public services usually obtain, when they are faithfully and firmly pursued with an honest devotion to the public good. If he should be re-elected, he will still more extensively possess the means of carrying into effect a wise and beneficent system of policy, foreign as well as domestic. And if he should be compelled to retire, he cannot but have the consciousness, that measures, long enough pursued to be found useful, will be persevered in; or, if abandoned, the contrast will reflect

---

of the Polish Diet, that the crown should continue elective.   1 Kent. Comm. Lect. 13, p. 256.   America has indulged the proud hope, that she shall avoid every danger of this sort, and escape at once from the evils of an hereditary, and of an elective monarchy.   Who, that loves liberty, does not wish success to her efforts?

[1] The Federalist, No. 71.

new honour upon the past administration of the government, and perhaps reinstate him in office. At all events, the period is not long enough to justify any alarms for the public safety.[1] The danger is not, that such a limited executive will become an absolute dictator; but, that he may be overwhelmed by the combined operations of popular influence and legislative power. It may be reasonably doubted, from the limited duration of this office, whether, in point of independence and firmness, he will not be found unequal to the task, which the constitution assigns him; and if such a doubt may be indulged, that alone will be decisive against any just jealousy of his encroachments.[2] Even in England, where an hereditary monarch with vast prerogatives and patronage exists, it has been found, that the house of commons, from their immediate sympathy with the people, and their possession of the purse-strings of the nation, have been able effectually to check all his usurpations, and to diminish his inflence. Nay, from small beginnings they have risen to be the great power in the state, counterpoising not only the authority of the crown, but the rank and wealth of the nobility; and gaining so solid an accession of influence, that they rather lead, than follow, the great measures of the administration.[3]

§ 1434. In comparing the duration of office of the president with that of the state executives, additional reasons will present themselves in favour of the former. At the time of the adoption of the constitution, the executive was chosen annually in some of the states; in others, biennially; and in others, triennially. In some

---

[1] 1 Tuck. Black. Comm. App. 318; Rawle on Const. ch. 31, p. 287 to 290.

[2] The Federalist, No. 71.

[3] The Federalist, No. 71.

of the states, which have been subsequently admitted
into the Union, the executive is chosen annually ; in
others, biennially ; in others, triennially ; and in others,
quadriennially. So that there is a great diversity of
opinion exhibited on the subject, not only in the early,
but in the later state constitutions in the Union.[1] Now,
it may be affirmed, that if, considering the nature of
executive duties in the state governments, a period of
office of two, or three, or even four years, has not been
found either dangerous or inconvenient, there are
very strong reasons, why the duration of office of the
president of the United States should be at least equal
to the longest of these periods. The nature of the
duties to be performed by the president, both at home
and abroad, are so various and complicated, as not only to
require great talents, and great wisdom to perform them
in any manner suitable to their importance and difficulty ;
but also long experience in office to acquire, what may
be deemed the habits of administration, and a steadiness,
as well as comprehensiveness, of view of all the bearings
of measures. The executive duties in the states are
few, and confined to a narrow range. Those of the
president embrace all the ordinary and extraordinary
arrangements of peace and war, of diplomacy and
negotiation, of finance, of naval and military operations,
and of the execution of the laws through almost infinite
ramifications of details, and in places at vast distances
from each other.[2] He is compelled constantly to take
into view the whole circuit of the Union ; and to master
many of the local interests and other circumstances,
which may require new adaptations of measures to meet

1 4 Elliot's Debates, App. 557 ; Dr. Leiber's Encyclopædia Americana, Art., *Constitutions* ; The Federalist, No. 39.
2 The Federalist, No. 72.

the public exigences. Considerable time must necessarily elapse before the requisite knowledge for the proper discharge of all the functions of his office can be obtained; and, after it is obtained, time must be allowed to enable him to act upon that knowledge so, as to give vigour and healthinesss to the operations of the government. A short term of office would scarcely suffice, either for suitable knowledge, or suitable action. And to say the least, four years employed in the executive functions of the Union would not enable any man to become more familiar with them, than half that period with those of a single state.[1] In short, the same general considerations, which require and justify a prolongation of the period of service of the members of the national legislature beyond that of the members of the state legislatures, apply with full force to the executive department. There have, nevertheless, at different periods of the government, been found able and ingenious minds, who have contended for an annual election of the president, or some shorter period, than four years.[2]

§ 1435. Hitherto our experience has demonstrated, that the period has not been found practically so long, as to create danger to the people, or so short, as to take away a reasonable independence and energy from the executive. Still it cannot be disguised, that sufficient

---

[1] 1 Kent. Comm. Lect. 13, p. 262.

[2] Mr. Senator Hillhouse, in April, 1808, proposed an annual election, among other amendments to the constitution; and defended the proposition in a very elaborate speech. The amendment, however, found no support. See Hillhouse's Speech, 12th April, 1808, printed at New Haven, by O. Steele & Co. The learned editor of Blackstone's Commentaries manifestly thought a more frequent election, than once in four years, desirable. 1 Tuck. Black. Comm. App. 328, 329.

time has scarcely yet elapsed to enable us to pronounce
a decisive opinion upon the subject; since the executive
has generally acted with a majority of the nation; and
in critical times has been sustained by the force of that
majority in strong measures, and in times of more
tranquillity, by the general moderation of the policy of
his administration.

§ 1436. Another question, connected with the duration of office of the president, was much agitated in
the convention, and has often since been a topic of
serious discussion; and that is, whether he should be
re-eligible to office. In support of the opinion, that
the president ought to be ineligible after one period
of office, it was urged, that the return of public officers
into the mass of the common people, where they would
feel the tone, which they had given to the administration
of the laws, was the best security the public could
have for their good behaviour. It would operate as
a check upon the restlessness of ambition, and at
the same time promote the independence of the executive. It would prevent him from a cringing subserviency to procure a re-election; or to a resort to
corrupt intrigues for the maintenance of his power.[1]
And it was even added by some, whose imaginations
were continually haunted by terrors of all sorts from the
existence of any powers in the national government,
that the re-eligibility of the executive would furnish an
inducement to foreign governments to interfere in our
elections, and would thus inflict upon us all the evils,
which had desolated, and betrayed Poland.[2]

[1] 3 Elliot's Debates, 99; Rawle on Const. ch. 31, p. 283; The Federalist, No. 72.
[2] See 2 Elliot's Debates, 357; Rawle on Const. ch. 31, p. 283.

§ 1437. In opposition to these suggestions it was stated, that one ill effect of the exclusion would be a diminution of the inducements to good behaviour. There are few men, who would not feel much less zeal in the discharge of a duty, when they were conscious, that the advantage of the station, with which it is connected, must be relinquished at a determinate period, than when they were permitted to entertain a hope of obtaining by their merit a continuance of it. A desire of reward is one of the strongest incentives of human conduct; and the best security for the fidelity of mankind is to make interest coincide with duty. Even the love of fame, the ruling passion of the noblest minds, will scarcely prompt a man to undertake extensive and arduous enterprises, requiring considerable time to mature and perfect, if they may be taken from his management before their accomplishment, or be liable to failure in the hands of a successor. The most, under such circumstances, which can be expected of the generality of mankind, is the negative merit of not doing harm, instead of the positive merit of doing good.[1] Another ill effect of the exclusion would be the temptation to sordid views, to peculation, to the corrupt gratification of favourites, and in some instances to usurpation. A selfish or avaricious executive might, under such circumstances, be disposed to make the most he could for himself, and his friends, and partisans, during his brief continuance in office, and to introduce a system of official patronage and emoluments, at war with the public interests, but well adapted to his own. If he were vain and ambitious, as well as avaricious and selfish, the transient possession of his honours would

---

[1] The Federalist, No. 72 ; 3 Elliot's Deb. 99 ; Id. 358.

depress the former passions, and give new impulses to the latter.   He would dread the loss of gain more, than the loss of fame; since the power must drop from his hands too soon to ensure any substantial addition to his reputation.[1]   On the other hand, his very ambition, as well as his avarice, might tempt him to usurpation; since the chance of impeachment would scarcely be worthy of thought; and the present power of serving friends might easily surround him with advocates for every stretch of authority, which would flatter his vanity, or administer to their necessities.

§ 1438.   Another ill effect of the exclusion would be depriving the community of the advantage of the experience, gained by an able chief magistrate in the exercise of office.   Experience is the parent of wisdom. And it would seem almost absurd to say, that it ought systematically to be excluded from the executive office. It would be equivalent to banishing merit from the public councils, because it had been tried.   What could be more strange, than to declare, at the moment, when wisdom was acquired, that the possessor of it should no longer be enabled to use it for the very purposes, for which it was acquired?[2]

§ 1439.   Another ill effect of the exclusion would be, that it might banish men from the station in certain emergencies, in which their services might be eminently useful, and indeed almost indispensable for the safety of their country.   There is no nation, which has not at some period or other in its history felt an absolute necessity of the services of particular men in particular stations; and perhaps it is not too much to say, as vital to the preservation of its political exist-

---

[1] The Federalist, No. 72; 2 Elliot's Debates, 358.
[2] The Federalist, No. 72; 3 Elliot's Debates, 99, 100.

ence. In a time of war, or other pressing calamity, the
very confidence of a nation in the tried integrity and
ability of a single man may of itself ensure a triumph.
Is it wise to substitute in such cases inexperience for
experience, and to set afloat public opinion, and change
the settled course of administration?[1] One should
suppose, that it would be sufficient to possess the right
to change a bad magistrate, without making the singular merit of a good one the very ground of excluding
him from office.

§ 1440. Another ground against the exclusion was
founded upon our own experience under the state governments of the utility and safety of the re-eligibility of
the executive. In some of the states the executive is
re-eligible; in others he is not. But no person has been
able to point out any circumstance in the administration of the state governments unfavourable to a re-election of the chief magistrate, where the right has constitutionally existed. If there had been any practical
evil, it must have been seen and felt. And the common practice of continuing the executive in office in
some of these states, and of displacing in others, demonstrates, that the people are not sensible of any
abuse, and use their power with a firm and unembar-
rassed freedom at the elections.

§ 1441. It was added, that the advantages proposed
by the exclusion, (1.) greater independence in the executive, (2.) greater security to the people, were not
well founded. The former could not be attained in
any moderate degree, unless the exclusion was made
perpetual. And, if it were, there might be many motives to induce the executive to sacrifice his indepen-

---

[1] The Federalist, No. 72; 2 Elliot's Debates, 99, 100.

dence to friends, to partisans, to selfish objects, and private gain, to the fear of enemies, and the desire to stand well with majorities. As to the latter supposed advantage, the exclusion would operate no check upon a man of irregular ambition, or corrupt principles, and against such men alone could the exclusion be important. In truth, such men would easily find means to cover up their usurpations and dishonesty under fair pretensions, and mean subserviency to popular prejudices. They would easily delude the people into a belief, that their acts were constitutional, because they were in harmony with the public wishes, or held out some specious, but false projects for the public good.

§ 1442. Most of this reasoning would apply, though with diminished force, to the exclusion for a limited period, or until after the lapse of an intermediate election to the office. And it would have equally diminished advantages, with respect both to personal independence, and public security. In short, the exclusion, whether perpetual or temporary, would have nearly the same effects; and these effects would be generally pernicious, rather than salutary.[1] Re-eligibility naturally connects itself to a certain extent with duration of office. The latter is necessary to give the officer himself the inclination and the resolution to act his part well, and the community time and leisure to observe the tendency of his measures, and thence to form an experimental estimate of his merits. The former is necessary to enable the people, when they see reason to approve of his conduct, to continue him in the station, in order to prolong the utility of his virtues and

[1] The Federalist, No. 72; Rawle on the Const. ch. 31, p. 288, 289.

talents, and to secure to the government the advantage of permanence in a wise system of administration.[1]

§ 1443. Still it must be confessed, that where the duration is for a considerable length of time, the right of re-election becomes less important, and perhaps less safe to the public. A president chosen for ten years might be made ineligible with far less impropriety, than one chosen for four years. And a president chosen for twenty years ought not to be again eligible, upon the plain ground, that by such a term of office his responsibility would be greatly diminished, and his means of influence and patronage immensely increased, so as to check in a great measure the just expression of public opinion, and the free exercise of the elective franchise. Whether an intermediate period, say of eight years, or of seven years, as proposed in the convention, might not be beneficially combined with subsequent ineligibility, is a point, upon which great statesmen have not been agreed; and must be left to the wisdom of future legislators to weigh and decide.[2] The

---

[1] The Federalist, No. 72.

[2] Mr. Jefferson appears to have entertained the opinion strongly, that the chief magistrate ought to be ineligible after one term of office. "Reason and experience tell us," says he, "that the chief magistrate will always be re-elected, if he may be re-elected. He is then an officer for life. This once observed, it becomes of so much consequence to certain nations to have a friend or a foe at the head of our affairs, that they will interfere with money and with arms, &c. The election of a president of America some years hence will be much more interesting to certain nations of Europe, than ever the election of a king of Poland was." (Letter to Mr. Madison in 1787, 2 Jeffer. Cor. 274, 275.) He added in the same letter: "The power of removing every fourth year by the vote of the people is a power, which they will not exercise; and if they were disposed to exercise it, they would not be permitted."* How little has this reasoning accorded with the fact!! In the memoir written by him towards the close of his life, he says: "My wish was, that the president

* See also 2 Jefferson's Corresp. 291, 439, 410, 443.

inconvenience of such frequently recurring elections of
the chief magistrate, by generating factions, combining
intrigues, and agitating the public mind, seems not
hitherto to have attracted as much attention, as it deserves. One of two evils may possibly occur from this
source; either a constant state of excitement, which
will prevent the fair operation of the measures of an
administration; or a growing indifference to the election, both on the part of candidates and the people,
which will surrender it practically into the hands of the
selfish, the office-seekers, and the unprincipled devo-
tees of power. It has been justly remarked by Mr.
Chancellor Kent, that the election of a supreme executive magistrate for a whole nation affects so many interests, addresses itself so strongly to popular passions,
and holds out such powerful temptations to ambition,
that it necessarily becomes a strong trial to public virtue, and even hazardous to the public tranquillity.[1]

§ 1444. The remaining part of the clause respects
the Vice-President. If such an officer was to be created, it is plain, that the duration of his office should
be co-extensive with that of the president. Indeed, as
we shall immediately see, the scheme of the government necessarily embraced it; for when it was decided,
that two persons were to be voted for, as president, it
was decided, that he, who had the greatest number of

should be elected for seven years, and be ineligible afterwards. This
term I thought sufficient to enable him, with the concurrence of the legislature, to carry through and establish any system of improvement he
should propose for the general good. But the practice adopted, I think,
is better, allowing his continuance for eight years, with a liability to be
dropped at half way of the term, making that a period of probation."
1 Jefferson's Corresp. 64, 65. See also 1 Tucker's Black. Comm. App.
328, 329.
[1] 1 Kent's Comm. Lect. 13, p. 257.

votes of the electors, after the person chosen as president, should be vice-president. The principal question, therefore, was, whether such an officer ought to be created. It has been already stated, that the original scheme of the government did not provide for such an officer. By that scheme, the president was to be chosen by the national legislature.[1] When afterwards an election by electors, chosen directly or indirectly by the people, was proposed by a select committee, the choice of a vice-president constituted a part of the proposition; and it was finally adopted by the vote of ten states against one.[2]

§ 1445. The appointment of a vice-president was objected to, as unnecessary and dangerous. As president of the senate, he would be entrusted with a power to control the proceedings of that body; and as he must come from some one of the states, that state would have a double vote in the body. Besides, it was said, that if the president should die, or be removed, the vice-president might, by his influence, prevent the election of a president. But, at all events, he was a superfluous officer, having few duties to perform, and those might properly devolve upon some other established officer of the government.[3]

§ 1446. The reasons in favour of the appointment were, in part, founded upon the same ground as the objections. It was seen, that a presiding officer must be chosen for the senate, where all the states were equally represented, and where an extreme jealousy might naturally be presumed to exist of the preponder-

1 Journal of Convention, 68, 92, 136, 224.
2 Journal of Convention, 323, 324, 333, 337.
3 See 2 Elliot's Deb. 359, 361 ; The Federalist, No. 68.

ating influence of any one state. If a member of the senate were appointed, either the state would be deprived of one vote, or would enjoy a double vote in case of an equality of votes, or there would be a tie, and no decision. Each of these alternatives was equally undesirable, and might lay the foundation of great practical inconveniences. An officer, therefore, chosen by the whole Union, would be a more suitable person to preside, and give a casting vote, since he would be more free, than any member of the senate, from local attachments, and local interests; and being the representative of the Union, would naturally be induced to consult the interests of all the states.[1] Having only a casting vote, his influence could only operate exactly, when most beneficial; that is, to procure a decision. A still more important consideration is the necessity of providing some suitable person to perform the executive functions, when the president is unable to perform them, or is removed from office. Every reason, which recommends the mode of election of the president, prescribed by the constitution, with a view either to dignity, independence, or personal qualifications for office, applies with equal force to the appointment of his substitute. He is to perform the same duties, and to possess the same rights; and it seems, if not indispensable, at least peculiarly proper, that the choice of the person, who should succeed to the executive functions, should belong to the people at large, rather than to a select body chosen for another purpose. If (as was suggested) the president of the senate, chosen by that body, might have been designated, as the constitutional substitute; it is

---

[1] 3 Elliot's Deb. 37, 38, 51, 52; The Federalist, No. 68.

by no means certain, that he would either possess so high qualifications, or enjoy so much public confidence, or feel so much responsibility for his conduct, as a vice-president selected directly by and from the people. The president of the senate would generally be selected from other motives, and with reference to other qualifications, than what ordinarily belonged to the executive department. His political opinions might be in marked contrast with those of a majority of the nation; and while he might possess a just influence in the senate, as a presiding officer, he might be deemed wholly unfit for the various duties of the chief executive magistrate. In addition to these considerations, there was no novelty in the appointment of such an officer for similar purposes in some of the state governments;[1] and it therefore came recommended by experience, as a safe and useful arrangement, to guard the people against the inconveniences of an interregnum in the government, or a devolution of power upon an officer, who was not their choice, and might not possess their confidence.

§ 1447. The next clause embraces the mode of election of the President and Vice-President; and although it has been repealed by an amendment of the constitution, (as will be hereafter shown,) yet it still deserves consideration, as a part of the original scheme, and more especially, as very grave doubts have been entertained, whether the substitute is not inferior in wisdom and convenience.

§ 1448. The clause is as follows: " Each state " shall appoint in such manner, as the legislature there- " of may direct, a number of electors, equal to the

---

1 The Federalist, No. 68.

" whole number of senators and representatives, to
" which the state may be entitled in the congress. But
" no senator, or representative, or person holding an
" office of trust or profit under the United States, shall
" be appointed an elector.

" The electors shall meet in their respective states,
" and vote by ballot for two persons, of whom one at
" least shall not be an inhabitant of the same state with
" themselves. And they shall make a list of all the
" persons voted for, and of the number of votes for each;
" which list they shall sign and certify, and transmit,
" sealed, to the seat of the government of the United
" States, directed to the president of the senate. The
" president of the senate shall, in the presence of the
" senate and house of representatives, open all the cer-
" tificates, and the votes shall then be counted. The
" person having the greatest number of votes shall be
" the president, if such number be a majority of the
" whole number of electors appointed; and if there be
" more than one, who have such majority and have an
" equal number of votes, then the house of representa-
" tives shall immediately choose by ballot one of them
" for president; and if no person have a majority, then
" from the five highest on the list the said house shall
" in like manner choose the president. But in choos-
" ing the president, the votes shall be taken by states,
" the representation from each state having one vote;
" a quorum for this purpose shall consist of a member
" or members from two-thirds of the states, and a ma-
" jority of all the states shall be necessary to a choice.
" In every case, after the choice of the president, the
" person having the greatest number of votes of the
" electors shall be the vice-president. But if there
" should remain two or more, who have equal votes,

" the senate shall choose from them by ballot the vice-
"president."

§ 1449. It has been already remarked, that originally in the convention the choice of the president was,
by a vote of eight states against two, given to the national legislature.[1] This mode of appointment, however, does not seem to have been satisfactory ; for a
short time afterwards, upon a reconsideration of the
subject, it was voted, by six states against three, one
being divided, that the president should be chosen by
electors appointed for that purpose ; and by eight states
against two, that the electors should be chosen by the
legislatures of the states.[2] Upon a subsequent discussion, by the vote of seven states against four, the
choice was restored to the national legislature.[3] Towards the close of the convention the subject was
referred to a committee, who reported a scheme,
in many respects, as it now stands. The clause,
as to the mode of choice by electors, was carried, by
the vote of nine states against two ; that respecting the time, and place, and manner of voting of the
electors, by ten states against one ; that respecting
the choice by the house of representatives, in case no
choice was made by the people, by ten states against
one.[4]

§ 1450. One motive, which induced a change of the
choice of the president from the national legislature,
unquestionably was, to have the sense of the people

---

[1] Journal of Convention, 68, 92, 136, 224, 225 ; Id. 286, 287.

[2] Journal of Convention, 190, 191.

[3] Id. 200. See Id. 286, 287.

[4] Journal of Convention, 324, 333, 334, 335, 336, 337. — The committee of the convention reported in favour of a choice by *the senate*, in case
there was none by the people. Journal of Convention, 325.

operate in the choice of the person, to whom so important a trust was confided. This would be accomplished much more perfectly by committing the right of
choice to persons, selected for that sole purpose at the
particular conjuncture, instead of persons, selected for
the general purposes of legislation.[1] Another motive
was, to escape from those intrigues and cabals, which
would be promoted in the legislative body by artful
and designing men, long before the period of the choice,
with a view to accomplish their own selfish purposes.[2]
The very circumstance, that the body entrusted with
the power, was chosen long before the presidential
election, and for other general functions, would facilitate every plan to corrupt, or manage them. It would
be in the power of an ambitious candidate, by holding
out the rewards of office, or other sources of patronage
and honour, silently, but irresistibly to influence a majority of votes; and thus, by his own bold and unprincipled conduct, to secure a choice, to the exclusion of the
highest, and purest, and most enlightened men in the
country. Besides; the very circumstance of the possession of the elective power would mingle itself with
all the ordinary measures of legislation. Compromises
and bargains would be made, and laws passed, to gratify particular members, or conciliate particular interests; and thus a disastrous influence would be shed
over the whole policy of the government. The president would, in fact, become the mere tool of the dominant party in congress; and would, before he occupied
the seat, be bound down to an entire subserviency to
their views.[3] No measure would be adopted, which

---

[1] The Federalist, No. 68.   [2] 2 Wilson's Law Lect. 187.
[3] Rawle on the Constitution, ch. 5, p. 58.

was not, in some degree, connected with the presidential election; and no presidential election made, but what would depend upon artificial combinations, and a degrading favouritism.[1] There would be ample room for the same course of intrigues, which has made memorable the choice of a king in the Polish diet, of a chief in the Venetian senate, and of a pope in the sacred college of the Vatican.

§ 1451. Assuming that the choice ought not to be confided to the national legislature, there remained various other modes, by which it might be effected; by the people directly; by the state legislatures; or by electors, chosen by the one, or the other. The latter mode was deemed most advisable; and the reasoning, by which it was supported, was to the following effect. The immediate election should be made by men, the most capable of analyzing the qualities adapted to the station, and acting under circumstances favourable to deliberation, and to a judicious combination of all the inducements, which ought to govern their choice. A small number of persons, selected by their fellow citizens from the general mass for this special object, would be most likely to possess the information, and discernment, and independence, essential for the proper discharge of the duty.[2] It is also highly important to afford as little opportunity, as possible, to tumult and disorder. These evils are not unlikely to occur in the election of a chief magistrate directly by the people, considering the strong excitements and interests, which such an occasion may naturally be presumed to produce. The choice of a number of persons, to

---

[1] See 1 Kent's Comm. Lect. 13, p. 261, 262.
[2] The Federalist, No. 68.

form an intermediate body of electors, would be far
less apt to convulse the community with any extraordinary or violent movements, than the choice of one,
who was himself the final object of the public wishes.
And as the electors chosen in each state are to assemble, and vote in the state, in which they are chosen,
this detached and divided situation would expose
them much less to heats and ferments, which might be
communicated from them to the people, than if they
were all convened at one time in one place.[1] The
same circumstances would naturally lessen the dangers
of cabal, intrigue, and corruption, especially, if congress
should, as they undoubtedly would, prescribe the same
day for the choice of the electors, and for giving their
votes throughout the United States. The scheme,
indeed, presents every reasonable guard against these
fatal evils to republican governments. The appointment of the president is not made to depend upon any
pre-existing body of men, who might be tampered with
beforehand to prostitute their votes; but is delegated
to persons chosen by the immediate act of the people,
for that sole and temporary purpose. All those persons,
who, from their situation, might be suspected of too
great a devotion to the president in office, such as senators, and representatives, and other persons holding
offices of trust or profit under the United States, are
excluded from eligibility to the trust. Thus, without
corrupting the body of the people, the immediate agents
in the election may be fairly presumed to enter upon
their duty free from any sinister bias. Their transitory existence, and dispersed situation would present
formidable obstacles to any corrupt combinations; and

---

1 The Federalist, No. 68 : 1 Kent's Comm. Lect. 13, p. 261, 262.

time, as well as means, would be wanting to accomplish, by bribery or intrigue of any considerable number, a betrayal of their duty.[1] The president, too, who should be thus appointed, would be far more independent, than if chosen by a legislative body, to whom he might be expected to make correspondent sacrifices, to gratify their wishes, or reward their services.[2] And on the other hand, being chosen by the voice of the people, his gratitude would take the natural direction, and sedulously guard their rights.[3]

---

[1] The Federalist, No. 68 ; 1 Tuck. Black. Comm. App. 326, 327 ; 2 Wilson's Law Lect. 187, 188, 189.

[2] Id.

[3] In addition to these grounds, it has been suggested, that a still greater and more insuperable difficulty against a choice directly by the people, as a single community, was, that such a measure would be an entire consolidation of the government of the country, and an annihilation of the state sovereignties, so far as concerned the organization of the executive department of the Union. This was not to be permitted, or endured ; and it would, besides, have destroyed the balance of the Union, and reduced the weight of the slave-holding states to a degree, which they would have deemed altogether inadmissible. 1 Kent's Comm. Lect. 13, p. 261. It is not perceived, how either of these results could have taken place, unless upon some plan, (which was never proposed,) which should disregard altogether the existence of the states, and take away all representation of the slave population. The choice might have been directly by the people without any such course. And in point of fact, such an objection, as that suggested by Mr. Chancellor Kent, to a choice by the people, does not seem to have occurred to the authors of the Federalist. If the choice had been directly by the people, each state having as many votes for president, as it would be entitled to electors, the result would have been exactly, as it now is. If each state had been entitled to one vote, only, then the state sovereignties would have been completely represented by the people of each state upon an equality. If the choice had been by the people in districts, according to the ratio of representation, then the president would have been chosen by a majority of the people in a majority of the representative districts. There would be no more a consolidation, than there now is in the house of representatives. In neither view could there be any injurious inequality bearing on the Southern states.

§ 1452. The other parts of the scheme are no less entitled to commendation. The number of electors is equal to the number of senators and representatives of each state ; thus giving to each state as virtual a repre- sentation in the electoral colleges, as that, which it en- joys in congress. The votes, when given, are to be transmitted to the seat of the national government, and there opened and counted in the presence of both houses. The person, having a majority of the whole number of votes, is to be president. But, if no one of the candidates has such a majority, then the house of representatives, the popular branch of the government, is to elect from the five highest on the list the person, whom they may deem best qualified for the office, each state having one vote in the choice. The person, who has the next highest number of votes after the choice of president, is to be vice-president. But, if two or more shall have equal votes, the senate are to choose the vice-president. Thus, the ultimate functions are to be shared alternately by the senate and representatives in the organization of the executive department.[1]

§ 1453. "This process of election," adds the Fed- eralist, with a somewhat elevated tone of satisfaction, "affords a moral certainty, that the office of president will seldom fall to the lot of a man, who is not in an eminent degree endowed with the requisite qualifica-

---

[1] Mr. Chancellor Kent has summed up the general arguments in fa- vour of an election by electors with great felicity. 1 Kent's Comm. Lect. 13, p. 261, 262. And the subject of the organization of the exec- utive department is also explained, with much clearness and force, by the learned editor of Blackstone's Commentaries, and by Mr. Rawle in his valuable labours. 1 Tucker's Black. Comm. App. 325 to 328; Rawle on Constitution, ch. 5, p. 51 to 55; 2 Wilson's Law Lectures, 186 to 189.

tions. Talents for low intrigue, and the little arts of popularity, may alone suffice to elevate a man to the first honours of a single state. But it will require other talents, and a different kind of merit to establish him in the esteem, and confidence of the whole Union, or of so considerable a portion of it, as will be necessary to make him a successful candidate for the distinguished office of president of the United States. It will not be too strong to say, that there will be a constant probability of seeing the station filled by characters pre-eminent for ability and virtue. And this will be thought no inconsiderable recommendation of the constitution by those, who are able to estimate the share, which the executive in every government must necessarily have in its good or ill administration." [1]

§ 1454. The mode of election of the president thus provided for has not wholly escaped censure, though the objections have been less numerous, than those brought against many other parts of the constitution, touching that department of the government. [2]

§ 1455. One objection was, that he is not chosen directly by the people, so as to secure a proper dependence upon them. And in support of this objection it has been urged, that he will in fact owe his appointment to the state governments; for it will become the policy of the states, which cannot directly elect a president, to prevent his election by the people, and thus to throw the choice into the house of representatives, where it will be decided by the votes of states. [3] Again, it was urged, that this very mode of choice by states in the house of representatives is most unjust

---

[1] The Federalist, No. 68.
[2] See The Federalist, No. 68; 2 Elliot's Debates, 360 to 363.
[3] 2 Elliot's Debates, 360, 361.

and unequal.   Why, it has been said, should Delaware,
with her single representative, possess the same vote
with Virginia, with ten times that number?[1]   Besides;
this mode of choice by the house of representatives will
give rise to the worst intrigues; and if ever the arts of
corruption shall prevail in the choice of a president,
they will prevail by first throwing the choice into the
house of representatives, and then assailing the virtue,
and independence of members holding the state vote,
by all those motives of honour and reward, which can
so easily be applied by a bold and ambitious candidate.[2]

§ 1456. The answer to these objections has been
already in a great measure anticipated in the preceding
pages.   But it was added, that the devolution of the
choice upon the house of representatives was inevitable, if there should be no choice by the people; and it
could not be denied, that it was a more appropriate
body for this purpose, than the senate, seeing, that the
latter were chosen by the state legislatures, and the
former by the people.   Besides; the connexion of the
senate with the executive department might naturally
produce a strong influence in favour of the existing
executive, in opposition to any rival candidate.[3]   The
mode of voting by states, if the choice came to the
house of representatives, was but a just compensation
to the smaller states for their loss in the primary election.   When the people vote for the president, it is
manifest, that the large states enjoy a decided advantage over the small states; and thus their interests may
be neglected or sacrificed.   To compensate them for
this in the eventual election by the house of represen-

---

1 1 Tucker's Black. Comm. App. 327.
2 1 Tucker's Black. Comm. App. 327, 328.
3 1 Tucker's Black. Comm. App. 327, 328.

tatives, a correspondent advantage is given to the small states. It was in fact a compromise.[1] There is no injustice in this; and if the people do not elect a president, there is a greater chance of electing one in this mode, than there would be by a mere representative vote according to numbers; as the same divisions would probably exist in the popular branch, as in their respective states.[2]

§ 1457. It has been observed with much point, that in no respect have the enlarged and liberal views of the framers of the constitution, and the expectations of the public, when it was adopted, been so completely frustrated, as in the practical operation of the system, so far as relates to the independence of the electors in the electoral colleges.[3] It is notorious, that the electors are now chosen wholly with reference to particular candidates, and are silently pledged to vote for them. Nay, upon some occasions the electors publicly pledge themselves to vote for a particular person; and thus, in effect, the whole foundation of the system, so elaborately constructed, is subverted.[4] The candidates for the presidency are selected and announced in each state long before the election; and an ardent canvass is maintained in the newspapers, in party meetings, and in the state legislatures, to secure votes for the favourite candidate, and to defeat his opponents. Nay, the state legislatures often become the nominating body, acting in their official capacities, and recommending by solemn resolves their own candidate to the other states.[5] So, that nothing is left to the electors after their choice,

---

[1] 2 Elliot's Debates, 364.   [2] Rawle on Constitution, ch. 5, p. 54.
[3] Rawle on Constitution, ch. 5, p. 57, 58.   [4] Ibid.
[5] Ibid. — A practice, which has been censured by some persons, as still more alarming, is the nomination of the president by members of

but to register votes, which are already pledged; and an exercise of an independent judgment would be treated, as a political usurpation, dishonourable to the individual, and a fraud upon his constituents.

§ 1458. The principal difficulty, which has been felt in the mode of election, is the constant tendency, from the number of candidates, to bring the choice into the house of representatives. This has already occurred twice in the progress of the government; and in the future there is every probability of a far more frequent occurrence. This was early foreseen; and, even in one of the state conventions, a most distinguished statesman, and one of the framers of the constitution, admitted, that it would probably be found impracticable to elect a president by the immediate suffrages of the people; and that in so large a country many persons would probably be voted for, and that the lowest of the five highest on the list might not have an inconsiderable number of votes.[1] It cannot escape the discernment of any attentive observer, that if the house of representatives is often to choose a president, the choice will, or at least may, be influenced by many motives, independent of his merits and qualifications. There is danger, that intrigue and cabal may mix in the rivalries and strife.[2] And the discords, if not the corruptions, generated by the occasion, will probably long outlive the immediate choice, and scatter their pestilential influences over all the great interests of the country. One fearful crisis was passed in the choice

congress at political meetings at Washington; thus, in the mild form of recommendation introducing their votes into the election with all their official influence. Rawle on Const. ch. 5, p. 58.

[1] Mr. Madison, 2 Elliot's Debates, 364.

[2] 1 Tucker's Black. Comm. App. 327; 1 Kent's Comm. Lect. 13, p. 261.

of Mr. Jefferson over his competitor, Mr. Burr, in 1801, which threatened a dissolution of the government, and put the issue upon the tried patriotism of one or two individuals, who yielded from a sense of duty their preference of the candidate, generally supported by their friends.[2]

§ 1459. Struck with these difficulties, it has been a favourite opinion of many distinguished statesmen, especially of late years, that the choice ought to be directly by the people in representative districts, a measure, which, it has been supposed, would at once facilitate a choice by the people in the first instance, and interpose an insuperable barrier to any general corruption or intrigue in the election. Hitherto this plan has not possessed extensive public favour. Its merits are proper for discussion elsewhere, and do not belong to these Commentaries.

§ 1460. The issue of the contest of 1801 gave rise

---

[1] 1 Kent's Comm. Lect. 13, p. 262.

[2] Allusion is here especially made to the late Mr. Bayard, who held the vote of Delaware, and who, by his final vote in favour of Mr. Jefferson, decided the election. It was remarked at the time, that in the election of Mr. Jefferson, in 1801, the votes of two or three states were held by persons, who soon afterwards received office from him. The circumstance is spoken of in positive terms by Mr. Bayard, in his celebrated Speech on the Judiciary, in 1802.* Mr. Bayard did not make it matter of accusation against Mr. Jefferson, as founded in corrupt bargaining. Nor has any such charge been subsequently made. The fact is here stated merely to show, how peculiarly delicate the exercise of such functions necessarily is; and how difficult it may be, even for the most exalted and pure executive, to escape suspicion or reproach, when he is not chosen directly by the people. Similar suggestions will scarcely ever fail of being made, whenever a distinguished representative obtains office after an election of president, to which he has contributed. The learned editor of Blackstone's Commentaries has spoken with exceeding zeal of the dangers arising from the intrigues and cabals of an election by the house of representatives. 1 Tucker's Black. Comm. App. 327.

* Debates on the Judiciary, printed by Whitney & Co., Albany, 1802, p. 418, 419.

to an amendment of the constitution in several respects, materially changing the mode of election of president. In the first place it provides, that the ballots of the electors shall be separately given for president and vice-president, instead of one ballot for two persons, as president; that the vice-president (like the president) shall he chosen by a majority of the whole number of electors appointed; that the number of candidates, out of whom the selection of president is to be made by the house of representatives, shall be three, instead of five; that the senate shall choose the vice-president from the two highest numbers on the list; and that, if no choice is made of president before the fourth of March following, the vice-president shall act as president.

§ 1461. The amendment was proposed in October, 1803, and was ratified before September, 1804,[1] and is in the following terms.

" The electors shall meet in their respective states,
" and vote by ballot for president and vice-president,
" one of whom, at least, shall not be an inhabitant of
" the same state with themselves; they shall name in
" their ballots the person voted for as president, and in
" distinct ballots the person voted for as vice-president;
" and they shall make distinct lists of all persons voted
" for as president, and of all persons voted for as vice-
" president, and of the number of votes for each; which
" lists they shall sign and certify, and transmit sealed
" to the seat of government of the United States;
" directed to the president of the senate; — the presi-
" dent of the senate shall, in the presence of the senate
" and house of representatives, open all the certificates,

" and the votes shall then be counted; the person hav-
" ing the greatest number of votes for president shall
" be the president, if such number be a majority of the
" whole number of electors appointed; and if no person
" have such majority, then from the persons having the
" highest numbers, not exceeding three, on the list of
" those voted for as president, the house of repre-
" sentatives shall choose immediately, by ballot, the
" president. But in choosing the president, the votes
" shall be taken by states, the representation from each
" state having one vote; a quorum for this purpose
" shall consist of a member, or members, from two-
" thirds of the states, and a majority of all the states
" shall be necessary to a choice. And if the house of
" representatives shall not choose a president, whenever
" the right of choice shall devolve upon them, before
" the fourth day of March next following, then the vice-
" president shall act as president, as in the case of the
" death or other constitutional disability of the presi-
" dent.

" The person, having the greatest number of votes
" as vice-president, shall be the vice-president, if such
" number be a majority of the whole number of elec-
" tors appointed; and if no person have a majority,
" then from the two highest numbers on the list, the
" senate shall choose the vice-president; a quorum for
" the purpose shall consist of two-thirds of the whole
" number of senators, and a majority of the whole
" number shall be necessary to a choice.

" But no person, constitutionally ineligible to the
" office of president, shall be eligible to that of vice-
" president of the United States."

§ 1462. This amendment has alternately been the
subject of praise and blame, and experience alone can

decide, whether the changes proposed by it are in all respects for the better, or the worse.[1] In some respects it is a substantial improvement. In the first place, under the original mode, the senate was restrained from acting, until the house of representatives had made their selection, which, if parties ran high, might be considerably delayed. By the amendment the senate may proceed to a choice of the vice-president, immediately on ascertaining the returns of the votes.[2] In the next place, under the original mode, if no choice should be made of a president by the house of representatives until after the expiration of the term of the preceding officer, there would be no person to perform the functions of the office, and an *interregnum* would ensue, and a total suspension of the powers of government.[3] By the amendment, the new vice-president would in such case act as president. By the original mode, the senate are to elect the vice-president by ballot; by the amendment, the mode of choice is left open, so that it may be *vivâ voce*. Whether this be an improvement, or not, may be doubted.

§ 1463. On the other hand, the amendment has certainly greatly diminished the dignity and importance of the office of vice-president. Though the duties remain the same, he is no longer a competitor for the presidency, and selected, as possessing equal merit, talents, and qualifications, with the other candidate. As every state was originally compelled to vote for two candidates (one of whom did not belong to the state)

---

[1] 1 Kent's Comm. Lect. 13, p. 262 ; Rawle on Const. ch. 5, p. 54, 55.

[2] Rawle on Const. ch. 5, p. 54 : 1 Kent's Comm. Lect. 13, p. 260.

[3] Mr. Rawle is of opinion, that the old vice-president would, under the old mode, act as president in case of a non-election of president. I cannot find in the constitution any authority for such a position. Rawle on Const. ch. 5, p. 54. See also Act of Congress, 1st March, 1792, ch. 8.

for the same office, a choice was fairly given to all other states to select between them; thus excluding the absolute predominance of any local interest, or local partiality.

§ 1464. In the original plan, as well as in the amendment, no provision is made for the discussion or decision of any questions, which may arise, as to the regularity and authenticity of the returns of the electoral votes, or the right of the persons, who gave the votes, or the manner, or circumstances, in which they ought to be counted. It seems to have been taken for granted, that no question could ever arise on the subject; and that nothing more was necessary, than to open the certificates, which were produced, in the presence of both houses, and to count the names and numbers, as returned. Yet it is easily to be conceived, that very delicate and interesting inquiries may occur, fit to be debated and decided by some deliberative body.[1] In fact, a question did occur upon the counting of the votes for the presidency in 1821 upon the re-election of Mr. Monroe, whether the votes of the state of Missouri could be counted; but as the count would make no difference in the choice, and the declaration was made of his re-election, the senate immediately withdrew; and the jurisdiction, as well as the course of proceeding in a case of real controversy, was left in a most embarrassing situation.

§ 1465. Another defect in the constitution is, that no provision was originally, or is now made, for a case, where there is an equality of votes by the electors for more persons, than the constitutional number, from which the house of representatives is to make the election. The language of the original text is, that

---

[1] See 1 Kent's Comm. Lect. 13, p. 258, 259.

the house shall elect "from the five highest on the list." Suppose there were six candidates, three of whom had an equal number; who are to be preferred? The amendment is, that the house shall elect "from the "persons having the highest numbers, not exceeding "three." Suppose there should be four candidates, two of whom should have an equality of votes; who are to be preferred? Such a case is quite within the range of probability; and may hereafter occasion very serious dissensions. One object in lessening the number of the persons to be balloted for from five to three, doubtless was, to take away the chance of any person having very few votes from being chosen president against the general sense of the nation.[1] Yet it is obvious now, that a person having but a very small number of electoral votes, might, under the present plan, be chosen president, if the other votes were divided between two eminent rival candidates; the friends of each of whom might prefer any other to such rival candidate. Nay, their very hostility to each other might combine them in a common struggle to throw the final choice upon the third candidate, whom they might hope to control, or fear to disoblige.

§ 1466. It is observable, that the language of the constitution is, that "each state shall appoint in such "manner, as the legislature thereof may direct," the number of electors, to which the state is entitled. Under this authority the appointment of electors has been variously provided for by the state legislatures. In some states the legislature have directly chosen the electors by themselves; in others they have been chosen by the people by a general ticket throughout the whole state; and in others by the people in electoral

---

[1] 2 Elliot's Debates, 362, 363.

districts, fixed by the legislature, a certain number of
electors being apportioned to each district.[1] No question has ever arisen, as to the constitutionality of either
mode, except that of a direct choice by the legislature.
But this, though often doubted by able and ingenious
minds,[2] has been firmly established in practice, ever
since the adoption of the constitution, and does not
now seem to admit of controversy, even if a suitable
tribunal existed to adjudicate upon it.[3] At present, in
nearly all the states, the electors are chosen either by
the people by a general ticket, or by the state legislature. The choice in districts has been gradually
abandoned; and is now persevered in, but by two
states.[4] The inequality of this mode of choice, unless
it should become general throughout the Union, is
so obvious, that it is rather matter of surprise, that it
should not long since have been wholly abandoned. In
case of any party divisions in a state, it may neutralize
its whole vote, while all the other states give an un-
broken electoral vote. On this account, and for the
sake of uniformity, it has been thought desirable by
many statesmen to have the constitution amended so, as
to provide for an uniform mode of choice by the people.

§ 1467. The remaining part of the clause, which
precludes any senator, representative, or person holding an office of trust or profit under the United States,
from being an elector, has been already alluded to, and
requires little comment. The object is, to prevent
persons holding public stations under the government
of the United States, from any direct influence in the

---

[1] 1 Tuck. Black. Comm. App. 326.
[2] See 3 Elliot's Debates, 100, 101.
[3] See 2 Wilson's Law Lect. 187.
[4] See Rawle on Const. ch. 5, p. 55.

choice of a president. In respect to persons holding office, it is reasonable to suppose, that their partialities would all be in favour of the re-election of the actual incumbent, and they might have strong inducements to exert their official influence in the electoral college. In respect to senators and representatives, there is this additional reason for excluding them, that they would be already committed by their vote in the electoral college ; and thus, if there should be no election by the people, they could not bring to the final vote either the impartiality, or the independence, which the theory of the constitution contemplates.

§ 1468. The next clause is, " The congress may " determine the time of choosing the electors, and the " day, on which they shall give their votes, which day " shall be the same throughout the United States."

§ 1469. The propriety of this power would seem to be almost self-evident. Every reason of public policy and convenience seems in favour of a fixed time of giving the electoral votes, and that it should be the same throughout the Union. Such a measure is calculated to repress political intrigues and speculations, by rendering a combination among the electoral colleges, as to their votes, if not utterly impracticable, at least very difficult ; and thus secures the people against those ready expedients, which corruption never fails to employ to accomplish its designs.[1] The arts of ambition are thus in some degree checked, and the independence of the electors against external influence in some degree secured. This power, however, did not escape objection in the general, or the state conventions, though the objection was not extensively insisted on.[2]

---

[1] 3 Elliot's Debates, 100. 101.
[2] Journal of Convention, 325, 331, 333, 335 ; 3 Elliot's Deb. 100, 101.

§ 1470. In pursuance of the authority given by this clause, congress, in 1792, passed an act declaring, that the electors shall be appointed in each state within thirty-four days, preceding the first Wednesday in December in every fourth year, succeeding the last election of president, according to the apportionment of representatives and senators then existing. The electors chosen are required to meet and give their votes on the said first Wednesday of December, at such place in each state, as shall be directed by the legislature thereof. They are then to make and sign three certificates of all the votes by them given, and to seal up the same, certifying on each, that a list of the votes of such state for president and vice-president is contained therein, and shall appoint a person to take charge of, and deliver, one of the same certificates to the president of the senate at the seat of government, before the first Wednesday of January then next ensuing ; another of the certificates is to be forwarded forthwith by the post-office to the president of the senate at the seat of government ; and the third is to be delivered to the judge of the district, in which the electors assembled.[1] Other auxiliary provisions are made by the same act for the due transmission and preservation of the electoral votes; and authenticating the appointment of the electors. The president's term of office is also declared to commence on the fourth day of March next succeeding the day, on which the votes of the electors shall be given.[2]

§ 1471. The next clause respects the qualifications of the president of the United States. " No person, " except a natural born citizen, or a citizen of the " United States at the time of the adoption of this con- " stitution, shall be eligible to the office of president.

---

[1] Act of 1st March, 1792, ch. 8. [2] Ibid.

"Neither shall any person be eligible to that office,
"who shall not have attained to the age of thirty-five
"years, and been fourteen years a resident within the
"United States."

§ 1472. Considering the nature of the duties, the
extent of the information, and the solid wisdom and
experience required in the executive department, no
one can reasonably doubt the propriety of some qualification of age. That, which has been selected, is the
middle age of life, by which period the character and
talents of individuals are generally known, and fully de-
veloped; and opportunities have usually been afforded
for public service, and for experience in the public
councils. The faculties of the mind, if they have not
then attained to their highest maturity, are in full vigour, and hastening towards their ripest state. The
judgment, acting upon large materials, has, by that time,
attained a solid cast; and the principles, which form
the character, and the integrity, which gives lustre
to the virtues of life, must then, if ever, have acquired
public confidence and approbation.[1]

§ 1473. It is indispensable, too, that the president
should be a natural born citizen of the United States;
or a citizen at the adoption of the constitution, and for
fourteen years before his election. This permission of a
naturalized citizen to become president is an exception from the great fundamental policy of all governments, to exclude foreign influence from their executive
councils and duties. It was doubtless introduced (for it
has now become by lapse of time merely nominal, and
will soon become wholly extinct) out of respect to
those distinguished revolutionary patriots, who were
born in a foreign land, and yet had entitled themselves

---

[1] See 1 Kent's Comm. Lect. 13, p. 273.

to high honours in their adopted country.[1]   A positive
exclusion of them from the office would have been unjust to their merits, and painful to their sensibilities.
But the general propriety of the exclusion of foreigners,
in common cases, will scarcely be doubted by any sound
statesman.   It cuts off all chances for ambitious foreigners, who might otherwise be intriguing for the
office ; and interposes a barrier against those corrupt
interferences of foreign governments in executive elections, which have inflicted the most serious evils upon the
elective monarchies of Europe.   Germany, Poland, and
even the pontificate of Rome, are sad, but instructive
examples of the enduring mischiefs arising from this
source.[2]   A residence of fourteen years in the United
States is also made an indispensable requisite for every
candidate ; so, that the people may have a full opportunity to know his character and merits, and that he
may have mingled in the duties, and felt the interests,
and understood the principles, and nourished the attachments, belonging to every citizen in a republican government.[3]   By "residence," in the constitution, is to be
understood, not an absolute inhabitancy within the
United States during the whole period ; but such an
inhabitancy, as includes a permanent domicil in the
United States.   No one has supposed, that a temporary absence abroad on public business, and especially
on an embassy to a foreign nation, would interrupt the
residence of a citizen, so as to disqualify him for
office.[4]   If the word were to be construed with such
strictness, then a mere journey through any foreign

[1] Journ. of Convention, 267, 325, 361.
[2] 1 Kent's Comm. Lect. 13, p. 255; 1 Tuck. Black. Comm. App. 323.
[3] Ibid.
[4] Rawle on Const. ch. 31, p. 287.

adjacent territory for health, or for pleasure, or a commorancy there for a single day, would amount to a disqualification.   Under such a construction a military or civil officer, who should have been in Canada during the late war on public business, would have lost his eligibility.   The true sense of residence in the constitution is fixed domicil, or being out of the United States, and settled abroad for the purpose of general inhabitancy, *animo manendi*, and not for a mere temporary and fugitive purpose, *in transitu.*

§ 1474. The next clause is, " In case of the removal " of the president from office, or his death, resignation, " or inability to discharge the duties of the said office, " the same shall devolve on the vice-president.   And " the congress may by law provide for the case of re-" moval, death, resignation, or inability of the president " and vice-president, declaring what officer shall then " act as president ; and such officer shall act accord-"ingly, until the disability be removed, or a president " shall be elected."

§ 1475. The original scheme of the constitution did not embrace (as has been already stated) the appointment of any vice-president, and in case of the death, resignation, or disability of the president, the president of the senate was to perform the duties of his office.[1] The appointment of a vice-president was carried by a vote of ten states to one.[2]   Congress, in pursuance of the power here given, have provided, that in case of the removal, death, resignation, or inability of the president and vice-president, the president of the senate *pro tempore,* and in case there shall be no president, then the speaker of the house of representatives for the

---

[1] Journal of Convention, p. 225, 226.   [2] Id. 324, 333, 337.

CH. XXXVI.] EXECUTIVE—VACANCY OF OFFICE. 335

time being shall act as president, until the disability be removed, or a president shall be elected.[1]

§ 1476. No provision seems to be made, or at least directly made, for the case of the non-election of any president and vice-president at the period prescribed by the constitution. The case of a vacancy by removal, death, or resignation, is expressly provided for; but not of a vacancy by the expiration of the official term of office. A learned commentator has thought, that such a case is not likely to happen, until the people of the United States shall be weary of the constitution and government, and shall adopt this method of putting a period to both, a mode of dissolution, which seems, from its peaceable character, to recommend itself to his mind, as fit for such a crisis.[2] But no absolute dissolution of the government would constitutionally take place by such a non-election. The only effect would be, a suspension of the powers of the executive part of the government, and incidentally of the legislative powers, until a new election to the presidency should take place at the next constitutional period, an evil of very great magnitude, but not equal to a positive extinguishment of the constitution. But the event of a non-election may arise, without any intention on the part of the people to dissolve the government. Suppose there should

---

[1] Act of 1st March, 1792, ch. 8, § 9. — If the office should devolve on the speaker, after the congress, for which the last speaker was chosen, had expired, and before the next meeting of congress, it might be a question, who is to serve, and whether the speaker of the house of representatives, then extinct, could be deemed the person intended. 1 Kent's Comm. Lect. 13, p. 260, 261. In order to provide for the exigency of a vacancy in the office of president during the recess of congress, it has become usual for the vice-president, a few days before the termination of each session of congress, to retire from the chair of the senate, to enable that body to elect a president *pro tempore* to be ready to act in any case of emergency. Rawle on Const. ch. 5, p. 57.

[2] 1 Tuck. Black. Comm. App. 320.

be three candidates for the presidency, and two for the vice-presidency, each of whom should receive, as nearly as possible, the same number of votes; which party, under such circumstances, is bound to yield up its own preference? May not each feel equally and conscientiously the duty to support to the end of the contest its own favorite candidate in the house of representatives? Take another case. Suppose two persons should receive a majority of all the votes for the presidency, and both die before the time of taking office, or even before the votes are ascertained by congress. There is nothing incredible in the supposition, that such an event may occur. It is not nearly as improbable, as the occurrence of the death of three persons, who had held the office of president, on the anniversary of our independence, and two of these in the same year. In each of these cases there would be a vacancy in the office of president and vice-president by mere efflux of time; and it may admit of doubt, whether the language of the constitution reaches them. If the vice-president should succeed to the office of president, he will continue in it until the regular expiration of the period, for which the president was chosen; for there is no provision for the choice of a new president, except at the regular period, when there is a vice-president in office; and none for the choice of a vice-president, except when a president also is to be chosen.[1]

§ 1477. Congress, however, have undertaken to provide for every case of a vacancy both of the offices of president and vice-president; and have declared, that in such an event there shall immediately be a new election made in the manner prescribed by the act.[2]

[1] See Rawle on Const. ch. 5, p. 56.
[2] Act of 1st March, 1792, ch. 8, § 11.

How far such an exercise of power is constitutional has never yet been solemnly presented for decision. The point was hinted at in some of the debates, when the constitution was adopted; and it was then thought to be susceptible of some doubt.[1] Every sincere friend of the constitution will naturally feel desirous of upholding the power, as far as he constitutionally may.[2] But it would be more satisfactory, to provide for the case by some suitable amendment, which should clear away every doubt, and thus prevent a crisis dangerous to our future peace, if not to the existence of the government.

§ 1478. What shall be the proper proof of the resignation of the president, or vice-president, or of their refusal to accept the office, is left open by the constitution. But congress, with great wisdom and forecast, have provided, that it shall be by some instrument in writing, declaring the same, subscribed by the party, and delivered into the office of the secretary of state.[3]

§ 1479. The next clause is, "The president shall, "at stated times, receive for his services a compensa- "tion, which shall neither be increased, nor diminish- "ed during the period, for which he shall have been "elected, and he shall not receive within that period "any other emolument from the United States, or any "of them."

§ 1480. It is obvious, that without due attention to the proper support of the president, the separation

[1] 2 Elliot's Debates, 359, 360.
[2] In the revised draft of the constitution, the clause stood: " And such officer shall act accordingly, until the disability be removed, *or the period for choosing another president arrive ;* " and the latter words were then altered, so as to read, " *until a president shall be elected.*" Journ. of Convention, 361, 382.
[3] Act of 1st March, 1792, ch. 8, § 11.

of the executive from the legislative department would be merely nominal and nugatory. The legislature, with a discretionary power over his salary and emolument, would soon render him obsequious to their will. A control over a man's living is in most cases a control over his actions. To act upon any other view of the subject would be to disregard the voice of experience, and the operation of the invariable principles, which regulate human conduct. There are, indeed, men, who could neither be distressed, nor won into a sacrifice of their duty. But this stern virtue is the growth of few soils; and it will be found, that the general lesson of human life is, that men obey their interests ; that they may be driven by poverty into base compliances, or tempted by largesses to a desertion of duty.[1] Nor have there been wanting examples in our own country of the intimidation, or seduction of the executive by the terrors, or allurements of the pecuniary arrangements of the legislative body.[2] The wisdom of this clause can scarcely be too highly commended. The legislature, on the appointment of a president, is once for all to declare, what shall be the compensation for his services during the time, for which he shall have been elected. This done, they will have no power to alter it, either by increase or diminution, till a new period of service by a new election commences. They can neither weaken his fortitude by operating upon his necessities, nor corrupt his integrity by appealing to his avarice. Neither the Union, nor any of its members, will be at liberty to give, nor will he be at liberty to receive, any other emolument. He can, of course, have

---

[1] The Federalist, No. 73 ; 1 Kent's Comm. Lect. 13, p. 263.

[2] The Federalist, No. 73 ; 1 Kent's Comm. Lect. 13, p. 263 ; 1 Tuck. Black. Comm. App. 323, 324.

no pecuniary inducement to renounce, or desert, the independence intended for him by the constitution.[1] The salary of the first president was fixed by congress at the sum of twenty-five thousand dollars per annum, and of the vice-president, at five thousand dollars.[2] And to prevent any difficulty, as to future presidents, congress, by a permanent act, a few years afterwards established the same compensation for all future presidents and vice-presidents.[3] So that, unless some great changes should intervene, the independence of the executive is permanently secured by an adequate maintenance ; and it can scarcely be diminished, unless some future executive shall basely betray his duty to his successor.

§ 1481. The next clause is, "Before he enters on " the execution of his office, he shall take the following " oath or affirmation : I do solemnly swear, (or affirm,) " that I will faithfully execute the office of President of " the United States, and will, to the best of my ability, " preserve, protect, and defend the constitution of the " United States."

§ 1482. There is little need of commentary upon this clause. No man can well doubt the propriety of placing a president of the United States under the most solemn obligations to preserve, protect, and defend the constitution. It is a suitable pledge of his fidelity and responsibility to his country ; and creates upon his conscience a deep sense of duty, by an appeal at once in the presence of God and man to the most sacred and solemn sanctions, which can operate upon the human mind.[4]

---

[1] The Federalist, No. 73.
[2] Act of 24th September, 1789, ch. 19.
[3] Act of 18th February, 1793, ch. 9.
[4] See Journal of Convention, 225, 296, 361, 383.

CHAPTER XXXVII.

EXECUTIVE — POWERS AND DUTIES.

§ 1483. HAVING thus considered the manner, in which the executive department is organized, the next inquiry is, as to the powers, with which it is entrusted. These, and the corresponding duties, are enumerated in the second and third sections of the second article of the constitution.

§ 1484. The first clause of the second section is, "The President shall be commander-in-chief of the "army and navy of the United States, and of the mili- "tia of the several states, when called into the actual "service of the United States.[1] He may require the "opinion in writing of the principal officer in each of "the executive departments, upon any subject relat- "ing to the duties of their respective offices. And he "shall have power to grant reprieves and pardons for "offences against the United States, except in cases of "impeachment."

§ 1485. The command and application of the public force, to execute the laws, to maintain peace, and to resist foreign invasion, are powers so obviously of an executive nature, and require the exercise of quali- ties so peculiarly adapted to this department, that a well-organized government can scarcely exist, when they are taken away from it.[2] Of all the cases and concerns of government, the direction of war most peculiarly demands those qualities, which distinguish

---

[1] See Journal of Convention, 225, 295, 362, 383.
[2] 1 Kent's Comm. Lect. 13, p. 264; 3 Elliot's Deb. 103.

the exercise of power by a single hand.[1] Unity of plan, promptitude, activity, and decision, are indispensable to success ; and these can scarcely exist, except when a single magistrate is entrusted exclusively with the power. Even the coupling of the authority of an executive council with him, in the exercise of such powers, enfeebles the system, divides the responsibility, and not unfrequently defeats every energetic measure. Timidity, indecision, obstinacy, and pride of opinion, must mingle in all such councils, and infuse a torpor and sluggishness, destructive of all military operations. Indeed, there would seem to be little reason to enforce the propriety of giving this power to the executive department, (whatever may be its actual organization,) since it is in exact coincidence with the provisions of our state constitutions ; and therefore seems to be universally deemed safe, if not vital to the system.

§ 1486. Yet the clause did not wholly escape animadversion in the state conventions. The propriety of admitting the president to be commander-in-chief, so far as to give orders, and have a general superintendency, was admitted. But it was urged, that it would be dangerous to let him command in person without any restraint, as he might make a bad use of it. The consent of both houses of congress ought, therefore, to be required, before he should take the actual command.[2] The answer then given was, that though the president might, there was no necessity, that he should, take the command in person ; and there was no probability, that he would do so, except in extraordinary emergencies, and when he was possessed

---

[1] The Federalist, No 74 ; 3 Elliot's Debates, 103.
[2] 2 Elliot's Debates, 365. See also 3 Elliot's Debates, 108.

of superior military talents.[1] But if his assuming the
actual command depended upon the assent of congress,
what was to be done, when an invasion, or insurrection
took place during the recess of congress? Besides ;
the very power of restraint might be so employed, as
to cripple the executive department, when filled by a
man of extraordinary military genius. The power of
the president, too, might well be deemed safe; since he
could not, of himself, declare war, raise armies, or call
forth the militia, or appropriate money for the purpose;
for these powers all belonged to congress.[2] In Great
Britain, the king is not only commander-in-chief of the
army, and navy, and militia, but he can declare war;
and, in time of war, can raise armies and navies, and
call forth the militia of his own mere will.[3] So, that (to
use the words of Mr. Justice Blackstone) the sole supreme government and command of the militia within
all his majesty's realms and dominions, and of all forces
by sea and land, and of all forts and places of strength,
ever was and is the undoubted right of his majesty;
and both houses or either house of parliament cannot, nor ought to pretend to the same.[4] The only
power of check by parliament is, the refusal of supplies;
and this is found to be abundantly sufficient to protect
the nation against any war against the sense of the
nation, or any serious abuse of the power in modern
times.[5]

---

[1] 2 Elliot's Debates, 366.   [2] 3 Elliot's Debates, 103.
[3] 3 Elliot's Debates, 103 ; 1 Black. Comm. 262, 408 to 421.
[4] 1 Black. Comm. 262, 263.
[5] During the war with Great Britain in 1812, it was questioned,
whether the president could delegate his right to command the militia,
by authorizing another officer to command them, when they were called
into the public service. (8 Mass. Reports, 548, 550.) If he cannot, this
extraordinary result would follow, that if different detachments of militia

§ 1487. The next provision is, as to the power of the president, to require the opinions in writing of the heads of the executive departments. It has been remarked, that this is a mere redundancy, and the right would result from the very nature of the office.[1] Still, it is not without use, as it imposes a more strict responsibility, and recognises a public duty of high importance and value in critical times. It has, in the progress of the government, been repeatedly acted upon; but by no president with more wisdom and propriety, than by President Washington.[2]

§ 1488. The next power is, "to grant reprieves and pardons." It has been said by the marquis Beccaria, that the power of pardon does not exist under a perfect administration of the laws; and that the admission of the power is a tacit acknowledgment of the infirmi-

---

were called out, he could not, except in person, command any of them; and if they were to act together, no officer could be appointed to command them in his absence. In the Pennsylvanian insurrection, in 1794, President Washington called out the militia of the adjacent states of New Jersey, Maryland, and Virginia, as well as of Pennsylvania, and all the troops, so called out, acted under the orders of the governor of Virginia, on whom the president conferred the chief command during his absence. Rawle on the Const. ch. 20, p. 193. It was a practical affirmation of the authority, and was not contested. See also 5 Marshall's Life of Washington, ch. 8, p. 580, 584, 588, 589.

[1] The Federalist, No. 74. See Journal of Convention, 225, 326, 342.

[2] Mr. Jefferson has informed us, that in Washington's administration, for measures of importance, or difficulty, a consultation was held with the heads of the departments, either assembled, or by taking their opinions separately in conversation, or in writing. In his own administration, he followed the practice of assembling the heads of departments, as a cabinet council. But he has added, that he thinks the course of requiring the separate opinion in writing of each head of a department is most strictly in the spirit of the constitution; for the other does, in fact, transform the executive into a directory. 4 Jefferson's Corresp. 143, 144.

ty of the course of justice.[1]   But if this be a defect at
all, it arises from the infirmity of human nature generally; and in this view, is no more objectionable, than
any other power of government ; for every such power,
in some sort, arises from human infirmity.   But if it be
meant, that it is an imperfection in human legislation to
admit the power of pardon in any case, the proposition
may well be denied, and some proof, at least, be required of its sober reality.   The common argument is,
that where punishments are mild, they ought to be certain; and that the clemency of the chief magistrate is
a tacit disapprobation of the laws.   But surely no man
in his senses will contend, that any system of laws can
provide for every possible shade of guilt, a proportionate
degree of punishment.   The most, that ever has been,
and ever can be done, is to provide for the punishment of
crimes by some general rules, and within some general
limitations.   The total exclusion of all power of pardon
would necessarily introduce a very dangerous power
in judges and juries, of following the spirit, rather than
the letter of the laws ; or, out of humanity, of suffering real offenders wholly to escape punishment; or
else, it must be holden, (what no man will seriously
avow,) that the situation and circumstances of the offender, though they alter not the essence of the offence,
ought to make no distinction in the punishment.[2]
There are not only various gradations of guilt in the
commission of the same crime, which are not susceptible of any previous enumeration and definition ; but the
proofs must, in many cases, be imperfect in their own
nature, not only as to the actual commission of the

[1] Beccaria, ch. 46; 1 Kent. Comm. Lect. 13, p. 265 ; 4 Black. Comm.
307 ; 2 Wilson's Law Lect. 193 to 198.
[2] 4 Black. Comm. 397.

offence, but also, as to the aggravating or mitigating circumstances. In many cases, convictions must be founded upon presumptions and probabilities. Would it not be at once unjust and unreasonable to exclude all means of mitigating punishment, when subsequent inquiries should demonstrate, that the accusation was wholly unfounded, or the crime greatly diminished in point of atrocity and aggravation, from what the evidence at the trial seemed to establish? A power to pardon seems, indeed, indispensable under the most correct administration of the law by human tribunals; since, otherwise, men would sometimes fall a prey to the vindictiveness of accusers, the inaccuracy of testimony, and the fallibility of jurors and courts.[1] Besides; the law may be broken, and yet the offender be placed in such circumstances, that he will stand, in a great measure, and perhaps wholly, excused in moral and general justice, though not in the strictness of the law. What then is to be done? Is he to be acquitted against the law; or convicted, and to suffer punishment infinitely beyond his deserts? If an arbitrary power is to be given to meet such cases, where can it be so properly lodged, as in the executive department?[2]

---

[1] 1 Kent's Comm. Lect. 13, p. 265.

[2] Mr. Chancellor Kent has placed the general reasoning in a just light. "Were it possible," says he "in every instance, to maintain a just proportion between the crime and the penalty, and were the rules of testimony and the mode of trial so perfect, as to preclude mistake, or injustice, there would be some colour for the admission of this (Beccaria's) plausible theory. But even in that case policy would sometimes require a remission of a punishment, strictly due for a crime certainly ascertained. The very notion of mercy implies the accuracy of the claims of justice."* What should we say of a government, which purported to act upon mere human justice, excluding all opera-

* 1 Kent's Comm. Lect. 13, p. 265.

§ 1489. Mr. Justice Blackstone says, that "in democracies, this power of pardon can never subsist; for, there, nothing higher is acknowledged, than the magistrate, who administers the laws; and it would be impolitic for the power of judging, and of pardoning to center in one and the same person. This (as the president Montesquieu, observes) [1] would oblige him very often to contradict himself, to make and unmake his decisions. It would tend to confound all ideas of right among the mass of the people, as they would find it difficult to tell, whether a prisoner was discharged by his innocence, or obtained a pardon through favour." [2] And hence, he deduces the superiority of a monarchical government; because in monarchies, the king acts in a superior sphere; and may, therefore, safely be trusted with the power of pardon, and it becomes a source of personal loyalty and affection. [3]

§ 1490. But, surely, this reasoning is extremely forced and artificial. In the first place, there is no more difficulty or absurdity in a democracy, than in a monarchy, in such cases, if the power of judging and pardoning be in the same hands; as if the monarch be at once the judge, and the person, who pardons. And Montesquieu's reasoning is in fact addressed to this very case of a monarch, who is at once the judge, and dispenser of pardons. [4] In the next place, there is no inconsistency in a democracy any more, than in a monarchy, in entrusting one magistrate with a power to try

tions of mercy in all cases? An inexorable government would scarcely be more praiseworthy, than a despotism. It would be intolerable and unchristian.

1 Montesq. Spirit of Laws, B. 6, ch. 5.
2 4 Black. Comm. 397, 398.
3 Ibid.   4 Montesq. B. 6, ch. 5.

the cause, and another with a power to pardon. The one power is not incidental to, but in contrast with the other. Nor, if both powers were lodged in the same magistrate, would there be any danger of their being necessarily confounded; for they may be required to be acted upon separately, and at different times, so as to be known as distinct prerogatives. But, in point of fact, no such reasoning has the slightest application to the American governments, or, indeed, to any others, where there is a separation of the general departments of government, legislative, judicial, and executive, and the powers of each are administered by distinct persons. What difficulty is there in the people delegating the judicial power to one body of magistrates, and the power of pardon to another, in a republic any more, than there is in the king's delegating the judicial power to magistrates, and reserving the pardoning power to himself, in a monarchy?[1]   In truth, the learned author, in his extreme desire to recommend a kingly form of government, seems on this, as on many other occasions, to have been misled into the most loose and inconclusive statements. There is not a single state in the Union, in which there is not by its constitution a power of pardon lodged in some one department of government, distinct from the judicial.[2] And the power of remitting penalties is in some cases, even in England, entrusted to judicial officers.[3]

§ 1491. So far from the power of pardon being in-

---

[1] Mr. Rawle's Remarks upon this subject are peculiarly valuable, from their accuracy, philosophical spirit, and clearness of statement. Rawle on Const. ch. 17, p. 174 to 177.

[2] 1 Tucker's Black. Comm. App. 331; 2 Wilson's Law Lect. 193 to 200.

[3] Bacon's Abridg. *Court of Exchequer*, B.

compatible with the fundamental principles of a republic, it may be boldly asserted to be peculiarly appropriate, and safe in all free states; because the power can
there be guarded by a just responsibility for its exercise.[1]   Little room will be left for favouritism, personal
caprice, or personal resentment. If the power should
ever be abused, it would be far less likely to occur in
opposition, than in obedience to the will of the people.
The danger is not, that in republics the victims of the
law will too often escape punishment by a pardon;
but that the power will not be sufficiently exerted in
cases, where public feeling accompanies the prosecution, and assigns the ultimate doom to persons, who
have been convicted upon slender testimony, or popular suspicions.

§ 1492. The power to pardon, then, being a fit one
to be entrusted to all governments, humanity and
sound policy dictate, that this benign prerogative should
be, as little as possible, fettered, or embarrassed. The
criminal code of every country partakes so much of
necessary severity, that, without an easy access to
exceptions in favour of unfortunate guilt, justice would
assume an aspect too sanguinary and cruel. The only
question is, in what department of the government it
can be most safely lodged; and that must principally
refer to the executive, or legislative department.
The reasoning in favour of vesting it in the executive
department may be thus stated. A sense of responsibility is always strongest in proportion, as it is undivided. A single person would, therefore, be most
ready to attend to the force of those motives, which

[1] Kent's Comm. Lect. 13, p. 266.

might plead for a mitigation of the rigour of the law; and the least apt to yield to considerations, which were calculated to shelter a fit object of its vengeance. The consciousness, that the life, or happiness of an offender was exclusively within his discretion, would inspire scrupulousness and caution; and the dread of being accused of weakness, or connivance, would beget circumspection of a different sort. On the other hand, as men generally derive confidence from numbers, a large assembly might naturally encourage each other in acts of obduracy, as no one would feel much apprehension of public censure.[1] A public body, too, ordinarily engaged in other duties, would be little apt to sift cases of this sort thoroughly to the bottom, and would be disposed to yield to the solicitations, or be guided by the prejudices of a few; and thus shelter their own acts of yielding too much, or too little, under the common apology of ignorance, or confidence. A single magistrate would be compelled to search, and act upon his own responsibility; and therefore would be at once a more enlightened dispenser of mercy, and a more firm administrator of public justice.

§ 1493. There are probably few persons now, who would not consider the power of pardon in ordinary cases, as best deposited with the president. But the expediency of vesting it in him in any cases, and especially in cases of treason, was doubted at the time of adopting the constitution; and it was then urged, that it ought at least in cases of treason to be vested in one, or both branches of the legislature.[2] That there are strong reasons, which may be assigned in favour of vesting the power in congress in cases of treason, need

---

[1] The Federalist, No. 74. See 2 Wilson's Law Lect. 198 to 200.
[2] 2 Elliot's Debates, 366; The Federalist, No. 74.

not be denied. As treason is a crime levelled at the
immediate existence of society, when the laws have
once ascertained the guilt of the offender, there would
seem to be a fitness in referring the expediency of an
act of mercy towards him to the judgment of the legislature.[1] But there are strong reasons also against it.
Even in such cases a single magistrate, of prudence
and sound sense, would be better fitted, than a numerous assembly, in such delicate conjunctures, to weigh
the motives for and against the remission of the punishment, and to ascertain all the facts without undue
influence. The responsibility would be more felt, and
more direct. Treason, too, is a crime, that will often
be connected with seditions, embracing a large portion
of a particular community; and might under such circumstances, and especially where parties were nearly
poised, find friends and favourites, as well as enemies
and opponents, in the councils of the nation.[2] So, that
the chance of an impartial judgment might be less
probable in such bodies, than in a single person at the
head of the nation.

§ 1494. A still more satisfactory reason is, that the
legislature is not always in session; and that their proceedings must be necessarily slow, and are generally
not completed, until after long delays. The inexpediency of deferring the execution of any criminal sentence, until a long and indefinite time after a conviction,
is felt in all communities. It destroys one of the best
effects of punishment, that, which arises from a prompt
and certain administration of justice following close
upon the offence. If the legislature is invested with

1 The Federalist, No. 74.
2 The Federalist, No. 74 ; Rawle on Const. ch. 17, p. 178.

the authority to pardon, it is obviously indispensable, that no sentence can be properly executed, at least in capital cases, until they have had time to act. And a mere postponement of the subject from session to session would be naturally sought by all those, who favoured the convict, and yet doubted the success of his application. In many cases delay would be equivalent to a pardon, as to its influence upon public opinion, either in weakening the detestation of the crime, or encouraging the commission of it. But the principal argument for reposing the power of pardon in the executive magistrate in cases of treason is, that in seasons of insurrection, or rebellion, there are critical moments, when a well-timed offer of pardon to the insurgents, or rebels, may restore the tranquillity of the Commonwealth; and if these are suffered to pass unimproved, it may be impossible afterwards to interpose with the same success. The dilatory process of convening the legislature, or one of the branches, for the purpose of sanctioning such a measure, would frequently be the loss of the golden opportunity. The loss of a week, of a day, or even of an hour may sometimes prove fatal. If a discretionary power were confided to the president to act in such emergencies, it would greatly diminish the importance of the restriction. And it would generally be impolitic to hold out, either by the constitution or by law, a prospect of impunity by confiding the exercise of the power to the executive in special cases; since it might be construed into an argument of timidity or weakness, and thus have a tendency to embolden guilt.[1] In point of fact, the power has always been found safe in the hands of the state executives in trea-

---

[1] The Federalist, No. 74; 3 Elliot's Debates, 105, 106, 107.

son, as well as in other cases; and there can be no
practical reason, why it should not be equally safe with
the executive of the Union.[1]

§ 1495. There is an exception to the power of pardon, that it shall not extend to cases of impeachment,
which takes from the president every temptation to
abuse it in cases of political and official offences by
persons in the public service. The power of impeachment will generally be applied to persons holding high
offices under the government; and it is of great consequence, that the president should not have the power
of preventing a thorough investigation of their conduct,
or of securing them against the disgrace of a public
conviction by impeachment, if they should deserve it.
The constitution has, therefore, wisely interposed this
check upon his power, so that he cannot, by any corrupt coalition with favourites, or dependents in high
offices, screen them from punishment.[2]

§ 1496. In England (from which this exception was
probably borrowed) no pardon can be pleaded in bar
of an impeachment. But the king may, after conviction upon an impeachment, pardon the offender. His
prerogative, therefore, cannot prevent the disgrace of a
conviction; but it may avert its effects, and restore the
offender to his credit.[3] The president possesses no
such power in any case of impeachment; and, as the
judgment upon a conviction extends no farther, than to
a removal from office, and disqualification to hold office,
there is not the same reason for its exercise after con-

[1] The Federalist, No. 64; 3 Elliot's Debates, 105, 106; 1 Tucker's
Black. Comm. App. 331.
[2] 1 Kent's Comm. Lect. 13, p. 266.
[3] 1 Tucker's Black. Comm. App. 331, 332; 4 Black. Comm. 399, 400.
See also Rawle on Const. ch. 17, p. 176; ch. 31, p. 293, 294.

viction, as there is in England; since (as we have seen) the judgment there, so that it does not exceed what is allowed by law, lies wholly in the breast of the house of lords, as to its nature and extent, and may, in many cases, not only reach the life, but the whole fortune of the offender.

§ 1497. It would seem to result from the principle, on which the power of each branch of the legislature to punish for contempts is founded, that the executive authority cannot interpose between them and the offender. The main object is to secure a purity, independence, and ability of the legislature adequate to the discharge of all their duties. If they can be overawed by force, or corrupted by largesses, or interrupted in their proceedings by violence, without the means of self-protection, it is obvious, that they will soon be found incapable of legislating with wisdom or independence. If the executive should possess the power of pardoning any such offender, they would be wholly dependent upon his good will and pleasure for the exercise of their own powers. Thus, in effect, the rights of the people entrusted to them would be placed in perpetual jeopardy. The constitution is silent in respect to the right of granting pardons in such cases, as it is in respect to the jurisdiction to punish for contempts. The latter arises by implication; and to make it effectual the former is excluded by implication.[1]

§ 1498. Subject to these exceptions, (and perhaps there may be others of a like nature standing on special grounds,) the power of pardon is general and unqualified, reaching from the highest to the lowest offences. The power of remission of fines, penalties, and forfeitures is

---

[1] Rawle on Constitution, ch. 17, p. 177.

also included in it; and may in the last resort be exercised by the executive, although it is in many cases by our laws confided to the treasury department.[1]   No law can abridge the constitutional powers of the executive department, or interrupt its right to interpose by pardon in such cases.[2]

§ 1499. The next clause is: "He (the president) "shall have power, by and with the advice and consent "of the senate, to make treaties, provided two thirds of "the senators present concur.   And he shall nominate, "and, by and with the advice and consent of the senate, "shall appoint ambassadors, other public ministers, "and consuls, judges of the Supreme Court, and all "other officers of the United States, whose appoint- "ments are not herein otherwise provided for, and "which shall be established by law.   But the congress "may by law vest the appointment of such inferior offi- "cers, as they think proper, in the president alone, in " the courts of law, or in the heads of departments."

§ 1500. The first power, "to make treaties," was not in the original draft of the constitution; but was afterwards reported by a committee; and after some ineffectual attempts to amend, it was adopted, in substance, as it now stands, except, that in the report the advice and consent of two thirds of the senators was not required to a treaty of peace. This exception was struck out by a vote of eight states against three. The principal struggle was, to require two thirds of the

---

1 Act of 3d of March, 1797, ch. 67 : Act of 11th of Feb. 1800, ch. 6.

2 Instances of the exercise of this power by the president, in remitting fines and penalties in cases, not within the scope of the laws giving authority to the treasury department, have repeatedly occurred; and their obligatory force has never been questioned.

whole number of members of the senate, instead of two thirds of those present.[1]

§ 1501. Under the confederation congress possessed the sole and exclusive power of "entering into treaties and alliances, provided, that no treaty of commerce shall be made, whereby the legislative power of the respective states shall be restrained from imposing such imposts and duties on foreigners, as their own people were subjected to; or from prohibiting the exportation or importation of any species of goods or commodities whatsoever." But no treaty or alliance could be entered into, unless by the assent of nine of the states.[2] These limitations upon the power were found very inconvenient in practice; and indeed, in conjunction with other defects, contributed to the prostration, and utter imbecility of the confederation.[3]

§ 1502. The power "to make treaties" is by the constitution general; and of course it embraces all sorts of treaties, for peace or war; for commerce or territory; for alliance or succours; for indemnity for injuries or payment of debts; for the recognition and enforcement of principles of public law; and for any other purposes, which the policy or interests of independent sovereigns may dictate in their intercourse with each other.[4] But though the power is thus general and unrestricted, it is not to be so construed, as to destroy the fundamental laws of the state. A power given by the constitution cannot be construed to authorize a destruction of other powers given in the same instrument. It must be con-

---

1 Journal of Convention, p. 225, 326, 339, 341, 342, 343, 362; The Federalist, No. 75.

2 Confederation, Art. 9.

3 The Federalist, No. 42.

4 See 5 Marshall's Life of Washington, ch. 8, p. 650 to 659.

strued, therefore, in subordination to it; and cannot supersede, or interfere with any other of its fundamental provisions.[1] Each is equally obligatory, and of paramount authority within its scope; and no one embraces a right to annihilate any other. A treaty to change the organization of the government, or annihilate its sovereignty, to overturn its republican form, or to deprive it of its constitutional powers, would be void; because it would destroy, what it was designed merely to fulfil, the will of the people. Whether there are any other restrictions, necessarily growing out of the structure of the government, will remain to be considered, whenever the exigency shall arise.[2]

§ 1503. The power of making treaties is indispensable to the due exercise of national sovereignty, and very important, especially as it relates to war, peace, and commerce. That it should belong to the national government would seem to be irresistibly established by every argument deduced from experience, from public policy, and a close survey of the objects of government. It is difficult to circumscribe the power within any definite limits, applicable to all times and exigencies, without impairing its efficacy, or defeating its purposes. The constitution has, therefore, made it general and unqualified. This very circumstance, however, renders it highly important, that it should be delegated in such

[1] See Woodeson's Elem. of Jurisp. p. 51.

[2] See 1 Tuck. Black. Comm. App. 332, 333; Rawle on Const. ch. 7, p. 63 to 76; 2 Elliot's Deb. 368, 369 to 379; Journal of Convention, p. 342; 4 Jefferson's Corresp. 2, 3. — Mr. Jefferson seems at one time to have thought, that the constitution only meant to authorize the president and senate to carry into effect, by way of treaty, *any power they might constitutionally exercise.* At the same time, he admits, that he was sensible of the weak points of this position. 4 Jefferson's Corresp. 498. What are such powers given to the president and senate? Could they make appointments by treaty?

a mode, and with such precautions, as will afford the highest security, that it will be exercised by men the best qualified for the purpose, and in the manner most conducive to the public good.[1]   With such views, the question was naturally presented in the convention, to what body shall it be delegated ?   It might be delegated to congress generally, as it was under the confederation, exclusive of the president, or in conjunction with him.   It might be delegated to either branch of the legislature, exclusive of, or in conjunction with him.   Or it might be exclusively delegated to the president.

§ 1504. In the formation of treaties, secrecy and immediate despatch are generally requisite, and sometimes absolutely indispensable.   Intelligence may often be obtained, and measures matured in secrecy, which could never be done, unless in the faith and confidence of profound secrecy.   No man at all acquainted with diplomacy, but must have felt, that the success of negotiations as often depends upon their being unknown by the public, as upon their justice or their policy.   Men will assume responsibility in private, and communicate information, and express opinions, which they would feel the greatest repugnance publicly to avow ;   and measures may be defeated by the intrigues and management of foreign powers, if they suspect them to be in progress, and understand their precise nature and extent.   In this view the executive department is a far better depositary of the power, than congress would be.   The delays incident to a large assembly ; the differences of opinion ; the time consumed in debate ; and the utter impossibility of secrecy, all combine to render them unfitted for the purposes of diplomacy.   And our

---

[1] The Federalist, No. 64.

own experience during the confederation abundantly demonstrated all the evils, which the theory would lead us
to expect.[1]   Besides ; there are tides in national affairs,
as well as in the affairs of private life.   To discern and
profit by them is the part of true political wisdom ; and
the loss of a week, or even of a day, may sometimes
change the whole aspect of affairs, and render negotiations wholly nugatory, or indecisive.   The loss of a
battle, the death of a prince, the removal of a minister,
the pressure or removal of fiscal embarrassments at the
moment, and other circumstances, may change the whole
posture of affairs, and ensure success, or defeat the best
concerted project.[2]   The executive, having a constant
eye upon foreign affairs, can promptly meet, and even
anticipate such emergencies, and avail himself of all the
advantages accruing from them ; while a large assembly
would be coldly deliberating on the chances of success,
and the policy of opening negotiations.   It is manifest,
then, that congress would not be a suitable depositary
of the power.

§ 1505. The same difficulties would occur from confiding it exclusively to either branch of congress.   Each
is too numerous for prompt and immediate action, and
secrecy.   The matters in negotiations, which usually
require these qualities in the highest degree, are the
preparatory and auxiliary measures ; and which are to
be seized upon, as it were, in an instant.   The president could easily arrange them.   But the house, or the
senate, if in session, could not act, until after great delays ; and in the recess could not act all.   To have
entrusted the power to either would have been to relinquish the benefits of the constitutional agency of the

_____

[1] The Federalist, No. 64.   [2] Id. No. 64.

president in the conduct of foreign negotiations. It is true, that the branch so entrusted might have the option to employ the president in that capacity; but they would also have the option of refraining from it; and it cannot be disguised, that pique, or cabal, or personal or political hostility, might induce them to keep their pursuits at a distance from his inspection and participation. Nor could it be expected, that the president, as a mere ministerial agent of such branch, would enjoy the confidence and respect of foreign powers to the same extent, as he would, as the constitutional representative of the nation itself; and his interposition would of course have less efficacy and weight.[1]

§ 1506. On the other hand, considering the delicacy and extent of the power, it is too much to expect, that a free people would confide to a single magistrate, however respectable, the sole authority to act conclusively, as well as exclusively, upon the subject of treaties. In England, the power to make treaties is exclusively vested in the crown.[2] But however proper it may be in a monarchy, there is no American statesman, but must feel, that such a prerogative in an American president would be inexpedient and dangerous.[3] It would be inconsistent with that wholesome jealousy, which all republics ought to cherish of all depositaries of power; and which, experience teaches us, is the best security against the abuse of it.[4] The check, which acts upon the mind from the consideration, that what is done is but preliminary, and requires the assent of other independent minds to give it a legal conclusiveness, is a restraint, which awakens caution, and compels to deliberation.

---

[1] The Federalist, No. 75.
[2] 1 Black. Comm. 257; The Federalist, No. 69.
[3] The Federalist, No. 75.   [4] Id. No. 75.

§ 1507. The plan of the constitution is happily adapted to attain all just objects in relation to foreign negotiations. While it confides the power to the executive department, it guards it from serious abuse by placing it under the ultimate superintendence of a select body of high character and high responsibility. It is indeed clear to a demonstration, that this joint possession of the power affords a greater security for its just exercise, than the separate possession of it by either.[1]   The president is the immediate author and finisher of all treaties; and all the advantages, which can be derived from talents, information, integrity, and deliberate investigation on the one hand, and from secrecy and despatch on the other, are thus combined in the system.[2]   But no treaty, so formed, becomes binding upon the country, unless it receives the deliberate assent of two thirds of the senate. In that body all the states are equally represented; and, from the nature of the appointment and duration of the office, it may fairly be presumed at all times to contain a very large portion of talents, experience, political wisdom, and sincere patriotism, a spirit of liberality, and a deep devotion to all the substantial interests of the country. The constitutional check of requiring two thirds to confirm a treaty is, of itself, a sufficient guaranty against any wanton sacrifice of private rights, or any betrayal of public privileges.   To suppose otherwise would be to suppose, that a representative republican government was a mere phantom; that the state legislatures were incapable, or unwilling to choose senators possessing due qualifications; and that the people would voluntarily confide power to those, who were ready to promote

---

[1] The Federalist, No. 75.   [2] Id. No. 64.

their ruin, and endanger, or destroy their liberties.
Without supposing a case of utter indifference, or utter
corruption in the people, it would be impossible, that
the senate should be so constituted at any time, as that
the honour and interests of the country would not be
safe in their hands. When such an indifference, or corruption shall have arrived, it will be in vain to prescribe
any remedy; for the constitution will have crumbled
into ruins, or have become a mere shadow, about which
it would be absurd to disquiet ourselves.[1]

§ 1508. Although the propriety of this delegation of
the power seems, upon sound reasoning, to be incontestible; yet few parts of the constitution were assailed
with more vehemence.[2] One ground of objection was,
the trite topic of an intermixture of the executive and
legislative powers; some contending, that the president ought alone to possess the prerogative of making
treaties; and others, that it ought to be exclusively
deposited in the senate. Another objection was, the
smallness of the number of the persons, to whom the
power was confided; some being of opinion, that the
house of representatives ought to be associated in its
exercise; and others, that two thirds of all the members of the senate, and not two thirds of all the members present, should be required to ratify a treaty.[3]

§ 1509. In relation to the objection, that the power
ought to have been confided exclusively to the president, it may be suggested in addition to the preceding
remarks, that, however safe it may be in governments,
where the executive magistrate is an hereditary monarch, to commit to him the entire power of making

---

[1] The Federalist, No. 64.
[2] See 2 Elliot's Debates, 367 to 379.
[3] The Federalist, No. 75.

treaties, it would be utterly unsafe and improper to entrust that power to an executive magistrate chosen for four years. It has been remarked, and is unquestionably true, that an hereditary monarch, though often the oppressor of his people, has personally too much at stake in the government to be in any material danger of corruption by foreign powers, so as to surrender any important rights or interests. But a man, raised from a private station to the rank of chief magistrate for a short period, having but a slender or moderate fortune, and no very deep stake in the society, might sometimes be under temptations to sacrifice duty to interest, which it would require great virtue to withstand. If ambitious, he might be tempted to seek his own aggrandizement by the aid of a foreign power, and use the field of negotiations for this purpose. If avaricious, he might make his treachery to his constituents a vendible article at an enormous price. Although such occurrences are not ordinarily to be expected; yet the history of human conduct does not warrant that exalted opinion of human nature, which would make it wise in a nation to commit its most delicate interests and momentous concerns to the unrestrained disposal of a single magistrate.[1] It is far more wise to interpose checks upon the actual exercise of the power, than remedies to redress, or punish an abuse of it.

§ 1510. The impropriety of delegating the power exclusively to the senate has been already sufficiently considered. And, in addition to what has been already urged against the participation of the house of representatives in it, it may be remarked, that the house of representatives is for other reasons far less fit, than the

---

[1] The Federalist, No. 75.

senate, to be the exclusive depositary of the power, or to hold it in conjunction with the executive. In the first place, it is a popular assembly, chosen immediately from the people, and representing, in a good measure, their feelings and local interests ; and it will on this account be more likely to be swayed by such feelings and interests, than the senate, chosen by the states through the voice of the state legislatures. In the next place, the house of representatives are chosen for two years only ; and the internal composition of the body is constantly changing so, as to admit of less certainty in their opinions, and their measures, than would naturally belong to a body of longer duration. In the next place, the house of representatives is far more numerous, than the senate, and will be constantly increasing in numbers so, that it will be more slow in its movements, and more fluctuating in its councils. In the next place, the senate will naturally be composed of persons of more experience, weight of character, and talents, than the members of the house. Accurate knowledge of foreign politics, a steady and systematic adherence to the same views, nice and uniform sensibility to national character, as well as secrecy, decision, and despatch, are required for a due execution of the power to make treaties. And, if these are not utterly incompatible with the genius of a numerous and variable body, it must be admitted, that they will be more rarely found there, than in a more select body, having a longer duration in office, and representing, not the interests of private constituents alone, but the sovereignty of states.

§ 1511. Besides; the very habits of business, and the uniformity and regularity of system, acquired by a long possession of office, are of great concern in all

cases of this sort. The senators from the longer duration of their office will have great opportunities of extending their political information, and of rendering
their experience more and more beneficial to their
country. The members are slowly changed; so, that
the body will at all times, from its very organization,
comprehend a large majority of persons, who have
been engaged for a considerable time in public duties,
and foreign affairs. If, in addition to all these reasons,
it is considered, that in the senate all the states are
equally represented, and in the house very unequally,
there can be no reasonable doubt, that the senate is in
all respects a more competent, and more suitable depositary of the power, than the house, either with, or without the co-operation of the executive. And most of
the reasoning applies with equal force to any participation by the house in the treaty-making functions. It
would add an unwieldly machinery to all foreign operations; and retard, if not wholly prevent, the beneficial purposes of the power.[1] Yet such a scheme has
not been without warm advocates. And it has been
thought an anomaly, that, while the power to make
war was confided to both branches of congress, the
power to make peace was within the reach of one,
with the co-operation of the president.[2]

§ 1512. But there will be found no inconsistency, or
inconvenience in this diversity of power. Considering
the vast expenditures and calamities, with which war
is attended, there is certainly the strongest ground for

---

[1] The Federalist, No. 64, 75. — In the convention a proposition was
made to add the house to the senate, in advising and consenting to treaties. But it was rejected by the vote of ten states against one. Journ.
of Convention, 339, 340.

[2] 1 Tuck. Black. Comm. App. 338, 339.

confiding it to the collected wisdom of the national councils. It requires one party only to declare war ; but it requires the co-operation and consent of both belligerents to make peace. No negotiations are necessary in the former case; in the latter, they are indispensable. Every reason, therefore, for entrusting the treaty-making power to the president and senate in common negotiations, applies *a fortiori* to a treaty of peace. Indeed, peace is so important to the welfare of a republic, and so suited to all its truest interests, as well as to its liberties, that it can scarcely be made too facile. While, on the other hand, war is at all times so great an evil, that it can scarcely be made too difficult. The power to make peace can never be unsafe for the nation in the hands of the president and two thirds of the senate. The power to prevent it, may not be without hazard in the hands of the house of representatives, who may be too much under the control of popular excitement, or legislative rivalry, to act at all times with the same degree of impartiality and caution. In the convention, a proposition to except treaties of peace from the treaty-making power was, at one time, inserted, but was afterwards deliberately abandoned.[1]

§ 1513. In regard to the objection, that the arrangement is a violation of the fundamental rule, that the legislative and executive departments ought to be kept separate; it might be sufficient to advert to the considerations stated in another place, which show, that the true sense of the rule does not require a total separation.[2] But, in truth, the nature of the power of making treaties indicates a peculiar propriety in the Union of the executive and the senate in the exercise of it.

[1] Journ. of Convention, 226, 325, 326, 341, 342.
[2] See Vol. II. § 524, et seq.

Though some writers on government place this power in the class of executive authorities ; yet, it is an arbitrary classification ; and, if attention is given to its operation, it will be found to partake more of the legislative, than of the executive character. The essence of legislation is to prescribe laws, or regulations for society ; while the execution of those laws and regulations, and the employment of the common strength, either for that purpose, or for the common defence, seem to comprize all the functions of the executive magistrate. The power of making treaties is plainly neither the one, nor the other. It relates, neither to the execution of subsisting laws, nor to the enactment of new ones ; and still less does it relate to the exertion of the common strength. Its objects are contracts with foreign nations, which have the force of law with us; but, as to the foreign sovereigns, have only the obligation of good faith. Treaties are not rules prescribed by the sovereign to his subjects ; but agreements between sovereign and sovereign. The treaty-making power, therefore, seems to form a distinct department, and to belong, properly, neither to the legislature, nor the executive, though it may be said to partake of qualities common to each. The president, from his unity, promptitude, and facility of action, is peculiarly well adapted to carry on the initiative processes ; while the senate, representing all the states, and engaged in legislating for the interests of the whole country, is equally well fitted to be entrusted with the power of ultimate ratification.[1]

§ 1514. The other objection, which would require a concurrence of two thirds of all the members of the

---

[1] The Federalist, No. 75.

senate, and not merely of two thirds of all present, is not better founded.[1] All provisions, which require more, than a majority of any body to its resolutions, have (as has been already intimated) a direct tendency to embarrass the operations of the government, and an indirect one to subject the sense of the majority to that of the minority. This consideration ought never to be lost sight of; and very strong reasons ought to exist to justify any departure from the ordinary rule, that the majority ought to govern. The constitution has, on this point, gone as far in the endeavour to secure the advantage of numbers in the formation of treaties, as can be reconciled either with the activity of the public councils, or with a reasonable regard to the sense of the major part of the community. If two thirds of the whole number of members had been required, it would, in many cases, from a non-attendance of a part, amount in practice to a necessity almost of unanimity. The history of every political establishment, in which such a principle has prevailed, is a history of impotence, perplexity, and disorder. Proofs of this position may be easily adduced from the examples of the Roman tribuneship, the Polish diet, and the states general of the Netherlands, and even from our own experience under the confederation.[2] Under the latter instrument the concurrence of nine states was necessary, not only to making treaties, but to many other acts of a less important character; and measures were often defeated by the non-attendance of members, sometimes by design, and sometimes by accident.[3] It is hardly possible, that a treaty could be ratified by surprise, or tak-

1 2 Elliot's Debates, 367 to 379.
2 The Federalist, No. 75 ; Id. No. 22.
3 Ibid. and 1 Elliot's Debates, 44, 45.

ing advantage of the accidental absence of a few members; and certainly the motive to punctuality in attendance will be greatly increased by making such ratification to depend upon the numbers present.[1]

§ 1515. The Federalist has taken notice of the difference between the treaty-making power in England, and that in America in the following terms: "The president is to have power, with the advice and consent of the senate, to make treaties, provided two thirds of the members present concur. The king of Great Britain is the sole and absolute representative of the nation, in all foreign transactions. He can, of his own accord, make treaties of peace, commerce, alliance, and of every other description. It has been insinuated, that his authority, in this respect, is not conclusive; and that his conventions with foreign powers are subject to the revision, and stand in need of the ratification of parliament. But, I believe, this doctrine was never heard of, till it was broached upon the present occasion. Every jurist of that kingdom, and every other man acquainted with its constitution, knows, as an established fact, that the prerogative of making treaties exists in the crown in its utmost plenitude; and that the compacts entered into by the royal authority have the most complete legal validity and perfection, independ-

---

[1] The Federalist, No. 75, 22 ; 2 Elliot's Debates, 368. — In the convention a proposition to require the assent of two thirds of all the members of the senate was rejected by the vote of eight states against three. Another to require, that no treaty shall be made, unless two thirds of the whole number of senators were present, was also rejected by the vote of six states against five. Another, to require a majority of all the members of the senate to make a treaty, was also rejected by the vote of six states against five. Another, to require, that all the members should be summoned, and have time to attend, shared a like fate, by the vote of eight states against three. Journal of Convention, 343, 344.

ent of any other sanction. The parliament, it is true, is sometimes seen employing itself in altering the existing laws, to conform them to the stipulations in a new treaty; and this may have, possibly, given birth to the imagination, that its co-operation was necessary to the obligatory efficacy of the treaty. But this parliamentary interposition proceeds from a different cause; from the necessity of adjusting a most artificial and intricate system of revenue and commercial laws to the changes made in them by the operation of the treaty ; and of adapting new provisions and precautions to the new state of things, to keep the machine from running into disorder. In this respect, therefore, there is no comparison between the intended power of the president, and the actual power of the British sovereign. The one can perform alone, what the other can only do with the concurrence of a branch of the legislature. It must be admitted, that, in this instance, the power of the federal executive would exceed that of any state executive. But this arises naturally from the exclusive possession, by the Union, of that part of the sovereign power, which relates to treaties. If the confederacy were to be dissolved, it would become a question, whether the executives of the several states were not solely invested with that delicate and important prerogative."[1]

§ 1516. Upon the whole it is difficult to perceive, how the treaty-making power could have been better deposited, with a view to its safety and efficiency. Yet it was declaimed against with uncommon energy, as dangerous to the commonwealth, and subversive of

---

[1] See also the opinion of Iredell J. in *Ware v. Hylton*, 3 Dall. 272 to 276.

public liberty.[1] Time has demonstrated the fallacy of such prophecies ; and has confirmed the belief of the friends of the constitution, that it would be, not only safe, but full of wisdom and sound policy. Perhaps no stronger illustration, than this, can be found, of the facility of suggesting ingenious objections to any system, calculated to create public alarm, and to wound public confidence, which, at the same time, are unfounded in human experience, or in just reasoning.

§ 1517. Some doubts appear to have been entertained in the early stages of the government, as to the correct exposition of the constitution in regard to the agency of the senate in the formation of treaties. The question was, whether the agency of the senate was admissible previous to the negotiation, so as to advise on the instructions to be given to the ministers ; or was limited to the exercise of the power of advice and consent, after the treaty was formed ; or whether the president possessed an option to adopt one mode, or the other, as his judgment might direct.[2] The practical exposition assumed on the first occasion, which seems to have occurred in President Washington's administration, was, that the option belonged to the executive to adopt either mode, and the senate might advise before, as well as after, the formation of a treaty.[3] Since that period, the senate have been rarely, if ever, consulted, until after a treaty has been completed, and laid before them for ratification.[4] When so laid before the senate, that body is in the habit of deliberating upon it, as, indeed, it does on all *executive* business, in secret,

1 2 Elliot's Debates, 367 to 379.
2 5 Marshall's Life of Washington, ch. 2, p. 223.
3 Executive Journal, 11th August, 1790, p. 60, 61.
4 Rawle on Const. ch. 7, p. 63.

and with closed doors. The senate may wholly reject
the treaty, or advise and consent to a ratification of part
of the articles, rejecting others, or recommend additional or explanatory articles. In the event of a partial ratification, the treaty does not become the law of
the land, until the president and the foreign sovereign
have each assented to the modifications proposed by
the senate.[1] But, although the president may ask the
advice and consent of the senate to a treaty, he is not
absolutely bound by it ; for he may, after it is given,

---

[1] Rawle on Const. ch. 7, p. 63, 64. — Before the ratification of treaties, it is common for the senate to require, and for the president to lay
before them, all the official documents respecting the negotiations, to
assist their judgment. But the house of representatives have no constitutional right to insist on the production of them ; and it is matter of
discretion with the president, whether to comply, or not, with the demand of the house, which is but in the nature of a request. In the case
of the British Treaty of 1794, President Washington refused to lay the
papers before the house of representatives, when requested by them so
to do. See his Message, 24th of March, 1796; 1 Tuck. Black. Comm.
App. 334 ; 5 Marshall's Life of Washington, ch. 8, p. 654 ; 4 Jefferson's
Corresp. 464, 465 ; Rawle on Const. ch. 16, p. 171.

In the early part of President Washington's administration, he occasionally met the senate in person, to confer with them on the executive
business confided to them by the constitution. But this practice was
found very inconvenient, and was soon abandoned. In June, 1813, the
senate appointed a committee to hold a conference with President
Madison, respecting his nomination of a minister to Sweden, then before
them for ratification. But he declined it, considering, that it was incompatible with the due relations between the executive, and other departments of the government.* It is believed, that the practice has been
ever since abandoned.

Mr. Jefferson and the cabinet, (with the exception of Mr. Hamilton,)
in President Washington's administration, seem to have been of opinion,
that neither branch of the legislature had a right to call upon the heads
of departments, except through calls on the president for information or
papers. (4 Jefferson's Corresp. 463, 464, 465.) The practice has, however, of late years, settled down in favour of making direct calls on the
heads of the departments. Rawle on Const. ch. 16, p. 171, 172.

* Sergeant on Const. ch. 31, (2d edition,) p. 371 ; 5 Niles's Register, 243, 290; Id. 276, 340 ;
2 Executive Journal, 354, 381, 382. See also 2 Executive Journal, 353, 354, 388, 389.

still constitutionally refuse to ratify it.   Such an occurrence will probably be rare, because the president will scarcely incline to lay a treaty before the senate, which he is not disposed to ratify.[1]

§ 1518. The next part of the clause respects appointments to office.   The president is to nominate, and by and with the advice and consent of the senate, to appoint ambassadors, other public ministers, and consuls, judges of the Supreme Court, and other officers, whose appointments are not otherwise provided for.

§ 1519. Under the confederation, an exclusive power was given to congress of " sending and receiving ambassadors." [2] The term "ambassador," strictly construed, (as would seem to be required by the second article of that instrument,) comprehends the highest grade only of public ministers ; [3] and excludes those grades, which the United States would be most likely to prefer, whenever foreign embassies may be necessary.   But under no latitude of construction could the term, " ambassadors," comprehend consuls.   Yet it was found necessary by congress to employ the inferior grades of ministers, and to send and receive consuls. It is true, that the mutual appointment of consuls might have been provided for by treaty ; and where no treaty existed, congress might perhaps have had the authority under the ninth article of the confederation, which conferred a general authority to appoint officers managing the general affairs of the United States.   But the admis-

---

[1] Rawle on the Constitution, ch. 20, p. 194, 195 ; 4 Jefferson's Correspondence, 317, 318.

[2] Article 9.

[3] An enumeration of the various grades and powers of foreign ministers properly belongs to a treatise on public law.   The learned reader, however, will find ample information in the treatises of Grotius, Vattel, Martens, and Wicquefort.

sion of foreign consuls into the United States, when not stipulated for by treaty, was no where provided for.[1] The whole subject was full of embarrassment and constitutional doubts; and the provision in the constitution, extending the appointment to other public ministers and consuls, as well as to ambassadors, is a decided improvement upon the confederation.

§ 1520. In the first draft of the constitution, the power was given to the president to appoint officers in all cases, not otherwise provided for by the constitution; and the advice and consent of the senate was not required.[2] But in the same draft, the power to appoint ambassadors and judges of the Supreme Court was given to the senate.[3] The advice and consent of the senate, and the appointment by the president of ambassadors, and ministers, consuls, and judges of the Supreme Court, was afterwards reported by a committee, as an amendment, and was unanimously adopted.[4]

§ 1521. The mode of appointment to office, pointed out by the constitution, seems entitled to peculiar commendation. There are several ways, in which in ordinary cases the power may be vested. It may be confided to congress; or to one branch of the legislature; or to the executive alone; or to the executive in concurrence with any selected branch. The exercise of it by the people at large will readily be admitted by all considerate statesmen, to be impracticable, and therefore need not be examined. The suggestions, already made upon the treaty-making power, and the inconveniences of vesting it in congress, apply with great force to that of vesting the power of appointment to office in the

[1] The Federalist, No. 42.
[2] Journ. of Convention, p. 225.   [3] Id. 223.
[4] Id. 325, 326, 340, 362.

same body. It would enable candidates for office to introduce all sorts of cabals, intrigues, and coalitions into congress ; and not only distract their attention from their proper legislative duties ; but probably in a very high degree influence all legislative measures. A new source of division and corruption would thus be infused into the public councils, stimulated by private interests, and pressed by personal solicitations. What would be to be done, in case the senate and house should disagree in an appointment ? Are they to vote in convention, or as distinct bodies ? There would be practical difficulties attending both courses ; and experience has not justified the belief, that either would conduce either to good appointments, or to due responsibility.[1]

§ 1522. The same reasoning would apply to vesting the power exclusively in either branch of the legislature. It would make the patronage of the government subservient to private interests, and bring into suspicion the motives and conduct of members of the appointing body. There would be great danger, that the elections at the polls might be materially influenced by this power, to confer, or to withhold favours of this sort.[2]

§ 1523. Those, who are accustomed to profound reflection upon the human character and human experience, will readily adopt the opinion, that one man of discernment is better fitted to analyze and estimate the peculiar qualities, adapted to particular offices, than any body of men of equal, or even of superior discernment.[3] His sole and undivided responsibility will naturally beget a livelier sense of duty, and a more ex-

---

1 See The Federalist, No. 76, 77.   2 Ibid.
3 The Federalist, No. 76; 2 Wilson's Law Lect. 191, 192.

act regard to reputation. He will inquire with more earnestness, and decide with more impartiality. He will have fewer personal attachments to gratify, than a body of men; and will be less liable to be misled by his private friendships and affections; or, at all events, his conduct will be more open to scrutiny, and less liable to be misunderstood. If he ventures upon a system of favoritism, he will not escape censure, and can scarcely avoid public detection and disgrace. But in a public body appointments will be materially influenced by party attachments and dislikes; by private animosities, and antipathies, and partialities; and will be generally founded in compromises, having little to do with the merit of candidates, and much to do with the selfish interests of individuals and cabals. They will be too much governed by local, or sectional, or party arrangements.[1] A president, chosen from the nation at large, may well be presumed to possess high intelligence, integrity, and sense of character. He will be compelled to consult public opinion in the most important appointments; and must be interested to vindicate the propriety of his appointments by selections from those, whose qualifications are unquestioned, and unquestionable. If he should act otherwise, and surrender the public patronage into the hands of profligate men, or low adventurers, it will be impossible for him long to retain public favour. Nothing, no, not even the whole influence of party, could long screen him from the just indignation of the people. Though slow, the ultimate award of popular opinion would stamp upon his conduct its merited infamy. No president, however weak, or credulous, (if such a per-

---

[1] The Federalist, No. 76.

son could ever under any conjuncture of circumstances obtain the office,) would fail to perceive, or to act upon admonitions of this sort. At all events, he would be less likely to disregard them, than a large body of men, who would share the responsibility, and encourage each other in the division of the patronage of the government.

§ 1524. But, though these general considerations might easily reconcile us to the choice of vesting the power of appointment exclusively in the president, in preference to the senate, or house of representatives alone; the patronage of the government, and the appointments to office are too important to the public welfare, not to induce great hesitation in vesting them exclusively in the president. The power may be abused; and, assuredly, it will be abused, except in the hands of an executive of great firmness, independence, integrity, and public spirit. It should never be forgotten, that in a republican government offices are established, and are to be filled, not to gratify private interests and private attachments; not as a means of corrupt influence, or individual profit; not for cringing favourites, or court sycophants; but for purposes of the highest public good; to give dignity, strength, purity, and energy to the administration of the laws. It would not, therefore, be a wise course to omit any precaution, which, at the same time, that it should give to the president a power over the appointments of those, who are in conjunction with himself to execute the laws, should also interpose a salutary check upon its abuse, acting by way of preventive, as well as of remedy.

§ 1525. Happily, this difficult task has been achieved by the constitution. The president is to nominate, and thereby has the sole power to select for office; but his nomination cannot confer office, unless approved by a majority of the senate. His responsibility and theirs is thus complete, and distinct. He can never be compelled to yield to their appointment of a man unfit for office; and, on the other hand, they may withhold their advice and consent from any candidate, who in their judgment does not possess due qualifications for office. Thus, no serious abuse of the power can take place without the co-operation of two co-ordinate branches, of the government, acting in distinct spheres; and, if there should be any improper concession on either side, it is obvious, that from the structure and changes, incident to each department, the evil cannot long endure, and will be remedied, as it should be, by the elective franchise. The consciousness of this check will make the president more circumspect, and deliberate in his nominations for office. He will feel, that, in case of a disagreement of opinion with the senate, his principal vindication must depend upon the unexceptionable character of his nomination. And in case of a rejection, the most, that can be said, is, that he had not his first choice. He will still have a wide range of selection; and his responsibility to present another candidate, entirely qualified for the office, will be complete and unquestionable.

§ 1526. Nor is it to be expected, that the senate will ordinarily fail of ratifying the appointment of a suitable person for the office. Independent of the desire, which such a body may naturally be presumed to feel, of having offices suitably filled, (when they cannot make the appointment themselves,) there will be a responsibility to public opinion for a rejection, which will overcome all common private wishes. Cases, indeed, may be imagined, in which the senate from party motives, from a spirit of opposition, and even from motives of a more private nature, may reject a nomination absolutely unexceptionable. But such occurrences will be rare. The more common error, (if there shall be any) will be too great a facility to yield to the executive wishes, as a means of personal, or popular favour. A president will rarely want means, if he shall choose to use them, to induce some members of such a body to aid his nominations ; since a correspondent influence may be fairly presumed to exist, to gratify such persons in other recommendations for office, and thus to make them indirectly the dispensers of local patronage. It will be, principally, with regard to high officers, such as ambassadors, judges, heads of departments, and other appointments of great public importance, that the senate will interpose to prevent an unsuitable choice. Their own dignity, and sense of character, their duty to their country, and their very title to office will be materially dependent upon a firm discharge of their duty on such occasions.[1]

§ 1527. Perhaps the duties of the president, in the discharge of this most delicate and important duty of his office, were never better summed up, than in the following language of a distinguished commentator.[2] "A proper selection and appointment of subordinate officers is one of the strongest marks of a powerful mind. It is a duty of the president to acquire, as far

[1] The Federalist, No. 76, 77 ; 1 Kent's Comm. Lect. 13, p. 269; Rawle on Const. ch. 14, p. 162, &c. ; 1 Tucker's Black. Comm. App. 340 to 343. — The whole reasoning of the Federalist, on this subject, is equally striking for its sound practical sense and its candour. I have freely used it in the foregoing summary. The Federalist, No. 76.
[2] Rawle on Const. ch. 14, p. 164.

CH. XXXVII.] EXECUTIVE — APPOINTMENTS. 379

as possible, an intimate knowledge of the capacities and characters of his fellow citizens; to disregard the importunities of friends; the hints or menaces of enemies; the bias of party, and the hope of popularity. The latter is sometimes the refuge of feeble-minded men; but its gleam is transient, if it is obtained by a dereliction of honest duty and sound discretion. Popular favour is best secured by carefully ascertaining, and strictly pursuing the true interests of the people. The president himself is elected on the supposition, that he is the most capable citizen to understand, and promote those interests; and in every appointment he ought to consider himself as executing a public trust of the same nature. Neither should the fear of giving offence to the public, or pain to the individual, deter him from the immediate exercise of his power of removal, on proof of incapacity, or infidelity in the subordinate officer. The public, uninformed of the necessity, may be surprised, and at first dissatisfied; but public approbation ultimately accompanies the fearless and upright discharge of duty."

§ 1528. It was objected by some persons, at the time of the adoption of the constitution, that this union of the executive with the senate in appointments would give the president an undue influence over the senate. This argument is manifestly untenable, since it supposes, that an undue influence *over* the senate is to be acquired by the power of the latter to *restrain* him. Even, if the argument were well founded, the influence of the president over the senate would be still more increased, by giving him the exclusive power of appointment; for then he would be wholly beyond restraint. The opposite ground was assumed by other persons, who thought the influence of the

senate over the president would by this means become
dangerous, if not irresistible.[1] There is more plausibility in this suggestion; but it proceeds upon unsatisfactory reasoning. It is certain, that the senate cannot,
by their refusal to confirm the nominations of the
president, prevent him from the proper discharge of his
duty. The most, that can be suggested, is, that they
may induce him to yield to their favourites, instead of
his own, by resisting his nominations. But if this should
happen in a few rare instances, it is obvious, that his
means of influence would ordinarily form a counter
check. The power, which can originate the disposal
of honours and emoluments, is more likely to attract,
than to be attracted by the power, which can merely
obstruct their course.[2] But in truth, in every system
of government there are possible dangers, and real
difficulties; and to provide for the suppression of all
influence of one department, in regard to another,
would be as visionary, as to provide, that human passions and feelings should never influence public measures. The most, that can be done, is to provide checks,
and public responsibility. The plan of the constitution

---

[1] A practical question of some importance arose soon after the constitution was adopted, in regard to the appointment of foreign ministers;
whether the power of the senate over the appointment gave that body
a right to inquire into the policy of making any such appointment, or
instituting any mission; or whether their power was confined to the
consideration of the mere fitness of the person nominated for the office.
If the former were the true interpretation of the senatorial authority,
then they would have a right to inquire into the motives, which should
induce the president to create such a diplomatic mission. It was after
debate decided by a small majority of the senate, in 1792, that they had
no right to enter upon the consideration of the policy, or fitness of the
mission. 5 Marshall's Life of Washington, ch. 5, p. 370, note. But the
senate have on several occasions since that time decided the other way;
and particularly in regard to missions to Russia and Turkey.

[2] The Federalist, No. 77.

seems as nearly perfect for this purpose, as any one can be ; and indeed it has been less censured, than any other important delegation of power in that instrument.[1]

---

[1] Whether the senate should have a negative on presidential appointments, was a question, upon which the members of the convention were much divided.   Mr. John Adams (afterwards president) was opposed to it ; and a friendly correspondence took place between him and Mr. Roger Sherman, of Connecticut, (one of the framers of the constitution,) upon the subject.   I extract from Mr. Pitkin's valuable History of the United States, the substance of the arguments urged on each side, as they present a general view of the reasoning, which had influence in the convention.

" To some general observations of Mr. Sherman in favour of this power in the senate, Mr. Adams made the following objections.

" ' The negative of the senate upon appointments,' he said ' is liable to the following objections.

" ' 1. It takes away, or at least it lessens the responsibility of the executive — our constitution obliges me to say, that it lessens the responsibility of the president.   The blame of an hasty, injudicious, weak, or wicked appointment, is shared so much between him and the senate, that his part of it will be too small.   Who can censure him, without censuring the senate, and the legislatures who appoint them ? all their friends will be interested to vindicate the president, in order to screen them from censure ; besides, if an impeachment is brought before them against an officer, are they not interested to acquit him, lest some part of the odium of his guilt should fall upon them, who advised to his appointment ?

" ' 2. It turns the minds and attention of the people to the senate, a branch of the legislature, in executive matters ; it interests another branch of the legislature in the management of the executive ; it divides the people between the executive and the senate : whereas all the people ought to be united to watch the executive, to oppose its encroachments, and resist its ambition.   Senators and representatives, and their constituents — in short, the aristocratical and democratical divisions of society, ought to be united, on all occasions, to oppose the executive or the monarchical branch, when it attempts to overleap its limits.   But how can this union be effected, when the aristocratical branch has pledged its reputation to the executive by consenting to an appointment ?

" ' 3. It has a natural tendency, to excite ambition in the senate.   An active, ardent spirit, in that house, who is rich, and able, has a great reputation and influence, will be solicited by candidates for office ; not to introduce the idea of bribery, because, though it certainly would force itself in, in other countries, and will probably here, when we

§ 1529. The other part of the clause, while it leaves to the president the appointment to all offices, not otherwise provided for, enables congress to vest the

grow populous and rich, yet it is not yet, I hope, to be dreaded. But ambition must come in, already. A senator of great influence will be naturally ambitious, and desirous of increasing his influence. Will he not be under a temptation to use his influence with the president, as well as his brother senators, to appoint persons to office in the several states, who will exert themselves in elections to get out his enemies or opposers, both in senate and house of representatives, and to get in his friends, perhaps his instruments? Suppose a senator, to aim at the treasury office, for himself, his brother, father, or son. Suppose him to aim at the president's chair, or vice-president's, at the next election — or at the office of war, foreign or domestic affairs, will he not naturally be tempted to make use of his whole patronage, his whole influence, in advising to appointments, both with president and senators, to get such persons nominated, as will exert themselves in elections of president, vice-president, senators, and house of representatives, to increase his interests, and promote his views? In this point of view, I am very apprehensive, that this defect in our constitution will have an unhappy tendency to introduce corruption of the grossest kinds, both of ambition and avarice, into all our elections. And this will be the worst of poisons to our constitution; it will not only destroy the present form of government, but render it almost impossible to substitute in its place any free government, even a better limited monarchy, or any other, than a despotism, or a simple monarchy.

" '4. To avoid the evil under the last head, it will be in danger of dividing the continent into two or three nations, a case that presents no prospect but of perpetual war.

" '5. This negative on appointments is in danger of involving the senate in reproach, obloquy, censure, and suspicion, without doing any good. Will the senate use their negative or not? — if not, why should they have it? — many will censure them for not using it — many will ridicule them, call them servile, &c., if they do use it. The very first instance of it will expose the senators to the resentment, not only of the disappointed candidate and all his friends, but of the president and all his friends; and those will be most of the officers of government, through the nation.

" '6. We shall very soon have parties formed — a court and country party — and these parties will have names given them; one party in the house of representatives will support the president and his measures and ministers — the other will oppose them — a similar party will be in the senate — these parties will struggle with all their art, perhaps with intrigue, perhaps with corruption at every election to increase their own

appointment of such inferior officers, as they may think proper, in the president, in the courts of law, or in the heads of departments. The propriety of this dis-

---

friends, and diminish their opposers. Suppose such parties formed in the senate, and then consider what factions, divisions, we shall have there, upon every nomination.

" ' 7. The senate have not time. You are of opinion, " that the concurrence of the senate in the appointment to office will strengthen the hands of the executive, and secure the confidence of the people, much better than a select council, and will be less expensive," but in every one of these ideas, I have the misfortune to differ from you. It will weaken the hands of the executive, by lessening the obligation, gratitude, and attachment of the candidate to the president, by dividing his attachment between the executive and legislature, which are natural enemies.

" ' Officers of government, instead of having a single eye, and undivided attachment to the executive branch, as they ought to have, consistent with law and the constitution, will be constantly tempted to be factious with their factious patrons in the senate. The president's own officers, in a thousand instances, will oppose his just and constitutional exertions, and screen themselves under the wings of their patrons and party in the legislature. Nor will it secure the confidence of the people; the people will have more confidence in the executive, in executive matters, than in the senate. The people will be constantly jealous of factious schemes in the senators to unduly influence the executive, and of corrupt bargains between the senate and executive, to serve each other's private views. The people will also be jealous, that the influence of the senate will be employed to conceal, connive, and defend guilt in executive officers, instead of being a guard and watch upon them, and a terror to them — a council selected by the president himself, at his pleasure, from among the senators, representatives, and nation at large, would be purely responsible — in that case, the senate, as a body, would not be compromised. The senate would be a terror to privy councillors — its honor would never be pledged to support any measure or instrument of the executive, beyond justice, law, and the constitution. Nor would a privy council be more expensive. The whole senate must now deliberate on every appointment, and, if they ever find time for it, you will find that a great deal of time will be required and consumed in this service. Then the president might have a constant executive council ; now he has none.

" ' I said, under the seventh head, that the senate would not have time. You will find, that the whole business of this government will be infinitely delayed, by this negative of the senate on treaties and appointments. Indian treaties and consular conventions have been

cretionary power in congress, to some extent, cannot well be questioned. If any discretion should be allowed, its limits could hardly admit of being exactly defined ;

---

already waiting for months, and the senate have not been able to find a moment of time to attend to them ; and this evil must constantly increase, so that the senate must be constantly sitting, and must be paid as long as they sit.

" ' But I have tired your patience. Is there any truth or importance in these broken hints and crude surmises, or not ? To me they appear well founded, and very important.'

" 'To these remarks Mr. Sherman replied, that he esteemed ' the provision made for appointments to office to be a matter of very great importance, on which the liberties and safety of the people depended, nearly as much as on legislation. If that was vested in the president alone, he might render himself despotic. It was a saying of one of the kings of England, " *that while the king could appoint the bishops and judges, he might have what religion and laws he pleased.*" To give that observation its full effect, they must hold their offices during his pleasure ; by such appointments, without control, a power might be gradually established, that would be more formidable than a standing army.

" ' It appears to me, that the senate is the most important branch in the government, for the aid and support of the executive, for securing the rights of the individual states, the government of the United States, and the liberties of the people. The executive is not to execute its own will, but the will of the legislature declared by the laws, and the senate, being a branch of the legislature, will be disposed to accomplish that end, and advise to such appointments, as will be most likely to effect it ; from their knowledge of the people in the several states, they can give the best information who are qualified for office. And they will, as you justly observe, in some degree lessen his responsibility, yet, will he not have as much remaining as he can well support ? and may not their advice enable him to make such judicious appointments, as to render responsibility less necessary ? no person can deserve censure, when he acts honestly according to his best discretion.

" 'The senators, being chosen by the legislatures of the states, and depending on them for re-election, will naturally be watchful to prevent any infringement of the rights of the states. And the government of the United States being federal, and instituted by a number of sovereign states for the better security of their rights, and advancement of their interests, they may be considered as so many pillars to support it, and by the exercise of the state governments, peace and good order may be preserved in the places most remote from the seat of the federal government, as well as at the centre.

and it might fairly be left to congress to act according to the lights of experience. It is difficult to foresee, or to provide for all the combinations of circumstances,

"'I believe this will be a better balance to secure the government, than three independent negatives would be.

"'I think you admit, in your Defence of the Governments of the United States, that even one branch might serve in a diplomatic government, like that of the Union ; but I think the constitution is much improved by the addition of another branch, and those of the executive and judiciary. This seems to be an improvement on federal government, beyond what has been made by any other states. I can see nothing in the constitution, that will tend to its dissolution, except the article for making amendments.

"'That the evils, that you suggest, may happen in consequence of the power vested in the senate, to aid the executive, appears to me to be but barely possible. The senators, from the provision made for their appointment, will commonly be some of the most respectable citizens in the states, for wisdom and probity, and superior to faction, intrigue, or low artifice, to obtain appointments for themselves, or their friends, and any attempts of that kind would destroy their reputation with a free and enlightened people, and so frustrate the end they would have in view. Their being candidates for re-election will probably be one of the most powerful motives (next to that of their virtue) to fidelity in office, and by that means alone would they hope for success. "He, that walketh uprightly, walketh surely," is the saying of a divinely inspired writer — they will naturally have the confidence of the people, as they will be chosen by their immediate representatives, as well as from their characters, as men of wisdom and integrity. And I see not why all the branches of government should not harmonize in promoting the great end of their institution, the good and happiness of the people.

"'The senators and representatives being eligible from the citizens at large, and wealth not being a requisite qualification for either, they will be persons nearly equal, as to wealth and other qualifications, so that there seems not to be any principle tending to aristocracy : which, if I understand the term, is a government by nobles, independent of the people, which cannot take place with us, in either respect, without a total subversion of the constitution. I believe the more this provision of the constitution is attended to, and experienced, the more the wisdom and utility of it will appear. As senators cannot hold any other office themselves, they will not be influenced, in their advice to the president, by interested motives. But it is said, they may have friends and kindred to provide for ; it is true they may, but when we consider their character and situation, will they not be diffident of nominating a friend, or relative, who may wish for an office, and be well qualified for it, lest it

which might vary the right to appoint in such cases. In one age the appointment might be most proper in the president; and in another age, in a department.

§ 1530. In the practical course of the government, there does not seem to have been any exact line drawn, who are, and who are not, to be deemed *inferior* officers in the sense of the constitution, whose appointment does not necessarily require the concurrence of the senate.[1] In many cases of appointments, congress have required the concurrence of the senate, where, perhaps, it might not be easy to say, that it was required by the constitution. The power of congress has been exerted

should be suspected to proceed from partiality? And will not their fellow members have a degree of the same reluctance, lest it should be thought they acted from friendship to a member of their body? so that their friends and connexions would stand a worse chance, in proportion to their real merit, than strangers. But if the president was left to select a council for himself, though he may be supposed to be actuated by the best motives — yet he would be surrounded by flatterers, who would assume the character of friends and patriots, though they had no attachment to the public good, no regard to the laws of their country, but influenced wholly by self-interest, would wish to extend the power of the executive, in order to increase their own; they would often advise him to dispense with laws, that should thwart their schemes, and in excuse plead, that it was done from necessity to promote the public good — they will use their own influence, induce the president to use his, to get laws repealed, or the constitution altered, to extend his powers and prerogatives, under pretext of advancing the public good, and gradually render the government a despotism. This seems to be according to the course of human affairs, and what may be expected from the nature of things. I think, that members of the legislature would be most likely duly to execute the laws, both in the executive and judiciary departments." *

[1] Rawle on Const. ch. 14, p. 163, 164; 1 Lloyd's Debates, 480 to 600; 2 Lloyd's Debates, 1 to 12; Sergeant on Const. ch. 29, (ch. 31.) — Whether the heads of departments are inferior officers in the sense of the constitution, was much discussed, in the debate on the organization of the department of foreign affairs, in 1789. The result of the debate seems to have been, that they were not. 1 Lloyd's Debates, 480 to 600; 2 Lloyd's Debates, 1 to 12; Sergeant on Const. ch. 29, (ch. 31.)

* 2 Pitkin's Hist. p. 285 to 291.

to a great extent, under this clause, in favour of the executive department. The president is by law invested, either solely, or with the senate, with the appointment of all military and naval officers, and of the most important civil officers, and especially of those connected with the administration of justice, the collection of the revenue, and the supplies and expenditures of the nation. The courts of the Union possess the narrow prerogative of appointing their own clerk, and reporter, without any farther patronage. The heads of department are, in like manner, generally entitled to the appointment of the clerks in their respective offices. But the great anomaly in the system is the enormous patronage of the postmaster general, who is invested with the sole and exclusive authority to appoint, and remove all deputy post-masters; and whose power and influence have thus, by slow degrees, accumulated, until it is, perhaps, not too much to say, that it rivals, if it does not exceed, in value and extent, that of the president himself. How long a power so vast, and so accumulating, shall remain without any check on the part of any other branch of the government, is a question for statesmen, and not for jurists. But it cannot be disguised, that it will be idle to impose constitutional restraints upon high executive appointments, if this power, which pervades every village of the republic, and exerts an irresistible, though silent, influence in the direct shape of office, or in the no less inviting form of lucrative contracts, is suffered to remain without scrutiny or rebuke. It furnishes no argument against the interposition of a check, which shall require the advice and consent of the senate to appointments, that the power has not hitherto been abused. In its own nature, the post-office establishment is susceptible of

abuse to such an alarming degree; the whole correspondence of the country is so completely submitted to
the fidelity and integrity of the agents, who conduct it;
and the means of making it subservient to mere state
policy are so abundant, that the only surprise is, that
it has not already awakened the public jealousy, and
been placed under more effectual control. It may be
said, without the slightest disparagement of any officer,
who has presided over it, that if ever the people are
to be corrupted, or their liberties are to be prostrated,
this establishment will furnish the most facile means,
and be the earliest employed to accomplish such a
purpose.[1]

§ 1531. It is observable, that the constitution makes
no mention of any power of removal by the executive
of any officers whatsoever. As, however, the tenure of
office of no officers, except those in the judicial department, is, by the constitution, provided to be during
good behaviour, it follows by irresistible inference, that
all others must hold their offices during pleasure, unless
congress shall have given some other duration to their
office.[2] As far as congress constitutionally possess
the power to regulate, and delegate the appointment of
"inferior officers," so far they may prescribe the term
of office, the manner in which, and the persons by
whom, the removal, as well as the appointment to office,
shall be made.[3] But two questions naturally occur
upon this subject. The first is, to whom, in the absence

---

[1] It is truly surprising, that, while the learned commentator on Blackstone has been so feelingly alive to all other exertions of national
power and patronage, this source of patronage should not have drawn
from him a single remark, except of commendation. 1 Tuck. Black.
Comm. App. 264, 341, 342.

[2] 1 Lloyd's Debates, 511, 512.

[3] See *Marbury v. Madison*, 1 Cranch, 137, 155.

of all such legislation, does the power of removal belong;
to the appointing power, or to the executive; to the
president and senate, who have concurred in the appointment, or to the president alone? The next is,
if the power of removal belongs to the executive, in
regard to any appointments confided by the constitution to him; whether congress can give any duration
of office in such cases, not subject to the exercise of
this power of removal?[1] Hitherto the latter has remained a merely speculative question, as all our legis-

[1] Another question occurred upon carrying into effect the act of congress of 1821, for reducing the military establishment. President
Monroe, on that occasion, contended, that he had a right, in filling the
original vacancies in the artillery, and in the newly created office of
adjutant general, to place in them any officer belonging to the whole
military establishment, whether of the staff, or of the line. " In filling
original vacancies," said he, " that is, offices newly created, it is my
opinion, that congress have no right, under the constitution, to impose
any restraint, by law, on the power granted to the president, so as to
prevent his making a free election for these offices from the whole body
of his fellow citizens." — " If the law imposed such a restraint, it would
be void." — " If the right of the president to fill these original vacancies,
by the selection of officers from any branch of the whole military establishment, was denied, he would be compelled to place in them officers
of the same grade, whose corps had been reduced, and they with them.
The effect, therefore, of the law, as to those appointments, would be to
legislate into office, men, who had been already legislated out of office,
taking from the president all agency in their appointment." — (Message,
12th April, 1822; 1 Executive Journal, 286.) The senate wholly disagreed to this doctrine, contending, that, as congress possessed the
power to make rules and regulations for the land and naval forces, they
had a right to make any, which they thought would promote the public
service. This power had been exercised from the foundation of the
government, in respect to the army and navy. Congress have a right
to fix the rule, as to promotions and appointments. Every promotion is
a new appointment, and is submitted to the senate for confirmation.
Congress, in all reductions of the army, have fixed the rules of reduc-
tion, and no executive had hitherto denied their rightful power so to do,
or hesitated to execute such rules, as had been prescribed. Sergeant
on Const. ch. 29, (ch. 31.)

lation, giving a limited duration to office, recognises the executive power of removal, as in full force.[1]

§1532. The other is a vastly important practical question; and, in an early stage of the government, underwent a most elaborate discussion.[2] The language of the constitution is, that the president " shall nomin-" ate, and, by and with the advice and consent of the " senate, appoint," &c. The power to nominate does not naturally, or necessarily include the power to remove; and if the power to appoint does include it, then the latter belongs conjointly to the executive and the senate. In short, under such circumstances, the removal takes place in virtue of the new appointment, by mere operation of law. It results, and is not separable, from the appointment itself.

§ 1533. This was the doctrine maintained with great earnestness by the Federalist;[3] and it had a most material tendency to quiet the just alarms of the overwhelming influence, and arbitrary exercise of this prerogative of the executive, which might prove fatal to the personal independence, and freedom of opinion of public officers, as well as to the public liberties of the country. Indeed, it is utterly impossible not to feel, that, if this unlimited power of removal does exist, it may be made, in the hands of a bold and designing

[1] In the debate in 1789 upon the bill for organizing the department for foreign affairs, (the department of state,) the very question was discussed; and the final vote seems to have expressed the sense of the legislature, that the power of removal by the executive could not be abridged by the legislature; at least, not in cases, where the power to appoint was not subject to legislative delegation. See 5 Marshall's Life of Washington, ch. 3. p. 196 to 200; 1 Lloyd's Debates, 351 to 366; Id. 450, 480 to 600; 2 Lloyd's Debates, 1 to 12.

[2] 1 Lloyd's Debates, 351, 366, 450, 480 to 600; 2 Lloyd's Debates, 1 to 12; 5 Marshall's Life of Washington, ch. 3, p. 196 to 200.

[3] The Federalist, No. 77.

man, of high ambition, and feeble principles, an instrument of the worst oppression, and most vindictive vengeance. Even in monarchies, while the councils of state are subject to perpetual fluctuations and changes, the ordinary officers of the government are permitted to remain in the silent possession of their offices, undisturbed by the policy, or the passions of the favourites of the court. But in a republic, where freedom of opinion and action are guaranteed by the very first principles of the government, if a successful party may first elevate their candidate to office, and then make him the instrument of their resentments, or their mercenary bargains; if men may be made spies upon the actions of their neighbours, to displace them from office; or if fawning sycophants upon the popular leader of the day may gain his patronage, to the exclusion of worthier and abler men, it is most manifest, that elections will be corrupted at their very source; and those, who seek office, will have every motive to delude, and deceive the people. It was not, therefore, without reason, that, in the animated discussions already alluded to, it was urged, that the power of removal was incident to the power of appointment. That it would be a most unjustifiable construction of the constitution, and of its implied powers, to hold otherwise. That such a prerogative in the executive was in its own nature monarchical and arbitrary; and eminently dangerous to the best interests, as well as the liberties, of the country. It would convert all the officers of the country into the mere tools and creatures of the president. A dependence, so servile on one individual, would deter men of high and honourable minds from engaging in the public service. And if, contrary to expectation, such men should be brought into office, they would be reduced to the necessity of sacrificing every principle of independence to the will of the chief magistrate, or of exposing themselves to the disgrace of being removed from office, and that too at a time, when it might no longer be in their power to engage in other pursuits.[1]

§ 1531. The Federalist, while denying the existence of the power, admits by the clearest implication the full force of the argument, thus addressed to such a state of executive prerogative. Its language is: *"The consent of that body* (the senate) *would be necessary to displace, as well as to appoint.* A change of the chief magistrate, therefore, could not occasion so violent, or so general a revolution in the officers of the government, as might be expected, if he were the sole disposer of offices. Where a man in any station had given satisfactory evidence of his fitness for it, a new president would be restrained from attempting a change in favour of a person, more agreeable to him, by the apprehension, that a discountenance of the senate might frustrate the attempt, and bring some degree of discredit upon himself. Those, who can best estimate the value of a steady administration, will be most disposed to prize a provision, *which connects the official existence of public men with the approbation or disapprobation of that body.* which, from the greater permanency of its own composition, will, in all probability, be less subject to inconstancy, than any other member of the government."[2] No man can fail to perceive the entire safety of the power of removal, if it must thus be exercised in conjunction with the senate.

---

[1] 5 Marshall's Life of Washington, ch. 3, p. 198 ; 1 Lloyd's Debates, 351, 366, 450, 480 to 600.

[2] The Federalist, No. 77.

§ 1535. On the other hand, those, who after the adoption of the constitution held the doctrine, (for before that period it never appears to have been avowed by any of its friends, although it was urged by its opponents, as a reason for rejecting it,) that the power of removal belonged to the president, argued, that it resulted from the nature of the power, and the convenience, and even necessity of its exercise. It was clearly in its nature a part of the executive power, and was indispensable for a due execution of the laws, and a regular administration of the public affairs. What would become of the public interests, if during the recess of the senate the president could not remove an unfaithful public officer? If he could not displace a corrupt ambassador, or head of department, or other officer engaged in the finances, or expenditures of the government? If the executive, to prevent a non-execution of the laws, or a non-performance of his own proper functions, had a right to suspend an unworthy officer from office, this power was in no respect distinguishable from a power of removal. In fact, it is an exercise, though in a more moderated form, of the same power. Besides; it was argued, that the danger, that a president would remove good men from office was wholly imaginary. It was not by the splendour attached to the character of a particular president like Washington, that such an opinion was to be maintained. It was founded on the structure of the office. The man, in whose favour a majority of the people of the United States would unite, to elect him to such an office, had every probability at least in favour of his principles. He must be presumed to possess integrity, independence, and high talents. It would be impossible, that he should abuse the patronage of the government, or his power of removal, to the base purposes of gratifying a party, or of ministering to his own resentments, or of displacing upright and excellent officers for a mere difference of opinion. The public odium, which would inevitably attach to such conduct, would be a perfect security against it. And, in truth, removals made from such motives, or with a view to bestow the offices upon dependents, or favourites, would be an impeachable offence.[1] One of the most distinguished framers of the constitution[2] on that occasion, after having expressed his opinion decidedly in favour of the existence of the power of removal in the executive, added: "In the first place he will be impeachable by this house before the senate for such an act of mal-administration; for I contend, that the wanton removal of meritorious officers would subject him to impeachment, and removal from his high trust."[3]

§ 1536. After a most animated discussion, the vote finally taken in the house of representatives was affirmative of the power of removal in the president, without any co-operation of the senate, by the vote of thirty-four members against twenty.[4] In the senate the clause in the bill, affirming the power, was carried by the casting vote of the vice-president.[5]

§ 1537. That the final decision of this question so made was greatly influenced by the exalted character of the president, then in office, was asserted at the time, and has always been believed. Yet the doctrine

---

[1] 1 Lloyd's Debates, 351, 366, 450, 480 to 600; 2 Lloyd's Debates, 1 to 12; 4 Elliot's Debates, 141 to 207; 5 Marsh. Life of Washington, ch. 3, p. 196 to 200.

[2] Mr. Madison, 1 Lloyd's Debates, 503.

[3] Ibid.

[4] 5 Marsh. Life of Washington, ch. 3, p. 199; 1 Lloyd's Debates, 599; 2 Lloyd's Debates, 12.

[5] Senate Journal, July 18, 1789, p. 42.

was opposed, as well as supported, by the highest talents and patriotism of the country. The public, however, acquiesced in' this decision; and it constitutes, perhaps, the most extraordinary case in the history of the government of a power, conferred by implication on the executive by the assent of a bare majority of congress, which has not been questioned on many other occasions.[1] Even the most jealous advocates of state rights seem to have slumbered over this vast reach of authority; and have left it untouched, as the neutral ground of controversy, in which they desired to reap no harvest, and from which they retired without leaving any protestations of title or contest.[2] Nor is this general acquiescence and silence without a satisfactory explanation. Until a very recent period, the power had been exercised in few cases, and generally in such, as led to their own vindication. During the administration of President Washington few removals were made, and none without cause; few were made in that of the first President Adams. In that of President Jefferson the circle was greatly enlarged; but yet it was kept within narrow bounds, and with an express disclaimer of the right to remove for differences of opinion, or otherwise, than for some clear public good. In the administrations of the subsequent presidents, Madison, Monroe, and J. Q. Adams, a general moderation and forbearance were exercised with the approbation of the country, and without disturbing the harmony of the system. Since the induction into office of President Jackson,

---

[1] 1 Kent's Comm. Lect. 14, p. 289, 290.

[2] Mr. Tucker in his Commentaries on Blackstone scarcely alludes to it. (See 1 Tucker's Black. Comm. App. 341.) On the other hand, Mr. Chancellor Kent has spoken on it with becoming freedom and pertinence of remark. 1 Kent's Comm. Lect. 14, p. 289, 290.

an opposite course has been pursued; and a system of removals and new appointments to office has been pursued so extensively, that it has reached a very large proportion of all the offices of honour and profit in the civil departments of the country. This is matter of fact; and beyond the statement of the fact [1] it is not the intention of the Commentator to proceed. This extraordinary change of system has awakened general attention, and brought back the whole controversy, with regard to the executive power of removal, to a severe scrutiny. Many of the most eminent statesmen in the country have expressed a deliberate opinion, that it is utterly indefensible, and that the only sound interpretation of the constitution is that avowed upon its adoption; that is to say, that the power of removal belongs to the appointing power.

---

[1] In proof of this statement, lest it should be questioned, it is proper to say, that a list of removals (confessedly imperfect) between the 4th of March, 1829, when President Jackson came into office, and the 4th of March, 1830, has been published, by which it appears, that, during that period, there were removed, eight persons in the diplomatic corps; thirty-six in the executive departments; and in the other civil departments, including consuls, marshals, district attorneys, collectors, and other officers of the customs, registers and receivers, one hundred and ninety-nine persons. These officers include a very large proportion of all the most lucrative offices under the national government. Besides these, there were removals in the post-office department, during the same period, of four hundred and ninety-one persons. (See Mr. Post-Master General Barry's Report of 24th of March, 1830.) This statement will be found in the National Intelligencer of the 27th of Sept., 1832, with the names of the parties (except post-masters;) and I am not aware, that it has ever been denied to be correct. It is impossible for me to vouch for its entire accuracy. It is not probable, that, from the first organization of the government, in 1789, down to 1829, the aggregate of all the removals made amounted to one third of this number. In President Washingto 's administration of eight years, only nine removals took place. See Mr. Clayton's Speech in the Senate, on the 4th of March, 1830.

§ 1538. Whether the predictions of the original advocates of the executive power, or those of the opposers of it, are likely, in the future progress of the government, to be realized, must be left to the sober judgment of the community, and to the impartial award of time. If there has been any aberration from the true constitutional exposition of the power of removal, (which the reader must decide for himself,) it will be difficult, and perhaps impracticable, after forty years' experience, to recall the practice to the correct theory. But at all events, it will be a consolation to those, who love the Union, and honour a devotion to the patriotic discharge of duty, that in regard to "inferior officers," (which appellation probably includes ninety-nine out of a hundred of the lucrative offices in the government,) the remedy for any permanent abuse is still within the power of congress, by the simple expedient of requiring the consent of the senate to removals in such cases.

§ 1539. Another point of great practical importance is, when the appointment of any officer is to be deemed complete. It will be seen in a succeeding clause, that the president is to "commission all the officers of "the United States." In regard to officers, who are removable at the will of the executive, the point is unimportant, since they may be displaced, and their commission arrested at any moment. But if the officer is not so removable, the time, when the appointment is complete, becomes of very deep interest.

§ 1540. This subject was very elaborately discussed in the celebrated case of *Marbury* v. *Madison*.[1] Marbury had been appointed a justice of the peace of the

---

[1] 1 Cranch's R. 137 ; S. C. 1 Peters's Cond. R. 270.

District of Columbia for five years, according to an act of congress, by President Adams, by and with the consent of the senate. His commission had been signed by the president, and was sealed, and deposited in the department of state at the time of Mr. Jefferson's accession to the presidency; and was afterwards withheld from him by the direction of the latter. An act of congress had directed the secretary of state to keep the seal of the United States; and to make out, and record, and affix the seal to all civil commissions to officers of the United States, to be appointed by the president, after he should have signed the same. Upon the fullest deliberation, the court were of opinion, that, when a commission has been signed by the president, the appointment is final and complete. The officer appointed has, then, conferred on him legal rights, which cannot be resumed. Until that, the discretion of the president may be exercised by him, as to the appointment; but, from that moment, it is irrevocable. His power over the office is then terminated in all cases, where by law the officer is not removable by him. The right to the office is then in the person appointed, and he has the absolute, unconditional power of accepting, or rejecting it. Neither a delivery of the commission, nor an actual acceptance of the office, is indispensable to make the appointment perfect.

§ 1541. The reasoning, upon which this doctrine is founded, cannot be better elucidated, than by using the very language of the opinion, in which it is promulgated. After quoting the words of the constitution, and laws above referred to, it proceeds as follows:

§ 1542. "These are the clauses of the constitution and laws of the United States, which affect this part of

the case. They seem to contemplate three distinct
operations : (1.) The nomination. This is the sole act
of the president, and is completely voluntary. (2.)
The appointment. This is also the act of the president;
and is also a voluntary act, though it can only be performed by and with the advice and consent of the senate. (3.) The commission. To grant a commission
to a person appointed, might perhaps be deemed a
duty enjoined by the constitution. ' He shall,' says that
instrument, 'commission all the officers of the United
States.' The acts of appointing to office, and commis-
sioning the person appointed, can scarcely be considered as one and the same; since the power to perform
them is given in two separate and distinct sections of
the constitution. The distinction between the appointment and the commission will be rendered more apparent, by adverting to that provision in the second section of the second article of the constitution, which
authorizes congress 'to vest, by law, the appointment
of such inferior officers, as they think proper, in the
president alone, in the courts of law, or in the heads of
departments;' thus contemplating cases, where the
law may direct the president to commission an officer
appointed by the courts, or by the heads of departments. In such a case, to issue a commission would
be apparently a duty distinct from the appointment, the
performance of which, perhaps, could not legally be
refused. Although that clause of the constitution,
which requires the president to commission all the
officers of the United States, may never have been
applied to officers appointed otherwise, than by himself; yet it would be difficult to deny the legislative
power to apply it to such cases. Of consequence the
constitutional distinction between the appointment to

an office, and the commission of an officer, who has been appointed, remains the same, as if in practice the president had commissioned officers appointed by an authority, other than his own. It follows, too, from the existence of this distinction, that, if an appointment was to be evidenced by any public act, other than the commission, the performance of such public act would create the officer; and, if he was not removable at the will of the president, would either give him a right to his commission, or enable him to perform the duties without it. These observations are premised solely for the purpose of rendering more intelligible those, which apply more directly to the particular case under consideration.

§ 1543. "This is an appointment made by the president, by and with the advice and consent of the senate, and is evidenced by no act but the commission itself. In such a case, therefore, the commission and the appointment seem inseparable ; it being almost impossible to show an appointment otherwise, than by proving the existence of a commission. Still the commission is not necessarily the appointment ; though conclusive evidence of it. But at what stage does it amount to this conclusive evidence? The answer to this question seems an obvious one. The appointment, being the sole act of the president, must be completely evidenced, when it is shown, that he has done every thing to be performed by him. Should the commission, instead of being evidence of an appointment, even be considered as constituting the appointment itself; still, it would be made, when the last act to be done by the president was performed, or, at farthest, when the commission was complete. The last act to be done by the president, is the signature of the commission.

He has then acted on the advice and consent of the
senate to his own nomination. The time for deliberation has then passed. He has decided. His judgment,
on the advice and consent of the senate concurring
with his nomination, has been made, and the officer is
appointed. This appointment is evidenced by an open,
unequivocal act; and being the last act required from
the person making it, necessarily excludes the idea of
its being, so far as respects the appointment, an inchoate
and incomplete transaction. Some point of time must
be taken, when the power of the executive over an
officer, not removable at his will, must cease. That
point of time must be, when the constitutional power
of appointment has been exercised. And this power
has been exercised, when the last act, required from
the person possessing the power, has been performed.
This last act is the signature of the commission. This
idea seems to have prevailed with the legislature, when
the act passed, converting the department of foreign
affairs into the department of state. By that act it is
enacted, that the secretary of state shall keep the seal
of the United States, 'and shall make out and record,
and shall affix the said seal to all civil commissions to
officers of the United States, to be appointed by the
president:' 'Provided, that the said seal shall not be
affixed to any commission, before the same shall have
been signed by the president of the United States;
nor to any other instrument or act, without the special
warrant of the president therefor.' The signature is a
warrant for affixing the great seal to the commission ;
and the great seal is only to be affixed to an instrument,
which is complete. It attests, by an act supposed to
be of public notoriety, the verity of the presidential
signature. It is never to be affixed, till the commission

all the weight, which it appears possible to give them,
is signed, because the signature, which gives force and
effect to the commission, is conclusive evidence, that
the appointment is made. The commission being
signed, the subsequent duty of the secretary of state is
prescribed by law, and not to be guided by the will of
the president. He is to affix the seal of the United
States to the commission, and is to record it. This is
not a proceeding, which may be varied, if the judgment
of the executive shall suggest one more eligible ; but
is a precise course accurately marked out by law, and
is to be strictly pursued. It is the duty of the secretary of state to conform to the law, and in this he is an
officer of the United States, bound to obey the laws.
He acts, in this respect, as has been very properly
stated at the bar, under the authority of law, and not
by the instructions of the president. It is a ministerial
act, which the law enjoins on a particular officer for a
particular purpose. If it should be supposed, that the
solemnity of affixing the seal is necessary, not only to
the validity of the commission, but even to the completion of an appointment ; still, when the seal is affixed, the appointment is made, and the commission is
valid. No other solemnity is required by law ; no
other act is to be performed on the part of government.
All, that the executive can do to invest the person with
his office, is done ; and unless the appointment be then
made, the executive cannot make one without the co-
operation of others. After searching anxiously for the
principles, on which a contrary opinion may be supported, none have been found, which appear of sufficient force to maintain the opposite doctrine. Such, as
the imagination of the court could suggest, have been
very deliberately examined, and after allowing them

they do not shake the opinion, which has been formed.

§ 1544. "In considering this question, it has been
conjectured, that the commission may have been assim-
ilated to a deed, to the validity of which delivery is
essential. This idea is founded on the supposition,
that the commission is not merely *evidence* of an appointment, but is itself the actual appointment ; a supposition by no means unquestionable. But, for the
purpose of examining this objection fairly, let it be
conceded, that the principle claimed for its support is
established. The appointment being, under the constitution, to be made by the president *personally*, the
delivery of the deed of appointment, if necessary to its
completion, must be made by the president also. It is
not necessary, that the livery should be made personally to the grantee of the office. It never is so made.
The law would seem to contemplate, that it should be
made to the secretary of state, since it directs the secretary to affix the seal to the commission, *after* it shall
have been signed by the president. If, then, the act of
livery be necessary to give validity to the commission,
is has been delivered, when executed and given to the
secretary for the purpose of being sealed, recorded, and
transmitted to the party. But in all cases of letters
patent, certain solemnities are required by law,
which solemnities are the evidences of the validity
of the instrument. A formal delivery to the person
is not among them. In cases of commissions the sign
manual of the president, and the seal of the United
States, are those solemnities. This objection, therefore,
does not touch the case.

§ 1545. "It has also occurred, as possible, and barely possible, that the transmission of the commission, and

the acceptance thereof, might be deemed necessary to complete the right of the plaintiff. The transmission of the commission is a practice directed by convenience, but not by law. It cannot therefore be necessary to constitute the appointment, which must precede it, and which is the mere act of the president. If the executive required, that every person, appointed to an office, should himself take means to procure his commission, the appointment would not be the less valid on that account. The appointment is the sole act of the president; the transmission of the commission is the sole act of the officer, to whom that duty is assigned, and may be accelerated, or retarded by circumstances, which can have no influence on the appointment. A commission is transmitted to a person already appointed; not to a person to be appointed, or not, as the letter enclosing the commission should happen to get into the post-office, and reach him in safety, or to miscarry.

§ 1546. "It may have some tendency to elucidate this point, to inquire, whether the possession of the original commission be indispensably necessary to authorize a person, appointed to any office, to perform the duties of that office. If it was necessary, then a loss of the commission would lose the office. Not only negligence, but accident or fraud, fire or theft, might deprive an individual of his office. In such a case, I presume, it could not be doubted, but that a copy from the record of the office of the secretary of state would be, to every intent and purpose, equal to the original. The act of congress has expressly made it so. To give that copy validity, it would not be necessary to prove, that the original had been transmitted, and afterwards lost. The copy would be complete evidence, that the original had existed, and that the appointment had been made ; but, not that the original had been transmitted. If, indeed, it should appear, that the original had been mislaid in the office of state, that circumstance would not affect the operation of the copy. When all the requisites have been performed, which authorize a recording officer to record any instrument whatever, and the order for that purpose has been given, the instrument is, in law, considered as recorded, although the manual labour of inserting it in a book kept for that purpose may not have been performed. In the case of commissions, the law orders the secretary of state to record them. When, therefore, they are signed and sealed, the order for their being recorded is given ; and whether inserted in the book, or not, they are in law recorded. A copy of this record is declared equal to the original, and the fees, to be paid by a person requiring a copy, are ascertained by law. Can a keeper of a public record erase therefrom a commission, which has been recorded ? Or can he refuse a copy thereof to a person demanding it on the terms prescribed by law ? Such a copy would, equally with the original, authorize the justice of peace to proceed in the performance of his duty, because it would, equally with the original, attest his appointment.

§ 1547. "If the transmission of a commission be not considered, as necessary to give validity to an appointment, still less is its acceptance. The appointment is the sole act of the president ; the acceptance is the sole act of the officer, and is, in plain common sense, posterior to the appointment. As he may resign, so may he refuse to accept. But neither the one, nor the other, is capable of rendering the appointment a nonentity. That this is the understanding of the govern-

406 CONSTITUTION OF THE U. STATES. [BOOK III.

ment is apparent from the whole tenor of its conduct.
A commission bears date, and the salary of the officer
commences, from his appointment; not from the
transmission, or acceptance of his commission. When
a person, appointed to any office, refuses to accept that
office, the successor is nominated in the place of the
person, who has declined to accept, and not in the
place of the person, who had been previously in office,
and had created the original vacancy. It is, therefore,
decidedly the opinion of the court, that, when a commission has been signed by the president, the appointment is made; and that the commission is complete,
when the seal of the United States has been affixed to
it by the secretary of state. Where an officer is removable at the will of the executive, the circumstance,
which completes his appointment, is of no concern;
because the act is at any time revocable; and the
commission may be arrested, if still in the office. But
when the officer is not removable at the will of the executive, the appointment is not revocable, and cannot
be annulled. It has conferred legal rights, which cannot be resumed. The discretion of the executive is to
be exercised, until the appointment has been made.
But having once made the appointment, his power over
the office is terminated in all cases, where, by law, the
officer is not removable by him. The right to the office is *then* in the person appointed, and he has the
absolute, unconditional power of accepting or rejecting
it. Mr. Marbury, then, since his commission was signed by the president, and sealed by the secretary of
state, was appointed; and as the law, creating the office, gave the officer a right to hold for five years, independent of the executive; the appointment was not
revocable but vested in the officer legal rights, which

are protected by the laws of his country. To withhold his commission, therefore, is an act deemed by the
court not warranted by law, but violative of a vested
legal right." [1]

---

[1] See also Rawle on the Constitution, ch. 14, p. 166 ; Sergeant on
Constitution, ch. 29, [ch. 31.] — The reasoning of this opinion would
seem to be, in a judicial view, absolutely irresistible ; and, as such, received at the time a very general approbation from the profession.
It was, however, totally disregarded by President Jefferson, who, on this,
as on other occasions, placed his right of construing the constitution
and laws, as wholly above, and independent of, judicial decision. In his
correspondence, he repeatedly alluded to this subject, and endeavoured to vindicate his conduct. In one of his letters he says, "In the case
of Marbury and Madison, the federal judges declared, that commissions,
signed and sealed by the president, were valid, although not delivered.
I deemed delivery essential to complete a deed, which, as long as it
remains in the hands of the party, is, as yet, no deed ; it is *in posse* only,
but not *in esse ;* and I withheld the delivery of the commission. They
cannot issue a mandamus to the president, or legislature, or to any of
their officers." * It is true, that the constitution does not authorize the
Supreme Court to issue a mandamus in the exercise of *original* jurisdiction, as was the case in *Marbury* v. *Madison ;* and it was so decided by
the Supreme Court. But the Act of Congress of 1789, ch. 20, § 13, had
actually conferred the very power on the Supreme Court, by providing,
that the Supreme Court shall have power " to issue writs of mandamus,
&c. to any courts appointed, or persons holding office under the authority of the United States." So, that the Supreme Court, in declining
jurisdiction, in effect declared, that the act of congress was, in this respect, unconstitutional. But no lawyer could doubt, that congress
might confer the power on any other court ; and the Supreme Court
itself might issue a mandamus in the exercise of its appellate jurisdiction. But the whole argument of President Jefferson proceeds on an
assumption, which is not proved. He says, delivery is essential to
a deed. But, assuming this to be correct in all cases, it does not
establish, that a commission is essential to every appointment, or that a
commission must, by the constitution, be by a deed ; or that an appointment to office is not complete, before the commission is sealed, or delivered. The question is not, whether a deed at the common law is perfect without a delivery ; but whether an appointment under the constitution is perfect without a delivery of a commission. If a delivery were
necessary, when the president had signed the commission, and delivered it to the secretary to be sealed and recorded, such delivery would be

* 4 Jefferson's Corresp. 317 ; Id. 75 ; Id. 372, 373.

§ 1548. Another question, growing out of appointments, is, at what time the appointee is to be deemed in office, whether from the time of his acceptance of the office, or his complying with the preliminary requisitions, (such, as taking the oath of office, giving bond for the faithful discharge of his duties, &c.) or his actual entry upon the duties of his office. This question may become of great practical importance in cases of removals from office, and also in cases, where by law officers are appointed for a limited term. It frequently happens, that no formal removal from office is made by the president, except by nominating another person to the senate, in place of the person removed, and without any notice to him. In such a case, is the actual incumbent in office *de facto* removed immediately upon the nomination of a new officer? If so, then all his subsequent acts in the office are void, though he may have no notice of the nomination, and may, from the delay to give such notice, go on for a month to perform its functions. Is the removal to be deemed complete only, when the nomination has been confirmed? Or, when notice is actually given to the incumbent? Or, when the appointee has accepted the

sufficient, for it is the final act required to be done by the president. But, in point of fact, the *seal* is not the seal of the president, but of the United States. The commission, sealed by the president, is not his deed ; and it does not take effect, as his deed. It is merely a verification of his act by the highest evidence. The doctrine, then, of deeds of private persons, at the common law, is inapplicable. It is painful to observe in President Jefferson's writings, the constant insinuations against public men and public bodies, who differ from his own opinions or measures, of being governed by improper or unworthy motives, or mere party spirit. The very letters here cited (4 Jefferson's Corresp. 75, 317, 372) afford illustrations, not to be mistaken ; and certainly diminish the value, which might otherwise be attributed to his criticisms.

office?[1] Hitherto this point does not seem to have received any judicial decision, and therefore must be treated as open to controversy. If the decision should be, that in such cases the nomination without notice creates a removal *de facto*, as well as *de jure*, it is obvious, that the public, as well as private individuals, may become sufferers by unintentional and innocent violations of law. A collector, for instance, may receive duties, may grant clearances to vessels, and may perform other functions of the office for months after such a nomination, without the slightest suspicion of any want of legal authority. Upon one occasion it was said by the Supreme Court, that " when a person appointed to any office (under the United States) refuses to accept that office, the successor is nominated in the place of the person, who has declined to accept, and not in the place of the person, who had been previously in office, and had created the original vacancy." [2] From this remark, it would seem to be the opinion of the court, that the office is completely filled in every case of vacancy, as soon as the appointment is complete ; independently of the acceptance of the appointee. If so, it would seem to follow, that the removal must, at all events, be complete, as soon as a new appointment is made.[3]

§ 1549. The next clause of the constitution is, " The " president shall have power to fill up all vacancies, that " may happen during the recess of the senate, by grant-

---

[1] See *Johnson* v. *United States*, 5 Mason's R. 425, 438, 439.

[2] *Marbury* v. *Madison*, 1 Cranch's R. 137 ; S. C. 1 Peters's Cond. R. 270.

[3] See *Johnson* v. *United States*, 5 Mason's R. 425, 438, 439 ; *United States* v. *Kirkpatrick*, 4 Wheat. R. 733, 734.

"ing commissions, which shall expire at the end of their "next session."

§ 1550. This clause was not in the first draft of the constitution ; but was afterwards inserted by an amendment, apparently without objection.[1] One of the most extraordinary instances of a perverse intention to misrepresent, and thereby to render odious the constitution, was in the objection, solemnly urged against this clause, that it authorized the president to fill vacancies in the senate itself, occurring during the recess ;[2] a power, which, in another clause of the constitution, was expressly confided to the state executive. It is wholly unnecessary, however, now to dwell upon this preposterous suggestion, since it does not admit of a doubt, that the power given to the president is applicable solely to appointments to offices under the United States, provided for by the constitution and laws of the Union. It is only another proof of the gross exaggerations, and unfounded alarms, which were constantly resorted to for the purpose of defeating a system, which could scarcely fail of general approbation, if it was fairly understood.[3]

§ 1551. The propriety of this grant is so obvious, that it can require no elucidation. There was but one of two courses to be adopted ; either, that the senate should be perpetually in session, in order to provide for the appointment of officers ; or, that the president should be authorized to make temporary appointments during the recess, which should expire, when the senate should have had an opportunity to act on the subject. The former course would have been at once burthensome to the senate, and expensive to the public. The latter combines convenience, promptitude of action, and general security.

---

[1] Journal of Convention, 225, 341.
[2] The Federalist, No. 67.   [3] Id. No. 67.

§ 1552. The appointments so made, by the very language of the constitution, expire at the next session of the senate ; and the commissions given by him have the same duration. When the senate is assembled, if the president nominates the same officer to the office, this is to all intents and purposes a new nomination to office ; and, if approved by the senate, the appointment is a new appointment, and not a mere continuation of the old appointment. So that, if a bond for fidelity in office has been given under the first appointment and commission, it does not apply to any acts done under the new appointment and commission.[1]

§ 1553. The language of the clause is, that the president shall have power to fill up *vacancies*, that may happen during the recess of the senate. In 1813, President Madison appointed and commissioned ministers to negotiate the treaty of peace of Ghent during the recess of the senate ; and a question was made, whether he had a constitutional authority so to do, there being no *vacancy* of any existing office ; but this being the creation of a new office. The senate, at their next session, are said to have entered a protest against such an exercise of power by the executive. On a subsequent occasion, (April 20, 1822,) the senate seem distinctly to have held, that the president could not create the office of minister, and make appointments to such an office during the recess, without the consent of the senate. By " vacancies " they understood to be meant vacancies occurring from death, resignation, promotion, or removal. The word " happen " had relation to some casualty, not provided for by law. If the senate are in session, when offices are created by law, which have not as yet been filled, and

[1] *United States v. Kirkpatrick*, 9 Wheat. R. 720, 733, 734, 735.

nominations are not then made to them by the president, he cannot appoint to such offices during the recess of the senate, because the vacancy does not happen during the recess of the senate. In many instances, where offices are created by law, special power is on this very account given to the president to fill them during the recess; and it was then said, that in no other instances had the president filled such vacant offices without the special authority of law.[1]

§ 1554. The next section of the second article is, " He (the president) shall from time to time give to " the congress information of the state of the Union, and " recommend to their consideration such measures, as " he shall judge necessary and expedient. He may, " on extraordinary occasions, convene both houses, or " either of them, and, in case of a disagreement between " them, with respect to the time of adjournment, he may " adjourn them to such time, as he shall think proper. " He shall receive ambassadors, and other public minis- " ters. He shall take care, that the laws be faithfully " executed; and shall commission all the officers of the " United States."

§ 1555. The first part, relative to the president's giving information and recommending measures to congress, is so consonant with the structure of the executive departments of the colonial and state governments, with the usages and practice of other free governments, with the general convenience of congress, and with a due share of responsibility on the part of the executive, that it may well be presumed to be above all real objection. From the nature and duties of the executive department, he must possess more extensive sources of

---

[1] Sergeant on Const. ch. 29, (ch. 31); 2 Executive Journal, p. 415, 500; 3 Executive Journal, 207

information, as well in regard to domestic as foreign affairs, than can belong to congress. The true workings of the laws ; the defects in the nature or arrangements of the general systems of trade, finance, and justice ; and the military, naval, and civil establishments of the Union, are more readily seen, and more constantly under the view of the executive, than they can possibly be of any other department. There is great wisdom, therefore, in not merely allowing, but in requiring, the president to lay before congress all facts and information, which may assist their deliberations ; and in enabling him at once to point out the evil, and to suggest the remedy. He is thus justly made responsible, not merely for a due administration of the existing systems, but for due diligence and examination into the means of improving them.[1]

§ 1556. The power to convene congress on extraordinary occasions is indispensable to the proper operations, and even safety of the government. Occasions may occur in the recess of congress, requiring the government to take vigorous measures to repel foreign aggres-

---

[1] See 1 Tuck. Black. Comm. App. 343, 344, 345 ; The Federalist, No. 78 ; Rawle on Const. ch. 16, p. 171. — The practice in the time of President Washington, and President John Adams was, for the president, at the opening of each session of congress to meet both Houses in person, and deliver a speech to them, containing his views on public affairs, and his recommendations of measures. On other occasions he simply addressed written messages to them, or either of them, according to the nature of the message. To the speeches thus made a written answer was given by each house ; and thus an opportunity was afforded by the opponents of the administration to review its whole policy in a single debate on the answer. That practice was discontinued by President Jefferson, who addressed all his communications to congress by written messages ; and to these no answers were returned.* The practice thus introduced by him has been ever since exclusively pursued by all succeeding presidents, whether for the better has been gravely doubted by some of our most distinguished statesmen.

* Rawle on Const. ch. 16, p. 171, 172, 173.

sions, depredations, and direct hostilities ; to provide
adequate means to mitigate, or overcome unexpected
calamities ; to suppress insurrections ; and to provide
for innumerable other important exigencies, arising out
of the intercourse and revolutions among nations.[1]

§ 1557. The power to adjourn congress in cases of
disagreement is equally indispensable ; since it is the
only peaceable way of terminating a controversy, which
can lead to nothing but distraction in the public councils.[2]

§ 1558. On the other hand, the duty imposed upon
him to take care, that the laws be faithfully executed,
follows out the strong injunctions of his oath of office,
that he will " preserve, protect, and defend the constitution." The great object of the executive department
is to accomplish this purpose ; and without it, be the
form of government whatever it may, it will be utterly
worthless for offence, or defence ; for the redress of
grievances, or the protection of rights ; for the happiness, or good order, or safety of the people.

§ 1559. The next power is to receive ambassadors
and other public ministers. This has been already
incidentally touched. A similar power existed under
the confederation ; but it was confined to receiving
" ambassadors," which word, in a strict sense, (as has
been already stated,) comprehends the highest grade
only of ministers, and not those of an inferior character.
The policy of the United States would ordinarily prefer
the employment of the inferior grades ; and therefore
the description is properly enlarged, so as to include all
classes of ministers.[3] Why the receiving of consuls

---

[1] See 1 Tuck. Black. Comm. App. 343, 344, 345 ; The Federalist, No.
78 ; Rawle on Const. ch. 16, p. 171.
[2] Id. ibid.   [3] The Federalist, No. 42.

was not also expressly mentioned, as the appointment
of them is in the preceding clause, is not easily to be
accounted for, especially as the defect of the confederation on this head was fully understood.[1] The power,
however, may be fairly inferred from other parts of the
constitution ; and indeed seems a general incident to
the executive authority. It has constantly been exercised without objection ; and foreign consuls have never
been allowed to discharge any functions of office, until
they have received the exequatur of the president.[2]
Consuls, indeed, are not diplomatic functionaries, or
political representatives of a foreign nation ; but are
treated in the character of mere commercial agents.[3]

§ 1560. The power to receive ambassadors and ministers is always an important, and sometimes a very
delicate function; since it constitutes the only accredited
medium, through which negotiations and friendly relations are ordinarily carried on with foreign powers. A
government may in its discretion lawfully refuse to receive an ambassador, or other minister, without its
affording any just cause of war. But it would generally
be deemed an unfriendly act, and might provoke hostilities, unless accompanied by conciliatory explanations.
A refusal is sometimes made on the ground of the bad
character of the minister, or his former offensive conduct, or of the special subject of the embassy not being
proper, or convenient for discussion.[4] This, however,
is rarely done. But a much more delicate occasion is,

[1] The Federalist, No. 42.
[2] Rawle on Const. ch. 24, p. 224, 225.
[3] Ibid. ; 1 Kent's Comm. Lect. 2, p. 40 to 44 ; The Indian Chief, 3
Rob. R. 22 ; The Bello Corunnes, 6 Wheat. R. 152, 168 ; Vivcash v.
Baker, 3 Maule & Selw. R. 284.
[4] 1 Kent's Comm. Lect. 2, p. 39 ; Rutherforth's Instit. B 2, ch. 9,
§ 20; Grotius, Lib. 2, ch. 8, § 1, 3, 4.

when a civil war breaks out in a nation, and two nations are formed, or two parties in the same nation, each claiming the sovereignty of the whole, and the contest remains as yet undecided, *flagrante bello.* In such a case a neutral nation may very properly withhold its recognition of the supremacy of either party, or of the existence of two independent nations; and on that account refuse to receive an ambassador from either.[1] It is obvious, that in such cases the simple acknowledgment of the minister of either party, or nation, might be deemed taking part against the other; and thus as affording a strong countenance, or opposition, to rebellion and civil dismemberment. On this account, nations, placed in such a predicament, have not hesitated sometimes to declare war against neutrals, as interposing in the war; and have made them the victims of their vengeance, when they have been anxious to assume a neutral position. The exercise of this prerogative of acknowledging new nations, or ministers, is, therefore, under such circumstances, an executive function of great delicacy, which requires the utmost caution and deliberation. If the executive receives an ambassador, or other minister, as the representative of a new nation, or of a party in a civil war in an old nation, it is an acknowledgment of the sovereign authority *de facto* of such new nation, or party. If such recognition is made, it is conclusive upon the nation, unless indeed it can be reversed by an act of congress repudiating it. If, on the other hand, such recognition has been refused by the executive, it is said, that congress may, notwithstanding, solemnly

1 1 Kent's Comm. Lect. 2, p. 39 ; Rawle on Const. ch. 20, p. 195 ; *Gelston* v. *Hoyt*, 3 Wheat. R. 324 ; *United States* v. *Palmer*, 3 Wheat. R. 630 ; Serg. on Const. ch. 28, p. 324, 325, (2d edit. ch. 30, p. 336, 337, 338.

acknowledge the sovereignty of the nation, or party.[1] These, however, are propositions, which have hitherto remained, as abstract statements, under the constitution; and, therefore, can be propounded, not as absolutely true, but as still open to discussion, if they should ever arise in the course of our foreign diplomacy. The constitution has expressly invested the executive with power to receive ambassadors, and other ministers. It has not expressly invested congress with the power, either to repudiate, or acknowledge them.[2] At all events, in the case of a revolution, or dismemberment of a nation, the judiciary cannot take notice of any new government, or sovereignty, until it has been duly recognised by some other department of the government, to whom the power is constitutionally confided.[3]

§ 1561. That a power, so extensive in its reach over our foreign relations, could not be properly conferred on any other, than the executive department, will admit of little doubt. That it should be exclusively confided to that department, without any participation of the senate in the functions, (that body being conjointly entrusted with the treaty-making power,) is

---

[1] Rawle on Constitution, ch. 20, p. 195, 196.

[2] It is surprising, that the Federalist should have treated the power of receiving ambassadors and other public ministers, as an executive function of little intrinsic importance. Its language is, "This, though it has been a rich theme of declamation, is more a matter of dignity, than of authority. It is a circumstance, which will be without consequence in the administration of the government. And it was far more convenient, that it should be arranged in this manner, than that there should be a necessity of convening the legislature, or one of its branches, upon every arrival of a foreign minister, though it were merely to take the place of a departed predecessor." The Federalist, No. 69.

[3] *United States* v. *Palmer*, 3 Wheat. R. 610, 634, 643; *Hoyt* v. *Gelston*, 3 Wheat. R. 246, 323, 324; *Rose* v. *Himely*, 4 Cranch, 441; The Divina Pastora, 4 Wheat. R. 52, and note 65; The Neustra Senora de la Caridad, 4 Wheat. R. 497.

not so obvious. Probably the circumstance, that in all foreign governments[1] the power was exclusively confided to the executive department, and the utter impracticability of keeping the senate constantly in session, and the suddenness of the emergencies, which might require the action of the government, conduced to the establishment of the authority in its present form.[2] It is not, indeed, a power likely to be abused; though it is pregnant with consequences, often involving the question of peace and war. And, in our own short experience, the revolutions in France, and the revolutions in South America, have already placed us in situations, to feel its critical character, and the necessity of having, at the head of the government, an executive of sober judgment, enlightened views, and firm and exalted patriotism.[3]

§ 1562. As incidents to the power to receive ambassadors and foreign ministers, the president is understood to possess the power to refuse them, and to dismiss those who, having been received, become obnoxious to censure, or unfit to be allowed the privilege, by their improper conduct, or by political events.[4] While, however, they are permitted to remain, as public functionaries, they are entitled to all the immunities and rights, which the law of nations has provided at once for their dignity, their independence, and their inviolability.[5]

§ 1563. There are other incidental powers, belonging to the executive department, which are necessarily implied from the nature of the functions, which are

[1] See 1 Black. Comm. 253.   [2] The Federalist, No. 69.
[3] See 5 Marshall's Life of Washington, ch. 6, p. 398, 399, 404, 405, 411, 412; 1 Tuck Black. Comm. App. 341.
[4] See 5 Marshall's Life of Washington, ch. 6, p. 443, 444; 7 Wait's State Papers, 282, 283, 302.
[5] 1 Kent's Comm. Lect. 2, p. 37, 38, 39.

confided to it. Among these, must necessarily be included the power to perform them, without any obstruction or impediment whatsoever. The president cannot, therefore, be liable to arrest, imprisonment, or detention, while he is in the discharge of the duties of his office; and for this purpose his person must be deemed, in civil cases at least, to possess an official inviolability. In the exercise of his political powers he is to use his own discretion, and is accountable only to his country, and to his own conscience. His decision, in relation to these powers, is subject to no control; and his discretion, when exercised, is conclusive. But he has no authority to control other officers of the government, in relation to the duties imposed upon them by law, in cases not touching his political powers.[1]

§ 1564. In the year 1793, president Washington thought it his duty to issue a proclamation, forbidding the citizens of the United States to take any part in the hostilities, then existing between Great Britain and France; warning them against carrying goods, contraband of war; and enjoining upon them an entire abstinence from all acts, inconsistent with the duties of neutrality.[2] This proclamation had the unanimous approbation of his cabinet.[3] Being, however, at variance with the popular passions and prejudices of the day, this exercise of incidental authority was assailed with uncommon vehemence, and was denied to be constitutional. It seems wholly unnecessary now to review

---

1 *Marbury* v. *Madison*, 1 Cranch. 137, S. C.; 2 Peters's Cond. R. 276, 277.

2 1 Wait's American State Papers, 44.

3 5 Marshall's Life of Washington, ch. 6, p. 404, 408.

the grounds of the controversy, since the deliberate sense of the nation has gone along with the exercise of the power, as one properly belonging to the executive duties.[1] If the P.esident is bound to see to the execution of the laws, and treaties of the United States; and if the duties of neutrality, when the nation has not assumed a belligerent attitude, are by the law of nations obligatory upon it, it seems difficult to perceive any solid objection to a proclamation, stating the facts, and admonishing the citizens of their own duties and responsibilities.[2]

§ 1565. We have seen, that by law the president possesses the right to require the written advice and opinions of his cabinet ministers, upon all questions connected with their respective departments. But, he does not possess a like authority, in regard to the judicial department. That branch of the government can be called upon only to decide controversies, brought before them in a legal form; and therefore are bound to abstain from any extra-judicial opinions upon points of law, even though solemnly requested by the executive.[3]

---

[1] Rawle on Const. ch. 20, p. 197. — The learned reader, who wishes to review the whole ground, will find it treated in a masterly manner, in the letters of Pacificus, written by Mr. Hamilton in favour of the power, and in the letters of Helvidius, written by Mr. Madison against it. They will both be found in the edition of the Federalist, printed at Washington, in 1818, and in Hallowell, in 1826, in the Appendix.

[2] 1 Tucker's Black. Comm. App. 346. — Both houses of Congress, in their answers to the President's speech at the ensuing session, approved of his conduct, in issuing the proclamation. — 1 Tucker's Black. Comm. App. 346.

[3] 5 Marshall's Life of Washington, ch. 6, p. 433, 441; Serg. Const. ch. 29, [ch. 31.] See also Hayburn's case, 2 Dall. R. 409, 410, and note; Marbury v. Madison, 1 Cranch. 137, 171. — President Washington, in 1793, requested the opinion of the Judges of the Supreme Court, upon the construction of the treaty with France, of 1778; but they declined

§ 1566. The remaining section of the fourth article, declaring that the President, Vice-President, and all civil officers of the United States shall be liable to impeachment, has been already fully considered in another place. And thus is closed the examination of the rights, powers, and duties of the executive department. Unless my judgment has been unduly biassed, I think it will be found impossible to hold from this part of the constitution a tribute of profound respect, if not of the liveliest admiration. All, that seems desirable in order to gratify the hopes, secure the reverence, and sustain the dignity of the nation, is, that it should always be occupied by a man of elevated talents, of ripe virtues, of incorruptible integrity, and of tried patriotism ; one, who shall forget his own interests, and remember, that he represents not a party, but the whole nation; one, whose fame may be rested with posterity, not upon the false eulogies of favourites, but upon the solid merit of having preserved the glory, and enhanced the prosperity of the country.[1]

---

to give any opinion, upon the ground stated in the text. 5 Marshall's Life of Washington, ch. 6, p. 433, 441.

[1] In consequence of President Jackson's Message, negativing the Bank of the United States, July 10, 1832, in which he advances the doctrine, that the decisions made by other departments of the government, including the Judiciary, and even by his predecessors in office in approving laws, are not obligatory on him ; the question has been a good deal agitated by statesmen and constitutional lawyers. The following extract from a letter, written by Mr. Madison to Mr. C. J. Ingersoll, on 25th of June, 1831, contains reasoning on this subject, worthy of the judgment of that great man.

"The charge of inconsistency between my objection to the constitutionality of such a bank, in 1791, and my assent, in 1817, turns to the question how far legislative precedents, expounding the constitution, ought to guide succeeding legislatures, and to overrule individual opinions.

"Some obscurity has been thrown over the question, by confounding it with the respect due from one legislature, to laws passed by preceding legislatures. But the two cases are essentially different. A constitution, being derived from a superior authority, is to be expounded and obeyed, not controlled or varied by the subordinate authority of a legislature. A law, on the other hand, resting on no higher authority, than that possessed by every successive legislature ; its expediency, as well as its meaning, is within the scope of the latter.

" The case in question has its true analogy, in the obligation arising from judicial expositions of the law on succeeding judges, the constitution being a law to the legislator, as the law is a rule of decision to the judge.

" And why are judicial precedents, when formed on due discussion and consideration, and deliberately sanctioned by reviews and repetitions, regarded as of binding influence, or rather of authoritative force, in settling the meaning of a law ? It must be answered, 1st, because it is a reasonable and established axiom, and the good of society requires, that the rules of conduct of its members, should be certain and known, which would not be the case if any judge, disregarding the decisions of his predecessors, should vary the rule of law, according to his individual interpretation of it. — Misera est servitus ubi jus aut vagum aut incognitum. 2d, because an exposition of the law publicly made, and repeatedly confirmed by the constituted authority, carries with it, by fair inference, the sanction of those, who, having made the law through their legislative organ, appear under such circumstances, to have determined its meaning through their judiciary organ.

" Can it be of less consequence, that the meaning of a constitution should be fixed and known, than that the meaning of a law should be so ? Can, indeed, a law be fixed in its meaning and operation, unless the constitution be so ? On the contrary, if a particular legislature, differing in the construction of the constitution, from a series of preceding constructions, proceed to act on that difference, they not only introduce uncertainty and instability in the constitution, but in the laws themselves ; inasmuch as all laws, preceding the new construction, and inconsistent with it, are not only annulled for the future, but virtually pronounced nullities from the beginning.

" But, it is said, that the legislator, having sworn to support the constitution, must support it in his own construction of it, however different from that put on by his predecessors, or whatever be the consequences of the construction. And is not the judge under the same oath to support the law ? yet, has it ever been supposed, that he was required, or at liberty, to disregard all precedents, however solemnly repeated and regularly observed ; and by giving effect to his own abstract and individual opinions, to disturb the established course of practice, in the business of the community ? Has the wisest and most conscientious judge ever scrupled to acquiesce in decisions, in which he

has been overruled by the matured opinions of the majority of his col-
leagues; and subsequently to conform himself thereto, as to authoritative expositions of the law? And is it not reasonable, that the same
view of the official oath should be taken by a legislator, acting under
the constitution, which is his guide, as is taken by a judge, acting under
the law, which is his?

"There is, in fact and in common understanding, a necessity of re-
garding a course of practice, as above characterized, in the light of
a legal rule of interpreting a law: and there is a like necessity of considering it a constitutional rule of interpreting a constitution.

"That there may be extraordinary and peculiar circumstances controlling the rule in both cases, may be admitted; but with such exceptions, the rule will force itself on the practical judgment of the most
ardent theorist. He will find it impossible to adhere to, and act officially upon his solitary opinions, as to the meaning of the law or constitution, in opposition to a construction reduced to practice, during a reasonable period of time; more especially, where no prospect existed of
a change of construction, by the public or its agents. And if a reasonable period of time, marked with the usual sanctions, would not bar the
individual prerogative, there could be no limitation to its exercise,
although the danger of error must increase with the increasing oblivion
of explanatory circumstances, and with the continual changes in the
import of words and phrases.

"Let it then be left to the decision of every intelligent and candid
judge, which, on the whole, is most to be relied on for the true and safe
construction of a constitution; that which has the uniform sanction of
successive legislative bodies through a period of years, and under the
varied ascendancy of parties; or that which depends upon the opinions of
every new legislature, heated as it may be by the spirit of party, eager
in the pursuit of some favourite object, or led astray by the eloquence
and address of popular statesmen, themselves, perhaps, under the influence of the same misleading causes.

"It was in conformity with the view here taken, of the respect due
to deliberate and reiterated precedents, that the bank of the United
States, though on the original question held to be unconstitutional, received the executive signature in the year 1817. The act originally
establishing a bank, had undergone ample discussions in its passage
through the several branches of the government. It had been carried
into execution throughout a period of twenty years, with annual legislative recognitions; in one instance, indeed, with a positive ramification
of it into a new state; and with the entire acquiescence of all the local
authorities, as well as of the nation at large; to all of which may be
added, a decreasing prospect of any change in the public opinion, adverse to the constitutionality of such an institution. A veto from the
executive under these circumstances, with an admission of the expediency and almost necessity of the measure, would have been a

defiance of all the obligations derived from a course of precedents, amounting to the requisite evidence of the national judgment and intention.

" It has been contended that the authority of precedents was in that case invalidated, by the consideration, that they proved only a respect for the stipulated duration of the bank, with a toleration of it, until the law should expire, and by the casting vote given in the senate by the Vice-President, in 1811, against a bill for establishing a National Bank, the vote being expressly given on the ground of unconstitutionality. But if the law itself was unconstitutional, the stipulation was void, and could not be constitutionally fulfilled or tolerated. And as to the negative of the senate, by the casting vote of the presiding officer; it is a fact well understood at the time, that it resulted not from an equality of opinions in that assembly, on the power of congress to establish a bank, but from a junction of those, who admitted the power, but disapproved the plan, with those who denied the power. On a simple question of constitutionality, there was a decided majority in favour of it."

There is also a very cogent argument, on the same side, in Mr. Webster's Speech in the senate, in July, 1832, on the Veto Message of the President.

CHAPTER XXXVIII.

JUDICIARY — ORGANIZATION AND POWERS.

§ 1567. THE order of the subject next conducts us to the consideration of the third article of the constitution, which embraces the organization and powers of the judicial department.

§ 1568. The importance of the establishment of a judicial department in the national government has been already incidentally discussed under other heads. The want of it constituted one of the vital defects of the confederation.[1] And every government must, in its essence, be unsafe and unfit for a free people, where such a department does not exist, with powers co-extensive with those of the legislative department.[2] Where there is no judicial department to interpret, pronounce, and execute the law, to decide controversies, and to enforce rights, the government must either perish by its own imbecility, or the other departments of government must usurp powers, for the purpose of commanding obedience, to the destruction of liberty.[3] The will

---

[1] The Federalist, No. 22; Cohens v. Virginia, 6 Wheat. R. 388; 1 Kent's Comm. Lect. 14, p. 277.

[2] The Federalist, No. 80; 1 Kent's Comm. Lect. 14, p. 277; Cohens v. Virginia, 6 Wheat. R. 384; 2 Wilson's Law Lect. ch. 3, p. 201; 3 Elliot's Deb. 143; Osborne v. Bank of United States, 9 Wheat. R. 818, 819. — Mr. Justice Wilson has traced out, with much minuteness of detail, the nature and character of the judicial department in ancient, as well as modern nations, and especially in England; and a perusal of his remarks will be found full of instruction. 2 Wilson's Law Lect. ch. 3, p. 201, &c.

[3] 1 Kent's Comm. Lect. 14, p. 277. — It has been finely remarked by Mr. Chief Justice Marshall, that "the judicial department has no will in any case. Judicial power, as contradistinguished from the power of

of those, who govern, will become, under such circumstances, absolute and despotic; and it is wholly immaterial, whether power is vested in a single tyrant, or in an
assembly of tyrants.   No remark is better founded in
human experience, than that of Montesquieu, that "there
is no liberty, if the judiciary power be not separated from
the legislative and executive powers." [1]   And it is no
less true, that personal security and private property
rest entirely upon the wisdom, the stability, and the
integrity of the courts of justice.[2]   If that government
can be truly said to be despotic and intolerable, in
which the law is vague and uncertain; it cannot but be
rendered still more oppressive and more mischievous,
when the actual administration of justice is dependent
upon caprice, or favour, upon the will of rulers, or the
influence of popularity.   When power becomes right,
it is of little consequence, whether decisions rest upon
corruption, or weakness, upon the accidents of chance,
or upon deliberate wrong.   In every well organized
government, therefore, with reference to the security
both of public rights and private rights, it is indispensable, that there should be a judicial department to
ascertain, and decide rights, to punish crimes, to administer justice, and to protect the innocent from injury
and usurpation.[3]

---

the laws, has no existence. Courts are the mere instruments of the
law, and can will nothing. When they are said to exercise a discretion,
it is a mere legal discretion, a discretion to be exercised in discerning
the course prescribed by law; and, when that is discerned, it is the duty
of the court to follow it. Judicial power is never exercised for the purpose of giving effect to the will of the judge; but always for the purpose
of giving effect to the will of the legislature; or, in other words, to the
will of the law." *

1 Montesquieu's Spirit of Laws, B. 11, ch. 6.
2 1 Kent's Comm. Lect. 14, p. 273.
3 Rawle on Constitution, ch. 21, p. 199.

* *Osborne v. Bank of United States.* 9 Wheat. R. 866.

§ 1569. In the national government the power is equally as important, as in the state governments. The laws and treaties, and even the constitution, of the United States, would become a dead letter without it. Indeed, in a complicated government, like ours, where there is an assemblage of republics, combined under a common head, the necessity of some controlling judicial power, to ascertain and enforce the powers of the Union, is, if possible, still more striking. The laws of the whole would otherwise be in continual danger of being contravened by the laws of the parts.[1] The national government would be reduced to a servile dependence upon the states ; and the same scenes would be again acted over in solemn mockery, which began in the neglect, and ended in the ruin, of the confederation.[2] Power, without adequate means to enforce it, is like a body in a state of suspended animation. For all practical purposes it is, as if its faculties were extinguished. Even if there were no danger of collision between the laws and powers of the Union, and those of the states, it is utterly impossible, that, without some superintending judiciary establishment, there could be any uniform administration, or interpretation of them. The idea of uniformity of decision by thirteen independent and co-ordinate tribunals(and the number is now advanced to twenty-four) is absolutely visionary, if not absurd. The consequence would necessarily be, that neither the constitution, nor the laws, neither the rights and powers of the Union, nor those of the states, would be the same in any two states. And there would be per-

---

1 The Federalist, No. 22 ; *Chisholm v. Georgia*, 2 Dall. 419, 474 ; ante, Vol. I. p. 216, 247 ; 3 Elliot's Deb. 142.

2 See *Cohens v. Virginia*, 6 Wheat. R. 384 to 390 ; Id. 402 to 404, 415 ; *Osborne v. Bank of United States*, 9 Wheat. R. 818, 819 ; ante, Vol. I. § 266, 267.

petual fluctuations and changes, growing out of the diversity of judgment, as well as of local institutions, interests, and habits of thought.[1]

§ 1570. Two ends, then, of paramount importance, and fundamental to a free government, are proposed to be attained by the establishment of a national judiciary. The first is a due execution of the powers of the government; 'and the second is a uniformity in the interpretation and operation of those powers, and of the laws enacted in pursuance of them. The power of interpreting the laws involves necessarily the function to ascertain, whether they are conformable to the constitution, or not; and if not so conformable, to declare them void and inoperative. As the constitution is the supreme law of the land, in a conflict between that and the laws, either of congress, or of the states, it becomes the duty of the judiciary to follow that only, which is of paramount obligation. This results from the very theory of a republican constitution of government; for otherwise the acts of the legislature and executive would in effect become supreme and uncontrollable, notwithstanding any prohibitions or limitations contained in the constitution; and usurpations of the most unequivocal and dangerous character might be assumed, without any remedy within the reach of the citizens.[2] The people would thus be at the mercy of their rulers,

1 *Martin v. Hunter*, 1 Wheat. R. 304, 345 to 349; The Federalist, No. 22.

2 The Federalist, No. 78, 80, 81, 82; 1 Tuck. Black. Comm. App. 355 to 360; 3 Elliot's Deb. 134. — This subject is very elaborately discussed in the Federalist, No. 78, from which the following extract is made:

" The complete independence of the courts of justice is peculiarly essential in a limited constitution. By a limited constitution, I understand one, which contains certain specified exceptions to the legislative authority; such, for instance, as that it shall pass no bills of attainder, no

in the state and national governments; and an omnipotence would practically exist, like that claimed for the British Parliament. The universal sense of America

ex post facto laws, and the like. Limitations of this kind can be preserved in practice no other way than through the medium of the courts of justice; whose duty it must be to declare all acts contrary to the manifest tenor of the constitution void. Without this, all the reservations of particular rights or privileges would amount to nothing.

"Some perplexity respecting the rights of the courts to pronounce legislative acts void, because contrary to the constitution, has arisen from an imagination, that the doctrine would imply a superiority of the judiciary to the legislative power. It is urged, that the authority, which can declare the acts of another void, must necessarily be superior to the one, whose acts may be declared void. As this doctrine is of great importance in all the American constitutions, a brief discussion of the grounds, on which it rests, cannot be unacceptable.

"There is no position, which depends on clearer principles, than that every act of a delegated authority, contrary to the tenor of the commission, under which it is exercised, is void. No legislative act, therefore, contrary to the constitution, can be valid. To deny this, would be to affirm, that the deputy is greater than his principal; that the servant is above his master; that the representatives of the people are superior to the people themselves; that men, acting by virtue of powers, may do, not only what their powers do not authorize, but what they forbid.

"If it be said, that the legislative body are themselves the constitutional judges of their own powers, and that the construction they put upon them is conclusive upon the other departments, it may be answered, that this cannot be the natural presumption, where it is not to be collected from any particular provisions in the constitution. It is not otherwise to be supposed, that the constitution could intend to enable the representatives of the people to substitute their *will* to that of their constituents. It is far more rational to suppose, that the courts were designed to be an intermediate body between the people and the legislature, in order, among other things, to keep the latter within the limits assigned to their authority. The interpretation of the laws is the proper and peculiar province of the courts. A constitution is, in fact, and must be regarded by the judges as a fundamental law. It must, therefore, belong to them to ascertain its meaning, as well as the meaning of any particular act proceeding from the legislative body. If there should happen to be an irreconcilable variance between the two, that which has the superior obligation and validity ought, of course, to be preferred: in other words, the constitution ought to be preferred to the statute; the intention of the people to the intention of their agents.

"Nor does the conclusion by any means suppose a superiority of the judicial to the legislative power. It only supposes, that the power of

has decided, that in the last resort the judiciary must decide upon the constitutionality of the acts and laws of the general and state governments, so far as they are

the people is superior to both; and that where the will of the legislature declared in its statutes, stands in opposition to that of the people declared in the constitution, the judges ought to be governed by the latter rather than the former. They ought to regulate their decisions by the fundamental laws, rather than by those, which are not fundamental.

"This exercise of judicial discretion, in determining between two contradictory laws, is exemplified in a familiar instance. It not uncommonly happens, that there are two statutes existing at one time, clashing in whole or in part with each other, and neither of them containing any repealing clause or expression. In such a case, it is the province of the courts to liquidate and fix their meaning and operation: so far as they can, by any fair construction, be reconciled to each other, reason and law conspire to dictate, that this should be done: where this is impracticable, it becomes a matter of necessity to give effect to one, in exclusion of the other. The rule, which has obtained in the courts for determining their relative validity is, that the last in order of time shall be preferred to the first. But this is a mere rule of construction, not derived from any positive law, but from the nature and reason of the thing. It is a rule not enjoined upon the courts by legislative provision, but adopted by themselves, as consonant to truth and propriety, for the direction of their conduct as interpreters of the law. They thought it reasonable, that between the interfering acts of an *equal* authority, that which was the last indication of its will, should have the preference.

"But in regard to the interfering acts of a superior and subordinate authority, of an original and derivative power, the nature and reason of the thing indicate the converse of that rule as proper to be followed. They teach us, that the prior act of a superior ought to be preferred to the subsequent act of an inferior and subordinate authority; and that accordingly, whenever a particular statute contravenes the constitution, it will be the duty of the judicial tribunals to adhere to the latter, and disregard the former.

"It can be of no weight to say, that the courts, on the pretence of a repugnancy, may substitute their own pleasure to the constitutional intentions of the legislature. This might as well happen in the case of two contradictory statutes; or it might as well happen in every adjudication upon any single statute. The courts must declare the sense of the law; and if they should be disposed to exercise *will* instead of *judgment*, the consequence would equally be the substitution of their pleasure to that of the legislative body. The observation, if it proved any thing, would prove, that there ought to be no judges distinct from that body."

The reasoning of Mr. Chief Justice Marshall on this subject in *Cohens*

capable of being made the subject of judicial controversy.[1] It follows, that, when they are subjected to the cognizance of the judiciary, its judgments must be conclusive; for otherwise they may be disregarded, and the acts of the legislature and executive enjoy a secure and

---

v. *Virginia*, (6 Wheat. R. 384 to 390,) has been already cited at large, ante Vol. I. p. 369 to 372. See also 6 Wheat. R. 413 to 423, and the Federalist, No. 22, on the same subject.

[1] 1 Kent's Comm. Lect. 20, p. 420 to 426. See also *Cohens* v. *Virginia*, 6 Wheat. R. 386 to 390. — The reasoning of the Supreme Court in *Marbury* v. *Madison*, (1 Cranch, 137,) on this subject is so clear and convincing, that it is deemed advisable to cite it in this place, as a corrective to those loose and extraordinary doctrines, which sometimes find their way into opinions possessing official influence.

"The question, whether an act, repugnant to the constitution, can become the law of the land, is a question deeply interesting to the United States; but, happily, not of an intricacy proportioned to its interest. It seems only necessary to recognise certain principles, supposed to have been long and well established, to decide it. That the people have an original right to establish, for their future government, such principles as, in their opinion, shall most conduce to their own happiness, is the basis, on which the whole American fabric has been erected. The exercise of this original right is a very great exertion; nor can it, nor ought it to be frequently repeated. The principles, therefore, so established, are deemed fundamental. And as the authority, from which they proceed, is supreme, and can seldom act, they are designed to be permanent. This original and supreme will organises the government, and assigns to different departments their respective powers. It may either stop here, or establish certain limits, not to be transcended by those departments.

"The government of the United States is of the latter description. The powers of the legislature are defined, and limited; and that those limits may not be mistaken, or forgotten, the constitution is written. To what purpose are powers limited, and to what purpose is that limitation committed to writing, if these limits may, at any time, be passed by those intended to be restrained? The distinction, between a government with limited and unlimited powers, is abolished, if those limits do not confine the persons, on whom they are imposed, and if acts prohibited, and acts allowed, are of equal obligation. It is a proposition too plain to be contested, that the constitution controls any legislative act repugnant to it; or, that the legislature may alter the constitution by an ordinary act. Between these alternatives there is no middle ground. The constitution is either a superior, paramount law, unchangeable by

irresistible triumph.[1]   To the people at large, therefore,
such an institution is peculiarly valuable ; and it ought to
be eminently cherished by them.   On its firm and inde-

---

ordinary means, or it is on a level with ordinary legislative acts, and, like
other acts, is alterable, when the legislature shall please to alter it.   If
the former part of the alternative be true, then a legislative act contrary to the constitution is not law ; if the latter part be true, then written
constitutions are absurd attempts, on the part of the people, to limit a
power, in its own nature illimitable.

"Certainly all those, who have framed written constitutions, contemplate them as forming the fundamental and paramount law of the nation,
and consequently the theory of every such government must be, that an
act of the legislature, repugnant to the constitution, is void.   This
theory is essentially attached to a written constitution, and is consequently to be considered by this court, as one of the fundamental principles of our society.   It is not, therefore, to be lost sight of in the further consideration of this subject.   If an act of the legislature, repugnant to the constitution, is void, does it, notwithstanding its invalidity,
bind the courts, and oblige them to give it effect?   Or, in other words,
though it be not law, does it constitute a rule as operative, as if it was a
law ?   This would be to overthrow in fact, what was established in theory ; and would seem, at first view, an absurdity too gross to be insisted
on.   It shall, however, receive a more attentive consideration.

"It is emphatically the province and duty of the judicial department
to say, what the law is.   Those, who apply the rule to particular cases,
must of necessity expound and interpret that rule.   If two laws conflict
with each other, the courts must decide on the operation of each.   So if
a law be in opposition to the constitution ; if both the law and the constitution apply to a particular case ; so that the court must either decide
that case conformably to the law, disregarding the constitution ; or conformably to the constitution, disregarding the law ; the court must determine, which of these conflicting rules governs the case.   This is of
the very essence of judicial duty.   If, then, the courts are to regard the
constitution ; and the constitution is superior to any ordinary act of the
legislature ; the constitution, and not such ordinary act, must govern the
case, to which they both apply.

"Those, then, who controvert the principle, that the constitution is to
be considered, in courts, as a paramount law, are reduced to the necessity of maintaining, that courts must close their eyes on the constitution
and see only the law.   This doctrine would subvert the very foundation

---

[1] 1 Kent's Comm. Lect. 20, p. 420 to 426.   See also 1 Tuck. Black.
Comm. App. 354 to 357 ; The Federalist, No. 3, 22, 80, 82 ; 2 Elliot's
Deb. 380.

pendent structure they may repose with safety, while
they perceive in it a faculty, which is only set in motion, when applied to; but which, when thus brought

of all written constitutions. It would declare, that an act, which, according to the principles and theory of our government, is entirely void,
is yet, in practice, completely obligatory. It would declare, that if the
legislature shall do, what is expressly forbidden, such act, notwithstanding the express prohibition, is in reality effectual. It would be giving
to the legislature a practical and real omnipotence, with the same breath,
which professes to restrict their powers within narrow limits. It is prescribing limits, and declaring, that those limits may be passed at pleasure. That it thus reduces to nothing, what we have deemed the greatest improvement on political institutions — a written constitution —
would of itself be sufficient, in America, where written constitutions
have been viewed with so much reverence, for rejecting the construction. But the peculiar expressions of the constitution of the United
States furnish additional arguments in favour of its rejection.

"The judicial power of the United States is extended to all cases,
arising under the constitution. Could it be the intention of those, who
gave this power, to say, that, in using it, the constitution should not be
looked into? That a case arising under the constitution should be
decided without examining the instrument, under which it arises? This
is too extravagant to be maintained. In some cases, then, the constitution must be looked into by the judges. And if they can open it at
all, what part of it are they forbidden to read, or to obey?

"There are many other parts of the constitution, which serve to illustrate this subject. It is declared, that 'no tax or duty shall be laid on
articles exported from any state.' Suppose a duty on the export of
cotton, of tobacco, or of flour; and a suit instituted to recover it. Ought
judgment to be rendered in such a case? ought the judges to close their
eyes on the constitution, and only see the law? The constitution declares, that 'no bill of attainder or *ex post facto* law shall be passed.' If,
however, such a bill should be passed, and a person should be prosecuted under it; must the court condemn to death those victims, whom the
constitution endeavours to preserve? 'No person,' says the constitution, 'shall be convicted of treason unless on the testimony of two witnesses to the same overt act, or on confession in open court.' Here the
language of the constitution is addressed especially to the courts. It
prescribes, directly for them, a rule of evidence not to be departed from.
If the legislature should change that rule, and declare *one* witness, or a
confession *out* of court, sufficient for conviction, must the constitutional
principle yield to the legislative act?

"From these, and many other selections, which might be made, it is
apparent, that the framers of the constitution contemplated that instru-

into action, must proceed with competent power, if
required to correct the error, or subdue the oppression
of the other branches of the government.[1]   Fortunately

---

ment, as a rule for the government of *courts*, as well as of the legislature. Why otherwise does it direct the judges to take an oath to support it? This oath certainly applies, in an especial manner, to their
conduct in their official character. How immoral to impose it on them,
if they were to be used as the instruments, and the knowing instruments
for violating what they swear to support! The oath of office, too, imposed by the legislature, is completely demonstrative of the legislative
opinion on this subject. It is in these words, 'I do solemnly swear, that
I will administer justice without respect to persons, and do equal right
to the poor and to the rich ; and that I will faithfully and impartially
discharge all the duties incumbent on me as   according to
the best of my abilities and understanding, agreeably to *the constitution*,
and laws of the United States.' Why does a judge swear to discharge
his duties agreeably to the constitution of the United States, if that constitution forms no rule for his government? if it is closed upon him, and
cannot be inspected by him? If such be the real state of things, this is
worse than solemn mockery. To prescribe, or to take this oath, becomes equally a crime.

"It is also not entirely unworthy of observation, that in declaring,
what shall be the *supreme* law of the land, the *constitution* itself is first
mentioned ; and not the laws of the United States generally, but those
only, which shall be made in *pursuance* of the constitution, have that
rank. Thus, the particular phraseology of the constitution of the United States confirms and strengthens the principle, supposed to be essential to all written constitutions, that a law repugnant to the constitution
is void; and that *courts*, as well as other departments, are bound by
that instrument."

In the Virginia Convention, Mr. Patrick Henry (a most decided oppo-
nent of the Constitution of the United States) expressed a strong opinion in favour of the right of the judiciary to decide upon the constitutionality of laws. His fears were, that the national judiciary was not so
organized, as that it would possess an independence sufficient for this
purpose. His language was: "The honourable gentleman did our judiciary honour in saying, that they had firmness enough to counteract
the legislature in some cases. Yes, sir, our judges opposed the acts of
the legislature. We have this land-mark to guide us. They had fortitude to declare, that they were the judiciary, and would oppose unconstitutional acts. Are you sure, that your federal judiciary will act thus?

---

[1] Rawle on Const. ch. 21, p. 199; Id. ch. 30, p. 275, 276; 1 Wilson's
Law Lect. 460, 461 ; 3 Elliot's Deb. 143; Id. 245; Id. 280.

too for the people, the functions of the judiciary, in deciding on constitutional questions, is not one, which it is at liberty to decline. While it is bound not to take jurisdiction, if it should not, it is equally true, that it must take jurisdiction, if it should. It cannot, as the legislature may, avoid a measure, because it approaches the confines of the constitution. It cannot pass it by, because it is doubtful. With whatever doubt, with whatever difficulties a case may be attended, it must decide it, when it arises in judgment. It has no more right to decline the exercise of a jurisdiction, which is given, than to usurp that, which is not given. The one, or the other would be treason to the constitution.[1]

§ 1571. The framers of the constitution, having these great principles in view, adopted two fundamental rules with entire unanimity; first, that a national judiciary ought to be established; secondly, that the national judiciary ought to possess powers co-extensive with

---

Is that judiciary so well constituted, and so independent of the other branches, as our state judiciary? Where are your land-marks in this government? I will be bold to say, you cannot find any. I take it, as the highest encomium on this country, that the acts of the legislature, if unconstitutional, are liable to be opposed by the judiciary." 2 Elliot's Debates, 248.

[1] *Cohens* v. *Virginia*, 6 Wheat. R. 404; 1 Wilson's Law Lect. 461, 462. — Mr. Justice Johnson, in *Fullerton* v. *Bank of United States*, (1 Peters's R. 604, 614,) says, " What is the course of prudence and duty, where these cases of difficult distribution as to power and right present themselves? It is to yield rather, than to encroach. The duty is reciprocal, and will no doubt be met in the spirit of moderation and comity. In the conflicts of power and opinion, inseparable from our many peculiar relations, cases may occur, in which the maintenance of principle and the constitution, according to its innate and inseparable attributes, may require a different course ; and when such cases do occur, our courts must do their duty." This is a very just admonition, when addressed to other departments of the government. But the judiciary has no authority to adopt any middle course. It is compelled, when called upon, to

those of the legislative department.[1]   Indeed, the latter
necessarily flowed from the former, and was treated,
and must always be treated, as an axiom of political
government.[2]   But these provisions alone would not
be sufficient to ensure a complete administration of
public justice, or to give permanency to the republic.
The judiciary must be so organized, as to carry into
complete effect all the purposes of its establishment.
It must possess wisdom, learning, integrity, independence, and firmness. It must at once possess the
power and the means to check usurpation, and enforce
execution of its judgments.   Mr. Burke has, with singular sagacity and pregnant brevity, stated the doctrine,
which every republic should steadily sustain, and conscientiously inculcate. "Whatever," says he, "is supreme in a state ought to have, as much as possible, its
judicial authority so constituted, as not only not to depend upon it, but in some sort to balance it.   It ought
to give security to its justice against its power.   It
ought to make its judicature, as it were, something
exterior to the state."[3]   The best manner, in which this
is to be accomplished, must mainly depend upon the
mode of appointment, the tenure of office, the compensation of the judges, and the jurisdiction confided
to the department in its various branches.

  § 1572. Let us proceed, then, to the consideration
of the judicial department, as it is established by the

decide, whether a law is constitutional, or not. If it declines to declare
it unconstitutional, that is an affirmance of its constitutionality.
  1 Journ. of Convention, 69, 98, 121, 137, 186, 188, 189, 212; The Federalist, No. 77, 78; 2 Elliot's Debates, 380 to 394; Id. 404.
  2 Cohens v. Virginia, 6 Wheat. R. 384; 1 Tucker's Black. Comm.
App. 350; The Federalist, No. 80; 2 Elliot's Debates, 380, 390, 404;
3 Elliot's Debates, 131, 143; Osborn v. Bank of United States, 9 Wheat.
R. 818, 819; 1 Kent's Comm. Lect. 14, p. 277.
  3 Burke's Reflections on the French Revolution.

constitution, and see, how far adequate means are provided for all these important purposes.

§ 1573. The first section of the third article is as follows: "The judicial power of the United States "shall be vested in one Supreme Court, and in such "inferior courts, as the congress may from time to time "ordain and establish. The judges, both of the su-"preme and inferior courts, shall hold their offices dur-"ing good behaviour; and shall at stated times receive "for their services a compensation, which shall not be "diminished during their continuance in office." To this may be added the clause in the enumeration of the powers of congress in the first article, (which is but a mere repetition,) that congress shall have power "to constitute tribunals inferior to the Supreme Court." [1]

---

[1] It is manifest, that the constitution contemplated distinct appointments of the judges of the courts of the United States. The judges of the Supreme Court are expressly required to be appointed by the president, by and with the advice and consent of the senate. They are, therefore, expressly appointed for that court, and for that court only. Can they be constitutionally required to act, as judges of any other court? This question (it now appears) was presented to the minds of the judges of the Supreme Court, who were first appointed under the constitution; and the chief justice (Mr. Jay) and some of his associates were of opinion, (and so stated to President Washington, in 1790, in a letter, which will be cited below at large,) that they could not constitutionally be appointed to hold any other court. They were, however, required to perform the duty of circuit judges in the circuit courts, until the year 1801; and then a new system was established. The latter was repealed in 1802: and the judges of the Supreme Court were again required to perform duty in the circuit courts. In 1803, the point was directly made before the Supreme Court; but the court were then of opinion, that the practice and acquiescence, for such a period of years, commencing with the organization of the judicial system, had fixed the construction, and it could not then be shaken. *Stuart v. Laird*, (1 Cranch's R. 299, 309.) That there have, notwithstanding, been many scruples and doubts upon the subject, in the minds of the judges of the Supreme Court, since that period, is well known. See 1 Paine's Cirt. Rep.

We here insert the letter of Mr. Chief Justice Jay and his associates,

§ 1574. In the convention, which framed the constitution, no diversity of opinion existed, as to the establishment of a supreme tribunal. The proposition

---

for which we are indebted to the editors of that excellent work, the American Jurist. It is in the number for October, 1830, (vol. 4, p. 294, &c.)

" The representation alluded to was in answer to a letter, addressed by General Washington to the court upon its organization, which we have therefore prefixed to it.

United States, April 3d, 1790.

" 'GENTLEMEN: I have always been persuaded, that the stability and success of the national government, and consequently the happiness of the people of the United States, would depend, in a considerable degree, on the interpretation of its laws. In my opinion, therefore, it is important, that the judiciary system should not only be independent in its operations, but as perfect, as possible, in its formation.

" ' As you are about to commence your first circuit, and many things may occur in such an unexplored field, which it would be useful should be known, I think it proper to acquaint you, that it will be agreeable to me to receive such information and remarks on this subject, as you shall from time to time judge it expedient to make.   GEO. WASHINGTON.

" ' The Chief Justice and Associate Justices
    of the Supreme Court of the United States.'

" ' SIR : We, the Chief Justice and Associate Justices of the Supreme Court of the United States, in pursuance of the letter, which you did us the honour to write, on the third of April last, take the liberty of submitting to your consideration the following remarks on the " Act to establish the Judicial Courts of the United States."

" ' It would doubtless have been singular, if a system so new and untried, and which was necessarily formed more on principles of theory, and probable expediency, than former experience, had, in practice, been found entirely free from defects.

" ' The particular and continued attention, which our official duties called upon us to pay to this act, has produced reflections, which at the time it was made and passed, did not, probably, occur in their full extent either to us or others.

" ' On comparing this act with the constitution, we perceive deviations, which, in our opinions, are important.

" ' The first section of the third article of the constitution declares, that "the judicial power of the United States shall be vested in one *Supreme* Court, and in such inferior courts, as the congress may, from time to time, ordain and establish."

was unanimously adopted.[1] In respect to the establishment of inferior tribunals, some diversity of opinion
was in the early stages of the proceedings exhibited.

" ' The second section enumerates the cases, to which the judicial
power shall extend. It gives to the Supreme Court original jurisdiction
in only *two* cases, but in all the others, vests it with *appellate* jurisdiction ; and that with such exceptions, and under such regulations, as the
congress shall make.

" ' It has long and very universally been deemed essential to the due
administration of justice, that some national court, or council should be
instituted, or authorized to examine the acts of the ordinary tribunals,
and ultimately, to affirm or reverse their judgments and decrees ; it being important, that these tribunals should be confined to the limits of
their respective jurisdiction, and that they should uniformly interpret
and apply the law in the same sense and manner.

" ' The appellate jurisdiction of the Supreme Court enables it to confine inferior courts to their proper limits, to correct their involuntary
errors, and, in general, to provide, that justice be administered accurately, impartially, and uniformly. These controlling powers were unavoidably great and extensive ; and of such a nature, as to render their
being combined with other judicial powers, in the same persons, unad-
visable.

" ' To the natural, as well as legal incompatibility of *ultimate* appellate jurisdiction, with original jurisdiction, we ascribe the exclusion of
the Supreme Court from the latter, except in two cases. Had it not
been for this exclusion, the unalterable, ever-binding decisions of this
important court, would not have been secured against the influences of
those predilections for individual opinions, and of those reluctances to
relinquish sentiments publicly, though, perhaps, too hastily given, which
insensibly and not unfrequently infuse into the minds of the most upright men, some degree of partiality for their official and public acts.

" ' Without such exclusion, no court, possessing the last resort of justice, would have acquired and preserved that public confidence, which
is really necessary to render the wisest institutions useful. A celebrated writer justly observes, that " next to doing right, the great object in
the administration of public justice should be to give public satisfaction."

" ' Had the constitution permitted the Supreme Court to sit in judgment, and finally to decide on the acts and errors, done and committed
by its own members, as judges of inferior and subordinate courts, much
room would have been left for men, on certain occasions, to suspect, that

---

A proposition to establish them was at first adopted. This was struck out by the vote of five states against four, two being divided; and a proposition was then

---

an unwillingness to be thought and found in the wrong, had produced an improper adherence to it; or that mutual interest had generated mutual civilities and tendernesses injurious to right.

" 'If room had been left for such suspicions, there would have been reason to apprehend, that the public confidence would diminish almost in proportion to the number of cases, in which the Supreme Court might *affirm* the acts of any of its members.

" 'Appeals are seldom made, but in doubtful cases, and in which there is, at least, much appearance of reason on both sides; in such cases, therefore, not only the losing party, but others, not immediately interested, would sometimes be led to doubt, whether the affirmance was entirely owing to the mere preponderance of right.

" 'These, we presume, were among the reasons, which induced the convention to confine the Supreme Court, and consequently its judges, to appellate jurisdiction. We say "consequently its judges," because the reasons for the one apply also to the other.

" 'We are aware of the distinction between a court and its judges; and are far from thinking it illegal or unconstitutional, however it may be inexpedient, to employ them for other purposes, provided the latter purposes be consistent and compatible with the former. But from this distinction it cannot, in our opinions, be inferred, that the judges of the Supreme Court may also be judges of inferior and *subordinate* courts, and be at the same time both the *controllers* and the *controlled.*

" 'The application of these remarks is obvious. The Circuit Courts established by the act are courts inferior and subordinate to the Supreme Court. They are vested with original jurisdiction in the cases, from which the Supreme Court is excluded; and to us it would appear very singular, if the constitution was capable of being so construed, as to exclude the court, but yet admit the judges of the court. We, for our parts, consider the constitution, as plainly opposed to the appointment of the same persons to both offices; nor have we any doubts of their legal incompatibility.

" 'Bacon, in his Abridgment, says, that "offices are said to be incompatible and inconsistent, so as to be executed by one person, when from the multiplicity of business in them, they cannot be executed with care and ability; or when their being subordinate, and interfering with each other, it induces a presumption they cannot be executed with impartiality and honesty; and this, my Lord Coke says, is of that importance, that if all offices, civil and ecclesiastical, &c. were only executed, each by different persons, it would be for the good of the commonwealth and

adopted, "that the national legislature be empowered to appoint inferior tribunals," by the vote of seven states against three, one being divided;[1] and ultimately this proposition received the unanimous approbation of the convention.[2]

---

advancement of justice, and preferment of deserving men. If a forester, by patent for his *life*, is made justice in Eyre of the same forest, *hac vice*, the forestership is become *void;* for these offices are incompatible, because the forester is *under the correction* of the justice in Eyre, and he cannot *judge himself*. Upon a mandamus to restore one to the place of town-clerk, it was returned, that he was elected mayor and sworn, and, therefore, they chose another town-clerk ; and the court were strong of opinion, that the offices were incompatible, because of the *subordination*. A coroner, made a sheriff, ceases to be a coroner ; so a parson, made a bishop, and a judge of the Common Pleas, made a judge of the King's Bench," &c.

"'Other authorities on this point might be added ; but the reasons, on which they rest, seem to us to require little elucidation, or support.

"'There is in the act another deviation from the constitution, which we think it incumbent on us to mention.

"'The second section of the second article of the constitution declares, that the president shall nominate, and by and with the advice and consent of the senate, "shall appoint judges of the Supreme Court, and *all* other officers of the United States, whose appointments are not *therein* otherwise provided for."

"'The constitution not having otherwise provided for the appointment of the judges of the inferior courts, we conceive, that the appointment of some of them, viz. of the Circuit Courts, by an act of the legislature, is a departure from the constitution, and an exercise of powers, which constitutionally and exclusively belong to the president and senate.

"'We should proceed, sir, to take notice of certain defects in the act relative to expediency, which we think merit the consideration of the congress. But, as these are doubtless among the objects of the late reference, made by the house of representatives to the attorney-general, we think it most proper to forbear making any remarks on this subject at present.

"'We have the honour to be most respectfully,

"'Sir, your obedient and humble servants.

"'The President of the United States.'"

[1] Journal of Convention, 69, 98, 99, 102, 137.

[2] Id. 188, 212.

§ 1575. To the establishment of one court of supreme and final jurisdiction, there do not seem to
have been any strenuous objections generally insisted
on in the state conventions, though many were urged
against certain portions of the jurisdiction, proposed by
the constitution to be vested in the courts of the United
States.[1] The principal question seems to have been of
a different nature, whether it ought to be a distinct co-
ordinate department, or a branch of the legislature.
And here it was remarked by the Federalist, that the
same contradiction of opinion was observable among
the opponents of the constitution, as in many other
cases. Many of those, who objected to the senate, as
a court of impeachment, upon the ground of an improper intermixture of legislative and judicial functions,
were, at least by implication, advocates for the propriety
of vesting the ultimate decision of all causes in the
whole, or in a part of the legislative body.[2]

§ 1576. The arguments, or rather suggestions, upon
which this scheme was propounded, were to the following effect. The authority of the Supreme Court
of the United States, as a separate and independent
body, will be superior to that of the legislature. The
power of construing the laws according to the spirit of
the constitution will enable that court to mould them
into whatever shape, it may think proper; especially,
as its decisions will not be in any manner subject to the
revision and correction of the legislative body. This
is as unprecedented, as it is dangerous. In Great
Britain the judicial power in the last resort resides in
the house of lords, which is a branch of the legislature.
And this part of the British government has been imi-

---

1 See 2 Elliot's Debates, 380 to 427.
2 The Federalist, No. 81.

tated in the state constitutions in general. The parliament of Great Britain, and the legislatures of the several states, can at any time rectify by law the exceptionable decisions of their respective courts. But the errors and usurpations of the Supreme Court of the United States will be uncontrollable, and remediless.[1]

§ 1577. The friends of the constitution, in answer to these suggestions, replied, that they were founded in false reasoning, or a misconception of fact. In the first place, there was nothing in the plan, which directly empowered the national courts to construe the laws according to the *spirit* of the constitution, or which gave them any greater latitude in this respect, than what was claimed and exercised by the state courts. The constitution, indeed, ought to be the standard of construction for the laws ; and wherever there was an opposition, the laws ought to give place to the constitution. But this doctrine was not deducible from any circumstance peculiar to this part of the constitution, but from the general theory of a limited constitution ; and, as far as it was true, it was equally applicable to the state governments.

§ 1578. So far as the objection went to the organization of the Supreme Court, as a distinct and independent department, it admitted of a different answer. It was founded upon the general maxim of requiring a separation of the different departments of government, as most conducive to the preservation of public liberty and private rights. It would not, indeed,

---

1 The Federalist, No. 81. — The learned reader will trace out, in subsequent periods of our history, the same objections revived in other imposing forms under the sanction of men, who have attained high ascendancy and distinction in the struggles of party.

absolutely violate that maxim, to allow the ultimate appellate jurisdiction to be vested in one branch of the legislative body.   But there were many urgent reasons, why the proposed organization would be preferable. It would secure greater independence, impartiality, and uniformity in the administration of justice.

§ 1579. The reasoning of the Federalist [1] on this point is so clear and satisfactory, and presents the whole argument in so condensed a form, that it supersedes all farther formal discussion.   " From a body, which had even a partial agency in passing bad laws, we could rarely expect a disposition to temper and moderate them in the application. The same spirit, which had operated in making them, would be too apt to influence their construction; still less could it be expected, that men, who had infringed the constitution, in the character of legislators, would be disposed to repair the breach in that of judges. Nor is this all. Every reason, which recommends the tenure of good behaviour for judicial offices, militates against placing the judiciary power, in the last resort, in a body composed of men chosen for a limited period. There is an absurdity in referring the determination of causes, in the first instance, to judges of permanent standing; in the last, to those of a temporary and mutable constitution. And there is a still greater absurdity in subjecting the decisions of men selected for the knowledge of the laws, acquired by long and laborious study, to the revision and control of men, who, for want of the same advantage, cannot but be deficient in that knowledge. The members of the legislature will rarely be chosen with a view to those qualifications, which fit men for the stations of judges; and as, on this account, there will be great

_____

[1] The Federalist, No. 81.

reason to apprehend all the ill consequences of defective information; so, on account of the natural propensity of such bodies to party divisions, there will be no less reason to fear, that the pestilential breath of faction may poison the fountains of justice. The habit of being continually marshalled on opposite sides, will be too apt to stifle the voice both of law and equity.

§ 1580. "These considerations teach us to applaud the wisdom of those states, who have committed the judicial power, in the last resort, not to a part of the legislature, but to distinct and independent bodies of men. Contrary to the supposition of those, who have represented the plan of the convention, in this respect, as novel and unprecedented, it is but a copy of the constitutions of New-Hampshire, Massachusetts, Pennsylvania, Delaware, Maryland, Virginia, North-Carolina, South-Carolina, and Georgia; and the preference, which has been given to these models, is highly to be commended.[1]

§ 1581. "It is not true, in the second place, that the parliament of Great Britain, or the legislatures of the particular states, can rectify the exceptionable decisions of their respective courts, in any other sense, than might be done by a future legislature of the United States. The theory, neither of the British nor the state constitutions, authorizes the revisal of a judicial sentence by a legislative act. Nor is there any thing in the proposed constitution, more than in either of them, by which it is forbidden. In the former, as in the latter, the impropriety of the thing, on the general principles of law and reason, is the sole obstacle. A legislature, without exceeding its province, cannot re-

---

[1] At the present time the same scheme of organizing the judicial power exists substantially in every state in the Union, except in N. York.

verse a determination, once made, in a particular case;
though it may prescribe a new rule for future cases.
This is the principle, and it applies, in all its consequences, exactly in the same manner and extent to the
state governments, as to the national government, now
under consideration. Not the least difference can be
pointed out in any view of the subject.

§1582. "It may, in the last place, be observed, that
the supposed danger of judiciary encroachments on
the legislative authority, which has been upon many
occasions reiterated, is, in reality, a phantom. Particular misconstructions and contraventions of the will of
the legislature may now and then happen; but they
can never be so extensive, as to amount to an inconvenience, or, in any sensible degree, to affect the order
of the political system. This may be inferred with
certainty from the general nature of the judicial power;
from the objects, to which it relates; from the manner,
in which it is exercised; from its comparative weakness; and from its total incapacity to support its usurpations by force. And the inference is greatly fortified
by the consideration of the important constitutional
check, which the power of instituting impeachments in
one part of the legislative body, and of determining
upon them in the other, would give to that body upon
the members of the judicial department. This is alone
a complete security. There never can be danger, that
the judges, by a series of deliberate usurpations on the
authority of the legislature, would hazard the united
resentment of the body intrusted with it, while this
body was possessed of the means of punishing their
presumption, by degrading them from their stations.
While this ought to remove all apprehensions on the
subject, it affords, at the same time, a cogent argument

for constituting the senate a court for the trial of impeachments."

§ 1583. In regard to the power of constituting inferior courts of the Union, it is evidently calculated to obviate the necessity of having recourse to the Supreme Court in every case of federal cognizance. It enables the national government to institute, or authorize, in each state or district of the United States, a tribunal competent to the determination of all matters of national jurisdiction within its limits. One of two courses only could be open for adoption ; either to create inferior courts under the national authority, to reach all cases fit for the national jurisdiction, which either constitutionally, or conveniently, could not be of original cognizance in the Supreme Court; or to confide jurisdiction of the same cases to the state courts, with a right of appeal to the Supreme Court. To the latter course solid objections were thought to apply, which rendered it ineligible and unsatisfactory. In the first place, the judges of the state courts would be wholly irresponsible to the national government for their conduct in the administration of national justice; so, that the national government would, or might be, wholly dependent upon the good will, or sound discretion of the states, in regard to the efficiency, promptitude, and ability, with which the judicial authority of the nation was administered. In the next place, the prevalency of a local, or sectional spirit might be found to disqualify the state tribunals for a suitable discharge of national judicial functions ; and the very modes of appointment of some of the state judges might render them improper channels of the judicial authority of the Union.[1]

---

[1] The Federalist, No. 81. See also *Cohens* v. *Virginia*, 6 Wheat. R. 386, 387.

State judges, holding their offices during pleasure, or from year to year, or for other short periods, would, or at least might, be too little independent to be relied upon for an inflexible execution of the national laws. What could be done, where the state itself should happen to be in hostility to the national government, as might well be presumed occasionally to be the case, from local interests, party spirit, or peculiar prejudices, if the state tribunals were to be the sole depositaries of the judicial powers of the Union, in the ordinary administration of criminal, as well as of civil justice? Besides; if the state tribunals were thus entrusted with the ordinary administration of the criminal and civil justice of the Union, there would be a necessity for leaving the door of appeal as widely open, as possible. In proportion to the grounds of confidence in, or distrust of the subordinate tribunals, ought to be the facility or difficulty of appeals. An unrestrained course of appeals would be a source of much private, as well as public inconvenience. It would encourage litigation, and lead to the most oppressive expenses.[1] Nor should it be omitted, that this very course of appeals would naturally lead to great jealousies, irritations, and collisions between the state courts and the Supreme Court, not only from differences of opinions, but from that pride of character, and consciousness of independence, which would be felt by state judges, possessing the confidence of their own state, and irresponsible to the Union.[2]

---

[1] The Federalist, No. 81.

[2] Mr. Rawle has remarked, that "the state tribunals are no part of the government of the United States. To render the government of the United States dependent on them, would be a solecism almost as great, as to leave out an executive power entirely, and to call on the states alone to enforce the laws of the Union." Rawle on Const. ch. 21, p. 200.

§ 1584. In considering the first clause of the third section, declaring, that "the judicial power of the Uni-"ted States shall be vested in one Supreme Court, and "in such inferior courts, as the congress may from time "to time ordain and establish," we are naturally led to the inquiry, whether congress possess any discretion, as to the creation of a Supreme Court and inferior courts, in whom the constitutional jurisdiction is to be vested. This was at one time matter of much discussion; and is vital to the existence of the judicial department. If congress possess any discretion on this subject, it is obvious, that the judiciary, as a co-ordinate department of the government, may, at the will of congress, be annihilated, or stripped of all its important jurisdiction; for, if the discretion exists, no one can say in what manner, or at what time, or under what circumstances it may, or ought to be exercised. The whole argument, upon which such an interpretation has been attempted to be maintained, is, that the language of the constitution, "shall be vested," is not imperative, but simply indicates the future tense. This interpretation has been overruled by the Supreme Court, upon solemn deliberation.[1] "The language of the third article," say the court, "throughout is manifestly designed to be mandatory upon the legislature. Its obligatory force is so imperative, that congress could not, without a violation of its duty, have refused to carry it into operation. The judicial power of the United States *shall be vested* (not may be vested) in one Supreme Court, and in such inferior courts, as congress

---

[1] See *Martin* v. *Hunter,* 1 Wheat. R. 304, 316. — The Commentator, in examining the structure and jurisdiction of the judicial department, is compelled by a sense of official reserve to confine his remarks chiefly to doctrines, which are settled, or which have been deemed incontrovertible, leaving others to be discussed by those, who are unrestrained by such considerations.

may, from time to time, ordain and establish.   Could congress have lawfully refused to create a Supreme Court, or to vest in it the constitutional jurisdiction? 'The judges, both of the supreme and inferior courts, *shall hold* their offices during good behaviour, and *shall*, at stated times, receive, for their services, a compensation, which shall not be diminished during their continuance in office.'   Could congress create or limit any other tenure of the judicial office?   Could they refuse to pay, at stated times, the stipulated salary, or diminish it during the continuance in office?   But one answer can be given to these questions; it must be in the negative.   The object of the constitution was to establish three great departments of government; the legislative, the executive, and the judicial department. The first was to pass laws, the second to approve and execute them, and the third to expound and enforce them.   Without the latter, it would be impossible to carry into effect some of the express provisions of the constitution.   How, otherwise, could crimes against the United States be tried and punished?   How could causes between two states be heard and determined? The judicial power must, therefore, be vested in some court by congress; and to suppose, that it was not an obligation binding on them, but might, at their pleasure, be omitted, or declined, is to suppose, that, under the sanction of the constitution, they might defeat the constitution itself. A construction, which would lead to such a result, cannot be sound.

§ 1585. "The same expression, 'shall be vested,' occurs in other parts of the constitution, in defining the powers of the other co-ordinate branches of the government.   The first article declares, that 'all legislative powers herein granted *shall be vested* in a congress of the United States.'   Will it be contended, that the legislative power is not absolutely vested? that the words merely refer to some future act, and mean only, that the legislative power may hereafter be vested? The second article declares, that ' the executive power *shall be vested* in a president of the United States of America.' Could congress vest it in any other person ; or, is it to await their good pleasure, whether it is to vest at all? It is apparent, that such a construction, in either case, would be utterly inadmissible. Why, then, is it entitled to a better support in reference to the judicial department?

§ 1536. "If, then, it is a duty of congress to vest the judicial power of the United States, it is a duty to vest the *whole judicial power*. The language, if imperative, as to one part, is imperative, as to all. If it were otherwise, this anomaly would exist, that congress might successively refuse to vest the jurisdiction in any one class of cases enumerated in the constitution, and thereby defeat the jurisdiction, as to all ; for the constitution has not singled out any class, on which congress are bound to act in preference to others.

§ 1587. "The next consideration is as to the courts, in which the judicial power shall be vested. It is manifest, that a supreme court must be established ; but whether it be equally obligatory to establish inferior courts, is a question of some difficulty. If congress may lawfully omit to establish inferior courts, it might follow, that, in some of the enumerated cases, the judicial power could nowhere exist. The supreme court can have original jurisdiction in two classes of cases only, viz. in cases affecting ambassadors, other public ministers and consuls, and in cases, in which a state is a party. Congress cannot vest any portion of the judicial power of the United States, except in courts ordained and established by itself; and if, in any of the

cases enumerated in the constitution, the state courts
did not then possess jurisdiction, the appellate jurisdiction of the supreme court (admitting that it could act
on state courts) could not reach those cases ; and, consequently, the injunction of the constitution, that the
judicial power ' *shall be vested*,' would be disobeyed.
It would seem, therefore, to follow, that congress are
bound to create some inferior courts, in which to vest
all that jurisdiction, which, under the constitution, is
exclusively vested in the United States, and of which
the Supreme Court cannot take original cognizance.
They might establish one or more inferior courts ; they
might parcel out the jurisdiction among such courts,
from time to time, at their own pleasure. But the
whole judicial power of the United States should be, at
all times, vested either in an original or appellate form,
in some courts created under its authority.

§ 1588. "This construction will be fortified by an
attentive examination of the second section of the third
article. The words are ' the judicial power *shall extend*,' &c. Much minute and elaborate criticism has
been employed upon these words. It has been argued,
that they are equivalent to the words 'may extend,'
and that ' extend ' means to widen to new cases not
before within the scope of the power. For the reasons, which have been already stated, we are of opinion,
that the words are used in an imperative sense. They
import an absolute grant of judicial power. They cannot have a relative signification applicable to powers
already granted ; for the American *people* had not made
any previous grant. The consitution was for a new
government, organized with new substantive powers,
and not a mere supplementary charter to a government
already existing. The confederation was a compact
between states ; and its structure and powers were

wholly unlike those of the national government. The constitution was an act of the people of the United States to supersede the confederation, and not to be ingrafted on it, as a stock through which it was to receive life and nourishment.

§ 1589. " If, indeed, the relative signification could be fixed upon the term 'extend,' it would not (as we shall hereafter see) subserve the purposes of the argument, in support of which it has been adduced. This imperative sense of the words ' shall extend,' is strengthened by the context. It is declared, that ' in all cases affecting ambassadors, &c., the supreme court *shall have* original jurisdiction.' Could congress withhold original jurisdiction in these cases from the supreme court? The clause proceeds — ' in all the other cases before mentioned the supreme court shall have appellate jurisdiction, both as to law and fact, with such exceptions, and under such regulations, as the congress shall make.' The very exception here shows, that the framers of the constitution used the words in an imperative sense. What necessity could there exist for this exception, if the preceding words were not used in that sense? Without such exception, congress would, by the preceding words, have possessed a complete power to regulate the appellate jurisdiction, if the language were only equivalent to the words ' may have ' appellate jurisdiction. It is apparent, then, that the exception was intended as a limitation upon the preceding words, to enable congress to regulate and restrain the appellate power, as the public interests might, from time to time, require.

§ 1590. " Other clauses in the constitution might be brought in aid of this construction ; but a minute examination of them cannot be necessary, and would occupy too much time. It will be found, that, whenever a particular object is to be effected, the language of the constitution is always imperative, and cannot be disregarded, without violating the first principles of public duty. On the other hand, the legislative powers are given in language, which implies discretion, as from the nature of legislative power such a discretion must ever be exercised." We shall presently see the important bearing, which this reasoning has upon the interpretation of that section of the constitution, which concerns the jurisdiction of the national tribunals.

§ 1591. The constitution has wisely established, that there shall be one Supreme Court, with a view to uniformity of decision in all cases whatsoever, belonging to the judicial department, whether they arise at the common law or in equity, or within the admiralty and prize jurisdiction; whether they respect the doctrines of mere municipal law, or constitutional law, or the law of nations. It is obvious, that, if there were independent supreme courts of common law, of equity, and of admiralty, a diversity of judgment might, and almost necessarily would spring up, not only, as to the limits of the jurisdiction of each tribunal; but as to the fundamental doctrines of municipal, constitutional, and public law. The effect of this diversity would be, that a different rule would, or might be promulgated on the most interesting subjects by the several tribunals; and thus the citizens be involved in endless doubts, not only as to their private rights, but as to their public duties. The constitution itself would or might speak a different language according to the tribunal, which was called upon to interpret it; and thus interminable disputes embarrass the administration of justice throughout the whole country.[1] But the same reason did not

---

[1] Dr. Paley's remarks, though general in their character, show a striking coincidence of opinion between the wisdom of the new, and the

apply to the inferior tribunals. These were, therefore, left entirely to the discretion of congress, as to their number, their jurisdiction, and their powers. Experience might, and probably would, show good grounds for varying and modifying them from time to time. It would not only have been unwise, but exceedingly inconvenient, to have fixed the arrangement of these courts in the constitution itself; since congress would have been disabled thereby from adapting them from time to time to the exigencies of the country.[2] But, whatever may be the extent, to which the power of congress reaches, as to the establishment of inferior tribunals, it is clear from what has been already stated, that all the jurisdiction contemplated by the constitu-

---

wisdom of the old world. Speaking on the subject of the necessity of one supreme appellate tribunal he says: "But, lastly, if several courts, co-ordinate to and independent of each other, subsist together in the country, it seems necessary, that the appeals from all of them should meet and terminate in the same judicature : in order, that one supreme tribunal, by whose final sentence all others are bound and concluded, may superintend and preside over the rest. This constitution is necessary for two purposes : — to preserve a uniformity in the decisions of inferior courts, and to maintain to each the proper limits of its jurisdiction. Without a common superior, different courts might establish contradictory rules of adjudication, and the contradiction be final and without remedy : the same question might receive opposite determinations, according as it was brought before one court or another, and the determination in each be ultimate and irreversible A common appellant jurisdiction prevents or puts an end to this confusion. For when the judgments upon appeals are consistent, (which may be expected, while it is the same court, which is at last resorted to,) the different courts, from which the appeals are brought will be reduced to a like consistency with one another. Moreover, if questions arise between courts independent of each other, concerning the extent and boundaries of their respective jurisdiction, as each will be desirous of enlarging its own, an authority, which both acknowledge, can alone adjust the controversy. Such a power, therefore, must reside somewhere, lest the rights and repose of the country be distracted by the endless opposition and mutual encroachments of its courts of justice."

2 See 2 Elliot's Debates, 380.

tion must be vested in some of its courts, either in an original, or an appellate form.

§ 1592. We next come to the consideration of those securities, which the constitution has provided for the due independence and efficiency of the judicial department.

§ 1593. The mode of appointment of the judges has necessarily come under review, in the examination of the structure and powers of the executive department. The president is expressly authorized, by and with the consent of the senate, to appoint the judges of the Supreme Court. The appointment of the judges of the inferior courts, is not expressly provided for; but has either been left to the discretion of congress, or silently belongs to the president, under the clause of the constitution authorizing him to appoint "all other officers of the United States, whose ap- "pointments are not herein otherwise provided for." [1] In the convention, a proposition at first prevailed, for the appointment of the judges of the Supreme Court by the senate, by a decided majority.[2] At a later period, however, upon the report of a committee, the appointment of the judges of the Supreme Court, was given to the president, subject to the advice and consent of the senate, by a unanimous vote.[3] The reasons for the change, were doubtless the same as those, which

---

[1] Whether the Judges of the inferior courts of the United States are such inferior officers, as the constitution contemplates to be within the power of congress, to prescribe the mode of appointment of, so as to vest it in the president alone, or in the courts of law, or in the heads of departments, is a point, upon which no solemn judgment has ever been had. The practical construction has uniformly been, that they are not such inferior officers. And no act of congress prescribes the mode of their appointment. See the American Jurist for October, 1830, vol. 4, art. V. p. 298.

[2] Journal of Convention, 69, 98, 121, 137, 186, 187, 195, 196, 211, 212.

[3] Id. 325, 326, 340.

led to the vesting of other high appointments in the executive department.[1]

§ 1594. The next consideration is the tenure, by which the judges hold their offices. It is declared that "the judges, both of the Supreme and In-

---

[1] The Federalist, No. 78. — Mr. Chancellor Kent has summed up the reasoning, in favour of an appointment of the judges by the executive, with his usual strength. "The advantages of the mode of appointment of public officers by the president and senate have been already considered. This mode is peculiarly fit and proper, in respect to the judiciary department. The just and vigorous investigation and punishment of every species of fraud and violence, and the exercise of the power of compelling every man, to the punctual performance of his contracts, are grave duties, not of the most popular character, though the faithful discharge of them, will certainly command the calm approbation of the judicious observer. The fittest men would probably have too much reservedness of manners, and severity of morals, to secure an election resting on universal suffrage. Nor can the mode of appointment by a large deliberative assembly be entitled to unqualified approbation. There are too many occasions, and too much temptation for intrigue, party prejudice, and local interests, to permit such a body of men to act, in respect to such appointments, with a sufficiently single and steady regard for the general welfare. In ancient Rome, the prætor was chosen annually by the people, but it was in the *comitia* by centuries; and the choice was confined to persons belonging to the patrician order, until the close of the fourth century of the city, when the office was rendered accessible to the plebeians; and when they became licentious, says Montesquieu, the office became corrupt. The popular elections did very well, as he observes, so long as the people were free, and magnanimous, and virtuous, and the public was without corruption. But all plans of government, which suppose the people will always act with wisdom and'integrity, are plainly Utopian, and contrary to uniform experience. Government must be framed for man, as he is, and not for man, as he would be, if he were free from vice. Without referring to those cases in our own country, where judges have been annually elected by a popular assembly, we may take the less invidious case of Sweden. During the diets, which preceded the revolution in 1772, the states of the kingdom sometimes appointed commissioners to act as judges. The strongest party, says Catteau, prevailed in the trials, that came before them; and persons condemned by one tribunal were acquitted by another." 1 Kent's Comm. Lect. 14, p. 273, 274, (2d edition, p. 291, 292.)

"ferior Courts shall hold their offices during good be-
"haviour." [1] Upon this subject, the Federalist has
spoken with so much clearness and force, that little
can be added to its reasoning. "The standard of
good behaviour, for the continuance in office of the
judicial magistracy, is certainly one of the most valuable of the modern improvements in the practice of
government. In a monarchy, it is an excellent barrier
to the despotism of the prince : in a republic, it is a no
less excellent barrier to the encroachments and oppressions of the representative body. And it is the best
expedient, which can be devised in any government, to
secure a steady, upright, and impartial administration of
the laws. Whoever attentively considers the different
departments of power, must perceive, that in a government, in which they are separated from each other,
the judiciary, from the nature of its functions, will always be the least dangerous to the political rights of
the constitution ; because it will be least in a capacity
to annoy, or injure them. The executive not only dis-
penses the honours, but holds the sword of the community. The legislature, not only commands the purse,
but prescribes the rules, by which the duties and rights
of every citizen are to be regulated. The judiciary, on
the contrary, has no influence over either the sword, or
the purse ; no direction either of the strength, or of
the wealth of the society ; and can take no active resolution whatever. It may truly be said to have neither
force, nor *will*, but merely judgment; and must ultimately depend upon the aid of the executive arm, for
the efficacious exercise even of this faculty.

[1] For the interpretation of the meaning of the words *good behaviour*,
see the judgment of Lord Holt, in *Harcourt* v. *Fox*; 1 Shower's R. 426,
506, 536. S. C. Shower's Cases in Parl. 158.

§ 1595. "This simple view of the matter suggests several important consequences. It proves incontestibly that the judiciary is, beyond comparison, the weakest of the three departments of power; that it can never attack with success either of the other two; and that all possible care is requisite to enable it to defend itself against their attacks. It equally proves, that, though individual oppression may now and then proceed from the courts of justice, the general liberty of the people can never be endangered from that quarter: I mean, so long as the judiciary remains truly distinct from both the legislature and executive. — For I agree, that 'there is no liberty, if the power of judging be not separated from the legislative and executive powers.' It proves, in the last place, that as liberty can have nothing to fear from the judiciary alone, but would have every thing to fear from its union with either of the other departments; that, as all the effects of such an union must ensue from a dependence of the former on the latter, notwithstanding a nominal and apparent separation; that as, from the natural feebleness of the judiciary, it is in continual jeopardy of being overpowered, awed, or influenced by its co-ordinate branches; that, as nothing can contribute so much to its firmness and independence, as *permanency in office*, this quality may, therefore, be justly regarded, as an indispensable ingredient in its constitution; and, in a great measure, as the *citadel* of the public justice and the public security."

§ 1596. "If then, the courts of justice are to be considered, as the bulwarks of a limited constitution against legislative encroachments; this consideration will afford a strong argument for the permanent tenure of judicial offices, since nothing will contribute, so much

as this, to that independent spirit in the judges, which
must be essential to the faithful performance of so
arduous a duty. This independence of the judges is
equally requisite to guard the constitution and the rights
of individuals from the effects of those ill humours,
which the arts of designing men, or the influence of
particular conjunctures, sometimes disseminate among
the people themselves; and which, though they speedily
give place to better information, and more deliberate
reflection, have a tendency, in the mean time, to occasion dangerous innovations in the government, and
serious oppressions of the minor party in the community. Though, I trust, the friends of the proposed
constitution will never concur with its enemies, in
questioning that fundamental principle of republican
government, which admits the right of the people to
alter or abolish the established constitution, whenever
they find it inconsistent with their happiness; yet it is
not to be inferred from this principle, that the representatives of the people, whenever a momentary inclination happens to lay hold of a majority of their constituents, incompatible with the provisions in the existing constitution, would, on that account, be justifiable
in a violation of those provisions; or that the courts
would be under a greater obligation to connive at infractions in this shape, than when they had proceeded
wholly from the cabals of the representative body.
Until the people have, by some solemn and authoritative act, annulled or changed the established form, it
is binding upon themselves collectively, as well as individually ; and no presumption, or even knowledge of
their sentiments, can warrant their representatives in a
departure from it, prior to such an act. But it is easy
to see, that it would require an uncommon portion of

fortitude in the judges to do their duty, as faithful guardians of the constitution, where legislative invasions of it have been instigated by the major voice of the community.

§ 1597. "But it is not with a view to infractions of the constitution only, that the independence of the judges may be an essential safeguard against the effects of occasional ill humours in the society. These sometimes extend no further, than to the injury of the private rights of particular classes of citizens by unjust and partial laws. Here, also, the firmness of the judicial magistracy is of vast importance, in mitigating the severity, and confining the operation of such laws. It not only serves to moderate the immediate mischiefs of those, which may have been passed; but it operates as a check upon the legislative body in passing them; who, perceiving that obstacles to the success of an iniquitous intention are to be expected from the scruples of the courts, are in a manner compelled by the very motives of the injustice they meditate, to qualify their attempts. This is a circumstance calculated to have more influence upon the character of our governments, than but few may imagine. The benefits of the integrity and moderation of the judiciary have already been felt in more states than one; and though they may have displeased those, whose sinister expectations they may have disappointed, they must have commanded the esteem and applause of all the virtuous and disinterested. Considerate men of every description ought to prize whatever will tend to beget or fortify that temper in the courts; as no man can be sure, that he may not be to-morrow the victim of a spirit of injustice, by which he may be a gainer to-day. And every man must now feel, that the inevitable tendency of such a spirit is to sap the foundations of public and private confidence, and to introduce in its stead universal distrust and distress.

§ 1598. "That inflexible and uniform adherence to the rights of the constitution, and of individuals, which we perceive to be indispensable in the courts of justice, can certainly not be expected from judges, who hold their offices by a temporary commission. Periodical appointments, however regulated, or by whomsoever made, would, in some way or other, be fatal to their necessary independence. If the power of making them was committed either to the executive or legislature, there would be danger of an improper complaisance to the branch, which possessed it; if to both, there would be an unwillingness to hazard the displeasure of either; if to the people, or to persons chosen by them for the special purpose, there would be too great a disposition to consult popularity to justify a reliance, that nothing would be consulted, but the constitution and the laws.

§ 1599. "There is yet a further and a weighty reason for the permanency of judicial offices, which is deducible from the nature of the qualifications they require. It has been frequently remarked with great propriety, that a voluminous code of laws is one of the inconveniencies necessarily connected with the advantages of a free government. To avoid an arbitrary discretion in the courts, it is indispensable, that they should be bound down by strict rules and precedents, which serve to define, and point out their duty in every particular case, that comes before them. And it will readily be conceived, from the variety of controversies, which grow out of the folly and wickedness of mankind, that the records of those precedents must unavoidably

swell to a very considerable bulk, and must demand
long and laborious study, to acquire a competent knowledge of them. Hence it is, that there can be but few
men in the society, who will have sufficient skill in the
laws to qualify them for the stations of judges. And
making the proper deductions for the ordinary de-
pravity of human nature, the number must be still
smaller of those, who unite the requisite integrity with
the requisite knowledge. These considerations ap-
prise us, that the government can have no great option
between fit characters; and that a temporary duration
in office, which would naturally discourage such characters from quitting a lucrative line of practice to accept a seat on the bench, would have a tendency to
throw the administration of justice into hands, less able,
and less well qualified to conduct it with utility and
dignity. In the present circumstances of this country,
and in those, in which it is likely to be for a long time
to come, the disadvantages on this score would be
greater, than they may at first sight appear; but it must
be confessed, that they are far inferior to those, which
present themselves under the other aspects of the
subject.

§ 1600. "Upon the whole, there can be no room to
doubt, that the convention acted wisely in copying
from the models of those constitutions, which have established *good behaviour*, as the tenure of judicial
offices in point of duration; and that, so far from being
blameable on this account, their plan would have been
inexcusably defective, if it had wanted this important
feature of good government. The experience of Great
Britain affords an illustrious comment on the excellence
of the institution."

§ 1601. These remarks will derive additional

strength and confirmation, from a nearer survey of the
judicial branch of foreign governments, as well as of
the several states composing the Union. In England,
the king is considered, as the fountain of justice; not
indeed as the author, but as the distributer of it; and
he possesses the exclusive prerogative of erecting
courts of judicature, and appointing the judges.[1] Indeed, in early times, the kings of England often in
person heard and decided causes between party and
party. But as the constitution of government became
m) e settled, the whole judicial power was delegated
to the judges of the several courts of justice; and any
attempt, on the part of the king, now to exercise it in
person, would be deemed an usurpation.[2] Anciently,
the English judges held their offices according to the
tenure of their commissions, as prescribed by the crown,
which was generally during the pleasure of the crown,
as is the tenure of office of the Lord Chancellor, the
judges of the courts of admiralty, and others, down to
the present day. In the time of Lord Coke, the
Barons of the Exchequer held their offices during good
behaviour, while the judges of the other courts of common law held them only during pleasure.[3] And it has
been said, that, at the time of the restoration of Charles
the Second, the commissions of the judges were during good behaviour.[4] Still, however, it was at the

1 1 Black. Comm. 267; 2 Hawk. B. 2, ch. 1, § 1, 2, 3; Com. Dig.
Prerogative, D. 28; Id. *Courts*, A.; Id. *Officers*, A.; Id. *Justices*, A.

2 Ibid; 1 Woodes. Lect. III, p. 87; 4 Inst. 70, 71; 2 Hawk. B. 2, ch.
1, § 2, 3; 1 Black. Comm. 41, and note by Christian.

3 4 Coke Inst. ch. 12, p. 117; Id. ch. 7, p. 75. — The tenure of office
of the Attorney and Solicitor General was at this period during good
behaviour; 4 Coke, Inst. 117.

4 1 Kent's Comm. Lect. 14, p. 275.

pleasure of the crown, to prescribe what tenure of office it might choose, until after the revolution of 1688; and there can be no doubt, that a monarch so profligate as Charles the Second, would avail himself of the prerogative, as often as it suited his political, or other objects.

§ 1602. It is certain, that this power of the crown must have produced an influence upon the administration, dangerous to private rights, and subversive of the public liberties of the subjects. In political accusations, in an especial manner, it must often have produced the most disgraceful compliances with the wishes of the crown; and the most humiliating surrenders of the rights of the accused.[1] The Statute of 13 Will. 3, ch. 2, provided, that the commissions of the judges of the courts of common law should not be as formerly *durante bene placito,* but should be *quam diu bene se gesserint,* and their salaries be ascertained, and established. They were made removeable, however, by the king, upon the address of both houses of parliament; and their offices expired by the demise of the king. Afterwards by a statute enacted in the reign of George the Third, at the earnest recommendation of the king, a noble improvement was made in the law, by which the judges are to hold their offices during good behaviour, notwithstanding any demise of the crown; and their full salaries are secured to them, during the continuance of their commissions.[2] Upon that occasion, the monarch made a declaration, worthy of perpetual

---

[1] See De Lolme, B. 2, ch. 16, p. 350 to 354, 362. — The State Trials before the year 1688 exhibit the most gross and painful illustrations of these remarks. Subserviency to the crown was so general in state prosecutions, that it ceased almost to attract public indignation.

[2] 1 Black. Comm. 267, 268.

remembrance, that "he looked upon the independence and uprightness of the judges, as essential to the impartial administration of justice; as one of the best securities of the rights and liberties of his subjects; and as most conducive to the honour of the crown."[1]   Indeed, since the independence of the judges has been secured by this permanent duration of office, the administration of justice has, with a single exception,[2] flowed on in England, with an uninterrupted, and pure, and unstained current.   It is due to the enlightened tribunals of that nation to declare, that their learning, integrity, and impartiality, have commanded the reverence and respect, as well of America, as Europe.[3]   The judges of the old parliaments of France (the judicial tribunals of that country) were, before the revolution, appointed by the crown; but they held their offices for life; and this tenure of office gave them substantial independence.   Appointed by the monarch, they were considered as nearly out of his power.   The most determined exertions of that authority against them only showed their radical independence.   They composed permanent bodies politic, constituted to resist arbitrary innovation; and from that corporate constitution, and from most of their powers they were well calculated to afford both certainty and stability to the laws.   They had been a safe asylum to secure their laws, in all the revolutions of human opinion.   They had saved that sacred deposit of the

---

1 1 Black. Comm. 267, 268.
2 Lord Macclesfield.
3 De Lolme has dwelt on this subject, with abundant satisfaction. (De Lolme, B. 2, ch. 16, p. 363 to 365.) The Eulogy of Emerigon has been often quoted, and indeed is as true, as it is striking. 2 Emerigon, 67, cited in 1 Marshall on Insurance, Preliminary Discourse, p. 30, note.

country during the reigns of arbitrary princes, and the struggles of arbitrary factions. They kept alive the memory and record of the constitution. They were the great security to private property, which might be said (when personal liberty had no existence,) to be as well guarded in France, as in any other country.[1]

§ 1603. The importance of a permanent tenure of office, to secure the independence, integrity, and impartiality of judges, was early understood in France. Louis the Eleventh, in 1467, made a memorable declaration, that the judges ought not to be deposed, or deprived of their offices, but for a forfeiture previously adjudged, and judicially declared by a competent tribunal. The same declaration was often confirmed by his successors; and after the first excesses of the French revolution were passed, the same principle obtained a public sanction. And it has now become incorporated, as a fundamental principle, into the present charter of France, that the judges appointed by the crown shall be irremoveable.[2] Other European nations have followed the same example;[3] and it is highly probable, that as the principles of free governments prevail, the necessity of thus establishing the independence of the judiciary will be generally felt, and firmly provided for.[4]

---

1 This is the very language of Mr. Burke in his Reflections on the French Revolution. See also De Lolme, B. 1, ch. 12, p. 159, note.

2 Merlin's Repertoire, art. *Juge*, No. 3.

3 1 Kent's Comm. Lect. 14, p. 275.

4 Dr. Paley's remarks on this subject are not the least valuable of his excellent writings. "The next security for the impartial administration of justice, especially in decisions, to which government is a party, is the independency of the judges. As protection against every illegal attack upon the rights of the subject by the servants of the crown is to be sought for from these tribunals, the judges of the land become not unfrequently the arbitrators between the king and the people ; on

§ 1604. It has sometimes been suggested, that, though in monarchial governments the independence of the judiciary is essential, to guard the rights of the subjects from the injustice and oppression of the crown ; yet that the same reasons do not apply to a republic, where the popular will is sufficiently known, and ought always to be obeyed.[1] A little consideration of the subject will satisfy us, that, so far from this being true, the reasons in favour of the independence of the judiciary apply with augmented force to republics ; and especially to such as possess a written constitution with defined powers, and limited rights.

§ 1605. In the first place, factions and parties are quite as common, and quite as violent in republics, as in monarchies ; and the same safeguards are as indispensable in the one, as in the other, against the encroachments of party spirit, and the tyranny of factions. Laws, however wholesome or necessary, are frequently the objects of temporary aversion, and popular odium, and sometimes of popular resistance.[2]

which account they ought to be independent of either ; or, what is the same thing, equally dependent upon both : that is, if they be appointed by the one, they should be removable only by the other. This was the policy, which dictated the memorable improvement in our constitution, by which the judges, who before the revolution held their offices during the pleasure of the king, can now be deprived of them only by an address from both houses of parliament ; as the most regular, solemn, and authentic way, by which the dissatisfaction of the people can be expressed. To make this independency of the judges complete, the public salaries of their office ought not only to be certain both in amount and continuance, but so liberal, as to secure their integrity from the temptation of secret bribes ; which liberality will answer, also, the further purpose of preserving their jurisdiction from contempt, and their characters from suspicion ; as well as of rendering the office worthy of the ambition of men of eminence in their profession."

1 4 Jefferson's Corresp. 287, 288, 289, 316, 352.
2 1 Kent's Comm. Lect. 14, p. 275.

Nothing is more facile in republics, than for demagogues, under artful pretences, to stir up combinations against the regular exercise of authority. Their selfish purposes are too often interrupted by the firmness and independence of upright magistrates, not to make them at all times hostile to a power, which rebukes, and an impartiality, which condemns them. The judiciary, as the weakest point in the constitution, on which to make an attack, is therefore, constantly that, to which they direct their assaults; and a triumph here, aided by any momentary popular encouragement, achieves a lasting victory over the constitution itself. Hence, in republics, those, who are to profit by public commotions, or the prevalence of faction, are always the enemies of a regular and independent administration of justice. They spread all sorts of delusion, in order to mislead the public mind, and excite the public prejudices. They know full well, that, without the aid of the people, their schemes must prove abortive ; and they, therefore, employ every art to undermine the public confidence, and to make the people the instruments of subverting their own rights and liberties.

§ 1606. It is obvious, that, under such circumstances, if the tenure of office of the judges is not permanent, they will soon be rendered odious, not because they do wrong; but because they refuse to do wrong; and they will be made to give way to others, who shall become more pliant tools of the leading demagogues of the day. There can be no security for the minority in a free government, except through the judicial department. In a monarchy, the sympathies of the people are naturally enlisted against the meditated oppressions of their ruler; and they screen his victims from his vengeance. His is the cause of one against the community.   But, in free governments, where the majority, who obtain power for the moment, are supposed to represent the will of the people, persecution, especially of a political nature, becomes the cause of the community against one.   It is the more violent and unrelenting, because it is deemed indispensable to attain power, or to enjoy the fruits of victory.   In free governments, therefore, the independence of the judiciary becomes far more important to the security of the rights of the citizens, than in a monarchy; since it is the only barrier against the oppressions of a dominant faction, armed for the moment with power, and abusing the influence, acquired under accidental excitements, to overthrow the institutions and liberties, which have been the deliberate choice of the people.[1]

§ 1607. In the next place, the independence of the judiciary is indispensable to secure the people against the intentional, as well as unintentional, usurpations of the executive and legislative departments.   It has been observed with great sagacity, that power is perpetually stealing from the many to the few; and the tendency of the legislative department to absorb all the other powers of the government has always been dwelt upon by statesmen and patriots, as a general truth, confirmed by all human experience.[2] If the judges are appointed at short intervals, either by the legislative, or the executive department, they will naturally, and, indeed, almost necessarily, become mere dependents upon the appointing power.   If they have any desire to obtain, or to hold office, they will at all times evince a desire to follow, and obey the will of the predominant power

[1] 1 Kent's Comm. Lect. 14, p. 275, 276.
[2] 1 Wilson's Law Lect. 461, 462, 463.

in the state. Justice will be administered with a faultering and feeble hand. It will secure nothing, but its own place, and the approbation of those, who value, because they control it. It will decree, what best suits the opinions of the day; and it will forget, that the precepts of the law rest on eternal foundations. The rulers and the citizens will not stand upon an equal ground in litigations. The favourites of the day will overawe by their power, or seduce by their influence; and thus, the fundamental maxim of a republic, that it is a government of laws, and not of men, will be silently disproved, or openly abandoned.[1]

§ 1608. In the next place, these considerations acquire (as has been already seen) still more cogency and force, when applied to questions of constitutional law. In monarchies, the only practical resistance, which the judiciary can present, is to the usurpations of a single department of the government, unaided, and acting for itself. But, if the executive and legislative departments are combined in any course of measures, obedience to their will becomes a duty, as well as a necessity. Thus, even in the free government of Great Britain, an act of parliament, combining, as it does, the will of the crown, and of the legislature, is absolute and omnipotent. It cannot be lawfully resisted, or disobeyed. The judiciary is bound to carry it into effect at every hazard, even though it should sub-

---

[1] It is far from being true, that the gross misconduct of the English Judges in many state prosecutions, while they held their offices during the pleasure of the crown, was in compliance only with the mere will of the monarch. On the contrary, they administered but too keenly to popular vengeance, acting under delusions of an extraordinary nature, sometimes political, sometimes religious, and sometimes arising from temporary prejudices.

vert private rights and public liberty.[1] But it is far
otherwise in a republic, like our own, with a limited
constitution, prescribing at once the powers of the
rulers, and the rights of the citizens.[2] This very circumstance would seem conclusively to show, that the independence of the judiciary is absolutely indispensable
to preserve the balance of such a constitution. In no
other way can there be any practical restraint upon the
acts of the government, or any practical enforcement of
the rights of the citizens.[3] This subject has been
already examined very much at large, and needs only
to be touched in this place. No man can deny the
necessity of a judiciary to interpret the constitution
and laws, and to preserve the citizens against oppression and usurpation in civil and criminal prosecutions.
Does it not follow, that, to enable the judiciary to fulfil
its functions, it is indispensable, that the judges should
not hold their offices at the mere pleasure of those,
whose acts they are to check, and, if need be, to declare

---

1 See 1 Black. Comm. 9 ; Woodeson's Elements of Jurisprudence,
Lect. 3, p. 48.

2 1 Wilson's Law Lect. 460, 461.

3 The remarks of Mr. Boudinot on this subject, in a debate in the
house of representatives, deserve insertion in this place, from his high
character for wisdom and patriotism. " It has been objected," says he,
" that, by adopting the bill before us, we expose the measure to be considered, and defeated by the judiciary of the United States, who may
adjudge it to be contrary to the constitution, and therefore void, and
not lend their aid to carry it into execution. This gives me no uneasi-
ness. I am so far from controverting this right in the judiciary, that it
is my boast, and my confidence. It leads me to greater decision on all
subjects of a constitutional nature, when I reflect, that, if from inattention, want of precision, or any other defect, I should do wrong, there is
a power in the government, which can constitutionally prevent the operation of a wrong measure from affecting my constituents. I am legislating for a nation, and for thousands yet unborn ; and it is the glory
of the constitution, that there is a remedy for the failures even of the
legislature itself."

void? Can it be supposed for a moment, that men holding their offices for the short period of two, or four, or even six years, will be generally found firm enough to resist the will of those, who appoint them, and may remove them?

§ 1609. The argument of those, who contend for a short period of office of the judges, is founded upon the necessity of a conformity to the will of the people. But the argument proceeds upon a fallacy, in supposing, that the will of the rulers, and the will of the people are the same. Now, they not only may be, but often actually are, in direct variance to each other. No man in a republican government can doubt, that the will of the people is, and ought to be, supreme. But it is the deliberate will of the people, evinced by their solemn acts, and not the momentary ebullitions of those, who act for the majority, for a day, or a month, or a year. The constitution is the will, the deliberate will, of the people. They have declared under what circumstances, and in what manner it shall be amended, and altered; and until a change is effected in the manner prescribed, it is declared, that it shall be the supreme law of the land, to which all persons, rulers, as well as citizens, must bow in obedience. When it is constitutionally altered, then and not until then, are the judges at liberty to disregard its original injunctions. When, therefore, the argument is pressed, that the judges ought to be subject to the will of the people, no one doubts the propriety of the doctrine in its true and legitimate sense.

§ 1610. But those, who press the argument, use it in a far broader sense. In their view, the will of the people, as exhibited in the choice of the rulers, is to be followed. If the rulers interpret the constitution differently from the judges, the former are to be obeyed, because they represent the opinions of the people ; and therefore, the judges ought to be removable, or appointed for a short period, so as to become subject to the will of the people, as expressed by and through their rulers.   But, is it not at once seen, that this is in fact subverting the constitution ?   Would it not make the constitution an instrument of flexible and changeable interpretation, and not a settled form of government with fixed limitations ?   Would it not become, instead of a supreme law for ourselves and our posterity, a mere oracle of the powers of the rulers of the day, to which implicit homage is to be paid, and speaking at different times the most opposite commands, and in the most ambiguous voices ?   In short, is not this an attempt to erect, behind the constitution, a power unknown, and unprovided for by the constitution, and greater than itself ?   What become of the limitations of the constitution, if the will of the people, thus inofficially promulgated, forms, for the time being, the supreme law, and the supreme exposition of the law ?   If the constitution defines the powers of the government, and points out the mode of changing them ; and yet, the instrument is to expand in the hands of one set of rulers, and to contract in those of another, where is the standard ?   If the will of the people is to govern in the construction of the powers of the constitution, and that will is to be gathered at every successive election at the polls, and not from their deliberate judgment, and solemn acts in ratifying the constitution, or in amending it, what certainty can there be in those powers ?   If the constitution is to be expounded, not by its written text, but by the opinions of the rulers for the time being, whose opinions are to prevail, the first, or the last? When, therefore, it is said, that the judges ought to be subjected to the will of the people, and to conform to their interpretation of the constitution, the practical meaning must be, that they should be subjected to the control of the representatives of the people in the executive and legislative departments, and should interpret the constitution, as the latter may, from time to time, deem correct.

§ 1611. But it is obvious, that elections can rarely, if ever, furnish any sufficient proofs, what is deliberately the will of the people, as to any constitutional or legal doctrines. Representatives and rulers must be ordinarily chosen for very different purposes; and, in many instances, their opinions upon constitutional questions must be unknown to their constituents. The only means known to the constitution, by which to ascertain the will of the people upon a constitutional question, is in the shape of an affirmative or negative proposition by way of amendment, offered for their adoption in the mode prescribed by the constitution. The elections in one year may bring one party into power; and in the next year their opponents, embracing opposite doctrines, may succeed; and so alternate success and defeat may perpetually recur in the same districts, and in the same, or different states.

§ 1612. Surely it will not be pretended, that any constitution, adapted to the American people, could ever contemplate the executive and legislative departments of the government, as the ultimate depositaries of the power to interpret the constitution ; or as the ultimate representatives of the will of the people, to change it at pleasure. If, then, the judges were appointed for two, or four, or six years, instead of during good behaviour, the only security, which the people would have for a due administration of public justice, and a firm support of the constitution, would be, that being dependent upon the executive for their appointment during their brief period of office, they might, and would represent more fully, for the time being, the constitutional opinion of each successive executive ; and thus carry into effect his system of government. Would this be more wise, or more safe, more for the permanence of the constitution, or the preservation of the liberties of the people, than the present system? Would the judiciary, then, be, in fact, an independent co-ordinate department ? Would it protect the people against an ambitious or corrupt executive ; or restrain the legislature from acts of unconstitutional authority ? [1]

§ 1613. The truth is, that, even with the most secure tenure of office, during good behaviour, the danger is not, that the judges will be too firm in resisting public opinion, and in defence of private rights or public liberties ; but, that they will be too ready to yield themselves to the passions, and politics, and prejudices of the day. In a monarchy, the judges, in the performance

[1] Mr. Jefferson, during the latter years of his life. and indeed from the time, when he became president of the United States, was a most strenuous advocate of the plan of making the judges hold their offices for a limited term of years only. He proposed, that their appointments should be for *four*, or *six* years, renewable by the president and senate. It is not my purpose to bring his opinions into review, or to comment on the terms, in which they are expressed. It is impossible not to perceive, that he entertained a decided hostility to the judicial department; and that he allowed himself in language of insinuation against the conduct of judges, which is little calculated to add weight to his opinions. He wrote on this subject apparently with the feelings of a partisan, and under influences, which his best friends will most regret. See 1 Jefferson's Corresp. 65, 66 ; 4 Jefferson's Corresp. 74, 75, 287, 288, 289, 317, 337, 352. His earlier opinions were of a different character. See Jefferson's Notes on Virginia, 195 ; Federalist, No. 48.

of their duties with uprightness and impartiality, will always have the support of some of the departments of the government, or at least of the people. In republics, they may sometimes find the other departments combined in hostility against the judicial ; and even the people, for a while, under the influence of party spirit and turbulent factions, ready to abandon them to their fate.[1] Few men possess the firmness to resist the torrent of popular opinion ; or are content to sacrifice present ease and public favour, in order to earn the slow rewards of a coscientious discharge of duty ; the sure, but distant, gratitude of the people ; and the severe, but enlightened, award of posterity.[2]

---

[1] An objection was taken in the Pennsylvania convention against the constitution of the United States, that the judges were not made sufficiently independent, because they might hold other offices. 3 Elliot's Debates, 300, 313, 314.

[2] Mr. (now Judge) Hopkinson has treated this subject, as he has treated every other, falling within the range of his forensic or literary labours, in a masterly manner. I extract the following passages from his Defence of Mr. Justice Chase, upon his Impeachment, as equally remarkable for truth, wisdom, and eloquence.

"The pure and upright adminstration of justice is of the utmost importance to any people ; the other movements of government are not of such universal concern. Who shall be president, or what treaties or general statutes shall be made, occupies the attention of a few busy politicians ; but these things touch not, or but seldom, the private interests and happiness of the great mass of the community. But the settlement of private controversies, the administration of law between man and man, the distribution of justice and right to the citizen in his private business and concern, comes to every man's door, and is essential to every man's prosperity and happiness. Hence I consider the judiciary of our country most important among the branches of government, and its purity and independence of the most interesting consequence to every man. Whilst it is honorably and fully protected from the influence of favour, or fear, from any quarter, the situation of a people can never be very uncomfortable or unsafe. But if a judge is for ever to be exposed to prosecutions and impeachments for his official conduct on the mere suggestions of caprice, and to be condemned by the mere voice of prejudice, under the specious name of common sense, can he hold

§ 1614. If passing from general reasoning, an appeal is made to the lessons of experience, there is every thing to convince us, that the judicial depart-

---

that firm and steady hand his high functions require? No; if his nerves are of iron, they must tremble in so perilous a situation. In England the complete independence of the judiciary has been considered, and has been found the best and surest safeguard of true liberty, securing a government of known and uniform laws, acting alike upon every man. It has, however, been suggested by some of our newspaper politicians, perhaps from a higher source, that although this independent judiciary is very necessary in a monarchy to protect the people from the oppression of a court, yet that in our republican institution the same reasons for it do not exist ; that it is indeed inconsistent with the nature of our government, that any part or branch of it should be independent of the people, from whom the power is derived. And, as the house of representatives come most frequently from this great source of power, they claim the best right of knowing and expressing its will; and of course the right of a controlling influence over the other branches. My doctrine is precisely the reverse of this.

" If I were called upon to declare, whether the independence of judges were more essentially important in a monarchy, or a republic, I should certainly say, in the latter, all governments require, in order to give them firmness, stability, and character, some permanent principle ; some settled establishment. The want of this is the great deficiency in republican institutions ; nothing can be relied upon ; no faith can be given, either at home or abroad, to a people, whose systems, and operations, and policy, are constantly changing with popular opinion ; if, however, the judiciary is stable and independent ; if the rule of justice between men rests on permanent and known principles, it gives a security and character to a country, which is absolutely necessary in its intercourse with the world, and in its own internal concerns. This independence is further requisite, as a security from oppression. History demonstrates, from page to page, that tyranny and oppression have not been confined to despotisms, but have been freely exercised in republics, both ancient and modern ; with this difference, — that in the latter, the oppression has sprung from the impulse of some sudden gust of passion or prejudice, while, in the former, it is systematically planned and pursued, as an ingredient and principle of the government ; the people destroy not deliberately, and will return to reflection and justice, if passion is not kept alive and excited by artful intrigue ; but, while the fit is on, their devastation and cruelty is more terrible and unbounded, than the most monstrous tyrant. It is for their own benefit, and to protect them from the violence of their own passions, that it is essential to have some firm, unshaken, independent, branch of government, able

ment is safe to a republic, with the tenure of office during good behaviour ; and that justice will ordinarily be best administered, where there is most independence. Of the state constitutions, five only out of twenty-four have provided for any other tenure of office, than during good behaviour ; and those adopted by the new states admitted into the Union, since the formation of the national government, have, with two or three exceptions only, embraced the same permanent tenure of office.[1] No one can hesitate to declare, that in the states, where the judges hold their offices during good behaviour, justice is administered with wisdom, moderation, and firmness; and that the public confidence has reposed upon the judicial department, in the most critical times, with unabated respect. If the same can be said in regard to other states, where the judges enjoy a less permanent tenure of office, it will not answer the reasoning, unless it can also be shown, that the judges have never been removed for political causes, wholly distinct from their own merit ; and yet have often deliberately placed themselves in opposition to the popular opinion.[2]

---

and willing to resist their phrenzy ; if we have read of the death of Seneca, under the ferocity of a Nero ; we have read too of the murder of a Socrates, under the delusion of a republic. An independent and firm judiciary, protected and protecting by the laws, would have snatched the one from the fury of a despot, and preserved the other from the madness of a people." 2 Chase's Trial, 18, 19, 20.

[1] Dr. Lieber's Encyclopedia Americana, Art. *Constitutions of the United States.*

[2] It affords me very great satisfaction to be able to cite the opinions of two eminent commentators on this subject, who, differing in many other views of constitutional law, concur in upholding the necessity of an independent judiciary in a republic. Mr. Chancellor Kent, in his Commentaries, says :

" In monarchical governments, the independence of the judiciary is essential to guard the rights of the subject from the injustice of the crown ; but in republics it is equally salutary, in protecting the constitution and

§ 1615. The considerations above stated lead to the conclusion, that in republics there are, in reality, stronger reasons for an independent tenure of office

laws from the encroachments and the tyranny of faction. Laws, however wholesome or necessary, are frequently the object of temporary aversion, and sometimes of popular resistance. It is requisite, that the courts of justice should be able, at all times, to present a determined countenance against all licentious acts ; and, to give them the firmness to do it, the judges ought to be confident of the security of their stations. Nor is an independent judiciary less useful, as a check upon the legislative power, which is sometimes disposed, from the force of passion, or the temptations of interest, to make a sacrifice of constitutional rights ; and it is a wise and necessary principle of our government, as will be shown hereafter in the course of these lectures, that legislative acts are subject to the severe scrutiny and impartial interpretation of the courts of justice, who are bound to regard the constitution, as the paramount law, and the highest evidence of the will of the people." 1 Kent's Comm. Lect. 14, p. 293, 294.

Mr. Tucker, in his Commentaries, makes the following remarks :

"The American constitutions appear to be the first, in which this absolute independence of the judiciary has formed one of the fundamental principles of the government. Doctor Rutherforth considers the judiciary, as a branch only of the executive authority ; and such, in strictness, perhaps, it is in other countries, its province being to advise the executive, rather than to act independently of it." " But, in the United States of America, the judicial power is a distinct, separate, independent, and co-ordinate branch of the government : expressly recognized as such in our state bill of rights, and constitution, and demonstrably so, likewise, by the federal constitution, from which the courts of the United States derive all their powers, in like manner, as the legislative and executive departments derive theirs. The obligation, which the constitution imposes upon the judiciary department, to support the constitution of the United States, would be nugatory, if it were dependent upon either of the other branches of the government, or in any manner subject to their control, since such control might operate to the destruction, instead of the support, of the constitution. Nor can it escape observation, that to require such an oath on the part of the judges, on the one hand, and yet suppose them bound by acts of the legislature, which may violate the constitution, which they have sworn to support, carries with it such a degree of impiety, as well as absurdity, as no man, who pays any regard to the obligations of an oath, can be supposed, either to contend for, or to defend.

"This absolute independence of the judiciary, both of the executive and the legislative departments, which I contend is to be found, both

by the judges, a tenure during good behaviour, than in a monarchy. Indeed, a republic with a limited constitution, and yet without a judiciary sufficiently inde-

in the letter, and spirit of our constitutions, is not less necessary to the liberty and security of the citizen, and his property, in a republican government, than in a monarchy. If, in the latter, the will of the prince may be considered, as likely to influence the conduct of judges created occasionally, and holding their offices only during his pleasure, more especially in cases, where a criminal prosecution may be carried on by his orders, and supported by his influence ; in a republic, on the other hand, the violence and malignity of party spirit, as well in the legislature, as in the executive, requires not less the intervention of a calm, temperate, upright, and independent judiciary, to prevent that violence and malignity from exerting itself ' to crush in dust and ashes ' all opponents to its tyrannical administration, or ambitious projects. Such an independence can never be perfectly attained, but by a *constitutional tenure of office*, equally independent of the frowns and smiles of the other branches of the government. Judges ought, not only to be incapable of holding any other office at the same time, but even of appointment to any but a judicial office. For the hope of favour is always more alluring, and generally more dangerous, than the fear of offending. In England, according to the principles of the common law, a judge cannot hold any other office ; and according to the practice there for more than a century, no instance can, I believe, be shown, where a judge has been appointed to any other, than a judicial office, unless it be the honorary post of privy counsellor, to which no emolument is attached. And even this honorary distinction is seldom conferred, but upon the chief justice of the king's bench, if I have been rightly informed. To this cause, not less than to the tenure of their offices *during good behaviour*, may we ascribe that pre-eminent integrity, which amidst surrounding corruption, beams with genuine lustre from the English courts of judicature, as from the sun through surrounding clouds and mists. To emulate both their wisdom and integrity is an ambition, worthy of the greatest characters in any country.

" If we consider the nature of the judicial authority, and the manner, in which it operates, we shall discover, that it cannot, of itself, oppress any individual ; for the executive authority must lend its aid in every instance, where oppression can ensue from its decisions : whilst, on the contrary, its decisions in favour of the citizen are carried into instantaneous effect, by delivering him from the custody and restraint of the executive officer, the moment, that an acquittal is pronounced. And herein consists one of the great excellencies of our constitution : that no individual can be oppressed, whilst this branch of the government remains independent, and uncorrupted : it being a necessary check

pendent to check usurpation, to protect public liberty, and to enforce private rights, would be as visionary and absurd, as a society organized without any restraints of law. It would become a democracy with unlimited powers, exercising through its rulers a universal despotic sovereignty. The very theory of a balanced republic of restricted powers presupposes some organized means to control, and resist, any excesses of authority. The people may, if they please, submit all power to their rulers for the time being ; but, then, the government should receive its true appellation and character. It would be a government of tyrants, elective, it is true, but still tyrants ; and it would become the more fierce, vindictive, and sanguinary, because it would perpetually generate factions in its own bosom, who could succeed only by the ruin of their enemies. It would be alternately characterized, as a reign of terror, and a reign of imbecillity. It would be as cor-

upon the encroachments, or usurpations of power, by either of the other."

"That absolute independence of the judiciary, for which we contend, is not, then, incompatible with the strictest responsibility; (for a judge is no more exempt from it, than any other servant of the people, according to the true principles of the constitution;) but such an independence of the other *co-ordinate* branches of the government, as seems absolutely necessary to secure to them the free exercise of their constitutional functions, without the hope of pleasing, or the fear of offending. And, as from the natural feebleness of the judiciary, it is in continual jeopardy of being overpowered, awed, or influenced by its co-ordinate branches, who have the custody of the purse and sword of the confederacy ; and as nothing can contribute so much to its firmness and independence, as permanency in office, this quality, therefore, may be justly regarded, as an indispensable ingredient in its constitution ; and in great measure, as the citadel of the public justice, and the public security." 1 Tuck. Black. Comm. App. 354, 356 to 360.

There is also a very temperate, and, at the same time, a very satisfactory elucidation of the same subject, in Mr. Rawle's work on the Constitution, (ch. 30.) It would be cheerfully extracted, if this note had not already been extended to an inconvenient length.

rupt, as it would be dangerous. It would form another model of that profligate and bloody democracy, which, at one time, in the French revolution, darkened by its deeds the fortunes of France, and left to mankind the appalling lesson, that virtue, and religion, genius, and learning, the authority of wisdom, and the appeals of innocence, are unheard and unfelt in the frenzy of popular excitement; and, that the worst crimes may be sanctioned, and the most desolating principles inculcated, under the banners, and in the name of liberty. In human governments, there are but two controlling powers; the power of arms, and the power of laws. If the latter are not enforced by a judiciary above all fear, and above all reproach, the former must prevail; and thus lead to the triumph of military over civil institutions. The framers of the constitution, with profound wisdom, laid the corner stone of our national republic in the permanent independence of the judicial establishment. Upon this point their vote was unanimous.[1] They adopted the results of an enlightened experience. They were not seduced by the dreams of human perfection into the belief, that all power might be safely left to the unchecked operation of the private ambition, or personal virtue of rulers. Nor, on the other hand, were they so lost to a just estimate of human concerns, as not to feel, that confidence must be reposed somewhere; if either efficiency, or safety are to be consulted in the plan of government. Having provided amply for the legislative and executive authorities, they established a balance-wheel, which, by its independent structure, should adjust the irregularities, and check the excesses of the occasional movements of the system.

[1] Journal of Convention, 100, 188.

§ 1616. In the convention a proposition was offered to make the judges removeable by the president, upon the application of the senate and house of representatives ; but it received the support of a single state only.[1]

§ 1617. This proposition doubtless owed its origin to the clause in the act of parliament, (13 Will. 3 ch. 2,) making it lawful for the king to remove the judges on the address of both houses of parliament, notwithstanding the tenure of their offices during good behaviour, established by the same act.[2] But a moment's reflection will teach us, that there is no just analogy in the cases. The object of the act of parliament was to secure the judges from removal at the mere pleasure of the crown ; but not to render them independent of the action of parliament. By the theory of the British constitution, every act of parliament is supreme and omnipotent. It may change the succession to the crown ; and even the very fundamentals of the constitution. It would have been absurd, therefore, to have exempted the judges alone from the general jurisdiction of this supreme authority in the realm. The clause was not introduced into the act, for the purpose of conferring the power on parliament, for it could not be taken away, or restricted ; but simply to recognize it, as a qualification of the tenure of office ; so that the judges should have no right to complain of any breach of an implied contract with them, and the crown should not be deprived of the means to remove an unfit judge, whenever parliament should in their discretion signify their assent. Besides ; in England the judges are not, and cannot be, called upon to de-

---

[1] Journ. of Convention, 206.   [2] 1 Black. Comm. 266.

cide any constitutional questions; and therefore there was no necessity to place them, and indeed there would have been an impropriety in placing them, even if it had been possible, (which it clearly was not) in a situation, in which they would not have been under the control of parliament.

§ 1618. Far different is the situation of the people of the United States. They have chosen to establish a constitution of government, with limited powers and prerogatives, over which neither the executive, nor the legislature, have any power, either of alteration or control. It is to all the departments equally a supreme, fundamental, unchangeable law, which all must obey, and none are at liberty to disregard. The main security, relied on to check any irregular, or unconstitutional measure, either of the executive, or the legislative department, was (as we have seen) the judiciary. To have made the judges, therefore, removable, at the pleasure of the president and congress, would have been a virtual surrender to them of the custody and appointment of the guardians of the constitution. It would have been placing the keys of the citadel in the possession of those, against whose assaults the people were most strenuously endeavouring to guard themselves. It would be holding out a temptation to the president and congress, whenever they were resisted in any of their measures, to secure a perfect irresponsibility by removing those judges from office, who should dare to oppose their will. In short, in every violent political commotion or change, the judges would be removed from office, exactly as the lord chancellor in England now is, in order, that a perfect harmony might be established between the operations of all the departments of government. Such a power would have been a signal proof of a solicitude to erect defences round the constitution, for the sole purpose of surrendering them into the possession of those, whose acts they were intended to guard against. Under such circumstances, it might well have been asked, where could resort be had to redress grievances, or to overthrow usurpations ? *Quis custodiet custodes ?*

§ 1619. A proposition of a more imposing nature was to authorize a removal of judges for inability to discharge the duties of their offices. But all considerate persons will readily perceive, that such a provision would either not be practised upon, or would be more liable to abuse, than calculated to answer any good purpose. The mensuration of the faculties of the mind has no place in the catalogue of any known art or science. An attempt to fix the boundary between the region of ability and inability would much oftener give rise to personal, or party attachments and hostilities, than advance the interests of justice, or the public good.[1] And instances of absolute imbecility would be too rare to justify the introduction of so dangerous a provision.

§ 1620. In order to avoid investigations of this sort, which must for ever be vague and unsatisfactory, some persons have been disposed to think, that a limitation of age should be assumed as a criterion of inability ; so that there should be a constitutional removal from office, when the judge should attain a certain age. Some of the state constitutions have adopted such a limitation. Thus, in New-York, sixty years of age is a disqualification for the office of judge ; and in some other states the period is prolonged to seventy. The value of these

---

[1] The Federalist, No. 79. See Rawle on Constitution, ch. 30, p. 278, 279.

provisions has never, as yet, been satisfactorily established by the experience of any state. That they have
worked mischievously in some cases is matter of public
notoriety. The Federalist has remarked, in reference
to the limitation in New-York,[1] " there are few at present, who do not disapprove of this provision. There is
no station, in which it is less proper, than that of a judge.
The deliberating and comparing faculties generally preserve their strength much beyond that period in men,
who survive it. And when, in addition to this circumstance, we consider how few there are, who outlive the
season of intellectual vigour, and how improbable it is,
that any considerable portion of the bench, whether
more or less numerous, should be in such a situation at
the same time, we shall be ready to conclude, that limitations of this sort have little to recommend them. In a

[1] The limitation of New-York struck from its bench one of the greatest
names, that ever adorned it, in the full possession of his extraordinary
powers. I refer to Mr. Chancellor Kent, to whom the jurisprudence of
New-York owes a debt of gratitude, that can never be repaid. He is at
once the compeer of Hardwicke and Mansfield. Since his removal
from the bench, he has composed his admirable Commentaries,* a work,
which will survive, as an honor to the country, long after all the perish-
able fabrics of our day shall be buried in oblivion. If he had not thus
secured an enviable fame since his retirement, the public might have
had cause to regret, that New-York should have chosen to disfranchise
her best citizens at the time, when their services were most important,
and their judgments most mature.

Even the age of seventy would have excluded from public service
some of the greatest minds which have belonged to our country. At
eighty, said Mr. Jefferson, Franklin was the ornament of human nature.
At eighty, Lord Mansfield still possessed in vigor his almost unrivalled
powers. If seventy had been the limitation in the constitution of the
United States, the nation would have lost seven years of as brilliant
judicial labors, as have ever adorned the annals of the jurisprudence of
any country.

* While the present work was passing through the press, a second edition has been published
by the learned author; and it has been greatly improved by his severe, acute, and accurate
judgment.

republic, where fortunes are not affluent, and pensions
not expedient, the dismission of men from stations, in
which they have served their country long and useful-
ly, and on which they depend for subsistence, and from
which it will be too late to resort to any other occupation for a livelihood, ought to have some better apology
to humanity, than is to be found in the imaginary danger
of a superannuated bench." [1]

§ 1621. It is observable, that the constitution has declared, that the judges of the inferior courts, as well as of
the Supreme Court, of the United States, shall hold their
offices during good behaviour. In this respect there is
a marked contrast between the English government
and our own. In England the tenure is exclusively confined to the judges of the superior courts, and does not
(as we have already seen) even embrace all of these. In
fact, a great portion of all the civil and criminal business
of the whole kingdom is performed by persons delegated, *pro hac vice*, for this purpose under commissions
issued periodically for a single circuit.[2] It is true, that
it is, and for a long period has been, ordinarily administered by the judges of the courts of King's Bench,
Common Pleas, and Exchequer ; but it is not so merely
virtute officii, but under special commissions investing
them from time to time with this authority in conjunction with other persons named in the commission.
Such are the commissions of oyer and terminer, of
assize, of gaol delivery, and of *nisi prius*, under which
all civil and criminal trials of matters of fact are had at
the circuits, and in the metropolis.[3] By the constitu-

---

[1] The Federalist, No. 79. See Rawle on Const. ch. 30, p. 278, 279.
[2] 1 Wilson's Law Lect. 463, 464 ; 2 Wilson's Law Lect. 258, 259.
[3] See 3 Black. Comm. 58, 59, 60.

tion of the United States all criminal and civil jurisdiction must be exclusively confided to judges holding their office during good behaviour; and though congress may from time to time distribute the jurisdiction among such inferior courts, as it may create from time to time, and withdraw it at their pleasure, it is not competent for them to confer it upon temporary judges, or to confide it by special commission. Even if the English system be well adapted to the wants of the nation, and secure a wise and beneficent administration of justice in the realm, as it doubtless does; still it is obvious, that, in our popular government, it would be quite too great a power, to trust the whole administration of civil and criminal justice to commissioners, appointed at the pleasure of the president. To the constitution of the United States, and to those, who enjoy its advantages, no judges are known, but such, as hold their offices during good behaviour.[1]

---

[1] 1 Wilson's Law Lect. 464, 465.—Mr. Tucker has spoken with a truly national pride and feeling on the subject of the national judiciary, in comparing it with that of England. "Whatever then has been said," says he, "by Baron Montesquieu, De Lolme, or Judge Blackstone, or any other writer, on the security derived to the subject from the independence of the judiciary of Great Britain, will apply at least as forcibly to that of the United States. We may go still further. In England the judiciary may be overwhelmed by a combination between the executive and the legislature. In America, (according to the true theory of our constitution,) it is rendered absolutely independent of, and superior to the attempts of both, to control, or crush it: First, by the tenure of office, which is during good behaviour; these words (by a long train of decisions in England, even as far back, as the reign of Edward the Third) in all commissions and grants, public or private, importing an office, or estate, for the life of the grantee, determinable only by his death, or breach of good behaviour. Secondly, by the independence of the judges, in respect to their salaries, which cannot be diminished. Thirdly, by the letter of the constitution, which defines and limits the powers of the several co-ordinate branches of the government; and the spirit of it, which forbids any attempt on the part of either to subvert the

§ 1622. The next clause of the constitution declares, that the judges of the supreme and inferior courts " shall, at stated times, receive for their services a com- " pensation, which shall not be diminished during their " continuance in office." Without this provision the other, as to the tenure of office, would have been utterly nugatory, and indeed a mere mockery. The Federalist has here also spoken in language so direct and convincing, that it supercedes all other argument.

§ 1623. " Next to permanency in office, nothing can contribute more to the independence of the judges, than a fixed provision for their support. The remark made in relation to the president is equally applicable here. In the general course of human nature, *a power over a man's subsistence amounts to a power over his will.* And we can never hope to see realized in practice the complete separation of the judicial from the legislative power, in any system, which leaves the former dependent for pecuniary resource on the occasional grants of the latter. The enlightened friends to good government in every state have seen cause to lament the want of precise and explicit precautions in the state constitutions on this head. Some of these indeed have declared, that *permanent* salaries should be established for the judges ; but the experiment has in some instances shown, that such expressions are not sufficiently definite to preclude legislative evasions. Something still more positive and unequivocal has been

constitutional independence of the others. Lastly, by that uncontrollable authority in all cases of litigation, criminal or civil, which from the very nature of things is exclusively vested in this department, and extends to every supposable case, which can affect the life, liberty, or property of the citizens of America, under the authority of the federal constitution, and laws, except in the case of an impeachment." 1 Tuck. Black. Comm. App. 353, 354.

evinced to be requisite. The plan of the convention
accordingly has provided, that the judges of the United
States " shall at *stated times* receive for their services a
compensation, which shall not be *diminished* during
their continuance in office."

§ 1624. "This, all circumstances considered, is the
most eligible provision, that could have been devised.
It will readily be understood, that the fluctuations in
the value of money, and in the state of society, rendered a fixed rate of compensation in the constitution inadmissible. What might be extravagant to-day, might in
half a century become penurious and inadequate. It
was therefore necessary to leave it to the discretion of
the legislature to vary its provisions in conformity to
the variations in circumstances; yet under such restrictions as to put it out of the power of that body to
change the condition of the individual for the worse. A
man may then be sure of the ground upon which he
stands; and can never be deterred from his duty by the
apprehension of being placed in a less eligible situation.
The clause, which has been quoted, combines both advantages. The salaries of judicial offices may from
time to time be altered, as occasion shall require; yet
so as never to lessen the allowance, with which any particular judge comes into office, in respect to him. It
will be observed, that a difference has been made by
the convention between the compensation of the president and of the judges. That of the former can neither
be increased, nor diminished. That of the latter can
only not be diminished. This probably arose from the
difference in the duration of the respective offices. As
the president is to be elected for no more than four
years, it can rarely happen, that an adequate salary,
fixed at the commencement of that period, will not

continue to be such to its end. But with regard to the judges, who, if they behave properly, will be secured in their places for life, it may well happen, especially in the early stages of the government, that a stipend, which would be very sufficient at their first appointment, would become too small in the progress of their service.

§ 1625. " This provision for the support of the judges bears every mark of prudence and efficacy ; and it may be safely affirmed, that together with the permanent tenure of their offices, it affords a better prospect of their independence, than is discoverable in the constitutions of any of the states, in regard to their own judges. The precautions for their responsibility are comprised in the article respecting impeachments. They are liable to be impeached for maleconduct by the house of representatives, and tried by the senate ; and, if convicted, may be dismissed from office, and disqualified for holding any other. This is the only provision on the point, which is consistent with the necessary independence of the judicial character ; and is the only one, which we find in our own constitution, in respect to our own judges." [1]

---

[1] Mr. Chancellor Kent has written a few brief but pregnant sentences on this subject; and he has praised the constitution of the United States, as in this respect an improvement upon all previously existing constitutions, in this, or in any other country. 1 Kent's Comm. Lect. 14, p. 276. In his second edition, (Id. p. 294,) he has in some measure limited the generality of expression of the first, by stating, that by the English act of settlement, of 12 & 13 Will. 3, it was declared, that the salaries of the judges should be ascertained and *established;* and by the statute 1 George 3, the salaries of the judges were absolutely secured to them, during the continuance of their commissions.* Still there remains a striking difference in favour of the American constitution, inasmuch as in England the compensation, as well as the tenure of office, is within

* See 1 Black. Comm. 267, 268.

§ 1626. Mr. Justice Wilson also has, with manifest satisfaction, referred to the provision, as giving a decided superiority to the national judges over those of England. " The laws," says he, " in England, respecting the independency of the judges, have been construed, as confined to those in the superior courts. In the United States, this independency extends to judges in courts inferior, as well as supreme. This independency reaches equally their salaries, and their commissions. In England, the judges of the superior courts do not now, as they did formerly, hold their commissions and their salaries at the pleasure of the crown ; but they still hold them at the pleasure of the parliament : the judicial subsists, and may be blown to annihilation, by the breath of the legislative department. In the United States, the judges stand upon the sure basis of the constitution : the judicial department is independent of the department of legislature. No act of congress can shake their commissions, or reduce their salaries. ' The judges, both of the supreme and inferior courts, shall hold their offices during good behaviour, and shall, at stated times, receive for their services a compensation, which shall not be diminished, during their continuance in office.' It is not lawful for the president of the United States to remove them on the address of the two houses of congress. They may be removed, however, as they ought to be, on conviction of high crimes and misdemeanours. The judges of the United States stand on a much more independent footing, than that on which the judges of England stand, with

the reach of the repealing power of parliament ; but in the national government it constitutes a part of the supreme fundamental law, unalterable, except by an amendment of the the constitution.

with regard to jurisdiction, as well as with regard to commissions and salaries. In many cases, the jurisdiction of the judges of the United States is ascertained, and secured by the constitution. As to these, the power of the judicial is co-ordinate with that of the legislative department. As to the other cases, by the necessary result of the constitution, the authority of the former is paramount to the authority of the latter."

§ 1627. It would be a matter of general congratulation, if this language had been completely borne out by the perusal of our juridical annals. But, unfortunately, a measure was adopted in 1802 under the auspices of president Jefferson,[1] which, if its constitutionality can be successfully vindicated, prostrates in the dust the independence of all inferior judges, both as to the tenure of their office, and their compensation for services, and leaves the constitution a miserable and vain delusion. In the year 1801, congress passed an act[2] reorganizing the judiciary, and authorizing the appointment of sixteen new judges, with suitable salaries, to hold the circuit courts of the United States, in the different circuits created by the act. Under this act the circuit judges received their appointments, and performed the duties of their offices, until the year 1802, when the courts, established by the act, were abolished by a general repeal of it by congress, without in the slightest manner providing for the payment of the salaries of the judges, or for any continuation of their offices.[3] The result of this act, therefore, is

---

[1] See Mr. Jefferson's Message, Dec. 8, 1801; 4 Wait's State Papers, p. 332.

[2] Act of 1801, ch. 75.

[3] Act of 8th of March, 1802, ch. 8.

(so far as it is a precedent,) that, notwithstanding the constitutional tenure of office of the judges of the inferior courts is during good behaviour, congress may, at any time, by a mere act of legislation, deprive them of their offices at pleasure, and with it take away their whole title to their salaries.[1] How this can be reconciled with the terms, or the intent of the constitution, is more, than any ingenuity of argument has ever, as yet, been able to demonstrate.[2] The system fell, because it was unpopular with those, who were then in possession of power; and the victims have hitherto remained without any indemnity from the justice of the government.

§ 1628. Upon this subject a learned commentator[3] has spoken with a manliness and freedom, worthy of himself and of his country. To those, who are alive to the just interpretation of the constitution; those, who, on the one side, are anxious to guard it against usurpations of power, injurious to the states; and those, who, on the other side, are equally anxious to

---

[1] See Sergeant on Const. ch. 30, [ch. 32.]

[2] The act gave rise to one of the most animated debates, to be found in the annals of congress; and was resisted by a power of argument and eloquence, which has never been surpassed. These debates were collected, and printed in a volume at Albany in 1802; and are worthy of the most deliberate perusal of every constitutional lawyer. The act may be asserted, without fear of contradiction, to have been against the opinion of a great majority of all the ablest lawyers at the time; and probably now, when the passions of the day have subsided, few lawyers will be found to maintain the constitutionality of the act. No one can doubt the perfect authority of congress to remodel their courts, or to confer, or withdraw their jurisdiction at their pleasure. But the question is, whether they can deprive them of the tenure of their office, and their salaries, after they have once become constitutionally vested in them. See 3 Tuck. Black. Comm. App. 22 to 25.

[3] Mr. Tucker, 1 Tuck. Black. Comm. App. 360; 3 Tuck. Black. Comm. App. 22 to 25.

prevent a prostration of any of its great departments
to the authority of the others ; the language can never
be unseasonable, either for admonition or instruction,
to warn us of the facility, with which public opinion
may be persuaded to yield up some of the barriers of
the constitution under temporary influences, and to
teach us the duty of an unsleeping vigilance to protect that branch, which, though weak in its powers, is
yet the guardian of the rights and liberties of the people. "It was supposed," says the learned author,
"that there could not be a doubt, that those tribunals, in which justice is to be dispensed, according to
the constitution and laws of the confederacy ; in
which life, liberty, and property are to be decided
upon ; in which questions might arise as to the constitutional powers of the executive, or the constitutional obligation of an act of the legislature ; and in
the decision of which the judges might find themselves
constrained by duty, and by their oaths, to pronounce
against the authority of either, should be stable and
permanent ; and not dependent upon the will of the
executive or legislature, or both, for their existence.
That without this degree of permanence, the tenure
of office during good behaviour could not secure to
that department the necessary firmness to meet unshaken every question, and to decide, as justice and
the constitution should dictate, without regard to consequences. These considerations induced an opinion,
which, it was presumed, was general, if not universal,
that the power vested in congress to erect, from time
to time, tribunals inferior to the supreme court, did
not authorize them, at pleasure, to demolish them.
Being built upon the rock of the constitution, their
foundations were supposed to partake of its perma-

nency, and to be equally incapable of being shaken by the other branches of the government. But a different construction of the constitution has lately prevailed. It has been determined, that a power to ordain and establish from time to time, carries with it a discretionary power to discontinue, or demolish. That although the tenure of office be *during good behaviour*, this does not prevent the separation of the office from the officer, by putting down the office; but only secures to the officer his station, upon the terms of good behaviour, so long as the office itself remains. Painful indeed is the remark, that this interpretation seems calculated to subvert one of the fundamental pillars of free governments, and to have laid the foundation of one of the most dangerous political schisms, that has ever happened in the United States of America." [1]

---

[1] Whether justices of the peace, appointed under the authority of the United States, are inferior courts, within the sense of the constitution, has been in former times a matter of some controversy, but has never been decided by the Supreme Court. They are doubtless officers of the government of the United States; but their duties are partly judicial, and partly executive or ministerial.* In these respects they have been supposed to be like commissioners of excise, of bankruptcy, commissioners to take depositions, and commissioners under treaties. And it has been said, that the constitution, in speaking of courts and judges, means those, who exercise all the regular and permanent duties, which belong to a court in the ordinary popular signification of the terms.†

At present the courts of the United States, organized under the constitution, consist of district courts, (one of which at least is established in every state in the Union,) of circuit courts, and of a Supreme Court, the latter being composed of seven judges. The judiciary act of 1789, ch. 20; and the judiciary act of 1802, ch. 31, are those, which make the general provisions for the establishments of these courts, and for their jurisdiction, original and appellate. Mr. Chancellor Kent has given a brief but accurate account of the examination of the courts of the United States. 1 Kent's Comm. Lect. 14, p. 279 to 285. [2d edit. p. 298 to 305.]

* *Wise* v. *Withers*, 3 Cranch's R. 336; S. C. 1 Peters's Cond. R. 552.
† Sergeant on Const. (2d edit.) ch. 32, p. 377, 378.

§ 1629. It is almost unnecessary to add, that, although the constitution has, with so sedulous a care, endeavoured to guard the judicial department from the overwhelming influence or power of the other co-ordinate departments of the government, it has not conferred upon them any inviolability, or irresponsibility for an abuse of their authority. On the contrary for any corrupt violation or omission of the high trusts confided to the judges, they are liable to be impeached, (as we have already seen,) and upon conviction removed from office. Thus, on the one hand, a pure and independent administration of public justice is amply provided for ; and, on the other hand, an urgent responsibility secured for fidelity to the people.

§ 1630. The judges of the inferior courts, spoken of in the constitution, do not include the judges of courts appointed in the territories of the United States under the authority, given to congress, to regulate the territories of the United States. The courts of the territories are not constitutional courts, in which the judicial power conferred by the constitution on the general government, can be deposited. They are legislative courts, created in virtue of the general sovereignty, which exists in the national government over its territories. The jurisdiction, with which they are invested, is not a part of the judicial power, which is defined in the third article of the constitution; but arises from the same general sovereignty. In legislating for them, congress exercises the combined powers of the general, and of a state government. Congress may, therefore, rightfully limit the tenure of office of the judges of the territorial courts, as well as their jurisdiction; and it has been accordingly limited to a short period of years.[1]

§ 1631. The second section of the third article contains an exposition of the jurisdiction appertaining to the judicial power of the national government. The first clause is as follows: "The judicial power shall "extend to all cases in law and equity arising under "this constitution, the laws of the United States, and "treaties made, or which shall be made, under their "authority; to all cases affecting ambassadors, other "public ministers, and consuls; to all cases of admi- "ralty and maritime jurisdiction; to controversies, to "which the United States shall be a party; to contro- "versies between two or more states; between a state "and citizens of another state; between citizens of "different states; between citizens of the same state, "claiming lands under grants of different states; and "between a state, or the citizens thereof, and foreign "states, citizens, or subjects."[2]

§ 1632. Such is the judicial power, which the constitution has deemed essential, in order to follow out one of its great objects stated in the preamble, "to establish justice." Mr. Chief Justice Jay, in his very

---

[1] *The American Insurance Company* v. *Canter*, 1 Peters's Sup. R. 511, 546.

[2] It has been very correctly remarked by Mr. Justice Iredell, that "the judicial power of the United States is of a peculiar kind. It is, indeed, commensurate with the ordinary legislative and executive powers of the general government, and the powers, which concern treaties. But it also goes further. When certain parties are concerned, although the subject in controversy does not relate to any special objects of authority of the general government, wherein the separate sovereignties of the separate states are blended in one common mass of supremacy; yet the general government has a judicial authority in regard to such subjects of controversy; and the legislature of the United States may pass all laws necessary to give such judicial authority its proper effect." *Chisholm* v. *Georgia*, 2 Dall. 433, 434; S. C. 2 Peters's Cond. R. 641.

able opinion, in *Chisholm* v. *The State of Georgia*,[1] has drawn up a summary of the more general reasoning, on which each of these delegations of power is founded. "It may be asked," said he, "what is the precise sense and latitude, in which the words '*to establish justice*,' as here used, are to be understood? The answer to this question will result from the provisions made in the constitution on this head. They are specified in the second section of the third article, where it is ordained, that the judicial power of the United States shall extend to ten descriptions of cases, viz. 1. To all cases arising under this constitution; because the meaning, construction, and operation of a compact ought always to be ascertained by all the parties, not by authority derived only from one of them. 2. To all cases arising under the laws of the United States; because, as such laws, constitutionally made, are obligatory on each state, the measure of obligation and obedience ought not to be decided and fixed by the party, from whom they are due, but by a tribunal deriving authority from both the parties. 3. To all cases arising under treaties made by their authority; because, as treaties are compacts made by, and obligatory on, the whole nation, their operation ought not to be affected, or regulated by the local laws, or courts of a part of the nation. 4. To all cases affecting ambassadors, or other public ministers, and consuls; because, as these are officers of foreign nations, whom this nation are bound to protect, and treat according to the laws of nations, cases affecting them ought only to be cognizable by national authority. 5. To all cases of admiralty and maritime jurisdiction; because, as the seas are the joint property

---

[1] 2 Dall. R. 419, 475; S. C. 2 Peters's Cond. R. 635, 671.

of nations, whose right and privileges relative thereto, are regulated by the law of nations and treaties, such cases necessarily belong to national jurisdiction. 6. To controversies, to which the United States shall be a party; because in cases, in which the whole people are interested, it would not be equal, or wise, to let any one state decide, and measure out the justice due to others. 7. To controversies between two or more states; because domestic tranquillity requires, that the contentions of states should be peaceably terminated by a common judicatory; and, because, in a free country, justice ought not to depend on the *will* of either of the litigants. 8. To controversies between a state and citizens of another state; because, in case a state (that is, all the citizens of it) has demands against some citizens of another state, it is better, that she should prosecute their demands in a national court, than in a court of the state, to which those citizens belong; the danger of irritation and criminations, arising from apprehensions and suspicions of partiality, being thereby obviated. Because, in cases, where some citizens of one state have demands against all the citizens of another state, the cause of liberty and the rights of men forbid, that the latter should be the sole judges of the justice due to the latter; and true republican government requires, that free and equal citizens should have free, fair, and equal justice. 9. To controversies between citizens of the same state, claiming lands under grants of different states; because, as the rights of the two states to grant the land are drawn into question, neither of the two states ought to decide the controversy. 10. To controversies between a state, or the citizens thereof, and foreign states, citizens, or subjects; because, as

every nation is responsible for the conduct of its
citizens towards other nations, all questions touching
the justice due to foreign nations, or people, ought to
be ascertained by, and depend on, national authority.
Even this cursory view of the judicial powers of the
United States leaves the mind strongly impressed
with the importance of them to the preservation of
the tranquillity, the equal sovereignty, and the equal
rights of the people."

§ 1633. This opinion contains a clear, and, as far
as it goes, an exact outline; but it will be necessary
to examine separately every portion of the jurisdiction here given, in order that a more full and comprehensive understanding of all the reasons, on which it
is founded, may be attained. And I am much mistaken, if such an examination will not display in a
more striking light the profound wisdom and policy,
with which this part of the constitution was framed.

§ 1634. And first, the judicial power extends to all
cases in law and equity, arising under the constitution, the laws, and the treaties of the United States.[1]
And by cases in this clause we are to understand criminal, as well as civil cases.[2]

§ 1635. The propriety of the delegation of jurisdiction, in "cases arising under the constitution," rests
on the obvious consideration, that there ought always
to be some constitutional method of giving effect to

1 In the first draft of the constitution the clause was, "the jurisdiction
of the Supreme Court shall extend to all cases arising under the laws
passed by the legislature of the United States;" the other words, "the
constitution," and "treaties," were afterwards added without any apparent objection. Journal of Convention, 226, 297, 298.

2 1 Tucker's Black. Comm. App. 420, 421; Cohens v. Virginia, 6
Wheat. R. 399; Rawle on Const. ch. 21, p. 226.

constitutional provisions.[1] What, for instance, would avail restrictions on the authority of the state legislatures, without some constitutional mode of enforcing the observance of them?[2] The states are by the

---

[1] *Cohens* v. *Virginia*, 6 Wheat. R. 415; Id. 402 to 404, *ante*, Vol. I. § 266, 267.

[2] Mr. Madison, in the Virginia Resolutions and Report, January, 1800, says, that "cases arising under the constitution," in the sense of this clause, are of two descriptions. One of these comprehends the cases growing out of the restrictions on the legislative power of the states, such as emitting bills of credit, making any thing but gold and silver a tender in payment of debts. "Should this prohibition be violated," says he, "and a suit *between citizens of the same state* be the consequence, this would be a case arising under the constitution before the judicial power of the United States. A second description comprehends suits between citizens and foreigners, or citizens of different states, to be decided according to the state or foreign laws; but submitted by the constitution to the judicial power of the United States; the judicial power being, in several instances, extended beyond the legislative power of the United States." [p. 28.] Mr. Tucker in his Commentaries uses the following language: "The judicial power of the federal government extends to all cases in law and equity arising under the constitution. Now, the powers granted to the federal government, or prohibited to the states, being all enumerated, the cases arising under the *constitution* can only be such, as arise out of some *enumerated* power delegated to the federal government, or prohibited to those of the several states. These general words include what is comprehended in the next clause, viz. cases arising under the laws of the United States. But, as contradistinguished from that clause, it comprehends some cases afterwards enumerated; for example, controversies between two or more states; between a state and foreign states; between citizens of the same state claiming lands under grants of different states: all which may arise under the *constitution*, and not under any law of the United States. Many other cases might be enumerated, which would fall strictly under this clause, and no other. As, if a citizen of one state should be denied the privileges of a citizen in another; so, if a person held to service or labour in one state, should escape into another and obtain protection there, as a free man; so, if a state should coin money, and declare the same to be a legal tender in payment of debt, the validity of such a tender, if made, would fall within the meaning of this clause. So also, if a state should, without the consent of congress, lay any duty upon goods imported, the question, as to the validity of such an act, if disputed, would come within the meaning of this clause, and not of any other.

504 CONSTITUTION OF THE U. STATES. [BOOK III.

constitution prohibited from doing a variety of things;
some of which are incompatible with the interests of
the Union; others with its peace and safety; others
with the principles of good government. The impo-
sition of duties on imported articles, the declaration
of war, and the emission of paper money, are examples of each kind. No man of sense will believe, that
such prohibitions would be scrupulously regarded,
without some effectual power in the government to
restrain, or correct the infractions of them.[1] The
power must be either a direct negative on the state
laws, or an authority in the national courts to overrule
such, as shall manifestly be in contravention to the
constitution. The latter course was thought by the
convention to be preferable to the former; and it is,
without question, by far the most acceptable to the
states.[2]

§ 1636. The same reasoning applies with equal
force to " cases arising under the laws of the United
States." In fact, the necessity of uniformity in the
interpretation of these laws would of itself settle
every doubt, that could be raised on the subject.
" Thirteen independent courts of final jurisdiction
(says the Federalist) over the same causes is a

In all these cases equitable circumstances may arise, the cognizance of
which, as well as such, as were strictly legal, would belong to the federal judiciary, in virtue of this clause." 1 Tuck. Black. Comm. App. 418,
419. See also 2 Elliot's Debates, 380, 383, 390, 400, 418, 419.

1 See 3 Elliot's Debates, 142.

2 The Federalist, No. 80. See also Id. No. 22; 2 Elliot's Debates,
389, 390. — The reasonableness of this extent of the judicial power is
very much considered by Mr. Chief Justice Marshall, in delivering the
opinion of the court, in *Cohens v. Virginia*, (6 Wheat. R. 413 to 423,)
from which some extracts will be made, in considering the appellate jurisdiction of the Supreme Court, in a future page.

Hydra in government, from which nothing but contradiction and confusion can proceed."[1]

§ 1637. There is still more cogency, if it be possible, in the reasoning, as applied to "cases arising under treaties made, or which shall be made, under the authority of the United States." Without this power, there would be perpetual danger of collision, and even of war, with foreign powers, and an utter incapacity to fulfil the ordinary obligations of treaties.[2] The want of this power was (as we have seen [3]) a most mischievous defect in the confederation; and subjected the country, not only to violations of its plighted faith, but to the gross, and almost proverbial imputation of punic insincerity.[4]

§ 1638. But, indeed, the whole argument on this subject has been already exhausted in the preceding part of these Commentaries, and therefore it may be dismissed without farther illustrations, although many humiliating proofs are to be found in the records of the confederation.[5]

---

1 The Federalist, No. 80 ; Id. No. 22 ; Id. No. 15 ; 2 Elliot's Debates, 389, 390 ; 3 Elliot's Debates, 142, 143. — In the Convention, which framed the constitution, the following resolution was unanimously adopted. "That the jurisdiction of the national judiciary shall extend to cases arising under laws passed by the general legislature, and to such other questions, as involve the national peace and harmony." Journ. of Convention, 188, 189.

2 The Federalist, No. 22, No. 80 ; 2 Elliot's Debates, 390, 400 ; The Federalist, No. 80. — The remarks of The Federalist, No. 80, on this subject will be found very instructive, and should be perused by every constitutional lawyer.

3 Ante, Vol. I. § 266, 267, 483, 484 ; 3 Elliot's Debates, 148, 280.

4 3 Elliot's Debates, 281.

5 Ante, Vol. I. § 266, 267, 483, 484 ; The Federalist, No. 22, No. 80 ; 1 Tuck. Black. Comm. App. 418, 419, 420. — This clause was opposed with great earnestness in some of the state conventions, and particularly in that of Virginia, as alarming and dangerous to the rights and

§ 1639. It is observable, that the language is, that "the judicial power shall extend to all cases *in law* and *equity*," arising under the constitution, laws, and treaties of the United States.[1] What is to be understood by "cases in law and equity," in this clause? Plainly, cases at the common law, as contradistinguished from cases in equity, according to the known distinction in the jurisprudence of England, which our ancestors brought with them upon their emigration, and with which all the American states were familiarly acquainted.[2] Here, then, at least, the constitution of the United States appeals to, and adopts, the common law to the extent of making it a rule in the pursuit of remedial justice in the courts of the Union.[3] If the remedy must be in law, or in equity, according to the course of proceedings at the common law, in cases arising under the constitution, laws, and treaties, of the United States, it would seem irresistibly

---

liberties of the states, since it would bring every thing within the vortex of the national jurisdiction. It was defended with great ability and conclusiveness of reasoning, as indispensable to the existence of the national government, and perfectly consistent with the safety and prerogatives of the states. See 2 Elliot's Debates, 380 to 427 ; 3 Elliot's Debates, 125, 128, 129, 133, 143 ; Id. 280 ; 4 Elliot's Debates, (Martin's Letter,) 45.

[1] See 3 Elliot's Debates, 127, 128, 129, 130, 133, 141, 143, 154.

[2] See *Robinson* v. *Campbell*, 3 Wheat. R. 212, 221, 223.

[3] It is a curious fact, that while the adoption of the common law, as the basis of the national jurisprudence, has been, in later times, the subject of such deep political alarm with some statesmen, the non-existence of it, as such a basis, was originally pressed by some of the ablest opponents of the constitution, as a principal defect. Mr. George Mason of Virginia urged, that the want of a clause in the constitution, securing to the people the enjoyment of the common law, was a fatal defect. 2 American Museum, 534 ; ante, Vol. I. p. 275. Yet the whole argument in the celebrated Resolutions of Virginia of January, 1800, supposes, that the adoption of it would have been a most mischievous provision.

to follow, that the principles of decision, by which these remedies must be administered, must be derived from the same source. Hitherto, such has been the uniform interpretation and mode of administering justice in civil cases, in the courts of the United States in this class of cases.[1]

§ 1640. Another inquiry may be, what constitutes a *case*, within the meaning of this clause. It is clear, that the judicial department is authorized to exercise jurisdiction to the full extent of the constitution, laws, and treaties of the United States, whenever any question respecting them shall assume such a form, that the judicial power is capable of acting upon it. When it has assumed such a form, it then becomes a case ; and then, and not till then, the judicial power attaches to it. A case, then, in the sense of this clause of the constitution, arises, when some subject, touching the constitution, laws, or treaties of the United States, is submitted to the courts by a party, who asserts his rights in the form prescribed by law.[2] In other words, a case is a suit in law or equity, instituted according to the regular course of judicial proceedings ; and, when it involves any question arising under the constitution, laws, or treaties of the United States, it is within the judicial power confided to the Union.[3]

---

[1] See *Cox & Dick* v. *United States*, 6 Peters's Sup. R. 172, 203 ; *Robinson* v. *Campbell*, 3 Wheat. R. 212. See Madison's Report, 7 January, 1800, p. 28, 29 ; *Chisholm's Executors* v. *Georgia*, 2 Dall. R. 419, 433, 437 ; S. C. 2 Cond. R. 635, 640, 642, per Iredell J. ; The Federalist, No. 80, No. 83.

[2] *Osborn* v. *The Bank of the United States*, 9 Wheat. R. 819. See Mr. Marshall's Speech on the case of Jonathan Robbins ; Bee's Adm. R. 277.

[3] See 1 Tuck. Black. Comm. App. 418, 419, 420 ; Madison's Virginia

§ 1641. Cases arising under the constitution, as contradistinguished from those, arising under the laws of the United States, are such as arise from the powers conferred, or privileges granted, or rights claimed, or protection secured, or prohibitions contained in the constitution itself, independent of any particular statute enactment. Many cases of this sort may easily be enumerated. Thus, if a citizen of one state should be denied the privileges of a citizen in another state ;[1] if a state should coin money, or make paper money a tender ; if a person, tried for a crime against the United States, should be denied a trial by jury, or a trial in the state, where the crime is charged to be committed ; if a person, held to labour, or service in one state, under the laws thereof, should escape into another, and there should be a refusal to deliver him up to the party, to whom such service or labour may be due ; in these, and many other cases, the question, to be judicially decided, would be a case arising under the constitution.[2] On the other hand, cases arising under the laws of the United States are such, as grow out of the legislation of congress, within the scope of their constitutional authority, whether they constitute the right, or privilege, or claim, or protection, or defence, of the party, in whole or in part, by whom they are asserted.[3] The same reasoning applies to cases arising under treaties. Indeed, wherever, in a judi-

Resolutions and Report, January, 1800, p. 28 ; *Marbury v. Madison*, 1 Cranch's R. 137, 173, 174 ; *Owing v. Norwood*, 5 Cranch, R. 344. See 2 Elliot's Debates, 418, 419.

[1] The Federalist, No. 80.
[2] 1 Tucker's Black. Comm. App. 418, 419 ; ante, Vol. II. §
[3] *Marbury v. Madison*, 1 Cranch, 137, 173, 174.

cial proceeding, any question arises, touching the validity of a treaty, or statute, or authority, exercised under the United States, or touching the construction of any clause of the constitution, or any statute, or treaty of the United States; or touching the validity of any statute, or authority exercised under any state, on the ground of repugnancy to the constitution, laws, or treaties, of the United States, it has been invariably held to be a case, to which the judicial power of the United States extends.[1]

§ 1642. It has sometimes been suggested, that a case, to be within the purview of this clause, must be one, in which a party comes into court to demand something conferred on him by the constitution, or a law, or a treaty, of the United States. But this construction is clearly too narrow. A case in law or equity consists of the right of the one party, as well as of the other, and may truly be said to arise under the constitution, or a law, or a treaty, of the United States, whenever its correct decision depends on the construction of either. This is manifestly the construction given to the clause by congress, by the 25th section of the Judiciary Act, (which was almost contemporaneous with the constitution,) and there is no reason to doubt its solidity or correctness.[2] Indeed, the main object of this clause would be defeated by any narrower construction; since the power was conferred for the purpose, in an especial manner, of

---

[1] See Judiciary Act of 1789, ch. 20, § 25; *Martin v. Hunter*, 1 Wheat. R. 304; *Cohens v. Virginia*, 6 Wheat. R. 264; *Osborn v. Bank of the United States*, 9 Wheat. R. 738; *Gibbons v. Ogden*, 9 Wheat. R. 1.

[2] *Cohens v. Virginia*, 6 Wheat. R. 378, 379, 391, 392. See also 1 Tuck. Black. Comm. App. 419, 420; Judiciary Act of 1789, ch. 20.

producing a uniformity of construction of the constitution, laws, and treaties of the United States.[1]

§ 1643. This subject was a good deal discussed in a recent case [2] before the Supreme Court, where one of the leading questions was, whether congress could constitutionally confer upon the bank of the United States, (as it has done by the seventh section of its charter,[3]) general authority to sue, and be sued in the circuit courts of the United States. It was contended, that they could not, because several questions might arise in such suits, which might depend upon the general principles of law, and not upon any act of congress. It was held, that congress did constitutionally possess the power, and had rightfully conferred it in that charter.

§ 1644. The reasoning, on which this decision was founded, cannot be better expressed, than in the very language, in which it was delivered by Mr. Chief Justice Marshall. "The question," said he, "is whether it (the case) arises under a law of the United States. The appellants contend, that it does not, because several questions may arise in it, which depend on the general principles of the law, not on any act of congress. If this were sufficient to withdraw a case from the jurisdiction of the federal courts, almost every case, although involving the construction of a law, would be withdrawn ; and a clause in the constitution, relating to a subject of vital importance to the government, and expressed in the most comprehensive terms, would be construed to mean almost nothing. There is scarcely any case, every part of which depends on the constitution, laws, or treaties of the United

1 The Federalist, No. 80 ; *Cohens v. Virginia*, 6 Wheat. R. 391, 392.
2 *Osborn v. Bank of the United States*, 9 Wheat. R. 738, 819, 820.
3 Act of 1816, ch, 44, § 7.

States. The questions, whether the fact, alleged as the foundation of the action, be real or fictitious ; whether the conduct of the plaintiff has been such as to entitle him to maintain his action ; whether his right is barred ; whether he has received satisfaction, or has, in any manner, released his claims ; are questions, some or all, of which may occur in almost every case ; and if their existence be sufficient to arrest the jurisdiction of the court, words, which seem intended to be as extensive, as the constitution, laws, and treaties of the Union, which seem designed to give the courts of the government the construction of all its acts, so far as they affect the rights of individuals, would be reduced to almost nothing." [1]

§ 1645. After adverting to the fact, that there is nothing in the constitution to prevent congress giving to inferiour courts original jurisdiction in cases, to which the appellate power of the Supreme Court may extend, he proceeds : " We perceive, then, no ground, on which the proposition can be maintained, that congress is incapable of giving the circuit courts original jurisdiction, in any case, to which the appellate jurisdiction extends. We ask, then, if it can be sufficient to exclude this jurisdiction, that the case involves questions depending on general principles ? A cause may depend on several questions of fact and law. Some of these may depend on the construction of a law of the United States ; others on principles unconnected with that law. If it be a sufficient foundation for jurisdiction, that the title or right, set up by the party, may be defeated by one construction of the constitution or law of the United

---

[1] *Osborn v. Bank of the United States*, 9 Wheat. R. 819, 820.

States, and sustained by the opposite construction, provided the facts necessary to support the action be made out, then all the other questions must be decided, as incidental to this, which gives that jurisdiction. Those other questions cannot arrest the proceedings. Under this construction, the judicial power of the Union extends effectively and beneficially to that most important class of cases, which depend on the character of the cause. On the opposite construction, the judicial power never can be extended to a whole case, as expressed by the constitution; but to those parts of cases only, which present the particular question involving the construction of the constitution or the law. We say it never can be extended to the whole case; because, if the circumstance, that other points are involved in it, shall disable congress from authorizing the courts of the Union to take jurisdiction of the original cause, it equally disables congress from authorizing those courts to take jurisdiction of the whole cause, on an appeal; and thus it will be restricted to a single question in that cause. And words obviously intended to secure to those, who claim rights under the constitution, laws, or treaties, of the United States, a trial in the federal courts, will be restricted to the insecure remedy of an appeal upon an insulated point, after it has received that shape, which may be given to it by another tribunal, into which he is forced against his will. We think, then, that when a question, to which the judicial power of the Union is extended by the constitution, forms an ingredient of the original cause, it is in the power of congress to give the circuit courts jurisdiction of that cause, although other questions of fact or of law may be involved in it."

§ 1646. " The case of the bank is, we think, a very strong case of this description. The charter of incorporation not only creates it, but gives it every faculty, which it possesses. The power to acquire rights of any description, to transact business of any description, to make contracts of any description, to sue on those contracts, is given and measured by its charter; and that charter is a law of the United States. This being can acquire no right, make no contract, bring no suit, which is not authorized by a law of the United States. It is not only itself the mere creature of a law, but all its actions, and all its rights are dependent on the same law. Can a being, thus constituted, have a case, which does not arise literally, as well as substantially, under the law? Take the case of a contract, which is put as the strongest against the bank. When a bank sues, the first question, which presents itself, and which lies at the foundation of the cause, is, has this legal entity a right to sue? Has it a right to come, not into this court particularly, but into any court? This depends on a law of the United States. The next question is, has this being a right to make this particular contract? If this question be decided in the negative, the cause is determined against the plaintiff; and this question, too, depends entirely on a law of the United States. These are important questions, and they exist in every possible case. The right to sue, if decided once, is decided for ever; but the power of congress was exercised antecedently to the first decision on that right; and if it was constitutional then, it cannot cease to be so, because the particular question is decided. It may be revived at the will of the party, and most probably would be renewed, were the tribunal to be changed. But the

question, respecting the right to make a particular
contract, or to acquire a particular property, or to
sue on account of a particular injury, belongs to
every particular case, and may be renewed in every
case.   The question forms an original ingredient in
every cause.   Whether it be in fact relied on, or not,
in the defence, it is still a part of the cause, and may
be relied on.   The right of the plaintiff to sue cannot depend on the defence, which the defendant may
choose to set up.   His right to sue is anterior to that
defence, and must depend on the state of things,
when the action is brought.   The questions, which
the case involves, then, must determine its character,
whether those questions be made in the cause or not.
The appellants say, that the case arises on the contract ; but the validity of the contract depends on a
law of the United States, and the plaintiff is compelled, in every case, to show its validity.   The case
arises emphatically under the law.   The act of congress is its foundation.   The contract could never
have been made, but under the authority of that act.
The act itself is the first ingredient in the case, is its
origin, is that, from which every other part arises.
That other questions may also arise, as the execution
of the contract, or its performance, cannot change
the case, or give it any other origin, than the charter
of incorporation.   The action still originates in, and
is sustained by, that charter.

§ 1647. "The clause, giving the bank a right to
sue in the circuit courts of the United States, stands
on the same principle with the acts authorizing officers of the United States, who sue in their own
names, to sue in the courts of the United States.
The post-master general, for example, cannot sue

under that part of the constitution, which gives jurisdiction to the federal courts, in consequence of the character of the party, nor is he authorized to sue by the judiciary act. He comes into the courts of the Union under the authority of an act of congress, the constitutionality of which can only be sustained by the admission, that his suit is a case arising under a law of the United States. If it be said, that it is such a case, because a law of the United States authorizes the contract, and authorizes the suit, the same reasons exist with respect to a suit brought by the bank. That, too, is such a case ; because that suit, too, is itself authorized, and is brought on a contract authorized by a law of the United States. It depends absolutely on that law, and cannot exist a moment without its authority.

§ 1648. " If it be said, that a suit brought by the bank may depend in fact altogether on questions, unconnected with any law of the United States, it is equally true with respect to suits brought by the post-master general. The plea in bar may be payment, if the suit be brought on a bond, or nonassumpsit, if it be brought on an open account, and no other question may arise, than what respects the complete discharge of the demand. Yet the constitutionality of the act, authorizing the post-master general to sue in the courts of the United States, has never been drawn into question. It is sustained singly by an act of congress, standing on that construction of the constitution, which asserts the right of the legislature to give original jurisdiction to the circuit courts, in cases arising under a law of the United States. The clause in the patent law, authorizing suits in the circuit courts, stands, we think, on the same principle. Such a suit is a case arising under a law of the United States. Yet the defendant may not, at the trial, question the validity of the patent, or make any point, which requires the construction of an act of congress. He may rest his defence exclusively on the fact, that he has not violated the right of the plaintiff. That this fact becomes the sole question made in the cause, cannot oust the jurisdiction of the court, or establish the position, that the case does not arise under a law of the United States.

§ 1649. "It is said, that a clear distinction exists between the party and the cause ; that the party may originate under a law, with which the cause has no connexion ; and that congress may, with the same propriety, give a naturalized citizen, who is the mere creature of a law, a right to sue in the courts of the United States, as give that right to the bank. This distinction is not denied ; and, if the act of congress was a simple act of incorporation, and contained nothing more, it might be entitled to great consideration. But the act does not stop with incorporating the bank. It proceeds to bestow upon the being it has made, all the faculties and capacities, which that being possesses. Every act of the bank grows out of this law, and is tested by it. To use the language of the constitution, every act of the bank arises out of this law. A naturalized citizen is indeed made a citizen under an act of congress, but the act does not proceed to give, to regulate, or to prescribe his capacities. He becomes a member of the society, possessing all the rights of a native citizen, and standing, in the view of the constitution, on the footing of a native. The constitution does not authorize congress to enlarge or abridge those rights. The simple power of the national legislature is to prescribe a uniform rule of naturalization, and the exercise of this power exhausts it, so far as respects the individual. The constitution then takes him up, and, among other rights, extends to him the capacity of suing in the courts of the United States, precisely under the same circumstances, under which a native might sue. He is distinguishable in nothing from a native citizen, except so far as the constitution makes the distinction. The law makes none. There is, then, no resemblance between the act incorporating the bank, and the general naturalization law. Upon the best consideration, we have been able to bestow on this subject, we are of opinion, that the clause in the act of incorporation, enabling the bank to sue in the courts of the Uuited States, is consistent with the constitution, and to be obeyed in all courts."[1]

§ 1650. Cases may also arise under laws of the United States by implication, as well as by express enactment; so, that due redress may be administered by the judicial power of the United States. It is not unusual for a legislative act to involve consequences, which are not expressed. An officer, for example, is ordered to arrest an individual. It is not necessary, nor is it usual, to say, that he shall not be punished for obeying this order. His security is implied in the order itself. It is no unusual thing for an act of congress to imply, without expressing, this very exemption from state control. The collectors of the revenue, the carriers of the mail, the mint

---

[1] *Osborn v. Bank of the United State,* 9 Wheat. R. 821 to 828. See also *Bank of the United States v. Georgia,* 9 Wheat. R. 904.

establishment, and all those institutions, which are public in their nature, are examples in point. It has never been doubted, that all, who are employed in them, are protected, while in the line of their duty ; and yet this protection is not expressed in any act of congress. It is incidental to, and is implied in, the several acts, by which those institutions are created ; and is secured to the individuals, employed in them, by the judicial power alone ; that is, the judicial power is the instrument employed by the government in administering this security.[1]

§ 1651. It has also been asked, and may again be asked, why the words, "cases in equity," are found in this clause ? What equitable causes can grow out of the constitution, laws, and treaties of the United States ? To this the general answer of the Federalist[2] seems at once clear and satisfactory. "There is hardly a subject of litigation between individuals, which may not involve those ingredients of *fraud, accident, trust,* or *hardship,* which would render the matter an object of equitable, rather than of legal jurisdiction, as the distinction is known and established in several of the states. It is the peculiar province, for instance, of a court of equity, to relieve against what are called hard bargains : these are contracts, in which, though there may have been no direct fraud or deceit, sufficient to invalidate them in a court of law ; yet there may have been some undue, and unconscionable advantage taken of the necessities, or misfortunes of one of the parties, which a

[1] *Osborn* v. *Bank of United States,* 9 Wheat. R. 865, 866 ; Id. 847, 848.

[2] The Federalist, No. 80. See also 1 Tuck. Black. Comm. App. 418, 419 ; 2 Elliot's Debates, 389, 390.

court of equity would not tolerate. In such cases, where foreigners were concerned on either side, it would be impossible for the federal judicatories to do justice, without an equitable, as well as a legal jurisdiction. Agreements to convey lands, claimed under the grants of different states, may afford another example of the necessity of an equitable jurisdiction in the federal courts. This reasoning may not be so palpable in those states, where the formal and technical distinction between LAW and EQUITY is not maintained, as in this state, where it is exemplified by every day's practice."

§ 1652. The next clause, extends the judicial power " to all cases affecting ambassadors, other " public ministers, and consuls." The propriety of this delegation of power to the national judiciary will scarcely be questioned by any persons, who have duly reflected upon the subject. There are various grades of public ministers, from ambassadors (which is the highest grade,) down to common resident ministers, whose rank, and diplomatic precedence, and authority, are well known, and well ascertained in the law and usages of nations.[1] But whatever may be their relative rank and grade, public ministers of every class are the immediate representatives of their sovereigns. As such representatives, they owe no subjection to any laws, but those of their own

---

[1] Three classes are usually distingnished in diplomacy ; 1. Ambassadors, who are the highest order, who are considered as personally representing their sovereigns ; 2. Envoys Extraordinary, and ministers plenipotentiary ; 3. Ministers resident, and ministers chargés d'affaires. Mere common chargés d'affaires, are deemed of still lower rank. Dr. Lieber's Encyclopedia Americana, art. *Ministers, Foreign.* Vattel, B. 4, ch. 6, § 71 to 74.

country, any more than their sovereign ; and their
actions are not generally deemed subject to the control of the private law of that state, wherein they are
appointed to reside. He, that is subject to the coercion of laws, is necessarily dependent on that power,
by whom those laws were made. But public ministers ought, in order to perform their duties to their
own sovereign, to be independent of every power,
except that by which they are sent ; and, of consequence, ought not to be subject to the mere municipal law of that nation, wherein they are to exercise
their functions.[1] The rights, the powers, the duties,

---

[1] 1 Black. Comm. 253; Vattel, B. 4, ch. 7, § 80, 81, 92, 99, 101 ;
1 Kent's Comm. Lect. 2, p. 37, 38, (2d edition, p. 38, 39.) — In the case
of the *Schooner Exchange* v. *M'Faddon*, (7 Cranch, 116, 138,) the Supreme Court state the grounds of the immunity of foreign ministers, in
a very clear manner, leaving the important question, whether that immunity can be forfeited by misconduct, open to future decision. " A
second case," (says Mr. Chief Justice Marshall, in delivering the opinion of the court,) " standing on the same principles with the first, is the
immunity, which all civilized nations allow to foreign ministers. Whatever may be the principle, on which this immunity is established, whether we consider him, as in the place of the sovereign he represents, or
by a political fiction suppose him to be extra-territorial, and, therefore,
in point of law, not within the jurisdiction of the sovereign, at whose
court he resides ; still, the immunity itself is granted by the governing
power of the nation, to which the minister is deputed. This fiction of
ex-territoriality could not be erected, and supported against the will of
the sovereign of the territory. He is supposed to assent to it.
" This consent is not expressed. It is true, that, in some countries,
and in this, among others, a special law is enacted for the case. But
the law obviously proceeds on the idea of prescribing the punishment
of an act previously unlawful, not of granting to a foreign minister a
privilege, which he would not otherwise possess.
" The assent of the sovereign to the very important and extensive
exemptions from territorial jurisdiction, which are admitted to attach to
foreign ministers, is implied from the considerations, that, without such
exemption, every sovereign would hazard his own dignity by employing
a public minister abroad. His minister would owe temporary and local
allegiance to a foreign prince, and would be less competent to the ob-

and the privileges of public ministers are, therefore, to be determined, not by any municipal constitutions, but by the law of nature and nations, which is equally obligatory upon all sovereigns, and all states.[1] What these rights, powers, duties, and privileges are, are inquiries properly belonging to a treatise on the law of nations, and need not be discussed here.[2] But it is obvious, that every question, in which these rights, powers, duties, and privileges are involved, is so intimately connected with the public peace, and policy, and diplomacy of the nation, and touches the dignity and interest of the sovereigns of the ministers concerned so deeply, that it would be unsafe, that they should be submitted to any other, than the highest judicature of the nation.

---

jects of his mission. A sovereign, committing the interests of his nation with a foreign power to the care of a person, whom he has selected for that purpose, cannot intend to subject his minister in any degree to that power; and, therefore, a consent to receive him implies a consent, that he shall possess those privileges, which his principal intended he should retain — privileges which are essential to the dignity of his sovereign, and to the duties he is bound to perform.

"In what cases a minister, by infracting the laws of the country, in which he resides, may subject himself to other punishment, than will be inflicted by his own sovereign, is an inquiry foreign to the present purpose. If his crimes be such, as to render him amenable to the local jurisdiction, it must be, because they forfeit the privileges annexed to his character; and the minister, by violating the conditions, under which he was received, as the representative of a foreign sovereign, has surrendered the immunities granted on those conditions; or, according to the true meaning of the original assent, has ceased to be entitled to them." See also 1 Black. Comm. 254, and Christian's note. (4); Vattel, B. 4, ch. 7, § 92, 99, 101 : Id. ch. 8, § 113, 114, 115, 116; Id. ch. 9, § 117, 119, 120, 121, 122, 123, 124; 1 Kent's Comm. Lect. 2.

1 *Ex parte Cabrera*, 1 Wash. Cir. R. 232.

2 Vattel discusses the subject of the rights, privileges, and immunities of foreign ambassadors very much at large, in B. 4, ch. 7, of his Treatise on the Law of Nations.

§ 1653. It is most fit, that this judicature should, in the first instance, have original jurisdiction of such cases,[1] so that, if it should not be exclusive, it might at least be directly resorted to, when the delays of a procrastinated controversy in inferior tribunals might endanger the repose, or the interests of the government.[2] It is well known, that an arrest of the Russian ambassador in a civil suit in England, in the reign of Queen Anne, was well nigh bringing the two countries into open hostilities; and was atoned for only by measures, which have been deemed, by her own writers, humiliating. On that occasion, an act of parliament was passed, which made it highly penal to arrest any ambassador, or his domestic servants, or to seize or distrain his goods; and this act, elegantly engrossed and illuminated, accompanied by a letter from the queen, was sent by an ambassador extraordinary, to propitiate the offended czar.[3] And a statute to the like effect exists in the criminal code established by the first congress, under the constitution of the United States.[4]

§ 1654. Consuls, indeed, have not in strictness a diplomatic character. They are deemed, as mere commercial agents; and therefore partake of the ordinary character of such agents; and are subject to the municipal laws of the countries, where they re-

---

[1] The Federalist, No. 80. See also 2 Elliot's Debates, 390, 400; The Federalist, No. 80; *Marbury* v. *Madison*, 1 Cranch, R. 137, 174, 175.

[2] 1 Tucker's Black. Comm. App. 361; *Ex parte Cabrera*, 1 Wash. Cirt. R. 232.

[3] 1 Black. Comm. 255, 256; 4 Id. 70.

[4] Act of 1790, ch. 36, § 26, 27; 1 Kent's Comm. Lect. 9, p. 170, 171, (2d edition, p. 182, 183.)

side.[1] Yet, as they are the public agents of the nation, to which they belong, and are often entrusted with the performance of very delicate functions of state, and as they might be greatly embarrassed by being subject to the ordinary jurisdiction of inferior tribunals, state and national, it was thought highly expedient to extend the original jurisdiction of the Supreme Court to them also.[2] The propriety of vesting jurisdiction, in such cases, in some of the national courts seems hardly to have been questioned by the most zealous opponents of the constitution.[3] And in cases *against* ambassadors, and other foreign ministers, and consuls, the jurisdiction has been deemed exclusive.[4]

---

[1] See Vattel, B. 2, ch. 2, § 31; Id. B. 4, ch. 6, § 75; Wicquefort, B. 1, § 5; 1 Kent's Comm. Lect. 2, p. 40, 43, [2d edition, p. 41 to 44;] 2 Brown's Adm. Law, ch. 14, p. 503; *Viveash* v. *Becker*, 3 Maule & Sel. R. 284; Rawle on Const. ch. 21, p. 224 to 226.

[2] The Federalist, No. 80; *Cohens* v. *Virginia*, 6 Wheat. R. 396; 1 Kent's Comm. Lect. 2, p. 44, (2d edition, p. 45;) Rawle on Const. ch. 24, p. 224 to 226.

[3] 2 Elliot's Debates, 383, 384, 418; 3 Id. 281; 1 Tucker's Black. Comm. App. 183. — Under the confederation no power existed in the national government, to punish any person for the violation of the rights of ambassadors, and other foreign ministers, and consuls. Congress, in November, 1781, recommended to the legislatures of the states, to pass laws punishing infractions of the law of Nations, committed by violating safe conducts, or passports granted by congress : by acts of hostility against persons in amity with the United States; by infractions of the immunities of ambassadors; by infractions of treaties, or conventions; and to erect a tribunal, or to vest one, already existing, with power to decide on offences against the law of nations; and to authorize suits for damages by the party injured, and for compensation to the United States, for damages sustained by them, from an injury done to a foreign power by a citizen. This, like other recommendations, was silently disregarded, or openly refused. See Journal of Congress, 23d of Nov. 1781, p. 234. Sergeant on Const. Introduction, p. 16, (2d edition.)

[4] Rawle on Constitution, ch. 21, p. 203; Id. ch. 24, p. 222, 223;

§ 1655. It has been made a question, whether this clause, extending jurisdiction to all cases *affecting* ambassadors, ministers, and consuls, includes cases of indictments found against persons for offering violence to them, contrary to the statute of the United States, punishing such offence. And it has been held, that it does not. Such indictments are mere public prosecutions, to which the United States and the offender only are parties; and which are conducted by the United States, for the purpose of vindicating their own laws, and the law of nations. They are strictly, therefore, cases affecting the United States; and the minister himself, who has been injured by the offence, has no concern in the event of the prosecution, or the costs attending it.[1] Indeed, it seems difficult to conceive, how there can be a case affecting an ambassador, in the sense of the constitution, unless he is a party to the suit on record, or is directly affected, and bound by the judgment.[2]

§ 1656. The language of the constitution is perhaps broad enough to cover cases, where he is not a party; but may yet be affected in interest. This peculiarity in the language has been taken notice of, in a recent case, by the Supreme Court.[3] "If a suit

---

1 Kent's Comm. Lect. 2, p. 44, (2d edition, p. 45); Id. Lect. 15, p. 294, 295, (2d edition, p. 314, 315); *Commonwealth* v. *Kosloff*, 5 Serg. & Rawle, 545; *Hall* v. *Young*, 3 Pick. R. 80; *United States* v. *Ortega*, 11 Wheat. R. 467, and Mr. Wheaton's note, Id. 469 to 475; *Manhardt* v. *Soderstrom*, 1 Binn. R. 138; *United States* v. *Ravara*, 2 Dall. R. 297; *Cohens* v. *Virginia*, 6 Wheat. R. 396, 397; *Osborn* v. *Bank of United States*, 9 Wheat. R. 820, 821; *Chisholm* v. *Georgia*, 2 Dall. R. 431, per Iredell, J.

1 *United States* v. *Ortega*, 11 Wheat. R. 467. See also *Osborn* v. *Bank of United States*, 9 Wheat. R. 854, 855.   2 Ibid.   3 4 Ibid.

be brought against a foreign minister," (said Mr. Chief Justice Marshall, in delivering the opinion of the court) "the Supreme Court alone has original jurisdiction, and this is shown on the record. But, suppose a suit to be brought, which affects the interest of a foreign minister, or by which the person of his secretary, or of his servant, is arrested. The minister does not, by the mere arrest of his secretary, or his servant, become a party to this suit; but the actual defendant pleads to the jurisdiction of the court, and asserts his privilege. If the suit affects a foreign minister, it must be dismissed, not because he is a party to it, but because it affects him. The language of the constitution in the two cases is different. This court can take cognizance of all cases 'affecting' foreign ministers; and, therefore, jurisdiction does not depend on the party named in the record. But this language changes, when the enumeration proceeds to states. Why this change? The answer is obvious. In the case of foreign ministers, it was intended, for reasons, which all comprehend, to give the national courts jurisdiction over all cases, by which they were in any manner affected. In the case of states, whose immediate, or remote interests were mixed up with a multitude of cases, and who might be affected in an almost infinite variety of ways, it was intended to give jurisdiction in those cases only, to which they were actual parties."

§ 1657. The next clause extends the judicial power "to all cases of admiralty and maritime jurisdiction."

§ 1658. The propriety of this delegation of power seems to have been little questioned at the time of adopting the constitution. "The most bigotted idol-

izers of state authority," said the Federalist,[1] "have
not thus far shown a disposition to deny the national
judiciary the cognizance of maritime causes.   These
so generally depend on the law of nations, and so
commonly affect the rights of foreigners, that they
fall within the considerations, which are relative to
the public peace."   The subject is dismissed with an
equally brief notice by Mr. Chief Justice Jay, in the
case of *Chisholm* v. *Georgia*, in the passage already
cited.[2]   It demands, however, a more enlarged examination, which will clearly demonstrate its utility
and importance, as a part of the national power.

§ 1659. It has been remarked by the Federalist, in
another place, that the jurisdiction of the court of admiralty, as well as of other courts, is a source of frequent and intricate discussions, sufficiently denoting
the indeterminate limits, by which it is circumscribed.[3]
This remark is equally true in respect to England and
America; to the high court of admiralty sitting in the
parent country; and to the vice-admiralty courts sitting in the colonies.   At different periods, the jurisdiction has been exercised to a very different extent;
and in the colonial courts it seems to have had boundaries different from those prescribed to it in England.   It has been exercised to a larger extent in
Ireland, than in England; and down to this very day
it has a most comprehensive reach in Scotland.[4]   The
jurisdiction claimed by the courts of admiralty, as
properly belonging to them, extends to all acts and

[1] The Federalist, No. 80.   See also 2 Elliot's Debates, 383, 384, 390,
418, 419.
[2] 2 Dall. R. 475; *ante* Vol. III. § 1633.
[3] The Federalist, No. 37.   See 1 Kent's Comm. Lect. 17.
[4] See *De Lovio* v. *Boit*, 2 Gallison's R. 398; 1 Kent's Comm. Lect. 17,
passim.

torts done upon the high seas, and within the ebb and
flow of the sea, and to all maritime contracts, that is,
to all contracts touching trade, navigation, or business
upon the sea, or the waters of the sea within the ebb
and flow of the tide. Some part of this jurisdiction
has been matter of heated controversy between the
courts of common law, and the high court of admiralty in England, with alternate success and defeat.
But much of it has been gradually yielded to the latter,
in consideration of its public convenience, if not of its
paramount necessity. It is not our design to go into
a consideration of these vexed questions, or to attempt any general outline of the disputed boundaries.
It will be sufficient in this place to present a brief
view of that, which is admitted, and is indisputable.[1]

§ 1660. The admiralty and maritime jurisdiction,
(and the word, "maritime," was doubtless added to
guard against any narrow interpretation of the preceding word, " admiralty,") conferred by the constitution, embraces two great classes of cases ; one dependent upon locality, and the other upon the nature
of the contract. The first respects acts or injuries
done upon the high sea, where all nations claim a

---

[1] Upon this subject the learned reader is referred to Sergeant on
Const. Law, ch. 21, and the authorities there cited ; to Gordon's Digest,
art. 763 to 792 ; to 1 Kent's Comm. Lect. 17, *passim* ; 2 Brown's Adm.
Law, ch. 4, 6, 12. Mr. Sergeant, in his introduction to the second edition of his very valuable work on Constitutional Law, (p. 3, 4, and note,)
seems to suppose, that the admiralty commission of the governor of
New-Hampshire, referred to in *De Lovio v. Boit*, 2 Gallison's R. 470,
471, might be an extension of the ordinary commissions of the colonial
admiralty judges. It is believed, that he is mistaken in this supposition.
In Stokes's History of the Colonies there is a commission similar in its
main clauses ; and Mr. Stokes says, that it was the usual form of the commissions. Stokes's Hist. of Colon. ch. 4, p. 166. See also Mr. Wheaton's Notes to the case of *United States v. Bevans*, 3 Wheat. R. 336,
357, 361, 365.

common right and common jurisdiction; or acts, or
injuries done upon the coast of the sea; or, at farthest,
acts and injuries done within the ebb and flow of the
tide. The second respects contracts, claims, and
services purely maritime, and touching rights and duties appertaining to commerce and navigation. The
former is again divisible into two great branches, one
embracing captures, and questions of prize arising
jure belli; the other embracing acts, torts, and injuries strictly of civil cognizance, independent of belligerent operations.[1]

§ 1661. By the law of nations the cognizance of
all captures, *jure belli,* or, as it is more familiarly
phrased, of all questions of prize, and their incidents,
belongs exclusively to the courts of the country, to
which the captors belong, and from whom they derive
their authority to make the capture. No neutral nation has any right to inquire into, or to decide upon,
the validity of such capture, even though it should
concern property belonging to its own citizens or
subjects, unless its own sovereign or territorial rights
are violated; but the sole and exclusive jurisdiction
belongs to the courts of the capturing belligerent.
And this jurisdiction, by the common consent of nations, is vested exclusively in courts of admiralty, possessing an original, or appellate jurisdiction. The
courts of common law are bound to abstain from any
decision of questions of this sort, whether they arise
directly or indirectly in judgment. The remedy
for illegal acts of capture is by the institution of
proper prize proceedings in the prize courts of the
captors.[2] If justice be there denied, the nation itself

[1] See *Martin v. Hunter,* 1 Wheat. R. 335.

[2] *Le Caux* v. *Eden,* Doug. R. 594; *Lindo* v. *Rodney,* Doug. R. 613,
note; *L'Invincible,* 1 Wheat. R. 238; *The Estrella,* 4 Wheat. R. 298;

becomes responsible to the parties aggrieved; and if every remedy is refused, it then becomes a subject for the consideration of the nation, to which the parties aggrieved belong, which may vindicate their rights, either by a peaceful appeal to negotiation, or a resort to arms.

§ 1662. It is obvious upon the slightest consideration, that cognizance of all questions of prize, made under the authority of the United States, ought to belong exclusively to the national courts. How, otherwise, can the legality of the captures be satisfactorily ascertained, or deliberately vindicated? It seems not only a natural, but a necessary appendage to the power of war, and negotiation with foreign nations. It would otherwise follow, that the peace of the whole nation might be put at hazard at any time by the misconduct of one of its members. It could neither restore upon an illegal capture; nor in many cases afford any adequate redress for the wrong; nor punish the aggressor. It would be powerless and palsied. It could not perform, or compel the performance of the duties required by the law of nations. It would be a sovereign without any solid attribute of sovereignty; and move *in vinculis* only to betray its imbecility. Even under the confederation, the power to decide upon questions of capture and prize was exclusively conferred in the last resort upon the national court of appeals.[1] But like all other powers conferred by that instrument, it was totally disregarded, wherever it interfered with state policy, or with extensive popular interests. We have seen, that the sentences of the

***

Bingham v. *Cabot,* 3 Dall. 19; *La Amistad de Rues,* 5 Wheat. R. 385; 1 Kent's Comm. Lect. 17, p. 334, (2 edition, p. 356.)

[1] Confederation, Art. 9.

national prize court of appeals were treated, as mere
nullities; and were incapable of being enforced, until
after the establishment of the present constitution.[1]
The same reasoning, which conducts us to the conclusion, that the national courts ought to have jurisdiction of this class of admiralty cases, conducts us
equally to the conclusion, that, to be effectual for the
administration of international justice, it ought to be
exclusive. And accordingly it has been constantly
held, that this jurisdiction is exclusive in the courts of
the United States.[2]

§ 1663. The other branch of admiralty jurisdiction,
dependent upon locality, respects civil acts, torts, and
injuries done on the sea, or (in certain cases) on waters of the sea, where the tide ebbs and flows, without
any claim of exercising the rights of war. Such are
cases of assaults, and other personal injuries; cases of
collision, or running of ships against each other; cases
of spoliation and damage, (as they are technically
called,) such as illegal seizures, or depredations upon
property; cases of illegal dispossession, or withholding possession from the owners of ships, commonly
called possessory suits; cases of seizures under municipal authority for supposed breaches of revenue,
or other prohibitory laws; and cases of salvage for
meritorious services performed in saving property,
whether derelict, or wrecked, or captured, or otherwise in imminent hazard from extraordinary perils.[3]

1 See *Penhallow* v. *Doane*, 3 Dall. R. 52; *Jennings* v. *Carson*, 4 Cranch
2; *ante*, Vol. I, §
2 See *Martin* v. *Hunter*, 1 Wheat. R. 345, 337; *United States* v. *Bevans*, 3 Wheat. R. 387; *Houston* v. *Moore*, 5 Wheat. R. 49; *Ogden* v.
Saunders, 12 Wheat. R. 278; 1 Kent's Comm. Lect. 17, p. 330 to 337,
[2 edition, p. 353 to 360.]
3 See *La Vengeance*, 3 Dall. R. 297; *Martin* v. *Hunter*, 1 Wheat. R.
335, 337; *The Sarah*, 8 Wheat. R. 391, 394; *McDonough* v. *Dannery*,

§ 1664. It is obvious, that this class of cases has, or may have, an intimate relation to the rights and duties of foreigners in navigation and maritime commerce. It may materially affect our intercourse with foreign states ; and raise many questions of international law, not merely touching private claims, but national sovereignty, and national reciprocity. Thus, for instance, if a collision should take place at sea between an American and a foreign ship, many important questions of public law might be connected with its just decision ; for it is obvious, that it could not be governed by the mere municipal law of either country. So, if a case of recapture, or other salvage service performed to a foreign ship, should occur, it must be decided by the general principles of maritime law, and the doctrines of national reciprocity. Where a recapture is made of a friendly ship from the hands of its enemy, the general doctrine now established is, to restore it upon salvage, if the foreign country, to which it belongs, adopts a reciprocal rule ; or to condemn it to the recaptors, if the like rule is adopted in the foreign country. And in other cases of salvage the doctrines of international and maritime law come into full activity, rather than those of any mere municipal code.[1] There is, therefore, a peculiar fitness in

---

3 Dall. R. 182 ; *The Blaireau,* 2 Cranch, 249 ; *The Amiable Nancy,* 3 Wheat. R. 546 ; *The General Smith,* 4 Wheat. R. 438 ; *Rose* v. *Himeley,* 4 Cranch, 241 ; *Manro* v. *Almeida,* 10 Wheat. R. 473 ; *The Apollon,* 9 Wheat. R. 362 ; *The Marianna Flora,* 11 Wheat. R. 1, 42 ; *The Fabius,* 2 Rob. R. 245 ; *The Thames,* 5 Rob. R. 345 ; *The St. Juan Baptista,* 5 Rob. R. 33, 40, 41 ; Abbott on Shipping, P. 2, ch. 4, note to American edition, 1829, p. 132, 133 ; *The Dundee,* 1 Hagg. Adm. R. 109 ; *The Ruckers,* 4 Rob. R. 73 ; 1 Kent's Comm. Lect. 17, p. 342 to 352, [2 edition, p. 365 to 377 ;] *The Agincourt,* 1 Hagg. R. 271.

[1] *The Santa Cruz,* 1 Rob. R. 50 ; *The San Francisco,* 1 Edw. R. 179 ; *The Adeline,* 9 Cranch, 244 ; 2 Wheat. R. App. 40 to 45 ; Abbott on Shipping, (Amer. edit. 1829,) P. 3, ch. 10, p. 397, 417, 422.

appropriating this class of cases to the national tribunals ; since they will be more likely to be there decided upon large and comprehensive principles, and
to receive a more uniform adjudication ; and thus to
become more satisfactory to foreigners.

§ 1665. The remaining class respects contracts,
claims, and services purely maritime. Among these
are the claims of material-men and others for repairs
and outfits of ships belonging to foreign nations, or to
other states ; [1] bottomry bonds for monies lent to ships
in foreign ports to relieve their distresses, and enable
them to complete their voyages ; [2] surveys of vessels
damaged by perils of the seas ; [3] pilotage on the high
seas ; [4] and suits for mariners' wages.[5] These, indeed, often arise in the course of the commerce and
navigation of the United States ; and seem emphatically to belong, as incidents, to the power to regulate
commerce. But they may also affect the commerce
and navigation of foreign nations. Repairs may be
done, and supplies furnished to foreign ships ; money
may be lent on foreign bottoms ; pilotage and mariners' wages may become due in voyages in foreign
employment ; and in such cases the general maritime
law enables the courts of admiralty to administer a
wholesome and prompt justice.[6] Indeed, in many of
these cases, as the courts of admiralty entertain suits

---

1 *The St. Jago de Cuba*, 9 Wheat. R. 409, 416 ; *The Aurora*, 1 Wheat.
R. 105.
  2 *The Aurora*, 1 Wheat. R. 96.
  3 *Janney* v. *Columbia Insurance Company*, 10 Wheat. R. 412, 415, 418.
  4 *The Anne*, 1 Mason's R. 508.
  5 *The Thomas Jefferson*, 10 Wheat. R. 428.
  6 *The Two Friends*, 1 Rob. R. 271 ; *The Helena*, 4 Rob. R. 3 ; *The
Jacob*, 4 Rob. R. 245 ; *The Gratitudine*, 3 Rob. R. 240 ; *The Favourite*,
2 Rob. R. 232 ; Abbott on Shipping, P. 2, ch. 3, p. 115, Story's note ;
Id. P. 4, ch. 4 ; *The Aurora*, 1 Wheat. R. 96.

in rem, as well as *in personam*, they are often the only courts, in which an effectual redress can be afforded, especially when it is desirable to enforce a specific maritime lien.[1]

§ 1666. So that we see, that the admiralty jurisdiction naturally connects itself, on the one hand, with our diplomatic relations and duties to foreign nations, and their subjects; and, on the other hand, with the great interests of navigation and commerce, foreign and domestic.[2] There is, then, a peculiar wisdom in giving to the national government a jurisdiction of this sort, which cannot be wielded, except for the general good; and which multiplies the securities for the public peace abroad, and gives to commerce and navigation the most encouraging support at home. It may be added, that, in many of the cases included in these latter classes, the same reasons do not exist, as in cases of prize, for an exclusive jurisdiction; and, therefore, whenever the common law is competent to give a remedy in the state courts, they may retain their accustomed concurrent jurisdiction in the administration of it.[3]

---

[1] *Manro* v. *Almeida*, 10 Wheat. R. 473; *The Merino*, 9 Wheat. R. 391, 416, 417; *The General Smith*, 4 Wheat. R. 438; *The Thomas Jefferson*, 10 Wheat. R. 428; *Sheppard* v. *Taylor*, 5 Peters's Sup. R. 675; 1 Kent's Comm. Lect. 17, p. 352 to 354, (2 edition, p. 378 to 381 ;) 2 Brown's Adm. Law, ch. 71.

[2] "The admiralty jurisdiction," said the Supreme Court in a celebrated case, "embraces all questions of prize and salvage, in the correct adjudication of which foreign nations are deeply interested. It embraces also maritime torts, contracts, and offences, in which the principles of the law and comity of nations often form an essential inquiry. All these cases, then, enter into the national policy, affect the national rights, and may compromit the national sovereignty." *Martin* v. *Hunter*, 1 Wheat. R. 335.

[3] Mr. Chancellor Kent and Mr. Rawle seem to think,* that the admiralty jurisdiction, given by the constitution, is in all cases necessarily

* 1 Kent's Comm. Lect. 17, p. 351, (2 edit. p. 377 ;) Rawle on the Const. ch. 21, p. 202. See also 1 Tucker's Black. Comm. App 181, 182 ; 2 Elliot's Deb. 390 ; 10 Wheat. R. 418.

§ 1667. We have been thus far considering the admiralty and maritime jurisdiction in civil cases only. But it also embraces all public offences, committed on the high seas, and in creeks, havens, basins, and bays within the ebb and flow of the tide, at least in such as are out of the body of any county of a state. In these places the jurisdiction of the courts of admiralty over offences is exclusive; for that of the courts of common law is limited to such offences, as are committed within the body of some county. And on the sea coast, there is an alternate, or divided

exclusive. But it is believed, that this opinion is founded in a mistake. It is exclusive in all matters of prize, for the reason, that at the common law this jurisdiction is vested in the courts of admiralty, to the exclusion of the courts of common law. But in cases, where the jurisdiction of the courts of common law and the admiralty are concurrent, (as in cases of possessory suits, mariners' wages, and marine torts,) there is nothing in the constitution, necessarily leading to the conclusion, that the jurisdiction was intended to be exclusive; and there is as little ground, upon general reasoning, to contend for it. The reasonable interpretation of the constitution would seem to be, that it conferred on the national judiciary the admiralty and maritime jurisdiction, exactly according to the nature and extent and modifications, in which it existed in the jurisprudence of the common law. Where the jurisdiction was exclusive, it remained so; where it was concurrent, it remained so. Hence, the states could have no right to create courts of admiralty, as such, or to confer on their own courts, the cognizance of such cases, as were exclusively cognizable in admiralty courts. But the states might well retain and exercise the jurisdiction in cases, of which the cognizance was previously concurrent in the courts of common law. This latter class of cases can be no more deemed cases of admiralty and maritime jurisdiction, than cases of common law jurisdiction. The judiciary act, of 1789, ch. 20, § 9, has manifestly proceeded upon this supposition; for, while it has conferred on the District Courts, "exclusive original cognizance of all civil causes of admiralty and maritime jurisdiction," it has, at the same time, saved "to the suitors, in all cases, the right of a common law remedy, where the common law is competent to give it." We shall, hereafter, have occasion to consider more at large, in what cases there is a concurrent jurisdiction in the national and state courts.

jurisdiction of the courts of common law, and admiralty, in places between high and low water mark; the former having jurisdiction when, and as far as the tide is out, and the latter when, and as far as the tide is in, *usque ad filum aquæ*, or to high water mark.[1] This criminal jurisdiction of the admiralty is therefore exclusively vested in the national government; and may be exercised over such crimes and offences, as congress may, from time to time, delegate to the cognisance of the national courts.[2] The propriety of vesting this criminal jurisdiction in the national government depends upon the same reasoning, and is established by the same general considerations, as have been already suggested in regard to civil cases. It is essentially connected with the due regulation, and protection of our commerce and navigation on the high seas, and with our rights and duties in regard to foreign nations, and their subjects, in the exercise of common sovereignty on the ocean. The states, as such, are not known in our intercourse with foreign nations, and not recognised as common sovereigns on the ocean. And if they were permitted to exercise criminal or civil jurisdiction thereon, there would be endless embarrassments, arising from the

---

[1] Constable's case, 5 Co. R. 106; 2 Instit. 51; 1 Black. Comm. 110; Hale in Harg. Law Tracts, pt. 1, ch. 3; Id. ch. 4, p. 10, 12, pt. 2, ch. 7, p. 88; 2 Hale, P. C. p. 13, &c.; 64 Com. Dig. *Navigation*, A. & B.; Id. *Admiralty*, E. J.; *United States v. Grush*, 5 Mason's R. 290; 1 Kent's Comm. Lect. 17, p. 337 to 342, [2d edition, p. 360 to 365;] *United States v. Bevans*, 3 Wheat. R. 336; Id. 357; Mr. Wheaton's notes, 357, 361, 365, 366, 368, 369; Beeve's case, 2 Leach. Cir. Cas. 1093, (4th edition;) Ryan & Russ. Cas. 243; 4 Tucker's Black. Comm. App. 7.

[2] *United States v. Bevans*, 3 Wheat. R. 356, 386 to 389; 4 Elliot's Deb. 290, 291; 1 Kent's Comm. Lect. 16, p. 319, 320, (2d edition, p. 339, 340;) Lect. 17, p. 337, (2d edition, p. 360.)

conflict of their laws, and the most serious dangers of perpetual controversies with foreign nations. In short, the peace of the Union would be constantly put at hazard by acts, over which it had no control; and by assertions of right, which it might wholly disclaim.[1]

§ 1668. The next clause extends the judicial power "to controversies, to which the United States shall be a party."[2] It scarcely seems possible to raise a rea-

---

[1] It has been made a question, whether the admiralty jurisdiction can be exercised within the territories of the United States by the judges of the territorial courts, appointed under the territorial governments, as they are appointed for a limited term only, and not during good behaviour. The decision has been in favour of the jurisdiction, upon the ground, (already suggested,) that congress have the exclusive power to regulate such territories, as they may choose; and they may confer on the territorial government such legislative powers, as they may choose. The courts appointed in such territories are not constitutional courts, in which the judicial powers conferred by constitution on the general government can be deposited. They are merely legislative courts; and the jurisdiction, with which they are invested, is not a part of the judicial power, defined in the third article of the constitution. The *American Insurance Company* v. *Canter*, 1 Peters's Sup. R. 511.

[2] Mr. Tucker, distinguishes between the word "cases," used in the preceding clauses, and the word "controversies," here used. The former he deems to include all suits, criminal as well as civil. The latter, as including such only, as are of a civil nature. As here applied, controversies "seem" (says he) "particularly appropriated to such disputes, as might arise between the United States, and any one or more states, respecting territorial or fiscal matters; or between the United States and their debtors, contractors, and agents. This construction is confirmed by the application of the word in the ensuing clauses, where it evidently refers to disputes of a civil nature only, such, for example, as may arise between two or more states, or between citizens of different states, or between a state and the citizens of another state, &c." 1 Tucker's Black. Comm. App. 420, 421. Mr. Justice Iredell, in his opinion in *Chisholm* v. *Georgia*, 2 Dall. R. 419, 431, 432, gives the same construction to the word "controversies," confining it to such as are of a civil nature.

In the original draft of the constitution, this clause, "controversies to which the United States shall be a party," was omitted. It was add-

sonable doubt, as to the propriety of giving to the
national courts jurisdiction of cases, in which the
United States are a party.[1] It would be a perfect
novelty in the history of national jurisprudence, as
well as of public law, that a sovereign had no authority to sue in his own courts. Unless this power
were given to the United States, the enforcement of
all their rights, powers, contracts, and privileges in
their sovereign capacity, would be at the mercy of
the states. They must be enforced, if at all, in the
state tribunals. And there would not only not be any
compulsory power over those courts to perform such
functions ; but there would not be any means of producing uniformity in their decisions. A sovereign without
the means of enforcing civil rights, or compelling the performance, either civilly or criminally, of
public duties on the part of the citizens, would be a
most extraordinary anomaly. It would prostrate the
Union at the feet of the states. It would compel the
national government to become a supplicant for justice
before the judicature of those, who were by other parts
of the constitution placed in subordination to it.[2]

§ 1669. It is observable, that the language used
does not confer upon any court cognizance of all controversies, to which the United States shall be a party,
so as to justify a suit to be brought against the United States without the consent of congress. And

ed afterwards without any apparent objection. Journal of Convention,
226, 297, 298.

[1] The Federalist, No. 80; 3 Elliot's Debates, 280, 281. See also
2 Elliot's Deb. 380, 383, 384, 389, 390, 400, 404.

[2] Mr. Sergeant, in his Introduction to his work on Constitutional Law,
has abundantly shown the mischief of such a want of power under the
confederation. See Serg. Const. Law, Introd. p. 15 to 18.

the language was doubtless thus guardedly introduced, for the purpose of avoiding any such conclusion. It is a known maxim, justified by the general sense and practice of mankind, and recognized in the law of nations, that it is inherent in the nature of sovereignty not to be amesnable to the suit of any private person, without its own consent.[1] This exemption is an attribute of sovereignty, belonging to every state in the Union; and was designedly retained by the national government.[2] The inconvenience of subjecting the government to perpetual suits, as a matter of right, at the will of any citizen, for any real or supposed claim or grievance, was deemed far greater, than any positive injury, that could be sustained by any citizen by the delay or refusal of justice. Indeed, it was presumed, that it never would be the interest or inclination of a wise government to withhold justice from any citizen. And the difficulties of guarding itself against fraudulent claims, and embarassing and stale controversies, were believed far to outweigh any mere theoretical advantages, to be derived from any attempt to provide a system for the administration of universal justice.

§ 1670. It may be asked, then, whether the citizens of the United States are wholly destitute of remedy, in case the national government should invade their rights, either by private injustice and injuries, or by public oppression? To this it may be answered, that in a general sense, there is a remedy in both cases. In

---

[1] The Federalist, No. 81. See *Chisholm* v. *Georgia*, 2 Dall. R. 419, 478, S. C.; 2 Peters's Cond. R. 635, 674; 1 Black. Comm. 241 to 243; *Cohens* v. *Virginia*, 6 Wheat. R. 380; Id. 411, 412.

[2] Mr. Locke strenuously contends for this exemption of the sovereign from judicial amesnability; and in this, he does but follow out the doctrines of Puffendorf, and other writers on the law of nations. See Locke on Government, Pt. 2, § 205; Puffendorf's Law of Nature and Nations, B. 8, ch. 10; Vattel, B. 1, ch. 4, § 49, 50.

regard to public oppressions, the whole structure of the government is so organized, as to afford the means of redress, by enabling the people to remove public functionaries, who abuse their trust, and to substitute others more faithful, and more honest, in their stead. If the oppression be in the exercise of powers clearly constitutional, and the people refuse to interfere in this manner, then indeed, the party must submit to the wrong, as beyond the reach of all human power; for how can the people themselves, in their collective capacity, be compelled to do justice, and to vindicate the rights of those, who are subjected to their sovereign control?[1]   If the oppression be in the exercise of unconstitutional powers, then the functionaries, who wield them, are amesnable for their injurious acts to the judicial tribunals of the country, at the suit of the oppressed.

§ 1671. As to private injustice and injuries, they may regard either the rights of property, or the rights of contract ; for the national government is *per se* incapable of any merely personal wrong, such as an assault and battery, or other personal violence. In regard to property, the remedy for injuries lies against the immediate perpetrators, who may be sued, and cannot shelter themselves under any imagined immunity of the government from due responsibility.[2]   If, therefore, any agent of the government shall unjustly invade the property of a citizen under colour of a public authority, he must, like every other violator of the laws, re-

---

[1] See on this subject, 1 Black. Comm. 243 to 245.

[2] See *Hoyt* v. *Gelston*, 3 Wheat. R. 246; *Osborn* v. *Bank of United States*, 9 Wheat. R. 738; *Marbury* v. *Madison*, 1 Cranch. 137, 164, 165; 3 Black. Comm. 255.

spond in damages. Cases, indeed, may occur, in which he may not always have an adequate redress, without some legislation by congress. As for example, in places ceded to the United States, and over which they have an exclusive jurisdiction, if his real estate is taken without, or against lawful authority. Here he must rely on the justice of congress, or of the executive department. The greatest difficulty arises in regard to the contracts of the national government; for as they cannot be sued without their own consent, and as their agents are not responsible upon any such contracts, when lawfully made, the only redress, which can be obtained, must be by the instrumentality of congress, either in providing (as they may) for suits in the common courts of justice to establish such claims by a general law, or by a special act for the relief of the particular party. In each case, however, the redress depends solely upon the legislative department, and cannot be administered, except through its favour. The remedy is by an appeal to the justice of the nation in that forum, and not in any court of justice, as matter of right.

§ 1672. It has been sometimes thought, that this is a serious defect in the organization of the judicial department of the national government. It is not, however, an objection to the constitution itself; but it lies, if at all, against congress, for not having provided, (as it is clearly within their constitutional authority to do,) an adequate remedy for all private grievances of this sort, in the courts of the United States. In this respect, there is a marked contrast between the actual right and practice of redress in the national government, as well as in most of the state governments, and the right and practice maintained under the British constitution. In England, if any person has, in point of

property, a just demand upon the king, he may petition him in his court of chancery (by what is called a
petition of right) where the chancellor will administer
right, theoretically as a matter of grace, and not upon
compulsion ;[1] but in fact, as a matter of constitutional
duty. No such judicial proceeding is recognised, as
existing in any state of this Union, as matter of constitutional right, to enforce any claim, or debt against a
state. In the few cases, in which it exists, it is matter
of legislative enactment.[2] Congress have never yet
acted upon the subject, so as to give judicial redress
for any non-fulfilment of contracts by the national government. Cases of the most cruel hardship, and intolerable delay have already occurred, in which meritorious creditors have been reduced to grievous suffering, and sometimes to absolute ruin, by the tardiness of
a justice, which has been yielded only after the humble
supplications of many years before the legislature.
One can scarcely refrain from uniting in the suggestion
of a learned commentator, that in this regard the constitutions, both of the national and state governments,
stand in need of some reform, to quicken the legislative action in the administration of justice ; and, that

---

[1] 1 Black. Comm. 243 ; Comyn's Dig. *Prerogative,* D. 78 to D. 85 ;
The Banker's case, 1 Freeman R. 331 ; S. C. 5 Mod. 29 ; 11 Harg.
State Trials, 137 ; Skinner's R. 601 ; 2 Dall. R. 437 to 445 ; S. C.
2 Peters's Cond. R. 642 to 646. But see *Macbeath* v. *Haldimand,* 1 T.
R. 172, 176, 177.

[2] A suit against the state has been allowed in Virginia* and Maryland, and some other states by statute. But it is intimated, that, even
when judgment has passed in favour of the claimant, he has sometimes
received no substantial benefit from the judgment, from the omission of
the legislature to provide suitable funds, or to make suitable appropriations to discharge the debt. 1 Tucker's Black. Comm. App. 352.

* 1 Tucker's Black. Comm. 243, note (5) ; *Chisholm* v. *Georgia,* 2 Dall. R. 419, 434, 435.

some mode ought to be provided, by which a pecuniary right against a state, or against the United States,
might be ascertained, and established by the judicial
sentence of some court; and when so ascertained and
established, the payment might be enforced from the
national treasury by an absolute appropriation.[1] Surely,
it can afford no pleasant source of reflection to an
American citizen, proud of his rights and privileges,
that in a monarchy the judiciary is clothed with ample
powers to give redress to the humblest subject in a
matter of private contract, or property against the crown;
and, that in a republic there is an utter denial of justice,
in such cases, to any citizen through the instrumentality
of any judicial process. He may complain; but he cannot compel a hearing. The republic enjoys a despotic
sovereignty to act, or refuse, as it may please; and is
placed beyond the reach of law. The monarch bows
to the law, and is compelled to yield his prerogative at
the footstool of justice.[2]

---

[1] 1 Tuck. Black. Comm. App. 352.

[2] Mr. Chief Justice Jay, in his opinion in the great case of *Chisholm's
Executors* v. *Georgia*, 3 Dall. R. 414, 474, (S. C. 2 Peters's Cond R. 635,
674,) takes a distinction between the case of the suability of a state, and
the suability of the United States, by a citizen under the constitution, affirming the former, and denying the latter. His reason is thus stated. " In
all cases of actions against states, or individual citizens, the national courts
are supported in all their legal and constitutional proceedings and judgments, by the arm of the executive powers of the United States. But
in cases of actions against the United States, there is no power, which
the courts can call to their aid. From this distinction, important conclusions are deducible ; and they place the case of a state, and the case of
the United States, in a very different view." In the case of *Macbeath*
v. *Haldimand*, (1 Term. Reports, 172.) Lord Mansfield seemed to intimate great doubts, whether a petition of right would lie in England in
any case, except of a private debt due from the crown ; and not for
debts contracted under the authority of parliament. Before the revolution, he said, " all the public supplies were given to the king, who, in

§ 1673. The next clause extends the judicial power "to controversies between two or more states; be-"tween a state and the citizens of another state; be-"tween citizens of different states, claiming lands un-"der grants of different states; and between a state "or the citizens thereof, and foreign states, citizens, or "subjects." Of these, we will speak in their order. And, first, "controversies between two or more states."[1] This power seems to be essential to the preservation of the peace of the Union. "History" (says the Federalist,[2]) gives us a horrid picture of the dissensions and private wars, which distracted and desolated Germany, prior to the institution of the imperial chamber by Maximilian, towards the close of the fifteenth century; and informs us at the same time of the vast influence of that institution, in appeasing the disorders, and establishing the tranquillity of the empire. This was a court invested with authority to decide finally all differences among the members of the Germanic body."[3]   But we need not go for illustrations to the history of other countries.   Our own has presented, in past times, abundant proofs of the irritating effects

---

his individual capacity contracted for all expenses. He alone had the disposition of the public money. But since that time, the supplies had been appropriated by parliament to particular purposes; *and now, whoever advances money for the public service, trusts to the faith of parliament.*" Id. 176. But see Buller J.'s opinion, in the same case. See also Mr. Justice Iredell's opinion in *Chisholm v. Georgia*, 2 Dall. R. 437 to 445.

[1] In the first draft of the constitution, the words were to controversies "between two or more states, *except such as shall regard territory or jurisdiction.*" The exception was subsequently abandoned. Journal of Convention, p. 226.

[2] The Federalist, No. 80.

[3] See also 1 Kent's Comm. Lect. 14, p. 277, 278, (2d edition, p. 295, 296;) 1 Robertson's Charles V. p. 183, 395, 397.

resulting from territorial disputes, and interfering claims of boundary between the states. And there are yet controversies of this sort, which have brought on a border warfare, at once dangerous to public repose, and incompatible with the public interests.[1]

§ 1674. Under the confederation, authority was given to the national government, to hear and determine, (in the manner pointed out in the article,) in the last resort, on appeal, all disputes and differences between two or more states concerning boundary, jurisdiction, or any other cause whatsoever.[2] Before the adoption of this instrument, as well as afterwards, very irritating and vexatious controveries existed between several of the states, in respect to soil, jurisdiction, and boundary; and threatened the most serious public mischiefs.[3] Some of these controversies were heard and determined by the court of commissioners, appointed by congress. But, notwithstanding these adjudications, the conflict was maintained in some cases, until after the establishment of the present constitution.[4]

§ 1675. Before the revolution, controversies between the colonies, concerning the extent of their rights of soil, territory, jurisdiction, and boundary, under their respective charters, were heard and determined before

---

[1] See Sergeant on Const. Introduction, p. 11 to 16; 2 Elliot's Deb. 418.

[2] Confederation, art. 9.

[3] 2 Elliot's Deb. 418; Sergeant on Const. Introduction, p. 11, 12, 13, 15, 16; 5 Journ. of Congress, 456; 7 Journ. of Congress, 364; 8 Journ. of Congress, 83; 9 Journ. of Congress, 64; 12 Journ. of Congress, 10, 52, 219, 220, 230.

[4] *New York v. Connecticut*, 4 Dall. R. 3; *Fowler v. Lindsey*, 3 Dall. R. 411; 3 Elliot's Deb. 281; 2 Elliot's Deb. 418.

the king in council, who exercised original jurisdiction therein, upon the principles of feudal sovereignty.[1] This jurisdiction was often practically asserted, as in the case of the dispute between Massachusetts and New Hampshire, decided by the privy council, in 1679;[2] and in the case of the dispute between New Hampshire and New York, in 1764.[3] Lord Hardwicke recognised this appellate jurisdiction in the most deliberate manner, in the great case of *Penn* v. *Lord Baltimore*.[4] The same necessity, which gave rise to it in our colonial state, must continue to operate through all future time. Some tribunal, exercising such authority, is essential to prevent an appeal to the sword, and a dissolution of the government. That it ought to be established under the national, rather than under the state, government; or, to speak more properly, that it can be safely established under the former only, would seem to be a position self-evident, and requiring no reasoning to support it.[5] It may justly be presumed, that under the national government in all controversies of this sort, the decision will be impartially made according to the principles of justice; and all the usual and most effectual precautions are taken to secure this impartiality, by confiding it to the highest judicial tribunal.[6]

§ 1676. Next; " controversies between a state and " the citizens of another state." " There are other

---

[1] 1 Black. Comm. 231.

[2] Ante, Vol. i, § 80; 1 Chalm. Annals, 489, 490; 1 Hutch. Hist. 319.

[3] Sergeant on Const. in Introduction, p. 5, 6; 3 Belknap's Hist. of New Hampshire, 296, App. 10.

[4] 1 Vesey's R. 444.

[5] The Federalist, No. 39. See also the remarks of Mr. Chief Justice Jay, ante, Vol. i, § 488, note; 2 Elliot's Debates, 418.

[6] The Federalist, No. 39, 80.

sources," says the Federalist,[1] "besides interfering claims of boundary, from which bickerings and animosities may spring up among the members of the Union. To some of these we have been witnesses in the course of our past experience. It will be readily conjectured, that I allude to the fraudulent laws, which have been passed in too many of the states. And though the proposed constitution establishes particular guards against the repetition of those instances, which have hitherto made their appearance ; yet it is warrantable to apprehend, that the spirit, which produced them, will assume new shapes, that could not be foreseen, nor specifically provided against. Whatever practices may have a tendency to distract the harmony of the states are proper objects of federal superintendence and control. It may be esteemed the basis of the Union, that 'the citizens of each state shall be entitled to all the privileges and immunities of citizens of the several states.' And if it be a just principle, that every government ought to possess the means of executing its own provisions by its own authority, it will follow, that, in order to the inviolable maintenance of that equality of privileges and immunities, to which the citizens of the Union will be entitled, the national judiciary ought to preside in all cases, in which one state, or its citizens, are opposed to another state, or its citizens. To secure the full effect of so fundamental a provision against all evasion and subterfuge, it is necessary, that its construction should be committed to that tribunal, which, having no local attachments, will be likely to be impartial between the different states and their citizens, and which, owing its official existence to the Union,

---

[1] The Federalist, No. 80.

will never be likely to feel any bias inauspicious to the principles, on which it is founded." It is added, " The reasonableness of the agency of the national courts in cases, in which the state tribunals cannot be supposed to be impartial, speaks for it. No man ought certainly to be a judge in his own cause, or in any cause, in respect to which he has the least interest or bias. This principle has no inconsiderable weight in designating the federal courts, as the proper tribunals for the determination of controversies between different states and their citizens." [1]

§ 1677. And here a most important question of a constitutional nature was formerly litigated; and that is, whether the jurisdiction given by the constitution in cases, in which a state is a party, extended to suits brought *against* a state, as well as *by* it, or was exclusively confined to the latter. It is obvious, that, if a suit could be brought by any citizen of one state against another state upon any contract, or matter of property, the state would be constantly subjected to judicial action, to enforce private rights against it in its sovereign capacity. Accordingly at a very early period numerous suits were brought against states by their creditors to enforce the payment of debts, or other claims. The question was made, and most elaborately considered in the celebrated case of *Chisholm v. Georgia;* [2] and the majority of the Supreme Court held, that the judicial power under the constitution applied equally to suits brought *by*, and *against* a state. The learned judges, on that occa-

---

[1] See also the remarks of Mr. Chief Justice Jay, in *Chisholm* v. *Georgia,* 2 Dall. R. 474, cited in the note, ante Vol. i. § 488.

[2] 2 Dall. R. 419; S. C, 2 Peters's Cond. R. 635. See also 1 Kent's Comm. Lect. 14, p. 278, (2d edit. p. 296, 297;) *Cohens* v. *Virginia* 6 Wheat. R. 381.

sion, delivered *seriatim* opinions, containing the grounds of their respective opinions. It is not my intention to go over these grounds, though they are stated with great ability and legal learning, and exhibit a very thorough mastery of the whole subject.[1] The decision created general alarm among the states; and an amendment was proposed, and ratified by the states,[2] by which the power was entirely taken away, so far as it regards suits brought *against* a state. It is in the following words: "The judicial power of the "United States shall not be construed to extend to "any suit in law, or equity, commenced or prosecuted "*against* one of the United States *by* citizens of "another state, or by citizens, or subjects of any "foreign state." This amendment was construed to include suits then pending, as well as suits to be commenced thereafter; and accordingly all the suits then pending were dismissed, without any further adjudication.[3]

---

1 Although the controversy is now ended, the opinions deserve a most attentive perusal, from their very able exposition of many constitutional principles. It is remarkable, that the Federalist (No. 81,) seems to have taken the opposite ground from the majority of the judges, holding, that the states were not suable, but might themselves sue under this clause of the constitution.* I confess it seems to me difficult to reconcile this position with the reasoning on the same subject in the preceding number, (80,) a part of which is quoted in the text, (§ 1676.) Mr. Justice Iredell, who dissented from the other judges of the Supreme Court, in *Chisholm* v. *Georgia*, put his opinion mainly on the ground, that it was a suit for a debt, for which no action lay, at least compulsively, at the common law against the crown, but at most, only a petition of right; and in America, whoever contracts with a state trusts to the good faith of the state.

2 In 1793; 3 Dall. R. 378.

3 *Hollingsworth* v. *Virginia*, 3 Dall. R. 378. — The history and reasons of this amendment are succinctly stated by Mr. Chief Justice Marshall, in *Cohens* v. *Virginia*, 6 Wheat. R. 406.

* See also 2 Elliot's Deb. 390, 391, 401, 405.

§ 1678. Since this amendment has been made, a question of equal importance has arisen ; and that is, whether the amendment applies to original suits only brought against a state, leaving the appellate jurisdiction of the Supreme Court in its full vigour over all constitutional questions, arising in the progress of any suit brought by a state in any state court against any private citizen or alien. But this question will more properly come under review, when we are considering the nature and extent of the appellate jurisdiction of the Supreme Court. At present, it is only necessary to state, that it has been solemnly adjudged, that the amendment applies only to original suits against a state; and does not touch the appellate jurisdiction of the Supreme Court to re-examine, on an appeal or writ of error, a judgment or decree rendered in any state court, in a suit brought originally by a state against any private person.[1]

§ 1679. Another inquiry suggested by the original clause, as well as by the amendment, is, when a state is properly to be deemed a party to a suit, so as to avail itself of, or to exempt itself from, the operation of the jurisdiction conferred by the constitution. To such an inquiry, the proper answer is, that a state, in the sense of the constitution, is a party only, when it is on the record as such ; and it sues, or is sued in its political capacity. It is not sufficient, that it may have an interest in a suit between other persons, or that its rights, powers, privileges, or duties, come therein incidentally in question. It must be in terms a plaintiff or defendant, so that the judgment, or decree may be binding upon it, as it is in common suits binding upon parties and privies. The point arose in

---

[1] *Cohens* v. *Virginia*, 6 Wheat. R. 264.

an early state of the government, in a suit between private persons, where one party asserted the land in controversy to be in Connecticut and the other in New York; and the court held, that neither state could be considered as a party.[1] It has been again discussed in some late cases; and the doctrine now firmly established is, that a state is not a party in the sense of the constitution, unless it appears on the record, as such, either as plaintiff or defendant. It is not sufficient, that it may have an interest in the cause, or that the parties before the court are sued for acts done, as agents of the state.[2] In short, the very immunity of a state from

---

[1] *Fowler* v. *Lindsey,* 3 Dall. R. 411; S. C. 1 Peters's Cond. R. 190, 191; *State of New York* v. *State of Connecticut,* 4 Dall. R. 1, 3 to 6; *United States* v. *Peters,* 5 Cranch's R. 115, 139; 1 Kent's Comm. Lect. 15, p. 302, (2d edit. p. 323.)

[2] The reasoning of Mr. Chief Justice Marshall in *Osborn* v. *Bank of United States,* (9 Wheat. R. 846, &c.) on this point is very full and satisfactory, and deserves to be cited at large. It is only necessary to premise, that the suit was a bill in equity brought by the Bank of the United States against Osborn and others, as state officers, for an injunction and other relief, they having levied a tax of one hundred thousand dollars on certain property of the bank, under a state law of the state of Ohio. "We proceed now," said the Chief Justice, "to the 6th point made by the appellants, which is, that if any case is made in the bill, proper for the interference of a court of chancery, it is against the state of Ohio, in which case the circuit court could not exercise jurisdiction.

"The bill is brought, it is said, for the purpose of protecting the bank in the exercise of a franchise, granted by a law of the United States, which franchise the state of Ohio asserts a right to invade, and is about to invade. It prays the aid of the court to restrain the officers of the state from executing the law. It is, then, a controversy between the bank and the state of Ohio. The interest of the state is direct and immediate, not consequential. The process of the court, though not directed against the state by name, acts directly upon it, by restraining its officers. The process, therefore, is substantially, though not in form, against the state, and the court ought not to proceed without making the state a party. If this cannot be done, the court cannot take jurisdiction of the cause.

"The full pressure of this argument is felt, and the difficulties it presents are acknowledged. The direct interest of the state in the suit, as

being made a party, constitutes, or may constitute, a
solid ground, why the suit should be maintained
against other parties, who act as its agents, or claim
under its title ; though otherwise, as the principal, it
might be fit, that the state should be made a party
upon the common principles of a court of equity.[1]

---

brought, is admitted ; and, had it been in the power of the bank to make
it a party, perhaps no decree ought to have been pronounced in the cause,
until the state was before the court.   But this was not in the power of
the bank.   The eleventh amendment of the constitution has exempted a
state from the suits of citizens of other states, or aliens ; and the very
difficult question is to be decided, whether, in such a case, the court may
act upon the agents employed by the state, and on the property in their
hands.

    " Before we try this question by the constitution, it may not be time
misapplied, if we pause for a moment, and reflect on the relative situation of the Union with its members, should the objection prevail.

    " A denial of jurisdiction forbids all inquiry into the nature of the case.
It applies to cases perfectly clear in themselves ; to cases, where the government is in the exercise of its best established and most essential
powers, as well as to those, which may be deemed questionable.   It asserts, that the agents of a state, alleging the authority of a law void in
itself, because repugnant to the constitution, may arrest the execution of
any law of the United States.   It maintains, that, if a state shall impose
a fine or penalty on any person employed in the execution of any law of
the United States, it may levy that fine or penalty by a ministerial officer, without the sanction even of its own courts ; and that the individual,
though he perceives the approaching danger, can obtain no protection
from the judicial department of the government.   The carrier of the
mail, the collector of the revenue, the marshal of a district, the recruit-
ing officer, may all be inhibited, under ruinous penalties, from the performance of their respective duties ; the warrant of a ministerial officer
may authorize the collection of these penalties ; and the person thus
obstructed in the performance of his duty, may indeed resort to his action for damages, after the infliction of the injury, but cannot avail himself of the preventive justice of the nation to protect him in the performance of his duties.   Each member of the Union is capable, at its will, of

---

    [1] *Osborn* v. *Bank of United States*, 9 Wheat. R. 738, 838 to 845; Id.
846 ; *The Governor of Georgia* v. *Madrazo*, 1 Peters's Sup. R. 110,
111, 122.

§ 1680. The same principle applies to cases, where a state has an interest in a corporation; as when it is a stockholder in an incorporated bank, the corporation is still suable, although the state, as such, is

attacking the nation, of arresting its progress at every step, of acting vigorously and effectually in the execution of its designs, while the nation stands naked, stripped of its defensive armour, and incapable of shielding its agent, or executing its laws, otherwise than by proceedings, which are to take place after the mischief is perpetrated, and which must often be ineffectual, from the inability of the agents to make compensation.

"These are said to be extreme cases; but the case at bar, had it been put by way of illustration in argument, might have been termed an extreme case; and, if a penalty on a revenue officer for performing his duty, be more obviously wrong, than a penalty on the bank, it is a difference in degree, not in principle. Public sentiment would be more shocked by the infliction of a penalty on a public officer for the performance of his duty, than by the infliction of this penalty on a bank, which, while carrying on the fiscal operations of the government, is also transacting its own business. But, in both cases, the officer levying the penalty acts under a void authority, and the power to restrain him is denied as positively in the one, as in the other.

"The distinction between any extreme case, and that which has actually occurred, if, indeed, any difference of principle can be supposed to exist between them, disappears, when considering the question of jurisdiction; for, if the courts of the United States cannot rightfully protect the agents, who execute every law authorized by the constitution, from the direct action of state agents in the collection of penalties, they cannot rightfully protect those, who execute any law.

"The question, then, is, whether the constitution of the United States has provided a tribunal, which can peacefully and rightfully protect those, who are employed in carrying into execution the laws of the Union, from the attempts of a particular state to resist the execution of those laws.

"The state of Ohio denies the existence of this power; and contends, that no preventive proceedings whatever, or proceedings against the very property, which may have been seized by the agent of a state, can be sustained against such agent, because they would be substantially against the state itself, in violation of the 11th amendment of the constitution.

"That the courts of the Union cannot entertain a suit brought against a state by an alien, or the citizen of another state, is not to be exempted from any action.[1]   The state does not, by becoming a corporator, identify itself with the corporation. The bank, in such a case, is not the state, although the state holds an interest in it. Nor will it

controverted. Is a suit, brought against an individual, for any cause whatever, a suit against a state, in the sense of the constitution?

" The 11th amendment is the limitation of a power supposed to be granted in the original instrument; and to understand accurately the extent of the limitation, it seems proper to define the power that is limited. The words of the constitution, so far as they respect this question, are, ' The judicial power shall extend to controversies between two or more states, between a state and citizens of another state, and between a state and foreign states, citizens, or subjects.' A subsequent clause distributes the power previously granted, and assigns to the Supreme Court original jurisdiction in those cases, in which ' a state shall be a party.' The words of the 11th amendment are, ' The judicial power of the United States shall not be construed to extend to any suit in law or equity, commenced or prosecuted against one of the United States, by citizens of another state, or by citizens or subjects of a foreign state.'

" The bank of the United States contends, that in all cases, in which jurisdiction depends on the character of the party, reference is made to the party on the record, not to one, who may be interested, but is not shown by the record to be a party. The appellants admit, that the jurisdiction of the court is not ousted by any incidental or consequential interest, which a state may have in the decision to be made, but is to be considered as a party, where the decision acts directly and immediately upon the state, through its officers.

" If this question were to be determined on the authorty of English decisions, it is believed, that no case can be adduced, where any person has been considered as a party, who is not made so in the record. But the court will not review those decisions, because it is thought a question growing out of the constitution of the United States, requires rather an attentive consideration of the words of that instrument, than of the decisions of analogous questions by the courts of any other country.

" Do the provisions, then, of the American constitution, respecting controversies, to which a state may be a party, extend, on a fair construction of that instrument, to cases in which the state is not a party on the record ? The first in the enumeration, is a controversy between two or more states. There are not many questions, in which a state would

<hr>

[1] *United States Bank v. Planters' Bank of Georgia*, 9 Wheat R. 904; *Bank of Com'th of Kentucky v. Wister*, 3 Peters's Sup. R. 318.

make any difference in the case, that the state has
the sole interest in the corporation, if in fact it creates
other persons corporators.[1]   An analogous case will
be found in the authority, given by an act of congress

---

be supposed to take a deeper or more immediate interest, than in those,
which decide on the extent of her territory.   Yet the constitution, not
considering the state as a party to such controversies, if not plaintiff or
defendant on the record, has expressly given jurisdiction in those between citizens claiming lands under grants of different states.   If each
state, in consequence of the influence of a decision on her boundary, had
been considered, by the framers of the constitution, as a party to that
controversy, the express grant of jurisdiction would have been useless.
The grant of it certainly proves, that the constitution does not consider
the state as a party in such a case.   Jurisdiction is expressly granted, in
those cases only, where citizens of the same state claim lands under
grants of different states.   If the claimants be citizens of different states,
the court takes jurisdiction for that reason.   Still, the right of the state
to grant is the essential point in dispute ; and in that point the state is
deeply interested.   If that interest converts the state into a party, there
is an end of the cause ; and the constitution will be construed to forbid
the circuit courts to take cognizance of questions, to which it was
thought necessary expressly to extend their jurisdiction, even when the
controversy arose between citizens of the same state.

   " We are aware, that the application of these cases may be denied,
because the title of the State comes on incidentally, and the appellants
admit the jurisdiction of the court, where its judgment does not act directly upon the property or interests of the state; but we deemed it of
some importance to show, that the framers of the constitution contemplated the distinction between cases, in which a state was interested, and
those, in which it was a party, and made no provision for a case of interest, without being a party on the record.   In cases, where a state is a
party on the record, the question of jurisdiction is decided by inspection.
If jurisdiction depend, not on this plain fact, but on the interest of the
state, what rule has the constitution given, by which this interest is to
be measured ?   If no rule be given, is it to be settled by the court ?   If
so, the curious anomaly is presented of a court examining the whole
testimony of a cause, inquiring into, and deciding on, the extent of a
state's interest, without having a right to exercise any jurisdiction in the
case.   Can this inquiry be made without the exercise of jurisdiction?

   " The next in the enumeration is a controversy between a state and
the citizens of another state.   Can this case arise, if the state be not a

---

[1] *Bank of Com'th of Kentucky* v. *Wister,* 3 Peters's Sup. R. 318.

to the postmaster-general, to bring suits in his official capacity. In such suits the United States are not understood to be a party, although the suits solely regard their interests. The postmaster-general does

---

party on the record? If it can, the question recurs, what degree of interest shall be sufficient to change the parties, and arrest the proceedings against the individual? Controversies respecting boundary have lately existed between Virginia and Tennessee, between Kentucky and Tennessee, and now exist between New-York and New-Jersey. Suppose, while such a controversy is pending, the collecting officer of one state should seize property for taxes belonging to a man, who supposes himself to reside in the other state, and who seeks redress in the federal court of that state, in which the officer resides. The interest of the state is obvious. Yet it is admitted, that in such a case the action would lie, because the officer might be treated as a trespasser, and the verdict and judgment against him would not act directly on the property of the state. That it would not so act, may, perhaps, depend on circumstances. The officer may retain the amount of the taxes in his hands, and, on the proceedings of the state against him, may plead in bar the judgment of a court of competent jurisdiction. If this plea ought to be sustained, and it is far from being certain, that it ought not, the judgment so pleaded would have acted directly on the revenue of the state, in the hands of its officer. And yet the argument admits, that the action, in such a case, would be sustained. But, suppose, in such a case, the party conceiving himself to be injured, instead of bringing an action sounding in damages, should sue for the specific thing, while yet in possession of the seizing officer. It being admitted in argument, that the action sounding in damages would lie, we are unable to perceive the line of distinction between that and the action of detinue. Yet the latter action would claim the specific article seized for the tax, and would obtain it, should the seizure be deemed unlawful.

"It would be tedious to pursue this part of the inquiry farther, and it would be useless, because every person will perceive, that the same reasoning is applicable to all the other enumerated controversies, to which a state may be a party. The principle may be illustrated by a reference to those other controversies, where jurisdiction depends on the party. But, before we review them, we will notice one, where the nature of the controversy is, in some degree, blended with the character of the party.

"If a suit be brought against a foreign minister, the Supreme Court alone has original jurisdiction, and this is shown on the record. But, suppose a suit to be brought, which affects the interest of a foreign minister, or by which the person of his secretary, or of his servant, is arrest-

not, in such cases, sue under the clause giving jurisdiction, " in controversies, to which the United States
shall be a party ; " but under the clause extending
the jurisdiction to cases arising under the laws of the
United States.[1]

ed. The minister does not, by the mere arrest of his secretary, or his
servant, become a party to this suit, but the actual defendant pleads to
the jurisdiction of the court, and asserts his privilege. If the suit affects
a foreign minister, it must be dismissed, not because he is a party to it,
but because it affects him. The language of the constitution in the two
cases is different. This court can take cognizance of all cases ' affecting' foreign ministers ; and, therefore, jurisdiction does not depend on
the party named in the record. But this language changes, when the
enumeration proceeds to states. Why this change? The answer is
obvious. In the case of foreign ministers, it was intended, for reasons,
which all comprehend, to give the national courts jurisdiction over all
cases, by which they were in any manner affected. In the case of
States, whose immediate or remote interests were mixed up with a multitude of cases, and who might be affected in an almost infinite variety
of ways, it was intended to give jurisdiction in those cases only, to which
they were actual parties.

" In proceeding with the cases, in which jurisdiction depends on the
character of the party, the first in the enumeration is, 'controversies to
which the United States shall be a party.' Does this provision extend
to the cases, where the United States are not named in the record, but
claim and are actually entitled to, the whole subject in controversy?
Let us examine this question. Suits brought by the postmaster-general
are for money due to the United States. The nominal plaintiff has no
interest in the controversy, and the United States are the only real party.
Yet, these suits could not be instituted in the courts of the Union, under
that clause, which gives jurisdiction in all cases, to which the United
States are a party ; and it was found necessary to give the court jurisdiction over them, as being cases arising under a law of the United
States.

" The judicial power of the Union is also extended to controversies
between citizens of different States ; and it has been decided, that the
character of the parties must be shown on the record. Does this provision depend on the character of those, whose interest is litigated, or of
those, who are parties on the record? In a suit, for example, brought
by or against an executor, the creditors or legatees of his testator are

[1] Osborn v. Bank of United States, 9 Wheat. R. 855, 856; Postmaster
General v. Early, 12 Wheat. R. 136, 149.

§ 1681. The reasoning, by which the general doctrine is maintained, is to the following effect. It is a sound principle, that, when a government becomes a partner in any trading company, it divests itself, so far

the persons really concerned in interest; but it has never been suspected, that, if the executor be a resident of another state, the jurisdiction of the federal courts could be ousted by the fact, that the creditors or legatees were citizens of the same state with the opposite party. The universally received construction in this case is, that jurisdiction is neither given nor ousted by the relative situation of the parties concerned in interest, but by the relative situation of the parties named on the record. Why is this construction universal? No case can be imagined, in which the existence of an interest out of the party on the record is more unequivocal, than in that, which has been just stated. Why, then, is it universally admitted, that this interest in no manner affects the jurisdiction of the court? The plain and obvious answer is, because the jurisdiction of the court depends, not upon this interest, but upon the actual party on the record. Were a state to be the sole legatee, it will not, we presume, be alleged, that the jurisdiction of the court, in a suit against the executor, would be more affected by this fact, than by the fact, that any other person, not suable in the courts of the Union, was the sole legatee. Yet, in such a case, the court would decide directly and immediately on the interest of the state.

"This principle might be further illustrated by showing, that jurisdiction, where it depends on the character of the party, is never conferred in consequence of the existence of an interest in a party not named; and by showing that, under the distributive clause of the 2d section of the 3d article, the Supreme Court could never take original jurisdiction, in consequence of an interest in a party not named in the record.

"But the principle seems too well established to require, that more time should be devoted to it. It may, we think, be laid down as a rule, which admits of no exception, that, in all cases where jurisdiction depends on the party, it is the party named in the record. Consequently, the 11th amendment, which restrains the jurisdiction granted by the constitution over suits against states, is, of necessity, limited to those suits, in which a state is a party on the record. The amendment has its full effect, if the constitution be construed, as it would have been construed, had the jurisdiction of the court never been extended to suits brought against a state, by the citizens of another state, or by aliens. The state not being a party on the record, and the court having jurisdiction over those, who are parties on the record, the true question is, not one of jurisdiction, but whether, in the exercise of its jurisdiction, the court ought to make a decree against the defendants; whether they are to be considered as having a real interest, or as being only nominal parties."

as concerns the transactions of that company, of its
sovereign character, and takes that of a private citizen.
Instead of communicating to the company its privileges and prerogatives, it descends to a level with
those, with whom it associates itself, and takes the
character, which belongs to its associates, and to the
business, which is transacted.   Thus, many states in
the Union, which have an interest in banks, are not
suable even in their own courts.   A state, which
establishes a bank, and becomes a stockholder in it,
and gives it a capacity to sue and be sued, strips itself of its sovereign character, so far as respects the
transactions of the bank, and waives all the privileges
of that character.   As a member of a corporation, a
government never exercises its sovereignty.   It acts
merely, as a corporator; and exercises no other power in the management of the affairs of the corporation,
than are expressly given by the incorporating act.
The United States held shares in the old bank of the
United States ; but the privileges of the government
were not imparted by that circumstance to the bank.
The United States were not a party to suits, brought
by or against the bank, in the sense of the constitution.
So, with respect to the present bank, suits brought
by or against it are not understood to be brought by
or against the United States.   The government, by
becoming a corporator, lays down its sovereignty, so
far as respects the transactions of the corporation ;
and exercises no power or privilege, which is not
derived from the charter.[1]   The reasoning admits of
further illustration.   A corporation is itself, in legal
contemplation, an artificial person, having a distinct

---

[1] *United States Bank* v. *Planters' Bank of Georgia*, 9 Wheat. R. 907,
908.

and independent existence from that of the persons composing it. · It is this personal, political, and artificial existence, which gives it the character of a body politic or corporate, in which may be vested peculiar powers and attributes, distinct and different from those belonging to the natural persons composing it.[1] Thus, the corporation may be perpetual, although the individuals composing it may in succession die. It may have privileges, and immunities, and functions, which do not, and cannot lawfully belong to individuals. It may exercise franchises, and transact business prohibited to its members, as individuals. The capacity to sue and be sued belongs to every corporation; and, indeed, is a function incident to it, independent of any special grant, because necessary to its existence.[2] It sues and is sued, however, not in the names of its members, but in its own name, as a distinct person. It acts, indeed, by and through its members, or other proper functionaries; but still the acts are its own, and not the private acts of such members or functionaries. The members are not only not parties to its suits in any legal sense, but they may sue it, or be sued by it, in any action, exactly as any stranger may sue it, or be sued by it. A state may sue a bank, in which it is a stockholder, just as any other stockholder may sue the same bank. The United States may sue the bank of the United States, and entitle themselves to a judgment for any debt due to them; and they may satisfy the execution, issuing on such a judgment, out of any property of the bank. Now it is plain, that this could not be done, if the state, or the United States, or any other stockholder

---

[1] See 1 Black. Comm. ch. 18, p. 467, 471, 475, 477.
[2] 1 Black. Comm. 475, 476.

were deemed a party to the record. It would be past all legal comprehension, that a party might sue himself, and be on both sides of the controversy. So, that any attempt to deem a state a party to a suit, simply because it has an interest in a suit, or is a stockholder in a corporation on the record, would be to renounce all ordinary doctrines of law applicable to such cases. The framers of the constitution must be presumed, in treating of the judicial department, to have used language in the sense, and with the limitations belonging to it in judicial usage. They must have spoken according to known distinctions, and settled rules of interpretation, incorporated into the very elements of the jurisprudence of every state in the Union.

§ 1682. It may, then, be laid down, as a rule, which admits of no exception, that in all cases under the constitution of the United States, where jurisdiction depends upon the party, it is the party named on the record. Consequently the amendment above referred to, which restrains the jurisdiction granted by the constitution over suits against states, is of necessity limited to those suits, in which a state is a party on the record. The amendment has its full effect, if the constitution is construed, as it would have been construed, had the jurisdiction never been extended to suits brought against a state by the citizens of another state, or by aliens.[1]

§ 1683. It has been doubted, whether this amendment extends to cases of admiralty and maritime juris-

---

1 *Osborn* v. *United States Bank*, 9 Wheat. R. 857, 858; *The Governor of Georgia* v. *Madrazo*, 1 Peters's Sup. R. 110, 122. — A state may be properly deemed a party, when it sues, or is sued by process, by or against the governor of the state in his official capacity. *The Governor of Georgia* v. *Madrazo*, 1 Peters's Sup. R. 110, 121 to 124.

diction, where the proceeding is *in rem*, and not *in personam*. There, the jurisdiction of the court is founded upon the possession of the thing; and if the state should interpose a claim for the property, it does not act merely in the character of a defendant, but as an actor. Besides; the language of the amendment is, th t " the judicial power of the United States shall not be 'construed to extend to any suit *in law or equity*." But a suit in the admiralty is not, correctly speaking, a suit in law, or in equity; but is often spoken of in contradistinction to both.[1]

§ 1684. Next. "Controversies between citizens of different states." Although the necessity of this power may not stand upon grounds quite as strong, as some of the preceding, there are high motives of state policy and public justice, by which it can be clearly vindicated. There are many cases, in which such a power may be indispensable, or in the highest degree expedient, to carry into effect some of the privileges and immunities conferred, and some of the prohibitions upon states expressly declared, in the constitution. For example; it is declared, that the citizens of each state shall be entitled to all the privileges and immunities of citizens of the several states. Suppose an attempt is made to evade, or withhold these privileges and immunities, would it not be right to allow the party aggrieved an opportunity of claiming them, in a contest with a citizen of the state, before a tribunal, at once national and impartial?[2] Suppose a state should pass a tender law,

---

[1] See *United States* v. *Blight*, 3 Hall's Law Journal, 197, 225; *The Governor of Georgia* v. *Madrazo*, 1 Peters's Sup. R. 124, and Id. 128, 129, 130, 131, 132, 133, the Opinion of Mr. Justice Johnson; *United States* v. *Peters*, 5 Cranch's R. 115, 139, 140.

[2] The Federalist, No. 80; Id. No. 42.

or law impairing the obligation of private contracts, or should in the course of its legislation grant unconstitutional preferences to its own citizens, is it not clear, that the jurisdiction to enforce the obligations of the constitution in such cases ought to be confided to the national tribunals? These cases are not purely imaginary. They have actually occurred; and may again occur, under peculiar circumstances, in the course of state legislation.[1] What was the fact under the confederation? Each state was obliged to acquiesce in the degree of justice, which another state might choose to yield to its citizens.[2] There was not only danger of animosities growing up from this source; but, in point of fact, there did grow up retaliatory legislation, to meet such real or imagined grievances.

§ 1685. Nothing can conduce more to general harmony and confidence among all the states, than a consciousness, that controversies are not exclusively to be decided by the state tribunals; but may, at the election of the party, be brought before the national tribunals. Besides; it cannot escape observation, that the judges in different states hold their offices by a very different tenure. Some hold during good behaviour; some for a term of years; some for a single year; some are irremovable, except upon impeachment; and others may be removed upon address of the legislature. Under such circumstances it cannot but be presumed, that there may arise a course of state policy, or state legislation, exceedingly injurious to the interests of the citi-

---

[1] See 2 Elliot's Debates, 391, 392, 401, 406; 3 Elliot's Debates, 142, 144, 277. 282.

[2] See *Chisholm* v. *Georgia*, 2 Dall. R. 474, 475, 476, per Mr. Chief Justice Jay; The Federalist, No. 80; 3 Elliot's Debates, 142, 144, 277, 282; *Martin* v. *Hunter*, 1 Wheat. R. 346, 347.

zens of other states, both as to real and personal property. It would require an uncommon exercise of candour or credulity to affirm, that in cases of this sort all the state tribunals would be wholly without state prejudice, or state feelings; or, that they would be as earnest in resisting the encroachments of state authority upon the just rights, and interests of the citizens of other states, as a tribunal differently constituted, and wholly independent of state authority. And if justice should be as fairly and as firmly administered in the former, as in the latter, still the mischiefs would be most serious, if the public opinion did not indulge such a belief. Justice, in cases of this sort, should not only be above all reproach, but above all suspicion. The sources of state irritations and state jealousies are sufficiently numerous, without leaving open one so copious and constant, as the belief, or the dread of wrong in the administration of state justice.[1] Besides; if the public confidence should continue to follow the state tribunals, (as in many cases it doubtless will,) the provision will become inert and harmless; for, as the party will have his election of the forum, he will not be inclined to desert the state courts, unless for some sound reason, founded either in the nature of his cause, or in the influence of state prejudices.[2] On the other hand, there can be no real danger of injustice to the other side in the decisions of the national tribunals; because the cause must still be decided upon the true principles of the local law, and not by any foreign jurisprudence.[3]

---

[1] See The Federalist, No. 80; 4 Dall. 474, 475, 476, per Mr. Chief Justice Jay; 1 Kent's Comm. Lect. 14, p. 276, (2 edit. p. 296); 3 Elliot's Debates, 141, 142, 144.

[2] See Rawle on Const. ch. 31, p. 204; 3 Elliot's Deb. 381, 382.

[3] 2 Elliot's Debates, 401, 402, 406.

There is another circumstance of no small importance, as a matter of policy; and that is, the tendency of such a power to increase the confidence and credit between the commercial and agricultural states. No man can be insensible to the value, in promoting credit, of the belief of there being a prompt, efficient, and impartial administration of justice in enforcing contracts.[1]

§ 1686. Such are some of the reasons, which are supposed to have influenced the convention in delegating jurisdiction to the courts of the United States in cases between citizens of different states. Probably no part of the judicial power of the Union has been of more practical benefit, or has given more lasting satisfaction to the people. There is not a single state, which has not at some time felt the influence of this conservative power; and the general harmony, which exists between the state courts and the national courts, in the concurrent exercise of their jurisdiction in cases between citizens of different states, demonstrates the utility, as well as the safety of the power. Indeed; it is not improbable, that the existence of the power has operated, as a silent, but irresistible check to undue state legislation; at the same time, that it has cherished a mutual respect and confidence between the state and national courts, as honourable, as it has been beneficent.

§ 1687. The next inquiry growing out of this part of the clause is, who are to be deemed citizens of different states within the meaning of it. Are all persons born within a state to be always deemed citizens of that state, notwithstanding any change of domicil; or does their citizenship change with their change of dom-

---

[1] 2 Elliot's Debates, 392, 406; 3 Elliot's Debates, 144; Id. 282.

icil? The answer to this inquiry is equally plain and satisfactory. The constitution having declared, that the citizens of each state shall be entitled to all privileges and immunities of citizens in the several states, every person, who is a citizen of one state, and removes into another, with the intention of taking up his residence and inhabitancy there, becomes *ipso facto* a citizen of the state, where he resides; and he then ceases to be a citizen of the state, from which he has removed his residence. Of course, when he gives up his new residence or domicil, and returns to his native, or other state residence or domicil, he reacquires the character of the latter. What circumstances shall constitute such a change of residence or domicil, is an inquiry, more properly belonging to a treatise upon public or municipal law, than to commentaries upon constitutional law. In general, however, it may be said, that a removal from one state into another, *animo manendi*, or with a design of becoming an inhabitant, constitutes a change of domicil, and of course a change of citizenship. But a person, who is a native citizen of one state, never ceases to be a citizen thereof, until he has acquired a new citizenship elsewhere. Residence in a foreign country has no operation upon his character, as a citizen, although it may, for purposes of trade and commerce, impress him with the character of the country.[1] To change allegiance is one thing; to change inhabitancy is quite another thing. The right and the power are not co-extensive in each case.[2] Every citizen of a state is *ipso facto* a citizen of the United States.[3]

---

[1] See 1 Kent's Comm. Lect. 4.
[2] See Rawle on Const. ch. 9, p. 87 to 100.
[3] Rawle on Const. ch. 9, p. 85, 86.

§ 1688. And a person, who is a naturalized citizen of the United States, by a like residence in any state in the Union, becomes *ipso facto* a citizen of that state. So a citizen of a territory of the Union by a like residence acquires the character of the state, where he resides.[1] But a naturalized citizen of the United States, or a citizen of a territory, is not a citizen of a state, entitled to sue in the courts of the United States in virtue of that character, while he resides in any such territory, nor until he has acquired a residence or domicil in the particular state.[2]

§ 1689. A corporation, as such, is not a citizen of a state in the sense of the constitution. But, if all the members of the corporation are citizens, their character will confer jurisdiction; for then it is substantially a suit by citizens suing in their corporate name.[3] And a citizen of a state is entitled to sue, as such, notwithstanding he is a trustee for others, or sues in *autre droit*, as it is technically called; that is, as representative of another. Thus, a citizen may sue, who is a trustee at law, for the benefit of the person entitled to the trust. And an administrator, and executor may sue for the benefit of the estate, which they represent; for in each of these cases it is their personal suit.[4] But if citizens, who are parties to a suit, are merely nominally so; as, for instance, if magistrates are officially required to

---

[1] See *Gassies* v. *Ballon*, 6 Peters's Sup. R. 761.

[2] *Hepburn* v. *Elszey*, 2 Cranch's 448; *Corporation of New-Orleans* v. *Winter*, 1 Wheat. R. 91; 1 Kent's Comm. Lect. 17, p. 360, (2 edition, p. 384.)

[3] *Hope Insurance Company* v. *Boardman*, 5 Cranch, 57; *Bank of United States* v. *Deveaux*, 5 Cranch, 61; *United States* v. *Planters' Bank*, 9 Wheat. R. 410.

[4] *Chappedelaine* v. *De Cheneaux*, 4 Cranch, 306; *Bank of United States* v. *Deveaux*, 5 Cranch, 61; *Childress* v. *Emory*, 8 Wheat. R. 668.

allow suits to be brought in their names for the use or benefit of a citizen or alien, the latter are deemed the substantial parties entitled to sue.[1]

§ 1690. Next. "Controversies between citizens of the same state, claiming lands under grants of different states." This clause was not in the first draft of the constitution, but was added without any known objection to its propriety.[2]   It is the only instance, in which the constitution directly contemplates the cognizance of disputes between citizens of the same state;[3] but certainly not the only one, in which they may indirectly upon constitutional questions have the benefit of the judicial power of the Union.[4]   The Federalist has remarked, that the reasonableness of the agency of the national courts in cases, in which the state tribunals cannot be supposed to be impartial, speaks for itself. No man ought certainly to be a judge in his own cause, or in any cause, in respect to which he has the least interest or bias.   This principle has no inconsiderable weight in designating the federal courts, as the proper tribunals for the determination of controversies between different states and their citizens.   And it ought to have the same operation in regard to some cases between citizens of the same state.   Claims to land under grants of different states, founded upon adverse pretensions of boundary, are of this description.   The courts of neither of the granting states could be expected to be unbiassed.   The laws may have even prejudged the question; and tied the courts down to decisions in favour of the grants of the state, to which they belonged.

1 *Brown* v. *Strode*, 5 Cranch, 303.
2 Journal of Convention, 226, 300.
3 The Federalist, No. 80.
4 *Cohens* v. *Virginia*, 6 Wheat. R. 390, 391, 392.

And where this has not been done, it would be natural, that the judges, as men, should feel a strong predilection for the claims of their own government.[1] And, at all events, the providing of a tribunal, having no possible interest on the one side, more than the other, would have a most salutary tendency in quieting the jealousies, and disarming the resentments of the state, whose grant should be held invalid. This jurisdiction attaches not only to grants made by different states, which were never united; but also to grants made by different states, which were originally united under one jurisdiction, if made since the separation, although the origin of the title may be traced back to an antecedent period.[2]

§ 1691. Next. "Controversies between a state, or the citizens thereof, and foreign states, citizens, or subjects." The Federalist[3] has vindicated this provision in the following brief, but powerful manner: "The peace of the whole ought not to be left at the disposal of a part. The Union will undoubtedly be answerable to foreign powers for the conduct of its members. And the responsibility for an injury ought ever to be accompanied with the faculty of preventing it. As the denial or perversion of justice by the sentences of courts is with reason classed among the just causes of war, it will follow, that the federal judiciary ought to have cognizance of all causes, in which the citizens of other countries are concerned. This is not less essential to the preservation of the public faith, than to the

[1] The Federalist, No. 80. See also Mr. Chief Justice Jay's Remarks, 4 Dall. 476, and *ante* vol. 3, § 1632.

[2] *Town of Pawlet* v. *Clarke*, 9 Cranch, 292 ; *Colson* v. *Lewis*, 2 Wheat. R. 377.

[3] The Federalist, No. 80. See also 3 Elliot's Debates, 283 ; 2 Elliot's Debates, 391.

security of the public tranquillity. A distinction may perhaps be imagined between cases arising upon treaties and the laws of nations, and those, which may stand merely on the footing of the municipal law. The former kind may be supposed proper for the federal jurisdiction; the latter for that of the states. But it is at least problematical, whether an unjust sentence against a foreigner, where the subject of controversy was wholly relative to the *lex loci*, would not, if unredressed, be an aggression upon his sovereign as well as one, which violated the stipulations of a treaty, or the general law of nations. And a still greater objection to the distinction would result from the immense difficulty, if not impossibility, of a practical discrimination between the cases of one complexion, and those of the other. So great a proportion of the controversies, in which foreigners are parties, involve national questions, that it is by far the most safe, and most expedient, to refer all those, in which they are concerned, to the national tribunals."

§ 1692. In addition to these suggestions, it may be remarked, that it is of great national importance to advance public, as well as private credit, in our intercourse with foreign nations and their subjects. Nothing can be more beneficial in this respect, than to create an impartial tribunal, to which they may have resort upon all occasions, when it may be necessary to ascertain, or enforce their rights.[1] Besides; it is not

---

[1] 3 Elliot's Debates, 142, 143, 144, 282, 283. — It is notorious, that this jurisdiction has been very satisfactory to foreign nations and their subjects. Nor have the dangers of state prejudice, and state attachment to local interests, to the injury of foreigners, been wholly imaginary. It has been already stated in another place, that the debts due to British subjects before the revolution, were never recovered, until after the adop-

wholly immaterial, that the law to be administered in cases of foreigners is often very distinct from the mere municipal code of a state, and dependent upon the law merchant, or the more enlarged consideration of international rights and duties, in a case of conflict of the foreign and domestic laws.[1] And it may fairly be presumed, that the national tribunals will, from the nature of their ordinary functions, become better acquainted with the general principles, which regulate subjects of this nature, than other courts, however enlightened, which are rarely required to discuss them.

§ 1693. In regard to controversies between an American and a foreign state, it is obvious, that the suit must, on one side at least, be wholly voluntary. No foreign state can be compelled to become a party, plaintiff or defendant, in any of our tribunals.[2] If, therefore, it chooses to consent to the institution of any suit, it is its consent alone, which can give effect to the jurisdiction of the court. It is certainly desirable to furnish some peaceable mode of appeal in cases, where any controversy may exist between an American and a foreign state, sufficiently important to require the grievance to be redressed by any other mode, than through the instrumentality of negotiations.[3]

§ 1694. The inquiry may here be made, who are to be deemed aliens entitled to sue in the courts of the United States. The general answer is, any person, who is not a citizen of the United States. A foreigner, who is naturalized, is no longer entitled to the character

tion of the constitution, by suits brought in the national courts. See *Ware* v. *Hylton*, 3 Dall. R. 199.

1 See 1 Tucker's Black. Comm. App. 421 ; 3 Elliot's Deb. 282, 283

2 See 2 Elliot's Deb. 391, 407 ; *Foster* v. *Nelson*, 2 Peters's R. 254, 307.

3 See 3 Elliot's Debates, 282, 283.

of an alien.[1] And when an alien is the substantial
party, it matters not, whether he is a suitor in his own
right; or whether he acts, as a trustee, or personal representative; or whether he is compellable by the local
law to sue through some official organ.[2] A foreign
corporation, established in a foreign country, all of
whose members are aliens, is entitled to sue in the
same manner, that an alien may personally sue in the
courts of the Union.[3] It is not sufficient to vest the
jurisdiction, that an alien is a party to the suit, unless
the other party be a citizen.[4] British subjects, born
before the American revolution, are to be deemed aliens;
and may sue American citizens, born before the revolution, as well as those born since that period. The
revolution severed the ties of allegiance; and made the
inhabitants of each country aliens to each other.[5] In
relation to aliens, however, it should be stated, that
they have a right to sue only, while peace exists between their country and our own. For if a war breaks
out, and they thereby become alien enemies, their right
to sue is suspended, until the return of peace.[6]

---

[1] Mr. Tucker supposes, that the several states still retain the power
of admitting aliens to become denizens of the state; but that they do
not thereby become citizens. (1 Tuck. Black. Comm. App. 365.) What
he means by denizens, he has not explained. If he means, that the
states may naturalize, so far as to make an alien a citizen of the state,
that may be well questioned. If he means only, that they may enable
aliens to hold lands, and enjoy certain other qualified privileges within
the state, that will not be denied.

[2] *Chappedelaine* v. *De Chenaux*, 4 Cranch, 306; *Brown* v. *Strode*,
5 Cranch, R. 303.

[3] *Society for Propagating the Gospel* v. *Town of New-Haven*, 8 Wheat.
R. 464.

[4] *Jackson* v. *Twentyman*, 2 Peters's Sup. R. 136.

[5] *Dawson's Lessee* v. *Godfrey*, 4 Cranch, 321; *Blight's Lessee* v. *Ro-
chester*, 7 Wheat. R. 535; *Inglis* v. *Trustees of Sailor's Snug Harbour*,
3 Peters's Sup. R. 126.

[6] 1 Kent's Comm. Lect. 3, p. 64, 65, (2 edition, p. 68, 69.)

§ 1695. We have now finished our review of the classes of cases, to which the judicial power of the United States extends. The next inquiry naturally presented is, in what mode it is to be exercised, and in what courts it is to be vested. The succeeding clause of the constitution answers this inquiry. It is in the following words. " In all cases affecting ambassa-" dors, other public ministers, and consuls, and those, in " which a state shall be a party, the Supreme Court " shall have *original* jurisdiction. In all the other cases " before mentioned, the Supreme Court shall have *ap-*" *pellate* jurisdiction, both as to law and fact, with such " exceptions and under such regulations, as the con-" gress shall make."[1]

§ 1696. The first remark arising out of this clause is, that, as the judicial power of the United States extends to all the cases enumerated in the constitution, it may extend to all such cases in any form, in which judicial power may be exercised. It may, therefore, extend to them in the shape of original, or appellate jurisdiction, or both; for there is nothing in the nature of the cases, which binds to the exercise of the one in

---

[1] In the first draft of the constitution, the words stood thus. "In cases of impeachment, cases affecting ambassadors, other public ministers, and consuls, and those, in which a state shall be a party, this jurisdiction (of the Supreme Court) shall be original. In all other cases before mentioned, *it shall be appellate*, with such exceptions and under such regulations, as the legislature may make. The legislature may assign any part of the jurisdiction above mentioned, (except the trial of the president of the United States) in the manner and under the limitations, which it shall think proper, to such inferior courts, as it shall constitute from time to time." It was varied to its present form by successive votes, in which there was some difference of opinion. Journal of Convention, p. 226, 227, 299, 300, 301.

preference to the other.[1]   But it is clear, from the language of the constitution, that, in one form or the other, it is absolutely obligatory upon congress, to vest all the jurisdiction in the national courts, in that class of cases at least, where it has declared, that it shall extend to " *all cases.*"[2]

§ 1697. In the next place, the jurisdiction, which is by the constitution to be exercised by the Supreme Court in an *original* form, is very limited, and extends only to cases affecting ambassadors, and other public ministers, and consuls, and cases, where a state is a party.   And congress cannot constitutionally confer on it any other, or further original jurisdiction. This is one of the appropriate illustrations of the rule, that the affirmation of a power in particular cases, excludes it in all others. The clause itself would otherwise be wholly inoperative and nugatory. If it had been intended to leave it to the discretion of congress, to apportion the judicial power between the supreme and inferior courts, according to the will of that body, it would have been useless to have proceeded further, than to define the judicial power, and the tribunals, in which it should be vested. Affirmative words often, in their operation, imply a negative of other objects, than those affirmed ; and in this case a negative, or exclusive sense, must be given to the words, or they have no operation at all. If the solicitude of the convention, respecting our peace with foreign powers, might induce a provision to be made, that the Supreme Court should have original jurisdiction in cases, which might

---

1 *Martin* v. *Hunter*, 1 Wheat. R. 333, 337, 338; *Osborn* v. *Bank of United States*, 9 Wheat. R. 820, 821.

2 Id. p. 328, 330, 336. — Upon this subject there is considerable discussion, in the case of *Martin* v. *Hunter*, (1 Wheat. R. 304, 313.)

be supposed to affect them ; yet the clause would have proceeded no further, than to provide for such cases, unless some further restriction upon the powers of congress had been intended. The direction, that the Supreme Court shall have appellate jurisdiction in all cases, with such exceptions, as congress shall make, will be no restriction, unless the words are to be deemed exclusive of original jurisdiction.[1] And accordingly, the doctrine is firmly established, that the Supreme Court cannot constitutionally exercise any original jurisdiction, except in the enumerated cases. If congress should confer it, it would be a mere nullity.[2]

§ 1698. But although the Supreme Court cannot exercise original jurisdiction in any cases, except those specially enumerated, it is certainly competent for congress to vest in any inferior courts of the United States original jurisdiction of all other cases, not thus specially assigned to the Supreme Court; for there is nothing in the constitution, which excludes such inferior courts from the exercise of such original jurisdiction. Original jurisdiction, so far as the constitution gives a rule, is co-extensive with the judicial power ; and except, so far as the constitution has made any distinction of it among the courts of the United States, it remains

<hr/>

[1] *Marbury* v. *Madison*, 1 Cranch, R. 174, 175; *Wiscart* v. *Dauchy*, 3 Dall. R. 321; *Cohens* v. *Virginia*, 6 Wheat. R. 392 to 395; Id. 400, 401 ; *Osborn* v. *Bank of United States*, 9 Wheat. R. 820, 821.

[2] Id. ibid. 1 Kent. Comm. Lect. 15, p. 294, 301, (2d edition, 314, 322;) *Wiscart* v. *Dauchy*, 3 Dall. R. 321. — Congress, by the judiciary act of 1789, ch. 20, § 13, did confer on the Supreme Court the authority to issue writs of mandamus, in cases warranted by the principles and usages of law, to persons holding office under the authority of the United States. But the Supreme Court, in 1801, held the delegation of power to be a mere nullity. *Marbury* v. *Madison*, 1 Cranch, R. 137, 173 to 180.

to be exercised in an original, or appellate form, or both, as congress may in their wisdom deem fit. Now, the constitution has made no distinction, except of the original and appellate jurisdiction of the Supreme Court. It has no where insinuated, that the inferior tribunals shall have no original jurisdiction. It has no where affirmed, that they shall have appellate jurisdiction. Both are left unrestricted and undefined. Of course, as the judicial power is to be vested in the supreme and inferior courts of the Union, both are under the entire control and regulation of congress.[1]

§ 1699. Indeed, it has been a matter of much question, whether the grant of original jurisdiction to the Supreme Court, in the enumerated cases, ought to be construed to give to that court exclusive original jurisdiction, even of those cases. And it has been contended, that there is nothing in the constitution, which warrants the conclusion, that it was intended to exclude the inferior courts of the Union from a concurrent original jurisdiction.[2] The judiciary act of 1789, (ch. 20, § 11, 13,) has manifestly proceeded upon the supposition, that the jurisdiction was not exclusive; but, that concurrent original jurisdiction in those cases might be vested by congress in inferior courts.[3] It has been strongly intimated, indeed, by the highest tribunal, on more than one occasion, that the original jurisdiction of the Supreme Court in those cases is exclusive;[4] but

---

1 *Martin* v. *Hunter*, 1 Wheat. R. 337, 338; *Osborn* v. *Bank of United States*, 9 Wheat. R. 820, 821; *Cohens* v. *Virginia*, 6 Wheat. R. 395, 396.
2 *United States* v. *Ravara*, 2 Dall. R. 297; *Chisholm* v. *Georgia*, 2 Dall. R. 419, 431, 436, per Iredell J. Sergeant on Const. ch. 2.
3 1 Kent. Comm. Lect. 15, p. 294, 295, (2d edition, p. 314, 315.)
4 See *Marbury* v. *Madison*, 1 Cranch, R. 137; *Martin* v. *Hunter*

the question remains to this hour without any authoritative decision.[1]

§ 1700. Another question of a very different nature is, whether the Supreme Court can exercise appellate jurisdiction in the class of cases, of which original jurisdiction is delegated to it by the constitution; in other words, whether the original jurisdiction excludes the appellate; and so, *e converso*, the latter implies a negative of the former. It has been said, that the very distinction taken in the constitution, between original and appellate jurisdiction, presupposes, that where the one can be exercised, the other cannot. For example, since the original jurisdiction extends to cases, where a state is a party, this is the proper form, in which such cases are to be brought before the Supreme Court; and, therefore, a case, where a state is a party, cannot be brought before the court, in the exercise of its appellate jurisdiction; for the affirmative here, as well as in the cases of original jurisdiction, includes a negative of the cases not enumerated.

§ 1701. If the correctness of this reasoning were admitted, it would establish no more, than that the Supreme Court could not exercise appellate jurisdiction in cases, where a state is a party. But it would by no means establish the doctrine, that the judicial power of the United States did not extend, in an appellate form, to such cases. The exercise of appellate jurisdiction is far from being limited, by the terms of the constitution, to the Supreme Court. There can be no

1 Wheat. R. 337, 338 ; *Osborn* v. *Bank of United States,* 9 Wheat. R. 820, 821 ; 1 Kent's Comm. Lect. 15, p. 294, 295, (2d edition, p. 314, 315 ;) *Cohens* v. *Virginia,* 6 Wheat. R. 395, 396, 397.

1 *United States* v. *Ortega,* 11 Wheat. R. 467 ; *Cohens* v. *Virginia,* 6 Wheat R. 396, 397.

doubt, that congress may create a succession of inferior tribunals, in each of which it may vest appellate, as well as original jurisdiction. This results from the very nature of the delegation of the judicial power in the constitution. It is delegated in the most general terms; and may, therefore, be exercised under the authority of congress, under every variety of form of original and appellate jurisdiction. There is nothing in the instrument, which restrains, or limits the power; and it must, consequently, subsist in the utmost latitude, of which it is in its nature susceptible.[1] The result then would be, that, if the appellate jurisdiction over cases, to which a state is a party, could not, according to the terms of the constitution, be exercised by the Supreme Court, it might be exercised exclusively by an inferior tribunal. The soundness of any reasoning, which would lead us to such a conclusion, may well be questioned.[2]

---

[1] *Martin* v. *Hunter*, 1 Wheat. R. 337, 338; *Osborn* v. *Bank of United States*, 9 Wheat. R. 820, 821; *Cohens* v. *Virginia*, 6 Wheat. R. 392 to 396.

[2] The Federalist, No. 82, has spoken of the right of congress to vest appellate jurisdiction in the inferior courts of the United States from state courts, (for it had before expressly affirmed that of the Supreme Court in such cases) in the following terms. " But could an appeal be made to lie from the state courts to the subordinate federal judicatories? This is another of the questions, which have been raised, and of greater difficulty, than the former. The following considerations countenance the affirmative. The plan of the convention, in the first place, authorizes the national legislature ' to constitute tribunals, inferior to the Supreme Court. It declares, in the next place, that ' the judicial power of the United States *shall be vested* in one Supreme Court, and in such inferior courts, as congress shall ordain and establish ;' and it then proceeds to enumerate the cases, to which this judicial power shall extend. It afterwards divides the jurisdiction of the Supreme Court into original and appellate, but gives no definition of that of the subordinate courts. The only outlines described for them are, that they shall

§ 1702. But the reasoning itself is not well founded. It proceeds upon the ground, that, because the character of the *party* alone, in some instances, entitles the Supreme Court to maintain original jurisdiction, without any reference to the nature of the case, therefore, the character of the *case*, which in other instances is made the very foundation of appellate jurisdiction, cannot attach. Now, that is the very point of controversy. It is not only not admitted, but it is solemnly denied. The argument might just as well, and with quite as much force, be pressed in the opposite direction. It might be said, that the appellate jurisdiction is expressly extended by the constitution to all cases in law and equity, arising under the constitution, laws, and treaties of the United States, and, therefore, in no such cases could the Supreme Court exercise original jurisdiction, even though a state were a party.

§ 1703. But this subject has been expounded in so masterly a manner by Mr. Chief Justice Marshall, in delivering the opinion of the Supreme Court in a very celebrated case,[1] that it will be more satisfactory to

---

be 'inferior to the Supreme Court,' and that they shall not exceed the specified limits of the federal judiciary. Whether their authority shall be original, or appellate, or both, is not declared. All this seems to be left to the discretion of the legislature. And this being the case, I perceive at present no impediment to the establishment of an appeal from the state courts to the subordinate national tribunals: and many advantages, attending the power of doing it, may be imagined. It would diminish the motives to the multiplication of federal courts, and would admit of arrangements, calculated to contract the appellate jurisdiction of the Supreme Court. The state tribunals may then be left with a more entire charge of federal causes; and appeals, in most cases, in which they may be deemed proper, instead of being carried to the Supreme Court, may be made to lie from the state courts to district courts of the Union."

[1] *Cohens* v. *Virginia*, 6 Wheat. R. 264, 392, *et seq.*

give the whole argument in his own language. "The constitution" (says he,) "gives the Supreme Court original jurisdiction in certain enumerated cases, and gives it appellate jurisdiction in all others. Among those, in which jurisdiction must be exercised in the appellate form, are cases arising under the constitution and laws of the United States. These provisions of the constitution are equally obligatory, and are to be equally respected. If a state be a party, the jurisdiction of this court is original; if the case arise under the constitution, or a law, the jurisdiction is appellate. But a case, to which a state is a party, may arise under the constitution, or a law of the United States. What rule is applicable to such a case? What, then, becomes the duty of the court? Certainly, we think, so to construe the constitution, as to give effect to both provisions, as far as it is possible to reconcile them, and not to permit their seeming repugnancy to destroy each other. We must endeavour so to construe them, as to preserve the true intent and meaning of the instrument.

§ 1704. "In one description of cases, the jurisdiction of the court is founded entirely on the character of the parties; and the nature of the controversy is not contemplated by the constitution. The character of the parties is every thing, the nature of the case nothing. In the other description of cases, the jurisdiction is founded entirely on the character of the case, and the parties are not contemplated by the constitution. In these, the nature of the case is every thing, the character of the parties nothing. When, then, the constitution declares the jurisdiction in cases, where a state shall be a party, to be original, and in all cases arising under the constitution, or a law, to be appellate, the

conclusion seems irresistible, that its framers designed
to include in the first class those cases, in which jurisdiction is given, because a state is a party; and to include in the second those, in which jurisdiction is given,
because the case arises under the constitution, or a law.
This reasonable construction is rendered necessary by
other considerations. That the constitution, or a law
of the United States, is involved in a case, and makes
a part of it, may appear in the progress of a cause, in
which the courts of the Union, but for that circumstance,
would have no jurisdiction, and which of consequence
could not originate in the Supreme Court. In such a
case, the jurisdiction can be exercised only in its appellate form. To deny its exercise in this form is to
deny its existence, and would be to construe a clause,
dividing the power of the Supreme Court, in such
manner, as in a considerable degree to defeat the power
itself. All must perceive, that this construction can be
justified, only where it is absolutely necessary. We
do not think the article under consideration presents
that necessity.

§ 1705. "It is observable, that in this distributive
clause no negative words are introduced. This observation is not made for the purpose of contending, that
the legislature may 'apportion the judicial power between the supreme and inferior courts, according to
its will.' That would be, as was said by this court in
the case of *Marbury* v. *Madison*, to render the distributive clause 'mere surplusage,' to make it 'form
without substance.' This cannot, therefore, be the
true construction of the article. But although the
absence of negative words will not authorize the legislature to disregard the distribution of the power
previously granted, their absence will justify a sound

construction of the whole article, so as to give every part its intended effect. It is admitted, that 'affirmative words are often, in their operation, negative of other objects, than those affirmed;' and that where 'a negative or exclusive sense, must be given to them, or they have no operation at all,' they must receive that negative, or exclusive sense. But where they have full operation without it; where it would destroy some of the most important objects, for which the power was created; then, we think, affirmative words ought not to be construed negatively.

§ 1706. "The constitution declares, that in cases, where a state is a party, the Supreme Court shall have original jurisdiction; but does not say, that its appellate jurisdiction shall not be exercised in cases, where, from their nature, appellate jurisdiction is given, whether a state be, or be not a party.[1] It may be conceded, that where the case is of such a nature, as to admit of its originating in the Supreme Court, it ought to originate there; but where, from its nature, it cannot originate in that court, these words ought not to be so construed, as to require it. There are many cases, in which it would be found extremely difficult, and subversive of the spirit of the constitution, to maintain the construction, that appellate jurisdiction cannot be exercised, where one of the parties might sue, or be sued in this court. The constitution defines the jurisdiction of the Supreme Court, but does not define that of the inferior courts. Can it be affirmed, that a state might not sue the citizen of another state in a Circuit Court? Should the Circuit Court decide for, or against its jurisdiction, should it dismiss the suit, or give judgment

---

[1] See 9 Wheat. R. 820, 821.

against the state, might not its decision be revised in the Supreme Court? The argument is, that it could not; and the very clause, which is urged to prove, that the Circuit Court could give no judgment in the case, is also urged to prove, that its judgment is irreversible. A supervising court, whose peculiar province it is to correct the errors of an inferior court, has no power to correct a judgment given without jurisdiction, because, in the same case, that supervising court has original jurisdiction. Had negative words been employed, it would be difficult to give them this construction, if they would admit of any other. But, without negative words, this irrational construction can never be maintained.

§ 1707. "So, too, in the same clause, the jurisdiction of the court is declared to be original, 'in cases affecting ambassadors, other public ministers, and consuls.' There is, perhaps, no part of the article under consideration so much required by national policy, as this; unless it be that part, which extends the judicial power 'to all cases arising under the constitution, laws, and treaties of the United States.' It has been generally held, that the state courts have a concurrent jurisdiction with the federal courts in cases, to which the judicial power is extended, unless the jurisdiction of the federal courts be rendered exclusive by the words of the third article. If the words, 'to all cases,' give exclusive jurisdiction in cases affecting foreign ministers, they may also give exclusive jurisdiction, if such be the will of congress, in cases arising under the constitution, laws, and treaties of the United States. Now, suppose an individual were to sue a foreign minister in a state court, and that court were to maintain its jurisdiction, and render judgment against the minister, could it be contended, that this court would be incapable of revising such judgment, because the constitution had given it original jurisdiction in the case? If this could be maintained, then a clause inserted for the purpose of excluding the jurisdiction of all other courts, than this, in a particular case, would have the effect of excluding the jurisdiction of this court in that very case, if the suit were to be brought in another court, and that court were to assert jurisdiction. This tribunal, according to the argument, which has been urged, could neither revise the judgment of such other court, nor suspend its proceedings; for a writ of prohibition, or any other similar writ, is in the nature of appellate process.

§ 1708. " Foreign consuls frequently assert, in our prize courts, the claims of their fellow subjects. These suits are maintained by them, as consuls. The appellate power of this court has been frequently exercised in such cases, and has never been questioned. It would be extremely mischievous to withhold its exercise. Yet the consul is a party on the record. The truth is, that, where the words confer only appellate jurisdiction, original jurisdiction is most clearly not given; but where the words admit of appellate jurisdiction, the power to take cognizance of the suit originally does not necessarily negative the power to decide upon it on an appeal, if it may originate in a different court. It is, we think, apparent, that to give this distributive clause the interpretation contended for, to give to its affirmative words a negative operation, in every possible case, would, in some instances, defeat the obvious intention of the article. Such an interpretation would not consist with those rules, which, from time immemorial, have guided courts in their construction of instruments brought under their consideration. It must, therefore, be discarded. Every part of the article must be taken into view, and that construction adopted, which will consist with its words, and promote its general intention. The court may imply a negative from affirmative words, where the implication promotes, not where it defeats, the intention.

§ 1709. "If we apply this principle, the correctness of which we believe will not be controverted, to the distributive clause under consideration, the result, we think, would be this; the original jurisdiction of the Supreme Court in cases, where a state is a party, refers to those cases, in which, according to the grant of power made in the preceding clause, jurisdiction might be exercised in consequence of the character of the party, and an original suit might be instituted in any of the federal courts ; not to those cases, in which an original suit might not be instituted in a federal court. Of the last description is every case between a state and its citizens, and, perhaps, every case, in which a state is enforcing its penal laws. In such cases, therefore, the Supreme Court cannot take original jurisdiction. In every other case, that is, in every case, to which the judicial power extends, and in which original jurisdiction is not expressly given, that judicial power shall be exercised in the appellate, and only in the appellate form. The original jurisdiction of this court cannot be enlarged, but its appellate jurisdiction may be exercised in every case, cognizable under the third article of the constitution in the federal courts, in which original jurisdiction cannot be exercised; and the extent of this judicial power is to be measured, not by giving the affirmative words of the distributive clause a negative operation in every possible case, but by giving their true meaning to the words, which define its extent. The counsel for the defendant in error urge, in opposition to this rule of construction, some *dicta* of the court, in the case of *Marbury* v. *Madison*.[1]

§ 1710. "It is a maxim not to be disregarded, that general expressions, in every opinion, are to be taken in connexion with the case, in which those expressions are used. If they go beyond the case, they may be respected, but ought not to control the judgment in a subsequent suit, when the very point is presented for decision. The reason of this maxim is obvious. The question actually before the court is investigated with care, and considered in its full extent. Other principles, which may serve to illustrate it, are considered in their relation to the case decided, but their possible bearing on all other cases is seldom completely investigated. In the case of *Marbury* v. *Madison*, the single question before the court, so far as that case can be applied to this, was, whether the legislature could give this court original jurisdiction in a case, in which the constitution had clearly not given it, and in which no doubt respecting the construction of the article could possibly be raised. The court decided, and we think very properly, that the legislature could not give original jurisdiction in such a case. But, in the reasoning of the court in support of this decision, some expressions are used, which go far beyond it. The counsel for Marbury had insisted on the unlimited discretion of the legislature in the apportionment of the judicial power; and it is against this argument, that the reasoning of the court is directed. They say, that, if such had been the intention of the article, 'it would certainly have been useless to

---

[1] 1 Cranch, R. 174, 175, 176.

proceed farther, than to define the judicial power, and the tribunals, in which it should be vested.' The court says, that such a construction would render the clause, dividing the jurisdiction of the court into original and appellate, totally useless; that 'affirmative words are often, in their operation, negative of other objects, than those which are affirmed; and, in this case, (in the case of *Marbury* v. *Madison*,) a negative or exclusive sense must be given to them, or they have no operation at all.' 'It cannot be presumed,' adds the court, 'that any clause in the constitution is intended to be without effect; and, therefore, such a construction is inadmissible, unless the words require it.'

§ 1711. "The whole reasoning of the court proceeds upon the idea, that the affirmative words of the clause, giving one sort of jurisdiction, must imply a negative of any other sort of jurisdiction, because otherwise the words would be totally inoperative; and this reasoning is advanced in a case, to which it was strictly applicable. If in that case original jurisdiction could have been exercised, the clause under consideration would have been entirely useless. Having such cases only in its view, the court lays down a principle, which is generally correct, in terms much broader, than the decision, and not only much broader, than the reasoning, with which that decision is supported, but in some instances contradictory to its principle. The reasoning sustains the negative operation of the words in that case, because otherwise the clause would have no meaning whatever, and because such operation, was necessary to give effect to the intention of the article. The effort now made is, to apply the conclusion, to which the court was conducted by that reasoning in the particular case, to one, in which the words have their full operation, when understood affirmatively, and in which the negative, or exclusive sense is to be so used, as to defeat some of the great objects of the article. To this construction the court cannot give its assent. The general expressions in the case of *Marbury* v. *Madison* must be understood with the limitations, which are given to them in this opinion; limitations, which in no degree affect the decision in that case, or the tenor of its reasoning. The counsel, who closed the argument, put several cases for the purpose of illustration, which he supposed to arise under the constitution, and yet to be, apparently, without the jurisdiction of the court. Were a state to lay a duty on exports, to collect the money and place it in her treasury, could the citizen, who paid it, he asks, maintain a suit in this court against such state, to recover back the money? Perhaps not. Without, however, deciding such supposed case, we may say, that it is entirely unlike that under consideration.

§ 1712. "The citizen, who had paid his money to his state, under a law that is void, is in the same situation with every other person, who has paid money by mistake. The law raises an assumpsit to return the money, and it is upon that assumpsit, that the action is to be maintained. To refuse to comply with this assumpsit may be no more a violation of the constitution, than to refuse to comply with any other; and as the federal courts never had jurisdiction over contracts between a state and its citizens, they may have none over this. But let us so vary the supposed case, as to give it a real resemblance to that under consideration. Suppose a citizen to refuse to pay this export duty, and a suit to be instituted for the purpose of compelling him to pay it. He pleads the constitution of the United States in bar of the action, notwithstanding which the court gives judgment against him. This would be a case arising under the constitution, and would be the very case now before the court.

§ 1713. "We are also asked, if a state should confiscate property secured by a treaty, whether the individual could maintain an action for that property? If the property confiscated be debts, our own experience informs us, that the remedy of the creditor against his debtor remains. If it be land, which is secured by a treaty, and afterwards confiscated by a state, the argument does not assume, that this title, thus secured, could be extinguished by an act of confiscation. The injured party, therefore, has his remedy against the occupant of the land for that, which the treaty secures to him; not against the state for money, which is not secured to him.

§ 1714. "The case of a state, which pays off its own debts with paper money, no more resembles this, than do those, to which we have already adverted. The courts have no jurisdiction over the contract. They cannot enforce it, nor judge of its violation. Let it be, that the act discharging the debt is a mere nullity, and that it is still due. Yet the federal courts have no cognizance of the case. But suppose a state to institute proceedings against an individual, which depended on the validity of an act emitting bills of credit: suppose a state to prosecute one of its citizens for refusing paper money, who should plead the constitution in bar of such prosecution. If his plea should be overruled, and judgment rendered against him, his case would resemble this; and, unless the jurisdiction of this court might be exercised over it, the constitution would be violated, and the injured party be unable to bring his case before that tribunal, to which the people of the United States have assigned all such cases. It is most true, that this court will not take jurisdiction, if it should not: but it is equally true, that it must take jurisdiction, if it should. The judiciary cannot, as the legislature may, avoid a measure, because it approaches the confines of the constitution. We cannot pass it by, because it is doubtful. With whatever doubts, with whatever difficulties, a case may be attended, we must decide it, if it be brought before us. We have no more right to decline the exercise of jurisdiction, which is given, than to usurp that, which is not given. The one or the other would be treason to the constitution. Questions may occur which we would gladly avoid; but we cannot avoid them. All we can do is, to exercise our best judgment, and conscientiously to perform our duty. In doing this, on the present occasion, we find this tribunal invested with appellate jurisdiction in all cases, arising under the constitution and laws of the United States. We find no exception to this grant, and we cannot insert one.

§ 1715. "To escape the operation of these comprehensive words, the counsel for the defendant has mentioned instances, in which the constitution might be violated without giving jurisdiction to this court. These words, therefore, however universal in their expression, must, he contends, be limited, and controlled in their construction by circumstances. One of these instances is, the grant by a state of a patent of nobility. The court, he says, cannot annul this grant. This may be very true; but by no means justifies the inference drawn from it. The article does not extend the judicial power to every violation of the constitution, which may possibly take place; but to 'a case in law or equity,' in which a right, under such law, is asserted

in a court of justice.   If the question cannot be brought
into a court, then there is no case in law or equity, and
no jurisdiction is given by the words of the article.
But if, in any controversy depending in a court, the cause
should depend on the validity of such a law, that would
be a case arising under the constitution, to which the
judicial power of the United States would extend.
The same observation applies to the other instances,
with which the counsel, who opened the cause, has
illustrated this argument.   Although they show, that
there may be violations of the constitution, of which
the courts can take no cognizance, they do not show,
that an interpretation more restrictive, than the words
themselves import, ought to be given to this article.
They do not show, that there can be ' a *case* in law or
equity,' arising under the constitution, to which the
judicial power does not extend.   We think, then, that,
as the constitution originally stood, the appellate jurisdiction of this court, in all cases arising under the constitution, laws, or treaties of the United States, was
not arrested by the circumstance, that a state was a
party."[1]

---

[1] Much reliance has occasionally been laid upon particular expressions of the Supreme Court, used incidentally in argument, to support the
reasoning, which is here so ably answered.   The reasoning in *Marbury*
v. *Madison*, (1 Cranch, R. 174, 175, 176,) has been cited, as especially
in point.   But the Supreme Court, in *Cohens* v. *Virginia*, (6 Wheat. R.
399 to 402) explained it in a satisfactory manner.   So, in other cases, it
is said by the Supreme Court, that "appellate jurisdiction is given to
the Supreme Court in all cases, where it has not original jurisdiction;"
and that "it may be exercised (by the Supreme Court) in all other cases,
than those, of which it has original cognizance."*   And again, "in
those cases, in which the original jurisdiction is given to the Supreme
Court, the judicial power of the United States cannot be exercised in

* *Martin* v. *Hunter*, 1 Wheaton's R. 337, 338.

§ 1716. The next inquiry is, whether the eleventh amendment to the constitution has effected any change of the jurisdiction, thus confided to the judicial power of the United States. And here again the most satisfactory answer, which can be given, will be found in the language of the same opinion.[1] After quoting the words of the amendment, which are, " the " judicial power of the United States shall not be " construed to extend to any suit in law or equity, " commenced or prosecuted against one of the states " by citizens of another state, or by citizens or sub- " jects of any foreign state," the opinion proceeds: " It is a part of our history, that, at the adoption of the constitution, all the states were greatly indebted; and the apprehension, that these debts might be prosecuted in the federal courts, formed a very serious objection to that instrument. Suits were instituted; and the court maintained its jurisdiction. The alarm was general; and, to quiet the appre-

---

its appellate form. ' *   Now, these expression, if taken in connexion with the context, and the general scope of the argument, in which they are to be found, are perfectly accurate.   It is only by detaching them from this connexion, that they are supposed to speak a language, inconsistent with that in *Cohens* v. *Virginia*, (6 Wheat. R. 392 to 399.)   The court, in each of the cases, where the language above cited is used, were referring to those classes of cases, in which original jurisdiction is given solely by the character of the *party*, i. e. a state, a foreign ambassador, or other public minister, or a consul.   In such cases, if there would be no jurisdiction at all, founded upon any other part of the constitutional delegation of judicial power, except that applicable to *parties*, the court held, that the appellate jurisdiction would not attach.   Why?   Plainly, because original jurisdiction only was given in such cases.   But where the constitution extended the appellate jurisdiction to a class of cases, embracing the particular suit, without any reference to the point, who were parties, there the same reasoning would not apply.

1 *Cohens* v. *Virginia*, 6 Wheat. R. 406 to 412.

Osborn v. Bank of United States, 9 Wheaton's R. 820.

hensions, that were so extens'vely entertained, this
amendment was proposed in Congress, and adopted
by the state legislatures. That its motive was not to
maintain the sovereignty of a state from the degrada-
tion, supposed to attend a compulsory appearance
before the tribunal of the nation, may be inferred
from the terms of the amendment. It does not comprehend controversies between two or more states,
or between a state and a foreign state. The jurisdiction of the court still extends to these cases; and
in these a state may still be sued. We must ascribe
the amendment, then, to some other cause, than the
dignity of a state. There is no difficulty in finding
this cause. Those, who were inhibited from commencing a suit against a state, or from prosecuting
one, which might be commenced before the adoption
of the amendment, were persons, who might probably
be its creditors. There was not much reason to fear,
that foreign or sister states would be creditors to any
considerable amount; and there was reason to retain
the jurisdiction of the court in those cases, because
it might be essential to the preservation of peace.
The amendment, therefore, extended to suits commenced, or prosecuted by individuals, but not to those
brought by states.

§ 1717. " The first impression made on the mind
by this amendment is, that it was intended for those
cases, and for those only, in which some demand
against a state is made by an individual in the courts
of the Union. If we consider the causes, to which it
is to be traced, we are conducted to the same conclusion. A general interest might well be felt in
leaving to a state the full power of consulting its
convenience in the adjustment of its debts, or of

other claims upon it; but no interest could be felt in so changing the relations between the whole and its parts, as to strip the government of the means of protecting, by the instrumentality of its courts, the constitution and laws from active violation.

§ 1718. "The words of the amendment appear to the court to justify and require this construction. The judicial power is not 'to extend to any suit in law or equity, commenced, or prosecuted against one of the United States by citizens of another state, &c.'

§ 1719. "What is a suit? We understand it to be the prosecution, or pursuit, of some claim, demand, or request. In law language, it is the prosecution of some demand in a court of justice. The remedy for every species of wrong is, says Judge Blackstone, 'the being put in possession of that right whereof the party injured is deprived.' 'The instruments, whereby this remedy is obtained, are a diversity of suits and actions, which are defined by the Mirror to be "the lawful demand of one's right;" or, as Bracton and Fleta express it, in the words of Justinian, *jus prosequendi in judicio, quod alicui debetur.* Blackstone then proceeds to describe every species of remedy by suit; and they are all cases, where the party suing claims to obtain something, to which he has a right.

§ 1720. "To commence a suit is to demand something by the institution of process in a court of justice; and to prosecute the suit, is, according to the common acceptation of language, to continue that demand. By a suit commenced by an individual against a state, we should understand process sued out by that individual against the state, for the purpose of establishing some claim against it by the judgment of a court; and the prosecution of that suit is its continuance. Whatever may be the stages of its progress, the actor is still the same. Suits had been commenced in the Supreme Court against some of the states before this amendment was introduced into Congress, and others might be commenced, before it should be adopted by the state legislatures, and might be depending at the time of its adoption. The object of the amendment was, not only to prevent the commencement of future suits, but to arrest the prosecution of those, which might be commenced, when this article should form a part of the constitution. It therefore embraces both objects; and its meaning is, that the judicial power shall not be construed to extend to any suit, which may be commenced, or which, if already commenced, may be prosecuted against a state by the citizen of another state. If a suit, brought in one court, and carried by legal process to a supervising court, be a continuation of the same suit, then this suit is not commenced nor prosecuted against a state. It is clearly in its commencement the suit of a state against an individual, which suit is transferred to this court, not for the purpose of asserting any claim against the state, but for the purpose of asserting a constitutional defence against a claim made by a state.

§ 1721. "A writ of error is defined to be a commission, by which the judges of one court are authorized to examine a record, upon which a judgment was given in another court, and, on such examination, to affirm, or reverse the same according to law. If, says my Lord Coke, by the writ of error the plaintiff may recover, or be restored to any thing, it may be released by the name of an action. In Bacon's

Abridgment, tit. *Error*, L. it is laid down, that
' where by a writ of error the plaintiff shall recover,
or be restored to any personal thing, as debt, damage, or the like, a release of all actions personal is a
good plea. And when land is to be recovered, or
restored in a writ of error, a release of actions real is
a good bar. But where by a writ of error the plaintiff
shall not be restored to any personal or real thing,
a release of all actions real or personal is no bar.'
And for this we have the authority of Lord Coke,
both in his Commentary on Littleton and in his
Reports. A writ of error, then, is in the nature of a
suit or action, when it is to restore the party, who
obtains it to the possession of any thing, which is
withheld from him, not when its operation is entirely
defensive. This rule will apply to writs of error from
the Courts of the United States, as well as to those
writs in England.

§ 1722. " Under the judiciary act, the effect of a
writ of error is simply to bring the record into Court,
and submit the judgment of the inferior tribunal to
re-examination. It does not in any manner act upon
the parties; it acts only on the record. It removes
the record into the supervising tribunal. Where,
then, a state obtains a judgment against an individual,
and the court, rendering such judgment, overrules a
defence, set up under the constitution, or laws of the
United States, the transfer of this record into the Supreme Court, for the sole purpose of inquiring, whether
the judgment violates the constitution or laws of the
United States, can, with no propriety, we think, be denominated a suit commenced, or prosecuted against
the state, whose judgment is so far re-examined. Nothing is demanded from the state. No claim against it,

of any description, is asserted or prosecuted. The
party is not to be restored to the possession of any
thing. Essentially, it is an appeal on a single point;
and the defendant, who appeals from a judgment rendered against him, is never said to commence, or prosecute a suit against the plaintiff, who has obtained the
judgment. The writ of error is given, rather than an
appeal, because it is the more usual mode of removing
suits at common law; and because, perhaps, it is more
technically proper, where a single point of law, and not
the whole case, is to be re-examined. But an appeal
might be given, and might be so regulated, as to effect
every purpose of a writ of error. The mode of removal is form, and not substance. Whether it be by
writ of error, or appeal, no claim is asserted, no demand
is made by the original defendant. He only asserts the
constitutional right, to have his defence examined by
that tribunal, whose province it is to construe the constitution and laws of the Union.

§ 1723. "The only part of the proceeding, which is
in any manner personal, is the citation. And what is
the citation? It is simply notice to the opposite party,
that the record is transferred into another court, where
he may appear, or decline to appear, as his judgment,
or inclination may determine. As the party, who has
obtained a judgment is out of court, and may, therefore, not know, that his cause is removed, common justice requires, that notice of the fact should be given him.
But this notice is not a suit, nor has it the effect of
process. If the party does not choose to appear, he
cannot be brought into court, nor is his failure to appear
considered as a default. Judgment cannot be given
against him for his non-appearance; but the judgment
is to be re-examined, and reversed, or affirmed, in like

manner, as if the party had appeared, and argued his cause.

§ 1724. "The point of view, in which this writ of error, with its citation, has been considered uniformly in the courts of the Union, has been well illustrated by a reference to the course of this court in suits instituted by the United States. The universally received opinion is, that no suit can be commenced, or prosecuted against the United States; that the judiciary act does not authorize such suits. Yet writs of error, accompanied with citations, have uniformly issued for the removal of judgments in favour of the United States into a superior court, where they have, like those in favour of an individual, been re-examined, and affirmed, or reversed. It has never been suggested, that such writ of error was a suit against the United States, and, therefore, not within the jurisdiction of the appellate court. It is, then, the opinion of the court, that the defendant, who removes a judgment, rendered against him by a state court, into this court, for the purpose of re-examining the question, whether that judgment be in violation of the constitution and laws of the United States, does not commence, or prosecute a suit against the state, whatever may be its opinion, where the effect of the writ may be to restore the party to the possession of a thing, which he demands."[1]

§ 1725. Another inquiry, touching the appellate jurisdiction of the Supreme Court, of a still more general character, is, whether it extends only to the inferior courts of the Union, constituted by congress, or reaches to cases decided in the state courts. This question

---

[1] See also *Governor of Georgia* v. *Madrazo*, 1 Peters's Sup. R. 128 to 131, per Johnson J.

has been made on several occasions; and has been
most deliberately weighed, and solemnly decided in
the Supreme Court. The reasoning of the court in
Martin v. *Hunter*,[1] (which was the first time, in which
the question was directly presented for judgment,) will
be here given, as it has been affirmed on more recent
discussions.[2]

§ 1726. "This leads us," says the court "to the
consideration of the great question, as to the nature
and extent of the appellate jurisdiction of the United
States. We have already seen, that appellate jurisdiction is given by the constitution to the Supreme Court
in all cases, where it has not original jurisdiction; subject, however, to such exceptions and regulations, as
congress may prescribe. It is, therefore, capable of
embracing every case enumerated in the constitution,
which is not exclusively to be decided by way of original jurisdiction. But the exercise of appellate jurisdiction is far from being limited by the terms of the
constitution to the Supreme Court. There can be no
doubt, that congress may create a succession of inferior
tribunals, in each of which it may vest appellate, as
well as original jurisdiction. The judicial power is
delegated by the constitution in the most general terms,
and may, therefore, be exercised by congress, under
every variety of form of appellate, or original jurisdiction. And as there is nothing in the constitution, which
restrains, or limits this power, it must, therefore, in all
these cases, subsist in the utmost latitude, of which, in
its own nature, it is susceptible.

§ 1727. "As, then, by the terms of the constitution,

1 1 Wheat. R. 304.
2 *Cohens* v. *Virginia*, 6 Wheat. R. 413 to 423.

the appellate jurisdiction is not limited, as to the Supreme Court, and as to this court it may be exercised in all other cases, than those, of which it has original cognizance, what is there to restrain its exercise over state tribunals in the enumerated cases? The appellate power is not limited by the terms of the third article to any particular courts. The words are, 'the judicial power (which includes appellate power,) shall extend *to all cases,*' &c., and 'in all other cases before mentioned, the Supreme Court shall have appellate jurisdiction.' It is the *case,* then, and not *the court,* that gives the jurisdiction. If the judicial power extends to the case, it will be in vain to search in the letter of the constitution for any qualification, as to the tribunal, where it depends. It is incumbent, then, upon those, who assert such a qualification, to show its existence by necessary implication. If the text be clear and distinct, no restriction upon its plain and obvious import ought to be admitted, unless the inference be irresistible.

§ 1728. "If the constitution meant to limit the appellate jurisdiction to cases pending in the courts of the United States, it would necessarily follow, that the jurisdiction of these courts would, in all the cases enumerated in the constitution, be exclusive of state tribunals. How, otherwise, could the jurisdiction extend to all cases, arising under the constitution, laws, and treaties of the United States, or, to *all cases* of admiralty and maritime jurisdiction? If some of these cases might be entertained by state tribunals, and no appellate jurisdiction, as to them, should exist, then the appellate power would not extend to *all,* but to *some,* cases. If state tribunals might exercise concurrent jurisdiction over all, or some of the other

classes of cases in the constitution, without control,
then the appellate jurisdiction of the United States
might, as to such cases, have no real existence, contrary to the manifest intent of the constitution. Under such circumstances, to give effect to the judicial
power, it must be construed to be exclusive; and
this, not only when the *casus fœderis* should arise directly; but when it should arise incidentally in cases
pending in state courts. This construction would
abridge the jurisdiction of such courts far more, than
has been ever contemplated in any act of congress.

§ 1729. " On the other hand, if, as has been contended, a discretion be vested in congress to establish, or not to establish, inferior courts at their own
pleasure, and congress should not establish such
courts, the appellate jurisdiction of the Supreme
Court would have nothing to act upon, unless it could
act upon cases pending in the state courts. Under
such circumstances it must be held, that the appellate
power would extend to state courts; for the constitution is peremptory, that it shall extend to certain
enumerated cases, which cases could exist in no
other courts. Any other construction, upon this
supposition, would involve this strange contradiction,
that a discretionary power, vested in congress, and
which they might rightfully omit to exercise, would
defeat the absolute injunctions of the constitution in
relation to the whole appellate power.

§ 1730. " But it is plain, that the framers of the
constitution did contemplate, that cases within the
judicial cognizance of the United States, not only
might, but would arise in the state courts in the exercise of their ordinary jurisdiction. With this view,
the sixth article declares, that ' this constitution, and

the laws of the United States, which shall be made in pursuance thereof, and all treaties made, or which shall be made, under the authority of the United States, shall be the supreme law of the land, and the judges, in every state, shall be bound thereby, any thing, in the constitution or laws of any state, to the contrary notwithstanding.' It is obvious, that this obligation is imperative upon the state judges in their official, and not merely in their private capacities. From the very nature of their judicial duties, they would be called upon to pronounce the law, applicable to the case in judgment. They were not to decide, merely according to the laws, or constitution of the state, but according to the constitution, laws, and treaties of the United States, — 'the supreme law of the land.'

§ 1731. "A moment's consideration will show us the necessity and propriety of this provision in cases, where the jurisdiction of the state courts is unquestionable. Suppose a contract, for the payment of money, is made between citizens of the same state, and performance thereof is sought in the courts of that state; no person can doubt, that the jurisdiction completely and exclusively attaches, in the first instance, to such courts. Suppose at the trial, the defendant sets up, in his defence, a tender under a state law, making paper money a good tender, or a state law, impairing the obligation of such contract, which law, if binding, would defeat the suit. The constitution of the United States has declared, that no state shall make any thing but gold or silver coin a tender in payment of debts, or pass a law impairing the obligation of contracts. If congress shall not have passed a law, providing for the removal of such a suit to the courts of the United States, must not the state court proceed to hear, and determine it? Can a mere plea in defence be, of itself, a bar to further proceedings, so as to prohibit an inquiry into its truth, or legal propriety, when no other tribunal exists, to whom judicial cognizance of such cases is confided? Suppose an indictment for a crime in a state court, and the defendant should allege in his defence, that the crime was created by an *ex post facto* act of the state, must not the state court, in the exercise of a jurisdiction, which has already rightfully attached, have a right to pronounce on the validity, and sufficiency of the defence? It would be extremely difficult, upon any legal principles, to give a negative answer to these inquiries. Innumerable instances of the same sort might be stated, in illustration of the position; and unless the state courts could sustain jurisdiction in such cases, this clause of the sixth article would be without meaning or effect; and public mischiefs, of a most enormous magnitude, would inevitably ensue.

§ 1732. "It must, therefore, be conceded, that the constitution, not only contemplated, but meant to provide for cases within the scope of the judicial power of the United States, which might yet depend before state tribunals. It was foreseen, that, in the exercise of their ordinary jurisdiction, state courts would, incidentally, take cognizance of cases arising under the constitution, the laws, and treaties of the United States. Yet to all these cases the judicial power, by the very terms of the constitution, is to extend. It cannot extend by original jurisdiction, if that has already rightfully and exclusively attached in the state courts, which (as has been already shown) may occur; it must, therefore, extend by appellate jurisdiction, or not at all. It would seem to follow, that the appellate power of the United States must, in such cases, extend to state tribunals; and, if in such cases, there is no reason, why it should not equally attach upon all others within the purview of the constitution. It has been argued, that such an appellate jurisdiction over state courts is inconsistent with the genius of our governments, and the spirit of the constitution. That the latter was never designed to act upon state sovereignties, but only upon the people; and that, if the power exists, it will materially impair the sovereignty of the states, and the independence of their courts. We cannot yield to the force of this reasoning; it assumes principles, which we cannot admit, and draws conclusions, to which we do not yield our assent.

§ 1733. "It is a mistake, that the constitution was not designed to operate upon states in their corporate capacities. It is crowded with provisions, which restrain, or annul the sovereignty of the states, in some of the highest branches of their prerogatives. The tenth section of the first article contains a long list of disabilities and prohibitions imposed upon the states. Surely, when such essential portions of state sovereignty are taken away, or prohibited to be exercised, it cannot be correctly asserted, that the constitution does not act upon the states. The language of the constitution is also imperative upon the states, as to the performance of many duties. It is imperative upon the state legislatures to make laws prescribing the time, places, and manner of holding elections for senators and representatives, and for electors of president and vice-president. And in these, as well as some other cases, congress have a right to revise, amend, or supercede the laws, which may be passed by state legislatures. When, therefore, the states are stripped of some of the highest attributes of sovereignty, and the same are given to the United States; when the legislatures of the states are, in some respects, under the control of congress, and, in every case, are, under the constitution, bound by the paramount authority of the United States; it is certainly difficult to support the argument, that the appellate power over the decisions of state courts is contrary to the genius of our institutions. The courts of the United States can, without question, revise the proceedings of the executive and legislative authorities of the states; and, if they are found to be contrary to the constitution, may declare them to be of no legal validity. Surely, the exercise of the same right over judicial tribunals is not a higher, or more dangerous act of sovereign power.

§ 1734. "Nor can such a right be deemed to impair the independence of state judges. It is assuming the very ground in controversy to assert, that they possess an absolute independence of the United States. In respect to the powers granted to the United States, they are not independent; they are expressly bound to obedience by the letter of the constitution; and, if they should unintentionally transcend their authority, or misconstrue the constitution, there is no more reason for giving their judgments an absolute and irresistible force, than for giving it to the acts of the other co-ordinate departments of state sovereignty. The argument urged from the possibility of the abuse of the revising power is equally unsatisfactory. It is always a doubtful course to argue against the use, or existence of a power, from the possibility of its abuse. It is still more difficult, by such an argument, to ingraft upon a general power a restriction, which is not to be found in the terms, in which it is given. From the very nature of things, the absolute right of decision, in the last resort, must rest somewhere. Wherever it may be vested, it is susceptible of abuse. In all questions of jurisdiction, the inferior, or appellate court, must pronounce the final judgment; and common sense, as well as legal reasoning, has conferred it upon the latter.

§ 1735. "It has been further argued against the existence of this appellate power, that it would form a novelty in our judicial institutions. This is certainly a mistake. In the articles of confederation, an instrument framed with infinitely more deference to state rights, and state jealousies, a power was given to congress, to establish 'courts for revising and determining, finally, *appeals* in all cases of captures.' It is remarkable, that no power was given to entertain *original* jurisdiction in such cases; and, consequently, the appellate power, (although not so expressed in terms,) was altogether to be exercised in revising the decisions of state tribunals. This was, undoubtedly, so far a surrender of state sovereignty. But it never was supposed to be a power fraught with public danger, or destructive of the independence of state judges. On the contrary, it was supposed to be a power indispensable to the public safety, inasmuch as our national rights might otherwise be compromitted, and our national peace be endangered. Under the present constitution, the prize jurisdiction is confined to the courts of the United States; and a power to revise the decisions of state courts, if they should assert jurisdiction over prize causes, cannot be less important, or less useful, than it was under the confederation. In this connexion, we are led again to the construction of the words of the constitution, 'the judicial power shall extend,' &c. If, as has been contended at the bar, the term ' extend' have a relative signification, and mean to widen an existing power, it will then follow, that, as the confederation gave an appellate power over state tribunals, the constitution enlarged, or widened that appellate power to all the other cases, in which jurisdiction is given to the courts of the United States. It is not presumed, that the learned counsel would choose to adopt such a conclusion.

§ 1736. "It is further argued, that no great public mischief can result from a construction, which shall limit the appellate power of the United States to cases in their own courts : first, because state judges are bound by an oath, to support the constitution of the United States, and must be presumed to be men of learning and integrity; and, secondly, because congress must have an unquestionable right to remove all cases, within the scope of the judicial power, from the state courts, to the courts of the United States, at any time before final judgment, though not after final judgment. As to the first reason, — admitting that the judges of the state courts are, and always will be, of as much learning, integrity, and wisdom, as those of the courts of the United States, (which we very cheerfully admit,) it does not aid the argument. It is manifest, that the constitution has proceeded upon a theory of its own, and given, and withheld powers according to the judgment of the

American people, by whom it was adopted. We can only construe its powers, and cannot inquire into the policy, or principles, which induced the grant of them. The constitution has presumed (whether rightly or wrongly, we do not inquire) that state attachments, state prejudices, state jealousies, and state interests, might sometimes obstruct, or control, or be supposed to obstruct, or control, the regular administration of justice. Hence, in controversies between states; between citizens of different states; between citizens, claiming grants under different states; between a state and its citizens, or foreigners; and between citizens and foreigners; it enables the parties, under the authority of congress, to have the controversies heard, tried, and determined before the national tribunals. No other reason, than that, which has been stated, can be assigned, why some, at least, of these cases should not have been left to the cognizance of the state courts. In respect to the other enumerated cases, — the cases arising under the constitution, laws, and treaties of the United States; cases affecting ambassadors and other public ministers; and cases of admiralty and maritime jurisdiction, — reasons of a higher and more extensive nature, touching the safety, peace, and sovereignty of the nation, might well justify a grant of exclusive jurisdiction.

§ 1737. "This is not all. A motive of another kind, perfectly compatible with the most sincere respect for state tribunals, might induce the grant of appellate power over their decisions. That motive is the importance, and even necessity, of *uniformity* of decisions throughout the whole United States upon all subjects within the purview of the constitution. Judges of equal learning and integrity, in different states, might differently interpret a statute, or a treaty of the United States, or even the constitution itself. If there were no revising authority to control these jarring and discordant judgments, and harmonise them into uniformity, the laws, the treaties, and the constitution of the United States, would be different in different states; and might, perhaps, never have precisely the same construction, obligation, or efficacy, in any two states. The public mischiefs, which would attend such a state of things, would be truly deplorable ; and it cannot be believed, that they could have escaped the enlightened convention, which formed the constitution. What, indeed, might then have been only prophecy, has now become fact; and the appellate jurisdiction must continue to be the only adequate remedy for such evils.

§ 1738. "There is an additional consideration, which is entitled to great weight. The constitution of the United States was designed for the common and equal benefit of all the people of the United States. The judicial power was granted for the same benign and salutary purposes. It was not to be exercised exclusively for the benefit of parties, who might be plaintiffs, and would elect the national forum; but also for the protection of defendants, who might be entitled to try their rights, or assert their privileges, before the same forum. Yet, if the construction contended for be correct, it will follow, that, as the plaintiff may always elect the state courts, the defendant may be deprived of all the security, which the constitution intended in aid of his rights. Such a state of things can, in no respect, be considered, as giving equal rights. To obviate this difficulty, we are referred to the power, which it is admitted, congress possess to remove suits from state courts, to the national courts; and this forms the second ground, upon which the argument, we are considering, has been attempted to be sustained.

§ 1739. "This power of removal is not to be found in express terms in any part of the constitution; if it be given, it is only given by implication, as a power necessary and proper to carry into effect some express power. The power of removal is certainly not, in strictness of language, an exercise of original jurisdiction; it presupposes an exercise of original jurisdiction to have attached elsewhere. The existence of this power of removal is familiar in courts, acting according to the course of the common law, in criminal, as well as in civil cases; and it is exercised before, as well as after judgment. But this is always deemed, in both cases, an exercise of appellate, and not of original jurisdiction. If, then, the right of removal be included in the appellate jurisdiction, it is only, because it is one mode of exercising that power; and as congress is not limited by the constitution to any particular mode, or time of exercising it, it may authorize a removal, either before, or after judgment. The time, the process, and the manner, must be subject to its absolute legislative control. A writ of error is, indeed, but a process, which removes the record of one court to the possession of another court, and enables the latter to inspect the proceedings, and give such judgment, as its own opinion of the law and justice of the case may warrant. There is nothing in the nature of the process, which forbids it from being applied by the legislature to interlocutory, as well as final judgments. And if the right of removal from state courts exist before judgment, because it is included in the appellate power, it must, for the same reason, exist after judgment. And if the appellate power, by the constitution, does not include cases pending in state courts, the right of removal, which is but a mode of exercising that power, cannot be applied to them. Precisely the same objections, therefore, exist as to the right of removal before judgment, as after; and both must stand, or fall together. Nor, indeed, would the force of the arguments on either side materially vary, if the right of removal were an exercise of original jurisdiction. It would equally trench upon the jurisdiction, and independence of state tribunals.

§ 1740. "The remedy, too, of removal of suits would be utterly inadequate to the purposes of the constitution, if it could act only on the parties, and not upon the state courts. In respect to criminal prosecutions, the difficulty seems admitted to be insurmountable; and in respect to civil suits, there would, in many cases, be rights without corresponding remedies. If state courts should deny the constitutionality of the authority to remove suits from their cognizance, in what manner could they be compelled to relinquish the jurisdiction? In respect to criminal cases, there would at once be an end of all control; and the state decisions would be paramount to the constitution. And though, in civil suits, the courts of the United States might act upon the parties; yet the state courts might act in the same way; and this conflict of jurisdictions would not only jeopard private rights, but bring into imminent peril the public interests. On the whole, the court are of opinion, that the appellate power of the United States does extend to cases pending in the state courts; and that the 25th section of the judiciary act, which authorizes the exercise of this jurisdiction in the specified cases, by a writ of error, is supported by the letter and spirit of the constitution. We find no clause in that instrument, which limits this power; and we dare not interpose a limitation, where the people have not been disposed to create one.

§ 1741. "Strong as this conclusion stands upon the general language of the constitution, it may still derive support from other sources. It is an historical fact, that this exposition of the constitution, extending its appellate power to state courts, was, previous to its adoption, uniformly and publicly avowed by its friends, and admitted by its enemies, as the basis of their respective reasonings, both in and out of the state conventions. It is an historical fact, that, at the time, when the judiciary act was submitted to the deliberations of the first congress, composed, as it was, not only of men of great learning and ability, but of men, who had acted a principal part in framing, supporting, or opposing that constitution, the same exposition was explicitly declared, and admitted by the friends, and by the opponents of that system. It is an historical fact, that the Supreme Court of the United States have, from time to time, sustained this appellate jurisdiction in a great variety of cases, brought from the tribunals of many of the most important states in the Union ; and that no state tribunal has ever breathed a judicial doubt on the subject, or declined to obey the mandate of the Supreme Court, until the present occasion. This weight of contemporaneous exposition by all parties, this acquiescence of enlightened state courts, and these judicial decisions of the Supreme Court, through so long a period, do, as we think, place the doctrine upon a foundation of authority, which cannot be shaken, without delivering over the subject to perpetual, and irremediable doubts."[1]

---

[1] The same subject is most elaborately considered in *Cohens v. Virginia*, (6 Wheat. R. 413 to 423,) from which the following extract is taken. After adverting to the nature of the national government, and its powers and capacities, Mr. Chief Justice Marshall proceeds as follows. "In a government so constituted, is it unreasonable, that the judicial power should be competent to give efficacy to the constitutional laws of the legislature? That department can decide on the validity of the constitution, or law of a state, if it be repugnant to the constitution, or to a law of the United States. Is it unreasonable, that it should also be empowered to decide on the judgment of a state tribunal, enforcing such unconstitutional law? Is it so very unreasonable, as to furnish a justification for controling the words of the constitution?

"We think it is not. We think that in a government, acknowledgedly supreme with respect to objects of vital interest to the nation, there is nothing inconsistent with sound reason, nothing incompatible with the nature of government, in making all its departments supreme, so far as respects those objects, and so far as is necessary to their attainment. The exercise of the appellate power, over those judgments of the state tribunals, which may contravene the constitution, or laws of the United States, is, we believe, essential to the attainment of those objects.

"The propriety of entrusting the construction of the constitution, and laws made in pursuance thereof, to the judiciary of the Union, has not, we believe, as yet been drawn into question. It seems to be a corollary from this political axiom, that the federal courts should either possess exclusive jurisdiction in such cases, or a power to revise the judgment rendered in them by the state tribunals. If the federal and state courts have concurrent jurisdiction in all cases arising under the constitution, laws, and treaties of the United States; and, if a case of this description, brought in a state court, cannot be removed before judgment, nor revised after judgment, then the construction of the constitution, laws, and treaties of the United States, is not confided particularly to their judicial department; but is confided equally to that department, and to the state courts, however they may be constituted. 'Thirteen independent courts,' says a very celebrated statesman, (and we have now, more than twenty such courts,) 'of final jurisdiction over the same causes, arising upon the same laws, is a hydra in government, from which, nothing but contradiction and confusion can proceed.'

"Dismissing the unpleasant suggestion, that any motives, which may not be fairly avowed, or which ought not to exist, can ever influence a state, or its courts, the necessity of uniformity, as well as correctness, in expounding the constitution and laws of the United States, would itself

§ 1742. Another inquiry is, whether the judicial power of the United States in any cases, and if in any, in

---

suggest the propriety of vesting in some single tribunal the power of deciding, in the last resort, all cases, in which they are involved.

"We are not restrained, then, by the political relation between the general and state governments, from construing the words of the constitution, defining the judicial power, in their true sense. We are not bound to construe them more restrictively than they naturally import.

"They give to the Supreme Court appellate jurisdiction in all cases, arising under the constitution, laws, and treaties of the United States. The words are broad enough to comprehend all cases of this description, in whatever court they may be decided. In expounding them, we may be permitted to take into view those considerations, to which courts have always allowed great weight in the exposition of laws.

"The framers of the constitution would naturally examine the state of things, existing at the time; and their work sufficiently attests, that they did so. All acknowledge, that they were convened for the purpose of strengthening the confederation, by enlarging the powers of the government, and by giving efficacy to those, which it before possessed, but could not exercise. They inform us, themselves, in the instrument they presented to the American public, that one of its objects was to form a more perfect Union. Under such circumstances, we certainly should not expect to find, in that instrument, a diminution of the powers of the actual government.

"Previous to the adoption of the confederation, congress established courts, which received appeals in prize causes, decided in the courts of the respective states. This power of the government, to establish tribunals for these appeals, was thought consistent with, and was founded on, its political relations with the states. These courts did exercise appellate jurisdiction over those cases, decided in the state courts, to which the judicial power of the federal government extended.

"The confederation gave to congress, the power 'of establishing courts, for receiving and determining, finally, appeals in all cases of captures.'

"This power was uniformly construed to authorize those courts to receive appeals from the sentences of state courts, and to affirm or reverse them. State tribunals are not mentioned; but this clause, in the confederation, necessarily comprises them. Yet the relation between the general and state governments was much weaker, much more lax, under the confederation, than under the present constitution; and the states being much more completely sovereign, their institutions were much more independent.

"The convention, which framed the constitution, on turning their

what cases, is exclusive in the courts of the United
States, or may be made exclusive at the election of

---

attention to the judicial power, found it limited to a few objects, but exercised, with respect to some of those objects, in its appellate form, over
the judgments of the state courts. They extend it, among other objects, to all cases arising under the constitution, laws, and treaties of
the United States; and in a subsequent clause declare, that in such
cases the Supreme Court shall exercise appellate jurisdiction. Nothing
seems to be given, which would justify the withdrawal of a judgment
rendered in a state court, on the constitution, laws, or treaties of the
United States, from this appellate jurisdiction.

" Great weight has always been attached, and very rightly attached,
to contemporaneous exposition. No question, it is believed, has arisen,
to which this principle applies more unequivocally, than to that now under consideration.

" The opinion of the *Federalist* has always been considered, as of
great authority. It is a complete commentary on our constitution; and
is appealed to by all parties, in the questions, to which that instrument has
given birth. Its intrinsic merit entitles it to this high rank; and the
part, two of its authors performed in framing the constitution, put it very
much in their power to explain the views, with which it was framed.
These essays having been published, while the constitution was before
the nation, for adoption or rejection, and having been written in answer
to objections, founded entirely on the extent of its powers, and on its
diminution of state sovereignty, are entitled to the more consideration,
where they frankly avow, that the power objected to is given, and
defend it.

" In discussing the extent of the judicial power, the *Federalist** says,
' Here another question occurs: what relation would subsist between
the national and state courts, in these instances of concurrent jurisdiction? I answer, that an appeal would certainly lie from the latter, to
the Supreme Court of the United States. The constitution in direct
terms gives an appellate jurisdiction to the Supreme Court, in all the
enumerated cases of federal cognizance, in which it is not to have an
original one, without a single expression to confine its operation to the
inferior federal courts. The objects of appeal, not the tribunals, from
which it is to be made, are alone to be contemplated. From this circumstance, and from the reason of the thing, it ought to be construed
to extend to the state tribunals. Either this must be the case, or the
local courts must be excluded from a concurrent jurisdiction in matters
of national concern, else the judicial authority of the Union may be

---

* The Federalist, No. 82.

Congress.   This subject was much discussed in the
case of *Martin* v. *Hunter.*[1]   On that occasion the
court said[2] " It will be observed, that there are two
classes of cases enumerated in the constitution, between which a distinction seems to be drawn.   The first
class includes cases arising under the constitution,
laws, and treaties of the United States; cases affect-

---

cluded at the pleasure of every plaintiff, or prosecutor.   Neither of
these consequences ought, without evident necessity, to be involved;
the latter would be entirely inadmissible, as it would defeat some of the
most important and avowed purposes of the proposed government, and
would essentially embarrass its measures.   Nor do I perceive any foundation for such a supposition.   Agreeably to the remark already made,
the national and state systems are to be regarded as *one whole*.   The
courts of the latter, will of course be natural auxiliaries to the execution of the laws of the Union; and an appeal from them will as naturally
lie to that tribunal, which is destined to unite, and assimilate the principles of natural justice, and the rules of national decision.   The evident
aim of the plan of the national convention is, that all the causes of the
specified classes shall, for weighty public reasons, receive their original
or final determination in the courts of the Union.   To confine, therefore, the general expressions, which give appellate jurisdiction to the
Supreme Court, to appeals from the subordinate federal courts, instead
of allowing their extension to the state courts, would be to abridge the
latitude of the terms, in subversion of the intent, contrary to every sound
rule of interpretation.'

" A contemporaneous exposition of the constitution, certainly of not
less authority, than that, which has been just cited, is the judiciary act
itself.   We know that in the congress, which passed that act, were
many eminent members of the convention, which formed the constitution.   Not a single individual, so far as is known, supposed that part of
the act, which gives the Supreme Court appellate jurisdiction over the
judgments of the state courts, in the cases therein specified, to be un-
authorized by the constitution."   The 25th section of the judiciary act,
of 1789, ch. 20, here alluded to, as contemporaneous construction of
the constitution, is wholly founded upon the doctrine, that the appellate jurisdiction of the Supreme Court may constitutionally extend over
causes in state courts.   See also 1 Kent's Comm. Lect. 15; Rawle on
Const. ch. 28; Sergeant on Const. ch. 7.

[1] 1 Wheat. R. 304, 333.
[2] Ibid. See also *Ex parte Cabrera*, 1 Wash. Cir. R. 232.

ing ambassadors, other public ministers, and consuls; and cases of admiralty and maritime jurisdiction. In this class the expression is, that the judicial power shall extend to *all cases*. But in the subsequent part of the clause, which embraces all the other cases of national cognizance, and forms the second class, the word '*all*' is dropped, seemingly *ex industria*. Here, the judicial authority is to extend to controversies, (not to *all* controversies) to which the United States shall be a party, &c. From this difference of phraseology, perhaps a difference of constitutional intention may, with propriety, be inferred. It is hardly to be presumed, that the variation in the language could have been accidental. It must have been the result of some determinate reason ; and it is not very difficult to find a reason, sufficient to support the apparent change of intention. In respect to the first class, it may well have been the intention of the framers of the constitution imperatively to extend the judicial power, either in an original, or appellate form, to *all cases* ; and, in the latter class, to leave it to congress to qualify the jurisdiction, original or appellate, in such manner, as public policy might dictate.

§ 1743. " The vital importance of all the cases, enumerated in the first class, to the national sovereignty, might warrant such a distinction. In the first place, as to cases arising under the constituton, laws, and treaties of the United States. Here the state courts could not ordinarily possess a direct jurisdiction. The jurisdiction over such cases could not exist in the state courts previous to the adoption of the constitution. And it could not afterwards be directly conferred on them ; for the constitution expressly requires the judicial power to be vested in courts ordained and established by the United States. This class of cases would embrace civil as well as criminal jurisdiction, and affect not only our internal policy, but our foreign relations. It would, therefore, be perilous to restrain it in any manner whatsoever, inasmuch as it might hazard the national safety. The same remarks may be urged as to cases affecting ambassadors, other public ministers, and consuls, who are emphatically placed under the guardianship of the law of nations. And as to cases of admiralty and maritime jurisdiction, the admiralty jurisdiction embraces all questions of prize and salvage, in the correct adjudication of which foreign nations are deeply interested; it embraces also maritime torts, contracts, and offences, in which the principles of the law and comity of nations often form an essential inquiry. All these cases, then, enter into the national policy, affect the national rights, and may compromit the national sovereignty. The original or appellate jurisdiction ought not, therefore, to be restrained; but should be commensurate with the mischiefs intended to be remedied, and, of course, should extend to all cases whatsoever.

§ 1744. " A different policy might well be adopted in reference to the second class of cases; for although it might be fit, that the judicial power should extend to all controversies, to which the United States should be a party; yet this power might not have been imperatively given, lest it should imply a right to take cognizance of original suits brought against the United States, as defendants in their own courts. It might not have been deemed proper to submit the sovereignty of the United States, against their own will, to judicial cognizance, either to enforce rights, or to prevent wrongs. And as to the other cases of the second class, they might well be left to be exercised under the exceptions and regulations, which congress might, in their wisdom, choose to apply. It is also worthy of remark, that congress seem, in a good degree, in the establishment of the present judicial system, to have adopted this distinction. In the first class of cases, the jurisdiction is not limited, except by the subject-matter; in the second, it is made materially to depend upon the value in controversy.

§ 1745. "We do not, however, profess to place any implicit reliance upon the distinction, which has here been stated, and endeavoured to be illustrated. It has the rather been brought into view in deference to the legislative opinion, which has so long acted upon, and enforced, this distinction. But there is, certainly, vast weight in the argument, which has been urged, that the constitution is imperative upon Congess to vest all the judicial power of the United States in the shape of original jurisdiction in the supreme and inferior courts, created under its own authority. At all events, whether the one construction or the other prevail, it is manifest, that the judicial power of the United States is unavoidably, in some cases, exclusive of all state authority, and in all others, may be made so at the election of congress. No part of the criminal jurisdiction of the United States can, consistently with the constitution, be delegated to state tribunals. The admiralty and maritime jurisdiction is of the same exclusive cognizance; and it can only be in those cases, where, previous to the constitution, state tribunals possessed jurisdiction independent of national authority, that they can now constitutionally exercise a concurrent jurisdiction. Congress, throughout the judicial act, and particularly in the 9th, 11th, and 13th sections, have legislated upon the supposition, that in all the cases, to which the judicial power of the United States extended, they might rightfully vest exclusive jurisdiction in their own courts."

§ 1746. The Federalist has spoken upon the same subject in the following terms. "The only thing in the proposed constitution, which wears the appearance of confining the causes of federal cognizance to the federal courts, is contained in this passage; 'The *judicial power* of the United States *shall be vested* in one supreme court, and in *such* inferior courts as the congress shall from time to time ordain, and establish.' This might either be construed to signify, that the supreme and subordinate courts of the union should alone have the power of deciding those causes, to which their authority is to extend; or simply to denote, that the organs of the national judiciary should be one supreme court, and as many subordinate courts, as congress should think proper to appoint; in other words, that the United States should exercise the judicial power, with which they are to be invested, through one supreme tribunal, and a certain number of inferior ones, to be instituted by them. The first excludes, the last admits, the concurrent jurisdiction of the state tribunals; and as the first would amount to an alienation of state power by implication, the last appears to me the most defensible construction.

§ 1747. "But this doctrine of concurrent jurisdiction, is only clearly applicable to those descriptions of causes, of which the state courts had previous cogniz- ance. It is not equally evident in relation to cases, which may grow out of, and be *peculiar* to, the constitution to be established : for not to allow the state courts a right of jurisdiction in such cases, can hardly be considered as the abridgement of a pre-existing authority. I mean not, therefore, to contend, that the United States, in the course of legislation upon the objects intrusted to their direction, may not commit the decision of causes arising upon a particular regulation to the federal courts solely, if such a measure should be deemed expedient ; but I hold, that the state courts will be divested of no part of their primitive jurisdiction further than may relate to an appeal. And I am even of opinion, that in every case, in which they were not expressly excluded by the future acts of the national legislature, they will of course take cognizance of the causes, to which those acts may give birth. This I infer from the nature of judiciary power, and from the general genius of the system. The judiciary power of every government looks beyond its own local or municipal laws, and, in civil cases, lays hold of all subjects of litigation between parties within its jurisdiction, though the causes of dispute are relative to the laws of the most distant part of the globe. Those of Japan, not less than of New York, may furnish the objects of legal discussion to our courts. When in addition to this we consider the state governments, and the national governments, as they truly are, in the light of kindred systems, and as parts of *one whole*, the inference seems to be conclusive, that the state courts would have a concurrent jurisdiction in all cases arising under the laws of the union, where it was not expressly prohibited." [1]

1 See The Federalist, No. 82. Id. 81.

§ 1748. It would be difficult, and perhaps not desirable, to lay down any general rules in relation to the cases, in which the judicial power of the courts of the United States is exclusive of the state courts, or in which it may be made so by congress, until they shall be settled by some positive adjudication of the Supreme Court. That there are some cases, in which that power is exclusive, cannot well be doubted ; that there are others, in which it may be made so by congress, admits of as little doubt ; and that in other cases it is concurrent in the state courts, at least until congress shall have passed some act excluding the concurrent jurisdiction, will scarcely be denied. [1] It seems to be admitted, that the jurisdiction of the courts of the United States is, or at least may be, made exclusive in all cases arising under the constitution, laws, and treaties of the United States ; [2] in all cases affecting ambassadors, other public ministers and consuls ; [3] in all cases (*in their character exclusive*) of admiralty and maritime jurisdiction ; [4] in controversies, to which the United States shall be a party ; in controversies between two or more states ; in

---

[1] See *Cohens* v. *Virginia*, 6 Wheat. R. 396, 397 ; 2 Elliot's Deb. 380, 381. See 11 Wheat. R. 472, note ; Rawle on Const. ch. 21 ; 1 Kent's Comm. Lect. 18, p. 370, &c. (2 edition, 395, &c.) ; 1 Tucker's Black. Comm. App. 181, 182, 183 ; *Governor of Georgia* v. *Madrazo*, 1 Peters's Sup. R. 128, 129, Per Johnson J.

[2] *Cohens* v. *Virginia*, 6 Wheat. R. 396, 397 ; *Houston* v. *Moore*, 5 Wheat. R. 25 to 28 ; Id. 69, 71 ; *Slocum* v. *Maybury* ; 2 Wheat. R. 1 ; *Hoyt* v. *Gelston*, 3 Wheat. R. 246, 311.

[3] The Federalist, No. 82 ; *Martin* v. *Hunter*, 1 Wheat. R. 336, 337.

[4] See 2 Elliot's Deb. 380 ; *Cohens* v. *Virginia*, 6 Wheat. R. 396, 397 ; *Martin* v. *Hunter*, 1 Wheat. R. 337, 373 ; *Houston* v. *Moore*. 5 Wheat. R. 49 ; *United States* v. *Bevans*, 3 Wheat. R. 387 ; Ante, Vol. III., § 1665 ; *Ogden* v. *Saunders*, 12 Wheat. R. 278, Johnson J. ; *Janney* v. *Columbian Ins. Co.*, 10 Wheat. R. 418.

controversies between a state and citizens of another state ; and in controversies between a state and foreign states, citizens, or subjects.[1] And it is only in those cases, where, previous to the constitution, state tribunals possessed jurisdiction, independent of national authority, that they can now constitutionally exercise a concurrent jurisdiction.[2] Congress, indeed, in the Judiciary Act of 1789, (ch. 20, § 9, 11, 13,) have manifestly legislated upon the supposition, that, in all cases, to which the judicial power of the United States extends, they might rightfully vest exclusive jurisdiction in their own courts.[3]

§ 1749. It is a far more difficult point, to affirm the right of congress to vest in any state court any part of the judicial power confided by the constitution to the national government. Congress may, indeed, permit the state courts to exercise a concurrent jurisdiction in many cases ; but those courts then derive no authority from congress over the subject-matter, but are simply left to the exercise of such jurisdiction, as is conferred on them by the state constitu-

---

[1] See 1 Tucker's Black. Comm. App. 181, 182, 183 ; 1 Kent's Comm. Lect. 18, p. 370, &c. (2 edit. p. 395 to 404.)

[2] *Martin* v. *Hunter*, 1 Wheat. R. 336, 337 ; The Federalist, No. 27, No. 82; *Houston* v. *Moore*, 5 Wheat. R. 49.

[3] Ibid. See 1 Peters's Sup. Ct. R. 128, 129, 130, per Johnson J.; *Ex parte Cabrera*, 1 Wash. Cir. R. 232. — It would seem, upon the common principles of the laws of nations, as ships of war of a government are deemed to be under the exclusive dominion and sovereignty of their own government, wherever they may be, and thus enjoy an extra territorial immunity, that crimes committed on board of ships of war of the United States, in port, as well as at sea, are exclusively cognizable, and punishable by the United States. The very point arose in *United States* v. *Bevans*, (3 Wheat. R. 336, 388); but it was not decided. The result of that trial, however, showed the general opinion, that the state courts had no jurisdiction ; as the law officers of the state declined to interfere, after the decision in the Supreme Court of the United States.

tion and laws. There are, indeed, many acts of congress, which permit jurisdiction over the offences therein described, to be exercised by state magistrates and courts ; but this (it has been said by a learned judge,[1]) is not, because such permission was considered to be necessary, under the constitution, to vest a concurrent jurisdiction in those tribunals ; but because the jurisdiction was exclusively vested in the national courts by the judiciary act ; and consequently could not be otherwise executed by the state courts. But, he has added, " for I hold it to be perfectly clear, that congress cannot confer jurisdiction upon any courts, but such as exist under the constitution and laws of the United States ; although the state courts may exercise jurisdiction in cases authorized by the laws of the state, and not prohibited by the exclusive jurisdiction of the federal courts." This latter doctrine was positively affirmed by the Supreme Court in *Martin* v. *Hunter* ;[2] and indeed seems, upon general principles, indisputable. In that case, the court said, " congress cannot vest any portion of the judicial power of the United States, except in courts, ordained and established by itself." [3]

---

[1] Mr. Justice Washington in *Houston* v. *Moore*, 5 Wheat. R. 27, 28 ; The Federalist, No. 27 ; Id. No. 82.

[2] 1 Wheaton's R. 330. See 1 Kent's Comm. Lect. 18, p. 375, (2 edit. p. 400.)

[3] Ibid. See also *Houston* v. *Moore*, 5 Wheat. R. 68, 69. See 1 Kent's Comm. Lect. 18, p. 375, &c. (2 edit. p. 400 to 404.) — The Federalist (No. 81) seems faintly to contend, that congress might vest the jurisdiction in the state courts, " to confer upon the existing courts of the several states the power of determining such causes, would, *perhaps,* be as much to ' constitute tribunals,' as to create new courts with the like power." But, how is this reconcileable with the context of the constitution ? " The judicial power of the United States shall be vested in one Supreme Court, and in such inferior courts, as congress may,

§ 1750. In regard to jurisdiction over crimes committed against the authority of the United States, it has been held, that no part of this jurisdiction can, consistently with the constitution, be delegated to state tribunals.[1] It is true, that congress has, in various acts, conferred the right to prosecute for offences, penalties, and forfeitures, in the state courts. But the latter have, in many instances, declined the jurisdiction, and asserted its unconstitutionality. And certainly there is, at the present time, a decided preponderance of judicial authority in the state courts against the authority of congress to confer the power.[2]

§ 1751. In the exercise of the jurisdiction confided respectively to the state courts, and those courts of the United States, (where the latter have not appellate jurisdiction,) it is plain, that neither can have any right to interfere with, or control, the operations of the other. It has accordingly been settled, that no state court can issue an injunction upon any judgment in a court of the United States ; the latter having an exclusive au-

---

from time to time, ordain and establish. The judges both of the Supreme and inferior courts, shall hold their offices during good behaviour," &c. Are not these judges of the inferior courts the same, in whom the jurisdiction is to be vested ? Who are to appoint them ? Who are to pay their salaries ? Can their compensation be diminished ? All these questions must be answered with reference to the same judges, that is, with reference to judges of the Supreme and inferior courts of the United States, and not of state courts. See also The Federalist, No. 45.

[1] *Martin* v. *Hunter*, 1 Wheat. R. 337 ; *Houston* v. *Moore*, 5 Wheat. R. 35, 69, 71, 74, 75.

[2] See Sergeant on Const. Law, ch. 27, (ch. 28 :) *United States*, v. *Campbell*, 6 Hall's Law Jour. 113 ; *United States* v. *Lathrop*, 17 John. R. 5 ; *Coruth* v. *Freely*, Virginia Cases, 321 ; *Ely* v. *Peck*, 7 Connecticut R. 239 ; 1 Kent's Comm. Lect. 18, p. 370, &c. (2 edit. p. 395 to 404.) But see 1 Tucker's Black. Comm. App. 181, 182 ; Rawle on Const. ch. 21.

thority over its own judgments and proceedings.[1]   Nor can any state court, or any state legislature, annul the judgments of the courts of the United States, or destroy the rights acquired under them;[2] nor in any manner deprive the Supreme Court of its appellate jurisdiction;[3] nor in any manner interfere with, or control the process (whether mesne or final) of the courts of the United States;[4] nor prescribe the rules or forms of proceeding, nor effect of process, in the courts of the United States ;[5] nor issue a mandamus to an officer of the United states, to compel him to perform duties, devolved on him by the laws of the United States.[6]   And although writs of *habeas corpus* have been issued by state judges, and state courts, in cases, where the party has been in custody under the authority of process of the courts of the United States, there has been considerable diversity of opinion, whether such an exercise of authority is constitutional ; and it yet remains to be decided, whether it can be maintained.[7]

§ 1752.   Indeed, in all cases, where the judicial power of the United States is to be exercised, it is for congress alone to furnish the rules of proceeding, to

1 *McKim* v. *Voorhis*, 7 Cranch's R. 279; 1 Kent's Comm. Lect. 19, p. 382 to 387, (2 edit. 409 to 412.)

2 *United States* v. *Peters*, 5 Cranch, 115; S. C. 2 Peters's Cond. R. 202; 1 Kent's Comm. Lect. 19, p. 382, &c. (2 edit. p. 409, &c.)

3 *Wilson* v. *Mason*, 1 Cranch, 94; S. C. 1 Peters's Cond. R. 242; 1 Kent's Comm. Lect. 19, p. 382, (2 edit. 409.)

4 *United States* v. *Wilson*, 8 Wheat. R. 253.

5 *Wayman* v. *Southard*, 10 Wheat. R. 1. 21, 22; *Bank of the United States* v. *Halstead*, 10 Wheat. R. 51.

6 *McClung* v. *Silliman*, 6 Wheat. R. 598.

7 See Sergeant on Const. Law, ch. 27, (ch. 28 ;) 1 Kent's Comm. Lect. 18, p. 375, (2 edit. p. 400.)   See 1 Tucker's Black. Comm. App. 291, 292.

direct the process, to declare the nature and effect of
the process, and the mode, in which the judgments,
consequent thereon, shall be executed.   No state legislature, or state court, can have the slightest right to
interfere ; and congress are not even capable of delegating the right to them.   They may authorize national
courts to make general rules and orders, for the purpose of a more convenient exercise of their jurisdiction;
but they cannot delegate to any state authority any
control over the national courts.[1]

§ 1753. On the other hand the national courts have
no authority (in cases not within the appellate jurisdiction of the United States) to issue injunctions to judgments in the state courts ;[2] or in any other manner to
interfere with their jurisdiction or proceedings.[3]

§ 1754. Having disposed of these points, we may
again recur to the language of the constitution for the
purpose of some farther illustrations.   The language
is, that " the Supreme Court shall have appellate juris-
" diction, both as to law and fact, with such exceptions,
" and under such regulations, as the congress shall
" make."

§ 1755. In the first place, it may not be without
use to ascertain, what is here meant by appellate jurisdiction ; and what is the mode, in which it may be
exercised.   The essential criterion of appellate jurisdiction is, that it revises and corrects the proceedings
in a cause already instituted, and does not create that

[1] *Wayman* v. *Southard*, 10 Wheat. R. 1 ; *Palmer* v. *Allen*, 7 Cranch,
R. 550; *Gibbons* v. *Ogden*, 9 Wheat. R. 207, 208; *Bank of the United
States* v. *Halstead*, 10 Wheat. R. 51.
[2] *Diggs* v. *Wolcott*, 4 Cranch, 178.   See 1 Kent's Comm. Lect. 15,
p. 301, (2 edit. 321.)
[3] *Ex parte Cabrera*, 1 Wash. Cir. R. 232; 1 Kent's Comm. Lect. 19,
p. 386, (2 edit. p. 411, 412.)

cause.[1] In reference to judicial tribunals, an appellate
jurisdiction, therefore, necessarily implies, that the subject matter has been already instituted in, and acted
upon, by some other court, whose judgment or proceedings are to be revised. This appellate jurisdiction
may be exercised in a variety of forms, and indeed in
any form, which the legislature may choose to prescribe ;[2] but, still, the substance must exist, before
the form can be applied to it. To operate at all, then,
under the constitution of the United States, it is not
sufficient, that there has been a decision by some officer, or department of the United states ; it might be
by one clothed with judicial authority, and acting in a
judicial capacity. A power, therefore, conferred by
congress on the Supreme Court, to issue a mandamus
to public officers of the United States generally, is not
warranted by the constitution ; for it is, in effect, under
such circumstances, an exercise of original jurisdiction.[3]
But where the object is to revise a judicial proceeding,
the mode is wholly immaterial ; and a writ of *habeas
corpus*, or mandamus, a writ of error, or an appeal, may
be used, as the legislature may prescribe.[4]

§ 1756. The most usual modes of exercising appellate jurisdiction, at least those, which are most known
in the United States, are by a writ of error, or by an
appeal, or by some process of removal of a suit from
an inferior tribunal. An appeal is a process of civil
law origin, and removes a cause, entirely subjecting

---

[1] *Marbury* v. *Madison*, 1 Cranch, R. 175, 176 ; S. C. 1 Peters's Cond.
R. 267, 282 ; The Federalist, No. 81 ; *Weston* v. *City Council of Charles-
ton*, 2 Peters's Sup. R. 449.
[2] Ibid.   [3] Ibid.
[4] Ibid ; *United States* v. *Hamilton*, 3 Dall. 17 ; *Ex parte Bollman*, 4
Cranch, R. 75 ; *Ex parte Kearney*, 7 Wheat. R. 38 ; *Ex parte Crane*,
5 Peters's Sup. R. 190.

the fact, as well as the law, to a review and a re-trial. A writ of error is a process of common law origin; and it removes nothing for re-examination, but the law.[1] The former mode is usually adopted in cases of equity and admiralty jurisdiction ; the latter, in suits at common law tried by a jury.

§ 1757. It is observable, that the language of the constitution is, that " the Supreme Court shall have " appellate jurisdiction, *both as to law and fact.*" This provision was a subject of no small alarm and misconstruction at the time of the adoption of the constitution, as it was supposed to confer on the Supreme Court, in the exercise of its appellate jurisdiction, the power to review the decision of a jury in mere matters of fact ; and thus, in effect, to destroy the validity of their verdict, and to reduce to a mere form the right of a trial by jury in civil cases. The objection was at once seized hold of by the enemies of the constitution ; and it was pressed with an urgency and zeal, which were well nigh preventing its ratification.[2] There is certainly some foundation, in the ambiguity of the language, to justify an interpretation, that such a review might constitutionally be within the reach of the appellate power, if congress should choose to carry it to that extreme latitude.[3] But, practically speaking, there was not the slightest danger, that congress would ever adopt such a course, even if it were within their

---

[1] *Wiscart* v. *Dauchy,* 3 Dall. R. 321 ; S. C. 1 Peters's Cond. R. 144 ; *Cohens* v. *Virginia,* 6 Wheat. R. 409 to 412.

[2] See 1 Elliot's Debates, 121, 122 ; 2 Elliot's Debates, 346, 380 to 410 ; Id. 413 to 427 ; 3 Elliot's Debates, 139 to 157 ; 2 Amer. Museum, 425 ; Id. 534 ; Id. 540, 548, 553 ; 3 Amer. Museum, 419, 420 ; 1 Tuck. Black. Comm. App. 351.

[3] 2 Elliot's Debates, 318, 347, 419 ; 3 Elliot's Debates, 140, 149 ; Rawle on Const. ch. 10, p. 135.

constitutional authority; since it would be at variance with all the habits, feelings, and institutions of the whole country. At least it might be affirmed, that congress would scarcely take such a step, until the people were prepared to surrender all the great securities of their civil, as well as of their political rights and liberties; and in such an event the retaining of the trial by jury would be a mere mockery. The real object of the provision was to retain the power of reviewing the fact, as well as the law, in cases of admiralty and maritime jurisdiction.[1] And the manner, in which it is expressed, was probably occasioned by the desire to avoid the introduction of the subject of a trial by jury in civil cases, upon which the convention were greatly divided in opinion.

§1758. The Federalist met the objection, pressed with much earnestness and zeal, in the following manner: "The propriety of this appellate jurisdiction has been scarcely called in question in regard to matters of law; but the clamours have been loud against it, as applied to matters of fact. Some well-intentioned men in this state, deriving their notions from the language and forms, which obtain in our courts, have been induced to consider it, as an implied supersedure of the trial by jury, in favour of the civil law mode of trial, which prevails in our courts of admiralty, probates, and chancery. A technical sense has been affixed to the term 'appellate,' which, in our law parlance, is commonly used in reference to appeals in the course of the civil law. But, if I am not misinformed, the same meaning would not be given to it in any part of New-England. There, an appeal from one jury to another is familiar

---

[1] 3 Elliot's Debates, 283.

both in language and practice, and is even a matter of course, until there have been two verdicts on one side. The word 'appellat.,' therefore, will not be understood in the same sense in New-England, as in New-York, which shows the impropriety of a technical interpretation, derived from the jurisprudence of a particular state. The expression, taken in the abstract, denotes nothing more, than the power of one tribunal to review the proceedings of another, either as to the law, or fact, or both. The mode of doing it may depend on ancient custom, or legislative provision; in a new government it must depend on the latter, and may be with, or without, the aid of a jury, as may be judged advisable. If, therefore, the re-examination of a fact, once determined by a jury, should in any case be admitted under the proposed constitution, it may be so regulated, as to be done by a second jury, either by remanding the cause to the court below for a second trial of the fact, or by directing an issue immediately out of the Supreme Court.

§ 1759. "But it does not follow, that the re-examination of a fact, once ascertained by a jury, will be permitted in the Supreme Court. Why may it not be said, with the strictest propriety, when a writ of error is brought from an inferior to a superior court of law in this state, that the latter has jurisdiction of the fact, as well as the law? It is true, it cannot institute a new inquiry concerning the fact, but it takes cognizance of it, as it appears upon the record, and pronounces the law arising upon it. This is jurisdiction of both fact and law; nor is it even possible to separate them. Though the common law courts of this state ascertain disputed facts by a jury, yet they unquestionably have jurisdiction of both fact and law; and accordingly,

when the former is agreed in the pleadings, they have
no recourse to a jury, but proceed at once to judgment.
I contend, therefore, on this ground, that the expressions, 'appellate jurisdiction, both as to law and fact,'
do not necessarily imply a re-examination in the Supreme Court of facts decided by juries in the inferior
courts.

§ 1760. "The following train of ideas may well be
imagined to have influenced the convention, in relation
to this particular provision. The appellate jurisdiction
of the Supreme Court, it may have been argued, will
extend to causes determinable in different modes, some
in the course of the *common law*, others in the course
of the *civil law*. In the former, the revision of the law
only will be, generally speaking, the proper province of
the Supreme Court; in the latter, the re-examination
of the fact is agreeable to usage; and in some cases, of
which prize causes are an example, might be essential
to the preservation of the public peace. It is therefore
necessary, that the appellate jurisdiction should, in certain cases, extend in the broadest sense to matters of
fact. It will not answer to make an express exception
of cases, which shall have been originally tried by a
jury, because in the courts of some of the states *all
causes* are tried in this mode; and such an exception
would preclude the revision of matters of fact, as well
where it might be proper, as where it might be improper. To avoid all inconveniences, it will be safest to
declare generally, that the Supreme Court shall possess
appellate jurisdiction, both as to law and *fact*, and that
this jurisdiction shall be subject to such *exceptions* and
regulations, as the national legislature may prescribe.
This will enable the government to modify it in such a
manner, as will best answer the ends of public justice
and security.

§ 1761. "This view of the matter, at any rate, puts it out of all doubt, that the supposed *abolition* of the trial by jury, by the operation of this provision, is fallacious and untrue. The legislature of the United States would certainly have full power to provide, that in appeals to the Supreme Court there should be no re-examination of facts, where they had been tried in the original causes by juries. This would certainly be an authorized exception; but if, for the reason already intimated, it should be thought too extensive, it might be qualified with a limitation to such causes only, as are determinable at common law in that mode of trial." [1]

§ 1762. These views, however reasonable they may seem to considerate minds, did not wholly satisfy the popular opinion; and as the objection had a vast influence upon public opinion, and amendments were proposed by various state conventions on this subject, congress at its first session, under the guidance of the friends of the constitution, proposed an amendment, which was ratified by the people, and is now incorporated into the constitution. It is in these words. "In suits at common law, where the value in controversy shall exceed twenty dollars, the right of a trial by jury shall be preserved. And no fact tried by a jury shall be otherwise re-examined in any court of the United States, than according to the rules of the common law." This amendment completely struck down the objection; and has secured the right of a trial by jury, in civil cases, in the fullest latitude of the common law.[2] Like the other amendments, proposed by the same congress, it was coldly received by the enemies of the

---

1 The Federalist, No. 81. See also The Federalist, No. 83.

2 See 1 Tuck. Black. Comm. App. 351; Rawle on Const. ch. 10, p. 135; *Bank of Hamilton* v. *Dudley*, 2 Peters's R. 492, 525.

constitution, and was either disapproved by them, or drew from them a reluctant acquiescence.[1] It weakened the opposition by taking away one of the strongest points of attack upon the constitution. Still it is a most important and valuable amendment; and places upon the high ground of constitutional right the inestimable privilege of a trial by jury in civil cases, a privilege scarcely inferior to that in criminal cases, which is conceded by all to be essential to political and civil liberty.[2]

---

[1] 5 Marshall's Life of Washington, ch. 3, p. 209, 210.

[2] It is due to the excellent statesmen, who framed the constitution, to give their reasons for the omission of any provision in the constitution, securing the trial by jury in civil cases. They were not insensible to its value; but the diversity of the institutions of different states on this subject compelled them to acquiesce in leaving it entirely to the sound discretion of congress. The Federalist, No. 83, has given an elaborate paper to the subject, which is transcribed at large, as a monument of admirable reasoning and exalted patriotism.

"The objection to the plan of the convention, which has met with most success in this state, is relative to *the want of a constitutional provision* for the trial by jury in civil cases. The disingenuous form, in which this objection is usually stated, has been repeatedly adverted to and exposed; but continues to be pursued in all the conversations and writings of the opponents of the plan. The mere silence of the constitution in regard to *civil causes*, is represented, as an abolition of the trial by jury; and the declamations, to which it has afforded a pretext, are artfully calculated to induce a persuasion, that this pretended abolition is complete and universal; extending not only to every species of civil, but even to *criminal causes*. To argue with respect to the latter, would be as vain and fruitless, as to attempt to demonstrate any of those propositions, which, by their own internal evidence, force conviction, when expressed in language adapted to convey their meaning.

"With regard to civil causes, subtleties almost too contemptible for refutation have been employed to countenance the surmise, that a thing, which is only *not provided for*, is entirely *abolished*. Every man of discernment must at once perceive the wide difference between *silence* and *abolition*. But, as the inventors of this fallacy have attempted to support it by certain *legal maxims* of interpretation, which they have perverted from their true meaning, it may not be wholly useless to explore the ground they have taken.

"The maxims, on which they rely, are of this nature: 'A specifica-

§ 1763. Upon a very recent occasion the true interpretation and extent of this amendment came before the Supreme Court for decision, in a case from

tion of particulars is an exclusion of generals ;' or, ' The expression of one thing is the exclusion of another.' Hence, say they, as the constitution has established the trial by jury in criminal cases, and is silent in respect to civil, this silence is an implied prohibition of trial by jury, in regard to the latter.

" The rules of legal interpretation are rules of *common sense*, adopted by the courts in the construction of the laws. The true test, therefore, of a just application of them, is its conformity to the source, from which they are derived. This being the case, let me ask, if it is consistent with common sense to suppose, that a provision obliging the legislative power to commit the trial of criminal causes to juries, is a privation of its right to authorize, or permit that mode of trial in other cases? Is it natural to suppose, that a command to do one thing is a prohibition to the doing of another, which there was a previous power to do, and which is not incompatible with the thing commanded to be done ? If such a supposition would be unnatural and unreasonable, it cannot be rational to maintain, that an injunction of the trial by jury, in certain cases, is an interdiction of it in others.

" A power to constitute courts is a power to prescribe the mode of trial ; and consequently, if nothing was said in the constitution on the subject of juries, the legislature would be at liberty, either to adopt that institution, or to let it alone. This discretion, in regard to criminal causes, is abridged by an express injunction ; but it is left at large in relation to civil causes, for the very reason, that there is a total silence on the subject. The specification of an obligation to try all criminal causes in a particular mode, excludes indeed the obligation of employing the same mode in civil causes, but does not abridge *the power* of the legislature to appoint that mode, if it should be thought proper. The pretence, therefore, that the national legislature would not be at liberty to submit all the civil causes of federal cognizance to the determination of juries, is a pretence destitute of all foundation.

" From these observations this conclusion results, that the trial by jury in civil cases would not be abolished : and that the use attempted to be made of the maxims, which have been quoted, is contrary to reason, and therefore inadmissible. Even if these maxims had a precise technical sense, corresponding with the ideas of those, who employ them upon the present occasion, which, however, is not the case, they would still be inapplicable to a constitution of government. In relation to such a subject, the natural and obvious sense of its provisions, apart from any technical rules, is the true criterion of construction.

Louisiana, where the question was, whether the Supreme Court could entertain a motion for a new trial, and re-examine the facts tried by a jury, that being

---

"Having now seen, that the maxims relied upon will not bear the use made of them, let us endeavour to ascertain their proper application. This will be best done by examples. The plan of the convention declares, that the power of congress, or, in other words, of the *national legislature*, shall extend to certain enumerated cases. This specification of particulars evidently excludes all pretension to a general legislative authority; because an affirmative grant of special powers would be absurd, as well as useless, if a general authority was intended.

"In like manner, the authority of the federal judicatures is declared by the constitution to comprehend certain cases particularly specified. The expression of those cases marks the precise limits, beyond which the federal courts cannot extend their jurisdiction; because the objects of their cognizance being enumerated, the specification would be nugatory, if it did not exclude all ideas of more extensive authority.

"These examples are sufficient to elucidate the maxims, which have been mentioned, and to designate the manner, in which they should be used.

"From what has been said, it must appear unquestionably true, that trial by jury is in no case abolished by the proposed constitution; and it is equally true, that in those controversies between individuals, in which the great body of the people are likely to be interested, that institution will remain precisely in the situation, in which it is placed by the state constitutions. The foundation of this assertion is, that the national judiciary will have no cognizance of them, and of course they will remain determinable, as heretofore, by the state courts only, and in the manner, which the state constitutions and laws prescribe. All land causes, except where claims under the grants of different states come into question, and all other controversies between the citizens of the same state, unless where they depend upon positive violations of the articles of union, by acts of the state legislatures, will belong exclusively to the jurisdiction of the state tribunals. Add to this, that admiralty causes, and almost all those, which are of equity jurisdiction, are determinable under our own government, without the intervention of a jury; and the inference from the whole will be, that this institution, as it exists with us at present, cannot possibly be affected, to any great extent, by the proposed alteration in our system of government.

"The friends and adversaries of the plan of the convention, if they agree in nothing else, concur at least in the value they set upon the trial by jury; or, if there is any difference between them, it consists in this: the former regard it, as a valuable safeguard to liberty; the latter

the practice under the local law, and there being an
act of congress, authorizing the courts of the United
States in Louisiana to adopt the local practice, with

---

represent it, as the very palladium of free government. For my own
part, the more the operation of the institution has fallen under my observation, the more reason I have discovered for holding it in high estimation ; and it would be altogether superfluous to examine, to what extent it deserves to be esteemed useful, or essential in a representative
republic, or how much more merit it may be entitled to, as a defence
against the oppressions of an hereditary monarch, than as a barrier to
the tyranny of popular magistrates in a popular government. Discussions of this kind would be more curious, than beneficial, as all are satisfied of the utility of the institution, and of its friendly aspect to liberty.
But I must acknowledge, that I cannot readily discern the inseparable
connexion between the existence of liberty, and the trial by jury in
civil cases. Arbitrary impeachments, arbitrary methods of prosecuting
pretended offences, arbitrary punishments upon arbitrary convictions,
have ever appeared to me the great engines of judicial despotism; and
all these have relation to criminal proceedings. The trial by jury in
criminal cases, aided by the *habeas corpus* act, seems therefore to be
alone concerned in the question. And both of these are provided for,
in the most ample manner, in the plan of the convention.

"It has been observed, that trial by jury is a safeguard against an
oppressive exercise of the power of taxation. This observation deserves
to be canvassed.

"It is evident, that it can have no influence upon the legislature, in
regard to the *amount* of the taxes to be laid, to the *objects*, upon which
they are to be imposed, or to the *rule*, by which they are to be apportioned. If it can have any influence, therefore, it must be upon the
mode of collection, and the conduct of the officers entrusted with the
execution of the revenue laws.

"As to the mode of collection in this state, under our own constitution, the trial by jury is in most cases out of use. The taxes are usually levied by the more summary proceeding of distress and sale, as in
cases of rent. And it is acknowledged on all hands, that this is essential to the efficacy of the revenue laws. The dilatory course of a trial
at law to recover the taxes imposed on individuals, would neither suit
the exigencies of the public, nor promote the convenience of the citizens. It would often occasion an accumulation of costs more burthensome, than the original sum of the tax to be levied.

"And, as to the conduct of the officers of the revenue, the provision
in favour of trial by jury in criminal cases, will afford the desired security. Wilful abuses of a public authority, to the oppression of the subject, and every species of official extortion, are offences against the

certain limitations. The Supreme Court held, that
no authority was given by the act to re-examine the
facts; and if it had been, an opinion was intimated of

---

government; for which the persons, who commit them, may be indicted
and punished according to the circumstance of the case.

"The excellence of the trial by jury in civil cases appears to depend
on circumstances, foreign to the preservation of liberty. The strongest
argument in its favour is, that it is a security against corruption. As
there is always more time, and better opportunity, to tamper with a
standing body of magistrates, than with a jury summoned for the occasion, there is room to suppose, that a corrupt influence would more easily
find its way to the former, than to the latter. The force of this consideration is, however, diminished by others. The sheriff, who is the sum-
moner of ordinary juries, and the clerks of courts, who have the nomination of special juries, are themselves standing officers, and, acting
individually, may be supposed more accessible to the touch of corruption, than the judges, who are a collective body. It is not difficult to
see, that it would be in the power of those officers to select jurors, who
would serve the purpose of the party, as well as a corrupted bench. In
the next place, it may fairly be supposed, that there would be less difficulty in gaining some of the jurors promiscuously taken from the public
mass, than in gaining men, who had been chosen by the government
for their probity and good character. But making every deduction for
these considerations, the trial by jury must still be a valuable check
upon corruption. It greatly multiplies the impediments to its success.
As matters now stand, it would be necessary to corrupt both court and
jury; for where the jury have gone evidently wrong, the court will generally grant a new trial, and it would be in most cases of little use to
practice upon the jury, unless the court could be likewise gained.
Here, then, is a double security; and it will readily be perceived, that
this complicated agency tends to preserve the purity of both institutions.
By increasing the obstacles to success, it discourages attempts to
seduce the integrity of either. The temptations to prostitution, which
the judges might have to surmount, must certainly be much fewer, while
the co-operation of a jury is necessary, than they might be, if they had
themselves the exclusive determination of all causes.

"Notwithstanding, therefore, the doubts I have expressed, as to the
essentiality of trial by jury in civil suits to liberty, I admit, that it is in
most cases, under proper regulations, an excellent method of determining questions of property; and that on this account alone it would be
entitled to a constitutional provision in its favour, if it were possible to
fix with accuracy the limits, within which it ought to be comprehended.
This, however, is in its own nature an affair of much difficulty; and

the most serious doubts of its constitutionality.   On
that occasion the court said: "The trial by jury is
justly dear to the American people.   It has always

---

men, not blinded by enthusiasm, must be sensible, that in a federal government, which is a composition of societies, whose ideas and institutions in relation to the matter materially vary from each other, the difficulty must be not a little augmented.   For my own part, at every new
view I take of the subject, I become more convinced of the reality of
the obstacles, which we are authoritatively informed, prevented the insertion of a provision on this head in the plan of the convention.

"The great difference between the limits of the jury trial, in different
states, is not generally understood.   And, as it must have considerable
influence on the sentence, we ought to pass upon the omission complained of, in regard to this point, an explanation of it is necessary.   In this
state, our judicial establishments resemble more nearly, than in any
other, those of Great Britain.   We have courts of common law, courts
of probates, (analogous in certain matters to the spiritual courts in England,) a court of admiralty, and a court of chancery.   In the courts of
common law only the trial by jury prevails, and this with some exceptions.   In all the others, a single judge presides, and proceeds in general, either according to the course of the canon, or civil law, without
the aid of a jury.   In New-Jersey there is a court of chancery, which
proceeds like ours, but neither courts of admiralty, nor of probates, in
the sense, in which these last are established with us.   In that state,
the courts of common law have the cognizance of those causes, which
with us are determinable in the courts of admiralty and of probates, and
of course the jury trial is more extensive in New-Jersey, than in New-
York.   In Pennsylvania this is perhaps still more the case ; for there is
no court of chancery in that state, and its common law courts have
equity jurisdiction.   It has a court of admiralty, but none of probates,
at least on the plan of ours.   Delaware has in these respects imitated
Pennsylvania.   Maryland approaches more nearly to New-York, as does
also Virginia, except that the latter has a plurality of chancellors.
North Carolina bears most affinity to Pennsylvania ; South Carolina to
Virginia.   I believe, however, that in some of those states, which have
distinct courts of admiralty, the causes depending in them are triable by
juries.   In Georgia there are none but common law courts, and an appeal of course lies from the verdict of one jury to another, which is
called a special jury, and for which a particular mode of appointment
is marked out.   In Connecticut they have no distinct courts, either of
chancery, or of admiralty, and their courts of probates have no jurisdiction of causes.   Their common law courts have admiralty, and, to a
certain extent, equity jurisdiction.   In cases of importance, their gene-

been an object of deep interest and solicitude, and every encroachment upon it has been watched with great jealousy. The right to such a trial is, it is be-

---

ral assembly is the only court of chancery. In Connecticut, therefore, the trial by jury extends in *practice* further, than in any other state yet mentioned. Rhode-Island is, I believe, in this particular, pretty much in the situation of Connecticut. Massachusetts and New-Hampshire, in regard to the blending of law, equity, and admiralty jurisdictions, are in a similar predicament. In the four eastern states, the trial by jury not only stands upon a broader foundation, than in the other states, but it is attended with a peculiarity unknown, in its full extent, to any of them. There is an appeal *of course* from one jury to another, till there have been two verdicts out of three on one side.

"From this sketch it appears, that there is a material diversity, as well in the modification, as in the extent of the institution of trial by jury in civil cases, in the several states; and from this fact, these obvious reflections flow: first, that no general rule could have been fixed upon by the convention, which would have corresponded with the circumstances of all the states; and, secondly, that more, or at least as much might have been hazarded, by taking the system of any one state for a standard, as by omitting a provision altogether, and leaving the matter, as has been done, to legislative regulation.

"The propositions, which have been made for supplying the omission, have rather served to illustrate, than to obviate the difficulty of the thing. The minority of Pennsylvania have proposed this mode of expression for the purpose, 'Trial by jury shall be as heretofore;' and this, I maintain, would be inapplicable and indeterminate. The United States, in their collective capacity, are the object, to which all general provisions in the constitution must be understood to refer. Now, it is evident, that though trial by jury, with various limitations, is known in each state individually, yet in the United States, *as such*, it is, strictly speaking, unknown; because the present federal government has no judiciary power whatever; and consequently there is no antecedent establishment, to which the term 'heretofore' could properly relate. It would, therefore, be destitute of precise meaning, and inoperative from its uncertainty.

"As, on the one hand, the form of the provision would not fulfil the intent of its proposers; so, on the other, if I apprehend that intent rightly, it would be in itself inexpedient. I presume it to be, that causes in the federal courts should be tried by jury, if in the state where the courts sat, that mode of trial would obtain in a similar case in the state courts; that is to say, admiralty causes should be tried in Connecticut by a jury, in New-York without one. The capricious operation of so

lieved, incorporated into, and secured in every state
constitution in the Union; and it is found in the constitution of Louisiana. One of the strongest objec-

---

dissimilar a method of trial in the same cases, under the same government, is of itself sufficient to indispose every well-regulated judgment
towards it. Whether the cause should be tried with, or without a jury,
would depend, in a great number of cases, on the accidental situation
of the court and parties.

"But this is not, in my estimation, the greatest objection. I feel a
deep and deliberate conviction, that there are many cases, in which the
trial by jury is an ineligible one. I think it so particularly in suits,
which concern the public peace with foreign nations; that is, in most
cases, where the question turns wholly on the laws of nations. Of this
nature, among others, are all prize causes. Juries cannot be supposed
competent to investigations, that require a thorough knowledge of the
laws and usages of nations; and they will sometimes be under the influence of impressions, which will not suffer them to pay sufficient regard to those considerations of public policy, which ought to guide their
inquiries. There would of course be always danger, that the rights of
other nations might be infringed by their decisions, so as to afford occasions of reprisal and war. Though the true province of juries be to
determine matters of fact, yet, in most cases, legal consequences are
complicated with fact in such a manner, as to render a separation impracticable.

"It will add great weight to this remark, in relation to prize causes,
to mention, that the method of determining them has been thought
worthy of particular regulation, in various treaties between different
powers of Europe, and that, pursuant to such treaties, they are determinable in Great Britain, in the last resort, before the king himself in
his privy council, where the fact, as well as the law, undergoes a re-
examination. This alone demonstrates the impolicy of inserting a fundamental provision in the constitution, which would make the state systems a standard for the national government in the article under consideration, and the danger of encumbering the government with any
constitutional provisions, the propriety of which is not indisputable.

"My convictions are equally strong, that great advantages result
from the separation of the equity from the law jurisdiction; and that
the causes, which belong to the former, would be improperly committed
to juries. The great and primary use of a court of equity is to give
relief *in extraordinary cases*, which are *exceptions* to general rules. To
unite the jurisdiction of such cases with the ordinary jurisdiction, must
have a tendency to unsettle the general rules, and to subject every case
that arises to a *special* determination; while a separation between the

tions, originally taken against the constitution of the United States, was the want of an express provision securing the right of trial by jury in civil cases. As

jurisdictions has the contrary effect of rendering one a sentinel over the other, and of keeping each within the expedient limits. Besides this, the circumstances, that constitute cases proper for courts of equity, are in many instances so nice and intricate, that they are incompatible with the genius of trials by jury. They require often such long and critical investigation, as would be impracticable to men called occasionally from their occupations, and obliged to decide, before they were permitted to return to them. The simplicity and expedition, which form the distinguishing characters of this mode of trial, require, that the matter to be decided should be reduced to some single and obvious point ; while the litigations, usual in chancery, frequently comprehend a long train of minute and independent particulars.

" It is true, that the separation of the equity from the legal jurisdiction is peculiar to the English system of jurisprudence ; the model, which has been followed in several of the states. But it is equally true, that the trial by jury has been unknown in every instance, in which they have been united. And the separation is essential to the preservation of that institution in its pristine purity. The nature of a court of equity will readily permit the extension of its jurisdiction to matters of law ; but it is not a little to be suspected, that the attempt to extend the jurisdiction of the courts of law to matters of equity will not only be unproductive of the advantages, which may be derived from courts of chancery on the plan, upon which they are established in this state ; but will tend gradually to change the nature of the courts of law, and to undermine the trial by jury, by introducing questions too complicated for a decision in that mode.

" These appear to be conclusive reasons against incorporating the systems of all the states, in the formation of the national judiciary, according to what may be conjectured to have been the intent of the Pennsylvania minority. Let us now examine, how far the proposition of Massachusetts is calculated to remedy the supposed defect.

" It is in this form : ' In civil actions between citizens of different states, every issue of fact, arising in *actions at common law*, may be tried by a jury, if the parties, or either of them, request it.'

" This, at best, is a proposition confined to one description of causes ; and the inference is fair, either that the Massachusetts convention considered that, as the only class of federal causes, in which the trial by jury would be proper ; or, that, if desirous of a more extensive provision, they found it impracticable to devise one, which would properly answer the end. If the first, the omission of a regulation, respecting so partial an object, can never be considered, as a material imperfection in the

soon as the constitution was adopted, this right was
secured by the seventh amendment of the constitution proposed by congress; which received an as-

---

system. If the last, it affords a strong corroboration of the extreme
difficulty of the thing.

"But this is not all. If we advert to the observations already made
respecting the courts, that subsist in the several states of the Union,
and the different powers exercised by them, it will appear, that there
are no expressions more vague and indeterminate, than those, which
have been employed to characterize *that* species of causes, which it is
intended shall be entitled to a trial by jury. In this state, the boundaries between actions at common law, and actions of equitable jurisdiction, are ascertained in conformity to the rules, which prevail in England upon that subject. In many of the other states, the boundaries are
less precise. In some of them every cause is to be tried in a court of
common law; and upon that foundation every action may be considered,
as an action at common law, to be determined by a jury, if the parties,
or either of them, choose it. Hence, the same irregularity and confusion would be introduced by a compliance with this proposition, that I
have already noticed, as resulting from the regulation proposed by the
Pennsylvania minority. In one state a cause would receive its determination from a jury, if the parties, or either of them, requested it; but
in another state, a cause exactly similar to the other must be decided
without the intervention of a jury, because the state tribunals varied,
as to common law jurisdiction.

"It is obvious, therefore, that the Massachusetts proposition cannot
operate, as a general regulation, until some uniform plan, with respect
to the limits of common law and equitable jurisdictions, shall be adopted
by the different states. To devise a plan of that kind is a task arduous
in itself, and which it would require much time and reflection to mature.
It would be extremely difficult, if not impossible, to suggest any general
regulation, that would be acceptable to all the states in the Union, or
that would perfectly quadrate with the several state institutions.

"It may be asked, why could not a reference have been made to the
constitution of this state, taking that, which is allowed by me to be a
good one, as a standard for the United States? I answer, that it is not
very probable the other states should entertain the same opinion of our
institutions, which we do ourselves. It is natural to suppose, that they
are more attached to their own, and that each would struggle for the
preference. If the plan of taking one state, as a model for the whole,
had been thought of in the convention, it is to be presumed, that the
adoption of it in that body would have been rendered difficult by the
predilection of each representation in favour of its own government;
and it must be uncertain, which of the states would have been taken,

sent of the people so general, as to establish its
importance, as a fundamental guarantee of the rights
and liberties of the people. This amendment de-

---

as the model. It has been shown, that many of them would be improper
ones. And I leave it to conjecture, whether, under all circumstances,
it is most likely, that New York, or some other state, would have been
preferred. But admit, that a judicious selection could have been
effected in the convention, still there would have been great danger of
jealousy and disgust in the other states, at the partiality, which had
been shown to the institutions of one. The enemies of the plan would
have been furnished with a fine pretext for raising a host of local prejudices against it, which perhaps might have hazarded, in no inconsiderable degree, its final establishment.

  "To avoid the embarrassments of a definition of the cases, which the
trial by jury ought to embrace, it is sometimes suggested by men of
enthusiastic tempers, that a provision might have been inserted for
establishing it in all cases whatsoever. For this, I believe, no precedent
is to be found in any member of the Union ; and the considerations,
which have been stated in discussing the proposition of the minority of
Pennsylvania, must satisfy every sober mind, that the establishment of
the trial by jury in *all* cases would have been an unpardonable error in
the plan.

  "In short, the more it is considered, the more arduous will appear
the task of fashioning a provision in such a form, as not to express too
little to answer the purpose, or too much to be advisable ; or which
might not have opened other sources of opposition to the great and
essential object of introducing a firm national government.

  "I cannot but persuade myself, on the other hand, that the different
lights, in which the subject has been placed in the course of these observations, will go far towards removing in candid minds the apprehensions they may have entertained on the point. They have tended to
show, that the security of liberty is materially concerned only in the
trial by jury in criminal cases, which is provided for in the most ample
manner in the plan of the convention ; that, even in far the greatest
proportion of civil cases, those, in which the great body of the community is interested, that mode of trial will remain in full force, as established in the state constitutions, untouched and unaffected by the plan
of the convention ; that it is in no case abolished by that plan ; and that
there are great, if not insurmountable difficulties in the way of making
any precise and proper provision for it, in the constitution for the United
States.

  "The best judges of the matter will be the least anxious for a constitutional establishment of the trial by jury in civil cases, and will be
the most ready to admit, that the changes, which are continually hap-

clares, that " in suits at common law, where the value
in controversy shall exceed twenty dollars, the right
of trial by jury shall be preserved ; and no fact, once
tried by a jury, shall be otherwise re-examined in
any court of the United States, than according to the

pening in the affairs of society, may render a different mode of determining questions of property preferable in many cases, in which that
mode of trial now prevails.   For my own part, I acknowledge myself to
be convinced, that even in this state it might be advantageously extended to some cases, to which it does not at present apply, and might
as advantageously be abridged in others.   It is conceded by all reasonable men, that it ought not to obtain in all cases.   The examples of innovations, which contract its ancient limits, as well in these states, as in
Great Britain, afford a strong presumption, that its former extent has
been found inconvenient ; and give room to suppose, that future experience may discover the propriety and utility of other exceptions.   I suspect it to be impossible in the nature of the thing to fix the salutary
point, at which the operation of the institution ought to stop ; and this
is with me a strong argument for leaving the matter to the discretion of
the legislature.
   " This is now clearly understood to be the case in Great Britain, and
it is equally so in the state of Connecticut.   And yet it may be safely
affirmed, that more numerous encroachments have been made upon the
trial by jury in this state since the revolution, though provided for by a
positive article of our constitution, than has happened in the same time
either in Connecticut, or Great Britain.   It may be added, that these
encroachments have generally originated with the men, who endeavour
to persuade the people, they are the warmest defenders of popular liberty, but who have rarely suffered constitutional obstacles to arrest
them in a favourite career.   The truth is, that the general genius of a
government is all, that can be substantially relied upon for permanent
effects.   Particular provisions, though not altogether useless, have far
less virtue and efficacy, than are commonly ascribed to them ; and the
want of them will never be with men of sound discernment a decisive
objection to any plan, which exhibits the leading characters of a good
government.
   " It certainly sounds not a little harsh and extraordinary to affirm, that
there is no security for liberty in a constitution, which expressly establishes a trial by jury in criminal cases, because it does not do it in civil
also; while it is a notorious fact, that Connecticut, which has been
always regarded, as the most popular state in the Union, can boast of
no constitutional provision for either."   The Federalist, No. 83.
   See also 2 Elliot's Debates, 346, 380 to 410 ; Id. 413 to 427 ; 3 Elliot's
Debates, 131, 132, 137, 141, 153 ; Id. 283, 284, 301, 302.

rules of the common law." At this time there were
no states in the Union, the basis of whose jurisprudence was not essentially that of the common law in
its widest meaning; and probably no states were
contemplated, in which it would not exist. The
phrase, 'common law,' found in this clause, is used in
contradistinction to equity, and admiralty, and maritime
jurisprudence. The constitution had declared, in the
third article, 'that the judicial power shall extend to
all cases in *law and equity* arising under this constitution, the laws of the United States, and treaties made,
or which shall be made under their authority,' &c., and
'to all cases of *admiralty and maritime jurisdiction.*'
It is well known, that in civil causes, in courts of equity
and admiralty, juries do not intervene; and that courts
of equity use the trial by jury only in extraordinary
cases to inform the conscience of the court. When,
therefore, we find, that the amendment requires, that
the right of trial by jury shall be preserved in suits at
common law, the natural conclusion is, that this distinction was present to the minds of the framers of the
amendment. By *common law* they meant, what the
constitution denominated in the third article 'law;'
not merely suits, which the *common* law recognized
among its old and settled proceedings, but suits, in
which *legal* rights were to be ascertained and determined, in contradistinction to those, in which equitable
rights alone were recognized, and equitable remedies
were administered; or in which, as in the admiralty, a
mixture of public law, and of maritime law and equity,
was often found in the same suit. Probably there
were few, if any, states in the Union, in which some
new legal remedies differing from the old common law
forms were not in use; but in which, however, the

trial by jury intervened, and the general regulations in other respects were according to the course of the common law. Proceedings in cases of partition, and of foreign and domestic attachment, might be cited, as examples variously adopted, and modified. In a just sense, the amendment then may well be construed to embrace all suits, which are not of equity and admiralty jurisdiction, whatever may be the peculiar form, which they may assume to settle legal rights. And congress seem to have acted with reference to this exposition in the judiciary act of 1789, ch. 20, (which was contemporaneous with the proposal of this amendment;) for in the ninth section it is provided, that 'the trial of issues in fact in the *district courts* in all causes, except civil causes of *admiralty and maritime jurisdiction*, shall be by jury;' and in the twelfth section it is provided, that 'the trial of issues in fact in the *circuit courts* shall in all suits, except those of *equity*, and of *admiralty* and *maritime jurisdiction*, be by jury.' And again, in the thirteenth section, it is provided, that 'the trial of issues in fact in the *supreme* court, *in all actions at law* against citizens of the United States, shall be by jury.'

§ 1764. "But the other clause of the amendment is still more important; and we read it, as a substantial and independent clause. 'No fact tried by a jury shall be otherwise re-examinable, in any court of the United States, than according to the rules of the common law.' This is a prohibition to the courts of the United States to re-examine any facts tried by a jury in any other manner. The only modes, known to the common law, to re-examine such facts, are the granting of a new trial by the court, where the issue was tried, or to which the record was properly returnable; or the award of a *venire facias de novo* by an appellate court, for some error of law, which intervened in the proceedings. The judiciary act of 1789, ch. 20, sec. 17, has given to all the courts of the United States 'power to grant new trials in cases, where there has been a trial by jury, for reasons, for which new trials have usually been granted in the courts of law.' And the appellate jurisdiction has also been amply given by the same act (sec. 22, 24) to this court, to redress errors of law; and for such errors to award a new trial in suits at law, which have been tried by a jury.

§ 1765. "Was it the intention of congress, by the general language of the act of 1824, to alter the appellate jurisdiction of this court, and to confer on it the power of granting a new trial by a re-examination of the facts tried by the jury? to enable it, after trial by jury, to do that in respect to the courts of the United States, sitting in Louisiana, which is denied to such courts, sitting in all the other states in the Union? We think not. No general words, purporting only to regulate the practice of a particular court, to conform its modes of proceeding to those prescribed by the state to its own courts, ought, in our judgment, to receive an interpretation, which would create so important an alteration in the laws of the United States, securing the trial by jury. Especially ought it not to receive such an interpretation, when there is a power given to the inferior court itself to prevent any discrepancy between the state laws, and the laws of the United States; so that it would be left to its sole discretion to supersede, or to give conclusive effect in the appellate court to the verdict of the jury.

§ 1766. "If, indeed, the construction contended for at the bar were to be given to the act of congress, we entertain the most serious doubts, whether it would not be unconstitutional. No court ought, unless the terms of an act rendered it unavoidable, to give a construction to it, which should involve a violation, however unintentional, of the constitution. The terms of the present act may well be satisfied by limiting its operation to modes of practice and proceeding in the court below, without changing the effect or conclusiveness of the verdict of the jury upon the facts litigated at the trial. Nor is there any inconvenience from this construction; for the party has still his remedy, by bill of exceptions, to bring the facts in review before the appellate court, so far as those facts bear upon any question of law arising at the trial; and if there be any mistake of the facts, the court below is competent to redress it, by granting a new trial." [1]

§ 1767. The appellate jurisdiction is to be "with such exceptions, and under such regulations, as the congress shall prescribe." But, here, a question is presented upon the construction of the constitution, whether the appellate jurisdiction attaches to the Supreme Court, subject to be withdrawn and modified by congress; or, whether an act of congress is necessary to confer the jurisdiction upon the court. If the former be the true construction, then the entire appellate jurisdiction, if congress should make no exceptions or regulations, would attach *proprio vigore* to the Supreme Court. If the latter, then, notwithstanding the imperative language of the constitution, the Supreme Court is lifeless, until congress have conferred power on it. And if congress may confer power, they may repeal it. So that the whole efficiency of the judicial power is left by the constitution wholly unprotected and inert, if congress shall refrain to act. There is certainly very

[1] *Parsons v. Bedford,* 3 Peters's R. 446 to 449.

strong grounds to maintain, that the language of the constitution meant to confer the appellate jurisdiction absolutely on the Supreme Court, independent of any action by congress; and to require this action to divest or regulate it. The language, as to the original jurisdiction of the Supreme Court, admits of no doubt. It confers it without any action of congress. Why should not the same language, as to the appellate jurisdiction, have the same interpretation? It leaves the power of congress complete to make exceptions and regulations; but it leaves nothing to their inaction. This construction was asserted in argument at an earlier period of the constitution.[1] It was at that time denied; and it was held by the Supreme Court, that, if congress should provide no rule to regulate the proceedings of the Supreme Court, it could not exercise any appellate jurisdiction.[2] That doctrine, however, has, upon more mature deliberation, been since overturned; and it has been asserted by the Supreme Court, that, if the judicial act (of 1789) had created the Supreme Court, without defining, or limiting its jurisdiction, it must have been considered, as possessing all the jurisdiction, which the constitution assigns to it. The legislature could have exercised the power possessed by it of creating a Supreme Court, as ordained by the constitution; and, in omitting to exercise the right of excepting from its constitutional powers, would have necessarily left those constitutional powers undiminished. The appellate powers of the Supreme Court are not given by the judicial act (of 1789). They are given by

[1] *Chisholm* v. *Georgia*, 2 Dall. 419, and Iredell J.'s Opinion, p. 432; S. C. 2 Peters's Cond. R. 635, 638.
[2] *Wiscast* v. *Dauchy*, 3 Dall. 321, 326; S. C. 1 Peters's Cond. R. 144, 146.

the constitution. But they are limited, and regulated by that act, and other acts on the same subject.[1] And where a rule is provided, all persons will agree, that it cannot be departed from.

§ 1768. It should be added, that, while the jurisdiction of the courts of the United States is almost wholly under the control of the regulating power of congress, there are certain incidental powers, which are supposed to attach to them, in common with all other courts, when duly organized, without any positive enactment of the legislature. Such are the power of the courts over their own officers, and the power to protect them and their members from being disturbed in the exercise of their functions.[2]

§ 1769. Although the judicial department under the constitution would, from the exposition, which has thus been made of its general powers and functions, seem above all reasonable objections, it was assailed with uncommon ardour and pertinacity in the state conventions, as dangerous to the liberties of the people, and the rights of the states; as unlimited in its extent, and undefined in its objects; as in some portions of its jurisdiction wholly unnecessary, and in others vitally defective. In short, the objections were of the most opposite characters; and, if yielded to, would have left it without a shadow of power, or efficiency.[3]

---

1 *Durousseau* v. *United States,* 6 Cranch, 307, 313, 314; *United States* v. *Moore,* 3 Cranch, 159, 170, 172.

2 *Ex parte Bollman,* 4 Cranch, 75; *Ex parte Kearney,* 7 Wheat. R. 38, 44; *Anderson* v. *Dunn,* 6 Wheat. R. 204.

3 See 2 Elliot's Debates, 380 to 427; 1 Elliot's Debates, 119 to 122; 3 Elliot's Debates, 125 to 145; 2 Amer. Museum, 422, 429, 435; 3 Amer. Museum, 62, 72; Id. 419, 420; Id. 534, 540, 546.

§ 1770. The Federalist has concluded its remarks on the judicial department in the following manner: "The amount of the observations hitherto made on the authority of the judicial department is this:— That it has been carefully restricted to those causes, which are manifestly proper for the cognizance of the national judicature; that, in the partition of this authority, a very small portion of original jurisdiction has been reserved to the Supreme Court, and the rest consigned to the subordinate tribunals; that the Supreme Court will possess an appellate jurisdiction, both as to law and fact, in all the cases referred to them, but subject to any *exceptions* and *regulations*, which may be thought advisable; that this appellate jurisdiction does, in no case, *abolish* the trial by jury; and that an ordinary degree of prudence and integrity in the national councils, will ensure us solid advantages from the establishment of the proposed judiciary, without exposing us to any of the inconveniences, which have been predicted from that source."[1]

§ 1771. The functions of the judges of the courts of the United States are strictly and exclusively judicial. They cannot, therefore, be called upon to advise the president in any executive measures; or to give extrajudicial interpretations of law; or to act, as commissioners in cases of pensions, or other like proceedings.[2]

1 The Federalist, No. 81. See on the Judiciary the Journal of Convention, p. 98, 99, 100, 188, 189, 295, 301.

2 5 Marshall's Life of Washington, ch. 6, p. 433, 441; Sergeant on Const. ch. 29, p. 363, (2 edit. ch. 31, p. 375); *Marbury* v. *Madison*, 1 Cranch, 171; *Dewhurst* v. *Coulthart*, 3 Dall. R. 409; *Hayburn's Case*, 2 Dall. R. 409, 410, and note Ibid., and p. 411; Sergeant on Const. ch. 33, p. 391, (ch. 34, p. 401, 2d edition.)

§ 1772. The next clause of the first section of the third article is : " The trial of all crimes, except in " cases of impeachment, shall be by jury ; and such " trial shall be held in the state, where such crimes " shall have been committed. But when not com- " mitted within any state, the trial shall be at such " place or places, as the congress may by law have di- " rected."

§ 1773. It seems hardly necessary in this place to expatiate upon the antiquity, or importance of the trial by jury in criminal cases. It was from very early times insisted on by our ancestors in the parent country, as the great bulwark of their civil and political liberties, and watched with an unceasing jealousy and solicitude. The right constitutes the fundamental articles of Magna Charta,[1] in which it is declared, *"nullus homo capiatur, nec imprisone- tur, aut exulet, aut aliquo modo destruatur, &c.; nisi per legale judicium parium suorum, vel per legem terræ;"* no man shall be arrested, nor imprisoned, nor banished, nor deprived of life, &c. but by the judgment of his peers, or by the law of the land. The judgment of his peers here alluded to, and com- monly called in the quaint language of former times a trial *per pais*, or trial by the country, is the trial by a jury, who are called the peers of the party accused, being of the like condition and equality in the state. When our more immediate ancestors removed to America, they brought this great privilege with them, as their birth-right and inheritance, as a part of that admirable common law, which had fenced round, and interposed barriers on every side against the ap-

---

[1] Magna Charta, ch. 29, (9 Henry 3d) ; 2 Inst. 45; 3 Black. Comm. 349; 4 Black. Comm. 349.

proaches of arbitrary power.[1]   It is now incorporated into all our state constitutions, as a fundamental right; and the constitution of the United States would have been justly obnoxious to the most conclusive objection, if it had not recognised, and confirmed it in the most solemn terms.

§ 1774. The great object of a trial by jury in criminal cases is, to guard against a spirit of oppression and tyranny on the part of rulers, and against a spirit of violence and vindictiveness on the part of the people.   Indeed, it is often more important to guard against the latter, than the former.   The sympathies of all mankind are enlisted against the revenge and fury of a single despot; and every attempt will be made to screen his victims.   But how difficult is it to escape from the vengeance of an indignant people, roused into hatred by unfounded calumnies, or stimulated to cruelty by bitter political enmities, or unmeasured jealousies? The appeal for safety can, under such circumstances, scarcely be made by innocence in any other manner, than by the severe control of courts of justice, and by the firm and impartial verdict of a jury sworn to do right, and guided solely by legal evidence and a sense of duty.   In such a course there is a double security against the prejudices of judges, who may partake of the wishes and opinions of the government, and against the passions of the multitude, who may demand their victim with a clamorous precipitancy. So long, indeed, as this palladium remains sacred and inviolable, the liberties of a free government cannot wholly fall.[2]   But to give it real efficiency, it must be

---

1 2 Kent's Comm. Lect. 24, p. 1 to 9, (2d edition, p. 1 to 12); 3 Elliot's Debates, 331, 399.

2 4 Black. Comm 349, 350.

preserved in its purity and dignity; and not, with a view to slight inconveniences, or imaginary burthens, be put into the hands of those, who are incapable of estimating its worth, or are too inert, or too ignorant, or too imbecile, to wield its potent armour. Mr. Justice Blackstone, with the warmth and pride becoming an Englishman living under its blessed protection, has said: "A celebrated French writer, who concludes, that because Rome, Sparta, and Carthage have lost their liberties, therefore those of England in time must perish, should have recollected, that Rome, Sparta, and Carthage, at the time, when their liberties were lost, were strangers to the trial by jury." [1]

§ 1775. It is observable, that the trial of all crimes is not only to be by jury, but to be held in the state, where they are committed. The object of this clause is to secure the party accused from being dragged to a trial in some distant state, away from his friends, and witnesses, and neighbourhood; and thus to be subjected to the verdict of mere strangers, who may feel no common sympathy, or who may even cherish animosities, or prejudices against him. Besides this; a trial in a distant state or territory might subject the party to the most oppressive expenses, or perhaps even to the inability of procuring the proper witnesses to establish his innocence. There is little danger, indeed, that con-

---

[1] 3 Black. Comm. 379. See also Id. 381. — I commend to the diligent perusal of every scholar, and every legislator, the noble eulogium of Mr. Justice Blackstone on the trial by jury. It is one of the most beautiful, as well as most forcible, expositions of that classical jurist. See 3 Black. Comm. 379, 380, 381; 4 Black. Comm. 349, 350. See also De Lolme, B. 1, ch. 13, B. 2, ch. 16. Dr. Paley's chapter on the administration of justice is not the least valuable part of his work on Moral Philosophy. See B. 6, ch. 8. See also 2 Wilson's Law Lect. P. 2, ch. 6, p. 305, &c.

gress would ever exert their power in such an oppressive, and unjustifiable a manner.[1] But upon a subject, so vital to the security of the citizen, it was fit to leave as little as possible to mere discretion. By the common law, the trial of all crimes is required to be in the county, where they are committed. Nay, it originally carried its jealousy still farther, and required, that the jury itself should come from the vicinage of the place, where the crime was alleged to be committed.[2] This was certainly a precaution, which, however justifiable in an early and barbarous state of society, is little commendable in its more advanced stages. It has been justly remarked, that in such cases to summon a jury, labouring under local prejudices, is laying a snare for their consciences ; and though they should have virtue and vigour of mind sufficient to keep them upright, the parties will grow suspicious, and indulge other doubts of the impartiality of the trial.[3] It was doubtless by analogy to this rule of the common law, that all criminal trials are required to be in the state, where committed. But as crimes may be committed on the high seas, and elsewere, out of the territorial jurisdiction of a state, it was indispensable, that, in such cases, congress should be enabled to provide the place of trial.

§ 1776. But, although this provision of a trial by jury in criminal cases is thus constitutionally preserved to all citizens, the jealousies and alarms of the opponents of the constitution were not quieted. They insisted, that a bill of rights was indispensable upon other subjects, and that upon this, farther auxiliary

1 See 2 Elliot's Debates, 399, 400, 407, 420.
2 2 Hale, P. C. ch. 24, p. 260, 264 ; Hawk, P. C., B. 2, ch. 25, § 34 ; 4 Black. Comm. 305.
3 3 Black. Comm. 383.

rights ought to have been secured.[1] These objections
found their way into the state conventions, and were
urged with great zeal against the constitution. They
did not, however, prevent the adoption of that instrument. But they produced such a strong effect upon
the public mind, that congress, immediately after their
first meeting, proposed certain amendments, embracing
all the suggestions, which appeared of most force; and
these amendments were ratified by the several states,
and are now become a part of the constitution. They
are contained in the fifth and sixth articles of the
amendments, and are as follows:

" No person shall be held to answer for a capital or
" otherwise infamous crime, unless on a presentment
" or indictment of a grand jury, except in cases arising
" in the land or naval forces, or in the militia, when in
" actual service, in time of war, or public danger : nor
" shall any person be subject, for the same offence, to be
" twice put in jeopardy of life or limb ; nor shall be com-
" pelled, in any criminal case, to be a witness against
" himself; nor be deprived of life, liberty, or property,
" without due process of law ; nor shall private property
" be taken for public use, without just compensation."

" In all criminal prosecutions, the accused shall en-
" joy the right to a speedy and public trial, by an im-
" partial jury of the state and district, wherein the
" crime shall have been committed; which district
" shall have been previously ascertained by law ; and
" to be informed of the nature and cause of the accusa-
" tion ; to be confronted with the witnesses against
" him ; to have compulsory process for obtaining wit-

---

[1] See 2 Elliot's Debates, 331, 380 to 427 ; 1 Elliot's Debates, 119, 120,
121, 122 ; 3 Elliot's Debates, 139, 140, 149, 153, 300.

"nesses in his favour; and to have the assistance of
"counsel for his defence."

§ 1777. Upon the main provisions of these articles
a few remarks only will be made, since they are almost self-evident, and can require few illustrations to
establish their utility and importance.

§ 1778. The first clause requires the interposition
of a grand jury, by way of presentment or indictment,
before the party accused can be required to answer to
any capital and infamous crime, charged against him.
And this is regularly true at the common law of all
offences, above the grade of common misdemeanors.
A grand jury, it is well known, are selected in the manner prescribed by law, and duly sworn to make inquiry,
and present all offences committed against the authority of the state government, within the body of the
county, for which they are impannelled. In the national courts, they are sworn to inquire, and present
all offences committed against the authority of the
national government within the state or district, for
which they are impannelled, or elsewhere within the
jurisdiction of the national government. The grand
jury may consist of any number, not less than twelve,
nor more than twenty-three ; and twelve at least must
concur in every accusation.[1] They sit in secret, and
examine the evidence laid before them by themselves.
A presentment, properly speaking, is an accusation
made *ex mero motu* by a grand jury of an offence upon their own observation and knowledge, or upon evidence before them, and without any bill of indictment
laid before them at the suit of the government.
An indictment is a written accusation of an offence

---

[1] 4 Black. Comm. 302, 306.

preferred to, and presented, upon oath, as true, by a grand jury at the suit of the government. Upon a presentment the proper officer of the court must frame an indictment, before the party accused can be put to answer it.[1] But an indictment is usually in the first instance framed by the officers of the government, and laid before the grand jury. When the grand jury have heard the evidence, if they are of opinion, that the indictment is groundless, or not supported by evidence, they used formerly to endorse on the back of the bill, "ignoramus," or we know nothing of it, whence the bill was said to be *ignored.* But now they assert in plain English, "not a true bill," or which is a better way, "not found;" and then the party is entitled to be discharged, if in custody, without farther answer. But a fresh bill may be preferred against him by another grand jury. If the grand jury are satisfied of the truth of the accusation, then they write on the back of the bill, "a true bill," (or anciently, " *billa vera.*") The bill is then said to be found, and is publicly returned into court ; the party stands indicted, and may then be required to answer the matters charged against him.[2]

§ 1779. From this summary statement it is obvious, that the grand jury perform most important public functions ; and are a great security to the citizens against vindictive prosecutions, either by the government, or by political partisans, or by private enemies. Nor is this all ;[3] the indictment must charge the time, and place, and nature, and circumstances, of the offence, with clearness and certainty ; so that the party

---

[1] 4 Black. Comm. 301, 302.

[2] 4 Black. Comm. 305, 306.

[3] See 1 Tuck. Black. Comm. App. 304, 305; Rawle on Const. ch. 10, p. 132.

may have full notice of the charge, and be able to make his defence with all reasonable knowledge and ability.

§ 1780. There is another mode of prosecution, which exists by the common law in regard to misdemeanors; though these also are ordinarily prosecuted upon indictments found by a grand jury. The mode, here spoken of, is by an information, usually at the suit of the government or its officers. An information generally differs in nothing from an indictment in its form and substance, except that it is filed at the mere discretion of the proper law officer of the government *ex officio*, without the intervention or approval of a grand jury.[1] This process is rarely recurred to in America; and it has never yet been formally put into operation by any positive authority of congress, under the national government, in mere cases of misdemeanor; though common enough in civil prosecutions for penalties and forfeitures.

§ 1781. Another clause declares, that no person shall be subject, "for the same offence, to be twice put "in jeopardy of life and limb." This, again, is another great privilege secured by the common law.[2] The meaning of it is, that a party shall not be tried a second time for the same offence, after he has once been convicted, or acquitted of the offence charged, by the verdict of a jury, and judgment has passed thereon for or against him. But it does not mean, that he shall not be tried for the offence a second time, if the jury have been discharged without giving any verdict; or, if, having given a verdict, judgment has been arrested upon it, or a new trial has been granted in his favour;

---

[1] 4 Black. Comm. 308, 309.
[2] Hawk. P. C., B. 2, ch. 35; 4 Black. Comm. 335.

for, in such a case, his life or limb cannot judicially be said to have been put in jeopardy.[1]

§ 1782. The next clause prohibits any person from being compelled, in any criminal case, to be a witness against himself, or being deprived of life, liberty, or property, without due process of law. This also is but an affirmance of a common law privilege. But it is of inestimable value. It is well known, that in some countries, not only are criminals compelled to give evidence against themselves, but are subjected to the rack or torture in order to procure a confession of guilt. And what is worse, it has been (as if in mockery or scorn) attempted to excuse, or justify it, upon the score of mercy and humanity to the accused. It has been contrived, (it is pretended,) that innocence should manifest itself by a stout resistance, or guilt by a plain confession ; as if a man's innocence were to be tried by the hardness of his constitution, and his guilt by the sensibility of his nerves.[2] Cicero, many ages ago,[3] though he lived in a state, wherein it was usual to put slaves to the torture, in order to furnish evidence, has denounced the absurdity and wickedness of the measure in terms of glowing eloquence, as striking, as they are brief. They are conceived in the spirit of Tacitus, and breathe all his pregnant and indignant sarcasm.[4] Ulpian, also, at a still later period in Roman jurisprudence, stamped the practice with severe reproof.[5]

---

[1] See *United States* v. *Haskell*, 4 Wash. Cir. R. 402, 410; *United States* v. *Perez*, 9 Wheat. R. 579; Hawk. P. C., B. 2, ch. 35, § 8; 1 Tuck. Black. Comm. App. 305; Rawle on the Constitution, ch. 10, p. 132, 133.

[2] 4 Black. Comm. 326 ; 3 Wilson's Law Lect. 154 to 159.

[3] Cicero, Pro Sulla, 28.

[4] Mr. Justice Blackstone quotes them in 4 Black. Comm. 326; 1 Tuck. Black. Comm. App. 304, 305 ; Rutherforth, Inst. B. 1, ch. 18, § 5.

[5] See 3 Wilson's Law Lect. 158 ; 1 Gilb. Hist. 249.

§ 1783. The other part of the clause is but an en-
largement of the language of magna charta, "*nec super
eum ibimus, nec super eum mittimus, nisi per legale judicium parium suorum, vel per legem terræ,*" neither
will we pass upon him, or condemn him, but by the lawful
judgment of his peers, or by the law of the land.   Lord
Coke says, that these latter words, *per legem terræ* (by
the law of the land,) mean by due process of law, that
is, without due presentment or indictment, and being
brought in to answer thereto by due process of the
common law.[1]   So that this clause in effect affirms the
right of trial according to the process and proceedings
of the common law.[2]

§ 1784. The concluding clause is, that private property shall not be taken for public use without just compensation.   This is an affirmance of a great doctrine
established by the common law for the protection of
private property.[3]   It is founded in natural equity, and
is laid down by jurists as a principle of universal law.[4]
Indeed, in a free government, almost all other rights
would become utterly worthless, if the government possessed an uncontrollable power over the private fortune
of every citizen.   One of the fundamental objects of
every good government must be the due administration
of justice; and how vain it would be to speak of such
an administration, when all property is subject to the
will or caprice of the legislature, and the rulers.[5]

---

[1] 2 Inst. 50, 51 ; 2 Kent's Comm. Lect. 24, p. 10, (2d edit. p. 13);
Cave's English Liberties, p. 19 ; 1 Tucker's Black. Comm. App. 304,
305.

[2] Ibid.

[3] 1 Black. Comm. 138, 139.

[4] 2 Kent's Comm. Lect. 24, p. 275, 276, (2d. edit. p. 339, 340); 3 Wilson's Law Lect. 203 ; *Ware v. Hylton*, 3 Dall. R. 194, 235 ; S. C. 1 Peters's Cond. R. 99, 111 ; 1 Black. Comm. 138, 139, 140.

[5] See 1 Tuck. Black. Comm. App. 305, 306 ; Rawle on Const. ch. 10,
p. 133.   See also *Van Horne v. Dorrance*, 2 Dall. 384.

§ 1785. The other article, in declaring, that the accused shall enjoy the right to a speedy and public trial by an impartial jury of the state or district, wherein the crime shall have been committed, (which district shall be previously ascertained by law,) and to be informed of the nature and cause of the accusation, and to be confronted with the witnesses against him, does but follow out the established course of the common law in all trials for crimes. The trial is always public; the witnesses are sworn, and give in their testimony (at least in capital cases) in the presence of the accused; the nature and cause of the accusation is accurately laid down in the indictment; and the trial is at once speedy, impartial, and in the district of the offence.[1] Without in any measure impugning the propriety of these provisions, it may be suggested, that there seems to have been an undue solicitude to introduce into the constitution some of the general guards and proceedings of the common law in criminal trials, (truly admirable in themselves) without sufficiently adverting to the consideration, that unless the whole system is incorporated, and especially the law of evidence, a corrupt legislature, or a debased and servile people, may render the whole little more, than a solemn pageantry. If, on the other hand, the people are enlightened, and honest, and zealous in defence of their rights and liberties, it will be impossible to surprise them into a surrender of a single valuable appendage of the trial by jury.[2]

§ 1786. The remaining clauses are of more direct significance, and necessity. The accused is entitled to

[1] See 4 Black. Comm. ch. 23 to ch. 28; Hawkins, P. C., B. 2, ch. 46, § 1; 1 Tuck. Black. Comm. App. 304, 305.
[2] See Rawle on Const. ch. 10, p. 128, 129.

have compulsory process for obtaining witnesses in his favour, and to have the assistance of counsel. A very short review of the state of the common law, on these points, will put their propriety beyond question. In the first place, it was an anciently and commonly received practice, derived from the civil law, and which Mr. Justice Blackstone says,[1] in his day, still obtained in France, though since the revolution it has been swept away, not to suffer the party accused in capital cases to exculpate himself by the testimony of any witnesses. Of this practice the courts grew so heartily ashamed from its unreasonable and oppressive character, that another practice was gradually introduced, of examining witnesses for the accused, but not upon oath ; the consequence of which was, that the jury gave less credit to this latter evidence, than to that produced by the government. Sir Edward Coke denounced the practice as tyrannical and unjust ; and denied, that, in criminal cases, the party accused was not to have witnesses sworn for him. The house of commons, soon after the accession of the house of Stuart to the throne of England, insisted, in a particular bill then pending, and, against the efforts both of the crown and the house of lords, caused a clause affirming the right, in cases tried under that act, of witnesses being sworn for, as well as against, the accused. By the statute of 7 Will. 3, ch. 3, the same measure of justice was established throughout the realm, in cases of treason ; and afterwards, in the reign of Queen Anne, the like rule was extended to all cases of treason and felony.[2] The right seems never to have been doubted, or denied, in cases of mere mis-

---

[1] 4 Black. Comm. 35 ; Rawle on Const. ch. 10, p. 128, 129.
[2] 4 Black. Comm. 359, 360 ; 3 Wilson's Law Lect. 170, 171 ; Hawk. P. C. ch. 46, § 160 ; 2 Hale P. C. 283.

demeanors.[1] For what causes, and upon what grounds this distinction was maintained, or even excused, it is impossible to assign any satisfactory, or even plausible reasoning.[2] Surely, a man's life must be of infinitely more value, than any subordinate punishment; and if he might protect himself against the latter by proofs of his innocence, there would seem to be irresistible reasons for permitting him to do the same in capital offences.[3] The common suggestion has been, that in capital cases no man could, or rather ought, to be convicted, unless upon evidence so conclusive and satisfactory, as to be above contradiction or doubt. But who can say, whether it be in any case so high, until all the proofs in favour, as well as against, the party have been heard? Witnesses for the government may swear falsely, and directly to the matter in charge; and, until opposing testimony is heard, there may not be the slightest ground to doubt its truth; and yet, when such is heard, it may be incontestible, that it is wholly unworthy of belief. The real fact seems to be, that the practice was early adopted into the criminal law in capital cases, in which the crown was supposed to take a peculiar interest, in base subserviency to the wishes of the latter. It is a reproach to the criminal jurisprudence of England, which the state trials, antecedently to the revolution of 1688, but too strongly sustain. They are crimsoned with the blood of persons, who were condemned to death, not only against law, but against the clearest rules of evidence.

---

[1] Hawk. P. C. ch. 46, § 159; 2 Hale P. C. 283; 1 Tuck. Black. Comm. App. 305.
[2] 2 Hale P. C. 283.
[3] Rawle on Const. ch. 10, p. 129, 130.

§ 1787. Another anomaly in the common law is, that in capital cases the prisoner is not, upon his trial upon the general issue, entitled to have counsel, unless some matter of law shall arise, proper to be debated. That is, in other words, that he shall not have the benefit of the talents and assistance of counsel in examining the witnesses, or making his defence before the jury. Mr. Justice Blackstone, with all his habitual reverence for the institutions of English jurisprudence, as they actually exist, speaks out upon this subject with the free spirit of a patriot and a jurist. This, he says, is "a rule, which, however it may be palliated under cover of that noble declaration of the law, when rightly understood, that the judge shall be counsel for the prisoner, that is, shall see, that the proceedings against him are legal, and strictly regular, seems to be not all of a piece with the rest of the humane treatment of prisoners by the English law. For upon what face of reason can that assistance be denied to save the life of a man, which is yet allowed him in prosecutions for every petty trespass." [1] The defect has indeed been cured in England in cases of treason ; [2] but it still remains unprovided for in all other cases, to, what one can hardly help deeming, the discredit of the free genius of the English constitution.

§ 1788. The wisdom of both of these provisions is, therefore, manifest, since they make matter of constitutional right, what the common law had left in a most imperfect and questionable state. [3] The right to have

---

[1] 4 Black. Comm. 355. — Mr. Christian in his note on the passage has vindicated the importance of allowing counsel in a strain of manly reasoning . 4 Black. Comm. 356, note 9.

[2] 4 B'lack. Comm. 356 ; 1 Tuck. Black. Comm. App. 305.

[3] 3 Wilson's Law Lect. 170, 171 ; 1 Tuck. Black. Comm. App. 305 ; Ra'gle on Const. ch. 10, p. 128, 129.

witnesses sworn, and counsel employed for the prisoner, are scarcely less important privileges, than the right of a trial by jury. The omission of them in the constitution is a matter of surprise; and their present incorporation is matter of honest congratulation among all the friends of rational liberty.

§ 1789. There yet remain one or two subjects connected with the judiciary, which, however, grow out of other amendments made to the constitution; and will naturally find their place in our review of that part of these Commentaries, which embraces a review of the remaining amendments.

CHAPTER XXXIX.

DEFINITION AND EVIDENCE OF TREASON.

§ 1790. The third section of the third article is as follows : " Treason against the United States shall con-" sist only in levying war against them, or in adhering " to their enemies, giving them aid and comfort. No "person shall be convicted of treason, unless on the "testimony of two witnesses to the same overt act, " or on confession in open court."

§ 1791. Treason is generally deemed the highest crime, which can be committed in civil society, since its aim is an overthrow of the government, and a public resistance by force of its powers. Its tendency is to create universal danger and alarm ; and on this account it is peculiarly odious, and often visited with the deepest public resentment. Even a charge of this nature, made against an individual, is deemed so opprobrious, that, whether just or unjust, it subjects him to suspicion and hatred ; and, in times of high political excitement, acts of a very subordinate nature are often, by popular prejudices, as well as by royal resentment, magnified into this ruinous importance.[1] It is, therefore, of very great importance, that its true nature and limits should be exactly ascertained ; and Montesquieu was so sensible of it, that he has not scrupled to declare, that if the crime of treason be indeterminate, that alone is sufficient to make any government degenerate into arbitrary

[1] 3 Wilson's Law Lect. ch. 5, p. 95, &c.

power.[1] The history of England itself is full of melancholy instruction on this subject. By the ancient common law it was left very much to discretion to determine, what acts were, and were not, treason; and the judges of those times, holding office at the pleasure of the crown, became but too often instruments in its hands of foul injustice. At the instance of tyrannical princes they had abundant opportunities to create *constructive* treasons ; that is, by forced and arbitrary constructions, to raise offences into the guilt and punishment of treason, which were not suspected to be such.[2] The grievance of these constructive treasons was so enormous, and so often weighed down the innocent, and the patriotic, that it was found necessary, as early as the reign of Edward the Third,[3] for parliament to interfere, and arrest it, by declaring and defining all the different branches of treason. This statute has ever since remained the pole star of English jurisprudence upon this subject. And although, upon temporary emergencies, and in arbitrary reigns, since that period, other treasons have been created, the sober sense of the nation has generally abrogated them, or reduced their power within narrow limits.[4]

§ 1792. Nor have republics been exempt from violence and tyranny of a similar character. The Federalist has justly remarked, that newfangled and artificial treasons have been the great engines, by

---

[1] Montesq. Spirit of Laws, B. 12, ch. 7 ; 4 Black. Comm. 75.

[2] 4 Black. Comm. 75 ; 3 Wilson's Law Lect. 96 ; 1 Tucker's Black. Comm. App. 275, 276.

[3] Stat. 25, Edw. 3, ch. 2 ; 1 Hale, P. C. 259.

[4] See 4 Black. Comm. 85 to 92 ; 3 Wilson's Law Lect. 96, 97, 98, 99 ; 1 Tuck. Black. Comm. App. 275.

which violent factions, the natural offspring of free governments, have usually wreaked their alternate malignity on each other.[1]

§ 1793. It was under the influence of these admonitions furnished by history and human experience, that the convention deemed it necessary to interpose an impassable barrier against arbitrary constructions, either by the courts, or by congress, upon the crime of treason. It confines it to two species; first, the levying of war against the United States ; and secondly, adhering to their enemies, giving them aid and comfort.[2] In so doing, they have adopted the very words of the Statute of Treason of Edward the Third ; and thus by implication, in order to cut off at once all chances of arbitrary constructions, they have recognized the well-settled interpretation of these phrases in the administration of criminal law, which has prevailed for ages.[3]

§ 1794. Fortunately, hitherto but few cases have occurred in the United States, in which it has been necessary for the courts of justice to act upon this important subject. But whenever they have arisen, the judges have uniformly adhered to the established doctrines, even when executive influence has exerted itself with no small zeal to procure convictions.[4] On one occasion only has the consideration of the question come before the Supreme Court; and we shall conclude what we have to say on this subject, with a short extract from the opinion delivered upon that

[1] The Federalist, No. 43 ; 3 Wilson's Law Lect. 96.

[2] See also Journ. of Convention, 221, 269, 270, 271.

[3] See 4 Black. Comm. 81 to 84 ; Foster, Cr. Law, Discourse I. But see 4 Tuck. Black. Comm. App. Note B.

[4] See 4 Jefferson's Corresp. 72, 75, 78, 83, 85, 86, 87, 88, 90, 101, 102, 103. See Burr's Trial in 1807 ; 3 Wilson's Law Lect. 100 to 106.

occasion. " To constitute that specific crime, for which the prisoners, now before the court, have been committed, war must be actually levied against the United States. However flagitious may be the crime of conspiring to subvert by force the government of our country, such conspiracy is not treason. To conspire to levy war, and actually to levy war, are distinct offences. The first must be brought into open action by the assemblage of men for a purpose treasonable in itself, or the fact of levying war cannot have been committed. So far has this principle been carried, that, in a case reported by Ventris, and mentioned in some modern treatises on criminal law, it has been determined, that the actual enlistment of men to serve against the government does not amount to levying war. It is true, that in that case the soldiers enlisted were to serve without the realm ; but they were enlisted within it, and if the enlistment for a treasonable purpose could amount to levying war, then war had been actually levied."

§ 1795. " It is not the intention of the court to say, that no individual can be guilty of this crime, who has not appeared in arms against his country. On the contrary, if war be actually levied, that is, if a body of men be actually assembled for the purpose of effecting by force a treasonable purpose, all those, who perform any part, however minute, or however remote from the scene of action, and who are actually leagued in the general conspiracy, are to be considered as traitors. But there must be an actual assembling of men for the treasonable purpose, to constitute a levying of war."[1]

---

[1] *Ex parte Bollman*, 4 Cranch, 126. See also *United States v. Burr*, 4 Cranch, 469 to 508, &c. ; Serg. on Const. ch. 30, (2 edit. ch. 32 ;) *People v. Lynch*, 1 John. R. 553.

§ 1796. The other part of the clause, requiring the testimony of two witnesses to the same overt act, or a confession *in open court*,[1] to justify a conviction is founded upon the same reasoning. A like provision exists in British jurisprudence, founded upon the same great policy of protecting men against false testimony, and unguarded confessions, to their utter ruin. It has been well remarked, that confessions are the weakest and most suspicious of all testimony ; ever liable to be obtained by artifice, false hopes, promises of favour, or menaces ; seldom remembered accurately, or reported with due precision ; and incapable, in their nature, of being disproved by other negative evidence.[2] To which it may be added, that it is easy to be forged, and the most difficult to guard against. An unprincipled demagogue, or a corrupt courtier, might otherwise hold the lives of the purest patriots in his hands, without the means of proving the falsity of the charge, if a secret confession, uncorroborated by other evidence, would furnish a sufficient foundation and proof of guilt. And wisely, also, has the constitution declined to suffer the testimony of a single witness, however high, to be sufficient to establish such a crime, which rouses against the victim at once private honour and public hostility.[3] There must, as there should, be a concurrence of two witnesses to the same overt, that is, open act of treason, who are above all reasonable exception.[4]

---

1 See *United States* v. *Fries*, Pamph. p. 171.
2 4 Black. Comm. 356, 357.
3 See 4 Black. Comm. 357, 358.
4 *United States* v. *Burr*, 4 Cranch, 469, 496, 503, 506, 507.

§ 1797. The subject of the power of congress to declare the punishment of treason, and the consequent disabilities, have been already commented on in another place.[1]

---

[1] See ante, Vol. III. § 1291 to 1296.

CHAPTER XL.

PRIVILEGES OF CITIZENS — FUGITIVES — SLAVES.

§ 1798. THE fourth article of the constitution contains several important provisions, some of which have been already considered. Among these are, the faith and credit to be given to state acts, records, and judgments, and the mode of proving them, and the effect thereof; the admission of new states into the Union; and the regulation and disposal of the territory, and other property of the United States.[1] We shall now proceed to those, which still remain for examination.

§ 1799. The first is, "The citizens of each state "shall be entitled to all privileges and immunities of "citizens in the several states." There was an article upon the same subject[2] in the confederation, which declared, "that the free inhabitants of each of these states, paupers, vagabonds, and fugitives from justice excepted, shall be entitled to all privileges and immunities of free citizens in the several states; and the people of each state shall, in every other, enjoy all the privileges of trade and commerce, subject to the same duties, impositions, and restrictions, as the inhabitants thereof respectively," &c.[3] It was remarked by the Federalist, that there is a strange confusion in this language. Why the terms, *free inhabitants*, are used in one part of the article, *free citizens* in another, and *people* in another; or what is meant by superadding

---

[1] See ante, Vol. III. § 1211 to 1230, § 1308 to 1315, and § 1316 to 1324.

[2] See 1 Tucker's Black. Comm. App. 365.

[3] Confederation, Art. 4.

to "all privileges and immunities of free citizens,"
"all the privileges of trade and commerce," cannot
easily be determined. It seems to be a construction,
however, scarcely avoidable, that those, who come
under the denomination of *free inhabitants* of a state,
although not citizens of such state, are entitled, in every
other state, to all the privileges of *free citizens* of the
latter ; that is to greater privileges, than they may be
entitled to in their own state. So that it was in the
power of a particular state, (to which every other state
was bound to submit,) not only to confer the rights of
citizenship in other states upon any persons, whom it
might admit to such rights within itself, but upon any
persons, whom it might allow to become *inhabitants*
within its jurisdiction.   But even if an exposition could
be given to the term, *inhabitants*, which would confine
the stipulated privileges to citizens alone, the difficulty
would be diminished only, and not removed.   The
very improper power was, under the confederation,
still retained in each state of naturalizing aliens in
every other state.[1]

§ 1800. The provision in the constitution avoids all
this ambiguity.[2]   It is plain and simple in its language ;
and its object is not easily to be mistaken.   Connected with the exclusive power of naturalization in the
national government, it puts at rest many of the difficulties, which affected the construction of the article of
the confederation.[3]   It is obvious, that, if the citizens of
each state were to be deemed aliens to each other, they
could not take, or hold real estate, or other privileges,

---

[1] The Federalist, No. 42. See also Id. No. 80; ante, Vol. III.
§ 1098.
[2] See Journ. of Convention, 222, 302.
[3] But see 1 Tuck. Black. Comm. App. 365.

except as other aliens. The intention of this clause was to confer on them, if one may so say, a general citizenship ; and to communicate all the privileges and immunities, which the citizens of the same state would be entitled to under the like circumstances.[1]

§ 1801. The next clause is as follows: "A person "charged in any state with treason, felony, or other "crime, who shall flee from justice, and be found in "another state, shall, on demand of the executive au-"thority of the state, from which he fled, be delivered "up, to be removed to the state having jurisdiction of "the crime." A provision, substantially the same, existed under the confederation.[2]

§ 1802. It has been often made a question, how far any nation is, by the law of nations, and independent of any treaty stipulations, bound to surrender upon demand fugitives from justice, who, having committed crimes in another country, have fled thither for shelter. Mr. Chancellor Kent considers it clear upon principle, as well as authority, that every state is bound to deny an asylum to criminals, and, upon application and due examination of the case, to surrender the fugitive to the foreign state, where the crime has been committed.[3] Other distinguished judges and jurists have entertained a different opinion.[4] It is not uncommon for treaties to contain mutual stipulations for the surrender of

---

[1] *Carfield* v. *Coryell*, 4 Wash. Cir. R. 371; Sergeant on Const. ch. 31, p. 384, (ch. 33, p. 393, 2 edit.): *Livingston* v. *Van Ingen*, 9 John. R. 507.

[2] Confederation, Art. 4.

[3] 1 Kent's Comm. Lect. 2, p. 36, (2 edit. p. 36, 37) ; Matter of Washburn, 4 John. Ch. R. 106; *Rex* v. *Ball*, 1 Amer. Jurist, 297 : Vattel, B. 2, § 76, 77 ; Rutherforth, Inst. B. 2, ch. 9, § 12.

[4] *Com'th.* v. *Deacon*, 10 Sergeant & Rawle, R. 125 ; 1 American Jurist. 297.

criminals ; and the United States have sometimes been a party to such an arrangement.[1]

§ 1803. But, however the point may be, as to foreign nations, it cannot be questioned, that it is of vital importance to the public administration of criminal justice, and the security of the respective states, that criminals, who have committed crimes therein, should not find an asylum in other states ; but should be surrendered up for trial and punishment. It is a power most salutary in its general operation, by discouraging crimes, and cutting off the chances of escape from punishment. It will promote harmony and good feelings among the states ; and it will increase the general sense of the blessings of the national government. It will, moreover, give strength to a great moral duty, which neighbouring states especially owe to each other, by elevating the policy of the mutual suppression of crimes into a legal obligation. Hitherto it has proved as useful in practice, as it is unexceptionable in its character.[2]

§ 1804. The next clause is, " No person held to ser-" vice or labor in one state under the laws thereof, " escaping into another, shall in consequence of any law " or regulation therein be discharged from such service " or labour; but shall be delivered up on the claim of " the party, to whom such service or labour may be " due." [3]

§ 1805. This clause was introduced into the constitution solely for the benefit of the slave-holding states,

---

[1] See Treaty with Great Britain of 1794, art. 27 ; *United States* v. *Nash,* Bees, Adm. R. 266.

[2] See 1 Kent's Comm. Lect. 2, p. 36, (2 edit. p. 36.) See Journ. of Convention, 222, 304.

[3] This clause in its substance was unanimously adopted by the Convention. Journ. of Convention, 307.

to enable them to reclaim their fugitive slaves, who should have escaped into other states, where slavery was not tolerated. The want of such a provision under the confederation was felt, as a grievous inconvenience, by the slave-holding states,[1] since in many states no aid whatsoever would be allowed to the owners ; and sometimes indeed they met with open resistance. In fact, it cannot escape the attention of every intelligent reader, that many sacrifices of opinion and feeling are to be found made by the Eastern and Middle states to the peculiar interests of the south. This forms no just subject of complaint ; but it should for ever repress the delusive and mischievous notion, that the south has not at all times had its full share of benefits from the Union.

§ 1806. It is obvious, that these provisions for the arrest and removal of fugitives of both classes contemplate summary ministerial proceedings, and not the ordinary course of judicial investigations, to ascertain, whether the complaint be well founded, or the claim of ownership be established beyond all legal controversy. In cases of suspected crimes the guilt or innocence of the party is to be made out at his trial; and not upon the preliminary inquiry, whether he shall be delivered up. All, that would seem in such cases to be necessary, is, that there should be *primâ facie* evidence before the executive authority to satisfy its judgment, that there is probable cause to believe the party guilty, such as upon an ordinary warrant would justify his commitment for trial.[2] And in the cases of fugitive slaves there would seem to be the same necessity of requir-

---

[1] 1 Tuck, Black. Comm. App. 366. See also Serg. on Const. ch. 31 p. 385, (ch. 33, p. 394 to 398, 2d edit.) *Glen* v. *Hodges*, 9 John. R. 67; *Commonwealth* v. *Halloway*, 2 Serg. & Rawle R. 306.

[2] See Serg. on Const. ch. 31 v. 385, 2d edit. ch. 33, p. 394.)

ing only *primâ facie* proofs of ownership, without putting the party to a formal assertion of his rights by a suit at the common law.   Congress appear to have acted upon this opinion ; and, accordingly, in the statute upon this subject have authorized summary proceedings before a magistrate, upon which he may grant a warrant for a removal.[1]

---

[1] Act of 12 Feb. 1793, ch. 51, (ch. 7) ; Serg. on Const. ch. 31, p. 387, (2d edit. ch. 33, p. 397, 398) ; *Glen* v. *Hodges*, 9 John. R. 62 ; *Wright* v. *Deacon*, 5 Serg. & R. 62 ; *Commonwealth* v. *Griffin*, 2 Pick. R. 11.

CHAPTER XLI.

GUARANTY OF REPUBLICAN GOVERNMENT — MODE
OF MAKING AMENDMENTS.

§ 1807. The fourth section of the fourth article is as
follows: "The United States shall guaranty to every
"state in this Union a republican form of government;
"and shall protect each of them against invasion; and
"on application of the legislature, or of the executive,
"when the legislature cannot be convened, against
"domestic violence."

§ 1808. The want of a provision of this nature was
felt, as a capital defect in the plan of the confederation,
as it might in its consequences endanger, if not overthrow, the Union. Without a guaranty, the assistance
to be derived from the national government in repelling
domestic dangers, which might threaten the existence
of the state constitutions, could not be demanded, as a
right, from the national government. Usurpation might
raise its standard, and trample upon the liberties of the
people, while the national government could legally do
nothing more, than behold the encroachments with
indignation and regret. A successful faction might
erect a tyranny on the ruins of order and law; while
no succour could be constitutionally afforded by the
Union to the friends and supporters of the government.[1] But this is not all. The destruction of the
national government itself, or of neighbouring states,
might result from a successful rebellion in a single state.
Who can determine, what would have been the issue, if

---

[1] The Federalist, No. 21.

the insurrection in Massachusetts, in 1787, had been successful, and the malecontents had been headed by a Cæsar or a Cromwell ?[1]   If a despotic or monarchical government were established in one state, it would bring on the ruin of the whole republic.   Montesquieu has acutely remarked, that confederated governments should be formed only between states, whose form of government is not only similar, but also republican.[2]

§ 1809. The Federalist has spoken with so much force and propriety upon this subject, that it super-cedes all further reasoning.[3]   " In a confederacy," says that work, " founded on republican principles, and com-posed of republican members, the superintending gov-ernment ought clearly to possess authority to defend the system against aristocratic or monarchical inno-vations.   The more intimate the nature of such a union may be, the greater interest have the members in the political institutions of each other ; and the greater right to insist, that the forms of government, under which the compact was entered into, should be *sub-stantially* maintained.

§ 1810. " But a right implies a remedy ; and where else could the remedy be deposited, than where it is deposited by the constitution?   Governments of dis-similar principles and forms have been found less adapted to a federal coalition of any sort, than those of a kindred nature.   ' As the confederate republic of Germany,' says Montesquieu, ' consists of free cities and petty states, subject to different princes, experi-ence shows us, that it is more imperfect, than that of

[1] The Federalist, No. 21.
[2] Montesq. B. 9, ch. 1, 2 ; 1 Tuck. Black. Comm. App. 366, 367. — This clause of guaranty was unanimously adopted in the convention. Journ. of Convention, 113, 189.
[3] The Federalist, No. 21.

Holland and Switzerland.' 'Greece was undone,' he
adds, ' as soon as the king of Macedon obtained a seat
among the Amphyctions.' In the latter case, no doubt,
the disproportionate force, as well as the monarchical
form of the new confederate, had its share of influence
on the events.

§ 1811. " It may possibly be asked, what need there
could be of such a precaution, and whether it may not
become a pretext for alterations in the state governments, without the concurrence of the states themselves.
These questions admit of ready answers. If the interposition of the general government should not be need-
ed, the provision for such an event will be a harmless
superfluity only in the constitution. But who can say,
what experiments may be produced by the caprice of
particular states, by the ambition of enterprising leaders, or by the intrigues and influence of foreign powers?
To the second question, it may be answered, that if the
general government should interpose by virtue of this
constitutional authority, it will be of course bound to
pursue the authority. But the authority extends no
further than to a *guaranty* of a republican form of government, which supposes a pre-existing government of
the form, which is to be guaranteed. As long therefore as the existing republican forms are continued by
the states, they are guaranteed by the federal constitution. Whenever the states may choose to substitute
other republican forms, they have a right to do so, and
to claim the federal guaranty for the latter. The only
restriction imposed on them is, that they shall not
exchange republican for anti-republican constitutions :
a restriction, which, it is presumed, will hardly be considered as a grievance.

§ 1812. "A protection against invasion is due from
every society, to the parts composing it. The latitude
of the expression here used, seems to secure each state
not only against foreign hostility, but against ambitious
or vindictive enterprises of its more powerful neighbours. The history both of ancient and modern confederacies proves, that the weaker members of the
union ought not to be insensible to the policy of this
article.

§ 1813. "Protection against domestic violence is
added with equal propriety. It has been remarked,
that even among the Swiss cantons, which, properly
speaking, are not under one government, provision is
made for this object ; and the history of that league
informs us, that mutual aid is frequently claimed and
afforded ; and as well by the most democratic, as the
other cantons. A recent and well-known event among
ourselves has warned us to be prepared for emergencies of a like nature.

§ 1814. "At first view, it might seem not to square
with the republican theory, to suppose, either that a
majority have not the right, or that a minority will have
the force, to subvert a government ; and consequently,
that the federal interposition can never be required, but
when it would be improper. But theoretic reasoning
in this, as in most other cases, must be qualified by the
lessons of practice. Why may not illicit combinations
for purposes of violence, be formed, as well by a majority of a state, especially a small state, as by a majority
of a county, or a district of the same state ; and if the
authority of the state ought in the latter case to protect the local magistracy, ought not the federal authority
in the former to support the state authority ? Besides ;
there are certain parts of the state constitutions, which

are so interwoven with the federal constitution, that a violent blow cannot be given to the one without communicating the wound to the other. Insurrections in a state will rarely induce a federal interposition, unless the number concerned in them bear some proportion to the friends of government. It will be much better, that the violence in such cases should be repressed by the superintending power, than that the majority should be left to maintain their cause by a bloody and obstinate contest. The existence of a right to interpose will generally prevent the necessity of exerting it.

§ 1815. "Is it true, that force and right are necessarily on the same side in republican governments? May not the minor party possess such a superiority of pecuniary resources, of military talents and experience, or of secret succours from foreign powers, as will render it superior also in an appeal to the sword? May not a more compact and advantageous position turn the scale on the same side, against a superior number so situated, as to be less capable of a prompt and collected exertion of its strength? Nothing can be more chimerical than to imagine, that, in a trial of actual force, victory may be calculated by the rules, which prevail in a census of the inhabitants, or which determine the event of an election! May it not happen, in fine, that the minority of *citizens* may become a majority of *persons*, by the accession of alien residents, of a casual concourse of adventurers, or of those, whom the constitution of the state has not admitted to the rights of suffrage? I take no notice of an unhappy species of population abounding in some of the states, who, during the calm of regular government, are sunk below the level of men ; but who, in the tempestuous scenes of civil violence, may emerge into the human character, and give a superiority of strength to any party, with which they may associate themselves.

§ 1816. "In cases where it may be doubtful, on which side justice lies, what better umpires could be desired by two violent factions, flying to arms and tearing the state to pieces, than the representatives of confederate states, not heated by the local flame? To the impartiality of judges they would unite the affection of friends. Happy would it be, if such a remedy for its infirmities could be enjoyed by all free governments; if a project equally effectual could be established for the universal peace of mankind!

§ 1817. " Should it be asked, what is to be the redress for an insurrection pervading all the states, and comprising a superiority of the entire force, though not a constitutional right? The answer must be, that such a case, as it would be without the compass of human remedies, so it is fortunately not within the compass of human probability; and that it is a sufficient recommendation of the federal constitution, that it diminishes the risk of a calamity, for which no possible constitution can provide a cure.

§ 1818. " Among the advantages of a confederate republic, enumerated by Montesquieu, an important one is, 'that should a popular insurrection happen in one of the states, the others are able to quell it. Should abuses creep into one part, they are reformed by those, that remain sound.' " [1]

§ 1819. It may not be amiss further to observe, (in the language of another commentator,) that every pretext for intermeddling with the domestic concerns of any state, under colour of protecting it against domestic

---

[1] The Federalist, No. 43.

violence, is taken away by that part of the provision, which renders an application from the legislature, or executive authority of the state endangered necessary to be made to the general government, before its interference can be at all proper. On the other hand, this article becomes an immense acquisition of strength, and additional force to the aid of any state government, in case of an internal rebellion, or insurrection against its authority. The southern states, being more peculiarly open to danger from this quarter, ought (he adds) to be particularly tenacious of a constitution, from which they may derive such assistance in the most critical periods.[1]

§ 1820. The fifth article of the constitution respects the mode of making amendments to it. It is in these words: "The congress, whenever two thirds of both "houses shall deem it necessary, shall propose amend-"ments to this constitution, or, on the application of "the legislatures of two thirds of the several states, "shall call a convention for proposing amendments, "which, in either case, shall be valid to all intents and "purposes, as part of this constitution, when ratified "by the legislatures of three fourths of the several "states, or by conventions in three fourths thereof, as "the one or the other mode of ratification may be pro-"posed by the congress; provided, that no amendment, "which may be made prior to the year one thousand "eight hundred and eight, shall in any manner affect "the first and fourth clauses in the ninth section of "the first article; and that no state, without its con-"sent, shall be deprived of its equal suffrage in the "senate." [2]

---

[1] 1 Tuck. Black. Comm. App. 367. See also Rawle on Const. ch. 32; 2 Elliot's Deb. 118, 119, 120; Journ. of Convention, p. 229, 311, 312.

[2] See Journ. of Convent 113; Id. 229, 313, 317, 318, 366, 386, 387, 388.

§ 1821. Upon this subject, little need be said to persuade us, at once, of its utility and importance. It is obvious, that no human government can ever be perfect; and that it is impossible to foresee, or guard against all the exigencies, which may, in different ages, require different adaptations and modifications of powers to suit the various necessities of the people. A government, forever changing and changeable, is, indeed, in a state bordering upon anarchy and confusion. A government, which, in its own organization, provides no means of change, but assumes to be fixed and unalterable, must, after a while, become wholly unsuited to the circumstances of the nation; and it will either degenerate into a despotism, or by the pressure of its inequalities bring on a revolution. It is wise, therefore, in every government, and especially in a republic, to provide means for altering, and improving the fabric of government, as time and experience, or the new phases of human affairs, may render proper, to promote the happiness and safety of the people. The great principle to be sought is to make the changes practicable, but not too easy; to secure due deliberation, and caution; and to follow experience, rather than to open a way for experiments, suggested by mere speculation or theory.

§ 1822. In regard to the constitution of the United States, it is confessedly a new experiment in the history of nations. Its framers were not bold or rash enough to believe, or to pronounce it to be perfect. They made use of the best lights, which they possessed, to form and adjust its parts, and mould its materials. But they knew, that time might develope many defects in its arrangements, and many deficiencies in its powers. They desired, that it might be open to improvement ; and under the guidance of the sober judgment and enlightened skill of the country, to be perpetually approaching nearer and nearer to perfection.[1] It was obvious, too, that the means of amendment might avert, or at least have a tendency to avert, the most serious perils, to which confederated republics are liable, and by which all have hitherto been ship-wrecked. They knew, that the besetting sin of republics is a restlessness of temperament, and a spirit of discontent at slight evils. They knew the pride and jealousy of state power in confederacies ; and they wished to disarm them of their potency, by providing a safe means to break the force, if not wholly to ward off the blows, which would, from time to time, under the garb of patriotism, or a love of the people, be aimed at the constitution. They believed, that the power of amendment was, if one may so say, the safety valve to let off all temporary effervescences and excitements ; and the real effective instrument to control and adjust the movements of the machinery, when out of order, or in danger of self-destruction.

§ 1823. Upon the propriety of the power, in some form, there will probably be little controversy. The only question is, whether it is so arranged, as to accomplish its objects in the safest mode ; safest for the stability of the government; and safest for the rights and liberties of the people.

§ 1824. Two modes are pointed out, the one at the instance of the government itself, through the instrumentality of congress; the other, at the instance of the states, through the instrumentality of a convention. Congress, whenever two thirds of each house shall

---

[1] The Federalist, No. 43.

concur in the expediency of an amendment, may propose it for adoption.[1] The legislatures of two thirds of the states may require a convention to be called, for the purpose of proposing amendments. In each case, three fourths of the states, either through their legislatures, or conventions, called for the purpose, must concur in every amendment, before it becomes a part of the constitution. That this mode of obtaining amendments is practicable, is abundantly demonstrated by our past experience in the only mode hitherto found necessary, that of amendments proposed by congress. In this mode twelve amendments have already been incorporated into the constitution. The guards, too, against the too hasty exercise of the power, under temporary discontents or excitements, are apparently sufficient. Two thirds of congress, or of the legislatures of the states, must concur in proposing, or requiring amendments to be proposed ; and three fourths of the states must ratify them. Time is thus allowed, and ample time, for deliberation, both in proposing and ratifying amendments. They cannot be carried by surprise, or intrigue, or artifice. Indeed, years may elapse before a deliberate judgment may be passed upon them, unless some pressing emergency calls for instant action. An amendment, which has the deliberate judgment of two-thirds of congress, and of three fourths of the states, can scarcely be deemed unsuited to the prosperity, or security of the republic. It must combine as much wisdom and experience in its favour, as ordinarily can belong to the management of any

---

[1] It has been held, that the approval of the president is not necessary to any amendment proposed by congress. *Hollingsworth* v. *Virginia*, 3 Dall. 378.

human concerns.[1]   In England the supreme power of the nation resides in parliament ; and, in a legal sense, it is so omnipotent, that it has authority to change the whole structure of the constitution, without resort to any confirmation of the people.   There is, indeed, little danger, that it will so do, as long as the people are fairly represented in it.   But still it does, theoretically speaking, possess the power ; and it has actually exercised it so far, as to change the succession to the crown, and mould to its will some portions of the internal structure of the constitution.[2]

§ 1825. Upon the subject of the national constitution, we may adopt without hesitation the language of a learned commentator. "Nor," says he, "can we too much applaud a constitution, which thus provides a safe and peaceable remedy for its own defects, as they may, from time to time, be discovered. A change of government in other countries is almost always attended with convulsions, which threaten its entire dis-

---

[1] The Federalist disposes of this article in the following brief, but decisive, manner : " That useful alterations will be suggested by experience, could not but be foreseen. It was requisite, therefore, that a mode for introducing them should be provided. The mode preferred by the convention seems to be stamped with every mark of propriety. It guards equally against that extreme facility, which would render the constitution too mutable ; and that extreme difficulty, which might perpetuate its discovered faults. It, moreover, equally enables the general, and the state governments to originate the amendment of errors, as they may be pointed out by the experience on one side, or the other. The exception, in favour of the equality of suffrage in the senate, was probably meant as a palladium to the residuary sovereignty of the states, implied and secured by that principle of representation in one branch of the legislature ; and was probably insisted on by the states particularly attached to that equality. The other exception must have been admitted on the same considerations, which produced the privilege defended by it." The Federalist, No. 43.

[2] See 1 Black. Comm. 90, 91, 146, 147, 151, 152, 160, 161, 162, 210 to 218.

solution ; and with scenes of horror, which deter
mankind from every attempt to correct abuses, or remove oppressions, until they have become altogether
intolerable.   In America we may reasonably hope, that
neither of these evils need be apprehended.   Nor is
there any reason to fear, that this provision in the
constitution will produce any instability in the government.   The mode, both of originating and ratifying
amendments, (in either mode, which the constitution
directs,) must necessarily be attended with such obstacles and delays, as must prove a sufficient bar against
light or frequent innovations.   And, as a further security against them, the same article further provides,
that no amendment, which may be made prior to the
year 1808, shall, in any manner affect those clauses of
the ninth section of the first article, which relate to the
migration or importation of such persons, as the states
may think proper to allow ; and to the manner, in
which direct taxes shall be laid ; and that no state
shall, without its consent, be deprived of its equal suffrage in the senate." [1]

---

[1] 1 Tuck. Black. Comm. App. 371, 372.

CHAPTER XLII.

PUBLIC DEBTS — SUPREMACY OF CONSTITUTION AND LAWS.

§ 1826. The first clause of the sixth article of the constitution is : " All debts contracted, and engage-" ments entered into before the adoption of this consti-" tution, shall be as valid against the United States, " under this constitution, as under the confederation." [1]

§ 1827. This can be considered in no other light, than as a declaratory proposition, resulting from the law of nations, and the moral obligations of society. Nothing is more clear upon reason or general law, than the doctrine, that revolutions in government have, or rather ought to have, no effect whatsoever upon private rights, and contracts, or upon the public obligations of nations.[2] It results from the first principles of moral duty, and responsibility, deducible from the law of nature, and applied to the intercourse and social relations of nations.[3] A change in the political form of a society ought to have no power to produce a dissolution of any of its moral obligations.[4]

§ 1828. This declaration was probably inserted in the constitution, not only as a solemn recognition of the obligations of the government resulting from na-

---

[1] See Journ. of Convention, 291.

[2] See *Jackson* v. *Luun*, 3 John. Cas. 109; *Kelly* v. *Harrison*, 2 John. Cas. 29; *Terrett* v. *Taylor*, 9 Cranch, 50.

[3] See Rutherforth, Inst. B. 2, ch. 9, § 1, 2; Id. ch. 10, § 14; Vattel, Prelim. Dis. § 2, 9: B. 2, ch. 1, § 1, ch. 5, § 64, ch. 14, § 214, 215, 216.

[4] The Federalist, No. 43; Rutherforth, Inst. B. 2, ch. 10, § 14, 15; Grotius, B. 2, ch. 9, § 8, 9.

tional law ; but for the more complete satisfaction and
security of the public creditors, foreign as well as domestic.　The articles of confederation contained a
similar stipulation in respect to the bills of credit emitted, monies borrowed, and debts contracted, by or under the authority of congress, before the ratification of
the confederation.[1]

§ 1829. Reasonable as this provision seems to be,
it did not wholly escape the animadversions of that
critical spirit, which was perpetually on the search to
detect defects, and to disparage the merits of the constitution.　It was said, that the validity of all engagements made *to*, as well as made *by*, the United States,
ought to have been expressly asserted.　It is surprising, that the authors of such an objection should have
overlooked the obvious consideration, that, as all engagements are in their nature reciprocal, an assertion
of their validity on one side, necessarily involves their
validity on the other; and that, as this article is but
declaratory, the establishment of it in debts entered
into by the government, unavoidably included a recognition of it in engagements with the government.[2]
The shorter and plainer answer is that pronounced by
the law of nations, that states neither lose any of their
rights, nor are discharged from any of their obligations,
by a change in the form of their civil government.[3]
More was scarcely necessary, than to have declared,
that all future contracts by and with the United States
should be valid, and binding upon the parties.

[1] 1 Tuck. Black. Comm. App. 268 ; Confederation, Art. 12.
[2] The Federalist, No. 43, No. 84.
[3] The Federalist, No. 84 ; Rutherforth, B. 2, ch. 10, § 14, 15 ; Grotius,
B. 2, ch. 9, § 8, 9.

§ 1830. The next clause is, "This constitution, "and the laws of the United States, which shall be "made in pursuance thereof, and all treaties made, or "which shall be made, under the authority of the United "States, shall be the supreme law of the land. And "the judges in every state shall be bound thereby, any "thing in the constitution or laws of any state to the "contrary notwithstanding."[1]

§ 1831. The propriety of this clause would seem to result from the very nature of the constitution. If it was to establish a national government, that government ought, to the extent of its powers and rights, to be supreme. It would be a perfect solecism to affirm, that a national government should exist with certain powers; and yet, that in the exercise of those powers it should not be supreme. What other inference could have been drawn, than of their supremacy, if the constitution had been totally silent? And surely a positive affirmance of that, which is necessarily implied, cannot in a case of such vital importance be deemed unimportant. The very circumstance, that a question might be made, would irresistibly lead to the conclusion, that it ought not to be left to inference. A law, by the very meaning of the term, includes supremacy. It is a rule, which those, to whom it is prescribed, are bound to observe. This results from every political association. If individuals enter into a state of society, the laws of that society must be the supreme regulator of their conduct. If a number of political societies enter into a larger political society, the laws, which the latter may enact, pursuant to the powers entrusted to it by its constitution, must necessarily be supreme over those

---

[1] See Journal of Convention, p. 222, 282, 293.

societies, and the individuals, of whom they are composed. It would otherwise be a mere treaty, dependent upon the good faith of the parties, and not a government, which is only another name for political power and supremacy. But it will not follow, that acts of the larger society, which are not pursuant to its constitutional powers, but which are invasions of the residuary authorities of the smaller societies, will become the supreme law of the land. They will be merely acts of usurpation, and will deserve to be treated as such. Hence we perceive, that the above clause only declares a truth, which flows immediately and necessarily from the institution of a national government.[1] It will be observed, that the supremacy of the laws is attached to those only, which are made in pursuance of the constitution; a caution very proper in itself, but in fact the limitation would have arisen by irresistible implication, if it had not been expressed.[2]

§ 1832. In regard to treaties, there is equal reason, why they should be held, when made, to be the supreme law of the land. It is to be considered, that treaties constitute solemn compacts of binding obligation among nations; and unless they are scrupulously obeyed, and enforced, no foreign nation would consent to negotiate with us; or if it did, any want of strict fidelity on our part in the discharge of the treaty stipulations would be visited by reprisals, or war.[3] It is, therefore, indispensable, that they should have the obli-

---

1 The Federalist, No. 33. See *Gibbons* v. *Ogden*, 9 Wheat. R. 210, 211; *McCulloch* v. *Maryland*, 4 Wheat. R. 405, 406. — This passage from the Federalist (No. 33) has been, for another purpose, already cited in Vol. I. § 340; but it is necessary to be here repeated to give due effect to the subsequent passages.

2 Ibid. See also 1 Tuck. Black. Comm. App. 369, 370.

3 See The Federalist, No. 64.

gation and force of a law, that they may be executed by the judicial power, and be obeyed like other laws. This will not prevent them from being cancelled or abrogated by the nation upon grave and suitable occasions; for it will not be disputed, that they are subject to the legislative power, and may be repealed, like other laws, at its pleasure;[1] or they may be varied by new treaties. Still, while they do subsist, they ought to have a positive binding efficacy as laws upon all the states, and all the citizens of the states. The peace of the nation, and its good faith, and moral dignity, indispensably require, that all state laws should be subjected to their supremacy. The difference between considering them as laws, and considering them as executory, or executed contracts, is exceedingly important in the actual administration of public justice. If they are supreme laws, courts of justice will enforce them directly in all cases, to which they can be judicially applied, in opposition to all state laws, as we all know was done in the case of the British debts secured by the treaty of 1783, after the constitution was adopted.[2] If they are deemed but solemn compacts, promissory in their nature and obligation, courts of justice may be embarrassed in enforcing them, and may be compelled to leave the redress to be administered through other departments of the government.[3] It is

---

[1] See Act of Congress, 7th July, 1798, ch. 84; *Talbot* v. *Seeman*, 1 Cranch, 1; *Ware* v. *Hylton*, 3 Dall. 361, Per Iredell J.

[2] *Ware* v. *Hylton*, 3 Dall. R. 199. See also *Gibbons* v. *Ogden*, 9 Wheat. R. 210, 211; Letter of Congress of 13th April, 1787; 12 Journ. of Congress, 32.

[3] See Iredell J.'s reasoning in *Ware* v. *Hylton*, 3 Dall. R. 270 to 277; 5 Marshall's Life of Washington, ch. 8, p. 652, 656; 1 Wait's State Papers, 45, 47, 71, 81, 145; Serg. on Const. ch. 21, p. 217, 218, ch. 33, p. 396, 397, (2d edit. ch. 21, p. 218, 219, ch. 34, p. 406, 407.) — " A

notorious, that treaty stipulations (especially those of the treaty of peace of 1783) were grossly disregarded by the states under the confederation. They were deemed by the states, not as laws, but like requisitions, of mere moral obligation, and dependent upon the good will of the states for their execution. Congress, indeed, remonstrated against this construction, as unfounded in principle and justice.[1] But their voice was not heard. Power and right were separated; the argument was all on one side; but the power was on the other.[2] It was probably to obviate this very difficulty, that this clause was inserted in the constitution;[3] and it would redound to the immortal honour of its authors, if it had done no more, than thus to bring treaties within the sanctuary of justice, as laws of supreme obligation.[4] There are, indeed, still cases, in which courts of justice can administer no effectual redress; as when the terms

---

treaty," said the Supreme Court, in *Foster* v. *Neilson,* 2 Peters's R. 314, "is in its nature a contract between two nations, not a legislative act. It does not generally effect of itself the object to be accomplished, especially so far, as its operation is infraterritorial; but is carried into execution by the sovereign power of the respective parties to the instrument. In the United States a different principle is established. Our constitution declares a treaty to be the law of the land. It is consequently to be regarded by courts of justice as equivalent to an act of the legislature, whenever it operates of itself without the aid of any legislative provision."

1 Circular Letter of Congress, 13th April, 1787; 12 Journ. of Congress, 32 to 36.

2 See the opinion of Iredell J. in *Ware* v. *Hylton,* 3 Dall. 270 to 277.

3 Id. 276, 277. See Journal of Convention, p. 222, 282, 283, 293.

4 The importance of this power has been practically illustrated by the redress afforded by courts of law in cases pending before them upon treaty stipulations. See *United States* v. *The Peggy,* 1 Cranch, 103; *Ware* v. *Hylton,* 3 Dall. R. 199, 244, 261; *United States* v. *Arradondo,* 6 Peters's R. 691; *Soulard* v. *Smith,* 4 Peters's Sup. R. 511; Case of *Jonathan Robbins,* 1 Hall's Journ. of Jurisp. 25; Bees Adm'rs Rep. 263; 5 Wheat. Rep. App.

of a stipulation import a contract, when either of the parties engages to perform a particular act the treaty addresses itself to the political, and not to the judicial, department ; and the legislature must execute the contract, before it can become a rule for the courts.[1]

§ 1833. It is melancholy to reflect, that, conclusive as this view of the subject is in favour of the supremacy clause, it was assailed with great vehemence and zeal by the adversaries of the constitution ; and especially the concluding clause, which declared the supremacy, "any thing in the constitution or laws of any state to "the contrary notwithstanding." [2]   And yet this very clause was but an expression of the necessary meaning of the former clause, introduced from abundant caution, to make its obligation more strongly felt by the state judges.   The very circumstance, that any objection was made, demonstrated the utility, nay the necessity of the clause, since it removed every pretence, under which ingenuity could, by its miserable subterfuges, escape from the controlling power of the constitution.

§ 1834. To be fully sensible of the value of the whole clause, we need only suppose for a moment, that the supremacy of the state constitutions had been left complete by a saving clause in their favour.   "In the first place, as these constitutions invest the state legislatures with absolute sovereignty, in all cases not excepted by the existing articles of confederation, all the authorities contained in the proposed constitution, so far as they exceed those enumerated in the confederation, would have been annulled, and the new

---

[1] *Foster* v. *Neilson*, 2 Peters's Sup. R. 254, 314. See also the Bello Corunnes, 6 Wheat. R. 171 ; Serg. on Const. ch. 33, p. 397, 398, 399, (ch. 34, p. 407, 408, 409, 410, 2d edit.)
[2] See The Federalist, No. 44, 64.

congress would have been reduced to the same impotent condition with their predecessors. In the next place, as the constitutions of some of the states do not even expressly and fully recognize the existing powers of the confederacy, an express saving of the supremacy of the former would, in such states, have brought into question every power contained in the proposed constitution. In the third place, as the constitutions of the states differ much from each other, it might happen, that a treaty or national law, of great and equal importance to the states, would interfere with some, and not with other constitutions, and would consequently be valid in some of the states, at the same time, that it would have no effect in others. In fine, the world would have seen, for the first time, a system of government founded on an inversion of the fundamental principles of all government; it would have seen the authority of the whole society everywhere subordinate to the authority of the parts; it would have seen a monster, in which the head was under the direction of the members." [1]

§ 1835. At an early period of the government a question arose, how far a treaty could embrace commercial regulations, so as to be obligatory upon the nation, and upon congress. It was debated with great zeal and ability in the house of representatives.[2] On the one hand it was contended, that a treaty might be made respecting commerce, as well as upon any other subject; that it was a contract between the two nations, which, when made by the president, by and with the consent of the senate, was binding

[1] The Federalist, No. 44.
[2] The question arose in the debate for carrying into effect the British Treaty of 1794.

upon the nation ; and that a refusal of the house of representatives to carry it into effect was breaking the treaty, and violating the faith of the nation.   On the other hand, it was contended, that the power to make treaties, if applicable to every object, conflicted with powers, which were vested exclusively in congress ;   that either the treaty making power must be limited in its operation, so as not to touch objects committed by the constitution to congress ; or the assent and co-operation of the house of representatives must be required to give validity to any compact, so far as it might comprehend these objects : that congress was invested with the exclusive power to regulate commerce ; that therefore, a treaty of commerce required the assent and co-operation of the house of representatives ;   that in every case, where a treaty required an appropriation of money, or an act of congress to carry it into effect, it was not in this respect obligatory, till congress had agreed to carry it into effect ; and, that they were at free liberty to make, or withhold such appropriation, or act, without being chargeable with violating the treaty, or breaking the faith of the nation.   In the result, the house of representatives adopted a resolution declaring, that the house of representatives do not claim any agency in making treaties ; but when a treaty stipulates regulations on any of the subjects submitted to the power of congress, it must depend for its execution, as to such stipulations, on a law or laws to be passed by congress ;   and that it is the constitutional right and duty of the house of representatives, in all such cases, to deliberate on the expediency or inexpediency of carrying such treaty into effect, and to determine and act thereon, as in their judgment may be most condu-

cive to the public good.   It is well known, that the
president and the senate, on that occasion, adopted a
different doctrine, maintaining, that a treaty once ratified became the law of the land, and congress were
constitutionally bound to carry it into effect.[1]   At the
distance of twenty years, the same question was again
presented for the consideration of both houses, upon
a bill to carry into effect a clause in the treaty of
1815 with Great Britain, abolishing discriminating
duties ; and, upon that occasion, it was most ably
debated. The result was, that a declaratory clause
was adopted, instead of a mere enacting clause, so

---

[1] See Journal of House of Representatives, 6th April, 1796; 5 Marshall's Life of Washington, ch 8, p. 650 to 659 ; Serg. on Const. ch. 33,
p. 401, (2d edit. ch. 34, p. 410, 411) ; 1 Debates on British Treaty,
by F. Bache, 1796, p. 374 to 386 ; 4 Elliot's Deb. 244 to 248. — President Washington, on this occasion, refused to deliver the papers respecting the British Treaty of 1794, called for by the house of representatives ;
and asserted the obligatory force of the treaty upon congress in the
most emphatic terms. He added, that he knew, that this was understood in the convention to be the intended interpretation, and he referred to the Journal of the Convention * to show, that a proposition was
made, " that no treaty should be binding on the United States, which
was not ratified by a law ; " and that it was explicitly rejected. (5 Marshall's Life of Washington, ch. 8, p. 654 to 653.)   At a much earlier
period, viz. in 1790, the same point came before the cabinet of President
Washington in a treaty proposed with the Creek Indians.   Upon that
occasion, there seems to have been no doubt in the minds of any of his
cabinet of the conclusiveness of a treaty containing commercial stipulations. Mr. Jefferson, on that occasion, firmly maintained it. A treaty,
(said he,) made by the president with the concurrence of two thirds of
the senate is the law of the land, and a law of a superior order, because it not only repeals past laws, *but cannot itself be repealed by future
ones.* The treaty then will legally control the duty act, and the act for
securing traders in this particular instance. Yet Mr. Jefferson afterwards, (in Nov. 1793,) seems to have fluctuated in opinion, and to have
been unsettled, as to the nature and extent of the treaty-making power.
4 Jefferson's Corresp. 497, 498.

* See Journal of Convention, p. 284, 325, 326, 339, 342, 343.

that the binding obligation of treaties was affirmatively settled.[1]

§ 1836. From this supremacy of the constitution and laws and treaties of the United States, within their constitutional scope, arises the duty of courts of justice to declare any unconstitutional law passed by congress or by a state legislature void. So, in like manner, the same duty arises, whenever any other department of the national or state governments exceeds its constitutional functions.[2] But the judiciary of the United States has no general jurisdiction to declare acts of the several states void, unless they are repugnant to the constitution of the United States, notwithstanding they are repugnant to the state constitution.[3] Such a power belongs to it only, when it sits to administer the local law of a state, and acts exactly, as a state tribunal is bound to act.[4] But upon this subject it seems unnecessary to dwell, since the right of all courts, state as well as national, to declare unconstitutional laws void, seems settled beyond the reach of judicial controversy.[5]

---

[1] Serg. on Const. ch. 33, p. 402, (2d edit. ch. 34, p. 411; 2 Elliot's Deb. 273 to 279. — Upon this occasion, a most admirable speech was delivered by the late William Pinkney, in which his great powers of reasoning and juridical learning had an ample scope. See Wheaton's Life of Pinkney, p. 517.

[2] *Marbury* v. *Madison*, 1 Cranch, 137, 176.

[3] *Calder* v. *Bull*, 3 Dall. R. 386; S. C. 1 Peters's Cond. R. 172, 177.

[4] *Satterlee* v. *Matthewson*, 2 Peters's Sup. R. 380, 413.

[5] See Serg. on Const. ch. 33, p. 391, (2d edit. ch. 34, p. 401); 1 Kent's Comm. Lect. 20, p. 420, 421, (2d edit. p. 448, 449, 450.)

CHAPTER XLIII.

§ 1837. The next clause is, " The senators and
"representatives before mentioned, and the members
" of the several state legislatures and all executive
" and judicial officers, both of the United States and
" of the several states, shall be bound by oath or
" affirmation to support the constitution.[1]   But no
" religious test shall ever be required as a qualifica-
" tion to any office or public trust under the United
" States."

§ 1838. That all those, who are entrusted with the
execution of the powers of the national government,
should be bound by some solemn obligation to the
due execution of the trusts reposed in them, and to
support the constitution, would seem to be a proposition too clear to render any reasoning necessary in
support of it.   It results from the plain right of society
to require some guaranty from every officer, that he will
be conscientious in the discharge of his duty.   Oaths
have a solemn obligation upon the minds of all reflecting men, and especially upon those, who feel a
deep sense of accountability to a Supreme being.   If,
in the ordinary administration of justice in cases of

---

[1] This clause, requiring an oath of the state and national functionaries to support the constitution, was at first carried by a vote of six states
against five ; but it was afterwards unanimously approved. Journ. of
Convention, p. 114, 197.   On the final vote, it was adopted by a vote of
eight states against one, two being divided. Id. 313. The clause respecting a religious test was unanimously adopted. Id. 313.

private rights, or personal claims, oaths are required of those, who try, as well as of those, who give testimony, to guard against malice, falsehood, and evasion, surely like guards ought to be interposed in the administration of high public trusts, and especially in such, as may concern the welfare and safety of the whole community. But there are known denominations of men, who are conscientiously scrupulous of taking oaths (among which is that pure and distinguished sect of Christians, commonly called Friends, or Quakers,) and therefore, to prevent any unjustifiable exclusion from office, the constitution has permitted a solemn affirmation to be made instead of an oath, and as its equivalent.

§ 1839. But it may not appear to all persons quite so clear, why the officers of the state governments should be equally bound to take a like oath, or affirmation; and it has been even suggested, that there is no more reason to require that, than to require, that all of the United States officers should take an oath or affirmation to support the state constitutions. A moment's reflection will show sufficient reasons for the requisition of it in the one case, and the omission of it in the other. The members and officers of the national government have no agency in carrying into effect the state constitutions. The members and officers of the state governments have an essential agency in giving effect to the national constitution. The election of the president and the senate will depend, in all cases, upon the legislatures of the several states; and, in many cases, the election of the house of representatives may be affected by their agency. The judges of the state courts will frequently be called upon to decide upon the constitution, and laws, and treaties of the United States ; and upon rights and claims growing out of them.   Decisions ought to be, as far as possible, uniform ; and uniformity of obligation will greatly tend to such a result.   The executive authority of the several states may be often called upon to exert powers, or allow rights, given by the constitution, as in filling vacancies in the senate, during the recess of the legislature ; in issuing writs of election to fill vacancies in the house of representatives ; in officering the militia, and giving effect to laws for calling them ; and in the surrender of fugitives from justice.   These, and many other functions, devolving on the state authorities, render it highly important, that they should be under a solemn obligation to obey the constitution.   In common sense, there can be no well-founded objection to it.   There may be serious evils growing out of an opposite course.[1]   One of the objections, taken to the articles of confederation, by an enlightened state, (New-Jersey,) was, that no oath was required of members of congress, previous to their admission to their seats in congress.   The laws and usages of all civilized nations, (said that state,) evince the propriety of an oath on such occasions ; and the more solemn and important the deposit, the more strong and explicit ought the obligation to be.[2]

§ 1840. As soon as the constitution went into operation, congress passed an act,[3] prescribing the time and manner of taking the oath, or affirmation, thus required, as well by officers of the several states, as of the United States.   On that occason, some

---

[1] The Federalist, No. 44 ; 1 Tuck. Black. Comm. App. 370, 371 ; Rawle on Constitution, ch. 19, p. 191, 192.

[2] 2 Pitk. Hist. 22 ; 1 Secret Journ. of Congress, June 25, 1778, p. 374.

[3] Act of 1st June, 1789, ch. 1.

scruple seems to have been entertained, by a few members, of the constitutional authority of congress to pass such an act.[1] But it was approved without much opposition. At this day, the point would be generally deemed beyond the reach of any reasonable doubt.[2]

§ 1841. The remaining part of the clause declares, that "no religious test shall ever be required, as a "qualification to any office or public trust, under the "United States." This clause is not introduced merely for the purpose of satisfying the scruples of many respectable persons, who feel an invincible repugnance to any religious test, or affirmation. It had a higher object; to cut off for ever every pretence of any alliance between church and state in the national government. The framers of the constitution were fully sensible of the dangers from this source, marked out in the history of other ages and countries; and not wholly unknown to our own. They knew, that bigotry was unceasingly vigilant in its stratagems, to secure to itself an exclusive ascendancy over the human mind; and that intolerance was ever ready to arm itself with all the terrors of the civil power to exterminate those, who doubted its dogmas, or resisted its infallibility. The Catholic and the Protestant had alternately waged the most ferocious and unrelenting warfare on each other; and Protestantism itself, at the very moment, that it was proclaiming the right of private judgment, prescribed boundaries to that right, beyond which if any one dared to pass, he must seal his rashness with the blood of martyr-

---

[1] Lloyd's Debates, 218 to 225; 4 Elliot's Debates, 139 to 141.

[2] See also *M'Culloh* v. *Maryland*, 4 Wheat. R. 415, 416.

dom.[1] The history of the parent country, too, could
not fail to instruct them in the uses, and the abuses
of religious tests. They there found the pains and
penalties of non-conformity written in no equivocal
language, and enforced with a stern and vindictive
jealousy.   One hardly knows, how to repress the
sentiments of strong indignation, in reading the cool
vindication of the laws of England on this subject,
(now, happily, for the most part abolished by recent
enactments,) by Mr. Justice Blackstone, a man, in
many respects distinguished for habitual moderation,
and a deep sense of justice.   " The second species,"
says he " of non-conformists, are those, who offend
through a mistaken or perverse zeal. Such were
esteemed by our laws, enacted since the time of the
reformation, to be papists, and protestant dissenters ;
both of which were supposed to be equally schis-
matics in not communicating with the national church ;
with this difference, that the papists divided from it
upon material, though erroneous, reasons ; but many
of the dissenters, upon matters of indifference, or, in
other words, upon no reason at all. Yet certainly
our ancestors were mistaken in their plans of compulsion and intolerance. The sin of schism, as such,
is by no means the object of temporal coercion and
punishment.   If, through weakness of intellect,
through misdirected piety, through perverseness and
acerbity of temper, or, (which is often the case,)
through a prospect of secular advantage in herding
with a party, men quarrel with the ecclesiastical
establishment, the civil magistrate has nothing to do
with it ; unless their tenets and practice are such, as

---

[1] See 4 Black. Comm. 44, 53, and ante, Vol. I, § 53.

threaten ruin or disturbance to the state. He is bound, indeed, to protect the established church; and, if this can be better effected, by admitting none but its genuine members to offices of trust and emolument, he is certainly at liberty so to do ; the disposal of offices being matter of favour and discretion. But, this point being once secured, all persecution for diversity of opinions, however ridiculous or absurd they may be, is contrary to every principle of sound policy and civil freedom. The names and subordination of the clergy, the posture of devotion, the materials and colour of the minister's garment, the joining in a known, or an unknown form of prayer, and other matters of the same kind, must be left to the option of every man's private judgment." [1]

§ 1842. And again : " As to papists, what has been said of the protestant dissenters would hold equally strong for a general toleration of them ; provided their separation was founded only upon difference of opinion in religion, and their principles did not also extend to a subversion of the civil government. If once they could be brought to renounce the supremacy of the pope, they might quietly enjoy their seven sacraments, their purgatory, and auricular confession ; their worship of reliques and images ; nay even their transubstantiation. But while they acknowledge a foreign power, superior to the sovereignty of the kingdom, they cannot complain, if the laws of that kingdom will not treat them upon the footing of good subjects." [2]

§ 1843. Of the English laws respecting papists, Montesquieu observes, that they are so rigorous,

---

[1] 4 Black. Comm. 52, 53.   [2] 4 Black. Comm. 54, 55.

though not professedly of the sanguinary kind, that
they do all the hurt, that can possibly be done in
cold blood.   To this just rebuke, (after citing it, and
admitting its truth,) Mr. Justice Blackstone has no
better reply to make, than that these laws are seldom exerted to their utmost rigour ; and, indeed, if
they were, it would be very difficult to excuse
them.[1]   The meanest apologist of the worst enormi-
ties of a Roman emperor could not have shadowed
out a defence more servile, or more unworthy of the
dignity and spirit of a freeman.   With one quotation
more from the same authority, exemplifying the nature and objects of the English test laws, this subject
may be dismissed.   " In order the better to secure
the established church against perils from non-
conformists of all denominations, infidels, Turks, Jews,
heretics, papists, and sectaries, there are, however,
two bulwarks erected, called the corporation and test-
acts.   By the former of which, no person can be
legally elected to any office relating to the government of any city or corporation, unless, within
a twelvemonth before, he has received the sacrament of the Lord's supper according to the rights
of the church of England ; and he is also enjoined to take the oaths of allegiance and supremacy,
at the same time, that he takes the oath of office ;
or, in default of either of these requisites, such election shall be void.   The other, called the test-act,
directs all officers, civil and military, to take the
oaths, and make the declaration against transubstantiation, in any of the king's courts at Westminster, or
at the quarter sessions, within six calendar months

---

[1] 4 Black. Comm. 57.

after their admission ; and also within the same time to receive the sacrament of the Lord's supper, according to the usage of the church of England, in some public church immediately after divine service and sermon ; and to deliver into court a certificate thereof signed by the minister and church-warden, and also to prove the same by two credible witnesses, upon forfeiture of 500*l*, and disability to hold the said office. And of much the same nature with these is the statute 7 Jac. I. c. 2., which permits no persons to be naturalized, or restored in blood, but such as undergo a like test ; which test, having been removed in 1753, in favour of the Jews, was the next session of parliament restored again with some precipitation." [1] It is easy to foresee, that without some prohibition of religious tests, a successful sect, in our country, might, by once possessing power, pass test-laws, which would secure to themselves a monopoly of all the offices of trust and profit, under the national government. [2]

§ 1844. The seventh and last article of the constitution is : " The ratification of the conventions of " nine states shall be sufficient for the establish-" ment of this constitution between the states so ratify-" ing the same."

§ 1845. Upon this article it is now wholly unnecessary to bestow much commentary, since the constitution has been ratified by all the states. If a ratification had been required of all the states, instead of nine, as a condition precedent, to give it life and motion, it is now known, that it would never have

---

[1] See also 2 Kent's Comm. Lect. 24, (2 edit.) p. 35, 36 ; Rawle on the Constitution, ch. 10, p. 121 ; 1 Tuck. Black. Comm. App. 296 ; 2 Tuck. Black. Comm. App. Note (G.), p. 3.

[2] See ante, Vol. II, § 621.

been ratified. North Carolina in her first convention rejected it ; and Rhode-Island did not accede to it, until more than a year after it had been in operation.[1] Some delicate questions, under a different state of things, might have arisen. What they were, and how they were disposed of at the time, is made known by the Federalist, in a commentary upon the article, which will conclude this subject.

§ 1846. "This article speaks for itself. The express authority of the people alone could give due validity to the constitution. To have required the unanimous ratification of the thirteen states, would have subjected the essential interests of the whole, to the caprice or corruption of a single member. It would have marked a want of foresight in the convention, which our own experience would have rendered inexcusable.

§ 1847. " Two questions of a very delicate nature present themselves on this occasion. (1.) On what principle the confederation, which stands in the solemn form of a compact among the states, can be superceded without the unanimous consent of the parties to it ? (2.) What relation is to subsist between the nine or more states ratifying the constitution, and the remaining few, who do not become parties to it ?

§ 1848. " The first question is answered at once, by recurring to the absolute necessity of the case ; to the great principle of self-preservation ; to the transcendent law of nature, and of nature's God, which declares, that the safety and happiness of society, are the objects, at which all political institutions

aim, and to which all such institutions must be sacrificed. Perhaps, also, an answer may be found, without searching beyond the principles of the compact
itself. It has been heretofore noted among the defects of the confederation, that, in many of the states,
it had received no higher sanction, than a mere legislative ratification. The principle of reciprocity
seems to require, that its obligation on the other
states should be reduced to the same standard. A
compact between independent sovereigns, founded
on acts of legislative authority, can pretend to no
higher validity, than a league or treaty between the
parties. It is an established doctrine, on the subject
of treaties, that all the articles are mutually conditions
of each other; that a breach of any one article is a
breach of the whole treaty; and that a breach, committed by either of the parties, absolves the others;
and authorizes them, if they please, to pronounce the
compact violated, and void. Should it unhappily be
necessary to appeal to these delicate truths, for a
justification for dispensing with the consent of particular states to a dissolution of the federal pact, will
not the complaining parties find it a difficult task to
answer the multiplied and important infractions, with
which they may be confronted? The time has been,
when it was incumbent on us all to veil the idea,
which this paragraph exhibits. The scene is now
changed, and with it, the part, which the same motives dictated.

§ 1849. "The second question is not less delicate;
and the flattering prospect of its being nearly hypothet-
ical, forbids an over-curious discussion of it. It is one
of those cases, which must be left to provide for itself.
In general, it may be observed, that although no politi-

cal relation can subsist between the assenting and dissenting states, yet the moral relations will remain uncancelled. The claims of justice, both on one side, and on the other, will be in force, and must be fulfilled; the rights of humanity must, in all cases, be duly and mutually respected ; whilst considerations of a common interest, and above all, the remembrance of the endearing scenes, which are past, and the anticipation of a speedy triumph over the obstacles to re-union, will, it is hoped, not urge in vain moderation on one side, and prudence on the other." [1]

§ 1850. And here closes our review of the constitution in the original form, in which it was framed for, and adopted by, the people of the United States. The concluding passage of it is, "Done in convention by the unanimous consent of all the states present, the seventeenth day of September, in the year of our Lord one thousand seven hundred and eighty-seven, and of the Independence of the United States of America, the twelfth." At the head of the illustrious men, who framed, and signed it, (men, who have earned the eternal gratitude of their country,) stands the name of GEORGE WASHINGTON, "President and Deputy from Virginia ;" a name, at the utterance of which envy is dumb, and pride bows with involuntary reverence, and piety, with eyes lifted to heaven, breathes forth a prayer of profound gratitude.

---

[1] The Federalist, No. 43.

CHAPTER XLIV.

AMENDMENTS TO THE CONSTITUTION.

§ 1851. WE have already had occasion to take notice of some of the amendments made to the constitution, subsequent to its adoption, in the progress of our review of the provisions of the original instrument. The present chapter will be devoted to a consideration of those, which have not fallen within the scope of our former commentaries.

§ 1852. It has been already stated, that many objections were taken to the constitution, not only on account of its actual provisions, but also on account of its deficiencies and omissions.[1] Among the latter, none were proclaimed with more zeal, and pressed with more effect, than the want of a bill of rights. This, it was said, was a fatal defect; and sufficient of itself to bring on the ruin of the republic.[2] To this objection several answers were given; first, that the constitution did in fact contain many provisions in the nature of a bill of rights, if the whole constitution was not in fact a bill of rights; secondly, that a bill of rights was in its nature more adapted to a monarchy, than to a government, professedly founded upon the will of the people, and executed by their immediate representatives and agents; and, thirdly, that a formal bill of rights, beyond what was contained in it, was wholly unnecessary, and might even be dangerous.[3]

---

[1] Vol. I., B. 3, ch. 2.

[2] 2 Amer. Museum, 423, 424, 425; Id. 435; Id. 534; Id. 540, 543, 546; Id. 553.

[3] The Federalist, No. 8; 3 Amer. Museum, 78, 79; Id. 559.

§ 1853. The first answer was supported by reference to the clauses in the constitution, providing for the judgment in cases of impeachment; the privilege of the writ of *habeas corpus;* the trial by jury in criminal cases ; the definition, trial, and punishment of treason ; the prohibition of bills of attainder, *ex post facto* laws, laws impairing the obligation of contracts, laws granting titles of nobility, and laws imposing religious tests.   All these were so many declarations of rights for the protection of the citizens, not exceeded in value by any, which could possibly find a place in any bill of rights.[1]

§ 1854. Upon the second point it was said, that bills of rights are in their origin stipulations between kings and their subjects, abridgments of prerogative in favour of privilege, and reservations of rights not surrendered to the prince.   Such was Magna Charta obtained by the barons, sword in hand, of King John. Such were the subsequent confirmations of that charter by succeeding princes.   Such was the petition of right assented to by Charles the First in the beginning of his reign.   Such, also, was the declaration of rights presented by the lords and commons to the prince of Orange in 1688, and afterwards put into the form of an act of parliament, called the bill of rights.[2] It is evident, therefore, that according to its primitive signification, a bill of rights has no application to constitutions professedly founded upon the power of the people, and executed by persons, who are immediately chosen by them to execute their will.   In our

---

[1] The Federalist, No. 84.

[2] Mr. Chancellor Kent has given an exact, though succinct history of the bills of rights, both in the mother country and the colonies, in 2 Kent's Comm. Lect. 24.

country, in strictness, the people surrender nothing; and as they retain every thing, they have no need of particular reservations.[1] "We, the people of the United States, to secure the blessings of *liberty* to ourselves and our posterity, do ordain and establish this constitution for the United States of America " — is a better recognition of popular rights, than volumes of those aphorisms, which make a principal figure in several of our state bills of rights, and which would sound much better in a treatise of ethics, than in a constitution of government.[2]

§ 1855. Upon the third point, it was said, that a minute detail of particular rights was certainly far less applicable to a constitution, designed to regulate the general political concerns of the nation, than to one, which had the regulation of every species of personal and private concerns. But (it was added) the argument might justly be carried further. It might be affirmed, that a bill of rights, in the sense and extent, which is contended for, was not only wholly unnecessary, but might even be dangerous. Such a bill would contain various exceptions to powers *not* granted; and on this very account might afford a colourable pretext to claim more than was granted.[3] For why (it might be asked) declare, that things shall not be done, which there is no power to do? Why, for instance, that the liberty of the press shall not be restrained, when no power is given, by which restrictions may be imposed? It is true, that upon sound reasoning a declaration of this sort could not fairly be construed to imply a regulating power; but it

[1] 1 Lloyd's Debates, 430, 431, 432.
[2] The Federalist, No. 84.
[3] 1 Lloyd's Debates, 433, 437.

might be seized upon by men disposed to usurpation, in order to furnish a plausible pretence for claiming the power. They might urge with a semblance of reason, that the constitution ought not to be charged with the absurdity of providing against an abuse of an authority, which was not given ; and that the provision against restraining the liberty of the press, afforded a clear implication, that a right to prescribe proper regulations concerning it, was intended to be vested in the national government.

§ 1856. It was further added, that in truth the constitution itself was, in every rational sense, and to every useful purpose, a bill of rights for the Union. It specifies, and declares the political privileges of the citizens in the structure and administration of the government. It defines certain immunities and modes of proceeding, which relate to their personal, private, and public rights and concerns. It confers on them the unalienable right of electing their rulers; and prohibits any tyrannical measures, and vindictive prosecutions. So, that, at best, much of the force of the objection rests on mere nominal distinctions, or upon a desire to make a frame of government a code to regulate rights and remedies.[1]

§ 1857. Although it must be conceded, that there is much intrinsic force in this reasoning,[2] it cannot in

---

[1] The Federalist, No. 84. See 1 Lloyd's Debates, 428, 429, 430; 3 Amer. Museum, 559.

[2] It had, beyond all question, extraordinary influence in the convention; for upon a motion being made to appoint a committee to prepare a bill of rights, the proposition was UNANIMOUSLY rejected. Journal of Convention, p. 369. This fact alone shows, that it was at best deemed a subject of doubtful propriety ; and that it formed no line of distinction between any of the parties in the convention. There will be found considerable reasoning on the subject in the debates in congress on the amendments proposed in 1789. See 1 Lloyd's Debates, 414 to 426; Id. 426 to 447.

candour be admitted to be wholly satisfactory, or conclusive on the subject. It is rather the argument of an able advocate, than the reasoning of a constitutional statesman. In the first place, a bill of rights (in the very sense of this reasoning) is admitted in some cases to be important; and the constitution itself adopts, and establishes its propriety to the extent of its actual provisions. Every reason, which establishes the propriety of any provision of this sort in the constitution, such as a right of trial by jury in criminal cases, is, *pro tanto*, proof, that it is neither unnecessary nor dangerous. It reduces the question to the consideration, not whether any bill of rights is necessary, but what such a bill of rights should properly contain. That is a point for argument, upon which different minds may arrive at different conclusions. That a bill of rights may contain too many enumerations, and especially such, as more correctly belong to the ordinary legislation of a government, cannot be doubted. Some of our state bills of rights contain clauses of this description, being either in their character and phraseology quite too loose, and general, and ambiguous; or covering doctrines quite debatable, both in theory and practice; or even leading to mischievous consequences, by restricting the legislative power under circumstances, which were not foreseen, and if foreseen, the restraint would have been pronounced by all persons inexpedient, and perhaps unjust.[1] Indeed, the rage of theorists to make constitutions a vehicle for the conveyance of their own crude, and visionary aphorisms of government, requires

---

[1] 2 Kent's Comm. Lect. 24, p. 6, (2d edition, p. 9,) and note Ibid.; 1 Lloyd's Debates, 431, 432.

to be guarded against with the most unceasing vigilance.[1]

§ 1858. In the next place, a bill of rights is important, and may often be indispensable, whenever it operates, as a qualification upon powers, actually granted by the people to the government.[2] This is the real ground of all the bills of rights in the parent country, in the colonial constitutions and laws, and in the state constitutions. In England, the bills of rights were not demanded merely of the crown, as withdrawing a power from the royal prerogative; they were equally important, as withdrawing power from parliament. A large proportion of the most valuable of the provisions in Magna Charta, and the bill of rights in 1688, consists of a solemn recognition, of limitations upon the power of parliament; that is, a declaration, that parliament *ought* not to abolish, or restrict those rights. Such are the right of trial by jury; the right to personal liberty and private property according to the law of the land; that the subjects ought to have a right to bear arms; that elections of members of parliament ought to be free; that freedom of speech and debate in parliament ought not to be impeached, or questioned elsewhere; and that excessive bail ought not to be required, nor excessive fines imposed, nor cruel or unusual punishments inflicted.[3] Whenever, then, a general power exists, or is granted to a government, which may in its actual exercise or abuse be dangerous to the people, there seems a peculiar

---

1 This whole subject is treated with great felicity and force by Mr. Chancellor Kent in his Commentaries; and the whole lecture will reward a most diligent perusal. 2 Kent's Comm. Lect. 24.

2 1 Lloyd's Debates, 429, 430, 431, 432.

3 See Magna Charta, ch. 29; Bill of Rights, 1688; 5 Cobbett's Parl. Hist. p. 110.

propriety in restricting its operations, and in excepting from it some at least of the most mischievous
forms, in which it may be likely to be abused. And
the very exception in such cases will operate with a
silent, but irresistible influence to control the actual
abuse of it in other analogous cases.[1]

§ 1859. In the next place, a bill of rights may be
important, even when it goes beyond powers supposed to be granted. It is not always possible to foresee the extent of the actual reach of certain powers,
which are given in general terms. They may be
construed to extend (and perhaps fairly) to certain
classes of cases, which did not at first appear to be
within them. A bill of rights, then, operates, as a
guard upon any extravagant or undue extension of
such powers. Besides; (as has been justly remarked,) a bill of rights is of real efficiency in controlling
the excesses of party spirit. It serves to guide, and
enlighten public opinion, and to render it more quick
to detect, and more resolute to resist, attempts to
disturb private rights. It requires more than ordinary hardihood and audacity of character, to trample
down principles, which our ancestors have consecrated with reverence; which we imbibed in our early
education; which recommend themselves to the judgment of the world by their truth and simplicity; and
which are constantly placed before the eyes of the
people, accompanied with the imposing force and
solemnity of a constitutional sanction. Bills of rights
are a part of the muniments of freemen, showing their
title to protection; and they become of increased
value, when placed under the protection of an inde-

---

[1] 1 Lloyd's Debates, 431, 432, 433, 434.

pendent judiciary instituted, as the appropriate guardian of the public and private rights of the citizens.[1]

§ 1860. In the next place, (it has been urged with much earnestness,) a bill of rights is an important protection against unjust and oppressive conduct on the part of the people themselves. In a government modified, like that of the United States, (said a great statesman,[2]) the great danger lies rather in the abuse of the community, than of the legislative body. The prescriptions in favour of liberty ought to be levelled against that quarter, where the greatest danger lies, namely, that which possesses the highest prerogative of power. But this is not found in the executive or legislative departments of government; but in the body of the people, operating by the majority against the minority. It may be thought, that all paper barriers against the power of the community are too weak to be worthy of attention. They are not so strong, as to satisfy all, who have seen and examined thoroughly the texture of such a defence. Yet, as they have a tendency to impress some degree of respect for them, to establish the public opinion in their favour, and to rouse the attention of the whole community, it may be one means to control the majority from those acts, to which they might be otherwise inclined.[3]

§ 1861. In regard to another suggestion, that the affirmance of certain rights might disparage others, or might lead to argumentative implications in favour of other powers, it might be sufficient to say, that such a course of reasoning could never be sustained upon any solid basis; and it could never furnish any just

---

[1] 1 Kent's Comm. Lect. 24, p. 5, 6, (2d edition, p. 8); 1 Lloyd's Debates, 429, 430, 431.

[2] Mr. Madison, 1 Lloyd's Deb. 431.   [3] Ibid.

ground of objection, that ingenuity might pervert, or usurpation overleap, the true sense. That objection will equally lie against all powers, whether large or limited, whether national or state, whether in a bill of rights, or in a frame of government. But a conclusive answer is, that such an attempt may be interdicted, (as it has been,) by a positive declaration in such a bill of rights, that the enumeration of certain rights shall not be construed to deny or disparage others retained by the people.[1]

§ 1862. The want of a bill of rights, then, is not either an unfounded or illusory objection. The real question is not, whether every sort of right or privilege or claim ought to be affirmed in a constitution; but whether such, as in their own nature are of vital importance, and peculiarly susceptible of abuse, ought not to receive this solemn sanction. Doubtless, the want of a formal bill of rights in the constitution was a matter of very exaggerated declamation, and party zeal, for the mere purpose of defeating the constitution.[2] But so far as the objection was well founded in fact, it was right to remove it by subsequent amendments; and congress have (as we shall see) accordingly performed the duty with most prompt and laudable diligence.[3]

1 Constitution, 9th Amendment; 1 Lloyd's Deb. 433.
2 The Federalist, No. 84. See also 2 Elliot's Deb. 65, 160, 243, 330, 331, 334, 344, 345, 346; 1 Jefferson's Corresp. 64; 2 Jefferson's Corresp. 274, 291, 344, 443, 459; 1 Tuck. Black. Comm. App. 308; 2 Amer. Museum, 334, 378, 424, 540; 3 Amer. Museum, 548, 559; 1 Lloyd's Deb. 423 to 437; 5 Marshall's Life of Washington, ch. 3, p. 207 to 210.
3 See 5 Marshall's Life of Washington, ch. 3, p. 207 to 210. — Congress, in the preamble to these amendments, use the following language: "The conventions of a number of the states having at the time of adopting the constitution expressed a desire, in order to prevent mis-

§ 1863. Let us now enter upon the consideration of the amendments, which, it will be found, principally regard subjects properly belonging to a bill of rights.

§ 1864. The first is, " Congress shall make no law " respecting an establishment of religion, or prohibit- " ing the free exercise thereof ; or abridging the free- " dom of speech, or of the press ; or the right of the " people peaceably to assemble, and to petition gov- " ernment for a redress of grievances."

§ 1865. And first, the prohibition of any establishment of religion, and the freedom of religious opinion and worship.

How far any government has a right to interfere in matters touching religion, has been a subject much discussed by writers upon public and political law. The right and the duty of the interference of government, in matters of religion, have been maintained by many distinguished authors, as well those, who were the warmest advocates of free governments, as those, who were attached to governments of a more arbitrary character.[1] Indeed, the right of a society or government to interfere in matters of religion will hardly be contested by any persons, who believe that piety, religion, and morality are intimately connected with the well being of the state, and indispensable to the administration of civil justice. The promulgation of

construction, or abuse of its powers, that further declaratory and restrictive clauses should be added ; and as extending the ground of public confidence in the government will best ensure the beneficent ends of its institution, &c. &c." 1 Tuck. Black. Comm. App. 269.

[1] See Grotius, B. 2, ch. 20, § 44 to 51 ; Vattell, B. 1, ch. 12, § 125, 126 ; Hooker's Ecclesiastical Polity, B. 5, § 1 to 10 ; Bynkershœck, 2 P. J. Lib. 2, ch. 18 ; Woodeson's Elem. Lect. 3, p. 49 ; Burlemaqui, Pt. 3, ch. 3, p. 171, and Montesq. B. 24, ch. 1 to ch. 8, ch. 14 to ch. 16, B. 25, ch. 1, 2, 2, 10, 11, 12.

the great doctrines of religion, the being, and attributes, and providence of one Almighty God; the
responsibility to him for all our actions, founded upon
moral freedom and accountability; a future state of
rewards and punishments; the cultivation of all
the personal, social, and benevolent virtues; — these
never can be a matter of indifference in any well ordered community.[1]   It is, indeed, difficult to conceive, how any civilized society can well exist without them.   And at all events, it is impossible for
those, who believe in the truth of Christianity, as a
divine revelation, to doubt, that it is the especial duty of government to foster, and encourage it among
all the citizens and subjects.   This is a point wholly
distinct from that of the right of private judgment in
matters of religion, and of the freedom of public worship according to the dictates of one's conscience.

§ 1866. The real difficulty lies in ascertaining the
limits, to which government may rightfully go in fos-
tering and encouraging religion.   Three cases may
easily be supposed.   One, where a government
affords aid to a particular religion, leaving all persons
free to adopt any other; another, where it creates
an ecclesiastical establishment for the propagation of
the doctrines of a particular sect of that religion, leaving a like freedom to all others; and a third, where
it creates such an establishment, and excludes all persons, not belonging to it, either wholly, or in part, from
any participation in the public honours, trusts, emoluments, privileges, and immunities of the state.   For
instance, a government may simply declare, that the
Christian religion shall be the religion of the state,

---

[1] See Burlemaqui, Pt. 3, ch. 3, p. 171, &c.; 4 Black. Comm. 43.

724 CONSTITUTION OF THE U. STATES. [BOOK III.

and shall be aided, and encouraged in all the varieties
of sects belonging to it ; or it may declare, that the
Catholic or Protestant religion shall be the religion of
the state, leaving every man to the free enjoyment of
his own religious opinions ; or it may establish the
doctrines of a particular sect, as of Episcopalians, as
the religion of the state, with a like freedom ; or it
may establish the doctrines of a particular sect, as exclusively the religion of the state, tolerating others to
a limited extent, or excluding all, not belonging to it,
from all public honours, trusts, emoluments, privileges,
and immunities.

§ 1867. Now, there will probably be found few
persons in this, or any other Christian country, who
would deliberately contend, that it was unreasonable,
or unjust to foster and encourage the Christian religion generally, as a matter of sound policy, as well
as of revealed truth.   In fact, every American colony,
from its foundation down to the revolution, with the
exception of Rhode Island, (if, indeed, that state be
an exception,) did openly, by the whole course of its
laws and institutions, support and sustain, in some
form, the Christian religion ; and almost invariably
gave a peculiar sanction to some of its fundamental
doctrines.   And this has continued to be the case in
some of the states down to the present period, without the slightest suspicion, that it was against the
principles of public law, or republican liberty.[1]   Indeed, in a republic, there would seem to be a peculiar propriety in viewing the Christian religion, as the
great basis, on which it must rest for its support and
permanence, if it be, what it has ever been deemed by

_____

[1] 2 Kent's Comm. Lect. 34, p. 35 to 37 ; Rawle on Const. ch. 10,
p. 121, 122.

its truest friends to be, the religion of liberty. Montesquieu has remarked, that the Christian religion is a
stranger to mere despotic power.   The mildness so
frequently recommended in the gospel is incompatible with the despotic rage, with which a prince punishes his subjects, and exercises himself in cruelty.[1]
He has gone even further, and affirmed, that the Protestant religion is far more congenial with the spirit
of political freedom, than the Catholic.   "When,"
says he, "the Christian religion, two centuries ago,
became unhappily divided into Catholic and Protestant, the people of the north embraced the Protestant,
and those of the south still adhered to the Catholic.
The reason is plain.   The people of the north have,
and will ever have, a spirit of liberty and independence, which the people of the south have not.   And,
therefore, a religion, which has no visible head, is
more agreeable to the independency of climate, than
that, which has one." [2]   Without stopping to inquire,
whether this remark be well founded, it is certainly
true, that the parent country has acted upon it with
a severe and vigilant zeal ; and in most of the colonies
the same rigid jealousy has been maintained almost
down to our own times.   Massachusetts, while she
has promulgated in her BILL OF RIGHTS the importance and necessity of the public support of religion,
and the worship of God, has authorized the legislature to require it only for Protestantism.   The language of that bill of rights is remarkable for its pointed affirmation of the duty of government to support
Christianity, and the reasons for it.   "As," says the

---

[1] Montesq. Spirit of Laws, B. 24, ch. 3.
[2] Montesq. Spirit of Laws, B. 24, ch. 5.

third article, "the happiness of a people, and the good order and preservation of civil government, essentially depend upon piety, relig on, and morality ; and as these cannot be generally diffused through the community, but by the institution of the public worship of God, and of public instructions in piety, religion, and morality; therefore, to promote their happiness and to secure the good order and preservation of their government, the people of this Commonwealth have a right to invest their legislature with power to authorize, and require, and the legislature shall from time to time authorize and require, the several towns, parishes, &c. &c. to make suitable provision at their own expense for the institution of the public worship of God, and for the support and maintenance of public *protestant* teachers of piety, religion, and morality, in all cases where such provision shall not be made voluntarily." Afterwards there follow provisions, prohibiting any superiority of one sect over another, and securing to all citizens the free exercise of religion.

§ 1868. Probably at the time of the adoption of the constitution, and of the amendment to it, now under consideration, the general, if not the universal, sentiment in America was, that Christianity ought to receive encouragement from the state, so far as was not incompatible with the private rights of conscience, and the freedom of religious worship. An attempt to level all religions, and to make it a matter of state policy to hold all in utter indifference, would have created universal disapprobation, if not universal indignation.[1]

---

[1] See 2 Lloyd's Deb. 195, 196.

§ 1869. It yet remains a problem to be solved in human affairs, whether any free government can be permanent, where the public worship of God, and the support of religion, constitute no part of the policy or duty of the state in any assignable shape. The future experience of Christendom, and chiefly of the American states, must settle this problem, as yet new in the history of the world, abundant, as it has been, in experiments in the theory of government.

§ 1870. But the duty of supporting religion, and especially the Christian religion, is very different from the right to force the consciences of other men, or to punish them for worshipping God in the manner, which, they believe, their accountability to him requires. It has been truly said, that " religion, or the duty we owe to our Creator, and the manner of discharging it, can be dictated only by reason and conviction, not by force or violence," [1]   Mr. Locke himself, who did not doubt the right of government to interfere in matters of religion, and especially to encourage Christianity, at the same time has expressed his opinion of the right of private judgment, and liberty of conscience, in a manner becoming his character, as a sincere friend of civil and religious liberty.   " No man, or society of men," says he, " have any authority to impose their opinions or interpretations on any other, the meanest Christian ; since, in matters of religion, every man must know, and believe, and give an account for himself." [2]   The rights of conscience are, indeed, beyond the just reach of any human power.   They are given by God, and cannot be encroached upon by human authority, without

---

[1] Virginia Bill of Rights, 1 Tuck. Black. Comm. App. 296 ; 2 Tuck. Black. Comm. App. note G. p. 10, 11.

[2] Lord King's Life of Locke, p. 373.

a criminal disobedience of the precepts of natural, as well as of revealed religion.

§ 1871. The real object of the amendment was, not to countenance, much less to advance Mahometanism, or Judaism, or infidelity, by prostrating Christianity ; but to exclude all rivalry among Christian sects, and to prevent any national ecclesiastical establishment, which should give to an hierarchy the exclusive patronage of the national government. It thus cut off the means of religious persecution, (the vice and pest of former ages,) and of the subversion of the rights of conscience in matters of religion, which had been trampled upon almost from the days of the Apostles to the present age.[1] The history of the parent country had afforded the most solemn warnings and melancholy instructions on this head ;[2] and even New-England, the land of the persecuted puritans, as well as other colonies, where the Church of England had maintained its superiority, would furnish out a chapter, as full of the darkest bigotry and intolerance, as any, which could be found to disgrace the pages of foreign annals.[3] Apostacy, heresy, and nonconformity had been standard crimes for public appeals, to kindle the flames of persecution, and apologize for the most atrocious triumphs over innocence and virtue.[4]

§ 1872. Mr. Justice Blackstone, after having spoken with a manly freedom of the abuses in the Romish church respecting heresy ; and, that Christianity had been deformed by the demon of persecution upon the continent, and that the island of Great Britain had

1 2 Lloyd's Deb. 195.
2 4 Black. Comm. 41 to 59.
3 Ante, Vol. I. § 53, 72, 74.
4 See 4 Black. Comm. 43 to 59.

not been *entirely* free from the scourge,[1] defends the
final enactments against nonconformity in England, in
the following set phrases, to which, without any material change, might be justly applied his own sarcas-
tic remarks upon the conduct of the Roman ecclesiastics in punishing heresy.[2] "For nonconformity to the
worship of the church," (says he,) "there is much
more to be pleaded than for the former, (that is, re-
viling the ordinances of the church,) being a matter of
private conscience, to the scruples of which our *present* laws have shown a very just, and Christian indulgence. For undoubtedly all persecution and oppression
of weak consciences, on the score of religious persua-
sions, are highly unjustifiable upon every principle of
natural reason, civil liberty, or sound religion. But
care must be taken not to carry this indulgence into
such extremes, as may endanger the national church.
There is always a difference to be made between

---

[1] "*Entirely*"! Should he not have said, *never* free from the scourge,
as more conformable to historical truth?

[2] 4 Black. Comm. 45, 46. — His words are : "It is true, that the sanc-
timonious hypocrisy of the Canonists went, at first, no further, than
enjoining penance, excommunication, and ecclesiastical deprivation for
heresy, though afterwards they proceeded to imprisonment by the ordinary, and confiscation of goods *in pios usus*. But in the mean time they
had prevailed upon the weakness of bigotted princes to make the civil
power subservient to their purposes, by making heresy not only a temporal, but even a capital offence ; the Romish Ecclesiastics determining,
without appeal, whatever they pleased, to be heresy, and shifting off to
the secular arm the odium and the drudgery of executions, with which
they themselves were too tender and delicate to intermeddle. Nay,
they pretended to intercede, and pray in behalf of the convicted heretic,
ut citra mortis periculum sententia circum eum moderatur, well knowing,
at the same time, that they were delivering the unhappy victim to certain death." 4 Black. Comm. 45, 46. Yet the learned author, in the
same breath, could calmly vindicate the outrageous oppressions of the
Church of England upon Catholics and Dissenters with the unsuspecting
satisfaction of a bigot.

toleration and establishment." [1]   Let it be remembered, that at the very moment, when the learned commentator was penning these cold remarks, the laws of
England merely tolerated protestant dissenters in their
public worship upon certain conditions, at once irritating and degrading ; that the test and corporation
acts excluded them from public and corporate offices,
both of trust and profit ; that the learned commentator avows, that the object of the test and corporation
acts was to exclude them from office, in common with
Turks, Jews, heretics, papists, and other sectaries ; [2]
that to deny the Trinity, however conscientiously dis-
believed, was a public offence, punishable by fine and
imprisonment; and that, in the rear of all these disabilities and grievances, came the long list of acts
against papists, by which they were reduced to a state
of political and religious slavery, and cut off from some
of the dearest privileges of mankind. [3]

§ 1873. It was under a solemn consciousness of
the dangers from ecclesiastical ambition, the bigotry of
spiritual pride, and the intolerance of sects, thus exemplified in our domestic, as well as in foreign annals,
that it was deemed advisable to exclude from the
national government all power to act upon the subject. [4]   The situation, too, of the different states

[1] 4 Black. Comm. 51, 52.   [2] 1 Black. Comm. 58.

[3] 1 Black. Comm. 51 to 59. — Mr. Tucker, in his Commentaries on
Blackstone, has treated the whole subject in a manner of most marked
contrast to that of Mr. J. Blackstone.   His ardour is as strong, as the
coolness of his adversary is humiliating, on the subject of religious liberty. 2 Tuck. Black. Comm. App. Note G. p. 3, &c. See also 4 Jefferson's Corresp. 103, 104 ; Jefferson's Notes on Virginia, 264 to 270 ;
1 Tuck. Black. Comm. App. 296.

[4] 2 Lloyd's Debates, 195, 196, 197. — "The sectarian spirit," said the
late Dr. Currie, "is uniformly selfish, proud, and unfeeling." (Edin-
burgh Review, April, 1832, p. 125.)

equally proclaimed the policy, as well as the necessity of such an exclusion. In some of the states, episcopalians constituted the predominant sect ; in others, presbyterians ; in others, congregationalists ; in others, quakers ; and in others again, there was a close numerical rivalry among contending sects. It was impossible, that there should not arise perpetual strife and perpetual jealousy on the subject of ecclesiastical ascendancy, if the national government were left free to create a religious establishment. The only security was in extirpating the power. But this alone would have been an imperfect security, if it had not been followed up by a declaration of the right of the free exercise of religion, and a prohibition (as we have seen) of all religious tests. Thus, the whole power over the subject of religion is left exclusively to the state governments, to be acted upon according to their own sense of justice, and the state constitutions ; and the Catholic and the Protestant, the Calvinist and the Arminian, the Jew and the Infidel, may sit down at the common table of the national councils, without any inquisition into their faith, or mode of worship.[1]

§ 1874. The next clause of the amendment respects the liberty of the press. " Congress shall make no law abridging the freedom of speech, or of the press."[2] That this amendment was intended to secure to every citizen an absolute right to speak, or write, or print, whatever he might please, without any responsibility, public or private, therefor, is a supposition too wild to

---

[1] See 2 Kent's Comm. Lect. 24, (2d edition, p. 35 to 37); Rawle on Const. ch. 10, p. 121, 122 ; 2 Lloyd's Deb. 195. See also Vol. II. § 621.

[2] In the convention a proposition was moved to insert in the constitution a clause, that " the liberty of the press shall be inviolably preserved ;" but it was negatived by a vote of six states against five. Journal of Convention, p. 377.

be indulged by any rational man. This would be to allow to every citizen a right to destroy, at his pleasure, the reputation, the peace, the property, and even the personal safety of every other citizen. A man might, out of mere malice and revenge, accuse another of the most infamous crimes; might excite against him the indignation of all his fellow citizens by the most atrocious calumnies; might disturb, nay, overturn all his domestic peace, and embitter his parental affections; might inflict the most distressing punishments upon the weak, the timid, and the innocent; might prejudice all a man's civil, and political, and private rights; and might stir up sedition, rebellion, and treason even against the government itself, in the wantonness of his passions, or the corruption of his heart. Civil society could not go on under such circumstances. Men would then be obliged to resort to private vengeance, to make up for the deficiencies of the law; and assassinations, and savage cruelties, would be perpetrated with all the frequency belonging to barbarous and brutal communities. It is plain, then, that the language of this amendment imports no more, than that every man shall have a right to speak, write, and print his opinions upon any subject whatsoever, without any prior restraint, so always, that he does not injure any other person in his rights, person, property, or reputation;[1] and so always, that he does not thereby disturb the public peace, or attempt to subvert the government.[2] It is neither more nor less, than an expansion of the great doctrine, recently

---

[1] 1 Tuck. Black. Comm. App. 297 to 299 : 2 Tuck. Black. Comm. App. 11 ; 2 Kent's Comm. Lect. 24, p. 16 to 26.

[2] Rawle on Const. ch. 10, p. 123, 124 ; 2 Kent's Comm. Lect. 24, p. 16 to 26 : De Lolme, B. 2, ch. 12, 13 : 2 Lloyd's Deb. 197, 198.

brought into operation in the law of libel, that every man shall be at liberty to publish what is true, with good motives and for justifiable ends. And with this reasonable limitation it is not only right in itself, but it is an inestimable privilege in a free government. Without such a limitation, it might become the scourge of the republic, first denouncing the principles of liberty, and then, by rendering the most virtuous patriots odious through the terrors of the press, introducing despotism in its worst form.

§ 1875. A little attention to the history of other countries in other ages will teach us the vast importance of this right. It is notorious, that, even to this day, in some foreign countries it is a crime to speak on any subject, religious, philosophical, or political, what is contrary to the received opinions of the government, or the institutions of the country, however laudable may be the design, and however virtuous may be the motive. Even to animadvert upon the conduct of public men, of rulers, or representatives, in terms of the strictest truth and courtesy, has been, and is deemed, a scandal upon the supposed sanctity of their stations and characters, subjecting the party to grievous punishment. In some countries no works can be printed at all, whether of science, or literature, or philosophy, without the previous approbation of the government; and the press has been shackled, and compelled to speak only in the timid language, which the cringing courtier, or the capricious inquisitor, should license for publication. The Bible itself, the common inheritance not merely of Christendom, but of the world, has been put exclusively under the control of government; and not allowed to be seen, or heard, except in a language unknown to the common inhabitants of the country.

To publish a translation in the vernacular tongue, has been in former times a flagrant offence.

§ 1876. The history of the jurisprudence of England, (the most free and enlightened of all monarchies,) on this subject, will abundantly justify this statement. The art of printing, soon after its introduction, (we are told,) was looked upon, as well in England, as in other countries, as merely a matter of state, and subject to the coercion of the crown. It was therefore regulated in England by the king's proclamations, prohibitions, charters of privilege, and licenses, and finally by the decrees of the court of Star Chamber; which limited the number of printers, and of presses, which each should employ, and prohibited new publications, unless previously approved by proper licensers. On the demolition of this odious jurisdiction, in 1641, the long parliament of Charles the First, after their rupture with that prince, assumed the same powers, which the Star Chamber exercised, with respect to licensing books; and during the commonwealth, (such is human frailty, and the love of power, even in republics!) they issued their ordinances for that purpose, founded principally upon a Star Chamber decree, in 1637. After the restoration of Charles the Second, a statute on the same subject was passed, copied, with some few alterations, from the parliamentary ordinances. The act expired in 1679, and was revived and continued for a few years after the revolution of 1688. Many attempts were made by the government to keep it in force; but it was so strongly resisted by parliament, that it expired in 1694, and has never since been revived.[1]   To this

---

[1] 4 Black. Comm. 152, note ; 2 Tucker's Black. Comm. App. Note G. p. 12, 13 ; De Lolme, B. 2, ch. 12, 13 ; 2 Kent's Comm. Lect. 24, (2d edition, p. 17, 18, 19.)

very hour the liberty of the press in England stands upon this negative foundation. The power to restrain it is dormant, not dead. It has never constituted an article of any of her numerous bills of rights; and that of the revolution of 1688, after securing other civil and political privileges, left this without notice, as unworthy of care, or fit for restraint.

§ 1877. This short review exhibits, in a striking light, the gradual progress of opinion in favour of the liberty of publishing and printing opinions in England, and the frail and uncertain tenure, by which it has been held. Down to this very day it is a contempt of parliament, and a high breach of privilege, to publish the speech of any member of either house, without its consent.[1] It is true, that it is now silently established by the course of popular opinion to be innocent in practice, though not in law. But it is notorious, that within the last fifty years the publication was connived at, rather than allowed; and that for a considerable time the reports were given in a stealthy manner, covered up under the garb of speeches in a fictitious assembly.

§ 1878. There is a good deal of loose reasoning on the subject of the liberty of the press, as if its inviolability were constitutionally such, that, like the king of England, it could do no wrong, and was free from every inquiry, and afforded a perfect sanctuary for every abuse; that, in short, it implied a despotic sovereignty to do every sort of wrong, without the slightest accountability to private or public justice. Such a notion is too extravagant to be held by any sound constitutional lawyer, with regard to the rights and duties belonging to governments generally, or to the state gov-

---

[1] See Comyn's Dig. *Parliament*, G. 9.

ernments in particular.   If it were admitted to be correct, it might be justly affirmed, that the liberty of the
press was incompatible with the permanent existence
of any free government.   Mr. Justice Blackstone has
remarked, that the liberty of the press, properly understood, is essential to the nature of a free state; but
that this consists in laying no *previous* restraints upon
publications, and not in freedom from censure for criminal matter, when published.   Every freeman has an
undoubted right to lay what sentiments he pleases before the public; to forbid this is to destroy the freedom
of the press.   But, if he publishes what is improper,
mischievous, or illegal, he must take the consequences
of his own temerity.   To subject the press to the
restrictive power of a licenser, as was formerly done
before, and since the revolution (of 1688), is to subject
all freedom of sentiment to the prejudices of one man,
and make him the arbitrary and infallible judge of all
controverted points in learning, religion, and government.   But to punish any dangerous or offensive writings, which, when published, shall, on a fair and impartial trial, be adjudged of a pernicious tendency, is necessary for the preservation of peace and good order, of
government and religion, the only solid foundations of
civil liberty.   Thus, the will of individuals is still left
free; the abuse only of that free will is the object of
legal punishment.   Neither is any restraint hereby laid
upon freedom of thought or inquiry; liberty of private
sentiment is still left; the disseminating, or making
public of bad sentiments, destructive of the ends of
society, is the crime, which society corrects.   A man
may be allowed to keep poisons in his closet; but not
publicly to vend them as cordials.   And after some
additional reflections, he concludes with this memorable

sentence: "So true will it be found, that to censure the licentiousness, is to maintain the liberty of the press."[1]

§ 1879. De Lolme states the same view of the subject; and, indeed, the liberty of the press, as understood by all England, is the right to publish without any previous restraint, or license; so, that neither the courts of justice, nor other persons, are authorized to take notice of writings intended for the press; but are confined to those, which are printed. And, in such cases, if their character is questioned, whether they are lawful, or libellous, is to be tried by a jury, according to due proceedings at law.[2] The noblest patriots of England, and the most distinguished friends of liberty, both in parliament, and at the bar, have never contended for a total exemption from responsibility, but have asked only, that the guilt or innocence of the publication should be ascertained by a trial by jury.[3]

---

[1] 1 Black. Comm. 152, 153; *Rex* v. *Burdett*, 4 Barn. & Ald. R. 95.— Mr. Justice Best in *Rex* v. *Burdett*, (4 Barn. & Ald. R. 95, 132,) said "my opinion of the liberty of the press is, that every man ought to be permitted to instruct his fellow subjects; that every man may fearlessly advance any new doctrines, provided he does so with proper respect to the religion and government of the country; that he may point out errors in the measures of public men; but, he must not impute criminal conduct to them. The liberty of the press cannot be carried to this extent, without violating another equally sacred right, the right of character. This right can only be attacked in a court of justice, where the party attacked has a fair opportunity of defending himself. Where vituperation begins, the liberty of the press ends."

[2] De Lolme, B. 2, ch. 12, 291 to 297.

[3] See also *Rex* v. *Burdett*, 4 Barn. & Ald. 95.— The celebrated act of parliament of Mr. Fox, giving the right to the jury, in trials for libels, to judge of the whole matter of the charge, and to return a general verdict, did not affect to go farther. The celebrated defence of Mr. Erskine, on the trial of the Dean of St. Asaph, took the same ground. Even Junius, with his severe and bitter assaults upon established au-

§ 1880. It would seem, that a very different view of the subject was taken by a learned American commentator, though it is not, perhaps, very easy to ascertain the exact extent of his opinions. In one part of his disquisitions, he seems broadly to contend, that the security of the freedom of the press requires, that it should be exempt, not only from previous restraint by the executive, as in Great Britain ; but, from legislative restraint also ; and that this exemption, to be effectual, must be an exemption, not only from the previous inspection of licensers, but from the subsequent penalty of laws.[1]   In other places, he seems as explicitly to admit, that the liberty of the press does not include the right to do injury to the reputation of another, or to take from him the enjoyment of his rights or property, or to justify slander and calumny upon him, as a private or public man.   And yet it is added, that every individual certainly has a right to speak, or publish his sentiments on the measures of government.   To do this without restraint,

---

thority and doctrines, stopped here. "The liberty of the press," (said he,) "is the palladium of all the civil, political, and religious rights of an Englishman, and the right of juries to return a general verdict in all cases whatsoever, is an essential part of our constitution." "The laws of England, provide as effectually, as any human laws can do, for the protection of the subject in his reputation, as well as in his person and property. If the characters of private men are insulted, or injured, a double remedy is open to them, by action and by indictment." — "With regard to strictures upon the characters of men in office, and the measures of government, the case is a *little* different. A *considerable* latitude must be allowed in the discussion of public affairs, or the liberty of the press will be of no benefit to society." But he no where contends for the right to publish seditious libels ; and, on the contrary, through his whole reasoning he admits the duty to punish those, which are really so.

[1] 2 Tuck. Black. Comm. App. 20 ; 1 Tuck. Black. Comm. App. 298, 299.

control, or *fear of punishment for so doing*, is that which constitutes the genuine freedom of the press.[1] Perhaps the apparent contrariety of these opinions may arise from mixing up, in the same disquisitions, a discussion of the right of the state governments, with that of the national government, to interfere in cases of this sort, which may stand upon very different foundations. Or, perhaps, it is meant to be contended, that the liberty of the press, in all cases, excludes public punishment for public wrongs; but not civil redress for private wrongs, by calumny and libels.

§ 1881. The true mode of considering the subject is, to examine the case with reference to a state government, whose constitution, like that, for instance, of Massachusetts, declares, that "the liberty of the press is essential to the security of freedom in a state; it ought not, therefore, to be restrained in this commonwealth." What is the true interpretation of this clause? Does it prohibit the legislature from passing any laws, which shall control the licentiousness of the press, or afford adequate protection to individuals, whose private comfort, or good reputations are assailed, and violated by the press? Does it stop the legislature from passing any laws to punish libels and inflammatory publications, the object of which is to excite sedition against the government, to stir up resistance to its laws, to urge on conspiracies to destroy it, to create odium and indignation against virtuous citizens, to compel them to yield up their rights, or to make them the objects of popular

---

[1] 2 Tuck. Black. Comm. App. 28 to 30; 1 Tuck. Black. Comm. App. 298, 299.

vengeance? Would such a declaration in Virginia (for she has, on more than one occasion, boldly proclaimed, that the liberty of the press ought not to be restrained,) prohibit the legislature from passing laws to punish a man, who should publish, and circulate writings, the design of which avowedly is to excite the slaves to general insurrection against their masters, or to inculcate upon them the policy of secretly poisoning, or murdering them? In short, is it contended, that the liberty of the press is so much more valuable, than all other rights in society, that the public safety, nay the existence of the government itself is to yield to it? Is private redress for libels and calumny more important, or more valuable, than the maintenance of the good order, peace, and safety of society? It would be difficult to answer these questions in favour of the liberty of the press, without at the same time declaring, that such a licentiousness belonged, and could belong only to a despotism; and was utterly incompatible with the principles of a free government.

§ 1882. Besides:—What is meant by restraint of the press, or an abridgment of its liberty? If to publish without control, or responsibility be its genuine meaning; is not that equally violated by allowing a private compensation for damages, as by a public fine? Is not a man as much restrained from doing a thing by the fear of heavy damages, as by public punishment? Is he not often as severely punished by one, as by the other? Surely, it can make no difference in the case, what is the nature or extent of the restraint, if all restraint is prohibited. The legislative power is just as much prohibited from one mode, as from another. And it may be asked, where is the

ground for distinguishing between public and private
amesnability for the wrong? The prohibition itself
states no distinction. It is general; it is universal.
Why, then, is the distinction attempted to be made?
Plainly, because of the monstrous consequences flowing from such a doctrine. It would prostrate all personal liberty, all private peace, all enjoyment of property,
and good reputation. These are the great objects, for
which government is instituted ; and, if the licentiousness of the press must endanger, not only these, but
all public rights and public liberties, is it not as plain,
that the right of government to punish the violators of
them (the only mode of redress, which it can pursue)
flows from the primary duty of self-preservation ? No
one can doubt the importance, in a free government, of a
right to canvass the acts of public men, and the tendency of public measures, to censure boldly the conduct of
rulers, and to scrutinize closely the policy, and plans
of the government. This is the great security of a
free government. If we would preserve it, public opinion must be enlightened ; political vigilance must be
inculcated ; free, but not licentious, discussion must be
encouraged. But the exercise of a right is essentially
different from an abuse of it. The one is no legitimate inference from the other. Common sense here
promulgates the broad doctrine, *sic utere tuo, ut non
alienum lædas ;* so exercise your own freedom, as not
to infringe the rights of others, or the public peace and
safety.

§ 1883. The doctrine laid down by Mr. Justice
Blackstone, respecting the liberty of the press, has
not been repudiated (as far as is known) by any solemn decision of any of the state courts, in respect to
their own municipal jurisprudence. On the contrary,

it has been repeatedly affirmed in several of the states, notwithstanding their constitutions, or laws recognize, that "the liberty of the press ought not to be restrained," or more emphatically, that "the liberty of the press shall be inviolably maintained." This is especially true in regard to Massachusetts, South-Carolina, and Louisiana.[1] Nay; it has farther been held, that the truth of the facts is not alone sufficient to justify the publication, unless it is done from good motives, and for justifiable purposes, or, in other words, on an occasion, (as upon the canvass of candidates for public office,) when public duty, or private right requires it.[2] And the very circumstance, that, in the constitutions of several other states, provision is made for giving the truth in evidence, in prosecutions for libels for official conduct, when the matter published is proper for public information, is exceedingly strong to show, how the general law is understood. The exception establishes in all other cases the propriety of the doctrine. And Mr. Chancellor Kent, upon a large survey of the whole subject, has not scrupled to declare, that "it has become a constitutional principle in this country, that every citizen may freely speak, write, and publish his sentiments on all subjects, *being responsible for the abuse of that right;* and, that no law can rightfully be passed, to restrain, or abridge the freedom of the press."[3]

§ 1884. Even with these reasonable limitations, it is not an uncommon opinion among European states-

---

1 *Commonwealth* v. *Clap,* 4 Mass. R. 163; *Commonwealth* v. *Blanding,* 3 Pick. R. 304 : The *State* v. *Lehre,* 2 Rep. Const. Court, 809 ; 2 Kent's Comm. Lect. 24, (2d edition, p. 17 to 24.)   2 Ibid.

3 1 Kent's Comm. Lect. 24, (2d edition, p. 17 to 24.) See also Rawle on Const. ch. 10, p. 123, 124.

men of high character and extensive attainments, that the liberty of the press is incompatible with the permanent existence of any free government; nay, of any government at all. That, if it be true, that free governments cannot exist without it, it is quite as certain, that they cannot exist with it. In short, that the press is a new element in modern society ; and likely, in a great measure, to control the power of armies, and the sovereignty of the people. That it works with a silence, a cheapness, a suddenness, and a force, which may break up, in an instant, all the foundations of society, and move public opinion, like a mountain torrent, to a general desolation of every thing within its reach.

§ 1885. Whether the national government possesses a power to pass any law, not restraining the liberty of the press, but punishing the licentiousness of the press, is a question of a very different nature, upon which the commentator abstains from expressing any opinion. In 1798, Congress, believing that they possessed a constitutional authority for that purpose, passed an act, punishing all unlawful combinations, and conspiracies, to oppose the measures of the government, or to impede the operation of the laws, or to intimidate and prevent any officer of the United States from undertaking, or executing his duty. The same act further provided, for a public presentation, and punishment by fine, and imprisonment, of all persons, who should write, print, utter, or publish any false, scandalous, and malicious writing, or writings against the government of the United States, or of either house of congress, or of the president, with an intent to defame them, or bring them into contempt, or disrepute, or to excite against them the hatred of the good people of the United States ; or to excite them to oppose any

law, or act of the president, in pursuance of law of
his constitutional powers; or to resist, or oppose, or defeat any law; or to aid, encourage, or abet any hostile
designs of any foreign nation against the United States.
And the same act authorized the truth to be given in
evidence on any such prosecution; and the jury, upon
the trial, to determine the law and the fact, as in other
cases.[1]

§ 1886. This act was immediately assailed, as unconstitutional, both in the state legislatures, and the
courts of law, where prosecutions were pending. Its
constitutionality was deliberately affirmed by the
courts of law; and in a report made by a committee
of congress. It was denied by a considerable number
of the states; but affirmed by a majority. It became
one of the most prominent points of attack upon the
existing administration; and the appeal thus made was,
probably, more successful with the people, and more
consonant with the feelings of the times, than any other
made upon that occasion. The act, being limited to
a short period, expired by its own limitation, in March,
1801; and has never been renewed. It has continued, down to this very day, to be a theme of reproach
with many of those, who have since succeeded to
power.[2]

---

1 Act of 14th July, 1798, ch. 91.
2 The learned reader will find the subject discussed at large in many
of the pamphlets of that day, and especially in the Virginia Report, and
Resolutions of the Virginia Legislature, in December, 1798, and January, 1800; in the Report of a Committee of congress on the Alien and
Sedition laws, on the 25th of February, 1799; in the Resolutions of the
legislatures of Massachusetts and Kentucky, in 1799; in Bayard's
Speech on the Judiciary act, in 1802; in Addison's charges to the grand
jury, in Pennsylvania, printed with his Reports; in 2 Tucker's Black.
Comm. App. note G. p. 11 to 30. It is surprising, with what facility men

§ 1886. The remaining clause secures "the right of "the people peaceably to assemble and to petition the "government for a redress of grievances."

§ 1887. This would seem unnecessary to be expressly provided for in a republican government, since it results from the very nature of its structure and institutions. It is impossible, that it could be practically denied, until the spirit of liberty had wholly disappeared, and the people had become so servile and debased, as to be unfit to exercise any of the privileges of freemen.[1]

§ 1888. The provision was probably borrowed from the declaration of rights in England, on the revolution of 1688, in which the right to petition the king for a redress of grievances was insisted on; and the right to petition parliament in the like manner has been provided for, and guarded by statutes passed before, as well as since that period.[2] Mr. Tucker has indulged himself in a disparaging criticism upon the phraseology of this clause, as savouring too much of that style of condescension, in which favours are supposed to be

---

glide into the opinion, that a measure is universally deemed unconstitutional, because it is so in their own opinion, especially if it has become unpopular. It has been often asserted, by public men, as the universal sense of the nation, that this act was unconstitutional; and that opinion has been promulgated recently, with much emphasis, by distinguished statesmen; as we have already had occasion to notice. What the state of public and professional opinion on this subject now is, it is, perhaps, difficult to determine. But it is well known, that the opinions then deliberately given by many professional men, and judges, and legislatures, in favour of the constitutionality of the law, have never been retracted. See Vol. III. § 1288, 1289, and note.

[1] See 2 Lloyd's Debates, 197, 198, 199.

[2] See 1 Black. Comm. 143; 5 Cobbett's Parl'y. Hist. p. 109, 110; Rawle on Const. ch. 10, p. 124; 3 Amer. Museum, 420; 2 Kent's Comm. Lect. 24, p. 7, 8.

granted.[1] But this seems to be quite overstrained;
since it speaks the voice of the people in the language
of prohibition, and not in that of affirmance of a right,
supposed to be unquestionable, and inherent.

§ 1889. The next amendment is: "A well regulated
"militia being necessary to the security of a free state,
"the right of the people to keep and bear arms shall
"not be infringed."

§ 1890. The importance of this article will scarcely
be doubted by any persons, who have duly reflected
upon the subject. The militia is the natural defence
of a free country against sudden foreign invasions, domestic insurrections, and domestic usurpations of power
by rulers. It is against sound policy for a free people
to keep up large military establishments and standing
armies in time of peace, both from the enormous expenses, with which they are attended, and the facile
means, which they afford to ambitious and unprincipled
rulers, to subvert the government, or trample upon the
rights of the people. The right of the citizens to keep
and bear arms has justly been considered, as the palladium of the liberties of a republic; since it offers a strong
moral check against the usurpation and arbitrary power
of rulers; and will generally, even if these are successful
in the first instance, enable the people to resist and
triumph over them.[2] And yet, though this truth would
seem so clear, and the importance of a well regulated
militia would seem so undeniable, it cannot be disguised, that among the American people there is a growing
indifference to any system of militia discipline, and a
strong disposition, from a sense of its burthens, to be rid

1 1 Tucker's Black. Comm. App. 299.
2 1 Tucker's Black. Comm. App. 300; Rawle on Const. ch. 10, p. 125;
2 Lloyd's Debates, 219, 220.

of all regulations. How it is practicable to keep the people duly armed without some organization, it is difficult to see. There is certainly no small danger, that indifference may lead to disgust, and disgust to contempt; and thus gradually undermine all the protection intended by this clause of our national bill of rights.[1]

§ 1891. A similar provision in favour of protestants (for to them it is confined) is to be found in the bill of rights of 1688, it being declared, "that the subjects, which are protestants, may have arms for their defence suitable to their condition, and as allowed by law."[2] But under various pretences the effect of this provision has been greatly narrowed; and it is at present in England more nominal than real, as a defensive privilege.[3]

§ 1892. The next amendment is: "No soldier shall "in time of peace be quartered in any house, without "the consent of the owner, nor in time of war, but in a "manner to be prescribed by law."

§ 1893. This provision speaks for itself. Its plain object is to secure the perfect enjoyment of that great right of the common law, that a man's house shall be his own castle, privileged against all civil and military intrusion. The billetting of soldiers in time of peace upon the people has been a common resort of arbitrary princes, and is full of inconvenience and peril. In the

[1] It would be well for Americans to reflect upon the passage in Tacitus, (Hist. IV. ch. 74): ".Nam neque quies sine armis, neque arma sine stipendiis, neque stipendia sine tributis, haberi queunt." Is there 'any escape from a large standing army, but in a well disciplined militia? There is much wholesome instruction on this subject in 1 Black. Comm. ch. 13, p. 408 to 417.
[2] 5 Cobbett's Parl. Hist. p. 110; 1 Black. Comm. 143, 144.
[3] 1 Tucker's Black. Comm. App. 300.

petition of right (4 Charles I.), it was declared by parliament to be a great grievance.[1]

§ 1894. The next amendment is: "The right of the "people to be secure in their persons, houses, papers, "and effects against unreasonable searches and seizures "shall not be violated; and no warrants shall issue, but "upon probable cause, supported by oath or affirma- "tion, and particularly describing the place to be search- "ed, and the person or things to be seized."

§ 1895. This provision seems indispensable to the full enjoyment of the rights of personal security, personal liberty, and private property. It is little more than the affirmance of a great constitutional doctrine of the common law. And its introduction into the amendments was doubtless occasioned by the strong sensibility excited, both in England and America, upon the subject of general warrants almost upon the eve of the American Revolution. Although special warrants upon complaints under oath, stating the crime, and the party by name, against whom the accusation is made, are the only legal warrants, upon which an arrest can be made according to the law of England;[2] yet a practice had obtained in the secretaries' office ever since the restoration, (grounded on some clauses in the acts for regulating the press,) of issuing general warrants to take up, without naming any persons in particular, the authors, printers, and publishers of such obscene, or seditious libels, as were particularly specified in the warrant. When these acts expired, in 1694, the same practice was continued in every reign, and under every administration, except the four last years of Queen Anne's

1 2 Cobbett's Parl. Hist. 375; Rawle on Const. ch. 10, p. 126, 127; 1 Tucker's Black. Comm. App. 300, 301; 2 Lloyd's Debates, 223.
2 And see Ex parte Burford, 3 Cranch, 447; 2 Lloyd's Deb. 226, 227.

reign, down to the year 1763. The general warrants, so issued, in general terms authorized the officers to apprehend all persons suspected, without naming, or describing any person in special. In the year 1763, the legality of these general warrants was brought before the King's Bench for solemn decision; and they were adjudged to be illegal, and void for uncertainty.[1]

---

[1] *Money* v. *Leach,* 3 Burr, 1743; 4 Black. Comm. 291, 292, and note ibid. See also 15 Hansard's Parl. Hist. 1398 to 1418, (1764); *Bell* v. *Clapp,* 10 John. R. 263; *Sailly* v. *Smith,* 11 John. R. 500; 1 Tucker's Black. Comm. App. 301; Rawle on Const. ch. 10, p. 127. — It was on account of a supposed repugnance to this article, that a vehement opposition was made to the alien act of 1798, ch. 75, which authorized the president to order all such aliens, as he should judge dangerous to the peace and safety of the United States, or have reasonable grounds to suspect of any treasonable, or secret machinations against the government to depart out of the United States; and in case of disobedience, punished the refusal with imprisonment. That law having long since passed away, it is not my design to enter upon the grounds, upon which its constitutionality was asserted or denied. But the learned reader will find ample information on the subject in the report of a committee of congress, on the petitions for the repeal of the alien and sedition laws, 25th of February, 1799; the report and resolutions of the Virginia legislature of 7th of January, 1800; Judge Addison's charges to the grand jury in the Appendix to his reports; and 1 Tucker's Black. Comm. App. 301 to 304; Id. 306. See also Vol. III. § 1288, 1289, and note.

Mr. Jefferson has entered into an elaborate defence of the right and duty of public officers to disregard, in certain cases, the injunctions of the law, in a letter addressed to Mr. Colvin in 1810.* On that occasion, he justified a very gross violation of this very article by General Wilkinson, (if, indeed, he did not authorize it,) in the seizure of two American citizens by military force, on account of supposed treasonable conspiracies against the United States, and transporting them, without any warrant, or order of any civil authority, from New-Orleans to Washington for trial. They were both discharged from custody at Washington by the Supreme Court, upon a full hearing of the case.† Mr. Jefferson reasons out the whole case, and assumes, without the slightest hesitation, the positive guilt of the parties. His language is: "Under these circumstances, was he (General Wilkinson) justifiable (1.) in seizing notorious conspirators? On this there can be but

* 4 Jefferson's Corresp. 149, 151.
† *Ex parte Bollman & Swartout,* 4 Cranch, 75 to 136.

A warrant, and the complaint, on which the same is founded, to be legal, must not only state the name of the party, but also the time, and place, and nature of the offence with reasonable certainty.[1]

§ 1896. The next amendment is: "Excessive bail "shall not be required; nor excessive fines imposed; "nor cruel and unusual punishments inflicted." This is an exact transcript of a clause in the bill of rights, framed at the revolution of 1688.[2] The provision would seem to be wholly unnecessary in a free government, since it is scarcely possible, that any department of such a government should authorize, or justify such atrocious conduct.[3] It was, however, adopted, as an admonition to all departments of the national government, to warn them against such violent proceedings, as had taken place in England in the arbitrary reigns of some of the Stuarts.[4] In those

---

two opinions; *one, of the guilty, and their accomplices;* the *other, that of all honest men!!!* (2.) In sending them to the seat of government, when the *written law* gave them a right to TRIAL BY JURY? The danger of their rescue, of their continuing their machinations, *the tardiness and weakness of the law, apathy of the judges, active patronage of the whole tribe of lawyers, unknown disposition of the juries,* an hourly expectation of the enemy, salvation of the city, and of the Union itself, which would have been convulsed to its centre, had that conspiracy succeeded; *all these constituted a law of necessity and self-preservation; and rendered the salus populi supreme over the* WRITTEN *law!!!*" Thus, the constitution is to be wholly disregarded, because Mr. Jefferson has no confidence in judges, or juries, or laws. He first assumes the guilt of the parties, and then denounces every person connected with the courts of justice, as unworthy of trust. Without any warrant or lawful authority, citizens are dragged from their homes under military force, and exposed to the perils of a long voyage, against the plain language of this very article; and yet three years after they are discharged by the Supreme Court, Mr. Jefferson uses this strong language.

[1] See *Ex parte Burford,* 3 Cranch, 447.
[2] 5 Cobbett's Parl. Hist. 110.
[3] 2 Elliot's Debates, 345.
[4] See 2 Lloyd's Debates, 225, 226; 3 Elliot's Debates, 345.

times, a demand of excessive bail was often made against persons, who were odious to the court, and its favourites; and on failing to procure it, they were committed to prison.[1] Enormous fines and amercements were also sometimes imposed, and cruel and vindictive punishments inflicted. Upon this subject Mr. Justice Blackstone has wisely remarked, that sanguinary laws are a bad symptom of the distemper of any state, or at least of its weak constitution. The laws of the Roman kings, and the twelve tables of the Decemviri, were full of cruel punishments; the Porcian law, which exempted all citizens from sentence of death, silently abrogated them all. In this period the republic flourished. Under the emperors severe laws were revived, and then the empire fell.[2]

§ 1897. It has been held in the state courts, (and the point does not seem ever to have arisen in the courts of the United States,) that this clause does not apply to punishments inflicted in a state court for a crime against such state; but that the prohibition is addressed solely to the national government, and operates, as a restriction upon its powers.[3]

§ 1898. The next amendment is: "The enumeration "in the constitution of certain rights shall not be con-"strued to deny, or disparage others retained by the "people." This clause was manifestly introduced to prevent any perverse, or ingenious misapplication of the well known maxim, that an affirmation in particular cases implies a negation in all others; and *é converso*, that

---

[1] Rawle on Const. ch. 10, p. 130, 131.
[2] 4 Black. Comm. 17. See De Lolme, B. 2, ch. 16, p. 366, 367, 368, 369.
[3] See *Barker v. The People*, 3 Cowen's R. 686; *James v. Commonwealth*, 12 Sergeant and Rawle's R. 220. See *Barron v. Mayor of Baltimore*, 7 Peters's R. (1833.)

a negation in particular cases implies an affirmation in all others.[1] The maxim, rightly understood, is perfectly sound and safe; but it has often been strangely forced from its natural meaning into the support of the most dangerous political heresies. The amendment was undoubtedly suggested by the reasoning of the Federalist on the subject of a general bill of rights.[2]

§ 1899. The next and last amendment is: "The "powers not delegated to the United States by the "constitution, nor prohibited by it to the states, are "reserved to the states respectively, or to the people."

§ 1900. This amendment is a mere affirmation of what, upon any just reasoning, is a necessary rule of interpreting the constitution. Being an instrument of limited and enumerated powers, it follows irresistibly, that what is not conferred, is withheld, and belongs to the state authorities, if invested by their constitutions of government respectively in them; and if not so invested, it is retained BY THE PEOPLE, as a part of their residuary sovereignty.[3] When this amendment was before congress, a proposition was moved, to insert the word "expressly" before "delegated," so as to read "the powers not *expressly* delegated to the United States by the constitution," &c. On that occasion it was remarked, that it is impossible to confine a government to the exercise of express powers. There must necessarily be admitted powers by implication, unless the constitution descended to the most minute details.[4] It is a general principle, that all corporate

---

1 See *ante*, Vol. I. § 448; The Federalist, No. 83.

2 The Federalist, No. 84; *ante*, Vol. III. § 1852 to 1857; 1 Lloyd's Debates, 433, 437; 1 Tucker's Black. Comm. App. 307, 308.

3 See 1 Tucker's Black. Comm. App. 307, 308, 309.

4 Mr. Madison added, that he remembered the word "expressly" had been moved in the Virginia Convention by the opponents to the ratifi-

bodies possess all powers incident to a corporate capacity, without being absolutely expressed. The motion was accordingly negatived.[1] Indeed, one of the great defects of the confederation was, (as we have already seen,) that it contained a clause, prohibiting the exercise of any power, jurisdiction, or right, not *expressly delegated*.[2] The consequence was, that congress were crippled at every step of their progress; and were often compelled by the very necessities of the times to usurp powers, which they did not constitutionally possess; and thus, in effect, to break down all the great barriers against tyranny and oppression.[3]

§ 1901. It is plain, therefore, that it could not have been the intention of the framers of this amendment to give it effect, as an abridgment of any of the powers granted under the constitution, whether they are express or implied, direct or incidental. Its sole design is to exclude any interpretation, by which other powers should be assumed beyond those, which are granted. All that are granted in the original instrument, whether express or implied, whether direct or incidental, are left in their original state. All powers not delegated, (not all powers not *expressly* delegated,) and not prohibited, are reserved.[4] The attempts, then, which have been made from time to time, to force upon this language an abridging, or restrictive influence, are utterly unfounded in any just rules of interpreting the words,

cation; and after a full and fair discussion, was given up by them, and the system allowed to retain its present form. 2 Lloyd's Debates, 234.

[1] 2 Lloyd's Deb. 243, 244; *McCulloh* v. *Maryland*, 4 Wheat. R. 407; *Martin* v. *Hunter*, 1 Wheat. R. 325; *Houston* v. *Moore*, 5 Wheat. R. 49; *Anderson* v. *Dunn*, 6 Wheat. R. 225, 226.

[2] Confederation, Article 2, *ante* Vol. I. § 230.

[3] The Federalist, No. 33, 38, 42, 44; *ante* Vol. I. § 269.

[4] *McCulloh* v. *Maryland*, 4 Wheat. R. 406, 407; ante Vol. I. § 433.

or the sense of the instrument.   Stripped of the ingenious disguises, in which they are clothed, they are
neither more nor less, than attempts to foist into the
text the word "expressly;" to qualify, what is general, and obscure, what is clear, and defined.   They
make the sense of the passage bend to the wishes and
prejudices of the interpreter; and employ criticism to
support a theory, and not to guide it.   One should suppose, if the history of the human mind did not furnish
abundant proof to the contrary, that no reasonable man
would contend for an interpretation founded neither in
the letter, nor in the spirit of an instrument.   Where is
controversy to end, if we desert both the letter and the
spirit?   What is to become of constitutions of government, if they are to rest, not upon the plain import of
their words, but upon conjectural enlargements and
restrictions, to suit the temporary passions and interests of the day?   Let us never forget, that our constitutions of government are solemn instruments, addressed to the common sense of the people and designed to
fix, and perpetuate their rights and their liberties.   They
are not to be frittered away to please the demagogues
of the day.   They are not to be violated to gratify the
ambition of political leaders.   They are to speak in the
same voice now, and for ever.   They are of no man's
private interpretation.   They are ordained by the
will of the people; and can be changed only by
the sovereign command of the people.

§ 1902. It has been justly remarked, that the erection of a new government, whatever care or wisdom
may distinguish the work, cannot fail to originate questions of intricacy and nicety; and these may in a particular manner be expected to flow from the establishment of a constitution, founded upon the total, or

partial incorporation of a number of distinct sovereignties. Time alone can mature and perfect so compound
a system ; liquidate the meaning of all the parts ; and
adjust them to each other in a harmonious and consistent whole.[1]

---

[1] The Federalist, No. 82. See also Mr. Hume's Essays, Vol. I. *Essay
on the Rise of Arts and Sciences.*

CHAPTER XLV.

CONCLUDING REMARKS.

§ 1903. WE have now reviewed all the provisions of the original constitution of the United States, and all the amendments, which have been incorporated into it. And, here, the task originally proposed in these Commentaries is brought to a close. Many reflections naturally crowd upon the mind at such a moment; many grateful recollections of the past; and many anxious thoughts of the future. The past is secure. It is unalterable. The seal of eternity is upon it. The wisdom, which it has displayed, and the blessings, which it has bestowed, cannot be obscured; neither can they be debased by human folly, or human infirmity. The future is that, which may well awaken the most earnest solicitude, both for the virtue and the permanence of our republic. The fate of other republics, their rise, their progress, their decline, and their fall, are written but too legibly on the pages of history, if indeed they were not continually before us in the startling fragments of their ruins. They have perished; and perished by their own hands. Prosperity has enervated them, corruption has debased them, and a venal populace has consummated their destruction. Alternately the prey of military chieftains at home, and of ambitious invaders from abroad, they have been sometimes cheated out of their liberties by servile demagogues; sometimes betrayed into a surrender of them by false patriots; and sometimes they have willingly sold them for a price to the despot, who has bidden highest for his victims. They have disregarded the warning voice of their best statesmen; and have persecuted, and driven from office their truest friends. They have listened to the fawning sycophant, and the base calumniator of the wise and the good. They have reverenced power more in its high abuses and summary movements, than in its calm and constitutional energy, when it dispensed blessings with an unseen, but liberal hand. They have surrendered to faction, what belonged to the country. Patronage and party, the triumph of a leader, and the discontents of a day, have outweighed all solid principles and institutions of government. Such are the melancholy lessons of the past history of republics down to our own.

§ 1904. It is not my design to detain the reader by any elaborate reflections addressed to his judgment, either by way of admonition or of encouragement. But it may not be wholly without use to glance at one or two considerations, upon which our meditations cannot be too frequently indulged.

§ 1905. In the first place, it cannot escape our notice, how exceedingly difficult it is to settle the foundations of any government upon principles, which do not admit of controversy or question. The very elements, out of which it is to be built, are susceptible of infinite modifications; and theory too often deludes us by the attractive simplicity of its plans, and imagination by the visionary perfection of its speculations. In theory, a government may promise the most perfect harmony of operations in all its various combinations. In practice, the whole machinery may be perpetually retarded, or thrown out of order by accidental mal-adjustments. In theory, a government may seem deficient in unity of design and symmetry of parts; and yet, in practice, it may work with astonishing accuracy and force for the general welfare. Whatever, then, has been found to work well in experience, should be rarely hazarded upon conjectural improvements. Time, and long and steady operation are indispensable to the perfection of all social institutions. To be of any value they must become cemented with the habits, the feelings, and the pursuits of the people. Every change discomposes for a while the whole arrangements of the system. What is safe is not always expedient; what is new is often pregnant with unforeseen evils, and imaginary good.

§ 1906. In the next place, the slightest attention to the history of the national constitution must satisfy every reflecting mind, how many difficulties attended its formation and adoption, from real or imaginary differences of interests, sectional feelings, and local institutions. It is an attempt to create a national sovereignty, and yet to preserve the state sovereignties; though it is impossible to assign definite boundaries in every case to the powers of each. The influence of the disturbing causes, which, more than once in the convention, were on the point of breaking up the Union, have since immeasurably increased in concentration and vigour. The very inequalities of a government, confessedly founded in a compromise, were then felt with a strong sensibility; and every new source of discontent, whether accidental or permanent, has since added increased activity to the painful sense of these inequalities. The North cannot but perceive, that it has yielded to the South a superiority of representatives, already amounting to twenty-five, beyond its due proportion; and the South imagines, that, with all this preponderance in representation, the other parts of the Union enjoy a more perfect protection of their interests, than her own. The

West feels her growing power and weight in the Union; and the Atlantic states begin to learn, that the sceptre must one day depart from them. If, under these circumstances, the Union should once be broken up, it is impossible, that a new constitution should ever be formed, embracing the whole Territory. We shall be divided into several nations or confederacies, rivals in power and interest, too proud to brook injury, and too close to make retaliation distant or ineffectual. Our very animosities will, like those of all other kindred nations, become more deadly, because our lineage, laws, and language are the same. Let the history of the Grecian and Italian republics warn us of our dangers. The national constitution is our last, and our only security. United we stand; divided we fall.

§ 1907. If these Commentaries shall but inspire in the rising generation a more ardent love of their country, an unquenchable thirst for liberty, and a profound reverence for the constitution and the Union, then they will have accomplished all, that their author ought to desire. Let the American youth never forget, that they possess a noble inheritance, bought by the toils, and sufferings, and blood of their ancestors; and capable, if wisely improved, and faithfully guarded, of transmitting to their latest posterity all the substantial blessings of life, the peaceful enjoyment of liberty, property, religion, and independence. The structure has been erected by architects of consummate skill and fidelity; its foundations are solid; its compartments are beautiful, as well as useful; its arrangements are full of wisdom and order; and its defences are impregnable from without. It has been reared for immortality, if the work of man may justly aspire to such a title. It may, nevertheless, perish in an hour by the folly, or corruption, or negligence of its only keepers, THE PEOPLE. Republics are created by the virtue, public spirit, and intelligence of the citizens. They fall, when the wise are banished from the public councils, because they dare to be honest, and the profligate are rewarded, because they flatter the people, in order to betray them.

INDEX.

A.

COSIMO is a specialty publisher for independent authors, not-for-profit organizations, and innovative businesses, dedicated to publishing books that inspire, inform, and engage readers around the world.

Our mission is to create a smart and sustainable society by connecting people with valuable ideas. We offer authors and organizations full publishing support, while using the newest technologies to present their works in the most timely and effective way.

COSIMO BOOKS offers fine books that inspire, inform and engage readers on a variety of subjects, including personal development, socially responsible business, economics and public affairs.

COSIMO CLASSICS brings to life unique and rare classics, representing a wide range of subjects that include Business, Economics, History, Personal Development, Philosophy, Religion & Spirituality, and much more!

COSIMO REPORTS publishes reports that affect your world, from global trends to the economy, and from health to geopolitics.

COSIMO B2B offers custom editions for historical societies, museums, companies and other organizations interested in offering classic books to their audiences, customized with their own logo and message. **COSIMO B2B** also offers publishing services to organizations, such as media firms, think tanks, conference organizers and others who could benefit from having their own imprint.